Praise for
The Wiley Blackwell Companion to Ancient Israel

I had begun to think that there were already too many handbooks, dictionaries, and encyclopedias of the biblical world on the market for yet another one. But reading through this new volume, superbly planned and organized by Susan Niditch, showed me how wrong I was. There is frankly nothing quite like it. In an exceptionally comprehensive way, it explores what ancient Israel was all about: the varied aspects of its culture and society, the multiple historical contexts in which it existed, and the range of perspectives, literary, archaeological, religious, social scientific, from which modern interpreters must understand it. The volume, thus, is not only a survey of the facts and features of Israel's history and culture, as is typical of many handbooks. Even more, it is a searching inquiry into how we know what we know or think we know: what are the major issues of interpretation and how to evaluate them. Editor Niditch has not been afraid to encourage differing points of view on these issues and the evidence for them from her contributors, which her cross-referencing throughout helps the reader to appreciate. And the contributors – a well-respected international group from junior to senior scholars – have not been afraid to be provocative in what they have to say. Unquestionably, this volume will become a cornerstone for all future work on the study of ancient Israel.

Peter Machinist, Harvard University

The Wiley Blackwell Companions to Religion

The Wiley Blackwell Companions to Religion series presents a collection of the most recent scholarship and knowledge about world religions. Each volume draws together newly-commissioned essays by distinguished authors in the field, and is presented in a style which is accessible to undergraduate students, as well as scholars and the interested general reader. These volumes approach the subject in a creative and forward-thinking style, providing a forum in which leading scholars in the field can make their views and research available to a wider audience.

Recently Published

The Blackwell Companion to Catholicism
Edited by James J. Buckley, Frederick Christian Bauerschmidt, and Trent Pomplun
The Blackwell Companion to Eastern Christianity
Edited by Ken Parry
The Blackwell Companion to the Theologians
Edited by Ian S. Markham
The Blackwell Companion to the Bible in English Literature
Edited by Rebecca Lemon, Emma Mason, John Roberts, and Christopher Rowland
The Blackwell Companion to the New Testament
Edited by David E. Aune
The Blackwell Companion to Nineteenth Century Theology
Edited by David Fergusson
The Blackwell Companion to Religion in America
Edited by Philip Goff
The Blackwell Companion to Jesus
Edited by Delbert Burkett
The Blackwell Companion to Paul
Edited by Stephen Westerholm
The Blackwell Companion to Religion and Violence
Edited by Andrew R. Murphy
The Blackwell Companion to Christian Ethics, Second Edition
Edited by Stanley Hauerwas and Samuel Wells
The Wiley Blackwell Companion to Practical Theology
Edited by Bonnie J. Miller-McLemore
The Wiley Blackwell Companion to Religion and Social Justice
Edited by Michael D. Palmer and Stanley M. Burgess
The Wiley Blackwell Companion to Chinese Religions
Edited by Randall L. Nadeau
The Wiley Blackwell Companion to African Religions
Edited by Elias Kifon Bongmba
The Wiley Blackwell Companion to Christian Mysticism
Edited by Julia A. Lamm
The Wiley Blackwell Companion to the Anglican Communion
Edited by Ian S. Markham, J. Barney Hawkins IV, Justyn Terry, and Leslie Nuez Steffensen
The Wiley Blackwell Companion to Interreligious Dialogue
Edited by Catherine Cornille
The Wiley Blackwell Companion to East and Inner Asian Buddhism
Edited by Mario Poceski
The Wiley Blackwell Companion to Latino/a Theology
Edited by Orlando O. Espn
The Wiley Blackwell Companion to Ancient Israel
Edited by Susan Niditch

The Wiley Blackwell Companion to Ancient Israel

Edited by

Susan Niditch

WILEY Blackwell

This edition first published 2016
© 2016 John Wiley & Sons Ltd

Registered Office
John Wiley & Sons Ltd, The Atrium, Southern Gate, Chichester, West Sussex, PO19 8SQ, UK

Editorial Offices
350 Main Street, Malden, MA 02148-5020, USA
9600 Garsington Road, Oxford, OX4 2DQ, UK
The Atrium, Southern Gate, Chichester, West Sussex, PO19 8SQ, UK

For details of our global editorial offices, for customer services, and for information about how to apply for permission to reuse the copyright material in this book please see our website at www.wiley.com/wiley-blackwell.

Library of Congress Cataloging-in-Publication Data

The Wiley Blackwell companion to ancient Israel / edited by Susan Niditch.
   pages cm
Includes bibliographical references and index.
ISBN 978-0-470-65677-8 (cloth)
1. Jews–History–To 70 A.D. 2. Judaism–History–Post-exilic period, 586 B.C.-210 A.D. 3. Jews–Palestine–Civilization. 4. Palestine–Social life and customs–To 70 A.D. 5. Palestine–History–To 70 A.D. 6. Bible–Criticism, interpretation, etc. I. Niditch, Susan, editor.
   DS121.W65 2016
   933–dc23
                                                                          2015017683

A catalogue record for this book is available from the British Library.

Cover image: © Kavram / Getty Images

Set in 10/12.5pt Photina by Aptara Inc., New Delhi, India
Printed and bound in Malaysia by Vivar Printing Sdn Bhd

1   2016

Contents

Notes on Contributors

Elizabeth Bloch-Smith is an archaeologist who has unearthed the lived cultures of the ancient Levant, including ancient Israel. Her publications include *Judahite Burial Practices and Beliefs about the Dead* and articles on Tel Dor, the goddess Astarte, Israelite religion, the role of material culture in transmitting notions of gender, and archaeological contributions to biblical studies. She has excavated in Israel, Cyprus, Turkey, Tunisia, and Connecticut.

David M. Carr is Professor of Old Testament at Union Theological Seminary in New York. He is the author of *Introduction to the Old Testament: Sacred Texts and Imperial Contexts* (2010), *The Formation of the Hebrew Bible* (2011) and, most recently, *Holy Resilience: The Bible's Traumatic Origins*.

Charles E. Carter is Professor of Religion at Seton Hall University in South Orange, NJ. In addition to Hebrew Bible and New Testament, his teaching and research interests are archaeology, environmental studies, and religion and film. He was the Catholic Biblical Society Visiting Scholar at the Pontifical Biblical Institute in Rome and the École Biblique in Jerusalem in 2002–3 and a Pew Scholar in the Carnegie Academy for the Scholarship of Teaching and Learning in 1999–2000. He chaired the Department of Religion from 1999 to 2009. From 2009 to 2014, he served as Associate Dean of the College of Arts and Sciences.

Ohad Cohen is a Semitic linguist and Hebrew Bible scholar. In his book *The Verbal Tense System in Late Biblical Hebrew Prose* (2013), he offered a systematic structural analysis of the verb in late Biblical Hebrew prose. In his recent publications he has conceptualized new ways to deal with some classical debates on the meaning of Biblical Hebrew verbal forms.

John J. Collins is Holmes Professor of Old Testament Criticism and Interpretation at Yale University. He has written widely on apocalyptic literature and the Dead Sea Scrolls. His most recent book is *The Oxford Handbook of Apocalyptic Literature* (2014). He has been president of the Catholic Biblical Association (1997) and president of the Society of

Biblical Literature (2002), and is currently general editor of the Anchor Bible Series for Yale University Press.

Tamara Cohn Eskenazi is The Effie Wise Ochs Professor of Biblical Literature and History at Hebrew Union College-Jewish Institute of Religion in Los Angeles. Her publications include *In an Age of Prose: A Literary Approach to Ezra-Nehemiah* and *The JPS Bible Commentary: Ruth* (National Jewish Book Award in Women's Studies, 2011). She is senior editor of *The Torah: A Women's Commentary*, winner of the National Jewish Book of the Year Award in 2008, and recipient of a National Endowment for the Humanities Fellowship for work on women's lives in the Persian period.

Avraham Faust is Professor of Archaeology at the Martin (Szusz) Department of Land of Israel Studies and Archaeology, Bar-Ilan University, Israel. He is the author of numerous books and articles covering various aspects of Israel's archaeology from the Early Bronze Age to the Byzantine period, with a special focus on Iron Age societies. He is currently directing the excavations at Tel 'Eton.

S. A. Geller is the Irma Cameron Milstein Professor of Hebrew Bible at the Jewish Theological Seminary in New York. He has also taught at York University in Toronto, Dropsie College in Philadelphia, and Brandeis University in Waltham, MA. He has worked in the field of biblical poetry and religion, and has published books and numerous articles in these areas, among them *Sacred Enigmas: Literary Religion in the Hebrew Bible* (1996) and, most recently, studies on the role of nature in biblical religion and other topics. He is currently completing a commentary on the Book of Psalms.

Matthew J. Goff is an Associate Professor in the Department of Religion at Florida State University. His research interests include the Dead Sea Scrolls and wisdom literature. His most recent book is *4QInstruction: A Commentary* (2013).

Edward L. Greenstein is Meiser Professor of Biblical Studies and Director of the Institute for Jewish Biblical Interpretation at Bar-Ilan University, Israel. He has edited the *Journal of the Ancient Near Eastern Society* since 1974 and has published widely in ancient Near Eastern and biblical studies. Recipient of numerous fellowships, he completed the essay in the present volume while a visiting senior research fellow at the Herzl Institute, Jerusalem.

John R. Huddlestun is Associate Professor of Religious Studies at the College of Charleston. He has published on the relationship of ancient Israel to Egypt, especially on conceptions of the River Nile. Prior to his career in academia, Professor Huddlestun worked as a professional musician, living in southern Europe and Israel.

Brad E. Kelle, Professor of Old Testament and Director of the M.A. in Religion Program at Point Loma Nazarene University, has served as the Chair of the Society of Biblical Literature's Warfare in Ancient Israel Consultation (2004–6) and Section (2007–12). He has written or edited a variety of works on ancient Israel, including *Ancient Israel at War 853–586 BC* (2007) and *Biblical History and Israel's Past: The Changing Study of the Bible and History* (co-authored with Megan Bishop Moore, 2011).

T. M. Lemos is Associate Professor of Hebrew Bible at Huron University College at Western University, Ontario. She has published in the areas of Israelite marriage customs, social structure, impurity practices, masculinity, and violence.

Bernard M. Levinson serves as Professor of Classical and Near Eastern Studies and of Law at the University of Minnesota, where he holds the Berman Family Chair in Jewish Studies and Hebrew Bible. His research focuses on biblical and cuneiform law, textual reinterpretation in the Second Temple period, and the relation of the Bible to Western intellectual history. The interdisciplinary significance of his work has been recognized with appointments to major national and international research institutes.

Theodore J. Lewis holds the Blum-Iwry Professorship in Near Eastern Studies at The Johns Hopkins University. He specializes in Northwest Semitic languages and religions, is general editor of the book series Writings from the Ancient World and past editor of the journals *Near Eastern Archaeology* and *Hebrew Annual Review*. He is the author of *Cults of the Dead in Ancient Israel and Ugarit*, and co-author of *Ugaritic Narrative Poetry* and is currently writing *The Religion of Ancient Israel* for the Yale Anchor Bible Reference Library series for which he was awarded a Guggenheim Fellowship.

Carol Meyers, the Mary Grace Wilson Professor of Religious Studies at Duke University, has lectured and published widely in biblical studies and archaeology. She co-edited *Women in Scripture*, a comprehensive look at all biblical women; and her latest book, *Rediscovering Eve* (2013), is a landmark study of women in ancient Israel. She has been a frequent consultant for media productions and has served as president of the Society of Biblical Literature.

Susan Niditch is the Samuel Green Professor of Religion at Amherst College. Her research and teaching on the cultures of ancient Israel draw upon the fields of folklore and oral studies and reflect particular interests in war, gender, the body and lived religion. Her most recent book is *The Responsive Self: Personal Religion in Biblical Literature of the Neo-Babylonian and Persian Periods*.

Song-Mi Suzie Park is Assistant Professor of Old Testament at Austin Presbyterian Theological Seminary in Austin, Texas. Her main research interests center on the literary and theological interpretations of the Hebrew Bible, especially concerning the politics of identity. The author of *Hezekiah and the Dialogue of Memory* (2015) and several articles, she is currently at work on a feminist commentary on the Book of 2 Kings.

Raymond F. Person, Jr is Professor of Religion at Ohio Northern University. He is the author of numerous books and articles, including *The Deuteronomic History and the Book of Chronicles: Scribal Works in an Oral World* (2010) and *Deuteronomy and Environmental Amnesia* (2014).

J. J. M. Roberts is Princeton Theological Seminary's W. H. Green Professor of Old Testament Literature Emeritus, retired after 25 years in that position. Prior to that he taught in the Near Eastern departments at the University of Toronto and The Johns Hopkins University, and the Department of Religion at Dartmouth College. He served on the New

Revised Standard Version committee, on a number of editorial boards, and has published widely.

Christopher A. Rollston is a historian of the ancient Near East, with primary focus on Northwest Semitic epigraphy of the First and Second Temple periods, scribal education, writing and literacy in antiquity, Hebrew Bible, and law and diplomacy in the ancient Near East. He works in more than a dozen ancient and modern languages. He holds the MA and PhD from The Johns Hopkins University and is currently the Associate Professor of Northwest Semitic Languages and Literatures in the Department of Classical and Near Eastern Languages at George Washington University. He is the editor of the journal *Maarav*, the co-editor of the *Bulletin of the American Schools of Oriental Research*, and a member of Phi Beta Kappa.

J. David Schloen is Associate Professor of Syro-Palestinian Archaeology in the Oriental Institute and the Department of Near Eastern Languages and Civilizations of the University of Chicago, where he is also an associated faculty member of the Divinity School. He specializes in the archaeology and history of the ancient Levant (Syria and Palestine) from ca. 3000 to 300 BCE. Over the past two decades he has conducted archaeological excavations in Israel and Turkey. He is currently completing a book entitled *The Bible and Archaeology: Exploring the History and Mythology of Ancient Israel*, which explains how ancient artifacts, inscriptions, and other archaeological discoveries shed light on biblical narratives.

Tina M. Sherman is a Ph.D. candidate in the Department of Near Eastern and Judaic Studies at Brandeis University in Waltham, Massachusetts. Her dissertation investigates the nature of metaphor in prophetic oracles of judgment, situating them within their ancient Near Eastern context.

Mark S. Smith is the Skirball Professor of Hebrew Bible and Ancient Near Eastern Studies at New York University. Specializing in Israelite religion and the Hebrew Bible, as well as the literature and religion of Late Bronze Ugarit, he is the author of many books, most recently *Poetic Heroes: The Literary Commemorations of Warriors and Warrior Culture in the Early Biblical World* and *How Human Is God? Seven Questions about God and Humanity in the Bible* (both 2014).

Francesca Stavrakopoulou is Professor of Hebrew Bible and Ancient Religion at the University of Exeter, UK. Her research focuses on religious and social practices in ancient Israel and Judah, and the portrayal of the past in the Hebrew Bible. Her books include *King Manasseh and Child Sacrifice* (2004), *Land of Our Fathers: The Roles of Ancestor Veneration in Biblical Land Claims* (2010), and *Religious Diversity in Ancient Israel and Judah* (with J. Barton, 2010).

Neal Walls is Associate Professor of Old Testament Interpretation at the Wake Forest University School of Divinity in North Carolina. He is the author of *The Goddess Anat in Ugaritic Myth* and *Desire, Discord, and Death*.

Steven Weitzman serves as the Ella Darivoff Director of the Herbert D. Katz Center for Advanced Judaic Studies at the University of Pennsylvania where he is also the Abraham M. Ellis Professor of Hebrew and Semitic Languages and Literatures in the Department of Religious Studies. Recent publications include *Solomon: The Lure of Wisdom* (2011); with John Efron and Matthias Lehmann, a second revised edition of the textbook *The Jews* (2014); and with co-editor Michael Morgan, *Rethinking the Messianic Idea in Judaism* (2014).

Robert R. Wilson is the Hoober Professor of Religious Studies and Professor of Old Testament at Yale University. He is the author of *Genealogy and History in the Biblical World* (1977), *Prophecy and Society in Ancient Israel* (1980), *Sociological Approaches to the Old Testament* (1984), and numerous articles on prophecy, historiography, and judicial practice in ancient Israel.

Benjamin G. Wright III is University Distinguished Professor in the Department of Religion Studies at Lehigh University in Bethlehem, PA. He specializes in the history and literature of Second Temple Judaism and Early Christianity, with particular interest in wisdom literature, the Septuagint and problems related to translation in antiquity, and the Dead Sea Scrolls. He has recently completed a commentary on the *Letter of Aristeas* for the series Commentaries on Early Jewish Literature.

Acknowledgments

I thank the Trustees of Amherst College and Dean Greg S. Call for supporting the production of this volume with a grant from the Faculty Research Award Program. I would also like to thank Stewart Moore for his excellent work as editorial assistant during the preparation of the manuscript. My friend and colleague Peter Machinist was extremely helpful as I compiled the roster of contributors. I also wish to express my appreciation to all the colleagues who contributed essays. I thank them for the quality of their work, for their patience, and for their perseverance. For me, a particularly fruitful and enjoyable part of this project involved the lectures, based on their essays, delivered by contributors in a variety of classroom and public settings at Amherst College. My students over several years benefited greatly from these interactions that deeply enriched our courses and offered contributors an opportunity to give their essays a trial run in front of intelligent and enthusiastic listeners. The responses of these audiences in turn contributed to the final versions of the essays. The lectures were made possible by the Amherst College Willis D. Wood Fund. Finally, I would like to thank Rebecca Harkin, Georgina Coleby, Ben Thatcher, and the other editors at Wiley Blackwell who commissioned and supported our work.

Editor's Introduction

The *Companion to Ancient Israel* offers a multifaceted entry into ancient Israelite culture. The orientation of the *Companion* is rooted in several approaches: the history of religion with its interests in worldviews, symbol systems, paradigms, and the benefits of comparative, cross-cultural study; the study of religion as lived, an approach that asks about the everyday lives of ordinary people, the material culture that they shape and experience, and the relationships between individuals and tradition; and cultural studies, with its emphasis on interdisciplinary work and methodological questions about our own assumptions as scholars.

The essays of the *Companion* are presented in three parts, but each of the chapters relates to others in the volume to reveal a range of perspectives, emphases, and ways of reading that point both to areas of consensus and lively debate within a framework of shared questions and concerns. A first group of articles explores how we know what we know. Authors describe and apply major tools and approaches employed by scholars to contextualize ancient Israel and Judah and to explore the Hebrew Bible, the great anthology of literature integral to issues in Israelite history and culture. Throughout, readers are urged to approach the sources of our knowledge with suspicion, aware of the benefits and limitations of methodological approaches deployed in the study of ancient Israel.

In chapter 1, Elizabeth Bloch-Smith skillfully introduces readers to the modern field of ancient Near Eastern archaeology, its techniques and goals, and its implications for the study of ancient Israel. She reviews the history of the field, drawing an important distinction between "biblical" and "ancient Israel." Bloch-Smith emphasizes the critical importance of material culture for a full appreciation of Israelite religion, literature, and society even while pointing to the limitations of this evidence and the challenges of interpretation. She judiciously describes developments and debates among scholars

The Wiley Blackwell Companion to Ancient Israel, First Edition. Edited by Susan Niditch.
© 2016 John Wiley & Sons, Ltd. Published 2016 by John Wiley & Sons, Ltd.

concerning chronology and other critical issues, providing a thoughtful counterpoint to other essays in this volume such as that of Avraham Faust.

Grappling with issues in ethnography, worldview, and literary form, Song-Mi Suzie Park discusses the peoples surrounding ancient Israel who are described in the Hebrew Bible as playing critical roles in Israelite foundation tales. Park not only reviews what is known and not known about the historical locations, ethnic identity, and cultural orientations of the Edomites, Ammonites, Moabites, and others but also explores what terms such as Canaanite and Amorite variously mean in Israelite tradition. She asks how the ancient biblical authors portray neighboring peoples and what these portrayals say about Israelites' own sense of cultural self-definition contoured either in contrast with or in relation to other groups. In the process, she not only delves into the nature of ancient historiography but also provides an excellent case study in the genesis of cultural memory.

An important part of this memory relates to Egypt. John R. Huddlestun asks about the significance of biblical references to Egypt for understanding Israelite history and cultural identity. Huddlestun discusses periods and situations in which cultural contact between ancient Egypt and Israel might have been possible, pointing to historical and literary implications, but he is duly cautious about direct literary borrowings and links. Throughout, he pays excellent attention to the comparative method, offering a thoughtful review and critique of the work of previous scholarship, exploring what this work and conclusions drawn from it reveal about the field of biblical studies and the cultural orientations of its contributors. In an essay that shares some interests with those of Park, Faust, and Stavrakopoulou, Huddlestun has us consider what the biblical portrayals of Egypt and Egyptians say about biblical writers, their worldviews and contexts.

In a wide-ranging essay, Steven Weitzman also explores scholarly approaches to the contexts of biblical literature and the significance of certain recurring methodological assumptions. Weitzman is particularly sensitive to the difficulties in matching ancient texts with social, political, and intellectual history – the ambiguities and complexities, the constructions, interpretations, and receptions to which questions about text and context are subject. In particular, he assesses the contributions of ancient Near Eastern comparative studies and archaeology, discussing the New Historicism, postmodernism in various guises, minimalism, and the ways in which attention to collective memory relates to the very nature of tradition as received and worldview in context. His essay reads well in tandem with those of Bloch-Smith, Park, Faust, and Niditch.

Susan Niditch explores the ways in which categories introduced by folklorist Alan Dundes, "texture" (style and use of language), "text" (content), and "context" (social and literary), inform genres within folk groups. She points to interdisciplinary borders where folklore meets biblical form-criticism and contemporary material culture meets ancient Near Eastern archaeology. A discussion of oral and written literature is followed by a set of biblical case studies that underscore the various ways in which awareness of folklore, the field and the international corpus of material studied, deepens and enriches our understanding of ancient Israelite cultures. Her observations concerning oral tradition serve as a counterpoint to those of David M. Carr who seeks to understand how the compositions of the Hebrew Bible emerged and were preserved as written works.

In a sophisticated essay that rejects simplistic views of biblical sources, David M. Carr offers a model for the formation of the Hebrew Bible, seeking to account for doublets, contradictions, and awkwardness in the received, preserved written tradition. Drawing his examples from various ancient Near Eastern and biblical works and focusing on Genesis 1–11, Carr posits the use of specific scribal techniques, such as joining, blending, expanding, and counterwriting. His case studies lead Carr to review and assess the state of source criticism and to carefully draw some wider conclusions about the formation of the Pentateuch and its "multivoiced" quality. Carr's work is well read in tandem with that of Raymond F. Person, Jr who points to an oral-traditional dynamic in the process of written composition.

Composition also raises questions about the very words chosen by authors, the syntax and style of their language, and a host of other linguistic criteria. Ohad Cohen introduces readers to the ways in which experts in linguistics offer suggestions for the dating, authorship, and context of various biblical compositions. After describing the sort of criteria considered by scholars in the study of ancient Hebrew, Cohen provides useful case studies to explore the ways in which these criteria might be used to situate pieces and portions of biblical literature.

The culture of ancient Israel and Judah is, as emphasized throughout this volume, part of a larger Levantine world, both in regard to the content and nature of the evidence and in regard to the very writing system that has allowed for the preservation of literary evidence. Introducing readers to the variations and developments that occur in writing systems with specific reference to the ancient Near East, Christopher A. Rollston provides an array of key texts, examines the genres of literature produced or preserved in writing, and explores their political, historical, and cultural significance. Rollston discusses the methodological challenges and implications of epigraphic work, pointing to scholarly debates about the chronology and meaning of individual inscriptions. Rollston not only allows readers to think in material terms about the nature of writing in the ancient world to which Israel belonged, but also about who has access to this skill at various levels of expertise.

All of the questions about form and function, context and comparison that occupy authors in Part I of the *Companion* remain relevant in Part II dealing with political history. Developments in scholarly approaches will be especially striking to those who were introduced to the history of ancient Israel via works of the mid-twentieth century when venerable scholars such as John Bright could virtually visualize Abraham and his family as they traveled the steppe, donkeys in tow. Instead, Avraham Faust approaches this early period by examining the ways in which evidence of material culture reveals means of defining one's own group over against neighboring groups. In the process, he provides an overview of directions and variations in the field of archaeology as it has influenced biblical and ancient Near Eastern studies and hotly debated questions concerning Israelite origins. Faust examines critically what is meant by ethnicity and offers a chronology and a cultural map for the historical emergence of Israel as a people and a form of self-definition. His work reprises some of the themes explored by Park in her socioliterary approach. Similarly, Brad E. Kelle explores the complex intersection between legend, history, propaganda, and historiography in discussing the period of the early kings as described in the Hebrew Scriptures and as elucidated by extrabiblical evidence, archaeological, epigraphic, and literary. He points to various "reading frames" employed by modern interpreters and to the possible social contexts, worldviews, and motivations that may have informed the work of ancient composers, all of which relate to particular and often contrasting views of an early monarchy. Also employing biblical, archaeological, and extrabiblical written sources, J. J. M. Roberts points to the challenges of historical reconstruction and the inner tensions and contradictions in available material, asking how we know what we know and why the information is preserved by various sources in a particular way. His work, like that of Brad E. Kelle, thus not only provides a valuable background essay for the study of Israelite and Judean history, but also a useful model in historical methodology.

Similarly, Charles E. Carter grapples with various and contrasting reconstructions of the neo-Babylonian and Persian periods with special interest in the ways in which scholars employ and assess archaeological data. He too points to the challenges faced by historians, and offers judicious suggestions for the demography of Persian-period Judea. He points to ways in which details concerning the size and distribution of population and other information, gleaned from concrete evidence of material culture, relate to biblical authors' portrayals of exile, return, and daily life experienced under colonialist control in Israel, Judah, and the Diaspora. His essay beautifully relates conceptually to chapters by Smith, Collins, Lewis, and Eskenazi while grappling with many of the issues in archaeology and interpretation discussed by Bloch-Smith, Schloen, and Faust. Finally, Matthew J. Goff describes the political and cultural history of the Hellenistic period, exploring key events and turning points, issues relating to Israel and Diaspora, to the Maccabean revolt, and to manifestations of an apocalyptic worldview. He explores how extant literature reflects and helped to shape varieties of Jewish identity, and he allows for creativity and complexity in Jewish encounters with Hellenistic settings and ideas.

Part III of the *Companion* delves into critical themes in ancient Israelite cultures. Readers will notice the ways in which contributors creatively draw upon the various methodologies explored by earlier essays, often applying an interdisciplinary and comparative approach to the theme they present. Essays by Neal Walls and Mark S. Smith deal with representations of God and the gods.

Neal Walls describes the rich mythological matrix to which belong representations of deities in the ancient Levant. His work in comparative religion and comparative literature underscores not only similarities in language, imagery, and narrative medium employed by Israelite and neighboring authors to express essentials of worldview but also points to important variations between the literary inventions of various contributors, revealing their unique and culturally specific orientations. The essay thus joins that of Park to explore ways in which groups define the self and the other through creative media, in this case through stories about the gods. Walls points not only to a range of views expressed by Yahwists concerning the gods and the God of Israel, but also traces developments over time. Attuned to ways in which the literary evidence reveals both shared traditions and lively diversity in critical aspects of culture and belief, this essay anticipates studies by Greenstein and Lewis dealing with verbal and visual art and beautifully transitions to issues in monotheism discussed by Mark S. Smith.

Mark S. Smith explores ideas concerning a singular god that reflect and inform both modern theological perspectives and the very definitions of monotheism that emerge from or are imposed upon ancient texts. Smith places the development of monotheism in a sociohistorical framework and within a history of ideas, drawing comparisons with developing worldviews of Israel's neighbors as they relate to divinity. Key background events include the rise of empires in the ancient Near East and the trauma of Assyrian and Babylonian conquests which focus attention on individual human responsibility and the unique role of a single national god within the larger universe.

Articles by Steven A. Geller, Robert R. Wilson, and John J. Collins deal with the mediation between the God of Israel and human beings. Steven Geller's study of priests and ritual operates on diachronic and synchronic levels, as he analyzes critical founding myths and the institutions they describe, including the priesthood itself. On the one hand, he is interested in what characterizes and holds together the priestly narrative that plays such a dominant role in the Pentateuch, for example, unifying motifs such as light and blood and narrative patterns associating holiness with danger. He is also interested in the disparate threads of tradition combined to emphasize such motifs and form these narrative patterns. Geller thus ranges from legal and ritual materials to the origin myths that serve as their framework, exploring the heroic characters who star in these myths, providing models for priestly roles as intermediaries in lived religion, real or imagined.

With a carefully articulated comparative approach, Robert R. Wilson introduces readers to prophecy as presented in Hebrew Bible, its functions, forms, and means of transmission. Drawing upon relevant ancient Near Eastern and international material, Wilson explores the roles of prophecy and prophets in ancient Israelite culture, attuned to the sociological frameworks in which prophets operated and the anthropological models that help to make sense of the phenomenon.

Sharing Wilson's interest in form and function, John J. Collins's study of apocalypticism attends to matters of genre and context. His analysis of apocalypticism deals with critical questions in the sociological study of religion concerning worldview and social movements. For Collins, the key to understanding this material is context, for example in regards to Daniel, persecutions under the colonialist rule of the Seleucid monarch Antiochus the Fourth. He engages with and assesses traits typical of apocalyptic orientations. In this way he provides insight into the particular sort of mediation between God and human and the particular relationship to history envisioned in apocalyptic works.

A second set of essays in Part III of the *Companion* deals with forms of social interaction. In a thoughtful piece, Francesca Stavrakopoulou questions the methodological assumptions that have informed the study of "household" religion and related terminology, for example "family religion," "popular religion," "women's religion." Rejecting simple dichotomies sometimes drawn between sacred and profane, popular and elite, Stavrakopoulou complicates matters, exploring the complex nature of the ancient sources themselves and the theoretical paradigms applied to the study of "household religion." She notes that such paradigms are too often influenced by normative attitudes and Western orientations. Concentrating on the setting of home and tomb and on practices related to these spaces and to the body, Stavrakopoulou explores the material dimensions of ancient Israelite religion and the ways in which religion is constructed and lived in social contexts.

Another aspect of social context concerns education and the transmission of knowledge in a culture that valorizes oral communication. Raymond F. Person, Jr considers the role of families and elites, scribal guilds and the state, and the educative function of liturgy, recitation, and festival contexts. He points to connections between education and gender roles, and emphasizes the ongoing importance of kinship and "family households" in ancient Israelite self-definition. Taking account of the social, economic, and ecological environments that influence the form and function of education, he points to ways in which memorization allows for multiformity and creativity in the transmission of tradition and reinforcement of cultural values.

With an approach that is both social scientific and humanistic, T. M. Lemos also explores kinship and community in ancient Israel. Like the essays by Park and Faust, this chapter evidences a deep interest in questions of cultural identity. Grappling with the terminology of kinship, Lemos explores the ways in which kinship, community, and society are understood and experienced in key periods of the social and political history of Israel and Judah and points to the ways in which the social landscape changes over time in response to changing political realities and how these changes are reflected in our sources. Like Francesca Stavrakopoulou, she makes readers aware of the methodological difficulties faced in such reconstructions of ancient history. Some particularly interesting threads in the essay deal with views of kinship and community in the Diaspora following the Babylonian conquest, attitudes to intermarriage in late biblical times, and the importance of wars in social change.

Bernard M. Levinson and Tina M. Sherman explore law and legal traditions in ancient Israel with attention to context on various levels: social, historical, narrative, and cross-cultural. Working comparatively within the biblical tradition and the wider world of the Levant, Levinson and Sherman raise questions about the relationship between extant biblical texts, as composed and framed, and actual ways of life, political institutions, and social bodies, noting that the understanding and application of law may have differed across segments of Israelite society. They explore the development of legal traditions over time, pointing to ways in which material has been reappropriated and altered, reflecting differing worldviews. Their study of law and legal traditions relates to and interweaves with many chapters of this volume including those concerned with kinship, priestly literature, economic life, and women's lives.

Focusing on the lives of women in ancient Israel, Carol Meyers examines in a sophisticated way textual, archaeological, and ethnographic sources. Taking account of the *Tendenz* of various biblical works, she notes that the Bible is a creation, in its current form, of male elites, even while the corpus may well reflect women's stories and concerns. Offhand references to material culture and daily life in biblical sources also reveal the possible realities of women's lives in various settings and periods. Meyers' work complements the essays on methodology and cultural reconstruction contributed to this volume by fellow archaeologists Elizabeth Bloch-Smith and Avraham Faust. Like Francesca Stavrakopoulou, Meyers points to the complex threads in women's religion in which public and private, official and unofficial overlap and interplay. Themes emphasized by Meyers include women's roles in education, the significance of female alliances, and women's economic activities and contributions.

With an explicit interest in the relevance of archaeological evidence for understanding economic realities and shifts in the Iron Age kingdoms of Israel and Judah, J. David Schloen offers a masterful overview of ancient Israelite history and historiography.

Working comparatively, he introduces readers to concepts in the field of economics that have been applied to preindustrial societies. He points to modes of economic integration, for example "reciprocity," "market exchange," "redistribution," and "householding," and explores how these concepts may apply to ancient Israel and Judah. Throughout, he takes account of the tendentiousness of sources, the fragmentary nature of evidence, and scholars' tendencies to employ anachronistic models. His work relates well to many chapters in this volume concerned with archaeology, social history, and the methodological challenges posed by evidence.

A final set of essays addresses artistic expression. With literary sensitivity and deep interest in the comparative study of ancient Near Eastern literatures, Edward L. Greenstein explores the ways in which ancient authors employed "artful language," paying special attention to the function of pieces of verbal art and pointing to their aesthetic and practical cultural roles. He also examines how composers of literature in their own cultural contexts defined various literary forms. Such forms may be distinguished not only by particulars of style, structure, content, or function but also, for example, by the presence of musical accompaniment. Greenstein underscores the importance of varieties of repetition in these literatures. Noting that "words have a mystique" in traditional cultures, he explores the worldviews behind the aesthetics, the relationship between authors and audiences, and the spectrum from oral to written styles. His essay relates well to chapters by Person, Weitzman, and Niditch in asking questions about the relationship between medium, meaning, and context and joins those of Huddlestun, Smith, Walls, and others in its attention to the interrelationships between cultures of the ancient Levant.

In her essay on Persian-period literature, Tamara Cohn Eskenazi thoughtfully analyzes the varied works in the portion of the Hebrew Bible called the Writings or Ketuvim. Attuned to matters of tradition and genre, Eskenazi points to the concerns and contexts that may explain the flowering of literature in this formative period and to ways in which these diverse writings reflect and helped to shape aspects of Jewish culture and identity. She suggests that the works provide a coping mechanism in a time of loss (e.g. Lamentations) and a source of renewal (e.g. Ezra-Nehemiah) and points to certain recurring features: the portrayal of daily life; the description of individual experience in the context of community identity; and the authors' interest in writing itself.

Benjamin G. Wright III explores the diverse corpus of Jewish Hellenistic literature, much of which was written by Greek-speaking Jews. A particularly informative set of writings in Hebrew, Greek, and Aramaic was preserved or composed by members of the Qumran community who took up self-imposed exile by the Dead Sea in the second century BCE. Wright describes how these various writings emerge in particular sociohistorical settings, reflecting and shaping different worldviews that all find a place under the "large tent" of Judaism. Wright pays special attention to matters of genre by setting up five categories of writings, each of which relates in a particular way to the inherited tradition and the earlier corpus of literature preserved in the Hebrew Bible.

Moving from verbal to nonverbal art, Theodore J. Lewis discusses ways in which Yahwistic divinity was imagined and represented. With a comparative and interdisciplinary approach, attention to questions of worldview, and engagement with questions concerning cultural representation and the inventiveness of human imagination, Lewis's essay relates well to many of the essays in the *Companion* volume. Areas explored include the links between written and visual representations of divinity, the ways in which attitudes to representation reflect the orientations of particular biblical writers, and the degree to which abstraction plays a role in representations of divinity.

Taken as a whole, these essays offer a fresh and creative analysis of critical and interrelated topics in the study of ancient Israel. They serve as an exciting window on contemporary dialog concerning the nature of ancient Israelite culture, its multiplicity, its complex relationships to the surrounding Levantine world, its literary and material aspects, and the challenges faced in describing and understanding this ancient culture in its vibrant, experienced, and situated forms.

Part I

Methodology: Questions, Concepts, Approaches, and Tools

A

Contextualizing Israelite Culture

CHAPTER 1

Archaeology
What It Can Teach Us

Elizabeth Bloch-Smith

Archaeological remains and biblical texts constitute independent witnesses to Israelite society. Physical remains offer extensive evidence for reconstructing "ancient Israel"; biblical texts form the basis for the literary construct "biblical Israel." Typically, information derived from the two is harmonized to reconstruct the ancient society. However, studying the data sets independently reveals discrepancies between the two, prompting renewed study of both.

Physical remains are inclusive, generally not manipulated by subsequent peoples, and immeasurably greater in scope than literary accounts. In contrast to texts, which are limited by religious and royal perspectives and agendas, material remains are generated by diverse human groups including rich and poor, males and females, adults and children, and urban and rural populations. These physical manifestations of society, labeled "material culture," enable reconstructing ancient Israelite society from the smallest constituent parts, phytoliths and pots, to integrated cultural systems (e.g., politics, religion and economy). Aspects of life such as daily work routines, the economic system, aesthetics, burial practices, tools and weapons, diet and health, while not the focus of biblical texts, are amply illustrated in the archaeological record.

Material remains permit absolute and relative dating, from specific features to general historical contexts. Unlike texts, for which dating remains a contentious issue, archaeology enables both synchronic and diachronic study of ancient Israel. Changes and developments in Israel including religious practices, which are a focus of the biblical text, are blurred by textual additions and revisions but remain distinct and differentiable in material remains. Archaeological studies enable biblicists to situate biblical Israel within the context of ancient Israel, to hear conversations and pronouncements of biblical authors and editors in their historical contexts.

Archaeology also suggests the period in which a text might have originated, if one accepts that the initial composition of a text derives meaning from historical reality. An

The Wiley Blackwell Companion to Ancient Israel, First Edition. Edited by Susan Niditch.
© 2016 John Wiley & Sons, Ltd. Published 2016 by John Wiley & Sons, Ltd.

argument for the importance of verisimilitude posits that texts written to convey Israel's history initially derived greater impact from known historical referents. By analogy, a text, either historical or satirical, set in the context of the Soviet-American Cold War would resonate for older Americans in a way that it does not for those now under 25. In today's American movies, the enemy is no longer a Soviet spy.

Introduction to Archaeological Methods of Excavation and Interpretation

Archaeology studies the lives and cultures of peoples of the past through retrieval and analysis of physical remains, in conjunction with written testimony, and in interaction with the natural environment. The process begins with a research agenda that determines where to survey and/or dig and the selection of excavation methods. For excavation, as opposed to survey, diachronic goals require smaller excavation areas dug down through multiple occupational phases, while synchronic goals necessitate greater horizontal exposure within a single occupational phase. Interest in detail, now down to the microscopic, forces a slow pace, while an interest in the "big picture" mandates faster excavation for the representative features. Most excavations pursue a combination of diachronic and synchronic goals, with different excavation methods for separate excavation areas. For ancient Israel, comparable to other ancient cultures, archaeological studies focus on single periods (synchronic) as well as developments over time (diachronic), on both the micro and the macro level.

Interpretation of the finds, undertaken both in the course of excavation and subsequently, constitutes the second step. The interpretive process, determining the specific use or function and symbolic value of material remains and architecture, entails several facets. To begin with, the archaeologist defines the research unit or context, such as a house/structure, the settlement, or the region. Archaeologists then look for patterned behavior within the defined unit, a repeating web of relationships among individual elements that establishes a general context and the place and meaning of specific items within that context. For example, a particular pot type that typically appears in a basement room of a house or the hold of a ship functions for storage or for transport. On a higher level of complexity, patterned behavior facilitates reconstructing regional practices or cultural systems (economic, political, social and religious).

A particular ornate column capital employed in elaborate buildings by nation-states both east and west of the Jordan River exemplifies a patterned behavior that conveys political meaning. The distinctively decorated capital signals internationally recognized elite status, probably royalty. At each level of complexity, from the individual item to the cultural system, the interpretation must account for both the range of available material remains and literary evidence.

Interpretation entails consideration of other ancient regional cultures, ancient texts and inscriptions, and ethnographic studies of comparable societies, keeping in mind that the comparative material derives from different cultural contexts. For ancient Israel, studies of contemporary, traditional Cypriot potters elucidate aspects of ancient pottery production. Our understanding of the biblical goddesses Asherah and Astarte draws on

Ugaritic and Phoenician evidence; the Bible refers to them but omits details. Whereas archaeology provides the physical remains, texts and inscriptions add mental components – beliefs and thoughts – as well as otherwise unattainable information such as people's names and specific dates of events. Other ancient cultures and ethnographic studies offer alternative societal models, which may be helpful in evaluating Israelite evidence.

Finally, interpretation benefits from studying the natural world with its resources and constraints such as topography, geology, climate, flora, fauna and water sources. Roads, water availability, and native plants and animals directly affect and determine societal aspects such as settlement location, subsistence strategies, and beliefs and practices stemming from human interaction with the natural environment. Israel's location of sacred sites on elevated ground, purification rituals, sacrificial offerings and the timing and offerings of agricultural and herding festivals exemplify religious features dependent on natural factors.

The archaeological endeavor – excavation and interpretation – is not without limitations. Some limitations stem from the paucity of available evidence. For example, the relatively poorly attested Late Bronze Age and Persian period, preceding and following the Israelite kingdoms of the Iron Age, are less well known than periods with more extensive remains. The small percentage of existent sites that have been excavated and published provide an incomplete, but hopefully representative, picture. The tendency to focus on tells – cities, towns, forts – leaves villages, hamlets, farmsteads and isolated activity areas less well represented and understood. Absolute dating, establishing specific years, persists as an archaeological Achilles' heel. Artifact and epigraphic typologies, datable items such as a royal scarab, and scientific methods such as 14C (carbon fourteen) dating currently provide a time frame but cannot pinpoint a year or even a decade. Archaeologists largely depend on texts for absolute dates. Sennacherib's inscribed and graphic depiction on the Nineveh palace walls of conquering the site of Lachish in 701 BCE correlates with and dates the Lachish Stratum III destruction. However, most of the time, no such explicit correspondence exists between material remains and texts or inscriptions.

The interpretive process further complicates reconstructing Israelite society. First, archaeological remains must be patterned to allow for interpretation, which necessitates multiple occurrences to detect a pattern. The obvious limitation of this interpretive strategy is that it elucidates a general pattern that marginalizes variation and unique occurrences. We reconstruct group but not individual or small-group behaviors. Second, for all our efforts at objectivity, interpretation remains a subjective endeavor colored by a mindset shaped by contemporary culture. For example, our form of government, whether a tribal-based society, a monarchy, or a democracy, may prejudice our understanding and reconstruction of ancient societies and their political structures. Third, vague terminology and inexplicit weighting of physical remains and literary evidence in the interpretive process complicate societal reconstructions. What is the reconstructed entity Merneptah's "Israel" (see below): archaeologically attested "ancient Israel"; "biblical Israel" as a national entity; "biblical Israel" as a religious ethnos; or a harmonized biblical-archaeological Israel, either national or religious? This shortcoming may be remedied through explicit methodological statements and explication of terminology employed.

"Biblical Israel" of the Text and "Ancient Israel" of the Archaeological Remains

A difference of opinion exists among archaeologists regarding the role of Israel in the southern Levant. Characterizing the two extremes, ethnocentric Biblical Archaeologists consider Israel as central and unique, while Syro-Palestinian Archaeologists view Israel as one of several regional kingdoms. The former stress the uniqueness of ancient Israel and rely heavily on the Bible as history to bolster their position. This approach stems from biblical archaeology of the 1950s (a cultural-historical approach), in which the canonical text had primacy of place and archaeology served to elucidate and verify the Bible. For the latter, Syro-Palestinian Archaeologists, the Bible constitutes a critically important cultural artifact that enhances understanding of the general culture but more specifically of those who composed, edited and transmitted the texts. This is not to minimize but to qualify use of biblical texts. Syro-Palestinian Archaeologists recognize that biblical texts and inscriptions contribute information irretrievable from material culture alone such as intangible facets of culture, beliefs and *mentalité* (e.g., ancestral stories, metaphors, myths of origins or qualifications for priesthood) plus specific information otherwise lost (e.g., tax assessments). Without texts, we might not know that Israelite society was patriarchal, patrilineal, and patrimonial. Both avenues of study, with the Bible either central or supplemental to the archaeological endeavor, contribute to the emerging picture of ancient and biblical Israel. However, the cultural presuppositions of each group, with consequent selectivity of cited data, must be kept in mind when utilizing publications and considering societal reconstructions.

The first extrabiblical reference to Israel comes from Pharaoh Merneptah's mention at the end of the thirteenth century BCE of "Israel" on a stele celebrating his conquests (for Merneptah, see also John Huddlestun's essay in this volume). Accordingly, studies of early Israel begin with the Iron Age I rural settlement in the Cisjordanian highlands, the biblical Israelite heartland. Scholarly consensus dates the southern Levantine Iron Age from ca. 1200–586 BCE. The periodization essentially remains as established by William Foxwell Albright in the early twentieth century CE, though specific beginning and ending dates are debated and varying historical monikers are used.

The approximately 400-year period of the Iron Age is divided into Iron I and Iron II, with further subdivisions. Dates for the subdivisions, dependent on events in Israel's history and so insignificant for Philistines, Transjordanian nations, and the Phoenicians, reflect the history and bias of the discipline (see also J. David Schloen's essay in this volume). Current debates regarding periodization perpetuate the biblical Israelite perspective. The Iron Age traditionally begins with the eclipse of eastern Mediterranean empires ca. 1200 BCE (A. Mazar 295–6). Israel Finkelstein and Nadav Na'aman propose revising the periodization in conformance with a more ethnocentric view of history by beginning the period ca. 1150 only after the Egyptian withdrawal with the emergence of regional cultures, including Israel (16). Changing dates to focus on Israelite events obscures the general eastern Mediterranean context in which Israel plays a minor part.

Based on Merneptah's testimony, archaeological studies of ancient Israel commence with the onset of the Iron Age. Iron I begins with extensive rural settlement in the central highlands (ca. 1200/1125–1000/900 BCE). Those who accept the canonical unilinear history of biblical Israel ("traditionalists") attribute these settlements to the "conquest and settlement" generations detailed in the books of Joshua and Judges. While settlement is evident, widespread conquests dated to a single period are unattested. Iron II has been variously divided based on biblical events and archaeological remains. Iron IIA (1000/930–900/840 BCE) represents the "united monarchy" for traditionalists who begin the period around 1000 BCE and credit David and Solomon with the intensified urbanization seen in this period (the "high chronology"). Advocates of a ca. 930 BCE start for the period (the "low chronology") attribute the spur in development to the northern Omride kings, Omri and Ahab, rather than David and Solomon (see Brad Kelle's essay in this volume). Iron IIB (900/840–722 BCE), the period of "the Divided Kingdom" for traditionalists, follows Iron IIA and continues to the fall of the northern kingdom of Israel to the Assyrians. Iron IIC (722–587/6 BCE) ends with the devastating Babylonian campaign of Nebuchadnezzar and the destruction of Jerusalem. Iron IIB and IIC dates are pegged to the specific years of historical events described in the Bible and noted in Assyrian and Babylonian royal annals. While debate continues over the absolute dates, archaeologists are refining our knowledge of the southern Levant by focusing on subphases within periods (e.g., Iron IA and IB), transitions and regional variations within periods.

The most basic units of our study remain elusive. Based on archaeological findings, even in conjunction with biblical testimony, self-defined members of the Israelite religious community remain indistinguishable from nonmembers (with the exception of the Philistines/Sea Peoples). Select items such as collar-rim storejars and pillared houses designated by contemporary scholars as markers of biblical Israelites lack distinctive Israelite markings and biblical mention as an ethnic marker. Furthermore, both the storejar and pillared house occur outside Israelite territory and their functional adaptation to a highland lifestyle favored use by non-Israelites as well as Israelites. Even abstinence from eating pig, an Israelite prohibition according to the Bible, characterized highland settlers of the preceding Late Bronze Age and so would not distinguish a biblical Israelite from any other highland non-Israelite predecessor or contemporary. Pig bones, indicative of human consumption, while retrieved in negligible quantities from both Bronze and Iron Age highland settlements, constitute nearly 20 percent of the faunal material from early Philistine sites situated in the coastal region and so distinguish Philistines from non-Philistines but not Israelites from "Canaanites" or other non-Israelites.

Given these limitations, is it possible to identify ancient and biblical Israelites in the archaeological record? Biblical texts regard select settlements as Israelite, including Dan on the northern border, the fortress at Lachish, and Jerusalem as the capital city of Judah. However, even within these royal and administrative settlements, houses and commercial establishments may have belonged to foreigners, including merchants and mercenaries. Unless clearly indicated to the contrary, settlements within the heartland of the Israelite and Judahite kingdoms are regarded as representative of biblical and ancient Israel even though they likely included non-Israelites.

Reconstructing Ancient and Biblical Israel from an Archaeological Perspective

Material remains elucidate ancient cultures from the individual item to the web of elements that demonstrate systemic behaviors such as economic and religious systems. On the most basic level, physical remains illustrate specific facets of ancient life. Examples range from flint sickle blades and city gate plans to personal stamp seals found in Jerusalem of King Zedekiah's court officials, Jucal, son of Shelemiah, and Gedaliah, son of Pashhur (Jer. 37:3; 38:1; E. Mazar 67–71). Current innovative work applies scientific techniques to the retrieval and analysis of archaeological remains, often at the microscopic level. Archaeobotanists determined that grains retrieved from the 604 BCE destruction level at Ashkelon included a high admixture of weeds (25 percent) and infestation by the granary weevil. Within the historical context, the excavators interpreted these findings as indicating haste in harvesting and poor storage facilities attributed to urgent preparations in anticipation of the Babylonian attack (Weiss et al. 595–6). In another example, residue analysis of Philistine cultic chalices excavated from a pit at Yavneh showed that the vessels functioned as incense altars to burn hallucination-inducing floral substances (Namdar et al. 169–70). Archaeology has traditionally served to verify site identification but the procedure suffers from circular reasoning. Based on the biblical narrative, scholars determine the site's period(s) of occupation and then search for a settlement in the appropriate vicinity that satisfies the dating criteria.

Archaeology's value for studying ancient Israel far exceeds site identification and illustration of details. On a higher level of cultural complexity, patterned remains demonstrate cultural systems – economic, political, social, religious and symbolic/ *mentalité*. For facets of society such as the economy, which are not the focus of the biblical text, archaeology provides much-needed evidence. Regarding religion, the Bible is a theological document and so generally regarded as Israel's definitive religious history. However, late Iron Age and subsequent perspectives retrojected into Israel's early history to explain the later course of events obscure or obfuscate both chronological developments and varying regional practices. Here archaeology plays a critical role as an independent witness. Datable material remains preserve actual religious practices, demonstrate chronological developments and regional variation, and provide the general historical contexts for the religious literary activity.

The Tel Arad temple exemplifies a disjunction between text and artifact; it illustrates praxis as opposed to promulgation and provides the context in which texts were written and to which they were responding. According to the Books of Kings, the late eighth- to late seventh-century BCE Judahite kings Hezekiah and Josiah tore down and defiled altars and high places to restrict worship with sacrifice to the Jerusalem temple (2 Kings 18:22; 23:5–20). However, the Bible omits mention of the royally sponsored temple with a sacrificial altar constructed within a Judahite military fort on the southern border at Arad. Seventh- to sixth-century BCE correspondence between the local commander Eliashib and his Jerusalem superior confirms both the fort's official status and Yahweh as the resident deity (Dobbs-Allsopp et al. 31–74). This alternative worship site consisted of a tripartite temple (ca. 12 × 16 meters), somewhat smaller than Solomon's Temple in Jerusalem, with an elevated, focal niche housing two incense altars and one, or more likely two, standing stones (*maṣṣēbâ/maṣṣēbôt*). The two incense altars, one larger than the other, enhance the likelihood of two stones displayed in the niche. The larger stone or stele stood 1 meter high, with flat faces, a rounded top, and smoothed sides retaining red paint. A second smaller stone of comparable shape was found plastered into the niche wall. In the courtyard, a large stone altar (ca. 2.5 meters square) accommodated animal sacrifices. Foundation and demise dates for the temple are debated. Construction occurred in the tenth or eighth century BCE and the *maṣṣēbâ/ôt* stood through the end of the eighth or as late as the sixth century BCE (Aharoni, "Excavations"; Aharoni, "Arad"; Ussishkin 149–51). All agree the temple functioned in the eighth century BCE. The existence of this royally sanctioned border temple conforms to the practice of marking and protecting borders with temples, as illustrated by the Israelite king Jeroboam's temples at Dan and Bethel (1 Kings 12:26–31). Depending on its dates, this temple outside of Jerusalem, in a royal fort and administrative center, suggests that Hezekiah and Josiah's alleged cultic reforms perhaps promoted royal oversight of the cult rather than exclusive worship in Jerusalem.

This temple challenges the canonical biblical picture of centralized worship of a single deity both in its very existence – an alternative, royally sponsored site of worship and sacrifice – and by the two stones standing in the niche. Some biblical passages recognize *maṣṣēbôt*/standing stones as part of the Yahwistic cult. Genesis 35:14 describes Jacob's *maṣṣēbâ* at Bethel and Isaiah 19:19–20 envisions a Yahwistic *maṣṣēbâ* erected on the border between Israel and Egypt. Passages in Deuteronomy that call for the smashing or otherwise eradication of *maṣṣēbôt* refer specifically to stones dedicated to foreign deities, not Yahweh (Deut. 7:5; 12:2–3). Most other passages prohibit the practice but do not identify the deity. No matter who the referent is, at some point or in some circles the practice that continued from the Bronze Age fell from favor (Lev. 26:1; Deut. 16:21–22; Mic. 5:12; 2 Kings 18:4; 23:14). Based on the Arad evidence, the stone itself may have become an object of worship and a challenge to Yahweh's exclusive residence in Jerusalem, prompting rejection of standing stones within certain segments of society.

Lacking explicit evidence naming the deities manifest in the stones, the identification of the larger and smaller stones respectively with the masculine god Yahweh and a female or lesser deity such as Asherah remains tentative and debated (Zevit 262; see further the essays by Mark Smith and Francesca Stavrakopoulou in this volume). Biblical and inscriptional testimonies associate Asherah with Yahweh and situate the goddess's symbol within Yahweh's temple in Jerusalem. Even if the supreme deity Yahweh has incorporated her and her powers (Smith 48), she retains a distinctive symbol known by her name. Inscriptions from the first quarter of the eighth century BCE from the desert caravanserai site of Kuntillet 'Ajrud invoke "Yahweh and his a/Asherah," "Yahweh of Teiman and [his] a/Asherah" and "Yahweh of Shomron (Samaria) and his a/Asherah" (Meshel; Dobbs-Allsopp et al. 285–97). From the last quarter of the eighth century BCE, an inscription or graffito from Khirbet el-Qom Tomb 3 also appeals to Yahweh and his a/Asherah (Dobbs-Allsopp et al. 408–14). Attestations to their relationship are not restricted to extrabiblical sources. 2 Kings acknowledges A/asherah manifest in the form of a wooden pole that stood and was worshipped within the Jerusalem temple; cultic reforms in the second half of the seventh century BCE attributed to Josiah mandated the destruction of temple objects dedicated to the goddess (2 Kings 21:7; 23:4, 6). Yahweh and A/asherah's association, as known from inscriptions and the Bible, explicitly in the Jerusalem temple, bolsters the argument for identifying the second, smaller stone in the Arad temple niche with the goddess.

Analyzing the biblical and archaeological data sets independently produces a different picture than that offered by those who advocate a composite picture. Harmonizing the evidence suggests that the Arad temple constituted royal infidelity, an abrogation of Jerusalem's cultic exclusivity. Comparable temples at the northern kingdom's border sites of Dan and Bethel were disparaged (1 Kings 12:28–30). Perhaps biblical authors omitted mention of the Arad temple in deference to the Davidic kings of Judah. Not harmonizing the two data sets yields a variant picture of this stage and of the general evolution of Yahwistic religion. Rather than viewing exclusive worship of Yahweh in the eighth- to sixth-century BCE Jerusalem temple as the norm, this temple illustrates Israelite worship, at disparate sites, of multiple deities manifest in physical forms, including standing stones. Biblical references to Israelites, including kings worshipping Baal, Asherah, the host of heaven, and the Queen of Heaven, in Jerusalem and at shrines throughout the country (2 Kings 23:4–6; Jer. 7:17–8; 44:17), suggest that Israelites of that period worshipped multiple deities. While select voices denounced polytheism as apostasy, it appears to have been common practice among the populace and royalty alike.

Might Judean pillar figurines (JPFs) also represent A/asherah? Their production began in the late tenth or ninth century BCE and ended in the early sixth century BCE, with their heyday in the eighth and seventh centuries BCE (see also Francesca Stavrakopoulou's essay in this volume). The earliest examples appeared at Tel Qasile on the coast, in the Shephelah, and at northern Negev sites but soon spread into the Israelite highlands (Kletter, *Figurines*, 40–1 and Appendix 1). The crude terracotta female image stands approximately 6 inches high, with a slightly flaring pole-shaped body, a prominent bosom supported by clasped hands, and either a pinched or a molded head. Petrography indicates regional production; Jerusalem and Tel Ira JPFs utilized Jerusalem vicinity terra-rossa clay and Negev loess clay respectively (Kletter, "Between text and theology," 188). Kletter cautiously estimates "a few dozen moulds for all the JPFs [heads]" (Kletter, *Figurines*, 52; "Between text and theology," 189). The small numbers of molds, petrographic evidence, plus regional differences in pillar manufacture and head depiction attest to regionalized production in the Jerusalem area and in the Negev rather than localized or individualized manufacture (Kletter, *Figurines*, 188–9).

Whom does the figurine portray? Circular reasoning claims this is not a plaything because toys are rarely attested in the ancient world, though JPFs have been interpreted as the ancient equivalent of a Barbie/Dolly Parton doll. The lack of clothing, relatively sudden appearance and end with Jerusalem's destruction, distribution throughout Judah, and managed production with limited variability suggest the figurine represents more than just a plaything. The fact that the anthropomorphic part of the figurine is naked (jewelry and makeup are occasionally added with paint but not clothing) argues for its divine status. Mortal women wore clothing; to be exposed was a source of shame and humiliation inflicted upon the likes of prisoners and the dead (Asher-Greve and

Sweeney 126–38; see also Gen. 3:10). Among goddesses, Asherah is the most likely identity as her symbol, a pole, stood in the Jerusalem temple during this period. While functioning as a stand, the pole or tree-shaped lower body of the JPF certainly evokes the goddess's symbol. Furthermore, Ugaritic texts inform us that Asherah mothered 70 children (KTU 1.4 vi:46, edited by Parker). The prominence of our figurine's mammary glands establishes her sex and links her to explicitly female biological activities – bearing children and lactation. This sexual role bolsters the identification of the figurine with Asherah. Alternatively, the figurine may represent an intercessory or "good luck" figure, perhaps a divinized ancestor. Israelites considered their deceased to be divine, 'ĕlōhîm (1 Sam. 28:13; Isa. 8:19) and tərāpîm, lifelike images of divinized ancestors, may have performed divinatory functions (Gen. 31:19, 30; 1 Sam. 19:13–16; Ezek. 21:26; Zech. 10:2). However, the controlled, centralized production and relative standardization of the figurines argue against their identification with individualized ancestors. While the identity of the figurine remains inconclusive, we may speculate about its function. Given the prominence of the bosom, perhaps royal authorities mass-produced these figurines to assert the positive value of women nursing their children, thereby promoting the health of the child and protecting mothers from medical complications accompanying pregnancies and births by reducing the frequency of pregnancies.

At the highest level of societal complexity, archaeologists reconstruct integrated systems. "Household archaeology," with combined social, economic, religious and political facets, exemplifies the approach and its application (see also the essay by Francesca Stavrakopoulou in this volume). Lawrence Stager's 1985 pioneering article modeled this approach to interpreting archaeological remains by incorporating perspectives from the social sciences, historiography and biblical studies. Stager presented Israel's settlements and dwellings as expressions of a social, political and economic settlement strategy for subsistence living in the Cisjordanian central highlands. Stager reconstructed a fully furnished and functioning highland pillared house; Carol Meyers fleshed out the individuals living and working in the house, focusing on women (see further Meyers' essay in this volume). Based on archaeological remains, ancient texts and iconography, Human Relations Area Files data (a database compiled by an academic consortium to study human cultures and societies around the world, past and present), and Middle Eastern studies, Meyers' 1990s work identified gendered labor groups, such as women who passed hours together in the tedious and time-consuming daily tasks of grinding grain and baking bread (Meyers 430–2).

More recently, Yuval Gadot and Assaf Yasur-Landau recreated life in late Iron I Megiddo based on a spacious house that violently burned and collapsed, trapping residents inside with all the house contents (Building 00/K/10; Level K-4). They reconstructed behavioral, social, economic and symbolic aspects to tease out the "habitus," the organizing "set of ideas, values and perceptions held by members of the society" (Gadot and Yasur-Landau 583). Four or five adults, one child and one infant died in the conflagration. For the authors, these individuals, presumed resident kin, constituted a joint or extended rather than a nuclear family. Spatial analysis, a study of the distribution of all objects from the nine rooms and courtyard, identified a kitchen, a storage room and activity areas for weaving (in conjunction with food preparation), with cultic objects scattered through the house. Exterior spaces served for flint knapping, the production of bone and antler tools, and the disposal of household trash. The excavators presume traditional gendered roles for the adults in the house. They note the food processing items found with the 30–40-year-old female in the central courtyard, though other items attest to a multifunction space. Similarly, the adult accompanied by a 0–5-year-old and a 5–7-year-old in a room devoted to cooking and weaving is suggested to be a woman. On the conceptual level, the authors distinguish between private and public space, between internal women's work spaces as private domain with limited and controlled access, and external or outside public space not subject to gendered work or restrictions (Gadot and Yasur-Landau 587–96). While the Bible presents and promotes domestic maintenance roles for women, including cooking, baking, spinning and weaving (Jer. 7:18; Lev. 26:26; 2 Kings 23:7; 2 Sam. 3:29), presuming the Megiddo individuals conform to these biblical dictates perpetuates the biblical gendered roles and obscures actual practices.

The Arad fort with its temple provides another locus of integrated systems, in this case, military, political, economic, administrative and religious. Army commanders taking orders from Jerusalem directed military operations in the region, including moving troops to counter Edom (Ostracon 24). The fort also served as a redistribution point for collected foodstuffs based on jar labels, inventories and receipts, and for the disbursement of bread, grain, flour, wine, vinegar and oil to Kittim mercenaries and others (Ostraca 1–14, 18, 22, 25, 31, 49 and 60). As a religious center, stones in the niche marked the manifestation of the deity/ies to whom sacrifices were offered on the courtyard altar. We lack information identifying the deity/ies worshipped in the early centuries but military correspondence of the late seventh and early sixth centuries BCE invokes only Yahweh (Ostraca 16, 18, 21).

The temple also served a critical function in the Israelite conception of where Yahweh was manifest, of national territorial boundaries, and of Yahweh's covenantal relationship with his people. This temple, comparable to Jeroboam's border temples, signified the deity's proprietary claim to the territory. Temples situated at national boundaries, such as Arad, marked the outermost of a series of concentric circles in which the deity was made manifest at borders and other liminal spaces. Beginning with the innermost circle or family home, sacred texts denoting divine presence were to be written on the doorpost of the house and on the compound gate, serving to demarcate internal, protected space from external space (Deut. 6:4–9). On the civic level, as at Tel Dan and Bethsaida, the deity and perhaps the divinized ancestors stood in the form of maṣṣēbôt or stele in the city gate, the liminal zone separating protected from vulnerable space (Biran). At the national level, temples including those at Dan, Bethel and Arad, and Isaiah's envisioned maṣṣēbâ (Isa. 19:19–20), delineated the boundary of Yahweh's territory and, by extension, his people. This proposed conceptualization demonstrates the need to consider archaeological remains in conjunction with literary evidence to reconstruct early Israelite beliefs.

One advantage of archaeological remains over textual evidence is the relative ease of determining dates. Excavated archaeological assemblages typically represent a single period of deposition datable by material culture such as local and imported pottery, distinctive items known from other contexts, architectural details, and by scientific techniques such as 14C dating. Subsequent intrusions are generally both identifiable and datable. By contrast, the repeated reworking of biblical texts complicates disentangling distinct literary strands and assigning dates. Although scholars have made such lofty claims for archaeology, the Arad Temple constitutes an obvious exception. The temple, which was excavated in the early 1960s, had partially collapsed into an underlying water channel, complicating the dating of the successive phases of construction, use and dismantling/destruction. Over the last half-century, improved excavation techniques and recording procedures, refined pottery typologies and scientific dating methods have significantly bettered the dating of archaeological remains.

Historical contexts dated by material culture may assist in identifying and dating biblical accounts if geopolitical reality or verisimilitude underlies the composition of texts. If so, the vicissitudes of Ammonite and Moabite control in Transjordan enable the dating of the composition of texts depicting Moab or Ammon as the threat or oppressor. Changes in settlement distribution, specific objects including pottery and statuary, inscribed items, and the Mesha Stele suggest that through the Iron IIB-C period (ca. ninth through the first quarter of the sixth century BCE), Moab followed by Ammon controlled the territory across the Jordan River from Jericho, rendering Moab (Iron IIB) and only subsequently Ammon (Iron IIC) a threat to the Israelites (Herr 150–1, 168–73; see also the essay by Song-Mi Suzie Park in this volume). This evidence parallels First Isaiah's view of an expansive Moab followed by Jeremiah's expanded Ammon (Isa. 15; compare Isa. 16:8–9 and Jer. 49:3 regarding Heshbon). Accordingly, the Judges 3 story of Ehud and Eglon, king of Moab, may derive from a period of Moabite dominance in Iron IIB, while Jephthah's battle with the Ammonites in Judges 11–12 more likely originates in late Iron IIB or Iron IIC.

The Mesha Stele, commemorating King Mesha of Moab's mid-ninth century BCE defeat of the king of Israel, refers to "the men of Gad" and their involvement with Israel.

> Now the men of Gad (had) dwelt in the land of 'Aṭarot from of old and the King of Israel built for (them) 'Aṭarot. And I fought against the city and took it and I killed all the people … and I caused men of Šaron and men of Maḥarot to dwell in it. (Mesha Inscription (MI), lines 10–13; trans. in Routledge 135–6)

Mesha's "men of Gad" are likely synonymous with the biblical tribe of Gad as they inhabited the same territory. Based on the Mesha Stele, it is arguable that the Gadites did not join Israel until the early ninth century BCE when the Omrides conquered the region and built the city of 'Aṭarot for them (MI, lines 10–11). The relationship ended abruptly with Mesha's conquest in the mid-ninth century BCE. According to this scenario, Gad affiliated with Israel for less than 50 years and only *after* the foundation of the northern kingdom. Biblical authors and editors selectively retrojected the tribe into premonarchic history (Gen. 30:11; Num. 1:14; Deut. 33:20–1). The Judges 5 call to battle includes the Transjordanian tribes of Reuben and Gilead but Gad does not appear among the ten tribes mentioned. Therefore, this list may predate Gad's Israelite affiliation in the early ninth century BCE.

As evident in examples cited, archaeological and biblical data are incomplete, subject to interpretation, and variously weighted in the interpretive process. These limitations give rise to varying reconstructions of both ancient and biblical Israel. Discussions of biblical Israel's ethnogenesis are illustrative. Did biblical Israel enter Canaan as a nation that was culturally distinct from the indigenous "Canaanites"; did it emerge in a relatively quick and radical departure from the indigenous culture; or was ethnogenesis and religious differentiation a gradual process? Avraham Faust, an archaeologist, exemplifies proponents of the appearance of a culturally distinct Israel in Iron I (see his essay in this volume). Faust argued that Merneptah's "Israel" aspired to an egalitarian ethos by the late thirteenth century BCE. The purported religious value was communicated through architecture and material culture that signaled no status differentiation such as the four-room house, undecorated pottery and simple burials (though none have been found in the central highlands), and is indicated by the absence of high status markers such as decorated and imported pottery. This aspiration, not an actualized reality but a shared ethos, distinguished highland Israelites from the Egypto-Canaanites and, later, the Philistines (Faust 159–63, 221–30).

Countering Faust's proposed egalitarian ethos, functional rather than ideological explanations attribute these same traits to the highland settlers' socioeconomic lifestyle. The quest for "early Israel" is further hampered by our inability to distinguish a "Canaanite" from an "early Israelite." If both peoples inhabited the central highlands, as the Bible describes, then Faust's ethos characterized Israelites and their neighbors alike and so does not serve as a distinguishing trait. Strikingly, Faust insists his "Israel" is biblical Israel based on geographical location but makes no mention of religion or lineage, the distinguishing features according to the Bible.

Raz Kletter also advocated the appearance of a fully formed Israel appearing on the scene, but took a different tack. He effectively eliminated the transitional phase of Iron I to argue for the appearance of a distinctive biblical Israel in Iron II. In discussing Iron I interments, Kletter assigned burials with form and finds derivative of Later Bronze Age culture to Late Bronze Age "Canaanites" and burials with affinities to Iron II practices to Iron II "Israelites," effectively eliminating continuity or overlap in Iron I to create a *de novo* distinctive Israel in Iron IIA (Kletter, "People"). Restoring the admittedly few Iron I tombs to their rightful chronological context demonstrates the gradual evolution of burial practices from the Late Bronze Age into Iron II (Bloch-Smith).

Proponents of the gradual emergence of biblical Israel focus on continuity of material culture from the Late Bronze Age into the Iron Age and especially the gradual evolution of religious beliefs and practices stemming from Israel's "Canaanite" or West Semitic heritage (Dever; Smith). Merneptah's late thirteenth-century BCE "Israel" (El worshippers) is not necessarily "biblical Israel" if the latter identifies itself as a community devoted to the worship of *Yahweh*. Relying primarily on Ugaritic and biblical texts, Mark Smith reconstructs a lengthy period of convergence and differentiation from the Late Bronze Age through the Iron Age leading to Israelite monotheism (see his essay in this volume). Smith notes continuity from the earlier into the later period evident in worship of the indigenous deities El, Baal and Asherah and in technical terminology for cultic sacrifices and personnel. Archaeological evidence substantiates Israel's continuation of Bronze Age cultic practices. High places/bāmôt, bull figurines, animal sacrifice on stone altars, standing stones, incense altars and the cherub throne exemplify Bronze Age elements featured in the early Israelite cult (Nakhai; Zevit). Both Tel Dan and Arad's sacred areas include elevated sacred space, standing stones, stone altars for sacrifice and incense altars (Biran; Aharoni, "Arad"). Biblical texts suggest the persistence of these practices at least until the cultic reforms attributed to the Judahite kings Hezekiah and Josiah in the late eighth and second half of the seventh century BCE respectively (2 Kings 18:4; 23:8, 12, 15). Both archaeology and texts support a reconstruction of a Late Bronze Age "Israel" (Merneptah's "Israel") that gradually becomes "biblical Israel" though assimilating or renouncing indigenous gods and religious practices for the exclusive worship of the foreign god Yahweh.

A second example revolves around the role of the canonical text in interpreting religious features, particularly those that deviate from the biblical ideal. Consider the horned-god stele from Bethsaida and the terracotta horned deities of Qitmit. From a biblical perspective, these depictions of horned gods, that recall Bronze Age horned deities, violate the commandment (of indeterminate date) forbidding images and so must represent foreign deities. Alternatively, given these objects' provenance from sites near or at Israel's and Judah's borders, respectively, they may be foreign-influenced Israelite depictions. Other evidence from these sites may be argued to support either position. In this example, the role of the Bible in the interpretive process dictated the outcome. Questions surrounding the horned deities and Israel's ethnogenesis illustrate the value of evaluating the physical evidence and literary testimony separately and explicitly acknowledging their relative roles in reconstructing Israelite society.

Archaeology offers an independent witness to and alternative perspective on ancient Israel, and the more perspectives, the better our chance of approximating historical reality. Viewing the archaeological and biblical pictures side by side shows convergences and differences. In addition, the archaeological picture fills in elements either omitted or sketchily drawn in the biblical portrait. The chronological schema afforded by archaeology assists in dating the composition of and later additions to biblical texts. Archaeology also provides a tangible experience of the world of ancient Israel, grounding and enlivening the Israelites and their neighbors with the physical remnants of their everyday lives. Through this engagement with the realia of ancient Israel, the significance of the ancient context, and, by extension, the modern context, comes to the fore in interpreting biblical texts.

Bibliography

Aharoni, Yohanan. "Excavations at Tel Arad: Preliminary report on the second season." *Israel Exploration Journal* 17 (1967): 233–49. Archaeological report detailing the temple remains.

Aharoni, Yohanan. "Arad: Its inscriptions and temple." *Biblical Archaeologist* 31 (1968): 2–32. Popular account of the temple and the inscriptions.

Asher-Greve, Julia and Deborah Sweeney. "On nakedness, nudity, and gender in Egyptian and Mesopotamian art." In Silvia Schroer (ed.), *Images and Gender: Contributions to the Hermeneutics of Reading Ancient Art* (pp. 125–76). Orbis Biblicus et Orientalis 220. Fribourg: Academic Press, 2006. Discussion of nakedness and nudity, functional and symbolic, among Israel's neighbors.

Biran, Avraham. "Sacred spaces: Of standing stones, high places and cult objects at Tel Dan." *Biblical Archaeology Review* 24 (1998): 38–45, 70. Popular account of the Tel Dan cultic remains.

Bloch-Smith, Elizabeth. "Resurrecting the Iron I dead." *Israel Exploration Journal* 54 (2004): 77–91. Response to Kletter, "People," regarding Iron I burials and their import.

Dever, William. "Cultural continuity, ethnicity in the archaeological record, and the question of Israelite origins." *Eretz Israel* 24 (1993): 22*–33*. A proponent of Israel's gradual adoption of religious practices favored in the Bible.

Dobbs-Allsopp, F. W., J. J. Roberts, C. L. Seow, and R. E. Whitaker. *Hebrew Inscriptions: Texts from the Biblical Period of the Monarchy with Concordance.* New Haven: Yale University Press, 2005. Hebrew inscriptions with English translations, transliterations, and commentary.

Faust, Avraham. *Israel's Ethnogenesis: Settlement, Interaction, Expansion and Resistance.* London: Equinox, 2006. A proponent of early Israel as a distinctive nation comparable to the biblical description.

Finkelstein, Israel and Nadav Na'aman. "Introduction: From nomadism to monarchy – the state of research in 1992." In Israel Finkelstein and Nadav Na'aman (eds), *From Nomadism to Monarchy: Archaeological and Historical Aspects of Early Israel* (pp. 9–17). Jerusalem: Yad Izhak Ben-Zvi and Israel Exploration Society, 1994. History and archaeology of premonarchic Israel.

Gadot, Yuval and Assaf Yasur-Landau. "Beyond finds: Reconstructing life in the courtyard building of Level K-4." In Israel Finkelstein, David Ussishkin, and Baruch Halpern (eds), *Megiddo IV: The 1998–2002 Seasons* (pp. 583–600). Tel Aviv: Institute of Archaeology, Tel Aviv University, 2006. An entry in the technical publication of the Megiddo 1998–2002 seasons.

Herr, Larry. "The Iron Age II period: Emerging nations." *Biblical Archaeologist* 60 (1997): 114–83. An overview of Iron II, southern Levantine archaeology.

Kletter, Raz. *The Judean Pillar-Figurines and the Archaeology of Asherah.* British Archaeological Reports International Series 636. Oxford: Tempus Reparatum, 1996. Technical report of Judean pillar-figurines.

Kletter, Raz. "Between text and theology: The pillar figurines from Judah and the Asherah." In A. Mazar and E. Mathias (eds), *Studies in the Archaeology of the Iron Age in Israel and Jordan* (pp. 177–214). Journal for the Study of the Old Testament, suppl. 331. Sheffield: Sheffield Academic Press, 2001.

Kletter, Raz. "People without burials? The lack of Iron I burials in the central highlands of Palestine." *Israel Exploration Journal* 52 (2002): 28–48. A proponent of early Israel as a distinctive nation comparable to the biblical description.

Mazar, Amihai. *Archaeology of the Land of the Bible 10,000–586 BCE.* New York: Doubleday, 1990. Overview of the archaeology of ancient Israel.

Mazar, Eilat. *The Palace of King David: Excavations at the Summit of the City of David: Preliminary Report of Seasons 2005–2007.* Jerusalem: Shoham Academic Research and Publication, 2009. Summary of Mazar's finds and her interpretations.

Meshel, Zev. *Kuntillet 'Ajrud: A Religious Centre from the Time of the Judean Monarchy on the Border of Sinai.* Jerusalem: Israel Museum, 1978. An illustrated museum catalog.

Meyers, Carol. "Material remains and social relations: Women's culture in agrarian households of the Iron Age." In William Dever and Seymour Gitin (eds), *Symbiosis, Symbolism, and the Power of the Past: Canaan, Ancient Israel, and Their Neighbors from the Late Bronze Age through Roman Palaestina* (pp. 425–44). Winona Lake, IN: Eisenbrauns, 2003. An archaeologically based reconstruction of women's lives in agrarian households.

Nakhai, Beth Alpert. *Archaeology and the Religions of Canaan and Israel.* Boston: American Schools of Oriental Research, 2001. Middle Bronze through Iron Age religious practices based on archaeological evidence.

Namdar, Dvory, Ronny Neumann, and Steve Weiner. "Residue analysis of chalices from the repository pit." In Raz Kletter, Irit Ziffer, and Wolfgang Zwickel (eds), *Yavneh I: The Excavation of the "Temple Hill" Repository Pit and the Cult Stands* (pp. 167–73). Fribourg: Academic Press, 2010. Technical residue analysis report.

Parker, Simon B. *Ugaritic Narrative Poetry*. Atlanta: Society of Biblical Literature, 1997. Collection of the most important epic poetry from Ugarit.

Routledge, Bruce Edward. *Moab in the Iron Age: Hegemony, Polity, Archaeology*. Philadelphia: University of Pennsylvania Press, 2004.

Smith, Mark. *The Early History of God: Yahweh and the Other Deities in Ancient Israel*. 2nd edn. Grand Rapids, MI: Eerdmans, 2002. Accessible discussion of evolution of Israelite religion.

Stager, Lawrence. "The archaeology of the family in ancient Israel." *Bulletin of the American Schools of Oriental Research* 260 (1985): 1–18. Archaeology, texts, and social science insights combined to reconstruct Israelite families and culture.

Ussishkin, David. "The date of the Israelite shrine at Arad." *Israel Exploration Journal* 38 (1988): 142–57. Challenges Aharoni's date for the Arad shrine.

Weiss, Ehud, Mordechai Kislev, and Yael Mahler-Slasky. "Plant remains." In Lawrence Stager, Daniel Master, and J. David Schloen (eds), *Ashkelon 3: The Seventh Century BC* (pp. 591–613). Winona Lake, IN: Eisenbrauns, 2011. Technical report in the Ashkelon excavation publication.

Zevit, Ziony. *The Religions of Ancient Israel: A Synthesis of Parallactic Approaches*. New York: Continuum, 2001. Comprehensive summary of evidence regarding religious practices with author's interpretations.

CHAPTER 2

Israel in Its Neighboring Context

Song-Mi Suzie Park

S tories told about neighboring peoples often say as much about the story-makers as they do about the groups who surround them. Tales of discord, rivalry and friendship all reveal a people's fears and aspirations – who they think they are and who they want to be. Comparison with the archaeological record may provide some reference when reading texts, but we must remember that this too is a story, albeit one composed of bones and potsherds. This essay examines the neighboring states around Israel and how these groups are described, depicted and characterized in the stories in the Hebrew Bible, which remains the main source of knowledge concerning these nations. Of particular focus will be narratives that describe the interactions between Israelite heroes and the eponymous ancestors of Israel's neighboring groups. These stories about familial relationships and interactions are not just entertaining tales, but important reflections of how Israel viewed and understood others and, therefore, itself. By looking at the sometimes inaccurate, biased narratives about these nations, what is revealed is not a historically precise account of these groups, but a self-portrait of Israel.

Amorites and the Canaanites

Israelite identity was formulated and maintained by contrasts drawn with the Canaanites and, by extension, the Amorites – two groups that are frequently confused in the biblical text. At points, the Amorites are envisioned as a subset of the Canaanites. For example, in the Table of Nations in Genesis 10, Canaan is said to be the grandson of Noah, the son of Ham, from whom the Jebusites, Amorites and Hivites, among others, are descended (Gen. 10:15–19). Other passages, however, depict the Amorites and the Canaanites as equivalent or interchangeable (e.g., Amos 2:10); while still other texts, such as Exodus 33:2, name the Amorites as one of the groups along with the Canaanites, Hittites and Jebusites that the Lord will drive out.

The question of distinction is related to questions of origins. The oldest references to Amorites in Mesopotamian literature refer to the Amorites as MART.TU in Sumerian

The Wiley Blackwell Companion to Ancient Israel, First Edition. Edited by Susan Niditch.
© 2016 John Wiley & Sons, Ltd. Published 2016 by John Wiley & Sons, Ltd.

or *Ammuru(m)* in Akkadian, meaning West. Most scholars maintain that the Amorites emigrated from Syria to Mesopotamia at the beginning of the second millennium (Liverani 106; Shoville 164–7) and, contrary to earlier understandings, consisted of both seminomadic and sedentary elements (Pitard, "Before Israel," 46). The origin of the Canaanites as well as the meaning of the name *Canaan* is more debated, however (Millard 34; Shoville 159). It is unclear whether the Canaanites were native to the region or immigrants, and if the latter, where this group came from. Some scholars even argue that Canaanite is a term used for Amorites who had settled earlier (Liverani 102).

Problems concerning national identity and origins, unsurprisingly, bleed into issues concerning the territorial boundaries of the Amorites and the Canaanites. The biblical text again conveys contradictory descriptions. At points, the land of the Amorites as well as other groups is distinguished from that of the Canaanites: "The Amalekites live in the land of the Negeb; the Hittites, the Jebusites, and the Amorites live in the hill country; and the Canaanites live by the sea, and along the Jordan" (Num. 13:29; cf. Deut. 1:7; Josh. 5:1). In Numbers 35:10, however, Canaan is used to refer to the Syro-Palestinian territory as a whole. Pitard writes that during the second millennium, the term Canaan was usually used to designate the area of Palestine west of the Jordan River, whose northern boundary "fluctuated between southern and central Lebanon" ("Before Israel," 40). Schoville, more broadly, states that the boundaries of Canaan, called *Retenu* in Middle Kingdom Egyptian texts (ca. 2000–1550 BCE) and *Kinahu/Kinanu* in the Amarna letters, "fluctuate over time and in relationship to the mighty powers of the ancient Near East" (Schoville 159–162).

While the history, origins and the exact identification of the Amorites and Canaanites remain shrouded in mystery, the biblical writer's feelings toward these groups are more certain. Indeed, the biblical writer emphasizes the longstanding roots of Canaan's depravity with a story in the primeval history (Gen. 1–12). Genesis 9 recounts how shortly after the flood, Ham, the father of Canaan, "looked upon the nakedness" of his father Noah who had fallen asleep naked, inebriated from wine. Though the exact nature of Ham's sin is not clearly stated in the text – interpretations range from Ham sexually violating his mother or father, castrating Noah, or merely shamefully looking at the body of his naked father (Sarna 66) – the narrative ends with an angry Noah placing a curse, not on his son Ham, but on Canaan, his grandson: "He said, 'Cursed be Canaan; lowest of slaves shall he be to his brothers'" (Gen. 9:25).

Through this story, the biblical writer shows how the ancestor of the Canaanites – and the Amorites who in the next chapter (Gen. 10) are said to have descended from Canaan – from the very beginning exhibited the characteristic lasciviousness of these groups. The message is that the Canaanites' sexual perversity is natural and ingrained and, hence, unalterable – an image solidified in other biblical narratives. The stories about Abimelech, who attempts to take Sarah and later Rebekah into his harem in Canaan (Gen. 20; 26:7–11), the destruction of Sodom and Gomorrah (Gen. 19:5–8), the rape of Dinah by Shechem (Gen. 34), and the misbehaving sons of Judah, Er and Onan, and his Canaanite wife (Gen. 38), all emphasize the consistent wantonness of the Canaanites (Sarna 64).

This image of the Canaanites as unchangeable deviants furthermore serves an important political function for the biblical writer, allowing him to justify calls for actions against the Canaanites that otherwise might have been deemed questionable. Scholars have noted how the frequent emphasis on Canaan as subservient to his brother as well as the wordplay on *k-n-'* (to be low) in Genesis 9 validates the occupation of Canaan by Israel. Indeed, the curse on Canaan by Noah, which concludes this account, places the blame for the oppression and conquest squarely on the Canaanites themselves. Because of their deviancy, they incurred the wrath and rejection of an ancient, pious figure such as Noah. Whatever follows in history, whether it be annihilation or slavery, is merely the fulfillment of a curse that Canaan brought down upon himself and his descendants.

This animosity is rooted in ideological and theological challenges posed by the presence of the Canaanites and the Amorites. Their presence in the land that Israel claimed as truly and rightfully theirs had to be explained. The curse in Genesis 9 attempts to address this problem by arguing that though the Canaanites were in the land first, it was never truly intended to be their property.

The sheer variety of justifications for the Israelite occupation of the land shows the extent of the ideological problem posed by the Canaanites and the Amorites. To mitigate this problem, the biblical writer attaches the Patriarchs of Israel to key sites in Canaan. For example, as many scholars have noticed, the purchase of the property and the burial of almost all of Israel's patriarchs and matriarchs at the Machpelah in Hebron (Gen. 23:19) centers around Israel's political claim to the land of Canaan (Stavrakopoulou 34–5). Similarly motivated are stories about the visitations, theophanic experiences and altar erections at key Canaanite holy sites by Abraham and Jacob, for example, Shechem (Gen. 12:6; Josh. 24:32 states that Joseph's bones are buried there) and Bethel (Gen. 12:8; 28:11–13; 35:1).

The placement of patriarchs in Canaanite territory goes hand in hand with the other claim, frequently made in the text, that God, the true owner of the land, had promised the territory to Israel's patriarchs and their descendants, unbeknownst to the Canaanites and Amorites: "And I will give to you, and to your offspring after you, the land where you are now an alien, all the land of Canaan, for a perpetual holding; and I will be their God" (Gen. 17:8, New Revised Standard Version (NRSV); cf. Exod. 6:4; 3:8; Lev. 25:38; Josh. 24:3; Ps. 105:11). Hence, it is not Israel, but God who commands that Israel annihilate and evict these groups (Exod. 34:11; 33:2): "You shall annihilate them – the Hittites and the Amorites, the Canaanites and the Perizzites, the Hivites and the Jebusites – just as the Lord your God has commanded" (Deut. 20:17, NRSV; cf. also Exod. 33:2; Num. 21:3; Zeph. 2:5). The removal of the Canaanites and Amorites and the acquisition of their territory was not the fault of Israel but the express will of God.

Why then is God so adamant that Israel expel and destroy these groups? The stories about the unalterable perversity of the Canaanites serves as a convenient excuse: First, because their deviancy is unchangeable, woven into the very fabric of their national character, there is no choice but to completely destroy them. Second, because of their ingrained perversity, these groups might be a bad influence on Israel (Judg. 2:12). Like a parent who frets that his child will be influenced by the bad children in the neighborhood, God lists for the Israelites the abominations for which the Canaanites were rejected from the land (Lev. 18:3ff; 20:1ff; Ps. 106). For good measure, God finishes off his admonition to Israel with the plea to not be like them: "You shall not follow the practices of the nation that I am driving out before you. Because they did all these things, I abhorred them" (Lev. 20:23, NRSV).

Interestingly, the list of abominations of which these groups are accused and which will thus act as an irresistible temptation to the Israelites are sexual abominations and religious unfaithfulness – two features which are closely linked in the mind of the biblical writer. So, for example, the condemnation of Israel as a lustful whore in Hosea, Ezekiel and various passages in the prophets (Hos. 1–3; Ezek. 16, 23; Jer. 2:24; Isa. 57:5) closely associates the worship of gods other than Yahweh with sexual infidelity. Indeed, the polemic against exogamous relationships between Israel and other groups (Gen. 28; Num. 25; Deut. 7:3–4), and, in particular, the Canaanites, stems, in part, from the association of sexuality and religious behavior. As it did for Solomon, intermarriage will lead to polytheism and the worship of other gods (1 Kings 11).

However, no matter how strong the command that Israel maintain social, sexual and religious separation from its neighbors nor how adamant the call for the complete and utter destruction of the Canaanites and the Amorites, the text admits that neither of these injunctions were ever fully executed. Rather, the Canaanites, Amorites and other groups are said to have continued to live on the land (Josh. 16:10; 17:12, 13; Judg. 1; 3:5), and that Israelites, even righteous ones, are said to have married non-Israelites (Gen. 38; Exod. 2:11–22; Ruth 1–4). These failures, at points, are explained as either the result of sheer disobedience on the part of Israel (Josh. 16; Judg. 1) or as a divine teaching tool – to continually test Israel's religious fidelity (Judg. 2:22–23) and/or to train Israel for war (Judg. 3:1).

This admission as well as the feeble excuses for Israel's failures hint that the lived reality was different and more complicated than that described and proscribed in the text. Indeed, comparative and archaeological data suggest that the biblical writer deliberately minimized the sociological and religious similarities between Israel and its neighboring groups (see also the essays of Elizabeth Bloch-Smith, Avraham Faust and Mark Smith in this volume). For example, texts from Ugarit (modern Ras Shamra), an important coastal town in Syria, show just how similar Yahweh was to the two main male Ugaritic deities, Baal and El. These gods are not only mentioned in the biblical text – the Israelites are condemned for their unfaithful worship of the baals who are Yahweh's chief rivals (Judg. 2:11–13) – but Yahweh himself, at times, is referred to as baal (Hos. 2:16) or with El epithets (El Olam in Gen. 21:33; El Elyon, Gen. 14:18–24; El Shaddai, Gen. 17:1; 28:3, etc.). The overlap in names along with parallel portrayals of Yahweh as both a young storm deity, like Baal, or as an otiose patriarchal ruler of the divine council, similar to El, hint of the religious development underlying Israel's deity. Miller even writes that Yahweh was "probably originally a cultic name of El as worshipped in the South" (Miller 2).

Moreover, the references at Kuntillet 'Ajrud and Khirbet el-Qom to "Yahweh and his 'ăšērâ," referring either to a cult object or to Yahweh's consort, again hint of Yahweh's resemblance, if not overlap, with El and maybe Baal whose consorts – Athirat and Anat, respectively – are both confused with Asherah (Miller 58–9). Ugaritic tales concerning Baal's battle with Yamm (literally "sea" or "ocean"), the symbol of chaos (Gen. 1; Exod. 15:1–18; Deut. 33:2–5, 26–29; Ps. 24, 68, 74), and about the sonless King Danel in the Aqhat myth, a narrative compared to that of Abraham and Sarah, echo motifs and themes found in the biblical corpus. These literary correlations, considered in the context of archaeological data, suggest that the lived religion of Israel was most likely polytheistic and very much part of the larger Canaanite culture (see also Elizabeth Bloch-Smith's essay in this volume).

Debates about the origin of Israel further complicate questions about the distinction between Israel and the other Canaanite groups. The earliest identification of Israel is found in the Merneptah Stele or Israel Stele from the thirteenth century BCE where the determinative references Israel as a people and not a city-state (see also John Huddlestun's essay in this volume). Questions about Israel's origins are complicated, however, by larger sociological issues concerning ethnicity and identity. Although there is no consensus about the origins of Israel, one hypothesis maintains that Israelites were originally Canaanites who developed a distinct self-consciousness centered on their religious devotion to Yahweh. Indeed, underlying the statement in Ezekiel 16:3 – "your origin and your birth were in the land of the Canaanites; your father was an Amorite, and your mother a Hittite" – might be a subtle acknowledgment of Israel's Canaanite and Amorite origin. The Merneptah reliefs at Karnak might lend further support to this view as they depict Israelites with the same clothing and hairstyle as the Canaanites (Stager 125).

Whether one agrees with this hypothesis or not, the Israelites living in the land of Canaan, surrounded by Canaanite culture, and speaking a similar language, were "frequently, and understandably pictured as absorbing customs and beliefs of Canaan ..." (Millard 48). These similarities shed further light on the animosity exhibited toward the Canaanites and the Amorites in the biblical text. The biblical writer emphasizes the differences between this group and Israel not only because its constructed history required justification, but also because such differences were fundamental to the formation and maintenance of Israelite identity. If the society, religion, stories and perhaps even the origins of Israel were acknowledged to be similar or related to those of the Canaanites, then the identity of Israel as a special and separate group chosen by Yahweh, an idea essential to Israel's self-understanding, would be undermined. No wonder that the biblical narrative so frequently juxtaposes Canaanites with Israelites; an Israelite is that which is *not* Canaanite or Amorite. Hence, the pleas in the text to not worship *their* gods, to not intermarry *with them*, to not follow *their* behavior and even to eradicate *them* convey this fear over the loss or weakening of Israelite identity. It is thus surprising that scholars have seen in Canaan an ever-changing cipher for other entities and groups necessary for the reinforcement of Israel's identity.

Philistines

The Israelite writer conveys a similar animosity toward the Philistines, a group regarded by the biblical writer as one of Israel's main adversaries, especially during the period of the Judges and the early monarchy. Indeed, the Philistines can almost be regarded as the Canaanites and Amorites of the pre- and early monarchic period. The Philistines, from which we get the word Palestine, were a motley amalgamation of people mainly from the Aegean, who settled in Canaan and blended with other groups in the region. The history and process of acculturation by the Philistines can be discerned by looking at changes in archaeological remains from the excavations at the Philistine Pentapolis (a coalition of five Philistine cities: Ashdod, Ashkelon, Gaza, Gath and Ekron) and throughout the Levant (Dothan and Dothan; A. Mazar 533–6; Stager 152–6). Especially important has been the study of Philistine pottery, which suddenly appears at Canaanite sites at the end of the Late Bronze period. The similarities between early Philistine monochrome vessels (called Mycenean IIIC:1b) and Mycenaean pottery from the Aegean region clearly show the path of migration taken by the Philistines. Moreover, archaeologists can trace the morphology of this earlier pottery into later related bichrome Philistine ware, which is also found throughout the Levantine area.

Both biblical and extrabiblical texts place the origins of the Philistines outside of Israel. Jeremiah 47:4 and Amos 9:7 state that the Philistines came from Caphtor, usually identified as the island of Crete (Howard 232; Kitchen 54–6), while the Table of Nations (Gen. 14:13–14) makes the Philistines the descendants of the Calushites, a group associated with the Sea People. Extrabiblical sources also link the Philistines with islands in the Aegean. The first mention of the Philistines is found in Egyptian inscriptions from the time of Rameses III (ca. 1184–1163 BCE), which describe sea and land battles with the Sea Peoples, among whom was a group called the "Peleset," usually identified with the Philistines. Egyptian reliefs from Medinet Habu from Rameses III's reign depict scenes of fierce battle between the Egyptian military and the Sea Peoples. The Sea Peoples, who first appeared during the time of Pharoah Merneptah (1208 BCE), seem to have been a coalition of various groups – among them the Peleset, Tjeker, Shekelesh, Denyen, Weshesh and Sherden – who came from islands or coastal areas in the Aegean to settle on the southeastern Mediterranean coast during a time of great upheaval and migration in the region (Dothan and Dothan 27).

Biblical stories tell of the complicated interactions between Israel and the Philistines as they intersected, clashed, and finally reached a point of tension-filled coexistence. Of particular interest are narratives in the Book of Judges describing the violent exchanges between the Philistines and Samson, a judge from the tribe of Dan – a tribe which, according to scholars, was likely forced to migrate north as a result of Philistine incursion and settlement (Stager 167). Not unlike the Greek Heracles, Samson is depicted as an impetuous, aggressive, feral culture hero who unbecoming to a Nazirite judge, tells riddles, performs inhuman acts of strength, and has a penchant for foreign women. Judges 14 tells of Samson's desire to wed a woman from the Philistine town of Timnah, a border region, which was the "first point of contact between the two cultures" (Stager 168). In a narrative saturated with sexual tension and latent aggression, Judges 14 describes how a pre-wedding groom's party filled with group bonding, celebration and joking escalates into a violent clash that serves to drive the two groups apart further. The event will culminate in the deaths of many Philistines, the burning of their fields, and the murder of the bride and her father.

The point of this narrative – to polemicize against intermarriage – at first seems quite apparent. However, though the marriage between Samson and his Philistine bride ends badly, this tale also shows that the intersection of the Israelites and Philistines resulted in exogamous relationships and cultural exchanges. In fact, this particular exogamous relationship is said to have been planned by Yahweh for his nefarious purposes (Judg. 14:4). Moreover, the depiction of an Israelite judge as a Greco-style hero in a story set soon after the invasion of the Aegean group conveys complicated ideas of identity.

The stories about Samson's interactions with the Philistines also show that these groups posed a serious cultural and military threat to the Israelites. Other narratives about Israel in the premonarchic period also testify to the martial abilities of the Philistines. The Philistines are said to be skilled archers (1 Sam. 31:2), infantrymen and makers of iron weapons (1 Sam. 13:19–22). Judges 1:18–19 states that Judah could not take possession of the coast because the Philistines had "chariots of iron" – a description confirmed by Egyptian inscriptions at Medinet Habu, which state that the Philistines were chariot-warriors.

The inadequacy of the Israelite military capabilities is evident in the Ark Narrative, which describes how the Israelites lost the ark of the covenant during a battle with the Philistines (1 Sam. 4–6). The ark, after being captured by the Philistines, is taken to Ashdod and placed in the temple of the Philistines' chief god, Dagon. When the statue of Dagon is found mutilated the next day and plague breaks out, the ark is passed around from one Philistine city to another until it is finally returned to Israel with offerings of five golden mice and golden tumors (1 Sam. 6:4). The message of the narrative is evident: Though the Israelites are militarily defeated and thus appear weaker than the Philistines, the god of Israel, Yahweh still reigns supreme, especially over the false god Philistine Dagon.

The attempt to assert a truer religious reality in the face of military defeat shows the seriousness of the threat posed by the Philistines. Indeed, biblical texts hint that the Israelite monarchy arose, in part, out of a need to combat the Philistines more effectively (Aharoni 286; Stager 170). Israel's first king, Saul from the tribe of Benjamin, is said to have continually battled the Philistines during his reign (1 Sam. 13; 14; 23:27–28) and eventually lost his life in battle against them (1 Sam. 31). The death and defeat of Saul was aided by the rise of David, whom the biblical text depicts as both colluding with and also waging war against the Philistines. One of the most famous events associated with David – though attributed to one of David's heroes in 2 Samuel 21:10 – concerns his fight with a Philistine named Goliath who comes to battle with a bronze helmet, a coat of bronze mail, bronze leg greaves, and a spear shaft "like a weaver's beam" (1 Sam. 17:5–7), most likely referring to a leash of cord wrapped around the shaft with loops for the fingers (Howard 241). This description of Goliath fits the depiction of Aegean warriors on the twelfth-century BCE "Warrior Vase" at Mycenae – further evidence that the origin of the Philistines is in the Aegean (Howard 241; Stager 169). Even after becoming king, David will continue to clash with the Philistines (2 Sam. 5:17; 8:1, 12; 21:15–22; 23:9–17; 1 Chr. 11:12–19; 14:8–17; 18:1; 20:4–8).

After the reign of David, however, there are some hints in the biblical text that Israelites and Philistines were able to coexist with each other, albeit uneasily. David himself at points is depicted as having cordial relations with Philistines (1 Sam. 27). Moreover, David seems to have had mercenaries and personal guards who were either Philistines or closely allied with them (2 Sam. 15:18–22). Indeed, Ittai the Gittite would remain loyal to David during his flight from Absalom (2 Sam. 15:19–22). Howard notes that though the Philistines would continue to battle with other Israelite and Judean kings after David (2 Kings 18:8; 2 Chr. 17:11), David seems to have "eliminated the Philistines' threat" (Howard 241). Even so, because of the threat they posed during the formation of the Israelite monarchy, the Philistines are remembered as Israel's enemy.

Moabites and Ammonites

Unlike the Canaanites and Philistines, who despite the historical record were imagined as primarily opposite or Other, the Israelites express a closer relationship with the
Ammonites and Moabites, though this closeness was a qualified one, and one that ultimately served the same purpose: to police and delineate Israelite identity. These groups
were viewed in the biblical text as distantly related to Israel through kinship – the descendants of an incestuous coupling of Abraham's nephew Lot and his daughters.

The close proximity of Moab and Ammon to each other and to Israel might have
led to a common origin story for both Ammon and Moab in the biblical text. Both
nations are in the Transjordan, with Ammon located in the area north of the Arnon
River (modern Wadi Mujib) and south of the Jabbok River (Wadi Zarqa), and the territory of Moab located between that of the Ammonites, which was to its the north, and
Edom, to its south in the plateau areas (the Plain of Moab) east of the Dead Sea. As with
all territories, however, the borders fluctuated over time, depending on the geopolitical
situation.

The origins of the people who came to make up Moab and Ammon are not completely known. The biblical narrative states that the Ammonites and the Moabites, having expelled the Rephaim (Deut. 2:10–11 and 20–21), were in Transjordan before the
arrival of the Israelites (Num. 21:24; Deut. 2:9, 19). Indeed, the Book of Numbers states
that Balak, the King of Moab (Num. 22–24), and the Amorite kings Sihon and Og (Num.
21:21–26, 33–35; Deut. 2:26–3:7) confront and attempt to block Israelites during their
wanderings. Archaeologists and historians propose, however, that these groups, like
Israel, emerged politically in the Iron Age. They speculate that the Ammonites and the
Moabites might have been part of the Amorite or Aramean migration or were originally Canaanites who fled into the highlands where they established distinct identities
(Younker 298). The similarities in the timing of the formation of these groups and Israel
might, in part, underlie the sense of familial ties professed by the biblical writer, though
it is unclear whether these groups should be connected to the Iron Age settlements in
the Israelite highlands, which scholars link with the origins of Israel.

Despite these similarities, however, the Ammonites and Moabites are configured as
distinct from the Israelites by way of a disparaging account of their origins and names
(Gen. 19:30–38). In Genesis, Lot, Abraham's nephew, follows his uncle into Canaan.
Lot, at first, is hinted at as a possible heir to Abraham, who is childless at this point.
However, a dispute over resources leads to the separation of uncle and nephew, and
Lot goes to settle in the area of Sodom and Gomorrah, which God destroys in Genesis
19 because of their wickedness. Lot and his daughters flee first to Zoar and then to the
hills, where the three take up residence in a cave. There the daughters get their father
drunk and in succession sleep with him and are impregnated. Names are given to both
the children referring to the incestuous act. The first child is called Moab, explained by
the biblical writer as meaning "from my father" in Hebrew, and the second, Ben-Ammi,
meaning "son of my kinsman" (Gen. 19:37–38). Though the historicity of the portrayal
of Ammon and Moab as close relations (also in Deut. 23:3) is questionable, the narrative clearly shows that the Israelite writer viewed the two nations as connected. This is
further supported by instances in the biblical text where the two nations are sometimes

confused. For example, the Israelite judge Jephthah erroneously refers to Chemosh, the god of Moab, as the deity of the Ammonites in Judges 11:12–28.

The Israelite origin story of Moab and Ammon not only links the two nations, but again utilizes sexual taboos to disparage the neighbor states. As with the tale of Noah and Ham, the story of Moab and Ammon's origins again connects wine, drunkenness and sexually deviant acts. Not only do the laws in Leviticus clearly forbid such incestuous relationships (Lev. 18:6), but the biblical writer conveys his disapproval of these groups by never again mentioning Lot. By concluding the stories of Abraham's nephew with that of the incestuous creation of two rival neighbors of Israel, the biblical writer conclusively answers in the negative the question of whether Lot would or could be the potential heir to the Abrahamic promise – a question that lingers throughout the Abrahamic Cycle until the birth of Isaac. The origin narrative of Ammon and Moab, hence, is used not only to belittle Ammon and Moab, but to contrast them to Israel, the pure and chosen nation of God. In a telling passage in Deuteronomy 23:2–3, right after forbidding those born of an illicit union from the Assembly of the Lord to the tenth generation, Moabites and Ammonites are also forbidden admittance to the tenth generation. The emphasis on Ammon and Moab's sexually debased roots are clear as the chapter also bars those with damaged genitalia as well as those of illegitimate birth (Deut. 23:1–4).

The origin account of Moab and Ammon exhibits complex and ambivalent feelings toward these groups. Genesis 19, though critical, at no point condemns the incestuous acts that occur. The narrative even conveys some underlying justifications for the daughters' action. As scholars have pointed out, the daughters do not act out of lust, but to ensure the survival of the human race in light of the catastrophe they had just witnessed. Moreover, the girls do not appear ashamed of what they have done but rather proudly give the children names that reflect the incestuous act. Lot, of course, cannot really be blamed as he is unaware of what has happened, and the daughters' action serves as a reversal of and just comeuppance for Lot's early offer to throw out his daughters to the townspeople.

Moreover, the many biblical references to Ammon and Moab as descendants of Lot, the nephew of Abraham (Deut. 2:9, 19; Ps. 83:9) clearly exhibit a sense of kinship with these nations. Indeed, the warm feelings between uncle and nephew are evident in Genesis 18:16–33 when Abraham is shown bargaining with God for the lives of his nephew and his family. The biblical text makes clear that Moab and Ammon owe their existence and survival to an Israelite patriarch. Furthermore, in contrast to attitudes to the Canaanites, the Israelites are explicitly told not to harass Moab and Ammon as God has designated for the descendants of Lot their particular territories (Deut. 2:9, 19; Judg. 11:15).

In the case of the Canaanites, sexual deviancy marks them as Other and justifies their conquest. In the case of Ammon and Moab, however, sexual deviancy and *sameness* or at least kinship are also used as justifications for conquest. This mixed portrayal of Ammon and Moab most likely results from the varying interactions among these countries and Israel during the time of the Israelite monarchy (B. Mazar; Rendsburg 109). Stories about the relatedness of these groups, for example, justify Israel's conquest of Moab and Ammon during the reign of David. In Numbers 24:17, a magician named Balaam, a figure also mentioned in an inscription from Tell Deir 'Alla, is hired by Moab to curse the invading Israelites. Instead of cursing the Israelites, however, Balaam foretells the conquest of Moab by an Israelite king, something which David accomplishes in 2 Samuel 8:2, 13–14. David will also colonize Ammon in 2 Samuel 10 after the Israelites' emissaries are humiliated by the Ammonite king Hanun. The story of Ruth, the famous Moabitess who is named as an ancestress of King David (Ruth 4), might also be an attempt to support Israel's colonization of Moab by emphasizing David's Moabite roots.

Contrary to the strong polemic against intermarriage expressed in parts of the biblical corpus (Num. 25:1; 1 Kings 11), David and Solomon appear to have had familial ties to Moab and Ammon. Intermarriage among the groups would have lent further political support for Israelite colonialism. During his flight from Saul, David leaves his parents with the king of Moab (1 Sam. 22:3), and the mother of Rehoboam who reigned in Israel after the death of his father, Solomon, is said to have been an Ammonite (1 Kings 14:21, 31). The long success of Israel's colonialism is attested by the Mesha Stele or the Moabite Stone (ca. 830 BCE), found in Dhiban, which commemorates Moab's independence from the control of the Omride dynasty during the reign of King Mesha. The biblical version of these events attributes Moab's success to child sacrifice (2 Kings 3:26–27).

Stories about Ammon and Moab's impure origins and about their familial ties to Israel served as a convenient excuse and justification for Israelite political and military actions against these nations. The biblical narrative tells how the Ammonites and the Moabites go out of their way to hinder their cousin nation from entering the Promised Land, even though their territories are protected by the Lord because of their kinship to Israel (Num. 21:21–26, 33–35; 21–24; Deut. 2:26–3:7). The harassment by these groups is said to have continued into the time of the settlement, and even served as an effective means by which God punished Israel for their infractions, the main violation being the Israelite worship of other gods, including those of Moab and Ammon (Judg. 10:16). Bespeaking their impure origins, these groups thus act as not only a territorial but also a spiritual hindrance to the Israelites (1 Kings 11:33). And as a result, intermarriage among the groups is strongly discouraged (1 Kings 11; Num. 25:1).

Judges 3, for example, tells of how Eglon, a Moabite king, was allowed to oppress the Israelites because of their wrongdoing until the rise of the left-handed Benjaminite judge Ehud. So too the Ammonites are said to have oppressed Israel until the time of Jephthah (Judg. 11). Even into the early monarchy, the Ammonites are said to have harassed the Israelites of Jabesh-Gilead until Saul came to their rescue (1 Kings 11). The stories of the unjustified hostility by Ammon and Moab as well as the emphasis on their lesser status all explain the need for Israelite defense against and conquest of these nations.

Edomites

Thus far we have seen how Israelites contrast themselves with other groups such as the Canaanites and Philistines in the starkest possible ways, although they find similarities and difference within commonality in their stories about the Ammonites and Moabites. The origins of the Edomites could not be closer to the Israelites, as the eponymous founders of both peoples shared a womb not just as siblings but as twins. This feeling of closeness no doubt again results from the close proximity of Edom to Israel and also to Ammon and Moab in the Transjordan area. Edom refers to the mountainous region that runs south from the Wadi el-Hasa in modern Jordan to the Gulf of Aqabah, east of the Wadi Arabah. The Wadi el-Hasa, which ends in the Dead Sea, was the ancient boundary between Moab and Edom.

The close kinship that the Israelite writer felt toward the Edomites is apparent in the origin story of Esau, the ancestor of Edom in Genesis 25:21. Rebekah, the barren wife of Isaac, quickly becomes pregnant with twins after her husband's prayer. When during her pregnancy Rebekah, alarmed by the movement inside her womb, goes to see the Lord (Gen. 25:22), God explains that her discomfort is caused by the presence of twins – twins who, the oracle goes on to say, will become two separate nations, namely Israel and Edom. God also cryptically replies that the greater will serve the lesser, or as it is usually translated, the elder will serve the younger. When it is time for the births of the twins, the competition between the brothers is emphasized in a wordplay on the name of Jacob, who comes out holding the heel ('āqēb) of Esau, his elder brother (Gen. 25:26).

Esau and Jacob's origin story therefore reflects both a sense of deep kinship and antagonism between Israel and Edom. Through the use of wordplay, the biblical writer emphasizes the national rivalry symbolized by the brothers and foretold in the oracle. As scholars have noted, Esau, the founder of Edom, is described as emerging from the womb red or 'admônî (Gen. 25:25), referring to the reddish Nubian sandstone prominent in the area of Edom (Bartlett 38; Sarna 180). In another play on words, the eponymous ancestor of Edom, of which Seir is a major region, is described as śē'ār or hairy. The hairy description might refer to the woody slopes of the Wadi Araba. The biblical description of Esau, the founder of Edom, as red and hairy might indicate that two areas, Seir and Edom, were originally distinct and only later unified and made indistinguishable (Bartlett 42–4; Hoglund 336). Though the Egyptian records from the fifteenth century BCE onward speak of encounters with a nomadic group called the *Shasu* in the area of Edom and Seir, the "nomads of Edom" and the "nomads of Seir" are described as two separate groups – a distinction upheld in Isaiah 21:1, though in other biblical passages the area is referred to as a unity (Num. 24:18; Judg. 5:14).

These plays on words in Genesis clearly show that Esau is not just Esau but also a symbol for Edom, Israel's rival nation. Moreover, the description of Esau is utilized to contrast Esau with Jacob, who is said to have come out smooth-skinned. Indeed, the twins are not just physically different but also greatly vary in character. Esau is described as an outdoorsy, overly masculine hunter, beloved by his father, while Jacob is stated to be the opposite: quiet and feminine with a preference for the indoors, and beloved of his mother (Gen. 25:27). Most importantly, Jacob is pictured as a shrewd long-term thinker who takes advantage of his brother's Esau short-sightedness to obtain the birthright of the firstborn (Gen. 25:29–34) and later, with the help of his mother, the blessing (Gen. 27:1–39).

By depicting Jacob and Esau as opposites, certain aspects of Israelite national qualities are stressed through contrast. This contrast is important as the twin births of Jacob and Esau to the same parents raises a question about the distinctiveness of the brothers and therefore the countries that will claim descent from them. The contrasting description of the twins, as well as the oracle, emphasize that though the twins Jacob and Esau (and thus Israel and Edom) seem equal, they are not really so. Rather, though Jacob is younger, his successful machinations and trickery show that he is the superior twin who has the favor of God, and hence, Israel is the superior, chosen nation. As with Ammon and Moab, the origin narratives of Edom emphasize the election of Israel and function to distinguish Israel from its neighbors.

However, the origin narrative depicting Esau as a twin of Jacob also indicates that the Israelite writer felt a very close kinship with the Edomites, a sense of connection conveyed by other passages. Job, the famous innocent sufferer, is said to be an Edomite and, in later traditions, even marries Dinah, Jacob's daughter. Not only is the territory of Edom, like that of the Ammonites and Moabites, guaranteed by God (Deut. 2:4–5, 8), but unlike these groups who are barred from the assembly of the Lord until the tenth generation, the Edomites are allowed admittance in the third generation (Deut. 23:4). In a telling note, Deuteronomy 23:8 explicitly states that the Israelites are not to "abhor an Edomite, for he is your brother." And this brotherhood will be frequently mentioned by the biblical writer (Deut. 2:4; 23:8; Num. 20:14; Obad. 10; Mal. 1:2) so that Nahum Sarna argues that the twinship of Esau and Jacob must "reflect authentic historical experience" – whether "shared memories of an early common ancestry, blood kinship, or treaty associations" (177). Bartlett argues that the emphasis on the kinship of Israel and Edom might be due to the fact that both groups, along with Ammon and Moab, "entered the land at much the same time," perhaps as part of the Aramean migration, though the origins of Edom, like other Transjordanian nations who sprang up during the Iron Age, remain shrouded in mystery (Bartlett 83).

Scholars have also proposed that this expression of close association between Israel and Edom resulted from a particular religious overlap between the two groups. Unlike with Moab and Ammon, whose head gods, Chemosh and Milcom, respectively, are condemned by the biblical writer (1 Kings 11:5, 7; 2 Kings 23:13), there is neither identification nor condemnation of Edom's god, nor even any mention of ritual actions on the part of the Edomites. Furthermore, the biblical writer does not seem surprised at the presence of Doeg the Edomite at the sanctuary of Nob in 1 Samuel 21:7. Instead, various biblical passages seem to point to Yahweh's home as located in Edom or Seir (Deut. 22:2; Judg. 5:4; Hab. 3:3; Isa. 63:1–6): "Lord, when you went out from Seir, when you marched from the region of Edom, the earth trembled and the heavens poured …" (Judg. 5:4). This has led scholars to argue that the Edomites might also have worshipped Yahweh along with other gods such as Qos, and that religious overlap might underlie the feeling of kinship expressed by the biblical writer (Bartlett 187–207; Hoglund 345–7).

As with Moab and Ammon, however, underlying the origin story of Edom with its emphasis on kinship and rivalry is a justification of the colonial actions of Israel under David (Rendsburg 108–9). By stressing Esau's inferiority and unchosen status, exemplified by his marriage to Hittite women (Gen. 26:34–45; 27:4) and the loss of the blessing and birthright to his superior younger twin brother, the origin narrative concerning Edom explains why its descendants had to submit to those of Jacob. Indeed, David defeats the Edomites and places garrisons throughout Edom to exert control over its neighbors (2 Sam. 8:13–14). Like Moab, the Edomites would not gain their independence until the reign of Jehoram of Judah ca. 845 BCE (2 Kings 8:20), about a century and a half later according to the biblical account. As with the curse of Canaan, the divine oracle in

Esau's story (Gen. 27:39–40) shows that the vassalage of Edom by Israel was destined and therefore natural and indisputable (Bartlett 85). Rendsburg suggests that the portrayal of Esau as Jacob's twin results from the firm grip that Israel had on Edom during the period of the united monarchy (109).

Esau's origin story not only justifies Edom's submission to Israel, but also acts as a critique of Edom's desire for independence. If his destiny is foretold and indeed confirmed by the interactions between Esau and Jacob, then Edom can be blamed for its unwillingness to accept its unchosen, inferior status, and any resistance can be dismissed as the result of unwarranted anger. The biblical writer goes out of his way to stress the quick-tempered, violent tendencies of Esau, who longs to kill his brother after Jacob's theft of the blessing (Gen. 27:41–42) and who, out of bitterness and jealousy, fails to act like a true brother to Jacob. Even after Jacob and Esau reconcile in Genesis 33, Jacob's desire to separate from his brother in his travels hints of lingering distrust and fear. The actions of Esau will set the pattern for his descendants, who will be criticized for being quick to violence and unbrotherly (Gen. 27:40; Amos 1:11–12), not even allowing Israel to pass through their land during its wanderings (Num. 20:14–21; Judg. 11:17–18; compare Deut. 2:1–8). Biblical writers bitterly remember the gloating and lack of familial sympathy expressed by Edom when the Babylonians besieged Jerusalem in 589–587 BCE (Jer. 40:11; Lam. 4:2; Ezek. 35; Ps. 137:7; Joel 4:19; Obad. 11–14), though what Edom exactly did remains unclear. In the postexilic era, the sense of brotherly betrayal will linger in the suspicion with which Idumean rulers, such as Herod the Great, were regarded. Edom will even come to be used as a reference to Rome.

Midianites

As with the Edomites, the Israelite writer expresses similar ambivalence toward the Midianites, a group said to have descended from the son of Abraham and Keturah, Abraham's third wife (Gen. 25:2). The depiction of the Midianites as the progeny of Keturah who are sent away by Abraham to settle in the east (Gen. 25:1–6) emphasizes both their relatedness to Israel and, perhaps, their unchosen status. Like the Ishmaelites, with whom the Midianites are sometimes confused (Gen. 37:25–36), the genealogy thus allows the biblical writer both to stress the commonality between Israel and Midian and to envision them, at points, as a threat.

The clearest expression of the association between the two groups is found in the story of Moses and his experiences in Midian. Moses, after killing an Egyptian, flees to the land of Midian, usually said to be located on the eastern shore of the Gulf of Aqaba in the northwestern Arabian Peninsula (now Hijaz). Because the group was nomadic (Num. 10:29; Gen. 36:35), it is difficult to ascertain the precise location of the territory of this group, which seems to have fluctuated over time. In Midian, Moses marries the daughter of a Midianite priest named Jethro (Reuel or Hobab in other sources), and, while tending sheep (a common vocation for many of Israel's leaders), has an encounter with a deity named Yahweh on the "mountain of God" in the form of a bush that is burning but not consumed (Exod. 3:1–4:17). Moses would later return to this mountain with the Israelites to receive the ten commandments (Exod. 19–20).

The biblical narrative further describes the friendly and close relationship between Moses and Jethro during Israel's wandering. Unlike other relatives and their descendants who opposed Israel during their time in the desert, the biblical text states that Jethro helped Moses establish a working judicial system (Exod. 18:13–27), guided the Israelites until they reached Canaan (Num. 10:29–32), and even offered sacrifices and burnt offerings to the Lord before joining Moses and the Israelite elders for a meal "in the presence of God" (Exod. 7:1–12).

These stories about Moses' experiences in Midian and his relationship with Jethro, the Midianite priest, have led scholars to argue that Yahwism, which was adopted by the Israelites, originally came from Midian (the Midianite/Kenite hypothesis). Indeed, intriguing details in the biblical text hint of a close connection between Yahwism and the area associated with Midian. For example, according to the earliest Hebrew poetry, the "mountain of God" where Moses receives the ten commandments and experiences the initial theophany, known as Mount Horeb or Sinai, seems to be located in the Arabian Peninsula, in an area connected to or in Midian (Judg. 5:4–5; Deut. 33:2; Hab. 3:3–7) (Stager 143–4). Moreover, in Egyptian sources, one of the territories of a group of tent-dwellers called the Shasu is designated as "the land of Shasu: Yhw3" or Yahweh. Thus, underlying the stories about Moses' marriage and interactions with Jethro might be authentic memories about the origins of Israel's religion in Midian.

The relationship between the two nations seems to have eventually deteriorated, however. Numbers 25:6–18, for example, describes how Phineas, a particularly zealous Aaronite, skewers both an Israelite man and his Midianite paramour, Cozbi, the daughter of Zur, the head of Midian, in one thrust when he finds them copulating in a tent near the tabernacle. In direct contrast to the friendlier accounts about Moses and his Midianite relations, Numbers 22:7 states that the elders of Moab and Midian hired Balaam to curse the Israelites during their wanderings. As a result of these two incidents, God commands Moses to annihilate the Midianites in Numbers 31:1–17, leading to the defeat of the five kings of Midian and also to the death of Balaam. Finally, Gideon in Judges 6–8 is said to have defeated the Midianites who were raiding and harassing the Israelites during the time of the Judges. As evident from the varying accounts of this group, Israel seems to have had conflicted feelings toward the Midianites.

Arameans

In a telling statement – "A wandering Aramean was my ancestor" (Deut. 26:5) – the Israelite writer professes a close connection between Israel and Aram. In contrast to attitudes toward other neighboring groups, the biblical writer expresses a sense of equanimity with Aram – the likely result of close political and cultural interactions between Israel and Aram in the monarchic period, especially during 900–730 BCE when the Kingdom of Aram became one of the most powerful states in the region. Aram would have a lasting influence on the culture of the ancient Near East with the spread of Aramaic, which would become the official diplomatic language of the Assyrian empire and the lingua franca of the Persian empire. Aramaic works such as the targumim, parts of Ezra and

Daniel, and the Elephantine texts, as well as works from Wadi el-Daliyeh and Qumran, all testify to the prevalence of this language.

In the Hebrew Bible, Aram is usually part of a compound name of different kingdoms (e.g., Aram-Damascus), mainly located north of Israel and east of the Jordan River. The earliest clear mention of the Arameans in Assyrian royal inscriptions from the twelfth century BCE shows that, like other neighboring groups of Israel, Aram emerged at the end of the Late Bronze Age (ca. 1200 BCE). Aram is also mentioned in Egyptian and Ugaritic texts and its capital kingdom, Damascus, is cited in the Amarna letters. The pre-twelfth century BCE origins of the Arameans, however, remain unclear. There may be some earlier references to this group in texts from Ebla from the third millennium BCE and in Ugaritic texts from the fourteenth century BCE, though these references are contested (Lipinski 26–40). Likewise debated is the nature of the relationship between Arameans and a seminomadic group called the Akhlamu who are mentioned in Mesopotamian texts from before the twelfth century BCE. The lack of archaeological evidence as well as newer understandings of anthropological/sociological patterns have also called into question the older, scholarly view that the Arameans were an invading, nomadic group from the Syrian desert. Rather, some scholars envision the Arameans as descendants of groups already present in northern Syria and upper Mesopotamia, such as the Amorites (Pitard, "Aramaeans," 208–10).

The biblical account provides four different accounts of the origin of the Arameans. Genesis 22:2 lists Aram, the eponymous ancestor of the Arameans, as the grandson of Abraham's brother Nahor, thus making Aram an equal of Israel or Jacob, who is the grandson of Abraham. In the later priestly Table of Nations in Genesis 10:22, Aram, along with Elam, Ashur (Assyria), and others, is said to be a son of Shem. The movement of Aram higher up in the genealogy indicates the growth of Aram's influence and power in Syro-Palestine in later periods. Perhaps a hint of Aram's influence on Israel can also be detected in the origin account in 1 Chronicles 7:34, which lists Aram as a descendant of one of Jacob's sons, Asher, and thus part of Israel. Finally, in a varying account, Amos 9:7 states that Yahweh brought the Arameans from an unknown place called Qir or Kir to their homeland.

Along with these origin accounts and the statement in Deuteronomy 26:5 wherein Jacob is said to have descended from a wandering Aramean, other stories in the Bible also indicate a close, albeit tension-filled relationship between Aram and Israel. Many of Israel's relations are said to be Aramean – Bethuel, the brother of Abraham (Gen. 25:20), Jacob's uncle Laban (Gen. 31:20), who is Bethuel's son, and the Israelite matriarchs Rebekah (Laban's sister), Rachel and Leah (Laban's daughters). The most telling account of the relationship between the two groups, however, is the lengthy narrative concerning Jacob, the eponymous ancestor of the Israelites, and Laban his uncle (Gen. 29–31).

Jacob, fearful of Esau after the theft of the blessing, flees to the house of his maternal uncle Laban in Aram Naharaim or Padan Aram in Haran where he agrees to work seven years for the hand of his cousin Rachel (Gen. 27:18–45). On the wedding night, in a trick that inverts Jacob's early theft of Esau's blessing, Laban switches Rachel, his younger daughter, for his elder daughter Leah (Gen. 29:18–27). This first ruse will be followed by a series of tricks between uncle and nephew with each trying to outdo and take advantage of the other (Gen. 29:25–31:16). In the end, Laban's desire to hold on to his wealth-producing nephew will force Jacob to flee with his family and property from his uncle in secret. A final agreement and oath-taking between Jacob and Laban mark- ing the groups' respective boundaries will conclude the cycle of stories.

If the stories about Laban reflect something about how the Israelite writer felt about the Arameans, then Israel viewed Aram both as a close relative and also as an adversary. In particular, the back and forth trickery between uncle and nephew seems to convey not only a feeling of rivalry and tension, but also a sense of parity. Indeed, some tales such as that of Laban's duping of Jacob on his wedding night and Jacob's flight from Laban's house suggest that Israel might have been, at times, fearful of Aram (Gen. 31:31), even viewing it as superior. Genesis 31:24 narrates that Laban let Jacob go because God came to him in a dream and warned him from saying anything good or bad to Jacob. Thus emphasized is the necessity of divine protection from the machinations of his Aramean uncle, Laban.

This fluctuating feeling of respect and animosity conveyed in the stories about Jacob and Laban seems to reflect the rather complicated relationship between Israel and Aram in the monarchic period. The two books of Samuel describe fights between Aram and Israel under King Saul (1 Sam. 14:47) as well as the defeat of the Aramean states of Zobah led by Hadadezer, son of Rehob, by King David (2 Sam. 8:3–16; 10:6–19). During the period of David's son Solomon, the biblical text also records the seizure of Aram Damascus, the primary Aramean kingdom, by Rezon, son of Eliada, from Hadadezer of Zobah (1 Kings 11:23–24), though it remains unclear whether Rezon seized Damascus away from Israel, Zobah or Edom.

After the death of Solomon, the relationship between Israel/Judah and Aram under Rezon and his descendants will continue to waver between hostility and collaboration – again mimicking the relationship between Jacob and Laban in Genesis (see also the discussion in J. J. M. Roberts' essay in this volume). 1 Kings 15:16–22, for example, describes how Aram, under Ben-Hadad I, son of Tab-Rimmon (biblical Ben-Hadad), in league with King Asa of Judah, attacked and captured several cities in the north- ern kingdom of Israel. With the rise of the Assyrian threat in the ninth century BCE, however, Assyrian texts such as the Monolith Inscription indicate that an alliance, led by Hadadezer of Damascus, with 12 other western states, including Israel under Ahab, effectively stopped Shalmaneser III of Assyria (858–24 BCE) from his westward expan- sion at the battle of Qarqar (853 BCE). Oddly, contradicting this account, 1 Kings 20 and 22 records a series of conflicts between Israel and Aram during this period (Pitard, "Aramaeans," 218–19; Campbell 296).

The most serious point of hostility between Aram and Judah, however, occurred after Hazael's usurpation of the throne of Damascus (ca. 842 BCE) following the death of Hadadezer (2 Kings 8:7–15). Though the extent of Aram's colonialism is debated, Haz- ael, during a period of Assyrian weakness, greatly expanded Aram's territories, subju- gating Israel and Judah (2 Kings 10:32–33; 13:3) and almost all the land west of the Jordan (2 Kings 12:17). Hazael is commonly thought to be the king who boasts about his victories over Israel and Judah in the Tel Dan Stela, an artifact famous for its mention of the "House of David." After decades of domination, Israel will regain its independence from Aram during the reign of Hazael's son, Ben Hadad (2 Kings 13:22–25). Though it is unclear, perhaps the stories about Jacob's fearful, secretive flight away from Laban is a subtle reference to this period of subjection.

Finally, with another resurgence of Assyria during the middle of the eighth century BCE, Aram under King Rezin will again try to form a new anti-Assyrian coalition of Syro-Palestinian states, going so far as to collude with Pekah of Israel, to remove Ahaz from power in Judah and to replace him with a puppet ruler named Tabeel (2 Kings 16:1–8; 2 Chr. 28:1–25; Isa. 7:1–17) – an event known as the Syro-Ephraimite War (734–731 BCE). Ahaz will appeal for help from Tiglath-pileser III, the ruler of Assyria, who will destroy Damascus in 732 BCE and execute Rezin. As with Jacob earlier, however, the prophet Isaiah states that it was actually Yahweh who had decreed Judah's protection from the plans of their devious Aramean relatives: "Take heed, be quiet, do not fear, and do not let your heart be faint because of these two smoldering stumps of firebrands, because of the fierce anger of Rezin and Aram and the son of Remaliah … It shall not stand, and it shall not come to pass …" (Isa. 7:4, 7, NRSV).

Conclusion

The biblical authors wrote stories about their neighbors as a way of asserting and policing Israelite identity. At times, as with the Canaanites and Amorites, and later with the Philistines, these neighbors were depicted as wholly at odds with Israel, even from their very origins. As a result, uncomfortable issues such as similarities of belief, cultural overlap, and marital union among the groups were downplayed in an effort to protect Israel's sense of itself. In the case of other groups, such as with the Ammonites, Moabites, Edomites and Midianites, stories about these nations' origins tended to emphasize and mythologize their closeness to Israel. This sense of kinship, however, was often used to distinguish Israel as well, by finding points of difference to reveal the divine election and religious purity of Israel. From here it was a short step to the justification of conquest. Lastly, with the Arameans, the stories about Jacob's interactions with his uncle Laban emphasized Israel's kinship with this group as a means by which to assert parity with this powerful kingdom. Moreover, the stories about Jacob and Laban's attempt to outtrick one another reflected the fluctuating relationship between Israel and Aram in the monarchic period, which wavered between cooperation and hostility.

The Bible presents a view of ancient Israel and its neighbors from the point of view of the Israelites. Not surprisingly, it is the Israelites themselves who constitute the protagonists of these narratives, with outside groups as antagonists or otherwise in supporting roles. Far from simple propaganda, however, we see in the Bible a group of people struggling to arrive at their own identity in a politically, morally, and psychologically challenging world.

Bibliography

Aharoni, Yohanan. *The Land of the Bible: A Historical Geography*. Philadelphia: Westminster Press, 1979. A classic work on the geography, history, and archaeology of ancient Palestine.

Bartlett, John R. *Edom and the Edomites*. Sheffield: Sheffield Academic Press, 1989. A book that provides a thorough overview of the archaeological, textual, and historical study of the Edomites.

Campbell, Edward E. "A land divided: Judah and Israel from the death of Solomon to the fall of Samaria." In Michael D. Coogan (ed.), *The Oxford History of the Biblical World* (pp. 273–319). Oxford: Oxford University Press, 1998. A clear presentation of the history of Israel in the period of the Divided Monarchy until the Judean Exile.

Dothan, Trude and Moshe Dothan. *People of the Sea: The Search for the Philistines*. New York: Macmillan, 1992. An overview of the history of scholarship and material culture of the Philistines with pictures and diagrams and suggestions for further reading.

Hoglund, Kenneth G. "Edomites." In Alfred J. Hoerth, Gerald L. Mattingly, and Edwin M. Yamauchi (eds), *Peoples of the Old Testament World* (pp. 335–48). Grand Rapids, MI: Baker, 1994. A succinct essay on the history, culture, religion, and biblical account of the Edomites.

Howard, David M. "Philistines." In Alfred J. Hoerth, Gerald L. Mattingly, and Edwin M. Yamauchi (eds), *Peoples of the Old Testament World* (pp. 231–50). Grand Rapids, MI: Baker, 1994. An essay that surveys the origins, history, and archaeological issues concerning the Philistines.

Kitchen, K. A. "The Philistines." In Dennis J. Wiseman (ed.), *Peoples of Old Testament Times* (pp. 53–78). Oxford: Clarendon, 1973. An essay on the history, culture, and religion of the Philistines.

Lipinski, Edward. *Arameans: Ancient History, Culture, Religion*. Leuven: Peeters, 2000. A thorough examination of the history, culture, and religion of the Arameans.

Liverani, Mario. "The Amorites." In Dennis J. Wiseman (ed.), *Peoples of Old Testament Times* (pp. 100–33). Oxford: Clarendon, 1973. An essay by a well-known historian on the history, origins and biblical account of the Amorites.

Mattingly, Gerald. "Moabites." In Alfred J. Hoerth, Gerald L. Mattingly, and Edwin M. Yamauchi (eds), *Peoples of the Old Testament World* (pp. 317–34). Grand Rapids, MI: Baker, 1994. A succinct summary of the history, culture and biblical description of the Moabites.

Mazar, Amihai. *Archaeology of the Land of the Bible: 10,000–586 BCE*. New York: Doubleday, 1990. A thorough overview of the major archaeological findings in the Levant to the time of the Exile.

Mazar, Benjamin. "The historical background of the Book of Genesis." *Journal of Near Eastern Studies* 28 (1969): 73–83. An important essay that examines the historical events reflected in the narratives in Genesis.

Millard, Allan R. "The Canaanites." In Dennis J. Wiseman (ed.), *Peoples of Old Testament Times* (pp. 29–52). Oxford: Clarendon, 1973. A slightly older, but useful essay on the history and origins of the Canaanites.

Miller, Patrick D. *Religion of Ancient Israel*. Louisville, KY: John Knox Press, 2000. A thorough overview of the religion of ancient Israel, including history and issues.

Pitard, Wayne E. "Arameans." In Alfred J. Hoerth, Gerald L. Mattingly, and Edwin M. Yamauchi (eds), *Peoples of the Old Testament World* (pp. 207–30). Grand Rapids, MI: Baker, 1994. An essay that provides a succinct but thorough overview of the history, culture, and religion of the Arameans.

Pitard, Wayne E. "Before Israel: Syria-Palestine in the Bronze Age." In Michael D. Coogan (ed.), *Oxford History of the Biblical World* (pp. 25–57). Oxford: Oxford University Press, 2001. A thorough essay on the history and archaeology of Syria-Palestine during the Bronze Age.

Rendsburg, Gary A. *The Redaction of Genesis*. Winona Lake, IN: Eisenbrauns, 1986. A monograph that examines the literary features as well as the redactional process of the stories in Genesis.

Sarna, Nahum. *Genesis: The Traditional Hebrew Text with New JPS Translation/Commentary*. Philadelphia: Jewish Publication Society, 1989. A classic commentary on Genesis by a prominent Jewish scholar.

Schoville, Keith N. "Canaanites and Amorites." In Alfred J. Hoerth, Gerald L. Mattingly, and Edwin M. Yamauchi (eds), *Peoples of the Old Testament World* (pp. 157–82). Grand Rapids, MI: Baker, 1994. An essay on the history, culture, and biblical descriptions of the Canaanites and the Amorites.

Stager, Lawrence E. "Before Israel: Syria-Palestine in the Bronze Age." In Michael D. Coogan (ed.), *Oxford History of the Biblical World* (pp. 123-176). Oxford: Oxford University Press, 2001. Important essay describing the theories and archaeological research on the origin of Israel.

Stavrakopoulou, Francesca. *Land of Our Fathers: The Roles of Ancestor Veneration in Biblical Land Claims*. New York: T&T Clark, 2010. A study of the ancestor veneration and territorial claims in the Hebrew Bible.

Younker, Randall W. "Ammonites." In Alfred J. Hoerth, Gerald L. Mattingly, and Edwin M. Yamauchi (eds), *Peoples of the Old Testament World* (pp. 293–316). Grand Rapids, MI: Baker, 1994. A clear and accessible essay on the history, culture, religion, and biblical accounts of the Ammonites.

CHAPTER 3

Ancient Egypt and Israel
History, Culture, and the Biblical Text

John R. Huddlestun

In any case it is now clear that social idealism, built up on lofty conceptions of character, the earliest known and in that age the *only* transcendentalism, arose in Egypt before 2000 BC and the actual books containing it were being read in Jerusalem by the men who produced those writings which we now call the Old Testament.

James Henry Breasted, *The Dawn of Conscience*

It is all the sort of vague general knowledge which any ancient tourist spending a few weeks in Egypt at almost any date after ca. 1600 might have acquired from his dragoman.

Thomas Eric Peet, *Egypt and the Old Testament*

One of the most striking results of this research was the large impact of Egyptian culture on Isaiah. … Isaiah becomes a much more significant locus of genuine Egyptian influence than has been thought heretofore … with knowledge of the Egyptian necromantic rites, their burial practices, and one of their national deities.

Christopher B. Hays, *Death … in First Isaiah*

Isaiah had no concrete knowledge of the religious practices of Egypt, save for the fact that the Egyptians, like all the neighbors of Israel, had many gods … [his] knowledge of Egypt and its culture was no different from that of the average educated person in the modern West of the peoples and cultures of the Far East, most probably even much less.

Shmuel Ahituv (in Shirun-Grumach)

The sages of Israel were not Egyptologists.

Michael V. Fox, "World Order and Ma'at"

W riting on "the sources of our moral heritage" in the quotation above, James Henry Breasted (d. 1935), one of the giants in the field of Egyptology, traces that Western heritage back to a period a thousand years before the birth of Israel, back to the social idealism and transcendentalism of the "Egyptian social prophets"

The Wiley Blackwell Companion to Ancient Israel, First Edition. Edited by Susan Niditch.
© 2016 John Wiley & Sons, Ltd. Published 2016 by John Wiley & Sons, Ltd.

(referring mostly, but not exclusively, to Egypt's wisdom tradition). Hundreds of years later, the author avers, the Hebrew prophets adopted the Egyptian social vision, along with its conception of a messianic age. Thus, the author speaks of the West's "two-fold legacy," first from Egypt and then from the Bible. Thomas Eric Peet, an English Egyptologist/archaeologist and contemporary of Breasted (d. 1934), is less charitable in his assessment of the Bible and Egypt. His comments on the lack of authentic Egyptian material behind the exodus narrative have been echoed by more recent scholars (Redford 410–12; Ahituv in Shirun-Grumach 132; Huddlestun, "Redactors," 224). The two quotes on Isaiah represent opposite ends of the comparative spectrum – one assuming very detailed knowledge and the other very little. The final quote sums up Fox's conclusions regarding the potential appropriation of the Egyptian concept of *Ma'at* in the biblical wisdom tradition, and raises the larger issue of the disparity between modern scholars and the ancient author in that the latter, in composing a given biblical passage or book, did not comb through Egyptian anthologies in search of appropriate material.

The above epigraphs serve as an entry point for the reader into the larger topic of ancient Egypt and Israel, their cultural and historical connections and how these might inform and illuminate the biblical text where Egyptian influence has been proposed. Conclusions regarding cultural influence vary, depending on the type of parallels proposed, as well as the nature of the evidence accepted and employed to support Egyptian influence. In the discussion to follow, we take up these topics with (1) a brief summary of key historical periods in the histories of Egypt and Israel where evidence of contact and transmission of knowledge about Egypt is thought to have been most likely; (2) some comments on the comparative method, its limitations, and some useful categories for parallels, illustrated by a critical survey of some scholarly proposals for Egyptian influence; and (3) some concluding comments.

Historical and Cultural Interaction

Evidence of contact between Egypt and the Levant can be found in a variety of contexts dating well before the more familiar period of Egyptian pharaonic history. Beginning in the early third millennium BCE, one finds imported items, both to and from the southern Levant. Egyptians imported needed materials from the Levant, including timber, olive oil, and wine. While relations with the Levant, both of a commercial and military nature, continue throughout the Old and Middle Kingdoms to varying degrees (Redford 29–122; survey in Bietak 417–32), it is in the Late Bronze Age with the Egyptian New Kingdom (ca. 1550–1175 BCE), and especially the Ramesside period, where Egypt had the most extensive direct and sustained contact with the inhabitants of Syria-Palestine. Thus this period is viewed by many as pivotal in the transmission of Egyptian cultural and religious traditions to the inhabitants of the north, especially via the coastal city-states where Egypt was the most active (e.g., Byblos), as well as a handful of important inland sites. In examining the textual and archaeological material, recent studies have demonstrated the complex and multifaceted nature of Egyptian control and influence.

Scholars have debated over how precisely to characterize the nature of Egyptian rule in the Levant during this period, employing a variety of terms and models to account for changes both in the archaeological record and Egyptian policy toward the northern territories (e.g., colonialism, direct rule, elite emulation, administrative imperialism). Regardless of terminology, the architectural, ceramic, and mortuary evidence from key sites such as Deir el-Balah, Aphek, and Tell Mor indicates the presence of Egyptians in a variety of capacities beyond a military role, including potters, sculptors, engravers (of inscriptions), artists, etc. (for terminology and models, see Higginbotham 6–16 and Morris 6–20).

These Canaanite city-states or towns were ruled by local vassals ("mayors" or "kings") under Egyptian authority (having taken an oath of loyalty to the king), but granted a fair amount of independence. Their duties included paying tribute and fulfilling requests from pharaoh for specific commodities; gathering corvée workers for cultivation of fields under Egyptian control (e.g., *ANET* 238, edited by Pritchard; *AEL* 2:34, edited by Lichtheim); absorbing the cost of housing and maintaining Egyptian garrison troops in their area; and keeping the king informed regarding important events in the region under their jurisdiction. Overseeing the city-states were "commissioners" sent out by order of the king to make the rounds, visiting various towns, bringing messages from the king, dealing with other matters relating to taxes or disputes regarding food supplies or garrison troops, and ultimately reporting back to the king (Redford 199–202; Higginbotham 50–1; and Morris 256–7, 271–6).

With the effective end of Egyptian domination of the Levant following the reign of Ramesses III in the mid-twelfth century, Egypt enters into a period characterized by political decentralization and instability, with competing dynasties and kingdoms, as well as the incursion and rule of outsiders – Libyans, Nubians, and Assyrians – the latter two nations having a significant impact on the affairs of Israel and especially Judah (Kitchen). Unlike the Ramesside period, our written Egyptian sources for involvement in the Levant decrease dramatically (the campaign of Shoshenq I being a notable exception), and we must rely on other material, namely, Egyptian or Egyptian-style objects discovered in the Levant, Assyrian and Babylonian royal inscriptions, and the biblical text (see Mumford for detailed lists and summaries).

With respect to Israel and Judah, Egyptian interaction in Levantine affairs is evident in the mid-ninth century with the battle of Qarqar (853 BCE), where the pharaoh Osorkon II supplied 1,000 troops as part of an anti-Assyrian coalition, and reemerges in the mid- to late eighth century with the rise of the Saite kingdom under Tefnakhte in the western Delta and the advent of the 25th Nubian Dynasty from the south. Kings of both Israel and Judah looked to Egypt to stave off Assyrian aggression. Hoshea's plea to King So of Egypt (in 2 Kings 17:4) may have been directed at the Saite kingdom (Redford 346) or, more likely, Osorkon IV in Tanis (Kitchen 372–3, 551, and xxxix), while Hezekiah's alliance with Egypt, repeatedly condemned by the prophet Isaiah, comes to a head in the events of 701 with Sennacherib's defeat of the anti-Assyrian coalition, including the Nubian ruler Shebitku, at the battle of Eltekeh (*ANET* 287–8).

Aside from the assumed Egyptian interaction that came with diplomatic contact and political alliances under Hezekiah, the growing evidence of Egyptian religious royal symbolism in the iconographic record has also been cited as indicative of Egyptian influence (whether direct or via Phoenician channels) in the eighth century (Keel and Uehlinger 248–81, 350–4). Egyptian control of the southern Levant reached its apex (for the Late Period, at least) in the closing decades of the seventh century – under the Judean kings Josiah and Jehoiakim – with the eclipse of Assyrian control concomitant with the resurgence of the 26th Saite Dynasty king Psammeticus I (a former Assyrian vassal). Evidence from Egyptian objects and inscriptions in the region indicate that Judah was an Egyptian vassal "successor state" under this Saite king (Schipper, "Egypt and the kingdom of Judah," 204–21; COS 3:132–3, edited by Hallo and Younger). This vassal relationship continued with Psammeticus's son and successor, Necho II (610–595), and ended with his defeat by the Babylonians in 605 (at Carchemish). Necho's actions regarding Judah on the eve of the Babylonian exile are well known from the biblical text (the death of Josiah and the appointment of vassal kings with payment of tribute; 2 Kings 23:28–35; summary in Redford 441–69).

In sum, three general time frames emerge where Egyptian presence and influence appears to be strongest in the Levant: the Ramesside period (19–20th Dynasties), which although removed in time from the biblical authors, could have left a cultural imprint (compare Schipper's "leftover" presence "whereby Egyptian motifs and parts of Egyptian religion become a part of the cultural heritage of Palestine": "Egypt and Israel," 35; similarly, Redford's "cultural baggage," that made its way to Judah via the Levantine coast: 393–4); the eighth century under Hezekiah; and the late seventh century with the eclipse of Neo-Assyrian control and the 26th Dynasty filling the gap (Redford in Lipschits et al. 285–91).

As for access and possible modes of transmission of cultural knowledge, Asiatics are mentioned and depicted throughout Egypt's long history. Both in temples and private tombs of the New Kingdom, one finds ceremonial processions of Asiatics from defeated territories bringing booty or gifts to the king in Egypt, including bound prisoners of war to work in private households or in the palace, temples, or funerary temple estates (for a letter regarding a lost Asiatic slave, see Redford 221–3; Morris 475–7). Asiatics also appear in Egyptian texts and reliefs in delegations of envoys, ambassadors, or vassals, some of whom may have been native Canaanites who were bilingual (see Morris 391, 479–81). The children of Canaanite vassals could be sent to Egypt to be raised there, brought up in royal institutions and thus acculturated to Egyptian life – a practice initiated under Thutmose III (ANET 239; Redford 198–9, 224; Morris 123–4). Acculturated Asiatics appear in a variety of occupations in the New Kingdom, with some rising to high-level positions in the Egyptian administration (e.g., cup bearer and later 19th Dynasty chancellor, Baya; Redford 225). Colonies or communities of Asiatics (merchants, mercenaries, Canaanite officials in Egyptian service, etc.) are attested in a number of sites in the Delta (Bietak 422–32).

A stellar example of Egyptian presence and influence is the northern site of Beth-Shean during the Ramesside period, where excavations have brought to light a wealth of Egyptian (and Egyptian-style) material (Panitz-Cohen and Mazar). Analysis of Egyptian and local Canaanite ceramic assemblages indicates not only that Egyptians resided at Beth-Shean, but that there was clear interaction and mutual influence between Egyptian and local Canaanite potters there, with some suggesting intermarriage. Excavators estimate that at least a quarter of the city's population may have been Egyptian (Panitz-Cohen and Mazar 17–23, 274–9, 465–7). On the religious side, scholars have long called attention to private stelae from the site depicting Egyptians worshiping Canaanite deities (*ANEP* nos 475, 487, edited by Pritchard; *ANET* 249; Higginbotham 236; Morris 250–1; Wimmer 1077). Although a number of temples have been excavated at Beth-Shean, earlier assumptions that these were functioning Egyptian ones (citing parallels from Egypt) have been called into question. Rather, the deities of these temples were Canaanite and were venerated by Egyptians (on temples, see especially Wimmer, as well as his essay in Shirun-Grumach 87–123; also Higginbotham 56–9, 290–301; Morris 727–31).

Aside from archaeological evidence, a key indication of cultural interaction and influence in both directions – Egyptians in the Levant and Asiatics in Egypt – is the presence of Semitic terms and loanwords in Egyptian and, conversely, Egyptian proper names and loanwords in Semitic languages. On the Egyptian side, Semitic terms dominate in areas relating to the military/warfare and topography/ecology, while Egyptian in Semitic languages includes, among other things, personal/proper names and various words relating to Egyptian topography and technology (see Hoch, especially 460–73; Muchiki; Wimmer in Shirun-Grumach 110).

The Comparative Enterprise

Their concept of the ancient Near East is a sort of timeless cultural stew in which everything from the first cities of Sumer to the arrival of Alexander the Great is muddled together.
Morton Smith, "The present state of Old Testament studies"

There is one aspect of scholarship that has remained constant from the earliest Near Eastern scribes and omen interpreters to contemporary academicians: the thrill of encountering a coincidence. … The thought that the patterns and interrelationships that he has patiently and laboriously teased out of his data might, in fact, exist …
Jonathan Z. Smith, "The bare facts of ritual"

Comparison is never innocent but is always interested.
Bruce Lincoln, "Theses on comparison"

It is somewhat ironic that the two foundational stories which feature Egypt as their primary literary setting – the Joseph story and exodus – have been shown to have little demonstrable connection to Egypt historically, given the lack of evidence for events described in Genesis and Exodus. Over the past decades, biblical scholarship generally has focused less on historical concerns per se, that is, the extent to which these stories reflect a historical reality of the time periods they purport to describe, and has turned more to literary and ideological analyses, and particularly issues of identity formation – all of which tell us more about the time period of the composition of the text (e.g., Greifenhagen; Redford 413–19, and his chapter, "The traditions surrounding 'Israel in Egypt,'" in Lipschits et al. 279–364). The average lay reader would no doubt be surprised to learn that those portions of the Hebrew Bible that appear most indebted to ancient

Egypt are not the grand master narratives of origins, where ideology is more prominent, but isolated passages that do not feature Egypt as their subject, such as two chapters in Proverbs, or a series of biblical verses in a psalm (more below).

The suggestion of Egyptian influence, most often of a textual nature, raises a host of questions for the scholar. For influence to be possible in any given case, one must be able to explain how the donor text or other (usually iconographic) material might have been transmitted to Canaan – particularly the coastal region where Egypt had a more vested interest – and then in what fashion or form the author had access to it. Is the borrowing direct or indirect? Did the biblical writer have access to an actual Egyptian text or a later Semitic version or adaptation of that text? Few today argue that the biblical writers actually knew Egyptian (Fox 763–4), but if they had access to Semitic versions or adaptations, these were produced by Semitic speakers (Phoenicians or Canaanites who learned the language in Egypt or Egyptian scribes in Canaan?) who did. Did the biblical writer intentionally employ Egyptian material, and if so who would have recognized this in the text? In the case of a subtle use of irony, allusion, or subversion of Egyptian idiom or ideology, is the biblical author writing only for the few literate elite who would appreciate this?

Moreover, why has this parallel been proposed and what does it contribute to our understanding of the biblical text? Not all comparisons are equal. Some can be motivated by a specific concern or agenda, for example to support a specific date for a biblical text. Others may argue against influence or offer alternative explanations based on perceived theological problems that arise with the notion of biblical authors borrowing from Mesopotamian or Egyptian material. In some cases, a scholarly article seems to have come about because its author – equipped with his or her handy anthology of ancient Near Eastern texts – happened to stumble on a passage that reminded them of a biblical text, a thrilling coincidence, as Jonathan Z. Smith characterizes it, that may or may not bear up to textual or historical scrutiny (see further Huddlestun, "Who is this?" 344–7). To what extent is the content of the proposed parallel geographically confined to Egypt, such that it cannot be accounted for otherwise? What if one encounters a mixture of traditions (as is often the case), where the biblical text seems to draw on innerbiblical and/or Canaanite imagery as well?

With the above information and questions in mind, we consider below some examples of proposed Egyptian influence in the biblical text. For the sake of convenience, these will be divided into three broad categories: first, cases where Egyptian influence or borrowing is highly likely; second, cases where Egyptian influence or borrowing cannot be ruled out, but is less likely and, in some cases, implausible; and third, cases where a commonly assumed Egyptian background is problematic, despite the Egyptian setting or application for the narrative or image.

Category 1

In 1923 the Egyptian wisdom text known as The Instruction or Teaching of Amenemope (British Museum papyrus 10474) was published. Following a prologue, the text

consists of 30 chapters devoted to various wisdom themes. These are referred to explicitly in the closing exhortation: "Look to these thirty chapters, they inform, they educate
… they make the ignorant wise" (*AEL* 2:162). The following year, the German Egyptologist Adolf Erman published a detailed comparative study of Amenemope and the
"Words of the Wise" contained in Proverbs 22–24 (particularly 22:17 through 23:11,
the section possessing the greatest number of similarities to the Egyptian text). In isolating a number of significant parallels, Erman argued that the writer/editor of Proverbs
22–24 drew from an incomplete Hebrew or Aramaic version of Amenemope, and had at
times "misunderstood" and "distorted" the Egyptian text (Bryce 17–19). Consequently,
like many who followed him, Erman proposed a variety of emendations to the Hebrew
text in order to bring it in line with the text of Amenemope, its Egyptian source. A key
element in the proposed link between the two texts was seen in Proverbs 22:20: "Have I
not written for you thirty (sayings)," where the problematic Hebrew *šlšwm* was believed
to be a corruption of *šəlōšîm*, "thirty," with reference to the same number at the end of
Amenemope.

Other scholars, following Erman's lead, identified additional parallels with Proverbs,
suggested further emendations to the Hebrew text to correspond with the Egyptian,
and more clearly defined or characterized the relationship between the two texts as
one of direct literary dependence (Bryce 19–28). By the end of the decade following
Erman's initial publication, the assumed "priority and influence" of Amenemope as a
source for reconstructing the Proverbs text had become "almost absolute" (Bryce 29–
30). Yet during this same period, contrary voices emerged to challenge this near consensus, even turning it on its head by proposing Egyptian dependence on a Semitic
original, whether a Canaanite-Hebrew document that lay behind both Amenemope
and Proverbs 22–24, or arguing that the Hebrew text of Proverbs itself was translated into Egyptian, but at times misunderstood; thus, the Hebrew could be used to
correct and reconstruct the Egyptian text. These proposals were fueled in part by theological presuppositions regarding the moral superiority of biblical thought, as well
as the presence of Semitisms in the language of Amenemope, which, it was argued,
betrayed translation from a Semitic original. Others have taken a third path by arguing
for a source common to both the Egyptian and biblical texts. None of these alternative
views has gained a foothold in biblical scholarship (the first in particular has been dis-
carded), while the views of Erman (with modifications) have generally stood the test of
time.

Any assertion of unambiguous dependence of Proverbs on Amenemope would hinge
on one's ability to demonstrate a sufficient number of specific parallels – in vocabulary,
ideas, images, and sequence of sayings – that could not otherwise be accounted for
except through the writer's knowledge of the Egyptian text or a Semitic version of it.
Bryce, in formulating his own ideas regarding the stages of assimilation of Egyptian
material, called attention to those parallel passages that seemed to be more than
coincidence. Like others before and after him, he compared the language of Proverbs
22:17–19 with the first chapter of the Egyptian text (following the Hebrew Masoretic
Text with two exceptions, indicated in italics; for Amenemope, see *AEL* 2:149, 153,
162):

Incline your ear and hear *my words*, and apply your heart to my knowledge. For it will be pleasant if you keep them in your belly, that they may be ready on your lips. In order that your trust may be in the Lord. Have I not made them known to you today, even you? Have I not written for you *thirty* (sayings) of counsel and knowledge? (Prov. 22:17–19, author's translation)

Give your ears, hear the sayings, give your heart to understand them. It profits to put them in your heart, Woe to him who neglects them! Let them rest in the casket of your belly, may they be bolted to your heart; When there rises a whirlwind of words, They'll be a mooring post for your tongue. (Amenemope, col. 3:9–16)

Look to these thirty chapters, They inform, they educate. (Amenemope, col. 27:6–7)

Do not befriend the angry man, nor go with a hothead, lest you learn his ways and become ensnared. (Prov. 22:24–25, author's translation)

Do not befriend the heated man, nor approach him for conversation … Do not allow him to cast words to ensnare you. (Amenemope, col. 11.12–15)

Bryce, followed by Fox, notes the similar terms that occur in both texts and in roughly the same order (following Fox 713):

Amenemope, column 3	*Proverbs, chapter 22*
9 give/set your ears	17b incline your ear
9 the things that are said	17b my words
10 give/set your heart	17c and set your heart
11 beneficial	18a pleasant
13 make them rest	18a if you keep them
13 in the casket of your belly	18a in your belly

The mention of thirty chapters occurs at the end of Amenemope, but this does not detract from the similarities. One image that stands out is the keeping or safeguarding of these words in the "belly" (Hebrew *beṭen*) or "box/casket of the belly" (Egyptian *ḥnw n ḥt*), a motif that occurs nowhere else in wisdom prologues, biblical or Egyptian. Shupak notes the rarity of this usage of *beṭen* in biblical literature (confined to wisdom texts in Job and Proverbs), and suggests it is Egyptian in origin. The Egyptian phrase "casket of the belly" finds its Hebrew counterpart in *ḥadrê bāṭen* ("rooms/chambers of the belly"), a phrase confined to Proverbs (18:8; 20:27, 30; and 26:22), which also makes an Egyptian origin highly likely (Shupak, *"Where Can Wisdom Be Found?"* 293–7). As with the Hebrew *beṭen*, the "angry man" or "hothead" occurs only in Proverbs (e.g., 15:18; 22:24; 29:22) and, again, is equivalent to the hot-tempered or "heated man" (Egyptian *šmm/ḥmm*) in Egyptian wisdom texts. This figure is especially prominent in Amenemope (chs 2–4, 9, 10), as opposed to other Egyptian texts, which further bolsters the case for Amenemope as the source. Moving beyond these two sections to 22:17–23:11 generally, Bryce (105) calls attention to the linguistic correspondences in the opening of six of the nine parallel sections (Prov. 22:22, 24, 29 and 23:1, 4, 10 being parallel to Amenemope 4:4, 11:13, 27:16, 23:13, 9:14, and 7:12 respectively).

More recently, the argument for dependence has been taken up most forcefully by Fox in a series of shorter publications and his commentary on Proverbs. In discussing links between the two works, the author notes that 15 out of the 24 verses in Proverbs 22:17–23:11 contain one or more strong parallels in Amenemope, while two other verses have thematic (rather than verbal) affinities. In addition, shared sequences bolster the case for dependence (Fox 754–5). Similarly, Shupak, whose study of Proverbs 22–24 identifies parallels with Egyptian wisdom literature as a whole, notes that its link to Amenemope is unique: "no other Egyptian wisdom work, including works published in recent years, contains such a large number of parallels to the Hebrew composition [Prov. 22:17–23:11]" ("Instruction," 214).

As for how, when, and in what form this process of transmission occurred, scholars have offered various historical scenarios, with most assuming the biblical author/editor possessed an Aramaic version of the Egyptian text. Few would dispute a scribal context for access, but the more traditional practice of appealing to the Solomonic period with its connections to Egypt is increasingly unlikely historically (Schipper, *Israel und Ägypten*, 11–82; Ash 126–30). Some prefer the eighth century under the reign of Hezekiah, citing the biblical reference to compilation of proverbs during this period, along with that king's pro-Egyptian policies, while others favor the seventh century (Fox 764; Schipper, "Egypt and Israel," 39–40). Still others have argued for the Persian period. Regardless of date, the extent to which modern scholarship has embraced the Egyptian source model can be seen in the reputable New American Bible's translation of Proverbs 22:19–20: "That your trust may be in the Lord, I make known to you the words of Amen-em-Ope. Have I not written for you the 'Thirty,' with counsels and knowledge ...?"

In addition to Proverbs 22–24 and Amenemope, biblical scholars and Egyptologists have long debated the possibility of Egyptian influence in Psalm 104 (bibliography in Dion; M. S. Smith, *God in Translation*, 69–70). Here one encounters similar language and themes, which could indicate specific knowledge of Egyptian solar hymns, yet the postulation of any link is hampered by the problem of access and transmission, as well as the large chronological gap that separates the Egyptian and biblical materials. In this case, scholarly studies have focused on a specific Egyptian text, the so-called Great Hymn to the Aten, found on the western wall of the Amarna tomb of Ay, a highly placed official under the pharaoh Akhenaten (*AEL* 2:96–100). This fourteenth-century hymn, a key text for Amarna theology (Assmann, "Akhanyati's theology"), extols the life-giving properties of the "living Aten" (the sun disk with its light/air), manifested solely through Akhenaten his son, who alone possesses the teaching revealed to him by the Aten. A key feature of the hymn and Amarna theology is the intentional omission of themes commonly found in traditional hymns with the sun god Amun: no solar passage through the underworld and thus no adoration of the arriving deity by its inhabitants, no confrontation with the serpent Apophis, and no victorious rising. The Aten is unique and alone, with no divine retinue accompanying him on the journey. Consequently, the hymn's primary focus is on creation and sustenance of life, with all dependent on the Aten. Here scholars have isolated verses 19–30 in Psalm 104, where both texts appear to share common ideas and images, including the following (versification of the hymn varies; I follow Assmann, "Akhanyati's theology," 171–5):

> sun sets/darkness/lions (Aten hymn lines 13–19 = Psalm vv. 20–21)
> the sun rises/people to work (Aten 24–31 = Psalm vv. 22–23)
> ships sail/fish-Leviathan (Aten 39–44 = Psalm vv. 25–26)
> dependence or needs of people/food (Aten 72 = Psalm vv. 27–28)
> hiding face/power over life and death (Aten 112–113 = Psalm vv. 29–30)

Given these and other parallels, some have concluded that "there is simply no alternative explanation for the concentration of contacts between these two poems heaped up in vv. 19–30" other than biblical borrowing (Dion 59; Redford 387–8; Assmann, "Akhanyati's theology," 167; contrast *AEL* 2:100 n3). Others counter that such themes can be found in other hymns both before and after the Amarna period (part of the new solar theology or religion, which predates Amarna, and formed the basis for later Ramesside solar religion; Assmann, *Egyptian Solar Religion*, 67–101), so one need not assume the Aten hymn as the only possible source. Moreover, some of the verses singled out in Psalm 104 possess good biblical parallels (e.g., God's hiding his face in 104:29 occurs also in Psalm 30:7, compared to the beaming face in Psalm 80:3, 7, and 19), so there is no compelling reason to see a link here with the Egyptian hymn, other than the more general idea of life and death in God's hands.

Scholars have sought for a means or mechanism by which these images from the hymn could have persisted or survived in some literary form (Semitic rather than Egyptian) in the Levant. The most widely accepted explanation points to the northern coastal city of Tyre and a fourteenth-century letter containing a hymn in praise of the Egyptian king, Akhenaten, written by that city's vassal ruler, Abimilki (Amarna letter 147). Scholars have long noted the close parallels between this letter and Egyptian solar hymns, which point to some knowledge among Canaanites (albeit fragmentary, to be sure) of solar themes and motifs, which could have survived in later periods in the Levant. Fortunately, one need not depend solely on earlier Late Bronze Age texts, given that the motifs in the Tyre letter/hymn are not unique to Amarna theology, but continue in hymns of the new solar theology. For example, sweet breath (of life), north wind, and opened/blocked noses, can be found in hymns and loyalist texts prior to Amarna and continue well after, down to the Persian period (at times grouped together, e.g., "sweet breath of the north wind" on a statue from the reign of Thutmose IV; *AEL* 2:94 for a shorter Amarna hymn; for post-Amarna examples, see Assmann, *Egyptian Solar Religion*, 113, 177, 181–5, 197). This allows for the possibility that these solar themes entered Canaanite literary tradition at a later period (eighth–seventh century?), a period where Egypt's influence in southern Canaan was significant, even if not at the same level as that in the Ramesside period.

Category II

The earlier chapters of the Book of Isaiah – the so-called First Isaiah – have received renewed attention over the past decades from Assyriologists interested in the writer's portrayal of the Neo-Assyrian empire, and especially its king. At issue is the use of Neo-Assyrian royal idiom, where the biblical writer adopts, alters and/or inverts common themes to his advantage in response to Assyrian dominion. The increasing evidence of Neo-Assyrian idiom in Isaiah naturally raises the question of similar Egyptian influence in oracles relating to Egypt (e.g., chs. 18–20, 30:1–7, 31:1–5), and in fact a number of scholars have argued that First Isaiah possessed specific knowledge of Egyptian texts and religious practices. To that end, a brief consideration of three cases – each drawing on different types of Egyptian material – provides some comparative perspective vis-à-vis the Assyrian studies.

Alviero Niccacci undertakes a historical and literary analysis of the oracles regarding Egypt and Kush in Isaiah 18–20. Two key assumptions govern the author's treatment of this material: (1) contrary to much of the scholarship on Isaiah, these chapters in their entirety date to the last decades of the eighth century (ca. 728–712), and thus should be interpreted in that historical context (215); and (2) the central Egyptian figure that informs much of the language behind Isaiah 18–20 is the Nubian ruler Piye (Piankhy, ca. 735–712) and his conquest of Middle Egypt and the Delta kingdoms, as narrated on the victory stela dated to his twenty-first year (ca. 716; *AEL* 3:66–84).

Leaving aside the historical problems that arise with the above assumptions, the author identifies a number of "genuine Egyptian motifs" in these three chapters (228). Most relevant to our immediate concern, Niccacci quotes portions of the victory stela of Piye, linking it to specific passages in the biblical text, although the nature of the relationship between First Isaiah and the Egyptian text is not clarified. For example, in Isaiah 19:16, a portion of the chapter usually dated much later than the eighth century, the author notes the expression "the Egyptians will be like women" and compares this to various passages in the Piye stela, which use the terms "bulls" and "women" to characterize the defeated in contrast to Piye: "Bull (Piye) attacking bulls (his enemies)" (line 72); "their legs were (like) the legs of women" (or perhaps "knees"), referring to the rulers who came to grovel before Piye at Athribis (lines 149–50); and in the closing three-line eulogy of praise, Piye is one who "makes bulls into women" (lines 157–8). Obviously, the term "bull" is not found in Isaiah's oracle, so one is left with the single reference to the defeated as women, a motif found elsewhere in the biblical text (as the author notes), as well as ancient Near Eastern treaty curse traditions (e.g., Jer. 51:30; Esharhaddon treaty, *ANET* 540). Given the common occurrence of the motif, there is no reason to think that First Isaiah was in any way influenced by the Piye stela or Egyptian idiom generally. The author's abrupt introduction of the term "bulls" vis-à-vis women in Isaiah appears to be motivated solely by a desire to create a link with the Egyptian text where none exists. If, on the other hand, one encountered in Isaiah a description of the defeated enemy, especially Egyptians, as bulls reduced to women or some reference to Piye or a nameless Egyptian king as a mighty bull, then Egyptian influence would be worth exploring.

Another example of the author's "genuine Egyptian motifs" in these three chapters involves a link between two verses in Isaiah (19:12, 17, proclaiming pharaoh's counselors to be fools) and the speech of Piye to his troops prior to their taking of Memphis (*AEL* 2:75–6). Here the author maintains that the biblical writer intentionally counters Egyptian "official royal ideology" with Piye's unwillingness to listen to the advice of his generals, preferring to act in accordance with the command of Amun. But the comparison is vague (the Egyptian text can be translated a variety of ways), and lacks the type of specific language common to both texts necessary to indicate knowledge of the Egyptian royal idiom that informs its composition; moreover, the author's quote omits a key portion of Piye's speech, one that undercuts his case for dependence. In the above examples, as with others not discussed here, there is no demonstrable evidence – certainly not of the type that one encounters with the Neo-Assyrian material – that the examples cited from any of these oracles in Isaiah must refer to Piye or echo language of his victory stela.

In another more recent study of Isaiah 19, Hilary Marlow rejects attempts to isolate or identify specific historical allusions or markers in the oracle against Egypt and instead focuses on its literary themes, form and structure. More specifically, Marlow's thesis is that 19:1–15 constitutes a literary unity, penned by the same author, contrary to those who have argued that verses 5–10 – on the failure of the Nile inundation and its aftermath – are a later addition. The primary evidence utilized by the author to support compositional unity is a handful of well-known literary texts of the late Middle Kingdom: the Prophecy of Neferti and the Admonitions of an Egyptian Sage (*AEL* 1:139–45, 149–63). Marlow calls attention to the literary topos of "national distress" in these texts (citing Lichtheim, but not important studies that appeared after her) and from this isolates what she sees as its two larger descriptive components: (1) "a lament over the land and the unpredictability of the Nile inundation," and (2) "a description of political and social strife" (232). These two elements, the author argues, are "not separate but interrelated" in the Egyptian texts, just as the seemingly disparate oracles in chapter 19 should also be considered a unity, with the two framing oracles dealing with social and political strife, while the inner verses 5–10 deal with the land and the Nile. Thus, drawing on the Egyptian texts as models, and especially the description of the land in Neferti, the author concludes, "it is not unreasonable to read Isaiah xix 1–15 as a whole unit, in which the author has *subverted* an ancient Egyptian literary form intended to reassure, and used it to pronounce judgment on Egypt" (Marlow 235, emphasis added).

Yet before one can argue that a literary form has been "subverted," one must first demonstrate that the biblical author actually possessed knowledge of that literary form or genre, and it is here that Marlow's case is wanting, given the lack of detailed analysis with a correlation of themes between Isaiah 19 and the Egyptian texts. Of the various themes present in the Egyptian topos of social upheaval, very few are found in Isaiah. More importantly, a key literary device in the Egyptian texts is that of social reversal (poor become rich, etc., expressed with the repeated line, "what is done is what is undone"), yet there is no evidence of this in Isaiah. For example, in Neferti, the Nile is said to be dry, yet a few lines later there is water, while in the stanza that follows, "desert flocks" (foreigners) drink from the river and enjoy its benefits (*AEL* 1:141). Based on the

Admonitions and Neferti, the lowly workers along the Nile in Isaiah should be among the wealthy(!).

The author acknowledges, but does not discuss, differences ("discontinuities") between the biblical and Egyptian texts. These are explained as the result of the biblical author's adapting "the Egyptian literary topos to his own purpose" (Marlow 234 n21). While this is possible, again the clear points of *continuity* between the biblical and Egyptian texts require further elucidation before one can speak of adaptation, especially with those verses that frame 19:5–10, given these too are said to derive from the Egyptian tradition (beyond a passing reference, there is no discussion of verses 11–14 and Neferti, verses that seem more at home in a wisdom, rather than lament, context). As it stands, the points of continuity are so sparse and general as to make the concept of subversion of a known Egyptian genre highly unlikely.

Lastly, Marlow's reference to First Isaiah's knowledge of Egyptian geography and the Nile is echoed by many before her, often in stronger terms. In the case of 19:5–10, however, we can compare the biblical writer's description of the failure of Nile inundations with what we know from narrative accounts of these throughout Egyptian history, which repeatedly emphasize famine (stretching from the Old Kingdom down to the so-called Famine Stela of the Late Period). Yet the description in Isaiah, even if a later addition (which appears more likely), lacks the usual Hebrew terms used of famine, hunger or starvation (and related terms that could indicate famine). Instead, the writer draws on traditional biblical phraseology relative to God's judgment (e.g., Jer. 14:1–6; Isa. 33:9, and the later Isaiah Apocalypse in chapter 24, especially vv. 4, 7), which argues against knowledge of historically low inundations and their aftermath or the textual traditions that describe them.

A recent study of death in First Isaiah by Christopher B. Hays fully explores the relevant Mesopotamian, Egyptian, and Canaanite materials, and concludes, among other things, that the impact of Egyptian culture on the biblical author is much greater than previously believed. Three Isaiah passages are singled out for analysis: Isaiah 19:11–14, where the author sees reference to an Egyptian "royal necromantic cult" (286–8); Isaiah 22:15–19, where the prophet's denunciation of Shebna relates more to the problem of his Egyptian-style tomb, the "focal point" of the diatribe (232–49); and Isaiah 28:1–22, where the author argues at length for an active cult to the Egyptian goddess Mut behind the covenant with death (288–323).

Confining ourselves to the last example (Isa. 28:1–22), the author maintains that the heretofore enigmatic covenant with death (Hebrew *mwt* in 28:15, 18) should be interpreted as a covenant with the Egyptian goddess Mut, relative to the pro-Egyptian stance assumed by some scholars in the chapter (although Egypt is not named in the text). This goddess and the rituals associated with her worship make the most sense, the author maintains, of the seemingly disparate images in the chapter. Among these the author cites the bilingual wordplay on the name itself, the appearance of Mut in biblical personal and geographical names, Mut's sheltering or protective role with the living, which then extended to the dead and the underworld, and flower garlands with group intoxication in festivals related to the goddess. Added to this is the iconographic evidence from the Iron Age in the Levant in the form of goddess amulets, some of which can be identified as Mut. Citing this and other evidence, the author concludes that "there existed an active cult of Mut in Isaiah's time," and that the Egyptian goddess "was sought out by Israelites, Judeans and others for blessings and protection, much as she was during the same period in Egypt" (Hays 293–4).

The author's proposal is a multifaceted one that involves a number of separate, but interlinking, components, all of which are brought together because of the reading of the Egyptian goddess Mut in 28:15 and 18. This identification emerges from the problems associated with reading the Canaanite figure Mot, where evidence is lacking for a covenant, the latter being a key point for the author, who speculates that pro-Egyptian Judean officials took an oath invoking Mut's protection in a treaty covenant ceremony in Jerusalem (Hays 307; the problems with reading Mot do not in themselves constitute evidence for Egyptian Mut). Thus, the only *direct* evidence for Mut in Isaiah resides in these two reinterpreted verses; the attending elements above are circumstantial and individually open to various interpretations, as the commentaries reveal, and do not require an Egyptian setting.

Moreover, in reading the author's lengthy survey of death in ancient Egypt, the modern reader senses a disconnect between this mass of information and what he or she encounters in the words of Isaiah. There is no clear, unambiguous language that the reader finds immediately recognizable from Egyptian mortuary practices, or that leads to the inescapable conclusion that the writer possessed specific knowledge of them. Earlier in his study, the author offers the important caveat that Egyptian cultural influence "is more often filtered or refracted through a native cultural lens so that it is less obvious" (Hays 65; cf. 303 on Mut), yet his appeal to Egyptian evidence and description of an active cult to Mut in Judah leave little room for filtering or refraction; the particulars of a refracted cult are not discussed. Nevertheless, given the iconographic evidence, which attests to some awareness of Mut in the Levant, the proposal for reading this Egyptian goddess behind the oracles in Isaiah 28 remains an intriguing possibility.

Category III

In our last category, we consider two biblical passages that feature Egypt as their literary setting: the plagues in Exodus 7–8, and the description of the Egyptian king Necho II in Jeremiah 46:7–8. With the water-to-blood plague, the majority of commentators and exegetes offer a naturalistic interpretation that links the blood to the reddish color of the Nile waters in inundation. Yet a closer examination of this naturalistic reading of the plague, specifically the assumption of a high inundation as catalyst for the plague cycle, is problematic. Moreover, situating the biblical narrative in its larger ancient Near Eastern context reveals this water-to-blood motif to be a common image outside Egypt, particularly in Mesopotamian campaign accounts, where the blood of the defeated flows in/like a river, signifying the total destruction of the enemy. Although rare in Egyptian literature, the image of the blood of the slain flowing was also familiar to the biblical authors (e.g., Ezek. 32:6; Isa. 15:9). There is thus no reason to assume an Egyptian setting as the only viable context for understanding this plague (Huddlestun, "Redactors").

Jeremiah 46 contains an oracle against Egypt, specifically directed at the Egyptian king Necho II concerning his defeat at the hands of the Babylonian king Nebuchadrezzar II in the battle of Carchemish in 605. In verses 7–8, the oracle appears to quote the words of Necho II in response to the rhetorical question, "Who is this that rises like the Nile, like rivers whose waters surge?" In reply, the pharaoh asserts, "I will rise, I will cover the land; I will wipe out towns and their inhabitants." Because the oracle concerns Egypt, commentators and others have assumed the image refers to the Nile inundation, that is, Necho will cover the lands of the enemy like the flood waters of the Nile. Yet this particular image of the Egyptian king as a raging Nile flood in battle is not found in Egyptian literature. It is, however, extremely common in Neo-Assyrian royal idiom with respect to the king in battle, and is applied to Sennacherib in Isaiah 8:7–8. One cannot help but conclude that the writer here has applied a Mesopotamian royal idiom to an Egyptian king (Huddlestun, "Who is this?" 360–3).

Concluding Comments

Coming back now to our three categories of potential Egyptian influence in the biblical text, the cases discussed above illustrate the uncertainties that confront the comparativist, even in cases where the evidence appears strongest. Any assertion of borrowing or influence must acknowledge the gap in our knowledge concerning the means by which the biblical author came to possess knowledge of Egypt and/or the relevant Egyptian source material. Moreover, each example involves, to varying degrees, a certain amount of speculation and circumstantial pleading. Nevertheless, some cases for influence and borrowing have been shown to be stronger than others. In the example of Amenemope and Proverbs, we have a sizable amount of material to compare (487 lines in Amenemope and 23 verses of Proverbs 22:17–23:11, where the parallels are most evident – not counting other passages in Proverbs that show possible influence), so one can obtain a reasonable idea of the relationship of the two in terms of the number or percentage of strong parallels that are difficult to explain without recourse to this specific Egyptian text. In addition, both texts belong to the well-established wisdom tradition/genre in the ancient Near East, one that emphasized learning and facilitated the transmission of texts, and in which the biblical writers were fully a part (Shupak, "Where Can Wisdom Be Found?").

With Psalm 104 and the hymn to the Aten, the amount of alleged common content is much smaller (11 biblical verses in the Psalm and roughly 25–30 lines in the Egyptian hymn, depending on one's versification and the extent of proposed influence). Nevertheless, given the parallel content in these few verses (especially vv. 20–21 on darkness, a rare motif in solar hymns outside Amarna; Assmann, Egyptian Solar Religion, 100–1), it is difficult to deny some type of literary dependence, although we can only speculate on what type of source the biblical writer had. The Egyptian solar themes in the Amarna letter from Tyre point to some Canaanite knowledge of the genre already in the fourteenth century BCE. But since some of these motifs continue down into the mid-first millennium in Egyptian literature, one could equally argue for a later date of transmission, for example, in the eighth–seventh centuries (or slightly later). Given the close thematic parallels and, in some cases, shared sequencing, these two examples fall into our first category, where Egyptian influence is highly likely, if not virtually certain.

With the cases relating to First Isaiah, the arguments for Egyptian influence do not focus on acknowledged similarities in specific language, sequence and context, such as we see above. Rather, in the first two cases with Isaiah 19, the appeal to Egyptian material (Egyptian royal ideology in the Piye stela and Middle Kingdom literary texts, especially Neferti) is more general in nature, and stems in part from debates regarding the date and historical context for the Isaiah oracles. In that sense, the search for parallels is not innocent (*pace* Lincoln), but seeks to demonstrate a particular position regarding the biblical text, namely an eighth-century date for Isaiah 18–20, and the compositional unity of Isaiah 19:1–15. In both cases, the proposed links between Isaiah and the Egyptian texts (a particular image of the enemy as women and royal ideology in the Piye stela, and the descriptions of social and political upheaval in the land) are not specific enough to allow the conclusion that the First Isaiah (assuming the same author throughout) had knowledge of these texts or the ideological and literary norms that governed their composition. This is not to say that the biblical author could not possess knowledge of Egyptian royal idiom and other literary traditions, only that the proposals above do not demonstrate this. More significantly, in the light of comparison with studies of Neo-Assyrian dependence, attempts to demonstrate the First Isaiah's use of comparable Egyptian idiom are problematic. (Note the Egyptian king does not speak or boast in First Isaiah, as is the case with the Assyrian king; e.g., Isa. 10:12–14). The third case is somewhat different in that the First Isaiah's knowledge of Egyptian religious practices is not based on Egyptian textual sources, but proposed new readings of heretofore problematic biblical passages (Isa. 22 and 28), coupled with iconographic material in the Levant. To that degree, the cases regarding Shebna's Egyptianized tomb and the covenant/cult of Mut may be characterized as more circumstantial, where the combination of elements read in a different light leads to a new understanding of the chapters. That Egyptian influence might be "less obvious" when translated into a Levantine context is an important point for any comparison. The problem, of course, is precisely how obvious does such influence have to be in order to qualify as such? A key contribution of Hays's study of death in First Isaiah is its scope, that is, drawing on evidence from throughout the ancient Near East to elucidate the biblical author's themes, images, and language relating to death. This leads us to our third category.

Our last category explores a less obvious, but no less significant, phenomenon in comparative studies, namely, the extent to which biblical writers might appropriate culturally and geographically disparate materials, that is, applying a common Neo-Assyrian image to an Egyptian king (Necho II) or adapting a common ancient Near Eastern image of defeat and destruction (well known in Mesopotamian royal idiom, but not in Egypt) to a particular Egyptian setting (the first plague in Exodus). In both cases, the modern interpreter must readjust his or her comparative lens when reading biblical and other ancient Near Eastern literature. Not being Egyptologists (or Assyriologists), the resourceful biblical writers did not adhere to such disciplinary boundaries in their search for the most apt metaphor or image to make their case. Neither should the modern scholar who reads them.

Bibliography

Ash, Paul. *David, Solomon and Egypt: A Reassessment.* Journal for the Study of the Old Testament, suppl. 297. Sheffield: Sheffield Academic Press, 1999. A survey of the evidence leads to the conclusion that there were "minimal relations" between the united monarchy and Egypt with no evidence of direct control or political influence.

Assmann, Jan. "Akhanyati's theology of light and time." *Proceedings of the Israel Academy of Sciences and Humanities* 7 (1992): 143–75. Analysis of the Great Hymn to the Aten from Amarna with some discussion of its relationship to Psalm 104.

Assmann, Jan. *Egyptian Solar Religion in the New Kingdom: Re, Amun and the Crisis of Polytheism.* Translated, revised and enlarged from German edn of 1983. London: Kegan Paul International, 1995. A seminal work on New Kingdom solar religion, including the emergence of new solar theology, the Amarna "heresy," and the Amun theology of the Ramesside period.

Bar, S., D. Kahn and J. J. Shirley (eds). *Egypt, Canaan and Israel: History, Imperialism, Ideology and Literature: Proceedings of a Conference at the University of Haifa, 3–7 May 2009.* Leiden: Brill, 2011. A collection of papers on a variety of topics dealing with Egypt, the Levant, and the biblical text, which illustrate the broad range of approaches taken by current scholarship in comparative studies.

Bietak, Manfred. "Egypt and the Levant." In Toby Wilkinson (ed.), *The Egyptian World* (pp. 417–48). London: Routledge, 2007. A nicely illustrated discussion of interactions and cross-influences between Egyptian and neighboring cultures with attention to material, artistic, commercial, and military dimensions.

Breasted, James Henry. *The Dawn of Conscience.* New York: Scribners, 1934. Classic maximalist reading of Egyptian-Israelite interaction.

Bryce, Glendon E. *A Legacy of Wisdom: The Egyptian Contribution to the Wisdom of Israel.* Cranbury, NJ: Associated University Presses, 1979. Surveys the history of scholarship on Proverbs and Amenemope with attention to the types/stages of transmission of Egyptian material.

Dion, Paul. "YHWH as storm-god and sun-god: The double legacy of Egypt and Canaan as reflected in Psalm 104." *Zeitschrift für die Alttestamentliche Wissenschaft* 103 (1979): 43–71. Examines both Canaanite and Egyptian elements in the psalm, arguing that some form of the hymn to the Aten was the source of inspiration for the psalmist.

Fox, Michael V. *Proverbs 1–9* (Anchor Bible 18A) and *Proverbs 10–31* (Anchor Bible 18B). New Haven: Yale University Press, 2007–2009. Provides up-to-date treatment of various scholarly issues and debates regarding the biblical book, with full analysis of the Egyptian context and background of Proverbs 22–24.

Fox, Michael V. "World Order and Ma'at: A Crooked Parallel." *Journal of the Ancient Near Eastern Society* 23 (1995), 37–48. Author adopts a more skeptical approach toward the identification of the Egyptian concept of Ma'at in Proverbs 1–9.

Greifenhagen, F. V. *Egypt on the Pentateuch's Ideological Map: Constructing Biblical Israel's Identity.* Journal for the Study of the Old Testament, suppl. 361. Sheffield: Sheffield Academic Press, 2002. Examines the multiple images of Egypt in the Pentateuch and the process by which the more pro-Egyptian stance was subordinated to a more negative one.

Hallo, W. H. and K. L. Younger (eds). *The Context of Scripture.* 3 vols. Leiden: Brill, 1997–2002. Recent collection of texts relevant to the study of the Hebrew Bible. Abbreviated as *COS*.

Hays, Christopher B. *Death in the Iron Age II and in First Isaiah.* Forschungen zum Alten Testament 79. Tübingen: Mohr Siebeck, 2011. A wide-ranging study of death in First Isaiah, which draws on ancient Near Eastern materials; the author emphasizes "the large impact of Egyptian culture" in the book.

Higginbotham, Carolyn R. *Egyptianization and Elite Emulation in Ramesside Palestine: Governance and Accommodation on the Imperial Periphery.* Leiden: Brill, 2000. An influential study of Egyptian rule in the Levant, which evaluates the evidence via two models (direct Egyptian control vs local elite emulation).

Hoch, James E. *Semitic Words in Egyptian Texts of the New Kingdom and Third Intermediate Period.* Princeton: Princeton University Press, 1994. The standard reference for all aspects of the linguistic study of the Semitic lexicon in Egyptian texts of this period.

Huddlestun, John R. "Who is this that rises like the Nile?" Some Egyptian texts on the inundation and a prophetic trope. In Astrid B. Beck et al. (eds), *Fortunate the Eyes That See: Essays in Honor of David Noel Freedman in Celebration of His Seventieth Birthday* (pp. 338–63). Grand Rapids, MI: Eerdmans, 1995. Surveys some Egyptian texts on the inundation with analysis of the image of pharaoh Necho in Jeremiah 46.

Huddlestun, John R. "Redactors, rationalists, and (bloodied) rivers: Some comments on the first biblical plague." In David Vanderhooft and Abraham Winitzer (eds), *Politics as Literature, Literature as Politics: Essays on the Ancient Near East in Honor of Peter Machinist* (pp. 211–25). Winona Lake, IN: Eisenbrauns, 2013. Argues against the naturalistic reading of the water-to-blood motif in the first plague as a uniquely Egyptian phenomenon.

Keel, Othmar and Christoph Uehlinger. *Gods, Goddesses, and Images of God in Ancient Israel.* Trans. from German edn of 1992. Minneapolis: Fortress, 1998. Seminal study of the iconographical evidence relating to ancient Israelite religion, with detailed surveys of Egyptian religious and royal symbolism in the ninth–eighth centuries.

Kitchen, Kenneth A. *The Third Intermediate Period in Egypt (1100–650 BC).* 2nd edn with supplement and 1995 Preface. Warminster, UK: Aris & Phillips, 1996. A leading reference work for this period of Egypt's history.

Lichtheim, Miriam (ed.). *Ancient Egyptian Literature: A Book of Readings.* 3 vols. Berkeley: University of California Press, 1973–1980. A standard anthology of Egyptian texts in translation. Abbreviated as *AEL*.

Lincoln, Bruce. "Theses on comparison." In Lincoln, *Gods and Demons, Priests and Scholars* (pp. 121–30). Chicago: University of Chicago Press, 2012. Discussion of some guiding principles for comparison by a leading scholar of religious studies.

Lipschits, Oded, Gary N. Knoppers, and Manfred Oeming (eds). *Judah and the Judeans in the Achaemenid Period: Negotiating Identity in an International Context.* Winona Lake, IN: Eisenbrauns, 2011. An important collection of essays dealing with identity issues in the Persian period, some relating to Egypt (especially by Redford, Lemaire, Quack, Becking, Wright).

Marlow, Hilary. "The lament over the River Nile – Isaiah xix 5–10 in its wider context." *Vetus Testamentum* 57 (2007): 229–42. Argues for the compositional unity of Isaiah 19 based on parallels in Egyptian Middle Kingdom literary texts.

Morris, Ellen Fowles. *The Architecture of Imperialism: Military Bases and the Evolution of Foreign Policy in Egypt's New Kingdom.* Leiden: Brill, 2005. A seminal study of Egyptian foreign policy in the New Kingdom period via analysis of fortresses and administrative headquarters erected in or near Nubia and the Levant.

Muchiki, Yoshiyuki. *Egyptian Proper Names and Loanwords in North-West Semitic.* Society of Biblical Literature Dissertation Series 173. Atlanta: Society of Biblical Literature, 1999. Surveys evidence for proper names and loanwords in Phoenician, Aramaic, Hebrew, etc., with very brief analysis of their cultural and religious significance.

Mumford, Gregory. "Egypto-Levantine relations during the Iron Age to early Persian periods (Dynasties 20 to 26)." In Thomas Schneider and Kasia Szpakowska (eds), *Egyptian Stories: A British Egyptological Tribute to Alan B. Lloyd on the Occasion of His Retirement* (pp. 225–88).

Münster: Ugarit-Verlag, 2007. Provides detailed lists and summaries of all known material relevant to Egypt's relations with the Levant in this period.

Niccacci, Alviero. "Isaiah XVII–XX from an Egyptological perspective." *Vetus Testamentum* 48 (1998): 214–38. Dates Isaiah 18–20 exclusively to the late eighth century and proposes examples of "genuine Egyptian motifs" in these oracles.

Panitz-Cohen, Nava and Amihai Mazar (eds). *Excavations at Tel Beth-Shean 1989–1996: Volume III: The 13th–11th Century BCE Strata in Areas N and S.* Jerusalem: Israel Exploration Society and Hebrew University of Jerusalem, 2009. Excavation report with essays on Egyptian and Egyptianized material at the site (pottery, small finds, scarabs, seals, inscribed objects, amulets, etc.).

Peet, Thomas Eric. *Egypt and the Old Testament.* Liverpool: Liverpool University Press, 1922. A historical survey of ancient Egypt and Israel by a British Egyptologist, who adopted a more critical stance toward the value of the biblical narrative.

Pritchard, James B. *Ancient Near East in Pictures Relating to the Old Testament (ANEP).* 2nd edn, with suppl. Princeton: Princeton University Press, 1969. Collection of visual sources from Mesopotamia, Egypt and elsewhere in the Near East relevant to the Hebrew Bible. Abbreviated as *ANEP*.

Pritchard, James B. (ed.). *Ancient Near Eastern Texts Relating to the Old Testament with Supplement.* 3rd edn. Princeton: Princeton University Press, 1969. Classic collection of ancient texts relevant to the study of the Hebrew Bible. Abbreviated as *ANET*.

Redford, Donald B. *Egypt, Canaan, and Israel in Ancient Times.* Princeton: Princeton University Press, 1992. A standard survey that examines all aspects of the relationship between Egypt and the Levant throughout their histories.

Schipper, Bernd Ulrich. *Israel und Ägypten in der Königszeit. Die kulturellen Kontakte von Salomo bis zum Fall Jerusalems.* Orbis Biblicus et Orientalis 170. Göttingen: Vandenhoeck & Ruprecht, 1999. A detailed exploration of the types of contact and influence (political, commercial, and personal) between Israel and Egypt during the period of the monarchy.

Schipper, Bernd Ulrich. "Egypt and the kingdom of Judah under Josiah and Jehoiakim." *Tel Aviv* 37 (2010): 200–26. Survey of the archaeological and inscriptional evidence relating to Judah during the closing decades of the seventh century under the 26th Dynasty.

Schipper, Bernd Ulrich. "Egypt and Israel: The ways of cultural contacts in the Late Bronze Age and Iron Age (20th–26th Dynasty)." *Journal of Ancient Egyptian Interconnections* 4 (2012): 30–47. Proposes two types of cultural contact between Egypt and the Levant: indirect influence in the earlier period, followed by more direct in the 25th–26th Dynasties.

Shirun-Grumach, Irene (ed.). *Jerusalem Studies in Egyptology.* Wiesbaden: Harrassowitz, 1998. A collection of papers dealing with a wide variety of topics on Egypt, the Levant, and the biblical text.

Shupak, Nili. *"Where Can Wisdom Be Found?" The Sage's Language in the Bible and in Ancient Egyptian Literature.* Orbis Biblicus et Orientalis 130. Göttingen: Vandenhoeck & Ruprecht, 1993. Seminal comparative study of terms and phrases in Egyptian and biblical wisdom literature.

Shupak, Nili. "The Instruction of Amenemope and Proverbs 22:17–24:22 from the perspective of contemporary research." In R. L. Troxel, K.G. Friebel, and D. N. Magary (eds), *Seeking Out the Wisdom of the Ancients: Essays Offered to Honor Michael V. Fox on the Occasion of his Sixty-Fifth Birthday* (pp. 203–20). Winona Lake, IN: Eisenbrauns, 2005. A survey of recent scholarship, which situates Proverbs 22–24 in its wider Egyptian wisdom context and argues for direct dependence on Amenemope.

Smith, Jonathan. "The bare facts of ritual." In Smith, *Imagining Religion: From Babylon to Jonestown* (pp. 53–65). Chicago: University of Chicago Press, 1982. A classic essay on the interpretation of ritual by a leading scholar of religious studies.

Smith, Mark S. *God in Translation: Cross-Cultural Recognition of Deities in the Biblical World.* Grand Rapids, MI: Eerdmans, 2010. Study of the relationships between polytheism and monotheism in the ancient world.

Smith, Morton. "The present state of Old Testament studies." *Journal of Biblical Literature* 88 (1969): 19–35. Critique of contemporary approaches to biblical research.

Wimmer, Stefan. "Egyptian temples in Canaan and Sinai." In Sarah Israelit-Groll (ed.), *Studies in Egyptology Presented to Miriam Lichtheim* (pp. 1065–99). 2 vols. Jerusalem: Magnes Press, 1990. An important survey of the evidence for Egyptian temples in the Levant (with follow-up essay in Shirun-Grumach, *Jerusalem Studies in Egyptology*).

CHAPTER 4

Text and Context in Biblical Studies
A Brief History of a Troubled Relationship

Steven Weitzman

> If we read a book which contains incredible or impossible narratives, or is written in a very obscure style, and if we know nothing of its author, nor of the time and occasion of its being written, we shall vainly endeavor to gain any certain knowledge of its true meaning. (Spinoza 111)

When these words were first published in 1670, no one so much as knew who their true author was. That would soon change, however, for they and the work in which they appeared – Spinoza's *Theologico-Political Treatise* – would go on to transform the field of biblical scholarship. Biblical interpreters at the time thought they already knew how to gain "certain knowledge" of the Bible's meaning. Spinoza challenged their certitude by endeavoring to factor into interpretation what we would call historical context: "the life, the conduct, and the studies of the author of each book, who he was, what was the occasion, and the epoch of his writing, whom did he write for, and in what language" – knowledge which could be partially reconstructed, he argued, and which exposed much of the biblical interpretation of his day as sheer fancy and anachronism. His attention to historical context was in fact essential to the interpretive revolution that Spinoza helped to initiate, a revolution that displaced the faith-based view of the Bible dominating Europe until that time, a view that looked to it as a source of contemporary religious and political norms, in favor of an empirically based view of the Bible as a human composition limited in relevance to the age in which it was produced.[1]

If Spinoza's effort to contextualize the Bible seems straightforward now, one reason is that we ourselves operate in a context shaped in part by what he and other historically minded biblical scholars initiated. But not everyone has been convinced that one needs to contextualize the Bible to understand it. In Spinoza's own day, those who resisted

The Wiley Blackwell Companion to Ancient Israel, First Edition. Edited by Susan Niditch.
© 2016 John Wiley & Sons, Ltd. Published 2016 by John Wiley & Sons, Ltd.

the historical contextualization of the Bible included his close associate Ludwig Meyer, perhaps the hidden opponent that the *Theologico-Political Treatise* was written to counter. Like Spinoza, Meyer recognized that the Bible was fundamentally obscure, but he did not look to historical context – to the author's intentions or occasion of composition – to resolve its meaning. What was necessary instead, he argued, was a knowledge of ideas that transcended the particular circumstances in which the Bible was written, ideas that were not time-bound and contingent but were eternal and universal. To understand the Bible according to Meyer, one need not engage in historical inquiry; on the contrary, one had to focus on what was timeless in the text, those aspects of it that transcended the context in which it was composed and were true in all possible settings.

Spinoza would seem to have won his debate with Meyer, at least within secular academe, but Meyer too has his modern-day counterparts, scholars who reject the idea that one needs to understand the author, time, and occasion of the Bible's composition to understand its meaning – though their indifference to historical context originates from a different intellectual orientation. In the final decades of the twentieth century, scholars became skeptical of the very possibility of historicizing the Bible. Knowledge that Spinoza thought was essential for determining the Bible's meaning – knowledge of who wrote it, when and in what circumstances – came be to be regarded by such scholars as beyond reach or simply beside the point, and what they proposed instead were modes of interpretation that did not require "extrinsic" knowledge of historical context but only an internal understanding of the text itself. In what follows, we will briefly survey this reaction against historical context in late twentieth-century biblical studies, and what has happened in its wake to Spinoza's project of reading the Bible in its historical context.

The Bible Displaced

It is one thing to claim that the meaning of biblical literature is context-dependent; it is another thing to try to define what it is that we mean by context. Context can overlap with what we mean by environment – the surroundings in which an organism operates or to which it responds – and indeed it has been defined by Ian Hodder as "the totality of the relevant environment" (143), but contexts do not exist in nature. They are constructions of the human imagination – artificial, ex post facto, an approximation of a real environment but selective and incomplete, like a museum display that artificially simulates the environment in which an object was originally used. As Robert Hume observes, a context is not a fact but a hypothesis which we use to explain texts, authors and situations (69). We use them to interpret texts, but they themselves come to exist only through interpretive construction, depending on abstraction, assemblage, judgments of relevance; furthermore, their contours vary depending on the perspective and goals of the interpreter.

The ambiguity and plasticity of context in general complicates what we mean by the historical context of the Bible. Spinoza had in mind the context in which its literature was written, but we now know that the composition of biblical books like Jeremiah spanned many centuries, and that it is often extremely difficult to distinguish the contributions of an original author or authors from later editors and copyists. Not a few scholars have given up on trying to contextualize the composition of the Bible, focusing instead on the historical contexts in which it came to be read. Though they will not be our focus here, biblical scholars have grown increasingly interested in the later meanings superimposed on the Bible over the history of its reception.

At the risk of appearing a little old-fashioned, my focus here will be on the Spinozan concept of context, the context(s) in which the Bible's authors lived and that is germane in one way or the other for understanding its composition and intended meaning. Narrowing what we mean by context, however, hardly simplifies things very much, for historical context in this sense can encompass not just historical facts, such as who the author was or when he lived, but conceivably any extratextual phenomenon deemed relevant for understanding the genesis and intended meaning of the text – events, literary influences, institutional sponsors, material conditions, and on and on. What aspects of the world beyond the biblical text – of that borderless context known as the ancient Near East for instance – do we need in order to understand its meaning, and where do we draw the line if we are not ready to consider everything as potentially relevant? The context of the Bible's composition remains elusive not just because we know so little about the world that produced the Bible but also because the concept of context itself is so slippery.

Consider what has befallen one of the best-known efforts by biblical scholarship to formulate a notion of context, the project known as "form criticism," which, among other goals, seeks to recover the *Sitz im Leben*, the "setting in life" out of which biblical literature developed and derived its original meaning and function. Developed in the early twentieth century by the German biblical scholar Hermann Gunkel, form criticism began from a sophisticated understanding of the relationship between texts and context, anticipating the philosophy of Wittgenstein, the speech act theory of J. L. Austin and sociolinguistics by recognizing that the meaning of words depends on how they are used in real-life social settings. By applying this insight to various genres reflected in biblical literature – most famously, the Psalms – Gunkel and later form critics were able to develop ingenious reconstructions of the underlying social settings out of which these genres developed, theories that had a profound influence on biblical scholarship. And yet, by the 1960s and 1970s, form criticism had gone into decline, and what happened to it, as critics have noted, is not simply that it became too speculative but that its practitioners found themselves drawn into the interpretive vortex of contextualization, now drawing ever more elaborate distinctions among various kinds of setting – the setting of performance, of transcription into writing, of reception, and so on. There never came a moment when form criticism was discredited; it simply seems to have exhausted itself in a never-ending quest for always elusive life-settings (Buss).

The difficulties encountered by form criticism are emblematic of a larger decontextualizing trend that beset biblical studies in the final decades of the twentieth century. In the centuries that followed Spinoza, Western scholarship had spectacular success in recovering the world in which the Bible was composed, deciphering ancient Near Eastern texts that illuminated its form and content and using archaeology to retrieve the geography, society and culture of ancient Israel. The results of all this effort are ably described elsewhere in this very volume, so suffice it to note here that scholars have demonstrated again and again the interpretive benefits of this kind of contextualization. By the end of the twentieth century, however, a countertrend had emerged from within academic biblical scholarship, a reaction against the effort to connect the Bible to extrabiblical reality. This resistance to historicizing the Bible cannot be traced to one particular argument, motivation or approach, but it happened to mirror a larger antihistoricizing trend in the humanities that crystalized in the same period.

One development that fed this skepticism was the reassessment of the archaeological evidence that had been used to connect the Bible to "facts on the ground." In the late 1960s and 1970s, as William Albright and other figures who had dominated biblical archaeology died, a crisis of confidence emerged in the field, a rising skepticism of what archaeology could reveal about the Hebrew Bible. Well-known discoveries that had seemed to confirm the historicity of the biblical account – the remnants of Solomon's kingdom at Megiddo and Hazor, as well as in the Negev where he allegedly had mining operations – proved upon reexamination to admit of other interpretations and to come from other periods, and scholars began to propose alternative reconstructions based on what they now perceived to be a *disjuncture* between the biblical testimony and the archaeological record (see Brad Kelle's essay in this volume). The best known – or most notorious – of these scholars are the so-called "minimalists," scholars like Thomas Thompson and Philip Davies who sought to "separate" the Bible from history, but they were not the only ones affected by this view. Already in the 1970s, leading archaeologists like William Dever, though later an opponent of the minimalists, distinguished what he was doing from earlier archaeologists who sought to use archaeology to prove a connection between the Bible and specific historical events. He and others began describing themselves as Syro-Palestinian archaeologists rather than biblical archaeologists in part to emphasize what they now saw as the disconnection between the biblical text and the archaeology, and the perception that, more often than not, they seem irrelevant for understanding one another (Dever 3–36; see also Elizabeth Bloch-Smith's essay in this volume).

And even those who had a more optimistic view of archaeology's potential to illumine the Bible could not escape the hermeneutical challenges of contextualization. Megan Moore has recently undertaken a survey of what she refers to as "non-minimalist" biblical historiography – histories written by scholars who believe that the Bible contains some reliable information about the past that it describes – and she finds great variety in how they connect the biblical testimony to the archaeological evidence. Some subordinate the biblical evidence to the archaeology, making sense of the Bible in light of the latter, but others insist that the archaeology can only be fully understood in light of the biblical text (Moore 126–30). There is still a widespread desire to connect the Bible to the archaeology – as witnessed by the popularity of the journal *Biblical Archaeology Review*, which in 2010 enjoyed a circulation of 176,000 according to the website Echo Media – but as Moore registers, there is currently no scholarly consensus about what makes one relevant for interpreting the other even for those convinced of such relevance.

Something similar undercut the relevance of ancient Near Eastern literature. Scholarship has continued to digest and to learn from it well into the twenty-first century, but as Mark Smith observes in a recent history of Ugaritic studies, even as new dictionaries and other tools were being published that facilitated the comparative study of the Bible, there also emerged in the 1960s, 1970s and 1980s new challenges to such comparison (Smith 163–9; see also the essays by John Huddlestun and Mark Smith in this volume). Scholars became increasingly aware of the perils of "parallelomania," the overextension of comparisons between the Bible and other ancient literatures as exemplified by the work of Mitchell Dahood, author of the Anchor Bible commentary on the book of Psalms, who used Ugaritic parallels to reconstruct many new readings of the Bible that seemed even to partisans of Ugaritic studies to be far-fetched. One scholar went so far as to remark that the failings of Dahood's parallels signaled the demise of Ugaritic as a resource for biblical studies (Brevard Childs, cited in Smith 163). Others responded to the overextension of ancient Near Eastern parallels by discontinuing their own use of such evidence, or by reexamining the so-called "comparative method" in ways that exposed its questionable premises and overreaching. Also contributing to the decline of the comparative method, finally, was the decline of new textual discoveries in the second half of the twentieth century to match those of the first three decades. Not that there were not new discoveries. In 1974–5, for example, archaeologists uncovered thousands of clay tablets at the Syrian site of Ebla which seemed at first to reveal many links to the biblical world, but this time, it turned out that the evidence was not as relevant as it initially seemed, for it became apparent that the connections were sensationalized, which in turn only reinforced the skepticism of those who believed the field had overstressed the value of such comparison.

Such developments need not have called the very act of contextualizing the Bible into question. Revision, refinement, and reassessment are inherent in any historical enterprise, and in the field of biblical scholarship, it has led in some cases to scholarship that is more aware of its own assumptions even as it pursues the project of historical contextualization (see, e.g., Machinist for an excellent effort to rethink a comparative approach to ancient Israel that is both self-aware and historicizing at the same time). But as it happens, doubts about form criticism, archaeology and the comparative method in biblical studies emerged in the field just in the period when the humanities in general were coming under the influence of certain literary theories that aimed to challenge conventional scholarly notions about how to relate texts and contexts, making the effort to connect them problematic not just in a contingent sense – an accidental reflection of what we happen to know or not know about a particular historical era – but necessarily so, as a problem that arises whenever one tries to anchor a text in a reality external to it.

The best-known of these theories, recognizable to anyone familiar with academic culture in the 1970s and 1980s, was an outgrowth of the posthumously published *Course in General Linguistics* by the Swiss linguist Ferdinand de Saussure, a seminal work of modern linguistics which helped to spawn both structuralism and poststructuralism by developing a way of analyzing language without reference to what Saussure called "external linguistic phenomena," to the things in the world to which language is referring or which can shape how it is used. What Saussure was interested in was the internal workings of language, how it worked as a system of signs whose power to signify was determined not by some inherent correspondence to whatever it is that it signified but through its contrastive relationship to other signs within the same linguistic system. Over the course of the twentieth century, Saussure's internal linguistic became a justification for a kind of textual hermeticism. Like language, literature came to be seen as a self-enclosed system that can be analyzed without reference to an external world. Recent scholars like Schalkwyk have argued that Saussure has been misconstrued, that he did not really advocate an unbridgeable rupture between language and the world. That, however, was how he was understood by scholars already primed by New Criticism to reject any kind of literary explanation that depended on or appealed to a reality external to the text. The New Criticism, an approach popular in the 1940s and 1950s, had tried to interpret texts solely based on the words on the page rather than in reference to the author's presumed intentions.

In some of its best-known forms, post-Saussureanism, better known as poststructuralism, argued for the dissolution of context altogether, or at least that was what its argument was understood to be in the broader academic culture. From Saussure's idea that the concept of something cannot exist independently of language, there emerged views such as the one ascribed to Jacques Derrida, that there is no access to the reality behind or beyond the text, not simply because we have no independent access to that reality but because there is no behind or beyond the text. To contextualize the text, to link its content to a real world behind the text – to the intention of an author, for instance – is to supplement it, to add something to the text without seeing that we do so, when there is nothing more than the writing itself. It was the effort to draw out the implications of this view that produced what has come to be known as the "linguistic turn," the rejection of the idea of language as a window onto a reality existing outside of or prior to language in favor of a "poststructuralist" view of reality as always linguistically mediated and therefore understandable only by means of an "intrinsic approach" – by analysis that aimed to understand language without considering to what it was referring in reality.

The influence of all this on biblical studies in the 1970s and 1980s is reflected in many corners of the field, but one example here may suffice to illustrate the larger reorientation that took place: the so-called literary approach to the Bible as developed by Meir Sternberg in his *The Poetics of Biblical Narrative*. Sternberg's approach is a descendant of Saussure's thinking, coming out of the Tel Aviv school of poetics, which was heir to Russian formalism, which itself grew as a development of Saussure's ideas, and it addressed the relevance of historical context in a typically Saussurean fashion.

Though paying lip service to the importance of historical context, Sternberg does not believe that we can actually reconstruct such a context. The "real world" out of which the Bible emerged is virtually inaccessible to us; we know almost nothing about it; and any sense of context that we can reconstruct is something we must infer from the text itself. However, this is a serious predicament only for those trying to learn something about "the real world behind the Bible," which was not Sternberg's goal. Ultimately, his focus was on the Bible not as a source of information about extratextual reality but as discourse – "the text itself as a pattern of meaning and effect" – and for such a project, information about the world outside the Bible is irrelevant. It might seem helpful to establish who wrote a particular biblical text, but even if such information were within reach, for Sternberg, it is beside the point for understanding the Bible as discourse, for the storyteller that matters from that perspective is not the author behind the text but the author projected by the text itself, a figure that only exists in and through language. For all its apparent openness to questions of historical context, Sternberg's approach turns out to be an offshoot of the "internal analysis" of language developed by Saussure.

It needs to be stressed that the problem of historicization that Sternberg was seeking a way around was not simply the problem of not knowing enough about the ancient past or the Bible's compositional history, a problem that Spinoza himself was perfectly ready to acknowledge limited our understanding of the Bible's meaning. That more information about the past does not alter the picture is shown by the fact that scholars of much better-documented periods also faced the disconnect between signs and referents that Sternberg is describing. It was certainly an option to ignore the implications of poststructuralism and this was an option that many biblical scholars exercised, but that response requires one to avoid engaging the implications of ideas that, in other fields, were transforming the nature of literary and historical interpretation. But if one takes this challenge seriously, what becomes of the historicizing project that Spinoza initiated? Should one simply give up on it, as Sternberg and others in this period seemed to be recommending? Some biblical scholars did so, but others, not so ready to abandon the Spinozan project or their own training in history and archaeology, began looking for ways to reassert the importance of historical context for understanding the Bible without, however, simply ignoring the implications of poststructuralism. As it happens, one such option emerged in the 1980s, arriving in what seemed like the nick of time to rescue biblical studies from the ahistoricism of recent literary theory. This approach came to be known as the New Historicism, and whether it proved to be the salvation of historicizing biblical scholarship in a decontextualizing age is the question to which we now turn.

New Historicism to the Rescue?

Biblical scholars were by no means the only ones in the final decades of the twentieth century wanting to break out of the confines of textuality pure of contextuality. The linguistic turn very quickly provoked a strong sense of dissatisfaction among scholars troubled by its isolation of texts from the world outside of them – from the agency of authors, from social practice, from the influence of politics and economic class. While some academic trends were making it difficult to move beyond texts into the world, intellectual influences coming from other directions – a lingering Marxism, social history, speech-act theory, anthropology, an emergent cultural studies – were pushing in the opposite direction, back toward the importance of setting and situation. Thus there began to appear calls for a return to contextualization – as in the first volume of the journal *Critical Inquiry*, where the Russian literary scholar Edward Wasiolek wrote of a need for a "new contextualism" that would draw "extrinsic" disciplines like sociology and anthropology back into the analysis of literary texts. This response was not a rejection of the linguistic turn wholesale. It often launched itself from poststructuralist premises, but it reformulated those premises in ways meant to revive the relevance of historical context for literary analysis, reasserting the text as a point of intersection with the world.

Some of the leading literary scholars of the era became involved in this project in one way or the other and their stature in the academy is due in part to the fact that their work addresses the threat that the linguistic turn poses to history and a historicizing view of literature. Their efforts to reformulate the relationship between texts and extratextual reality, recently surveyed by Spiegel, are too varied and complexly developed to survey here, ranging from efforts to redefine the category of the real, to shifting the focus from signs and texts to practice and performance, to going back to the foundational moment of the linguistic turn, the writing of Saussure himself, and challenging the way it has been understood. For an illustration, however, it may suffice to zero in on the work of just one of these figures, the Shakespearean scholar Stephen Greenblatt, whose publications in the 1980s inaugurated the New Historicism, or what he himself called "cultural poetics."

Greenblatt was heir to some of the anticontextualizing trends of the 1960s and 1970s, not to mention the New Criticism of an earlier era of literary scholarship, but his thinking was also shaped by the more recent thinking of figures like Michel Foucault, whom Greenblatt encountered at Berkeley in the 1970s and whose work introduced new ways of interconnecting discourse and historical context (as in Foucault's notion of the *episteme*, the unconscious assumptions of an era that precondition what can and cannot be said). Absorbing such influences into an intellectual style that was far more accessible than much of French literary theory at the time, Greenblatt sought to develop an approach that, while not disavowing the assumptions and moves of poststructuralism, nonetheless aimed to reconnect texts to historical reality, to actual people, to everyday life:

> we wanted to find in the past real bodies and living voices, and if we knew that we could not find these – the bodies having long mouldered away and the voices fallen silent – we could at least seize upon those traces that seemed to be close to actual experience … We wanted to recover in our literary criticism a confident conviction of reality, without giving up on the power of literature to sidestep or evade the quotidian and without giving up the minimally sophisticated understanding that any text depends upon the absence of the bodies and voices that it represents. (Greenblatt, in Gallagher and Greenblatt, 30–1)

There is some poststructuralist hedging here – Greenblatt does not dare to aspire to recovering reality itself but only a "confident conviction of reality" because he knows from the theory of his day that that reality itself is inaccessible: the bodies have moldered away and the voices have fallen silent. But remnants of these past presences survive, "traces" that bring one "close to actual experience," and his interest in recovering that experience is why his approach is as much anthropological as literary: his goal, as he puts it elsewhere, was to put literary texts back in touch with the "lived life … that had been progressively refined out of the most sophisticated literary studies."

What Greenblatt has in mind when he refers to culture is roughly equivalent to what we have been calling historical context, but he has a distinctive understanding of how texts interact with that context. A culture as he defines it functions as a "set of limits" within which social (or literary) behavior must be contained, establishing boundaries that delimit the range of possibility. In this sense it is hard to distinguish from what earlier scholars might have referred to as "background" or "milieu." What seems to be of much greater interest to Greenblatt, however, is how culture functions as "the regulator and guarantor of movement" – how individual writers improvise within the constraints imposed by culture and how they interact with other aspects of that culture through acts of acquisition, negotiation and circulation. Historical context in this way of thinking is not an inert or stable background on which authors draw or against which their work can be framed; it is a kind of economy in which authors participate as consumers, producers, brokers and poachers of resources shared with a community.

Critics of New Historicism have questioned New Historicism's claim to be new. Even if there is some truth to this criticism, however, it fails to recognize the timeliness of New Historicism, how it seeks to address the particular predicament in which literary scholarship found itself by reviving the quest for historical context *from within* the post-Saussurean view so dominant in the 1960s and 1970s. Greenblatt casts his work as, in part, a reaction against the ahistoricism of post-Saussurean theory, but he does not reject its tenets altogether, instead appropriating its orientation for his own purposes, as we can see even in the references cited above – in Greenblatt's definition of culture as a "system of signs" or his Derridean description of the textual remnants of the past as "traces." It is that effort at mediation – neither completely to reject what was implicitly defined as Old Historicism nor to embrace a New Critical position but to develop an approach between these options – that made his project so relevant for scholars in the 1980s and 1990s who were torn between historicizing impulses and the ahistoricism of contemporary literary theory.

As we have noted, Greenblatt was by no means the only scholar involved in this quest, but his work proved exceptionally resonant and not simply because he is a masterful writer. To understand this resonance, we might invoke Greenblatt's own description of resonance as "the power of the displayed object to reach beyond its formal boundaries to a larger world, to evoke in the viewer the complex, dynamic cultural forces from which it has emerged and for which – as metaphor or more simply as metonym – it may be taken by a viewer to stand" (Greenblatt, "Resonance," 19–20). Greenblatt's work resonated, I suspect, because it functioned as such a metonym, combining within it an array of contradictory forces that came to converge on each other in the 1980s, including the anticontextualism of New Criticism and poststructuralism joined now with the contextualizing impulses of Marxist criticism, anthropology, and postcolonialism. The result of all this effort was not necessarily theoretically defensible or even coherent if one examined it too closely. Greenblatt was not operating as a philosopher; and the cogency of his positions are issues that scholars debate even now. To identify the theoretical shortcomings of New Historicism required engaging in precisely the theorizing of which scholarship was tiring, however, and what it was looking for at the time was something other than more theory, a way to move forward without ignoring the legacy of poststructuralism but that would nonetheless allow for a reengagement with historical reality. Greenblatt modeled a way to do this. In some ways, his work seemed a rejection of literary theory, written in an accessible, level-headed style that eschewed the indecipherability associated with deconstructionism and embracing a return to history; in other ways, his project was an effort to extend that theory to the notion of historical context itself, preserving key tenets of poststructuralism by redefining all of culture as a signifying system.

Did biblical scholars at the time also recognize New Historicism's potential to recast the relationship between texts and historical context? At least a few did. In 1997 the journal *Biblical Interpretation* devoted a special volume to New Historicism edited by Stephen Moore that included essays on Deuteronomy and Jonah. The *Cambridge Companion to Biblical Interpretation*, published in 1998, included a chapter on New Historicism by Robert Carroll that identified the minimalists as New Historicists, and a few years later, in 2002, Fortress Press, which publishes a series of handbooks that aim to introduce various methods of biblical study to a nonspecialist audience, added a volume on the New Historicism written by Gina Hens-Piazza that aimed to make its approach accessible to a broad scholarly audience. As Hens-Piazza points out, the appeal of New Historicism for biblical scholars was not only that it offered a solution to an interpretive problem – how to rehistoricize texts without abandoning the legacy of poststructuralism – but also that it could remedy a sociological problem as well, potentially overcoming the divide between literary and historical scholars of the Bible:

> Literary analysis frequently involves setting aside the research and conclusions of historical critics. Different approaches to interpretation engender polarization on the determinacy and indeterminacy of meaning … New Historicism, on the other hand, abandons such specialization. It crosses boundaries separating the different disciplinary specializations and ignores the boundaries separating the world of the text and the world of the reader. (Hens-Piazza 18–19)

At the time that she wrote this, biblical studies can be said to have been riven in two by the disjuncture between signs and referents. On one side were literary scholars like Sternberg who regarded the pursuit of referents, of the world that generated biblical literature or to which it referred, as irrelevant. On the other were scholars interested in that world – those trained to use Assyriology, Ugaritology, epigraphy, and archaeology to situate biblical literature within a specific time and place – who could be dismissive of the literary approach as "ahistorical." The first tended to be located in Comparative Literature or Religious Studies departments, the other in Near Eastern languages departments, and they tended not to engage the other seriously. New Historicism offered a way to mediate between these perspectives, reasserting the value of historical context even as it redefined the relationship between texts and contexts in light of literary theory.

That was the promise of New Historicism, but I think it is fair to say, from the vantage point of more than a decade later, that that promise remains unfulfilled. New Historicism never really took root in biblical studies in the way that, say, structuralism or deconstructionism had. Only a handful of scholars adopted it as an approach, and their efforts have had little discernible impact on how scholars today relate the Hebrew Bible to its historical and cultural context – and this is something of a surprise given the resonance of New Historicism in other fields. Of course, recovering the world of Shakespeare poses different historiographical problems than those faced by those seeking to recover the world of the Hebrew Bible, but the topics that engage Greenblatt – the interactions between rulers and their subjects, for instance, or the intersections of literature and ritual – are certainly not irrelevant for biblical studies. Why then did his approach to the challenges of contextualization have so little impact on the field?

One likely reason is very practical – our poor knowledge of the historical context in which biblical literature was composed, however we define that context. New Historicism's ultimate goal is to render the boundary between text and context a porous one, but before it can do so, it must have a sense of what that context is, independent of its manifestation in the text, and it usually reconstructs this context in the same way that old-fashioned historicism does, through nonliterary documents – deeds, memoirs, private letters, diaries – which it treats as less processed, more transparent reflections of reality than a literary text like a Shakespearean play. A biblical scholar has very little of that kind of evidence. Texts cannot be dated with precision; authors are unknown; and the resulting, irresolvable debate over such issues makes it nearly impossible to draw the kinds of connections that New Historicism aspires to draw. An example is the aforementioned minimalists, who have been described as New Historicists but who are focused on a historical period for which the evidence doesn't allow for the kind of connections that New Historicism makes for much later periods of literary history. The minimalists look to late biblical books like Ezra and Nehemiah to argue for a new way of contextualizing biblical literature (that most of it is a fictionalization of collective identity born in the Persian or Hellenistic periods rather than the work of the preexilic period), but Ezra and Nehemiah do not offer a lot of information, and they are fraught with their own historiographical problems, so that, as Sara Japhet has argued, they simply cannot bear the weight that the minimalists place on them as a basis for reconstructing the historical context in which other biblical texts were composed. Largely because of this dearth of evidence, the minimalists have a far easier time stressing the disjuncture between signs and their referents – between what Philip Davies refers to as "Biblical Israel," the Israelites as represented in the Bible, versus "Ancient Israel," the real-life historical people beyond the text – than they do in constructing an alternative way of interconnecting texts and history, the essential New Historicist project.

But even if biblical scholarship had more evidence to work with than it does, it is still doubtful that it would have been able to assimilate successfully a New Historicist orientation, not because of its own shortcomings but because of New Historicism's shortcomings. The aspect of New Historicism that I myself find especially elusive is its understanding of how exactly texts relate to their historical contexts. It rejects a simplistic binary approach to this relationship, one that distinguishes neatly between texts and their contexts or between literary foregrounds and historical backgrounds, but neither does it completely collapse one into the other, repeatedly invoking realities that go beyond the boundaries of texts – real bodies, real voices, real selves. But if texts and contexts are distinguishable things, what exactly is the connection between them? To some critics, New Historicism has not succeeded in developing a clear-cut answer to this question despite its rhetorical adroitness. The connections that New Historicism asserts seem arbitrary – any literary text is potentially relatable to any social practice, and there is little to rule one connection in and another out. Greenblatt denies he is advocating an "anything goes" approach, but the critique does expose a vulnerability in New Historicism: what connects a text to a context in a New Historicist reading is not a causal relationship but some other, vaguer kind of relationship.

Greenblatt's efforts to explain this relationship have not clarified matters all that much. In *Shakespearean Negotiations*, he sought to define what it is that connects texts to the world, a relationship he describes as the circulation of social energy. Social energy, derived from the ancient rhetorical concept of *enargeia*, refers to the power to produce, shape and organize physical and mental experiences, and according to Greenblatt, it is a capacity that texts absorb from the surrounding culture, entering a text through the author's appropriation of modes of discourse and symbolic resources from the larger culture. The New Historicist task is to detect this social energy in a text, and then follow its circulation through the culture, to track where it comes from in the culture, be that source religion, the state, or experiences like the discovery of the New World.

This then is what connects a text to the world according to New Historicism – not direct contact between an author and some aspect of his environment but a more diffuse kind of power that flows through culture like electricity in a grid. But of course, Greenblatt is not talking about energy in a literal sense, and he himself admits that it cannot really be observed: "the term implies something measurable, yet I cannot provide a convenient and reliable formula for isolating a single, stable quantum for examination" (*Shakespearean Negotiations*, 6). The concept is a conceit, a way of describing a dynamic relationship between texts and the world but not an explanation for that relationship, and its formulation has raised as many questions as it has answered, to the point that it is far from clear that it has any real advantage over causality, influence, and other concepts that scholars use to describe the relationship between texts and their environments. Here and there, Greenblatt himself suggests an analogy between his approach and magical thinking, and building on such suggestions, I would argue that New Historicism itself depends on what James Frazer described as sympathetic magic, a magic based on the belief that there are invisible forces that connect people and things otherwise not in a position to influence each other. Social energy resembles this kind of invisible force, I would contend: more an imaginative projection than a description of how texts interact with the world or each other.

If New Historicism has failed to take root in biblical studies, in other words, it is not simply because biblical scholars lack the kind of evidence that would allow them to apply it productively. It is also because, even for scholars who shared Greenblatt's desire to reconnect texts and history, New Historicism did not really move things forward as much as it seemed to initially. In many ways, it continued on the trajectory of poststructuralism, making historical context even more elusive by exposing the search for background, influences, and causes as quixotic and superficial, but what it offers as an alternative – texts connected to the world via the circulation of social energy – has not held up to scrutiny in its own right.

While New Historicism may have failed to overcome the chasm between texts and the world, however, that chasm remains, and the evidence for this is that there are at least some biblical scholars still struggling to bridge it, who seem dissatisfied with the conventional way that scholars contextualize the Bible and are looking for new ways to understand the relationship between its texts and the historical reality in which they were composed. These efforts have not congealed into a discrete school or approach that can be given a label, and certainly not one that can rival the influence that New Historicism enjoyed in the 1980s and 1990s, but the very fact that such efforts continue means that the goal that New Historicists were after – to bridge "internal" and "external" approaches to discourse – is still something that biblical scholars pursue. We conclude this survey with a look at one such effort that has taken shape in the first decade of the twenty-first century, not to advocate for its approach but to show that biblical scholarship is still striving to rethink the relationship between texts and historical contexts in light of the challenge to historical contextualization mounted at the end of the twentieth century.

Down Memory Lane

Although the concept of social energy may not hold up under close scrutiny, it exemplifies one of the strategies that scholars have developed to bridge texts and historical contexts, the idea of some kind of mediating agent that exists both inside and outside of language and that can therefore connect it to extralinguistic reality. New Historicism's efforts to identify this medium have not resonated for most biblical scholars, but the field is developing alternatives that might be able to do the same work.

One of those possible alternatives is memory, or more precisely the concept of "collective memory" as first formulated by the sociologist Maurice Halbwachs – the memories of groups that cannot be explained only in terms of individual psychology but are shared by communities and are cultivated through social interaction and communal practices and symbols. There were two key aspects of Halbwachs' notion especially germane for the issue on which we are focused:

1   collective memory develops within specific social groups – families, nations, religious communities – and its formation must therefore always be understood within the context of the kind of community in which it takes shape – how it is organized, what its interests and needs are, how it relates to outsiders, how the group changes over time.
2   collective memory is constantly changing to reflect the evolving identity and needs of the remembering groups, and to change in this way, it must be shaped and reshaped in ways that resemble the fictional process: gaps must be filled in, coherent plot-lines formed, traditions invented to make the past more meaningful for the group to whom the memory belongs.

Like fiction, collective memory can also withhold information to achieve its ends, discarding or suppressing certain aspects of the past if these clash with a group's present-day self-image and needs (see also the essay by Raymond Person in this volume).

The concept of collective memory was formulated by Halbwachs in a study first published in 1941, but it has only recently begun to have an impact on biblical studies, penetrating the field in the last decade largely through the influence of a book by the Egyptologist Jan Assmann, *Moses the Egyptian: The Memory of Egypt in Western Monotheism*, which champions what Assman refers to as mnemohistory, the study of the past as it is remembered rather than as it actually happened. From there, the influence of collective memory flowed into the work of biblical scholars who have been productive in the last decade. An excellent example is the work of Ron Hendel, who applies the concept of "collective memory" to the stories of Abraham, the Exodus, and Solomon's reign.

Approaching the Bible as a repository of collective memory might not seem at first to be directly relevant to the struggle we have been tracing in this chapter. Originating not from literary studies or historiography but from sociology, its embrace is more obviously a reaction against the concept of myth as employed in the study of ancient narrative. Myth is often placed in opposition to history, a false representation of the past that is meant to help people understand the world but that does not correspond to reality. Collective memory is meant to stand somewhere between the extremes of history and myth, responding to real circumstances, places and events but through the prism of imagination and group identity. To use Hendel's *Remembering Abraham* as an example, its effort to distinguish in the Bible what is historical from what is a later fiction is not exactly new – there have been scholars engaged in this project for some time now. What the concept of "collective memory" adds to this is a way to mediate between these opposing options, to engage the Bible as a register of an extratextual reality while at the same time acknowledging its depiction of the past as a fictionalized construction.

Another way to understand the appeal of collective memory, however, is to recognize that it offers a potential solution to the problem with which we have been wrestling here, a way to reformulate the relationship between texts and historical context. Memory as Halbwachs conceptualized it can be analogized to "the text" as understood by a poststructuralist. It exists only within language, combining impressions, feelings, and experiences into a coherent whole through the mediation of language. As Halbwachs puts it: "one cannot in fact think about the events of one's past without discoursing upon them" (53). Memory here is not only analogous to language; it depends on it, and does not exist apart from it, only becoming meaningful by attaching itself to signs (or "names" as Halbwachs calls them). In this regard, collective memory overlaps with what later scholars call a text, only existing within the structure of language, but on the other hand, collective memory is also tied to an external world, not representing the past as it actually happened but very responsive to the environment in which it itself is taking shape.

What I am suggesting, in other words, is that collective memory offers the kind of compromise that New Historicism was after, a potential point of intersection between a text and an extratextual context. It is anachronistic to describe collective memory as a signifying system, but even as formulated by Halbwachs, it exists only within language, while at the same time also being context-dependent, connected to and influenced by people, events, and practices that exist outside of language. This is what allows biblical scholars like Hendel to position collective memory as a *mediation* between myth and history: it is not just that collective memory combines truth and falsehood, but that it combines elements of language and reality, of textuality and the external world, in ways that seem to overcome the gap that poststructuralism inserts between them.

Is "collective memory" the long sought-after solution to the challenges of historical contextualization with which we have been struggling? It functions much as social energy does in Greenblatt's approach, bridging the realms of discourse and extratextual reality, but it avoids some of that concept's shortcomings, or at least seems to. Social energy sounds at first like a scientific concept, a kind of physics, but as Greenblatt explains, it is really a rhetorical conceit and cannot actually be observed. Collective memory cannot be directly observed either but with an impressive lineage that goes back to Durkheim, it has gained widespread acceptance as a real social phenomenon, like government or the economy, an abstraction but one that is clearly manifest in specific ways in specific places and times. Despite such acceptance, however, collective memory does suffer from its share of problems. Halbwachs acknowledged that it is only individuals who actually remember, but he does not provide a clear explanation for how collective memories are formed. Critics like Gedi and Elam find that he merely blurs the relationship between the two rather than explaining how they actually interact. The intersubjective processes by which collective memory is formed and disseminated remain difficult to trace or understand: this is in contrast to individual memory whose workings can now be at least partially observed through the observation of brain activity and understood in light of what we know about neurology.

For reasons such as these, I am not endorsing the notion of collective memory as the solution to the problems of contextualization with which we have been grappling, and if we had more time we might consider some alternative ways in which present-day scholars are trying to contextualize biblical literature (see, for example, Moore and Sherwood 41–3: partisans of poststructuralism who claim to have never disavowed an interest in history but advocate turning the focus to the context of biblical studies itself, "the cultural and historical forces that had formed the discipline"). What the embrace of this concept does suggest, however, is that biblical scholars today have not simply returned to a pretheoretical state, seeking some way to combine an understanding of the Bible as discourse with a recognition of how that discourse has been "touched by the real" – shaped by a reality external to language. We have the texts themselves, and we know something of the world from which they originated; the challenge has always been how to bridge these, how to move from within a text and its construction of reality to a real-life outside and back again. The embrace of collective memory, whatever this notion's shortcomings, shows a biblical scholarship still striving to address the complexities of that connection, not simply to establish the fact of a connection but to flesh out the relationship in a way that resists a blinkered view of how texts relate to contexts but that also resists giving up on the project of historical contextualization.

My guess is that a majority of those who regard themselves as critical biblical scholars today would probably still judge Spinoza to have been correct: if we know nothing of a biblical text's author, nor of the time and circumstances in which that text is written, most would probably agree with Spinoza that "we shall vainly endeavor to gain any certain knowledge of its true meaning" (111). But for those who keep in mind the recent intellectual history that we have tried to review here, it remains an open question whether there is any way for such an effort *not* to be a vain endeavor, whether a scholar these days can realistically aspire to knowing the time and circumstances of the Bible's composition without a large degree of self-delusion. The approach Spinoza pioneered is surviving the challenges posed by poststructuralism, but its debate with the modern-day successors to Meyer is likely to continue, especially now that it has become clear that determining the context of the Bible generates nearly as many hermeneutical riddles as its text does.

Note

1   I would like to thank Ronald Hendel for his constructive feedback in response to an earlier version of this essay.

Bibliography

Assmann, Jan. *Moses the Egyptian: The Memory of Egypt in Western Monotheism*. Cambridge, MA: Harvard University Press, 1998. An effort by a leading Egyptologist to apply the concept of mnemohistory, a concept akin to collective memory, to Moses.

Burke, Peter. "Context in context." *Common Knowledge 8* (2002): 152–77. A brief intellectual history of the concept of "context."

Buss, Martin J. "The idea of *Sitz im Leben*: History and critique." *Zeitschrift für die Alttestamentliche Wissenschaft 90* (1978): 157–70. Examines how form criticism addresses the issue of context and its relevance for understanding the formation of biblical genres.

Carroll, Robert P. "Poststructuralist approaches: New historicism and post-modernism." In John Barton (ed.), *The Cambridge Companion to Biblical Interpretation* (pp. 50–66). Cambridge: Cambridge University Press, 1998. A review of recent approaches to the Bible that conflates New Historicism with the "minimalist" approach to biblical history.

Davies, Philip. *In Search of "Ancient Israel."* Sheffield: Sheffield Academic Press, 1992. A typical example of the so-called "minimalist" school of biblical historiography.

Dever, William. *Recent Archaeological Discoveries and Biblical Research*. Seattle: University of Washington Press, 1990. A work by a leading archaeologist that captures the growing disjuncture between biblical studies and Syro-Palestinian archaeology.

Gallagher, Catherine and Stephen Greenblatt. *Practicing New Historicism*. Chicago: University of Chicago Press, 2000. Includes reflections on the rise of New Historicism.

Gedi, Noa and Yigal Elam. "Collective memory: What is it?" *History and Memory 8* (1996): 30–50. A critical assessment of the concept of "collective memory."

Greenblatt, Stephen. *Shakespearean Negotiations: The Circulation of Social Energy in Renaissance England*. Berkeley: University of California Press, 1988. Among other things a kind of manifesto of New Historicism.

Greenblatt, Stephen. "Resonance and wonder." *Bulletin of the American Academy of Arts and Sciences 43* (2004): 11–34. An essay on the power of objects displayed in a museum, and their ability to attract attention.

Halbwachs, Maurice. *On Collective Memory*, trans. and ed. Lewis A. Coser. Chicago: University of Chicago Press, 1992. Includes a translation of a classic work from 1941, *La topographie légendaire des évangiles en terre sainte. Étude de mémoire collective*, that introduces the notion of "collective memory."

Hendel, Ronald S. *Remembering Abraham*. Oxford: Oxford University Press, 2005. Draws on collective memory studies to address challenges in biblical historiography.

Hens-Piazza, Gina. *The New Historicism*. Minneapolis: Fortress, 2002. An accessible introduction to New Historicism for scholars of the Bible.

Hodder, Ian. *Reading the Past*. 2nd edn. Cambridge: Cambridge University Press, 1991. Seminal text of postprocessual archaeology, which seeks better ways of understanding the people who left behind archaeological remains.

Hume, Robert D. *Reconstructing Contexts: The Aims and Principles of Archaeo-Historicism*. Oxford: Oxford University Press, 1999. A reaction against New Historicism that reexamines how historians relate texts to historical contexts.

Japhet, Sara. "Was the history of Israel 'invented' during the Persian period?" *Cathedra 100* (2001): 109–20. A critique of biblical "minimalism."

Machinist, Peter. "The question of distinctiveness in ancient Israel: An essay." In Mordechai Cogan and Israel Epha'al (eds), *Ah Assyria: Studies in Assyrian History and Ancient Near Eastern Historiography Presented to Hayim Tadmor* (pp. 196–212). Jerusalem: Magness Press, 1991. A self-aware effort to rethink the relationship between ancient Israel and its Ancient Near Eastern environs.

Moore, Megan Bishop. *Philosophy and Practice in Writing a History of Ancient Israel.* New York: T&T Clark, 2006. Examines the presuppositions of recent historiography in the field of biblical studies.

Moore, Stephen D. and Yvonne Sherwood. *The Invention of the Biblical Scholar.* Minneapolis: Fortress, 2011.

Preuss, James S. *Spinoza and the Irrelevance of Biblical Authority.* Cambridge: Cambridge University Press, 2001. A rereading of Spinoza that reframes his biblical criticism as a debate with Ludwig Meyer.

Rowlett, Lori L. *Joshua and the Rhetoric of Violence: A New Historicist Analysis.* Sheffield: Sheffield Academic Press, 1996. An early, disappointing attempt to apply New Historicism to biblical narrative.

Schalkwyk, David. *Literature and the Touch of the Real.* Newark: University of Delaware Press, 2004. An effort to rethink the relationship between texts and reality in light of New Historicism, deconstruction and analytic philosophy

Smith, Mark S. *Untold Stories: The Bible and Ugaritic Studies in the Twentieth Century.* Peabody, MA: Hendrickson, 2001. A history of Ugaritic studies that traces its relationship to biblical studies.

Spiegel, Gabrielle M. *Practicing History: New Directions in Historical Writing after the Linguistic Turn.* New York: Routledge, 2005. Explores the turn back to history in the wake of poststructuralism.

Spinoza, Baruch. *A Theologico-Political Treatise*, trans. R. H. M. Elwes. Mineola, NY: Dover, 2004. A foundational work of modern, historicist biblical studies.

Sternberg, Meir. *The Poetics of Biblical Narrative.* Bloomington: Indiana University Press, 1987. An ambitious effort to develop a literary approach to the Hebrew Bible that seeks, in effect, to bypass questions of historical context.

Thompson, Thomas L. *The Mythic Past: Biblical Archaeology and the Myth of Israel.* New York: Basic Books, 1999. Another example of biblical "minimalism."

Wasiolek, Edward. "Wanted: A new contextualism." *Critical Inquiry 1* (1975): 623–39. An early harbinger of the turn back to history that would lead to New Historicism.

B

Hebrew Bible and Tracking Israelite History and Culture

CHAPTER 5

Folklore and Israelite Tradition
Appreciation and Application

Susan Niditch

The Essence of Folklore

To paraphrase a question posed by the great biblicist Hermann Gunkel, "What has folklore to do with the Bible?" For contemporary Westerners the term "folklore" evokes certain genres, for example, folktales, legends, epics, myths, proverbs, and riddles. Some might also think to include material such as the ballads collected by Child or contemporary folk music or the sort of traditional art one often sees assessed on the popular American PBS program *Antiques Roadshow*. Folklorists have long discussed how to define folklore and questioned whether the categories listed above are accurate designations for forms of folklore in one or another cultural tradition (see Ben-Amos, "Analytical categories"; Niditch, *Folklore*: 67–87). Nevertheless, even allowing for these complexities, it would seem at the outset that folklore, both the material and the way in which it is studied, might well be relevant to the study of ancient Israelite culture.

The Hebrew Bible includes a whole book devoted to traditional sayings (Proverbs) and another that preserves and perhaps parodies such sayings (Ecclesiastes). Individual sayings are scattered throughout the Bible in ways that reveal possible performance contexts for their deployment. Riddles are mentioned in various biblical contexts, Samson's riddle being the best known. The Bible begins with an elegant account of the creation of the world, tracing a pattern from murky and sterile chaos to an orderly and fecund cosmos rich in plant and animal life and a first human pair – surely the stuff of myth, as is the tale of the great flood concerning Noah in Genesis 6–9. Stories about certain types of heroes abound in the Hebrew Bible, tricksters such as Jacob and Rebecca, strongmen such as Samson, warriors such as David who slays Goliath the man-giant in a biblical version of what folklorists call the "dragon-slayer motif." The Hebrew Bible, in short, is rich in folk literature. Folklore, moreover, includes much more than verbal genres, written or oral. Folk creations can be silent and dramatic, a kind of theater, or an item of

The Wiley Blackwell Companion to Ancient Israel, First Edition. Edited by Susan Niditch.

material culture. The folklore of ancient Israel is thus reflected not only in the various literary inventions preserved in the Bible but also in its ritual descriptions and in the difficult-to-interpret artifacts unearthed by archaeologists.

Dan Ben-Amos emphasizes that "folklore is not an aggregate of things, but … a communicative process," and he explores this communicative process in terms of three foci: "a body of knowledge," a phrase invoking content, wisdom, and tradition; "a mode of thought," that is, a way of thinking informed by a particular worldview; and "a kind of art," which suggests matters of style, tone, and aesthetics ("Toward a definition," 9, 5). Similarly, folklorist Alan Dundes has us consider folklore in terms of "text," that is, its content, "texture," its style, and "context" (16).

While folk genres may reflect certain universal human concerns and modes of expressing them (hence the ability to recognize what seems to be a proverb in someone else's tradition), folklore is always set in contexts, and contexts come in various forms: a group's shared social or cultural context; the more specific performance or rhetorical setting of a piece, the way it is employed, and where it is physically located; the role and attitude of the particular folk artist; and the expectations of the audience, the receivers of and participants in folklore. Thus as students of ancient Israelite literature, exploring the story of Noah, we might think in terms of shared human psychoanalytical associations between water and creation, of specific ancient Near Eastern and Israelite versions of the flood story and their possible performance contexts, of the literary setting of the biblical Genesis, and of the form, content, and messages of the specific version now preserved in Genesis 6–9.

Folklore is intimately related to performance. The Hebrew Bible alludes to performance settings in ancient Israel when describing the ways in which prophets address the people or perform dramatic symbolic actions, in interactive genres like the *māšāl* which can include parables, proverbs, and oracles (see Niditch, *Folklore*, 67–87), in instructions for ritual action, and in allusions to actual musical performance. Qualities of performance suggest oral production, but these characteristics, rooted in oral performance, also characterize traditional-style examples of verbal folklore that are preserved, and which may have been composed, in writing, as scholars of early and oral literatures increasingly emphasize. Indeed, classicist Gregory Nagy notes that oral works can become quite fixed and written works can be quite open to variation, as scribes engage in performance-like activity in the very act of writing, so that a work "is regenerated in each act of copying" (69). The qualities associated with but not confined to orally composed literature include the presence of repetition and the use of formulas, economy in expression, and metonymy. Each of these related qualities and terminology applied to them require some unpacking, and each is applicable and relevant to an appreciation of material folk culture as well.

In traditional or folk forms, repetition is valorized. In what Albert B. Lord calls economy or thrift, similar content is often expressed in variations upon shared language in verbal forms or similar actions or artistic motifs in nonverbal forms. For the epic literature he studies, Lord defines formula as "a group of words which is regularly employed under the same metrical conditions to express a given essential idea" (30). Metrical considerations may or may not be relevant to the use of formulaic language in one or another biblical genre but the notion of creating ideas and images in similar rather than different language is at the heart of folk literature. Thus when a ruler, be it Pharaoh or Nebuchadnezzar, faces a difficult conundrum, the biblical writers have him "call to his wise men, magicians, etc." Similarly, folk art, for example a quilt or a weathervane, will be the artisan's own version of an expected set of visual content. This concept of formulicity and thrift applies to the hundreds of Iron Age II Judean female figurines that relate to women's fertility (see Elizabeth Bloch-Smith's essay in this volume). Lord also notes that the repetitions may consist of "formula patterns," recognizable and recurring frameworks that can be filled out or specified in various ways (44).

The ruler in the example above may call to magicians, wise men, and enchanters or to dream-interpreters and counselors. He may be labeled a king or referred to by his name but the essential formula pattern "ruler + call term + helpers" remains recognizable, signaling a sort of content that deals with finding solutions to difficult problems and the role of the specially inspired to assist. These sorts of repetition can unify one epic or tale or, like the phrase about calling to magicians, appear throughout the tradition and serve to emphasize key recurring cultural themes.

A formula or formula pattern that recurs within the extant corpus of Israelite literature and that unifies and reflects the larger tradition evidences a characteristic that John Foley calls "metonymy" or imminent referentiality (11–13, 252). A brief allusion in imagery or recurring language can bring to bear on a piece of folklore the larger tradition of which it is a part. Thus the epithet for Yahweh, the recurring phrase "Bull of Jacob," is related to a particular iconography of ancient Near Eastern deities and to myths associated with them. It brings to bear on any passage notions of God's power, warrior status, and fecundity, even if the surrounding text is not about war or creation.

Another variety of repetition as it relates to folklore involves the presence of what Robert Alter has called "type scenes" whereby a plot or a scene will regularly consist of a recurring and expected set of motifs (*Art*, 47–62). One begins to see that in formulaic language and in formulaic content, recurring structures are critical whether in syntax, words used, or content conveyed.

In the case of the call to the wise man mentioned above, in an Israelite context the listener or reader knows that the savvy helper will not emerge from among the king's wise men but will be an unexpected outsider, wiser than any member of the establishment. Ritual patterns or examples of folk art similarly are composed of conventionalized constellations of motifs or accord with certain familiar patterns. Such recurring constellations in literature, rooted in oral worlds, are not, it is important to emphasize, merely means of holding attention or accommodating those who cannot consult a libretto. Such repetitions reinforce and convey essential cultural meaning and message – meanings and messages shared by an artist and audience.

Folklorists emphasize reception, the ongoing interaction of creators and receivers of material who share cultural assumptions. The preservers, composers, and creators of these materials are to be viewed as artists and performers who work within a traditional setting in which audiences have certain expectations for the ways stories go, heroes act, wives are wooed, rituals are performed, and so on. In ancient Israelite tradition, no decent hero has an easy birth or childhood. His mother is a barren woman (Isaac, Jacob, Samuel, Samson) or he himself is exposed to danger and death in infancy (Moses, Ishmael). When the hero finds himself at a well, a wife is in his future (Moses, Jacob, Eliezer for Isaac). Important scenes and stories, important combinations of motifs whether literary or visual, oral or written, exist in multiplicity, each one being a fresh version of a shared type. Like a musical score, the tradition is rich in variations.

To view the Bible as folklore and the ancient Israelites as participants in various folk groups is to be concerned not only with the form and setting of many types of biblical literature, epigraphic texts, and tactile archaeological discoveries, but is also to treat these materials as means by which Israelite identity, in its complexity and variousness, was reflected and constructed by creative members of Israelite folk groups. In any culture, each of us belongs to more than one folk group at once. In ancient Judea, for example, a person might belong to women of a particular age cohort; to those of priestly ancestry; to those who dwell in an urban setting; and so on. Particular types of folklore might emerge in each of these groups, while a larger fund of material appeals to all Israelites. The works of the Hebrew Bible are expressed in traditional media, revealing ways in which a variety of contributors and receivers participated in the process of cultural self-definition. Objects such as the standing stones discussed by Elizabeth Bloch-Smith in this volume are also conventionalized and traditional in form, location, and function. The field of folklore, however, is often misrepresented by scholars of the Bible and sometimes misapplied to the texts, textures, and contexts of ancient Israelite culture, while the benefits of comparative work with an international corpus of folklore is often not appreciated (for more on comparative studies, see the essays of John Huddlestun and Steven Weitzman in this volume). Such misapplications, misrepresentations, and missed opportunities come in various forms.

Resistance to Folklore and Misunderstanding

A first category of those who misunderstand folklore might be called "the deniers." To reprise the paraphrase from Gunkel with which this essay begins, these scholars suggest that the Bible is not folklore, that as Gunkel writes about narrative in the Hebrew Scriptures, "the Bible hardly contains a folktale anywhere. The elevated and rigorous spirit of biblical religion tolerated the folktale as such at almost no point and this near eradication from the holy tradition is one of the great acts of biblical religion" (*Folktale*, 33). Gunkel's view is informed by a conviction that folklore is the purview of the unsophisticated, the illiterate (in a bad, low-status sense), the superstitious. And yet ironically, Gunkel is exquisitely informed and influenced by the field of folklore as practiced in his time. In his study of Genesis, he employs Axel Olrik's classic "laws of epic," which point to a set of traits in content, typical of traditional style narrative (Gunkel, *Legends*, 46–72). Gunkel sensitively points to repetition, variation, and multiplicity in versions in biblical literary forms. He is especially attuned to contexts in which forms of folklore such as sayings or curses or ritual actions thrive and are recreated, in which authors and audiences coparticipate in the production of folklore. Similarly, Robert Alter claims to study "Samson without folklore," but his beautiful literal translations, his attention to the economical "delimited vocabulary" of the Bible (*The Five Books of Moses*, xxv), his work with "type scenes" (*The Art of Biblical Narrative*), and his psychoanalytical perspective ("Samson without folklore") could well find a home in folklore studies. Indeed folklore is a quintessential interdiscipline informed not only by literary and structuralist studies but also by psychology, anthropology, sociology, women's studies, and other areas all of which explore culture and identity, ways of understanding groups and the place of individuals within them. In appreciation of the sophistication and depth of biblical literature, Gunkel and Alter both feel the need to reject the notion that the Bible is a rich repository of folklore, and yet what we have begun to show is that folklore is integral to all cultures, comes in a wide array of genres, and emerges in various contexts: oral and written, verbal and visual, material and nonmaterial, urban and rural, culture-wide or group-specific. It is authors' and audiences' awareness of and immersion in the tradition and its literary forms that make the particular versions of tales or sayings or riddles now preserved in the Hebrew Bible so richly meaningful and communicative, culture-creating, and culture-revealing.

A second category of those who misrepresent folklore comes under the heading of oral versus written, and relates to the understanding of verbal media. Albert B. Lord notes that the formula is not a mechanical wooden device for making lines of proper length and rhythm but a meaning-rich component of characterization, tone, and message, a means of thematic emphasis and a reflection of aesthetics. Repetition is richness if one understands the register, nor is there just one oral register. There can be switches of register in one work to reflect content, character, and message. The choices made in the use of these flexible compositional devices matter. As noted earlier, Lord writes of formula patterns that could be filled in various ways. He is attuned to the artistry of composers, some of whom were more gifted than others. Variations matter and what is not repeated is as important as what is. Lord's work has often been misrepresented by his critics and inflexibly applied to various works of traditional literature by his fans.

In his little book *Homeric Questions*, Gregory Nagy provides a list of the ten most misunderstood things about Lord's theory of oral composition. These include, for example, the notion that "the poet has only one way of saying it" (25) or that "meter makes the poet say it that way" (23) or that "the Iliad is so unified it can't be oral" (26) and the related "Homer must have been able to write" or that there is one simple "world of Homer" (20), ignoring the rolling quality of the development of the Homeric tradition and the ancient and ongoing nature of the tradition.

Lord's work has led to a host of useful but less than satisfying searches for oral roots of biblical works. William Whallon and Robert C. Culley, for example, carefully explore the possibility that biblical poetry exhibits oral-compositional roots. David Gunn assesses possible oral roots of the biblical battle report. The authors themselves, however, express some disappointment with their results. The degree of formulicity is not high enough to "prove" oral composition. But the work of all these excellent scholars is very valuable in revealing the traditional style textures and texts of Israelite literature. The aesthetic is indeed related to matters of worldview and cultural context. It turns out that the issue of provable oral composition is a bit of a red herring, as is the sharp divide that Lord himself imagines between oral worlds and literate worlds, oral compositions and works created in writing.

Biblicists have partaken of their own view of the great divide and have expressed a rigid view of the evolution of written from oral works. The form-critical approach is grounded in the notion that early, simpler oral works are eventually written down and complicated by literate sophisticated writers. The former are primitive, the latter complex. We find such assumptions in the writing of Hermann Gunkel and Claus Westermann and in a host of other biblicists' work. This point of view sometimes leads to a pastoral romanticization of early contributors to the traditions, picturing them sitting by the fire, the sound of bleating sheep in the background (Gunkel, *Legends*, 41). It also leads to a distaste for the notion of an oral world background to the Hebrew Bible as too unsophisticated and demeaning of the great writerly tradition.

In fact, orally composed works can be long or short, created by people who can read and write or by those who can read but not write. Written traditional-style literature can be meant to be read aloud while orally composed works are set in writing by means of dictation or recreated in writing through memory. Writers can imitate oral style. Written works, their plots and characters, enter the oral end of the spectrum and vice versa. Once writing and reading are around a culture or even nearby, even if only practiced by elites, the two ways of imagining and creating literature influence one another and belong on a sliding scale or continuum, as Ruth Finnegan has shown. Nor does oral style serve as a certain marker of relative chronology. For example, a work that is more oral in style because of its formulaic qualities may have been composed later than a work in which language is varied and nonformulaic. Issues in texture and content say a good deal about authors' interests, settings, about ethnic genres and audiences, but the relative degree of "orality" is not a simple matter of chronology. Oral works and oral-style works are created and recreated even when writing is common. It is moreover no simple matter to distinguish between the orally composed work and the written work imitating orally composed works. Indeed in the Hebrew Bible it is impossible to do so. All is now written and yet all I would argue partakes of varying traditional-style registers.

If one reads John Foley's many works or the essays published in the last decade in the journal *Oral Tradition*, one sees this scholarly orientation to the interplay between oral and written. Increasingly one sees an emphasis on the role of memory in the oral-literate interplay as it affects the composition, preservation, and reception of traditional-style literatures (Carr). A number of recent works, in fact, grapple in various original and complex ways with the relationship between the oral and the written in the genesis of the biblical tradition (see the essay by Raymond Person in this volume).

A final category that points to a lack of conviction concerning the relevance of folklore to the study of ancient Israelite culture comes under the heading of "so what?" To put the question more fully, what does one learn from a folkloristic approach to biblical literature and Israelite culture that one cannot derive from the more usual methods of good biblical scholarship? Such methods include attention to philological detail, concern with questions of style, attention to structure, content, and sociohistorical context, engagement with material evidence obtained from archaeological work, and the use of innerbiblical and ancient Near Eastern comparisons to shed light on the Israelite case. Form-critical techniques in biblical scholarship, so well practiced by Gunkel, Westermann, and others, with their emphasis on genre and performance contexts, seem to steal the folklorist's agenda. What, then, distinguishes the application of folklore to ancient Israel in our efforts to understand extant cultural products preserved in the Hebrew Bible or those uncovered by archaeological means and the people who produced and received them as meaningful and expressive cultural communication? What do we see as folklorists that might not be apparent from a more typical biblicist's perspective? Answers to these questions and the implications of understanding folklore for the study of ancient Israel are provided by a series of case studies drawn from the traditional literature of the Hebrew Bible.

Applications

A first example is provided by an approach to the tale of creation concerning the first woman, the snake, and the first man in Genesis 2–3. Acculturated by Augustine or Milton or C. S. Lewis, many of us come to this tale as a story of mankind's fall. If one approaches the story with fresh eyes, however, paying attention to its text or narrative pattern one begins to see that the tale is not about original sin or woman's shortcomings, but tells about an ideal world with certain divinely set boundaries, the breaching of those boundaries or prohibitions, and the emergence of reality. And if one engages in comparative work with a range of international folklore, made possible by a resource such as the Type and Motif Indices of folklore (Thompson), but also nowadays enabled by simple Google online searches, such as under "myths about the origins of death," one begins to see that Genesis 2–3 is a tale about cultural emergence, explaining how the workaday world came to be ordered, and what Israelites (at least some Israelites) understood to be the place of men and women in that world.

Among the Gê of Brazil, for example, is a relevant and revealing tale about the loss of an ideal world situation. As the story goes, once corn grew beautifully and required no cultivation or hard work on the part of humans. One of the early human beings, however, cuts her hand on a corn stalk and, in pain, insults the deity who had planted the perfect and plentiful corn. The "father of the spirits" then refuses to continue to provide the corn. Human beings must work and tend to the corn, and the results are not always bountiful (Wilbert and Simoneau 153–4). Thus terms are set for daily existence in that native Brazilian culture. The underlying pattern shared by Genesis 2–3 and the Gê tale is ideal/paradise; implicit or explicit interdiction; interdiction broken; onset of reality. Not only does this outline characterize a fund of international tales, but is also found two more times in Genesis 1–11 in the story of the sons of God who take human wives (6:14) and in the story of the Tower of Babel in which human beings attempt to reach heaven (11:1–11). In the Israelite versions of this traditional pattern, breaching the boundary between divine and human, whether by eating of God's tree, by sexual encounter, or by spatial means, ironically leads to becoming more this-worldly and to the loss of paradise. Limits are set on life and various sorts of antipathy may accompany forms of differentiation: divine versus human, male versus female, animal versus human, one ethnic group versus another.

It is the way the pattern about ideal and reality is specified that tells us most about a particular culture and the concerns of a composer within that tradition. The version of the creation tale told in Genesis 2–3, for example, suggests a particular emphasis on agricultural matters, an androcentric society in which roles for men and women are clearly delineated, a view accepting of reality, and one in which there is no belief in some sort of paradise after death. Israelites' recreations and enjoyment of universal story patterns, however, also say a great deal on a shared humanistic level, providing a counterbalance to overtheologizing. All versions of this pattern show a human concern with the hardships of daily life, the relationship between human and divine, and the limits we face. These tales of origin retold by people in various cultures make reality more bearable by showing how it came about in settings and situations beyond their control. As Alan Dundes has noted, "folklore provides a socially sanctioned framework for the expression of critical anxiety-producing problems as well as a cherished artistic vehicle for communicating ethos and worldview" (9).

The awareness of shared international versions of narrative patterns is also a bulwark against excessive historicization. If the description of a battle in the Hebrew Bible, its prosecution, setting, and heroes, comports with those of epic war traditions around the world, one should hesitate to derive too much actual history from the events and protagonists as described. The French medieval *Song of Roland*, for example, does center around actual historical figures such as Charlemagne and is set in the context of a historically verifiable event, the eighth-century Battle of Roncesvalles, but the structure of the narrative and its characters have been presented in accordance with traditional narrative patterns; these patterns rather than history dominate the construction of the tale and the personalities of its heroic combatants. Robert Doran makes a similar case concerning the ordering of history in the Hellenistic Jewish work Second Maccabees. Awareness of the power of these traditional and formulaic patterns and attention to the existence of variants – multiple versions of identifiable, recurring combinations of language and content – bring us to a second case study. How does the field of folklore relate to and make us reconsider important methodological approaches in biblical studies: source criticism, text criticism, and redaction criticism?

Well before the nineteenth century, scholars of the Hebrew Bible posited the existence of written sources behind the now redacted or put-together whole, the biblical corpus (see the essay by David Carr in this volume). In particular, scholars have looked for evidence of documents running from Genesis through Deuteronomy and have suggested that four main sources have been combined, each with a particular style and orientation reflecting varying dates and authorship (see Carr in this volume for a full discussion of J, E, P and D). This documentary hypothesis, often associated with the work of the great German scholar Julius Wellhausen, has been variously applied and understood. Scholars have disagreed about the date of each source and about its extent and content. They have questioned whether individuals or groups lie behind the sources and disagreed about the number of sources. Nevertheless, a documentary hypothesis of some kind still dominates biblical scholarship, and its basic methodological assumptions also inform the understanding of layers in other biblical works. Common to all these suggestions is an emphasis on written sources or sources set in memory (see Baden; Carr, *Writing*; and Carr, this volume).

On the one hand, I agree that many sources lie behind the Hebrew Bible. The priestly material in Exodus, Leviticus, and Numbers, with its interests in ritual patterns, purities, priestly rights, obligations, and accoutrements such as clothing and ritual instruments, most clearly seem to indicate the purview of priests and material that priestly sources would seek to preserve in writing, although as Carr notes (this volume) there is evidence of more than one priestly source in the Pentateuch. The existence of identifiable Yahwist and Elohist sources is much more problematical (Carr, this volume).

The work of students of folklore in early and oral literatures, however, gives us pause concerning the suggestion articulated by Joel S. Baden that "four originally independent documents … have been combined into the single text of the canonical Pentateuch" (246). He views this conclusion as addressing "why the Pentateuch is incoherent" (249). This incoherence involves the presence of doublets, contradictions in content, and a lack of narrative continuity (246–7). The student of cultural settings in which the oral medium is valorized raises logistical questions about the way in which such a complex combining of set, written documents would take place (Niditch, *Oral World*, 60–77). Documentary hypotheses, earlier and contemporary versions, do not fully grapple with problems in the cut- or copy-and-paste views of biblical formation that are at odds with what we know about the logistics of writing and attitudes to literacy in the ancient world (Niditch, *Oral World*, 110–14, 116–17).

Even more important from a folkloristic perspective are questions about ancient Israelites' attitudes to the biblical tradition as preserved. Do ancient readers and composers not notice the doublets, the contradictions, and the awkward transitions? Or is the Bible itself more like an anthology or library than a book and do the supposed examples of "incoherence," in fact, exemplify the qualities of variation, repetition, and multiplicity which are characteristic of traditional-style literature? Whatever our view of sources, we have to account for the present aesthetic of Genesis, for example, which allows that the world is created and recreated several times, which provides two versions of Abraham's covenant-making in chapters 15 and 17, and which preserves two scenes of divine promise-making at the end of the flood account in chapters 8 and 9. The field of folklore alerts modern readers to the importance of this aesthetic of variation and repetition in ancient Israel as a reflection of worldview and literary sensibilities, firmly rooted in a traditional-style culture. Source-critical approaches often fail to take account of this aesthetic.

The emphasis on variants found in folklore studies also suggests an alternate approach to text-criticism, one of the staples of biblical scholarship. On a most basic level, text-critical decisions affect what scholars deem the texture and text of a work to be. In the exercise of text criticism, scholars consult various biblical manuscript traditions, preserved in Hebrew and/or in translation languages, to select or reconstruct a best or even original version of the text. The biblical book of Judges provides examples of the relevance of folklore methodologies for text-critical questions.[1]

The date of actual, extant manuscripts of Judges in Hebrew and various ancient translations is often quite late relatively speaking. For example, the Vaticanus Codex dates to the fourth century CE. Another fairly complete manuscript is the Greek Alexandrinus Codex which dates to the fifth century. The variations between Vaticanus (the so-called B text of Judges) and Alexandrinus (the so-called A text) have been of central interest to scholars engaged in text-critical analysis. In addition, an "Old Latin" (OL) version of Judges is believed to reflect a translation into Latin of an earlier "Old Greek" (OG) translation of a Hebrew version that antedates Hebrew traditions underlying Vaticanus and Alexandrinus. An extant Old Latin version of the whole book of Judges, except for the last chapter and a half, is available in the Lyons Manuscript (fifth or sixth century).

The discovery of ancient Hebrew biblical manuscripts in the caves around the Dead Sea provides further valuable information. Several fragments of Judges have been found in manuscripts whose scripts date them to the first century BCE.

The variety in the inherited manuscript traditions leads scholars in different directions. An approach that has come to dominate biblical studies suggests there was once, essentially, a single written version of Judges that branched out into different textual traditions, leading to various readings, variations in content. An alternate approach would suggest, to the contrary, that a great plethora of textual traditions – various ways Judges was written down – was eventually homogenized, either under conscious pressure from a politically controlling group who preferred one version and suppressed the rest, or through a less consciously directed effort. Some of the variant texts and their readings managed to survive, revealing a hint of what was once an even greater variety of manuscript traditions.

One need not merely speculate about some of the variants that existed in the tradition. Within the Hebrew Masoretic textual tradition preserved by medieval scribes and considered authoritative within Judaism, there is evidence of variation that has been embraced rather than edited away. Judges 1 contains, for example, three differing notices about the disposition of Jerusalem (1:7, 8, 21) and two different implied versions of the conquest of Hebron, one involving a leadership role for Judah at verse 10 and another for Caleb at verse 20. Joshua plays the role in Joshua 11:21 and Caleb in Joshua 15:13–14. A work such as Judges no doubt existed in multiple versions, even once its various stories were combined along the lines with which we are now familiar. Oral versions of larger or smaller portions of Judges would have existed side by side with accounts that were written down.

A model for this phenomenon of multiplicity is offered by the Qumran corpus, which contains two editions of Jeremiah, two editions of Exodus, variant editions of Numbers, and two possible editions of Psalms. As a student of the place of manuscripts in largely oral worlds, I am less inclined to reconstruct a whole text, to build it, however judiciously, from the limited number of available manuscripts. Nor do I seek an original or Ur-text for Judges. I worry about the artificiality of such a process and believe it more true to life to assume that there were always multiple versions of the tradition before the Common Era. Instead of thinking of scribes and translators as copyists and modern-style translators aiming for literal accuracy, we might regard them as composers, capable of creating additions in traditional style, of glossing scribal errors, of expanding upon ambiguous phrases, and of preserving oral traditions. This approach leads to an appreciation of interesting instances of traditional variation, for example a reference to a judge and his activities formulaically described at Judges 17:1 in the Old Latin not mentioned in the Masoretic Text or the Septuagint: "Asemada, the son of Annan, and he slaughtered of foreigners six hundred men beside the animals, and the Lord made Israel safe." The suggestion that the notion of an original or best text is contrary to a culture in which narratives exist in multiplicity challenges and complicates some very basic assumptions of biblical text criticism and deepens our appreciation for the literature as received by different communities.

In addition to making us reconsider aspects of source and text criticism as typically practiced among scholars of ancient Israel, the field of folklore adds an important dimension to biblical redaction criticism, the study of how disparate materials behind the Hebrew Bible, oral and written, have been combined. An example is offered by the last 11 chapters of the prophecies attributed to the sixth century BCE Ezekiel. Ezekiel 38–48 seems initially to be composed of an odd combination of material.

Ezekiel 38–39 describes an exciting battle waged by Gog of Magog, a nonidentifiable, mythological enemy, leading a host of nations in an apocalyptic world war in which Gog and his allies are defeated by God and Israel is restored. Ezekiel 40–48, however, is a strongly architectonic description of the new temple to be rebuilt after the Babylonian conquest in 587/6 BCE. Measurements are offered and building plans described in a kind of blueprint (see, e.g., chs 40–42). Furnishings and accoutrements are described (e.g., 40:38–43) and hierarchical information is provided about where various groups in Israel are allowed within the holy locus (see, e.g., 40:44–47; 42:13–15). Sabbaths, festivals, and rituals are described (45:21–25; 45:13; 46:4–15), all with attention to various sorts of status and place. Boundaries in "allotments of the holy portions" in chapter 48 reflect and map a social structure. God's glory is aroused (43:1–3) and fills the temple (44:4), and life-giving waters flow forth from the holy place (ch. 47). The temple thus serves as a kind of microcosm, a virtual ancient Israelite mandala. How do these two passages, the battle with Gog and the description of the temple, relate if at all to one another? Can we make suggestions about the ultimate arrangement of these materials in the current form of Ezekiel or are they simply awkwardly combined, disparate sources?

The war account and the temple description actually go beautifully together if one considers the victory-enthronement pattern that characterizes a host of ancient Near Eastern tales of world-creation with its pattern of battle, victory and housebuilding. The last ten chapters of Ezekiel have been composed and combined in response to this traditional pattern. The battle is followed by victory and celebration in chapters 38–39 and then in chapters 40–48 comes the building of the deity's abode, a cosmos over which he rules, in which he is enthroned, and from which his power emanates. This pattern characterizes the plot of ancient Near Eastern creation epics such as the Mesopotamian *Enuma elish* and informs a host of biblical works such as Exodus 15 and Zechariah 9. Thus a traditional and recurring narrative pattern provides the template for redaction, and awareness of the workings of such patterns enriches the exploration of redactional questions and helps to explain the inherited form of portions of the Hebrew Scriptures.

A final case study involves formulaic language. Albert B. Lord's emphasis on formula patterns and compositional technique attunes us to the textures and content of several examples of the description of heroes in the Israelite tradition, leading to better translation and to critical questions about cultural identity. The ancient song Judges 5 has a chiastic thematic structure that juxtaposes the activities of the divine warrior and his minions with the activities of human heroes. At the center of the piece is a description – indeed a traditional catalog of Israelite warriors – that might be compared with Iliad 3:160–244. This example is one of a number of biblical passages in which translators have often ignored the traditional nature and form of the material and instead provided forced translations that suit the scholars' own interpretation of the text.

The problem begins with a word of three letters, *lamed, mem, heh*. Most modern biblicists translate "why" for the opening of verse 16. This translation of *lamed, mem, heh*

admittedly is typical in the Hebrew Bible but leads the translators to use forced translations of all the verbs in order to describe various tribes as cowardly and unwilling to
fight. In the New Revised Standard Version (NRSV) translation, for example, the singer
asks Reuben, the tribe referenced in verse 15, "Why did you tarry among the sheep-
folds to hear the piping for flocks?" In turn this leads the translator to translate verse
17 "Gilead stayed beyond the Jordan, and Dan, why did he abide with the ships. Asher
sat still at the coast of the sea, settling down by the landings." The verbs in verses 16
and 17, however, most commonly refer not to delaying or tarrying or sitting still but to
residing, dwelling, and literally plying one's tent. The NRSV translation ill suits the final
entry in the description of warriors at verse 18 in which Zebulun and Naphtali's bravery
is described and is jarring in light of the structure of the song in which a condemnation
of those who do not participate in the battle comes at a later point in the passage at
verse 23.

Frank Moore Cross, however, offers a brilliant resolution to this problem. He suggests
that *lmh* is best read not as "why," as is most common in Biblical Hebrew, but as an
example of the "emphatic lamed extended by -*ma* known from Ugaritic" (235 n74) and
so translates "verily." The many discussions seeking to explain why Reuben, Gilead, Dan,
and Asher supposedly hold back from the fighting and the somewhat forced translations
that accompany them thus become unnecessary.

The catalog listing the members of this confederation is a traditional topos found several times in ancient Hebrew literature in genealogies, testaments, or other forms. Constituted by brief notices about heroes or groups, which sometimes appear singly – in the
annunciation form, for example – the catalog serves a critical cultural function in asserting group identity. It says essentially, this is how we are constituted, who our ancestor
heroes are. Here is a slice of our history as we understand it. In Judges 5, various groups
are described, where they dwell, what their occupations are, and how brave they are.
These parts map the whole, the people Israel with its disparate parts, characteristics,
and geographic origins (on translation, see Niditch, *Judges*, 74, 79–80).

> 16   Verily you dwell between the settlements
>   to hear the whistling for the flocks.
>   Concerning the divisions in Reuben,
>   great are the stout of heart.
> 17   Gilead in the Transjordan plies his tent,
>   and Dan, verily, he resides in ships.
>   Asher dwells on the shore of the sea
>   and on its promontories, he plies his tent.
> 18   Zebulun is a people whose soul taunts Death
>   and Naphtali on the heights of the open country.

Comparisons might be drawn with Genesis 49:13 and 16:12. A traditional catalog formula "tribe + location + tenting/residing" characterizes the references from Genesis and
those concerning Gilead, Dan, and Asher in Judges 5:17. These descriptive formulas are
building blocks of tradition.

This in turn brings us to another example, language concerning Ishmael, brother of Isaac, son of Abraham, and ancestor hero of the Ishmaelites. Hagar, Ishmael's mother-to-be, has fled from her oppressive mistress Sarah. Sarah has come to resent the concubine who gains new status, having conceived her husband Abraham's child in an ancient form of maternal surrogacy. The deity intervenes with the woman, who is marginalized and alone, declaring in traditional biblical-style content that the son of such a woman will indeed be a hero, a typical motif in the biographies of heroes. She need not fear.

> He will be a wild ass of a man,
> his hand will be in everything
> and everyone's hand will be in his,
> and next to his kin he will ply his tent.

Once again, Genesis 16:12 has generally been mistranslated to create a forced and negative portrait of Ishmael, but the verse really refers to his whereabouts and occupation, as is usual in this formula pattern. NRSV is typical of such negative translations: "He shall be a wild ass of a man, with his hand against everyone, and everyone's hand against him; and he shall live at odds with his kin." Implied is that being like a "wild ass" is bad, that Ishmael and his kin are violent aggressors and troublemakers who disrupt society. The modern translators expect the Israelite writers to condemn Ishmaelites, to draw differences between themselves as good citizens and their neighbors as antisocial marauding wildmen, the dangerous ethnic "Other." What, however, if we point out that biblical heroes are regularly compared to fecund, wild, macho animals such as bulls, strong donkeys (Gen. 49:14), and ravenous wolves (49:27)? It is a positive thing to use such metaphors.

The word "wild ass" connotes fertility, sexual liveliness and machismo. In an admittedly negative context, the prophet Jeremiah uses the female wild ass to develop the metaphor of Israel as a loose woman on the prowl who deserts her husband, Yahweh, to seek lovers, that is, other gods. She never tires (Jer. 2:24). I would suggest, however, that what is bad for the goose is good for the gander. The deity himself is known by the epithet "the Bull of Jacob," which in English Bibles is frequently translated "the Mighty One of Jacob." As Patrick D. Miller has shown, however, Yahweh as divine warrior, like his Canaanite counterpart Baal, is a horned, fertile, virile bull. In Deuteronomy 33:17, Joseph is positively compared to a first-born bull/a horned wild ox in images of warrior prowess. Similarly, in the Blessing of Jacob, the tribe/hero Issachar is called a strong or boney donkey (Gen. 49:14–15). The catalog concerning Issachar is similar in content and structure to Genesis 16:12, describing his manly quality via an animal metaphor, the location where he dwells, and the kind of work he does.

The virile Ishmael and hence future Ishmaelites are traders and make their dwelling place near Israel. In biblical material the Ishmaelites are known as traders par excellence – we recall for example their presence in the tale of Joseph (see especially Gen. 37:25–28). The imagery of Genesis 16:12 thus comports with the larger tradition or mythology about Ishmaelites. This material is of a kind with the descriptions of heroes/tribes in Judges 5:15–17 explored above with the component parts of hero's name/ethnic identity, location and occupation. This sort of formula can be a part of a catalog in a victory song as in Judges 5, an annunciation of a hero to be born as in Genesis 16, or a prophetic testament, as the patriarch Jacob is said to bless his sons before his death and thereby predict and describe the future roles of the groups descended from them (Gen. 49). Such works have significance for the political outlook and worldview of their authors, of those who deploy these formula patterns, saying something about their own views of Israelite identity while the composers conform to the shared conventions of pan-Israelite traditional literature. The founding hero of the Ishmaelites is presented positively. Here and in Genesis 21, another scene of divine rescue for the future hero and his mother, one feels as if one were in another group's foundation myth.

What is this material doing in the Hebrew Scriptures? Whose tradition is it and what is the larger cultural context to which it belongs? John W. Wright is interested in the Persian period Judaism reflected in late biblical literature, specifically in the ways in which the genealogies of 1 Chronicles present Yehud or Judah as a "familial/patronage system … an ethnos, with power distributed by real or fictitious familial/kinship ties" (73; see further the essay by Tamara Cohn Eskenazi in this volume). Wright links this function of genealogies with a reminder that in traditional states, polities are demarcated by porous frontiers rather than the sharper boundaries of modern states. Among such "traditional states, borders per se did not demarcate, or create, a sole sovereign state; territoriality instead was bounded by the much more porous concept of frontiers … in which multiple powers … make various claims over particular bodies in different situations" (72). The fictive links created by genealogies, reinforced by traditional catalogs or predictions about newborn or soon-to-be-born heroes, help to map an Israelite sense of ethnicity, a view of Israelites' place within a geographic setting, their historical location – in short, their very identity. Catalogs of heroes in Genesis, Deuteronomy, and Judges and the annunciation concerning Ishmael help to define a whole Israel made out of a mixed multitude and to incorporate neighboring others into the family or history of Israel, defining the people, its cultural and geographic frontiers, and its interactions with and relationships to neighboring groups (see also the essay by Song-Mi Suzie Park in this volume).

Findings

An overview of the field of folklore has addressed issues of definition and methodology, pointing to major emphases and areas of great relevance to the appreciation of ancient Israelite culture. Our study points to some misunderstandings and misrepresentations of folklore and provides several case studies, applying the insights of folklorists to the traditional literature of the Hebrew Bible. We ask what can be learned from the perspective of folklore studies that might otherwise be missed, how the approaches of folklore and awareness of comparative folk material can enrich the appreciation of Israelite tradition and provide alternatives, supplements or correctives to more typical treatments of biblical scholarship. Key recurring themes emphasize the importance of patterning, repetition, variation and multiplicity in traditional material, all of which warn against impositions of normative theologies upon biblical narratives and against overhistoricization.

The orientation of folklore challenges us to reconsider the way in which we approach manuscript variations and offers nuanced ways in which to assess the redaction history of texts, their translation, the nature of sources and the significance of the doublets, contradictions and seeming literary "incoherence" that source criticism seeks to explain. Thinking as folklorists is to ask questions about the "anxiety-producing" problems that provide the communicative contexts for forms of folklore and to think always about the role of artists and their audiences.

Note

1   This discussion of text-critical issues is drawn from the more fully framed introduction to Niditch, *Judges*.

Bibliography

Alter, Robert. *The Art of Biblical Narrative*. New York: Basic Books, 1981. An influential work exploring the characteristics of ancient Israelite narrative.

Alter, Robert. "Samson without folklore." In Susan Niditch (ed.), *Text and Tradition: The Hebrew Bible and Folklore* (pp. 47–56). Semeia Studies. Atlanta: Scholars Press, 1990. A psychoanalytical study of tales of Samson.

Alter, Robert. *The Five Books of Moses: A Translation with Commentary*. New York: W. W. Norton, 2004. A felicitous and thoughtful translation of the Pentateuch that captures the cadences of the Hebrew.

Baden, Joel S. *The Composition of the Pentateuch: Renewing the Documentary Hypothesis*. New Haven: Yale University Press, 2012. A study that argues for the existence of identifiable, written sources that were combined into the Pentateuch.

Ben-Amos, Dan. "Toward a definition of folklore in context." In A. Paredes and R. Bauman (eds), *Toward New Perspectives in Folklore* (pp. 3–15). Austin: University of Texas Press, 1972. An influential essay that offers a complex, performance-based definition of folklore.

Ben-Amos, Dan. "Analytical categories and ethnic genres." In Dan Ben-Amos (ed.), *Folklore Genres* (pp. 214–42). Austin: University of Texas Press, 1976. A study in genre that takes account of cultural context and the folk group.

Carr, David M. *Writing on the Tablet of the Heart: Origins of Scripture and Literature*. New York: Oxford University Press, 2005. An original study that explores the scribal cultures of the ancient Near East in the context of questions about memory, writing and orality.

Cross, Frank Moore. *Canaanite Myth and Hebrew Epic: Essays in the History of the Religion of Israel*. Cambridge, MA: Harvard University Press, 1973. Wide-ranging and influential contributions to the study of ancient Israel by a preeminent scholar of the Bible and the ancient Near East.

Culley, Robert C. *Oral Formulaic Language in the Biblical Psalms*. Near East and Middle East Series 4. Toronto: University of Toronto Press, 1967. A careful and thoughtful exploration of the oral-traditional qualities of biblical poetry.

Doran, Robert. *2 Maccabees: A Critical Commentary*. Hermeneia. Minneapolis: Fortress, 2012. An important new translation and commentary that deals with questions of genre, history and historiography.

Dundes, Alan. *Interpreting Folklore*. Bloomington: Indiana University Press, 1980. A masterful discussion of folklore theory that explores the field and the folk, addressing questions concerning a variety of folk genres and contexts.

Finnegan, Ruth H. *Literacy and Orality*. Oxford: Blackwell, 1988. An examination of the interplay between orality and writing in traditional African cultures with special attention to issues of genre.

Foley, John Miles. *Immanent Art: From Structure to Meaning in Traditional Oral Epic*. Bloomington: Indiana University Press, 1991. An influential study in comparative literature, influenced both by Lord's formulaic theory and Isser's reception theory.

Gunkel, Hermann. *The Legends of Genesis*. New York: Schocken, 1966. A translation of the introduction to Gunkel's masterful commentary to Genesis.

Gunkel, Hermann. *The Folktale in the Old Testament*. Sheffield: Almond Press, 1987. Originally published as *Das Märchen im Alten Testament*. Tübingen: J. B. C. Mohr, 1917. An innovative study of ancient Israelite narrative that exemplifies an astute awareness of the field of folklore as practiced in the early twentieth century.

Gunn, David. "The battle report: Oral or scribal convention?" *Journal of Biblical Literature* 93 (1974): 513–18. A thoughtful contribution to questions concerning oral-style conventions in ancient Israelite literature.

Lord, Albert B. *The Singer of Tales*. New York: Atheneum, 1968. The classic presentation of Lord and Milman Parry's theory of oral-formulaic composition.

Miller, Patrick D. "Animal names as designations in Ugaritic and Hebrew." *Ugarit-Forschungen 2* (1970): 177–86. This comparative study indicates that the epithet for Yahweh often translated "the Mighty One of Jacob" has the underlying meaning "Bull of Jacob."

Nagy, Gregory. *Homeric Questions*. Austin: University of Texas, 1996. A thoughtful presentation of Lord's theories and misunderstandings of them.

Niditch, Susan. *Folklore and the Hebrew Bible*. Minneapolis: Fortress, 1993. An introduction to the field of folklore studies as it relates to biblical literature.

Niditch, Susan. *Oral World and Written Word: Ancient Israelite Literature*. Louisville, KY: Westminster John Knox, 1996. A study of the interplay between the oral and the written in Israelite tradition.

Niditch, Susan. *Judges: A Commentary*. Old Testament Library. Louisville, KY: Westminster John Knox, 2008. A commentary informed by the field of folklore providing additional bibliography by Niditch and others.

Olrik, Axel. "Epic laws of folk narrative." In Alan Dundes (ed.), *The Study of Folklore* (pp. 129–41). Englewood Cliffs, NJ: Prentice-Hall, 1965. A classic study of key traits exhibited by an international fund of folk narrative.

Thompson, Stith (ed. and trans.). *The Types of the Folktale*. Folklore Fellows Communications 184. Helsinki: Suomalainen Tiedeakatemia (expanded edition of Antii Aarne's Verzeichnis). A compendium of folk narrative patterns compiled in the historic-geographic method of folklore studies.

Westermann, Claus. *Genesis: A Commentary*. 3 vols. Minneapolis: Augsburg, 1984–6. A masterful three-volume translation and commentary, informed by form-critical technique.

Whallon, William. *Formula, Character, and Context*. Center for Hellenic Studies. Cambridge, MA: Harvard University Press, 1969. A fine comparative study of traditional-style literature, one portion of which is devoted to evidence of formulaic composition in the Hebrew Bible.

Wilbert, Johannes and Karin Simoneau. *Folk Literature of the Gê Indians*, vol. 2. Los Angeles: UCLA Latin American Publications, 1984. A collection of tales from the Gê of Brazil.

Wright, John W. "The borders of Yehud and the genealogies of Chronicles." In Oded Lipschits and Manfred Oeming (eds), *Judah and the Judeans in the Persian Period* (pp. 67–89). Winona Lake, IN: Eisenbrauns, 2006. A thoughtful treatment of the role of genealogies in the formation and reinforcement of cultural identity.

CHAPTER 6

The Formation of the Hebrew Bible
Sources, Compositional Layers, and Other Revisions

David M. Carr

Because the Bible as we have it now is a *written* text, we typically bring modern assumptions about writing to bear on our ideas about its formation. But such modern assumptions can be misleading. Most contemporary readers are used to reading books by clearly identified authors. These authors have authorial rights over what is published in their name. If you are reading a given novel that is attributed to a particular author and find out that someone secretly revised and expanded on that novel, a natural reaction is to want to find a version of that novel with that novelist's original words. Moreover, the novelist or his or her publisher would have a right to sue anyone who republished their work in expanded and revised form without permission. These sorts of ideas about authorship, authorial rights and the integrity of a written work represent *our* modern assumptions about how written works should be/are produced. But they are not the assumptions that stand behind the Hebrew Bible.

To begin, biblical narratives like the Book of Genesis were originally *anonymous*. To be sure, later tradition attributes the books of Genesis through Deuteronomy to Moses, and other historical books are attributed to other authors. Nevertheless, ancient Near Eastern narratives like the Pentateuch (Genesis–Deuteronomy) were generally anonymous, and the earliest manuscripts of biblical narratives do not attribute them to any author at all. Moreover, there are features in the Pentateuch – such as the description at the end of Deuteronomy of Moses' own death and burial – which are not consistent with the idea that Moses wrote them.

So how, one might ask, did someone get the idea that Moses wrote these books? Perhaps the most persuasive explanation builds on *when* we first see claims of Mosaic

The Wiley Blackwell Companion to Ancient Israel, First Edition. Edited by Susan Niditch.
© 2016 John Wiley & Sons, Ltd. Published 2016 by John Wiley & Sons, Ltd.

authorship of the Pentateuch in datable Jewish works. It turns out that Jewish authors started to claim that Moses wrote the Pentateuch around the time that Judaism was most intensely engaged in cultural contact and competition with an ancient Greek culture that was particularly focused on authors, above all on Homer and the Greek epics (the Iliad and the Odyssey) attributed to him. Jews encountering this Greek culture asserted that Moses was an author yet more ancient than the Greek Homer, and the Pentateuch written by him was more ancient than Homer's epics. Of course, by now this belief that Moses wrote the Pentateuch is itself very old, and many Christians and Jews assume it to be an ancient truth. Nevertheless, this idea of Mosaic authorship of the whole Pentateuch is an imposition of Greek ideas about authorship and literary worth onto a Hebrew text that was written under other assumptions.

This article is an introduction to several centuries of biblical scholarship that have developed another perspective on the writing of the Pentateuch and other biblical books, a perspective grounded in a combination of data within the biblical text and evidence from ancient manuscripts about how scribes of the ancient Near East produced literary works. We now know that the scribes who wrote the Hebrew Bible did not just preserve texts like the Pentateuch, but revised and (often) expanded on them. Of course, they valued such ancient traditions. Indeed, their valuing of such traditions is one reason they wrote them down. Yet their writing of such traditions was part of a broader process of memorization, oral performance and (frequently) expansion upon such traditions (see also the essay by Susan Niditch in this volume). Thus the initial writing down of a given story did not mean that it stayed as it was. It was just the beginning.

Forms of Ancient Revision of Texts

Let us turn now to consider what scholars have learned about how ancient scribes actually treated the texts that they received. One major advance in recent research on the formation of ancient texts has been the study of certain ancient manuscripts where we can directly study the different stages through which these texts have grown. In cases like these we have what appears to be an early stage (or stages) of a given text, and then we have one or more later stages where that text has been expanded with additions or combined with another text. In some such cases, we actually have manuscripts that help us trace the growth of a biblical book. In other cases, the ancient text in question is a nonbiblical book from Mesopotamia or an early Jewish text that underwent one or more stages of expansion or recombination. In either situation, these ancient *documented* cases of scribal revision can help balance the modern assumptions described above about single authorship of texts and authorial rights. Over and over again, we see that ancient texts were revised over long periods of time. It is clear that these texts had many authors, but these authors – especially revisers – remained largely anonymous.

So, what sorts of changes are documented in ancient manuscripts? There are four main ways that scribes modified ancient traditions with which they worked: *joining* separate stories about different events end-to-end into a new longer narrative, *blending* (or "conflating") parallel narratives about the same set of events into a new combined whole, *expanding on* an existing text through adding newly composed material, and *counterwriting* an earlier narrative so that the new narrative in some way contradicts and aims to replace the older narrative on which it is modeled. Before turning to the Bible itself, let me note an example of each sort of documented growth in turn.

An example of "joining" comes from one of the best-documented cases of growth, the Mesopotamian epic of Gilgamesh. This epic was written in the ancient language of Akkadian and traces the journey of a Sumerian king, Gilgamesh, from his first formative friendship through a series of stories about his search for immortality in the wake of his friend's death. We do not have all the sources of these stories in the form of written documents. Nevertheless, there are a few surviving written compositions in the ancient language of Sumerian that present individual episodes in the life of Gilgamesh and may form part of the background of separate episodes now found in the full epic of Gilgamesh. If so, the author of the epic of Gilgamesh drew freely on the narrative motifs of these stories about Gilgamesh to write a longer story about him, joining them end-to-end into a larger whole.

But sometimes it appears that scribes wanted to combine stories about the *same* event or figure into the same text. In these cases, it was not possible to just join stories end-to-end. The narratives had to be blended. "Conflation" is when ancient scribes blended texts about the same event into each other to produce a mixed whole. One of the best cases of this is the creation of combined narratives about Jesus out of the parallel narratives about him in the canonical gospels. An ancient example of this is the *Diatessaron* which was created by the early Syrian church father Tatian out of the gospels of Matthew, Mark, Luke and John. When Tatian created this *Diatessaron*, he did not use every last bit of these canonical gospels. That would have produced a repetitive and nonsensical narrative! Rather he produced a very mixed form of the narratives shared by Matthew, Mark and Luke, while preserving relatively more of the distinctively different narratives about Jesus found in John (G. F. Moore in Tigay 255). For a while his *Diatessaron* was read as the preferred form of the Christian gospel in Syrian churches before almost all copies of it were burned as heretical. And this form of combination did not just happen in early Christianity. We have, for example, ancient manuscripts of the Pentateuch that selectively blend parts of Deuteronomy into the parts of Exodus and Numbers that Deuteronomy is said to review, while also inserting elements from Exodus and Numbers into relevant parts of Deuteronomy (Tigay in Tigay 61–83).

Perhaps our best-documented type of scribal revision is expansion, where ancient scribes would preserve all or most of an ancient text, but add new material to it composed by the scribe to explain, revise or augment that ancient text. A good example of this is found in the Hebrew Bible itself with the revision and expansion of large sections of Samuel–Kings in 1 Chronicles 10–2 Chronicles 36:21. To be sure, Chronicles does not preserve all of Samuel–Kings, leaving out, for example, some embarrassing episodes from the life of David, its hero. But it preserves much of Samuel–Kings, sometimes expanding that material with priestly and other traditions central to its interests. Another, more controversial, example is the documentation of two different editions of the Book of Jeremiah in ancient manuscripts: a shorter version reflected in an ancient Greek translation of Jeremiah and some Hebrew manuscripts found at the Dead Sea, and a version that is about 20 percent longer found in the standard Jewish manuscripts of Jeremiah. Though the latter standard version of Jeremiah is the one translated in most English Bibles, many scholars (myself included) believe this standard version of Jeremiah to be an *expansion* and reorganization of a shorter version of Jeremiah like that reflected in the Old Greek and Dead Sea manuscripts (Emanuel Tov in Tigay 212–37). The technical term that biblical scholars use for such scribal expansion on an earlier tradition is *redaction*, and there is widespread evidence for such "redaction" in documented cases of ancient textual growth.

As we look over the bulk of ancient evidence for scribal practices, it is clear that scribes *generally* aimed to preserve ancient traditions, even if they sometimes changed them. Yet we see a few cases where scribes appear to have *counterwritten* traditions that they aimed to contradict. In these cases, they modeled a new text on an older one whose claims they aimed to refute. An initial example of this would be the way a text called the Lagash King list was modeled on and yet competes with the older and better known Sumerian King list, with a focus on its list of kings after the flood (likely its oldest part). The Lagash king list reorients this list of postflood kings to focus on rulers of Lagash. Notably the first chapters of Genesis contain an ancient Israelite rewriting of this Sumerian king list tradition too, now featuring nonroyal figures like Adam and Noah and attributing lifespans to the preflood figures that are much reduced from the Sumerian kinglist, even if most of the lifespans in Genesis 5 are centuries longer than normal lifespans now.

Thus the Hebrew Bible was formed in an ancient Near Eastern context where scribes often revised ancient texts in concrete ways: joining, conflating/blending, expanding/redacting and/or counterwriting them. As suggested above, such revision in our contemporary, author-focused world might be viewed as a corruption of an original text, a wrong done to a text and its author that would require correction and could be subject to a copyright lawsuit. Yet an overview of documented cases of scribal revision suggests a very different attitude toward textual revision in ancient contexts. There it was the texts that no one cared about that were particularly likely to be left as is, gathering dust in the corner of some temple or scribal study. Meanwhile, scribes changed the texts that they most cherished, read and performed in their cultures. Especially in the early stages of their formation, valued texts such as Gilgamesh in ancient Mesopotamia or the Torah/Pentateuch in ancient Judaism were recombined, expanded upon and gradually transformed into a distillate of centuries of tradition and reflection. Rather than being by a single author, these important ancient texts were multivoiced. Thus the Pentateuch and other ancient texts were formed from the traditional memories and insights of generations of scribes.

Examples of Scribal Revision in Genesis 1–11

So far I have written generally about the fact *that* the Pentateuch and other parts of the Hebrew Bible were formed over time, but have not discussed many specifics of *how* they were reshaped. In what follows I will focus particularly on the first 11 chapters of Genesis to show how these chapters in the Bible reflect all four of the above-described processes of scribal change. This discussion will prepare for a broader discussion of how other parts of the Bible likewise were formed over time.

I start with evidence in Genesis 1–11 for the process of *joining* originally separate traditions about different episodes end-to-end into a single narrative. One major clue that this sort of thing has happened occurs in Genesis 4:17. After the first couple, Adam and Eve, had the first children, Cain and Abel, and Cain has been condemned to a life of wandering for having killed his brother, Abel (Gen. 4:1–16), Genesis 4:17 says, "Cain had intercourse with his wife, and she conceived and gave birth to Enoch." Attentive readers often are puzzled by this. Where did Cain's wife come from? Apparently, the genealogy of which Genesis 4:17 is a part was not originally written to continue a story of human origins where Cain was the only remaining son of the first human family. And this is not the only sign of originally separate origins for the genealogy found in Genesis 4:17–24. The genealogy speaks toward its conclusion of how Cain's great-grandson Lamech gave birth to the founders of nomadic life, music and craftwork (Gen. 4:19–22). This claim about Lamech's other sons as founders does not seem to take account of the fact that all of humanity except Lamech's son Noah is described later in Genesis as dying in the flood (Gen. 6–8). Signs such as this suggest that the genealogy in Genesis 4:17–24 once stood apart from the stories that precede and follow it, only being combined with the story of Adam and Eve, Cain and Abel and the flood, at a point after its original composition.

We also have some clues in Genesis 1–11 that parts of it were expanded, or to use the term from biblical scholarship, redacted. Just after the flood that kills all humanity there is a story about Noah being the first to plant a vineyard and (later) get drunk on the grapes it produced (Gen. 9:20–21). As sometimes happens when people get quite drunk, Noah is said to have taken off his clothes and passed out in his tent. The oldest of his sons, Ham, sees Noah lying naked in the tent and tells his brothers, Shem and Japheth. They then walk backward into the tent (to avoid seeing their father naked) and cover him up. This is where the puzzle of the story appears. Noah wakes up in the story, hears what happened to him, and pronounces a curse on the *son* of Ham, Canaan. The angry reaction is not a real puzzle, since the seeing of a male's nakedness was tantamount to having sex with that man. For example, Leviticus 18 lists forbidden sex acts between family members as cases where someone "reveals the nakedness" of someone else. Indeed, some have speculated, going beyond the evidence in Genesis 9:20–24, that Ham's seeing of his father's nakedness implies he actually did have sex with his father. But what is particularly strange about this text is that Noah curses Ham's *son* and not Ham himself. Why redirect the curse toward Ham's son when Ham was the wrongdoer? The identity of that son here, Canaan, provides a possible historical answer. Although the original version of this story probably featured a curse of Ham, a scribe may have redacted that story so that the curse now focused on Ham's son, Canaan. Why? Because Canaan is seen as the father of the nations that will eventually be conquered and displaced by the Israelites when they enter the land. Having Noah curse *Canaan* in Genesis 9:25–27 would be a way to anticipate the story of conquest of the Canaanites that comes much later in the Book of Joshua. Confirmation that some scribes modified parts of Genesis in this way comes in the very next chapter when an initial list of Canaan's individual children in Genesis 10:15 (see the similar lists in 10:8, 13, 21, 24) has been expanded with a list of nations that would be displaced in the story of the conquest (Gen. 10:16–18a; similar lists in Gen. 15:19–21; Deut. 7:1; Josh. 3:10; 5:1, etc.). Apparently a scribal redactor, anticipating the story of conquest, revised parts of Genesis 9 and 10 so that the roots of the destruction of the Canaanite nations could already be found in a form of Noah's curse revised to focus on Canaan (9:25–27) and on the nations that descended from him (10:16–18; see Carr 161–3).

So far I have discussed joining and redaction. There also is substantial evidence that Genesis 1–11 was formed through the conflation of two parallel narratives that *both* described the creation of life and its later destruction in a flood. Scholars have seen evidence for this for centuries, starting with a German pastor, Henning Bernard Witter. Three hundred years ago, in 1711, he noticed ways that the story of creation in Genesis 1 both doubled and diverged from the story of creation in Genesis 2 in ways that suggested the two were originally separate sources, each of which described creation, albeit in a different order: plants>animals>humans [both male and female] in Genesis 1 versus plants>the first [male] human>animals>then the first female human in Genesis 2. Just a few decades later, in 1753, a doctor in King Louis XIV's court, Jean Astruc, saw the same clues in the Genesis creation narratives, but noticed similar duplications and differences between other parts of Genesis, including the genealogies in Genesis 4 and 5 and parallel elements in the narrative of the flood in Genesis 6–9. Let us take a closer look at these clues, since they have played an important role in biblical scholarship.

I start with the genealogies in Genesis 4 and 5, both of which detail a series of generations between the first human and Noah, the progenitor of all of postflood humanity. If one skims these chapters, it is easy to miss that almost all of the names in the Genesis 4 genealogy appear in some form, even if slightly modified, in the Genesis 5 genealogy. Here is a chart showing the similarities (names are given in Hebrew transliteration):

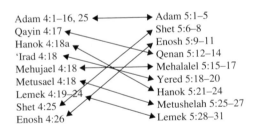

This sort of duplication and difference would be strange in a narrative written by one person at one time. Rather, this seems another example of the process of conflation where two texts covering the same events/people have been combined into one. In this case, the two texts have been mostly put one after the other, though scholars long have supposed that the fragment about Noah's naming found in Genesis 5:29 probably originated in a continuation of the genealogy that now ends with Lamech in Genesis 4:24 and only later was inserted into the Genesis 5 genealogy.

As we continue to the flood narrative, there is evidence of a far more intricate process of conflation. God perceives a problem with humanity twice (Gen. 6:5–7 and 6:12); Noah is described as an exception to this problem twice (Gen. 6:8 and 6:9); God announces twice to Noah God's plans to destroy the world and tells him to save some of the animals (Gen. 6:13–21 and 7:1–4); Noah is described briefly as complying with God's instructions twice (Gen. 6:22 and 7:5); Noah and his family enter the ark twice

(Gen. 7:7 and 7:13); and the duplications continue through to God's doubled promise not to bring a flood again (Gen. 8:21–22 and 9:8–17). Notably, one of the two divine promises not to bring a flood is prompted by God's appreciation of a sacrifice of animals by Noah (Gen. 8:20). Only one of the sets of doublets noted above describes Noah as bringing extra pairs of sacrifice-appropriate animals ("clean") that he could have sacrificed later without wiping out entire species (Gen. 7:2). The other set of doublets insists that he brought only one pair of each kind of animal on the ark (Gen. 6:19–20; also 7:15–16). This and other clues have suggested to the majority of scholars that Genesis 6–9 represents the combination of two flood narratives that were originally separate: one that describes Noah as bringing extra clean animals on the ark to prepare for his eventual sacrifice in 8:20 and God's promise to restore creation in 8:21–22 (including Gen. 6:1–9; 7:1–2, 3b–5, 7, 10, 12, 17, 22–23a; 8:2b–3a, 6–12, 13b, 20–22); and another that describes Noah as bringing only one pair each of animals that climaxes in the covenant of the rainbow in Genesis 9:8–17 (including Gen. 6:9*–22; 7:6, 11, 13–16a, 18–21, 23*–24; 8:1–2a, 3b–5, 14–19; 9:1–17; the rest is redaction joining the two strands; see Carr 48–62).

Furthermore, scholars have put these observations together to suggest that Genesis 1–11 is a conflation of two overall strands that described creation and flood. The older of the two strands originally started with the Garden of Eden story (Gen. 2:4b–3:24) and the Cain and Abel story in Genesis 4:1–16, continued with the genealogy of Cain in Genesis 4:17–24, and continued further with the strand of the flood narrative that climaxes with Noah's sacrifice. Notably, this strand often uses the term Yahweh to refer to God, a term often translated in English as LORD. For this reason, scholars often refer to these materials as "Yahwistic" or "J" (because some of the scholars to discover this source were German and rendered the "Y" sound with the letter J). The later strand of Genesis 1–11 originally began with the narrative of creation in seven days in Genesis 1:1–2:3, continued with the genealogy in the bulk of Genesis 5, and then continued further with the strand of the flood narrative that climaxes in the covenant of the rainbow in Genesis 9:8–17. This strand refers here to God with the Hebrew term "Elohim," which is rendered as "God" in most English translations. For over a century scholars have referred to this strand as Priestly or "P," because this source continues through the rest of the Pentateuch and includes a number of specifically priestly texts found in Exodus through Numbers. These two stories of creation and flood, "J" and "P," were originally separate from one another before they were conflated into the combined primeval history we now have in Genesis 1–9 (Carr 62–77).

These reflections on two source strands in Genesis 1–9 lead to a way that the first chapters of Genesis illustrate the fourth way that scribes revised ancient texts, through *counterwriting* them. For a close examination shows that the P strand appears to have been written, in part, to counter the account of creation and flood found in J. To be sure, P appears to have been written separately from J; otherwise we would not see now such extensive duplication in P of almost every element in J. Nevertheless, the originally separate P document opposes numerous specific aspects of the J document that it parallels. Let us focus here on ways that the Priestly creation account in Genesis 1:1–2:3 echoes and responds to parts of the Yahwistic Garden of Eden story in Genesis 2:4–3:24. Where the Yahwistic creation story starts "on the day that Yhwh created earth and heaven"

(Gen. 2:4b), the Priestly account makes claims to go even further back and puts heaven first by saying "In the *beginning* of God's creation of heaven and earth" (Gen. 1:1). The most prominent contrasts come when both narratives describe the creation and destiny of humanity. The Yahwistic story describes God as crafting the first human almost like a human potter, then breathing the divine breath into him to make him a "living being" (Gen. 2:7). The Priestly story shares the idea of humans partaking of divinity, but in it God simply speaks the first humans into existence, decreeing that they, both male and female, should bear God's "image and likeness" (Gen. 1:26–27; see also the discussion of this passage in the essay by Christopher Rollston in this volume). Then, where the Yahwistic story describes the *curses* that follow humans seeking to be "like God" (Gen. 3:5–7, 16–19) and depicts God as afraid that humans might become too godlike (Gen. 3:22–24), the Priestly story follows up its account of creation by saying that God simply *blessed* the humans (1:28) and pronounced that their creation was "very good" (Gen. 1:31). Now, of course, the P and J stories stand together in one conflated biblical narrative (Gen. 1–3), so that the Yahwistic story of creation and punishment (Gen. 2:4b–3:24) is a continuation and balance to the Priestly story of the creation of humans in God's image (Gen. 1:26–31). Originally, however, it is likely that the Priestly account was designed to counterwrite and *replace* the older Yahwistic creation narrative to which it responds (Smith 129–38; compare Susan Niditch's essay in this volume).

These ideas about joining, redaction, conflation and counterwriting in Genesis 1–9 are not new. Indeed, as mentioned before, scholars first discovered what we now call "J" and "P" in Genesis 1–11 over 300 years ago, and it is safe to say that this insight has stood the test of time. Virtually all scholars doing historical research on the Hebrew Bible continue to distinguish these strands from one another. Consider: this time-tested theory of sources was developed in biblical studies about the same time as Benjamin Franklin "discovered" electricity and Isaac Newton discovered the laws of motion. The theory of sources in Genesis represents the very earliest, foundational stage of "scientific" study of the Bible. This theory only remains relatively unknown in the general public because many religious communities find such ideas of multiple authorship threatening to their faith, while many secular schools avoid religious subjects.

Study of the Formation of the Pentateuch

So far I only have described some basic theories about the formation of Genesis 1–9, focusing particularly on the centuries-old finding that these first chapters of Genesis were formed through the combination of two, originally separate source strands now termed "J" and "P." Yet biblical research has come quite a long way in the centuries since this original discovery and arrived at a number of conclusions about how the rest of Genesis, indeed the rest of the Hebrew Bible, was formed. In particular, scholars have continued to be fascinated with study of the formation of the Pentateuch.

If there is one assured result of such scholarship, it concerns the identification of a broader Priestly layer that starts with the P layer discussed above in Genesis 1–9 (see also S. A. Geller's essay in this volume). For Genesis, this layer includes much of the genealogy of postflood nations in Genesis 10; all of the genealogy connecting Noah's son

Shem to Abraham's father, Terah (Gen. 11:10–27); the covenant of circumcision with Abraham in Genesis 17 along with some other texts about Abraham (e.g., Gen. 16:3, 15–16); other death notices and genealogies in Genesis (e.g., Gen. 25:7–20; 35:22–37:2); a few narratives about Jacob (e.g., Gen. 26:34–5; 27:46–28:9; 35:9–15) and perhaps fragments about Joseph (e.g., Gen. 41:46; 45:19–21; 47:5–11). Moving beyond Genesis, P includes the genealogy with which Exodus begins (Exod. 1:1–5); the second call of Moses (Exod. 6:2–13) and four of the plagues that follow (Exod. 7:19–22; 8:5–7, 15–19; 9:8–12; 11:9–10) and Passover, followed by a strand of the Red Sea story (Exod. 12:1–20, 28, 40–51; 14:1–4, 8–10, 15–28, 21–3, 26, 28–9); the divine instruction to set up and staff the wilderness sanctuary (Exod. 24:15–31:18) and human compliance to those instructions (Exod. 35–40; Lev. 8–9), along with numerous other sacrificial and purity regulations (e.g., Lev. 1–7, 11–15); the regulation of the camp before departure from Sinai (Num. 1:1–10:28) and parts of several narratives that follow (e.g., a strand of the spies story: Num. 13:1–17a, 21, 25–6, 32–3; 14:1–3, 5–10, 26–38). Closely related to this are the regulations about the people's holiness found particularly in Leviticus 16–26, but with related material elsewhere (e.g., Exod. 31:12–17). The material in Leviticus 16–26 was once thought to be a pre-Priestly "Holiness code" that was used as a source by the authors of P, but now many think it to be a relatively later layer of redaction that extends priestly laws of purity to the people as a whole. Either way (as source or as later redaction), this "Holiness layer" can be understood to be part of "P" quite broadly conceived.

Notably, numerous parts of this Priestly layer continue the pattern already seen in Genesis 1 (cf. Gen. 2–3) of responding to and countering earlier non-Priestly narratives. For example, the Priestly story of Jacob's *hearing* a divine promise at Bethel and anointing a pillar there (Gen. 35:9–15) counters an earlier account where Jacob *sees* God at Bethel and founds a "house of God" there (Gen. 28:10–22). Likely by the time that the Priestly version of the Bethel story was written it was no longer seen as appropriate for a patriarch like Jacob to found a temple outside Jerusalem and sacrifice at it. Therefore, the Priestly author wrote a new version of the Jacob story that lacked such elements (Gen. 35:9–15). Another example comes in the story of Israel at Mount Sinai. The older non-Priestly account tells a story about how the people recruited Aaron, a major ancestor of the high priesthood, to build a golden calf for them while Moses was on the mountain receiving the tablets (Exod. 32:1–6), an example of idol worship which Moses responds to by chastising Aaron (Exod. 32:21–24) and then recruiting the Levites to kill as many of their countrypeople as they can (Exod. 32:25–29). This picture of priestly Aaron as an idolater and of the priestly Levites as consecrated in their brothers' blood (Exod. 32:29) hardly would have sat well with the authors of the Priestly document. They told a different version of the Sinai story, one that moved simply from God's instructions for the sanctuary and ordination of Aaron and his sons (Exodus 25–31) to the Israelites' compliance with those instructions (Exod. 35–40; Lev. 8–9). As in the case of other Priestly, counterwritten texts, this Priestly account of Sinai would have performed best at cleansing Aaron and the Levites' name if it *replaced* the non-Priestly characterization of Aaron as an idolater and the Levites as murderers. Nevertheless, here again the Priestly Sinai story has been combined in our biblical text with the non-Priestly version it originally was meant to obliterate.

As mentioned above, scholars have reached a long-term consensus on the basic contents of P (broadly understood also to include Holiness materials), indeed one that has not varied by much since an influential analysis of P was published by the German scholar Theodor Nöldeke in 1869. Insofar as there is substantial dispute about this Priestly source now, it focuses mainly on the extent to which major parts of P might not have been part of a separate source, but instead were written from the outset as a *redaction* to balance or expand on earlier non-Priestly materials. The whole idea that P originally was a separate source fits texts like Genesis 1–9 well, where the Priestly layer duplicates and parallels so many parts of the non-Priestly material that it is difficult to understand why a scribal editor would *expand* on an existing text with so many duplications. Yet there are other parts of the Pentateuch where the Priestly material does show the character of an expansion, indeed an expansion that depends for its meaning on the way it responds to and follows up on an earlier non-Priestly story in the same narrative. For example, some have seen the Priestly story of Moses being forbidden to enter the land because of speaking to the people and then striking a rock for water (Num. 20:10–11; rather than speaking to the rock as God ordered in Num. 20:8) as a play on an earlier story about bringing water from a rock in Exodus 17:1–7, where Moses successfully brought water from a rock by striking it when ordered by God (Exod. 17:5–7). If so, then this would be a case where a Priestly story, Numbers 20:1–13, never stood apart from the non-Priestly Moses story (Exod. 17:1–7) which it follows. And scholars have proposed that other parts of the broader Priestly layer likewise may not have been part of a separate P source, especially those portions of P that occur after the climactic building of the wilderness sanctuary (Exodus 35–40).

Yet let us look now at the other strand that was discussed in Genesis 1–9: the Yahwistic source. It is not as clear as it once seemed to be just how far this source extends. To be sure, scholars once had broad agreement on the existence of a Yahwistic source that started with the stories of creation and curse in the J strand of Genesis 1–9, continued with stories of blessing on Abraham and his heirs starting in Genesis 12:1–3, and extended even to elements of similar blessing found in the story of Balaam in Numbers (e.g., Num. 22:6, 12; 24:1). Nevertheless, during the last few decades, an increasing number of scholars have noticed ways that the J story of creation and flood is only loosely connected to the following ancestral stories by the promise to Abraham in Gen. 12:1–3, and the following ancestral stories barely relate back to the primeval history either. Rather than being part of the same Yahwistic source, an increasing number of scholars believe that the Yahwistic story of creation and flood found in parts of Genesis 1–9 may once have stood separate from the stories about Abraham and other ancestors that now follow it, only later being joined to those stories by way of the Genesis 12:1–3 promise. If this is true, the earliest "J" source probably extended only up through the end of the primeval history. As such, it corresponded in outline and preoccupations to an earlier Mesopotamian story of creation and flood, the Atrahasis Epic, on which it may have been modeled (Carr 234–47; see also Edward Greenstein's essay in this volume).

As we move later into Genesis and the rest of the Pentateuch, it is difficult to define a scholarly consensus on the specific shaping of what might be neutrally termed "Non-Priestly" material (the material in the Pentateuch not assigned to the broad Priestly layer). Again, there once was a consensus that the non-Priestly portions of

Genesis–Exodus and Numbers could be assigned to two early sources, the Yahwist (discussed above) and yet a third source beginning in Genesis 20–22 called the Elohist (for "Elohim," the Hebrew divine designation often used in it). And indeed, there are important ways in which the "Elohistic" stories about Abraham found in Genesis 20–22 duplicate and diverge from stories about Abraham in Genesis 12–19 where "Yahweh" ("LORD" in English translations) is the preferred designation for God. For example, the story of Abraham passing Sarai off as his sister in Genesis 12:10–20 (see also Isaac in Gen. 26:1, 7–11) is paralleled by an Elohistic story of Abraham doing the same in Genesis 20:1–18, and the non-Priestly story of the expulsion of Hagar in Genesis 16:1–2, 4–14 parallels some parts of the story of her expulsion in Genesis 21:8–19. These indicators have led some scholars, even to the present day, to argue that the formation of the Pentateuch is best explained as the result of conflation of three sources – the Priestly source (P), a Yahwist source (J), and an Elohist source (E) – along with the addition of Deuteronomy at the end (D). This theory about J, E, D and P sources is referred to as "the documentary hypothesis" and is still taught in many textbooks.

At the same time, especially in Europe, a majority of specialists now doubt whether this is the best way to reconstruct the formation of the Pentateuch, especially its non-Priestly portions (Dozeman and Schmid). These specialists are struck with the basic differences between major blocks of the Pentateuch (e.g., primeval history, stories of the patriarchs, Moses story) and the extent to which these blocks are connected loosely with each other by brief connecting passages and a few cross-references. This has led many recent Pentateuchal scholars to suppose that the non-Priestly portions of the Pentateuch were formed by a mix of joining and redaction rather than conflation. They doubt that there ever existed a long Yahwistic or Elohistic source. Instead, they suggest that the earliest sources of the Pentateuch may have been an early, independent Jacob story along with a separate Moses story and possibly separate Abraham and/or primeval history traditions. Only at a relatively late stage, suggest these scholars, did these stories about different eras get joined by scribes who were particularly focused on the theme of promise and blessing. These scribes joined these separate, nonparallel stories end-to-end into a longer non-Priestly narrative, partly by adding layer upon layer of linking texts focused on promise, blessing and other themes. It was this complex narrative, then, that the Priestly authors counterwrote in composing their originally separate Priestly source.

By now the nonspecialist may be wondering what sort of clarity can be found in all this. Indeed, some biblical scholars sometimes share this sentiment and see such discord in Pentateuchal scholarship as a sign that no clarity can emerge in debates about biblical sources (see Steven Weitzman's essay in this volume). Nevertheless, it remains safe to say that some basic results, such as the distinction of Priestly materials from non-Priestly materials, have stood the test of time and remain assured. In addition, the last century of biblical scholarship has produced an increasing perception of the relative independence of major blocks of the Pentateuch from one another (e.g., primeval history, Jacob story, Joseph story, Moses story), even if scholars would date the linking of these blocks to different points.

Finally, these debates do help highlight a very important truth to keep in mind about all discussion of biblical formation: scholarly ideas about sources, redaction, etc., behind the Bible are *hypotheses*. They are attempts to explain data in the biblical text with imaginative models. They are not proven truth. There was a time a few decades ago when both students and scholars thought they could speak of J, E, D and P sources as if we had actual copies of such sources available somewhere for inspection and analysis. The truth is that *none* of these sources has ever been discovered in a manuscript. Some such sources, such as the P source and the Book of Deuteronomy, seem more clearly identifiable as distinct and separate. Others, such as J and E, are now doubted by many. None, however, is a given whole, and the more one attempts to identify the precise details of any source or redactional layer, the blurrier the picture becomes. *That* the Pentateuch was formed over time through a combination of joining, conflation, redaction and counter-writing is absolutely clear. The existence of some sort of Priestly source is also clear, as is the distinction of Deuteronomy from much of what precedes it. Beyond that, it appears that scholars are not able to achieve consensus.

The Formation of Other Parts of the Hebrew Bible

Having ended discussion of the Pentateuch on that sober note, let us turn briefly to study of the formation of other parts of the Hebrew Bible. Already I have mentioned the broad consensus among scholars that 1 Chronicles 10–2 Chronicles 36 represents a large-scale revision/redaction of some form of the text we now know as 1–2 Samuel and 1–2 Kings. It now seems likely that the version of Samuel–Kings used by the Chronicler was not identical to any known version of 1–2 Samuel and 1–2 Kings, but it seems clear that the author of Chronicles knew a version of Samuel and Kings that was virtually identical to major portions of the biblical books we now know as 1–2 Samuel and 1–2 Kings. Moreover, through comparison with Samuel–Kings we can clearly see certain additions made by the Chronicler to those materials, such as in the extensive lists of temple officials said to be appointed by David before turning over the kingdom to his son, Solomon (1 Chr. 23–27).

With Chronicles one can rely somewhat on comparison with Samuel–Kings, but with most other biblical books we are dependent on data within the text, much as was the case for the prehistory of the Pentateuch. For example, scholars long have supposed that the books of Deuteronomy, Joshua, Judges, 1–2 Samuel and 1–2 Kings once were part of an originally separate "Deuteronomistic History." Some have gone on to argue that this history was composed in at least two main stages: (1) an initial stage that started with some form of Deuteronomy and culminated in the rediscovery of that lawbook and Josiah's reform based on it (2 Kings 22:1–23:25); and then (2) an exilic redaction (or redactions) of that Josianic history that extended it to the exile (2 Kings 23:26–25:30) and added some exilic elements to previous books as well (e.g., Deut. 30:1–14). In addition, some have made compelling arguments that parts of these historical books go back to earlier sources, such as a set of conquest narratives associated with the central hill country embedded in Joshua 2–9, a "book of deliverers" found in parts of Judges 3:12–9:55, a narrative about the ark of the covenant seen in 1 Samuel 4:1–7:1 and 2 Samuel 6:2–23 or a narrative about the succession to King David in 2 Samuel 9–20; 1 Kings 1–2 (the "Succession Narrative"). As in the case of the documentary hypothesis, some of these older theories now are subject to intense debate, and some scholars would even question the extent to which Deuteronomy through 2 Kings once formed a coherent, originally separate Deuteronomistic History.

Scholars also have explored the formation of poetic books, such as psalms and prophets. For example, attentive readers as early as Martin Luther and the great Jewish commentator Rashi long ago noticed an important shift occurring at chapter 40 of the Book of Isaiah. By 1775 the German scholar Johann Christoph Döderlein proposed that Isaiah 40–66 does not originate from the eighth-century prophet Isaiah. Instead, he and others attributed this material to a sixth-century "Second Isaiah" (often known in Latin as Deutero-Isaiah), and this position has persuaded most scholars, mainly because chapters 40–55 presuppose a time after the fall of Jerusalem and refer to the rise of Cyrus, a sixth-century Persian king, as having occurred already (Isa. 44:28; 45:1). Subsequent scholarship has identified a potential "Isaiah memoir" standing behind chapters 6–8 of Isaiah, another collection of early Isaiah material behind Isaiah 28–32, and various layers of late fifth-century or later redactions of Isaiah, especially in Isaiah 56–66. Some also would see an early collection of Jeremiah sayings behind Jeremiah 1–25, but it is increasingly unclear how well one can distinguish distinct early collections of Jeremiah material from multiple layers of redaction.

Nevertheless, in some cases, scholars now can base their arguments about the growth of biblical books in part on actual manuscript evidence. Already above I mentioned some evidence in Jeremiah manuscripts that might help scholars identify the very latest layers of redaction of the Book of Jeremiah, in this case layers of scribal redaction that produced the standard Masoretic edition of Jeremiah that is translated in most Bibles. Another possible example comes from the books of Ezra-Nehemiah. Just 30 years after Astruc proposed his theory of interwoven sources for the Book of Genesis, Johann David Michaelis argued in 1783 that the books of Ezra and Nehemiah were composed out of two main sources: a memoir of Nehemiah found primarily in Nehemiah 1:1–7:4 and parts of Nehemiah (12–)13 and a history of rebuilding found in the Book of Ezra and concluding with Ezra's elevation of the Torah in Nehemiah 8. In this case he could support this argument by the fact that the early Jewish historian Josephus seems to know both of these sources in separate forms (Josephus, *Antiquities*, 11:159–83), and we actually have a Greek translation of the rebuilding-Ezra history in the Septuagint known as 1 Esdras. To be sure, some scholars would interpret this data in other ways. Nevertheless, this may be an instance where one can build a case for biblical sources based both on data internal to the biblical text and on external sources and references (Böhler).

Conclusion

The main point of this article is that the Hebrew Bible is a much more complex text than many initially suppose. We do not know exactly how it was formed over time, and specific theories about this or that source or redaction often are disputed. Nevertheless, some theories have proven more durable than others (e.g., the distinction of P and non-P), and the broader discussion has established beyond a doubt *that* the Bible underwent significant changes over time. Much of the Bible's prehistory, of course, is rooted in the rich and broad set of oral traditions on which it is based. It was, after all, written within the context of a culture primarily oriented toward orality. Moreover, even once written down, such writing was used to support an ongoing process of memorization and performance that meant it remained open to change in complex and often untraceable ways (see Susan Niditch's essay in this volume). Indeed, the Bible's oral-written fluidity may be one reason scholars have had trouble reaching assured results about some aspects of its prehistory.

Even if we do not know precisely how or when every biblical text developed, knowledge of this broader process can improve one's reading of the Bible in at least two ways. First, we can feel less compelled to harmonize each part of the Bible with each other part, trying to make the Bible sound as if it represents just one voice or perspective. Rather, the starting point needs to be that the Bible is multivoiced. Read within its ancient context, this is not a criticism, but a reflection of the text's importance. Second, the more we are sensitized to different voices in the text, such as the P creation text (Gen. 1:1–2:3) versus the J creation text (Gen. 2:4–3:24), the more we can read such biblical texts (e.g., Genesis 1–3) like duets or choral compositions rather than as solo works plagued with contradictions. In place of vain attempts at harmonization, we can explore how these different sources now work together as part of the Bible's complex, multivoiced whole. The multivoiced character of the Bible, in other words, ceases being a threat to the Bible's inspiration and becomes an interpretive opportunity.

Bibliography

Bailey, Lloyd R. *The Pentateuch*. Nashville: Abingdon, 1981. The first chapter of this book (pp. 13–59) provides a good introduction to problems surrounding Mosaic authorship, source-critical criteria, and two models for the formation of the Pentateuch.

Böhler, Dieter. "On the relationship between textual and literary criticism: The two recensions of the book of Ezra: Ezra-Neh (MT) and 1 Esdras (LXX)." In A. Schenker (ed.), *The Earliest Text of the Hebrew Bible* (pp. 35–50). Atlanta: Society of Biblical Literature, 2003. A succinct survey of a longer German-language work analyzing the relation of 1 Esdras to Ezra-Nehemiah.

Campbell, Anthony F. and Mark A. O'Brien. *Sources of the Pentateuch: Texts, Introductions, Annotations*. Minneapolis: Fortress, 2003. A helpful presentation of the documentary hypothesis.

Carr, David. *Reading the Fractures of Genesis: Historical and Literary Approaches*. Louisville, KY: Westminster, 1996. A study of the formation of Genesis including an overview of the arguments advanced for different theories.

Dozeman, Thomas B. and Konrad Schmid. *Farewell to the Yahwist? The Composition of the Pentateuch in Recent European Interpretation*. Atlanta: Society of Biblical Literature, 2006. An introduction for English-language readers to recent European Pentateuchal scholarship on the origins of the non-Priestly portions of the Pentateuch.

Gertz, Jan Christian with Angelika Berlejung, Konrad Schmid, and Markus Witte. *The T&T Clark Handbook of the Old Testament: An Introduction to the Literature, Religion, and History of the Old Testament*. London: T&T Clark, 2012. German original 2010. A judicious synthesis of recent research on the Old Testament from a European perspective, including various forms of redaction and source criticism of individual books.

Habel, Norman C. *Literary Criticism of the Old Testament*. Philadelphia: Fortress, 1971. Though fairly old, this book provides a good introduction to the types of reasoning used in analysis of Genesis 1–9 and summarized more briefly in this article.

Schmid, Konrad. *The Old Testament: A Literary History*, trans. L. Maloney. Minneapolis: Fortress, 2012. A synthesis of European scholarship on the formation of the Hebrew Bible.

Ska, Jean-Louis. *Introduction to Reading the Pentateuch*, trans. P. Dominique. Winona Lake, IN: Eisenbrauns, 2006 (Italian original 1998). An introduction both to the modes of reasoning of source critics and some recent developments in Pentateuchal source criticism.

Smith, Mark S. *The Priestly Vision of Genesis 1*. Minneapolis: Fortress, 2010. A detailed scholarly study of Genesis 1:1–2:3 and ways that it comments on the older creation story that follows.

Tigay, Jeffery (ed.). *Empirical Models for Biblical Criticism*. Philadelphia: University of Pennsylvania Press, 1985. An excellent collection of essays on documented cases of scribal revision.

CHAPTER 7

Linguistics and the Dating of Biblical Literature

Ohad Cohen

In this chapter, we will examine how linguistics is used to evaluate biblical texts from a historical perspective. There is wide scholarly consensus that the Hebrew Bible is a conglomeration of multifarious texts that were written over the course of many generations (for linguistic aspects of this, see Hornkohl). Nevertheless, the linguistic literature on Biblical Hebrew tends sometimes to refer to all parts of this canon as a single coherent linguistic unit. For this reason, one can find researchers who classify, say, prose from Genesis, juridical passages from Leviticus (both of which date to the classical era), a psalm dated to the Second Temple period, and the wisdom literature in Ecclesiastes under the same analytical framework. However, ignoring the Hebrew Bible's various strata and the different contexts in which they were created is liable to result in misguided conclusions about its language. In the pages that follow, the term classical Biblical Hebrew is interchangeable with First Temple Hebrew; and late Biblical Hebrew is synonymous with Second Temple Hebrew.

Among the perils of studying Biblical Hebrew through the prism of linguistics are several methodological obstacles that pertain to the development of the modern field of biblical research; in addition, there is the multilayered nature of the corpus. An attempt by scholars to break away from the theological premise that the disparate books of the Hebrew Bible constitute a single harmonious cultural and textual whole essentially gave rise to the modern field (see also the essay by David Carr in this volume).

Until the late nineteenth century linguists did not draw a sharp distinction between diachronic accounts – historical surveys that track the changes to a language over time – and synchronic accounts – overarching snapshots of a language at a given point in time. In the early 1800s, Gesenius (28–30) compiled an extensive list of "late" words and phrases that characterize the Second Temple period. Approximately 75 years later, Driver published the first study on the differences between classical and late Biblical Hebrew. Despite these first buds of a diachronic consciousness, nineteenth-century

The Wiley Blackwell Companion to Ancient Israel, First Edition. Edited by Susan Niditch.
© 2016 John Wiley & Sons, Ltd. Published 2016 by John Wiley & Sons, Ltd.

scholars did not fully fathom the methodological ramifications of this categorization. The primary architect and standard bearer of the synchronic/diachronic dichotomy was the linguist Ferdinand de Saussure (1857–1913). However, it would take many years for his approach to seep into the field of Biblical Hebrew research. Consequently, all the important grammar books – be they from the early or late twentieth century – are lacking in this regard (e.g., Gesenius, Kautzsch, and Cowley; Joüon; Bergsträsser; Joüon and Muraoka; Waltke and O'Connor).

The second obstacle, as above mentioned, is connected to the multitiered nature of the biblical corpus itself. Not only does the Bible comprise many works, but individual books often contain various layers of editing. Put differently, even after grappling with the corpus's gradual development, the researcher must still untangle a slew of editorial knots in specific texts. A case in point is the Book of Isaiah. The opening words of this book attribute its 66 chapters to the seer "Isaiah son of Amoz, who prophesied concerning Judah and Jerusalem in the reigns of Uzziah, Jotham, Ahaz, and Hezekiah, kings of Judah" (Isa. 1:1). Be that as it may, most scholars agree that only the first 39 chapters pertain to Isaiah son of Amoz, whereas the rest of the book describes the enterprise of a postexilic prophet (or prophets) who is usually referred to as Deutero-Isaiah (Baltzer 1–44). Therefore, upon making the transition from chapter 39 to 40, which usually appear on the same page of a Bible, the reader jumps – often unwittingly – about 200 years forward in time. This example, though, is merely the tip of the iceberg in all that concerns the Bible's editorial complexity.

The extant linguistic information in the biblical texts also presents certain difficulties. The phonetic system that is in place for the entire corpus is uniform, as most of the existing vowel points and accents are the labor of the Masoretes – Jewish scribes who were active between the sixth and ninth centuries CE. In many respects, the Masoretic diacritical marks are faithful to the ancient linguistic reality. That said, can we be sure that this tradition accurately reflects the Bible's original language and the text's evolution from the beginning of the First Temple period to the latter stages of the Second?

In all likelihood, there were numerous phonetic changes to the Bible over the ages. For instance, it is reasonable to assume that by the time of the Masoretes, there was no longer a distinction between the pharyngeal *het* (articulated from the pharynx) and the velar *het* (articulated with the back of the tongue touching or held close to the soft palate); otherwise the scribes would have diacritically marked the phonetic difference between these consonants, just as they did for the *šin* right (שׁ = sh) and *śin* left (s = שׂ). The Septuagint's second-century BCE transliterations of Hebrew names demonstrate that at one point there was indeed a distinction between these two phonemes. For example, the *het* in חנה = Avva (1 Samuel 1:2) is transliterated with the Greek letter A; and חירם = Χιραμ (2 Samuel 5:11) is spelled with the Greek χ (see Blau's seminal article).

At the outset of modern research, scholars realized that Biblical Hebrew harbors numerous signs of diachronic evolution. According to the majority of standard accounts, the linguistic Rubicon is the Babylonian exile. To wit, the major dividing line in the language's development is the transition from the First to the Second Temple period (see the essay by Charles Carter in this volume). These insights notwithstanding, the research on late Biblical Hebrew did not truly mature until the mid-1900s. During the field's nascent stages, researchers distinguished between the two eras by virtue of their linguistic instincts and, to some extent, their knowledge of the political changes that followed in the wake of the Babylonian exile. The long years of exile in an Aramaic-speaking environment and the emergence of Aramaic as the administrative tongue of the Persian empire had a profound impact on late Biblical Hebrew. The following passage from the Book of Nehemiah attests to the external linguistic influences on this language:

Example 1

גַּם בַּיָּמִים הָהֵם רָאִיתִי אֶת הַיְּהוּדִים הֹשִׁיבוּ נָשִׁים אַשְׁדֳּדִיּוֹת עַמֳּנִיּוֹת מוֹאֲבִיּוֹת: וּבְנֵיהֶם חֲצִי מְדַבֵּר אַשְׁדּוֹדִית וְאֵינָם מַכִּירִים לְדַבֵּר יְהוּדִית וְכִלְשׁוֹן עַם וָעָם

Also at that time, I saw that Jews had married Ashdodite, Ammonite, and Moabite women; a good number of their children spoke the language of Ashdod and the language of those various peoples, and did not know how to speak Judean. (Neh. 13:23–24, New Jewish Publication Society (NJPS))

While scholars are hard-pressed to pin down the nature of "the language of Ashdod," it is evident that the linguistic milieu during the return to Zion differed from that of the classical era.

The first monograph that was fully dedicated to the linguistic characterization of Biblical Hebrew's two strands was Kropat's early twentieth-century book on the syntax of Chronicles. However, nearly five decades would pass before another linguist took the baton. This interregnum perhaps stems from the discovery of Ugaritic in the 1920s, which diverted scholarly attention to archaic Hebrew and its resemblance to the new-found language. What is more, the research on Second Temple Hebrew was hobbled by a shortage of adequate methodological tools for distinguishing between the two epochs. Be that as it may, the startling discovery of the Dead Sea Scrolls in the late 1940s triggered a major about-face. As soon as the parchments from Qumran were unveiled, it was obvious to biblical scholars that a rare opportunity had fallen into their lap to acquaint themselves with Second Temple Hebrew from a firsthand source.

In 1959, Kutscher published *The Language and Linguistic Background of the Isaiah Scroll*. Within this framework, he articulated two principles that would have a marked impact on research into late Biblical Hebrew. Linguistically speaking, Kutscher demonstrated that the corresponding Masorah precedes the scrolls, even though the latter were written nearly one thousand years before the earliest Masoretic manuscripts of the Hebrew Bible. Secondly, he outlined the methodological criteria for determining the linguistic properties of the late biblical texts. The establishment of these guidelines indeed constituted a turning point in the research. Another watershed mark was Bendavid's *Biblical Hebrew and Mishnaic Hebrew*. In this two-volume work, the author explored a wide range of linguistic phenomena that set Biblical Hebrew apart from the language of the Sages. Shortly after, Hurvitz published *The Transition Period in Biblical Hebrew* (1972). Following in Kutscher's footsteps, he improved the methods for establishing linguistic antecedence and subsequence in the Bible. These pioneering works launched a bevy of articles on the lexicon and syntax of late Biblical Hebrew and the Dead Sea Scrolls.

In the pages to come, we will focus on the main historical development which occurred in late Biblical Hebrew as compared to classical Biblical Hebrew. By doing so, we wish to illustrate the unique diachronic developments in the Hebrew language during each of the biblical periods. Understanding this process enhances our capacity to date the various texts of the Bible. The linguistic developments in Biblical Hebrew (BH) during the Second Temple period can be summarized into two main categories: (A) external influences and (B) internal developments. The external influences can be divided into the following three languages:

1 Persian influence   Although Persian influence upon Biblical Hebrew is limited mostly to a small number of loanwords, it plays an important role in the historical linguistic perspective. Persian loanwords abound in the incontestably late prose writings, plus occasional occurrences in Qoheleth, Canticles and Psalms (see also the essay by Tamara Cohn Eskenazi in this volume). It is important to stress that Persian words are not to be found in the Pentateuch at all! Put differently, the presence of a Persian loanword in a specific biblical text is a strong argument for its late dating.

2 Aramaic influence   Two geopolitical processes stand at the basis of Aramaic influence upon Hebrew during the Second Temple period. The first was the long years of exile in an Aramaic-speaking environment and the second was the emergence of Aramaic as the administrative tongue of the Persian empire. These two processes had a profound impact on late Biblical Hebrew. The critical point of contact between Hebrew and Aramaic is to be found after the Babylonian exile in the sixth century BCE. Hebrew texts from this period exhibit clear and diverse instances of Aramaic influence. However, not every seeming "Aramaism" in Biblical Hebrew necessarily indicates genuine Aramaic influence. Moreover, not every instance of genuine Aramaic influence is necessarily late. When dating texts based on Aramaic influence, one should determine, first, whether or not there is real Aramaic influence and, second, whether this influence is late.

Hurvitz's methodological criteria for isolating linguistic Aramaic features distinctively characteristic of late Biblical Hebrew are:

a   *Late distribution* The biblical documentation of the Aramaic component should be characteristic of distinctively late biblical texts (Esther, Daniel, Ezra and Nehemiah and the nonsynoptic parts of Chronicles).

b   *Linguistic opposition* An Aramaic element's exclusively late distribution in the Hebrew Bible is not in and of itself sufficient grounds for its classification as a linguistic feature distinctively characteristic of late Biblical Hebrew. Thus, one should demonstrate that the Aramaic component deviates from standard language usage in the earlier books of the Old Testament.

c   *Extrabiblical sources* A given late Aramaic element is considered distinctively characteristic of late Biblical Hebrew if it is also employed in late extrabiblical sources, such as the Dead Sea Scrolls, Rabbinic literature, biblical Aramaic, the book of Ben Sira, the Aramaic *Targumim*, or Second Temple period epigraphic sources.

The *accumulation* of linguistic features mentioned above is what makes a specific linguistic feature distinctively characteristic of late Biblical Hebrew.

3 Presence of Mishnaic Hebrew components   The exact relationship between Biblical Hebrew and Mishnaic Hebrew is still under debate in the scholarly research. However, it is clear that one of the differences between the First and Second Temple periods in the Bible is that the latter has a significant presence of linguistic Mishnaic Hebrew components.

With these observations in mind, we can now turn to the question of how linguistic data is employed in the service of dating biblical texts. For example, some researchers consider Psalm 144 as an amalgamation of two different songs (e.g., Hurvitz, *The Transition Period*). Verses 1–11 are a victory hymn praising the Lord for his salvation during a war against foreign enemies. Verses 12–15, on the other hand, describe the prosperity of the homeland. Putting aside these differences in the content, the question is whether the language of the song in the final four verses of Psalm 144 can teach us something about its historical background.

Example 2

אֲשֶׁר בָּנֵינוּ כִּנְטִעִים מְגֻדָּלִים בִּנְעוּרֵיהֶם, בְּנוֹתֵינוּ כְזָוִיֹּת מְחֻטָּבוֹת תַּבְנִית הֵיכָל:
מְזָוֵינוּ מְלֵאִים מְפִיקִים מִזַּן אֶל זַן, צֹאונֵנוּ מַאֲלִיפוֹת מְרֻבָּבוֹת בְּחוּצוֹתֵינוּ:

[We] whose sons are as **plants (nəṭīʿîm)** grown up in their youth;
[whose] daughters are as **corner-pillars (zāwiyyōt)** carved after the fashion of a palace;
[Whose] garners are full, affording all manner of **store (zan)**;
[whose] sheep increase by thousands and ten thousands in our fields. (Ps. 144:12–13, author's translation)

While in verses 1–11 there are no late linguistic phenomena, in verses 12–15 we can find all the three described components, namely Aramaic influence, Persian influence and Mishnaic Hebrew influence:

זָוִיֹּת **(zāwiyyōt) (verse 12)**   The word זוית (zwyt) (corner) is an Aramaic word. It appears many times in the Aramaic translations of the Bible. Furthermore, the biblical books from the First Temple period use other words such as פנה, מקצוע, צלע, קצה in related Hebrew contexts:

Example 3

וְעָשִׂיתָ קַרְנֹתָיו עַל אַרְבַּע **פִּנֹּתָיו**
וְתַעֲבֵיד קַרְנוֹהִי עַל אַרְבַּע **זָוְיָתֵיהּ**

(Onkelos, an Aramaic biblical translation ("Targum"))

And you shall make the horns of it upon the four **corners** (Exod. 27:2)
(pinnōtāw, Hebrew; zāwəyātēh[h], Aramaic)

Outside the book of Psalms זוית (*zwyt*) appears in the Bible only once in the book of Zechariah (9:15), and it is common in Mishnaic Hebrew. In order to define a late Aramaic influence on Biblical Hebrew, three components should be identified: late distribution, linguistic opposition, and extrabiblical sources. As we can see, in the above example, these three components exist and therefore זוית (*zwyt*) should be considered a late Aramaic influence.

זַן (zan) (verse 13)   The word זן (*zn*) (species) is a Persian word that entered Hebrew probably through Aramaic. As explained before, the presence of a Persian word in a biblical text is a very strong argument for its late dating. Moreover, if we check the distribution of this word in the Bible we will see that outside Psalms, it appears only in Second Temple period texts (Chronicles). In the First Temple period texts, we can find the word מין (*myn*) in the same meaning:

Example 4

עֹשֶׂה פְּרִי לְמִינוֹ

עָבֵיד פֵּירִין לִזְנֵיהּ

(Onkelos)

[B]earing fruit after **its kind** (*mînô*, Hebrew; *zənēhʰ*, Aramaic) (Gen. 1:11)

נְטָעִים (naṭî'îm) (verse 12)   The word נטעים (*nṭ'ym*) is a plural form for the biblical word נטע (*nṭ'*). This word belongs to the common word pattern called segolates. The regular plural of this word pattern in Biblical Hebrew is נְטָעִים (*naṭā'îm*) (קְטָלִים/*qəṭālîm* pattern). The pattern נְטָעִים (*naṭî'îm*) (קְטִלִים/*qəṭîlîm* pattern) is the regular plural pattern of this group in Rabbinical Hebrew. The word נְטָעִים (*naṭî'îm*) in this passage is the only occurrence in the Bible of this word that uses this pattern. As aforementioned, the presence of Mishnaic components in Biblical Hebrew is another sign of late language.

Internal Developments

The diachronic standpoint is based on the assumption that the use of any linguistic marker is likely to erode over time. In this part, we will endeavor to delineate one of the changes, namely the use of the infinitive construct *liqtol*, which marked the transition from the classical era to the Second Temple period.[1]

In Biblical Hebrew there are two infinitive forms that are distinguished from each other both from a morphological perspective and by their grammatical role. In First Temple Biblical Hebrew the infinitive construct is a nominal verb form (a verb form that can function like a noun), and is frequently used as an adverb. In different contexts it may be translated in many different ways: for example, the infinitive לִכְתֹּב (*liktōb*) may be translated "to write," "in order to write," "in writing," or "by writing," depending on the context. In the following example the infinitive לִסְפֹּר (*lispōr*) is used as an adverb, translated "to count." Note that here the main verb תּוּכַל (*tûkal*) comes first and is then continued by the infinitive.

Example 5

וַיּוֹצֵא אֹתוֹ הַחוּצָה וַיֹּאמֶר הַבֶּט נָא הַשָּׁמַיְמָה וּסְפֹר הַכּוֹכָבִים אִם תּוּכַל **לִסְפֹּר** אֹתָם

And He brought him outside, and said: "Look now toward heaven, and count the stars, if you be able **to count (infinitive/adverb)** them." (Gen. 15:5, author's translation)

The use of the Hebrew infinitive construct as an independent verbal form (i.e., the equivalent of a regular verb) constitutes one of the most significant diachronic events of the Second Temple period. That said, the infinitive's role as a substitute for verbs prompted a major shift away from its classical roles. Out of the infinitive construct's 486 occurrences in the Second Temple prose, 104 (21.39 percent) fill various predicative roles of this sort (Cohen 211–36).

One of the infinitive construct's uses is the signification of commandments and the language of the law. However, the fact that the Second Temple texts largely comprise narrative material, rather than juridical contexts, hinders comparisons to early Biblical Hebrew in all that concerns this usage. Owing primarily to its abundance of legal compendiums, the Dead Sea Scrolls have contributed immensely to the research of late Biblical Hebrew. For instance, the texts from Qumran shed light on the infinitive forms in Esther 8:10–13:

Example 6

וַיִּכְתֹּב בְּשֵׁם הַמֶּלֶךְ אֲחַשְׁוֵרֹשׁ וַיַּחְתֹּם בְּטַבַּעַת הַמֶּלֶךְ וַיִּשְׁלַח סְפָרִים בְּיַד הָרָצִים בַּסּוּסִים רֹכְבֵי הָרֶכֶשׁ הָאֲחַשְׁתְּרָנִים בְּנֵי הָרַמָּכִים: אֲשֶׁר נָתַן הַמֶּלֶךְ לַיְּהוּדִים אֲשֶׁר בְּכָל עִיר וָעִיר **לְהִקָּהֵל וְלַעֲמֹד** עַל נַפְשָׁם **לְהַשְׁמִיד וְלַהֲרֹג וּלְאַבֵּד** אֶת כָּל חֵיל עַם וּמְדִינָה הַצָּרִים אֹתָם טַף וְנָשִׁים וּשְׁלָלָם **לָבוֹז**:

He had them written in the name of King Ahasuerus and sealed with the king's signet. Letters were dispatched by mounted couriers, riding steeds used in the king's service, bred of the royal stud, [letters] that the king has given to the Jews of every city [saying:] "**[They] shall assemble (infinitive/command?)** and **fight (infinitive/ command?)** for their lives; if any people or province attacks them, **[they] shall destroy, massacre**, and **exterminate (infinitive/command?)** its armed force together with women and children, and **plunder (infinitive/command?)** their possessions. (Esth. 8:10–11, NJPS (modified))

There are serious question marks concerning the function of the infinitive forms in this passage. Do they serve as complements of the infinitive verb נָתַן ("permitted to"), or are they independent verbal forms? A comparison with the language of the law in the Dead Sea Scrolls suggests that they are independent modal forms. Here is an example from The Community Rule (1QS) from the Dead Sea Scrolls:

Example 7

אלה החוקים למשכיל **להתהלך** בם עם כול חי לתכון עת ועת ולמשקל איש ואיש **לעשות** את
רצון אל ככול הנגלה לעת בעת...

These are the statutes for the Instructor. **[He] shall conduct (infinitive/command)** himself by them with every living person, guided by the precepts appropriate to each era and the value of each person: **[He] shall carry out (infinitive/command)** the will of God according to what has been revealed for each period of history… (1QS 9:12–13)

This string of commandments does not open with a main verb. Instead, it begins by informing the reader of a list of laws for the "Instructor." That the infinitives in the passage from Esther are independent modal forms is bolstered by the fact that the Bible's template for promulgating laws is echoed in several verses of The Community Rule (whose readership was certainly familiar with the Hebrew Scriptures). In some contexts where classical biblical texts of this sort employ *yiqtol* (this form is sometimes called "imperfect" or "future"[2]), the authors of the Rule availed themselves of infinitive forms. For instance:

Example 8

לֹא **תָסוּר** מִן הַדָּבָר אֲשֶׁר יַגִּידוּ לְךָ יָמִין וּשְׂמֹאל (דברים י"ז 11)

You must not deviate (*yiqtol*/law) from the verdict that they announce to you neither to the right nor to the left. (Deut. 17:11, NJPS (modified))

Example 9

ולא **לסור** מחוקי אמתו ללכת ימין ושמאול

[They] must not deviate (infinitive/law) from His unerring laws neither to the right nor the left. (1QS 1:15)

Against this backdrop, the infinitives in Esther 8 should be interpreted as independent modal forms that expand upon the king's edict. Determining whether these infinitives are independent predicates or adverbial forms is far from simple. Nevertheless, given the prevalence of this usage throughout the Second Temple period, they appear to be independent verbal forms that denote a general instruction, rather than adverbial complements. The similarities between the above-noted passages in The Community Rule and the Book of Esther should come as no surprise, for they all contain a set of instructions. Just as the infinitive forms signify the juridical content of the Rule, the succession in Esther should be viewed as the content of Ahasuerus' directive.

Another set of instructions in the Rule opens with the words "וזה **הסרך** לאנשי היחד", "and this is the Rule" (1QS 5:1ff.). This sort of introductory phrase is already familiar to us from early biblical chains of laws that begin with "וזאת התורה", "and this is the Instruction" (Deut. 4:44) and whose subsequent directives are conveyed via *yiqtol* and *wəqātal* (the converted perfect). For example:

Example 10

וַיְדַבֵּר יְהוָה אֶל מֹשֶׁה לֵּאמֹר: צַו אֶת אַהֲרֹן וְאֶת בָּנָיו לֵאמֹר **זֹאת תּוֹרַת הָעֹלָה** הִוא הָעֹלָה עַל מוֹקְדָה עַל הַמִּזְבֵּחַ כָּל הַלַּיְלָה עַד הַבֹּקֶר וְאֵשׁ הַמִּזְבֵּחַ **תּוּקַד** בּוֹ: **וְלָבַשׁ** הַכֹּהֵן מִדּוֹ בַד…

The LORD spoke to Moses, saying: Command Aaron and his sons thus: **This is the ritual of the burnt offering**: The burnt offering itself **shall remain (yiqtol/law)** where it is burned upon the altar all night until morning, while the fire on the altar is kept going on it. The priest **shall dress (wəqātal/law)** in linen raiment … (Lev. 6:1–3, NJPS)

Yet another function of the infinitive is the marking of iterative actions in the past – a role that was also filled by *yiqtol* and *wəqātal* during the First Temple period. In the passages below, *wayyiqtol* (also known as the "converted imperfect") and *qātal* (also known as the "past" or "perfect") forms set the temporal framework by expressing iterative actions in the past:

Example 11

וַיָּבִיאוּ אֶת אֲרוֹן הָאֱלֹהִים וַיַּצִּיגוּ אֹתוֹ בְּתוֹךְ הָאֹהֶל אֲשֶׁר נָטָה לוֹ דָּוִיד... וַיִּתֵּן לִפְנֵי אֲרוֹן יְהוָה מִן הַלְוִיִּם
מְשָׁרְתִים וּלְהַזְכִּיר וּלְהוֹדוֹת וּלְהַלֵּל לַיהוָה אֱלֹהֵי יִשְׂרָאֵל:

They brought (wayyiqtol/narrative past) in the Ark of God and **set (wayyiqtol/narrative past)** it up inside the tent that David had pitched for it … And **He appointed Levites (wayyiqtol/narrative past)** to minister before the Ark of the LORD, **and [they] used to invoke (infinitive/iterative past) [the name of], praise (infinitive/iterative past), and extol (infinitive/iterative past)** the LORD God of Israel. (1 Chr. 16:1–4, NJPS (modified))

This passage exemplifies the late biblical era's transition from narrative successions that were denoted by *wayyiqtol* to habitual actions signified by infinitive forms. In classical Hebrew, such chains are marked by substituting *wayyiqtol* for *yiqtol* and *wəqātal* forms:

Example 12

וַיִּתְנַצְּלוּ בְנֵי יִשְׂרָאֵל אֶת עֶדְיָם מֵהַר חוֹרֵב: וּמֹשֶׁה יִקַּח אֶת הָאֹהֶל וְנָטָה לוֹ מִחוּץ לַמַּחֲנֶה הַרְחֵק מִן הַמַּחֲנֶה
וְקָרָא לוֹ אֹהֶל מוֹעֵד...

So the Israelites **remained (wayyiqtol/narrative past)** stripped of the finery from Mount Horeb on. Now Moses **would take (yiqtol/iterative past)** the Tent **and pitch (wəqātal/iterative past)** it outside the camp, at some distance from the camp. And he **called (wəqātal/iterative past)** it the Tent of Meeting …(Exod. 33:6–7, NJPS (modified))

Like classical *yiqtol* and *wəqātal* forms, the infinitives in the Second Temple period Hebrew also express the habitual present:

Example 13

וְהֵם וּבְנֵיהֶם עַל הַשְּׁעָרִים לְבֵית יְהוָה לְבֵית הָאֹהֶל לְמִשְׁמָרוֹת: לְאַרְבַּע רוּחוֹת יִהְיוּ הַשֹּׁעֲרִים מִזְרָח יָמָּה
צָפוֹנָה וָנֶגְבָּה: וַאֲחֵיהֶם בְּחַצְרֵיהֶם לָבוֹא לְשִׁבְעַת הַיָּמִים מֵעֵת אֶל עֵת עִם אֵלֶּה:

They and their descendants were in charge of the gates of the House of the LORD, that is, the House of the Tent, as guards. The gatekeepers were on the four sides, east, west, north, and south; and their kinsmen in their villages **join (infinitive/habitual present)** them every seven days, according to a fixed schedule. (1 Chr. 9:23–25, NJPS (modified))

The adverbial phrase מֵעֵת אֶל עֵת underscores the point that "their kinsmen" arrive on a regular (habitual) basis. The following verses enable us to compare the ways in which the habitual present was expressed in negative sentences in each of the two periods under review:

Example 14

וַיֹּאמֶר לָבָן **לֹא יֵעָשֶׂה** כֵן בִּמְקוֹמֵנוּ לָתֵת הַצְּעִירָה לִפְנֵי הַבְּכִירָה:

Laban said, "**It is not (yiqtol/habitual present)** the practice in our place to marry off the younger before the older." (Gen. 29:26, NJPS)

Example 15

וּבְנֵי רְאוּבֵן בְּכוֹר יִשְׂרָאֵל כִּי הוּא הַבְּכוֹר וּבְחַלְּלוֹ יְצוּעֵי אָבִיו נִתְּנָה בְּכֹרָתוֹ לִבְנֵי יוֹסֵף בֶּן יִשְׂרָאֵל **וְלֹא לְהִתְיַחֵשׂ** לַבְּכֹרָה:

The sons of Reuben the first-born of Israel. (He was the first-born; but when he defiled his father's bed, his birthright was given to the sons of Joseph son of Israel, so **he is not reckoned (infinitive/habitual present)** as first-born in the genealogy.) (1 Chr. 5:1, NJPS)

Example 14 represents the standard pattern of early Biblical Hebrew in which the habitual present (custom) is denoted by *yiqtol*. The structure of the verse from 1 Chronicles is a revised version of the classical pattern, as *yiqtol* has been supplanted by an infinitive. In the Second Temple period, the infinitive also delineated a space's geographical boundaries within the framework of the habitual present/general truth:

Example 16

וַיִּתְפַּלֵּל אֵלָיו וַיֵּעָתֶר לוֹ וַיִּשְׁמַע תְּחִנָּתוֹ וַיְשִׁיבֵהוּ יְרוּשָׁלַ͏ִם לְמַלְכוּתוֹ וַיֵּדַע מְנַשֶּׁה כִּי יְהוָה הוּא הָאֱלֹהִים: וְאַחֲרֵי כֵן בָּנָה חוֹמָה חִיצוֹנָה לְעִיר דָּוִיד מַעְרָבָה לְגִיחוֹן בַּנַּחַל **וְלָבוֹא** בְשַׁעַר הַדָּגִים **וְסָבַב** לָעֹפֶל וַיַּגְבִּיהֶהָ מְאֹד וַיָּשֶׂם שָׂרֵי חַיִל בְּכָל הֶעָרִים הַבְּצֻרוֹת בִּיהוּדָה:

He prayed to Him, and He granted his prayer, heard his plea, and returned him to Jerusalem to his kingdom. Then Manasseh knew that the LORD alone was God. Afterward he built the outer wall of the City of David west of Gihon in the wadi and **[it] touches (infinitive/general truth)** the Fish Gate, and **it encircles (wəqātal/general truth)** the Ophel; he raised it very high. He also placed army officers in all the fortified towns of Judah. (2 Chr. 33:13–14, NJPS (modified))

This usage is also familiar to us from classical Hebrew, where *yiqtol* and *wəqātal* assume this role:

Example 17

וַיֵּצֵא הַגּוֹרָל לִבְנֵי יוֹסֵף מִיַּרְדֵּן יְרִיחוֹ לְמֵי יְרִיחוֹ מִזְרָחָה הַמִּדְבָּר עֹלֶה מִירִיחוֹ בָּהָר בֵּית אֵל: **וְיָצָא** מִבֵּית אֵל לוּזָה **וְעָבַר** אֶל גְּבוּל הָאַרְכִּי עֲטָרוֹת: **וְיָרַד** יָמָּה אֶל גְּבוּל הַיַּפְלֵטִי...

The portion that fell by lot to the Josephites ran from the Jordan at Jericho – from the waters of Jericho east of the wilderness. From Jericho it ascended through the hill country to Bethel. From Bethel **it ran (*wəqātal*/general truth)** to Luz **and passed (*wəqātal*/general truth)** on to the territory of the Archites at Ataroth, **descended (*wəqātal*/general truth)** westward to the territory of the Japhletites... (Josh. 16:1–3, NJPS (modified))

Just as the shift in Joshua from the narrative to the description of the border is marked by the transition from *wayyiqtol* (i.e., וַיֵּצֵא) to *wəqātal*, the shift in 2 Chronicles (Example 16) from Manasseh's concrete actions to the description of the wall is marked by a transition from *wayyiqtol* to infinitive and *wəqātal* forms.

We can now return to the question of how linguistic data is employed in the service of dating biblical texts. Yet another classical usage of *yiqtol* and *wəqātal* is the signification of future tense. In the ensuing passage from 2 Chronicles, a late biblical work, this function is carried out by an infinitive.

Example 18

עַתָּה אַל תַּקְשׁוּ עָרְפְּכֶם כַּאֲבוֹתֵיכֶם תְּנוּ יָד לַיהוָה וּבֹאוּ לְמִקְדָּשׁוֹ אֲשֶׁר הִקְדִּישׁ לְעוֹלָם וְעִבְדוּ אֶת יְהוָה אֱלֹהֵיכֶם וְיָשֹׁב מִכֶּם חֲרוֹן אַפּוֹ: כִּי בְשׁוּבְכֶם עַל יְהוָה אֲחֵיכֶם וּבְנֵיכֶם לְרַחֲמִים לִפְנֵי שׁוֹבֵיהֶם **וְלָשׁוּב** לָאָרֶץ הַזֹּאת כִּי חַנּוּן וְרַחוּם יְהוָה אֱלֹהֵיכֶם וְלֹא יָסִיר פָּנִים מִכֶּם אִם תָּשׁוּבוּ אֵלָיו:

Now do not be stiff-necked like your fathers; submit yourselves to the LORD and come to His sanctuary, which He consecrated forever, and serve the LORD your God so that His anger may turn back from you. If you return to the LORD, your brothers and children will be regarded with compassion by their captors, **and will return (infinitive/future)** to this land; for the LORD your God is gracious and merciful; He will not turn His face from you if you return to Him. (2 Chr. 30:8–9, NJPS)

The next verse is taken from the Book of Ruth, the dating of which is the subject of debate. Perhaps the text's language gives hints as to which of the biblical eras it belongs?

Example 19

וְהָיָה לָךְ לְמֵשִׁיב נֶפֶשׁ **וּלְכַלְכֵּל** אֶת שֵׂיבָתֵךְ כִּי כַלָּתֵךְ אֲשֶׁר אֲהֵבַתֶךְ יְלָדַתּוּ, אֲשֶׁר הִיא טוֹבָה לָךְ מִשִּׁבְעָה בָּנִים

And he will renew your life and (**he) will sustain (infinitive/future)** your old age; for he is born of your daughter-in-law, who loves you, and is better to you than your seven sons. (Ruth 4:15, NJPS (modified))

In the late biblical passage from 2 Chronicles (Example 18), Hezekiah's missive opens with several orders to the Kingdom of Israel's subjects. Its second verse enumerates the rewards that await them should they heed the king's words and "return to the LORD." In consequence, "ולשוב" should be interpreted as denoting the future. The same can be said for the use of the infinitive form in Ruth. Our knowledge, then, that infinitive constructs are a Second Temple period usage is clearly pertinent to any chronological analysis of this book.

Our comparison between the First and Second Temple periods demonstrates that Biblical Hebrew was in constant flux. From a diachronic standpoint, the transition between these two corpora attests to myriad dynamic changes. The prominent trends that drew our attention to the corpus's linguistic flexibility were both external influences (Persian, Aramaic and Mishnaic Hebrew) and internal developments (the use of the infinitive construct). As we have seen, these sorts of linguistic observations can help scholars date chronologically ambiguous parts of the Bible.

Notes

1 This part is predicated on my book *The Verbal Tense System in Late Biblical Hebrew Prose* (Harvard Semitic Studies 63), esp. chapter 8. I would like to thank Avi Aronsky for his fine editing of this part.
2 The linguistic terminology in the field of the verbal forms is weighed down by a surfeit of terms that are ascribed to each and every form. We have chosen a classification method that refers exclusively to structure, rather than meaning, in which the names are primarily based on elementary inflected forms from the *qtl* root. Every term is essentially an abridgement of all the persons and verbal stems that are likely to appear in that same pattern. For example, the *yiqtol* form (third person singular) is used to denote all the persons: אקטל ,תקטל ,יקטל ,נקטל, יקטלו etc.

Bibliography

Baltzer, Klaus. *Deutero-Isaiah*. Minneapolis: Fortress, 1999. Commentary on the text of Isaiah 40–66.

Bauer, Hans and Pontus Leander. *Historische Grammatik der hebräischen Sprache des Alten Testaments*. Tübingen: Halle, 1922. Classic reference grammar.

Bendavid, Abba. *Biblical Hebrew and Mishnaic Hebrew*. 2 vols. Tel Aviv: Dvir, 1967–71 [Hebrew]. A historical survey of the Hebrew language.

Bergsträsser, Gotthelf. *Hebräische Grammatik*. 2 vols. Leipzig: Vogel, 1918–29. Repr. in 1 vol., Hildesheim: Olms, 1962. Classic reference grammar.

Blau, Joshua. "On polyphony in Biblical Hebrew." *Proceedings of the Israel Academy of Sciences and Humanities* 6 (1983): 105–83. An article on the history of Hebrew phonology.

Cohen, Ohad. *The Verbal Tense System in Late Biblical Hebrew Prose*. Harvard Semitic Studies 63. Winona Lake, IN: Eisenbrauns, 2013. A full description of the usages of verbs in late Biblical Hebrew prose.

Driver, S. R. *An Introduction to the Literature of the Old Testament*. 9th edn. Edinburgh, 1913.

Durham, John I. *Exodus*. Word Biblical Commentary Series. Waco, TX: Word Books, 1987. A commentary with bibliographic references for each literary unit.

Gesenius, W., E. Kautzsch and A. E. Cowley. *Gesenius' Hebrew Grammar*. Oxford: Clarendon, 1910. Classic reference grammar.

Hornkohl, Aaron. "Biblical: Periodization." In G. Khan et al. (eds), *The Encyclopedia of Hebrew Language and Linguistics*, vol. 1 (pp. 315–25). Leiden: Brill, 2013. An encyclopedia entry, and a good summary of the question of biblical periodization.

Hurvitz, Avi. *The Transition Period in Biblical Hebrew: A Study of Post-exilic Hebrew and Its Implications for the Dating of Psalms*. Jerusalem: Mossad Harav Kook and Bialik Institute, 1972 [Hebrew]. Hurvitz's first monograph concerning late Biblical Hebrew.

Hurvitz, Avi. "Hebrew and Aramaic in the biblical period: The problem of 'Aramaisms' in linguistic research on the Hebrew Bible." In I. Young (ed.), *Biblical Hebrew: Studies in Typology and Chronology* (pp. 24–37). London: T&T Clark, 2003. An article concerning the question of Aramaic influence in the Bible.

Joüon, Paul. *Grammaire de l'hebreu biblique*. Rome: Pontifical Biblical Institute, 1923. The French original version of the Joüon-Muraoka grammar below.

Joüon, Paul and Takamitsu Muraoka. *A Grammar of Biblical Hebrew*. Rome: Pontifical Biblical Institute Press, 2006. The most up-to-date reference grammar of Biblical Hebrew.

Kropat, Arno. *Die Syntax des Autors der Chronik*. Giessen: Töpelmann, 1909. The first monograph on late Biblical Hebrew.

Kutscher, Edward Yechezkel. *The Language and Linguistic Background of the Isaiah Scroll (1QIsᵃ)*. Jerusalem: Magnes Press, 1959 [Hebrew]. English trans., Leiden: Brill, 1974. On the dialect of the Dead Sea Scrolls.

Saussure, Ferdinand de. *Cours de linguistique générale*, ed. T. D. Mauro. Paris: Payot, 1972. Introduction to general linguistics.

Waltke, Bruce K. and Michael P. O'Connor. *An Introduction to Biblical Hebrew Syntax*. Winona Lake, IN: Eisenbrauns, 1990. A reference grammar, and a very good introduction to Hebrew syntax.

CHAPTER 8

Epigraphy
Writing Culture in the Iron Age Levant

Christopher A. Rollston

Laying the Groundwork

Writing began around 3200 BCE in the great power centers of the ancient Near East, Mesopotamia and Egypt, and so is not only a very important technology, but also a very old technology (Kramer; Michalowski; Huehnergard and Woods; Loprieno). Broadly speaking, there are two major subdivisions of ancient writing systems: non-alphabetic writing systems and alphabetic writing systems. The writing systems used in Mesopotamia and Egypt were nonalphabetic. Around 1800 BCE, alphabetic writing began, probably invented by Semites in Egypt who were familiar with the Egyptian writing system. The writing systems used to write Phoenician, Hebrew, Aramaic, Greek and Latin were alphabetic writing systems. Writing systems can be succinctly described as a graphic means of attempting to record language (i.e., speech).

An alphabet can be defined as a writing system in which one grapheme (letter) is used to represent one phoneme (the smallest meaningful unit of sound). Some alphabetic writing systems in antiquity exclusively represented consonantal morphemes (e.g., Early Alphabetic, Phoenician, and, for the most part, Ugaritic), but other alphabetic writing systems have letters to represent vowels as well as consonants (e.g., Greek, Latin). Some alphabetic writing systems were primarily consonantal, but did attempt to represent some vowels by using consonantal letters to signify certain long vowels (e.g., Old Hebrew, Old Aramaic, Moabite, Ammonite).

Thus, within Old Hebrew (an alphabetic writing system), the letter *bet* represents the phoneme /b/, the letter *zayin* represents the phoneme /z/ and the letter *yod* represents the phoneme /y/. Within alphabetic writing systems, the number of letters is rather small, normally in the range of 20 to 40 letters. Thus, the Old Hebrew alphabet has 22 letters, the Classical Greek alphabet has 24, and the Classical Armenian alphabet has 36 (and later, 38).

The Wiley Blackwell Companion to Ancient Israel, First Edition. Edited by Susan Niditch.
© 2016 John Wiley & Sons, Ltd. Published 2016 by John Wiley & Sons, Ltd.

Sometimes there is a very close correspondence in an alphabetic writing system between a phoneme and the letter used to represent that phoneme. Languages such as this, for example modern German, are referred to as having a "shallow orthography." An old adage for German is that if you can pronounce a word correctly in German, you can also spell it correctly. This is because there is such a close correspondence between the phonemes in German and the letters used to represent those phonemes. Languages in which there is often not such a close correspondence between the letters used to represent the phonemes and the phonemes themselves are said to have a "deep orthography," for example, modern French and English. It should be remembered that the term "orthography" is a technical term to refer to spelling conventions in a writing system (Rollston, "Scribal education," 48–9).

In the nonalphabetic systems of writing used in ancient Mesopotamia (for the Sumerian and Akkadian languages) and in ancient Egypt, the signs used to write these languages were primarily (a) logographic (with a sign capable of representing an entire word), and (b) syllabic (with a sign capable of representing a syllable). In addition, within the Mesopotamian and Egyptian writing systems, a sign could sometimes be used (before or after a word) to signify something about the nature of a word. These are called (c) determinatives. For example, within a Mesopotamian or Egyptian text with a list of gods and goddesses, the names of each of these deities is often accompanied by a determinative to indicate that the name is that of a deity.

Significantly, nonalphabetic writing systems routinely have several hundred signs (but not all will be used in any given chronological horizon or location). This is the case for Mesopotamian cuneiform and also for Egyptian hieroglyphs. For this reason, the writing systems used in Mesopotamia and Egypt were quite complicated to learn and arguably required several years of formal training. Alphabetic writing systems are easier to learn, but it should be emphasized that becoming proficient in one's first alphabetic writing system was not simple and even this arguably required a few years of training for proficiency (Rollston, "Scribal education," 48–50).

The Focus: Iron Age Inscriptions in the Levant

There is a fairly substantial, growing corpus of Iron Age inscriptions from the Levant (Naveh, *Early History*; Cross, *Leaves*). Most of these inscriptions were written in an alphabetic script and most are written in a Northwest Semitic language. Among the Northwest Semitic languages of the Iron Age are Phoenician, Old Hebrew, Old Aramaic, Moabite, Ammonite, Edomite and Philistine. Although the alphabet was invented in around 1800 BCE, the linear alphabet was not standardized during the first few centuries of its usage (contrast the alphabetic cuneiform used at Late Bronze Age Ugarit and its environs). During the first few centuries of its usage, there was dramatic variation in the stance and position of the letters of the alphabet. That is, the letters could "lean" heavily in one direction or the other, or they could even be rotated as much as 90 or 180 degrees, or more. And they could "face" in different directions as well. In addition, there was also variation in terms of the direction of writing. To be precise, during the early centuries of the linear alphabet's use, the text of an inscription could be written (and thus would have to be read) from right to left ("sinistrograde"), from left to right ("dextrograde"), boustrophedon (one line sinistrograde and the next line dextrograde, and the next line sinistrograde, etc.) or in vertical columns. Moreover, the number of consonants in this early alphabet could range up to almost as high as 30. However, by around the eleventh century BCE, the number of consonantal graphemes had been reduced to 22, the direction of writing was consistently sinistrograde, and the stance and the direction of the letters was quite consistent as well. The preferable term for the linear alphabet prior to the standardization is "Early Alphabetic" (or "Proto-Sinaitic" or "Proto-Canaanite") and the term for the alphabet after the standardization is "Phoenician" (Naveh, *Early History*, 42).

The reason for using the term "Phoenician" for this alphabet is because this standardized form of the alphabet is first attested at Phoenician archaeological sites and because the Phoenician language is the language of these inscriptions. In addition, it was the ancient Phoenician language that had 22 consonantal phonemes (in contrast to Aramaic and Hebrew, which had more than 22 consonantal phonemes). Therefore, it seems most reasonable to posit that the Phoenicians standardized the alphabet. It should also be noted that there is a strong tradition among Greek writers of antiquity to affirm that the Phoenicians were responsible for the origins of the alphabet (although, as stated above, technically speaking the Phoenicians were responsible for standardizing the alphabet, rather than inventing it).

There are many possible ways to discuss the inscriptional evidence for "writing culture" in the Iron Age Levant (Niditch; Schniedewind; van der Toorn; Rollston, *Writing and Literacy*). For the purposes of this article, I have chosen to provide a synopsis of some of the most important types of inscriptional documents, as a means of demonstrating the breadth, depth, and nature of writing in the Iron Age Levant. The predominant focus of this article will be on monumental inscriptions, but there will be some discussion of nonmonumental inscriptions as well. The intent is to provide the reader with a concrete sense for the sorts of documents that were produced in the Levant during the Iron Age, that is, a sense for "writing culture" (see also the essay by Edward Greenstein in this volume). Unless otherwise noted, the translations in this article are mine, although there are times when they will differ only modestly from the *editio princeps* (the first modern publication of an ancient text) or a recent reedition.

Of Kings and Kingdoms: Monumental Inscriptions of the Iron Age

Writing in the Iron Age Levant was an activity of the elite (Young, "Israelite Literacy: Part I" and "Part II"; Rollston, "Scribal education"; "Phoenician script"; *Writing and Literacy*). Much of the populace in the ancient Near East was agricultural and pastoral. For those working in the fields, there was normally neither the time available for formal education in writing nor a particularly strong need for thorough knowledge of a writing system. The same holds true for the artisans, that is, vocations such as carpentry, blacksmithing, and pottery production (Rollston, "Ben Sira"). Of course, some merchants in antiquity might have found a need for a knowledge of the most basic aspects of a writing system, but I suspect that the number of merchants in the Iron Age Levant with fluency and sophistication in both reading and writing was small (Rollston, "Ben Sira"; "Phoenician script"). Writing was primarily, I believe the epigraphic evidence reveals, the realm of officialdom, that is, scribes, military and governmental officials, and priests (Fox; see also the essays of S. A. Geller and of Bernard Levinson and Tina Sherman in this volume). Among the most impressive written materials from the ancient Iron Age Levant are monumental inscriptions.

The term "monumental inscription" is often used to refer to inscriptions commissioned by kings and high officials and which were intended to be permanent, enduring and (to some degree) public. Often these inscriptions were carved into stone. Within monumental inscriptions, the scribe or stonemason who was doing the chiseling would attempt to ensure that the lines of the inscription were fairly straight, of approximately the same length, and with fairly consistent spacing between the letters. The letters of a monumental inscription are normally carefully formed, in terms of the morphology and the stance of the letters. Naturally, there is some variation, but the variation is modest and falls within fairly narrow parameters.

Monumental Inscriptions about Military Conquests: Tel Dan (Old Aramaic) and Mesha (Moabite)

The Tel Dan Stele is written in the Old Aramaic language and in the Phoenician script, that is, the prestige script used to write both Phoenician and Aramaic at that time. Although it is not a particularly long inscription, and although it is not entirely preserved, it is quite impressive. Moreover, its contents are interesting and also representative of the standard content of victory stelae in general.

Based on the historical content and the paleography, this inscription can be dated rather confidently to the ninth century BCE. Tel Dan was an Israelite site at this time. The person who commissioned this stele was an Aramean king whom most scholars identify as Hazael of Damascus (Biran and Naveh; cf. Athas). This Aramaic inscription was placed on Israelite soil by the winners of a war, as a reminder to the Israelites of a major military defeat.

The preserved portion of the stele begins with an obscure reference to cutting (perhaps about the making of a treaty, or about the breach of a treaty), and then mentions that "my father went up against him in war … and my father lay down and he went to his fathers." That is, the stele contains reference (but without preserved details, per se) to the history that antedates Hazael's own kingship and conquest. Among the things mentioned is the death of his father ("he lay down and went to his fathers" is a standard idiom for this). The inscription then moves into the reason for Hazael's war against Israel and Judah, namely, "the king of Israel had gone formerly into the land of my father" (i.e., territorial encroachment by Israel). The term "formerly" is used here to indicate that this happened prior to Hazael's coronation. The inscription then moves into a discussion of Hazael's rise to kingship. "As for me, Hadad made me king and Hadad went before me (in battle)."

It is useful to reflect for a moment on the fact that in the ancient Near Eastern world, kings often affirmed that they had come to the throne at the behest of, and with the support of, their God or their Gods (in this case, the Aramean Storm God "Hadad"). Along those lines, consider also, for example, the Old Aramaic Stele of Zakir, King of Hamat and Luat. This inscription hails from the late ninth or very early eighth centuries BCE. It begins with these words, "I am Zakir, King of Hamat and Lu'at. I was a humiliated man, but Ba'lshamayin rescued me, and Ba'lshamayin arose with me, and Ba'lshamayin made me king." Similarly, within the Old Aramaic Panamuwa Inscription of the eighth century BCE, the following words are etched into stone, "I am Panamuwa the son of Qarli, king of Ya'diya, who erected this stele for Hadad. In my youth, the gods Hadad and 'Il and Rešep and Rakab-'il and Šamaš rose up in support of me. And into my hands, Hadad and 'Il, and Rakab-'il, and Šamaš, and Rešep placed the scepter of dominion." Similar motifs are present in the Hebrew Bible, for example, with regard to King David's rise to power (1 Sam. 16–2 Sam. 4). Kings in the ancient Levant (and the ancient Near East in general) were fond of affirming that they rose to power with the support of the heavens.

Continuing with the content of the Tel Dan Stele, this Old Aramaic inscription also recounts some of Hazael's victories. But because this portion of the inscription is not well preserved, the precise contents cannot be discerned. Some details, nevertheless, are preserved. Namely, Hazael states that he killed King Jehoram son of Ahab the king of Israel and that he killed King Ahaziah son of Jehoram king of the House of David (i.e., Judah). Only a few words of the remainder of the stele are preserved after this. But the fact that Hazael states that he was responsible for the deaths of King Jehoram of Israel and King Ahaziah of Judah is very important. Particularly striking is the fact that within the Hebrew Bible, there is reference to King Jehu being responsible for slaying King Jehoram of Israel and King Ahaziah of Judah, after he (Jehu) had usurped the throne from King Jehoram (2 Kings 9). The following text from the Hebrew Bible may be relevant in this regard: "And it shall be that the one who escapes from the sword of Hazael, Jehu will slay, and the one who escapes from the sword of Jehu, Elisha shall slay" (1 Kings 19:17). Based on the data at hand, it seems that Hazael (the usurper of the throne of Damascus) and Jehu (the usurper of the throne of Israel) had formed an alliance. Thus, it should come as no surprise that a Hebrew text attributes the death of both Jehoram and Ahaziah to Jehu and an Aramaic text attributes the death of both to Hazael. Based on the content and context (Israelite soil) of this stele, it may be that Jehu was the junior member of the alliance, or it may be that at some point the alliance between Hazael and Jehu was fractured. Evidence of both could be marshaled (see J. J. M. Roberts's essay in this volume). In any case, the Tel Dan Stele is a paradigmatic example of a victory stele, where a king claims victory over an enemy, on the enemy's territory, and then leaves a stele to remind the conquered of their military losses. And all of this happens with the support and the assistance of heaven itself, according to many of these inscriptions. The "writing culture" of the Levantine world focused heavily on victories on enemy territory and the Tel Dan Stele is a fine exemplar of this.

The Mesha Stele (dating to the ninth century BCE) is among the longest and most impressive of all Iron Age Northwest Semitic inscriptions (Dearman). Within this inscription, King Mesha of Moab provides his patronymic ("son of Kemoshyat") and refers to himself as a "Daibonite." Then, he states that Kemosh (the national god of Moab, 1 Kings 11:7) had been "angry" with Moab and had allowed Moab to be subjected to the hegemony of King Omri of Israel. Omri's son and successor (not named in the inscription) had desired to continue with the same "foreign policy." However, Mesha affirms that Kemosh "returned" and assisted Mesha in numerous military campaigns against Israel, resulting in the restoration of much territory to Moab (e.g., Nebo, Yaḥaṣ). Of significance is the fact that the material about Mesha detailed in the Mesha Stele parallels some of the material in the Hebrew Bible (2 Kings 3:4–8; see J. J. M. Roberts's essay in this volume). Before turning from this component of the Mesha Stele, it is worth emphasizing that just as the Mesha Stele declares that Kemosh was angry with his people and dire consequences resulted, so also the Hebrew Bible states that Yahweh was angry at times with his people and this resulted in dire consequences for Israel and Judah (e.g., Judg. 3–4; 2 Kings 17, 23). Thus, the ancient epigraphic record provides us with a window into ancient notions about the results of divine anger and divine mercy and this sheds light on the broader context of the Hebrew Bible. Continuing with the content of the Mesha Stele, it is stated that in addition to killing many people, Mesha "took the vessels of Yahweh" (the national god of Israel) and "dragged these vessels before Kemosh." The practice of removing the cult objects of vanquished foes to one's own territory was a common practice in the ancient Near East (cf. 1 Sam. 4–6; 2 Sam. 6; Kutsko 103–23).

It should be noted that the function of the Mesha Stele can be distinguished from that of the Tel Dan Stele, at least to some degree. For example, the Mesha Stele was erected in traditional Moabite territory and was intended to laud the Moabite king for his victories over a former suzerain. In addition, within the Mesha Stele, there is substantial attention devoted to "public works" projects, something that would be predictable for an inscription that would be intended primarily for the Moabite citizenry (on this, see below). In contrast, the Tel Dan Stele was placed on Israelite territory by a victorious foreign king. Again, the epigraphic material in the Tel Dan Stele and the Mesha Stele reveals something about the sorts of epigraphic texts which kings in the Iron Age Levant were commissioning, namely, texts about victories over enemies. Obviously, this is a particularly important aspect of writing culture in the Iron Age Levant.

Treaty Texts: Sefire (Old Aramaic)

Within the ancient Near East, kings engaged in battles, as demonstrated by the historical content of the Tel Dan Stele and the Mesha Stele. And, of course, kings would also find it useful at times to make treaties and alliances. The international treaty text from Sefire is a priceless document in this regard (Fitzmyer). The Sefire Treaty is written in the Old Aramaic language and in a stunningly beautiful script. Of interest, though not at all unique, the script of this inscription is written in *scripta continua*, that is, without word dividers of any sort. The Sefire Inscriptions can be dated with substantial certitude to the mid-eighth century BCE, based on historical data present in them.

There were two types of treaties in ancient times, vassal treaties and parity treaties. Within the latter, both parties are, at least at some level, equals. Within a vassal treaty, however, the parties to the treaty are not equal. There is a superior member (the suzerain) and an inferior member (the vassal). Within such treaties, the suzerain sets most of the terms and the vassal is called upon to meet those terms (Cohen and Westbrook).

Within the Sefire Treaty, King Mati'el of Arpad (a region in North Syria) is (arguably) a vassal of King Bar-Ga'yah of a neighboring region. The text of the Sefire Treaty consists of an introduction, stipulations, list of gods, and curses. Within the introduction, the parties are introduced and the treaty is said to be binding for Bar-Ga'yah and Mati'el and also for their sons and grandsons. Within ancient Near Eastern treaties, the gods and goddesses of the parties are named as witnesses and the Sefire Inscriptions are paradigmatic in this regard. The Sefire Inscriptions invoke a number of deities, including Marduk, Nabu, Nergal, Shamash, Kur, Sin, Zarpanit, Nikkar, Hadad of Aleppo, 'El, and 'Elyan.

Stipulations of the suzerain are a fundamental component of a vassal treaty, and the Sefire Inscriptions contain various statements that fall within this domain. There is, for example, reference to the fact that Mati'el must surrender any person that may "utter evil" against Bar-Ga'yah so that he might take appropriate measures. Fugitives that might flee to Mati'el for sanctuary must be surrendered as well, that is, extradition was part of this treaty. Moreover, any ambassador that might be sent by or to Bar-Ga'yah must be granted safe passage, without exception. Although the treaty generally discourages Mati'el from becoming involved in problems arising out of succession in Bar-Ga'yah's realm, there is a statement that Mati'el must make a punitive campaign against any of Bar-Ga'yah's relatives ("brothers" or "sons") or high officials that attempt to usurp his throne. Naturally, any attempt by Mati'el to assassinate Bar-Ga'yah is affirmed to be a fundamental breach of the treaty. Indeed, deviation from any of the stipulations is considered to be a demonstration that the vassal is unfaithful (šqr).

Curses are pronounced against Mati'el should he prove unfaithful. Among the curses that are mentioned are things such as the following: "May Mati'el be blinded" and "may his wives be stripped and the wives of his sons and nobles," and "may Arpad and her associated cities be burned with fire," and "may Hadad sow them with salt and weeds, and may they not be mentioned again." Moreover, things such as the following are also included: "may seven nurses suckle a young boy, but may he not have his fill," and "though seven mares suckle a colt, may it not be sated," and "may the locusts devour Arpad for seven years." Blessings are also present, such as "may the gods keep all evil away from his day and from his house." Curses are also pronounced upon any that might wish to efface or destroy the text of the treaty: "may he and his son die in terrible torment." Promises such as "if you obey, then I shall not be able to raise a hand against you" are present. Diplomatic texts are attested in various parts of the ancient Near East, particularly the Late Bronze Age materials from Amarna (Moran). The Sefire Treaty texts demonstrate that ancient rulers were making and breaking international treaties during the Iron Age Levant as well.

The King's Public Works and Pious Deeds

There seems to have been a premium put on public works in antiquity. This is quite understandable, as the king was not only supposed to be distinguished in battle and capable of negotiating treaties in the international realm; he was also supposed to be the great benefactor of his people. For this reason, ancient inscriptions from the Iron Age Levant will often detail the king's great public works (Green).

The Tell Miqne (Ekron) Temple Inscription (Phoenician of Philistia)

The monumental inscription from Tel Miqne is particularly impressive. This stele weighs around 100 kilograms and is 60 × 39 × 26 centimeters (Gitin et al.) and it was found in a Philistine temple, namely, Temple Complex 650. It can be dated to the seventh century BCE with substantial certainty. The inscription can be read as follows: "The Temple (which) Achish the son of Padi, the son of Yasad, the son of Ada, the son of Ya'ir, the prince of Ekron built for Ptgyh his Lordess. May she bless him and may she guard him, and may she lengthen his days and may she bless his land." There has been substantial discussion about the deity mentioned here, and it must be conceded that the reading of the letter *gimel* is not absolutely certain. But it is certain that a goddess (not a god) is referred to, because the word *'dt* is feminine, namely, "Lordess" (not "Lord"). Among the most important aspects of this inscription is that it is a marvelous statement about the building activity of a Philistine king, namely, his building a sacred temple. And for this inscription to be found in the remains of the temple itself, preserved so well, is particularly welcome. It should also be emphasized that kings were often active in such ventures, and were pleased to be able to boast about such pious actions, with the hope that both heaven and earth would see.

The personal names of this inscription are also of interest and merit some reference. For example, King Padi of Ekron is mentioned in the annals of Sennacherib and in these annals it is stated that the Judean King Hezekiah had (with the complicity of the elites in Ekron) deposed Padi and imprisoned him in Jerusalem. From the context of Sennacherib's discussion, it is readily apparent that Padi had not joined the coalition of Levantine states that had formed against Sennacherib: hence the ire of various alliance members, including Hezekiah. Nevertheless, Sennacherib's punitive campaign in 701 BCE was successful and he was able to destroy 46 fortified cities of Judah, kill the elites of Ekron who had surrendered Padi, demand the release of Padi from Jerusalem and restore him to the throne of Ekron (cf. 2 Kings 18–19; Isa. 36–38). This "Padi" of the Tel Miqne Inscription is arguably the father of King Achish who built the Philistine temple at Ekron. In any case, the Tel Miqne Inscription is a paradigmatic dedication inscription, replete with the stated and customary request for long life and blessings for the king.

The Public Works of King Mesha (Moabite)

Some reference has been made to the military successes of King Mesha of Moab, but it is important to emphasize in this context that his public works are also a strong component of this inscription. For example, Mesha states that "I built Ba'l-Maon and I made a water reservoir in it, and I built Qiryatēn." Later, Mesha states that he went up against Yaḥaṣ and seized it to augment the territory of Dibon and he built "Qarḥoh, the walls of the lower acropolis and the walls of the upper acropolis." And he goes on and states that "I myself built its gates and I myself built its towers and I myself built its royal palaces and I myself made the retaining walls of the water reservoir for the water spring within the city … and I built ʿAroʿer and the surfaced road at the ʿArnon." As noted, it was believed that kings should excel in public works and Mesha certainly contends that he did just that.

The Public Works of King Amminadab: The Tell Siran Bronze Bottle (Ammonite)

Similar in content, though diminutive in size (measuring just 10 cm long), is the Tell Siran Bottle (Aufrecht 203–11). It was found during a salvage expedition in Amman (Jordan). Because Amman was the capital of the Iron Age kingdom of Ammon, this inscription is of particular importance for a number of reasons, not the least of which is the fact that it provides a sequence of three Iron Age Ammonite kings. At the time of discovery it was still sealed with a pin, and contained dried barley and wheat. This inscription consists of eight lines and the letters have all been executed with care. The script is Ammonite as is also the language, and it is normally dated convincingly to the sixth century BCE. Word dividers are sometimes used in this inscription, but not with absolute consistency (as is quite common).

The person that commissioned this inscription is "Amminadab king of the Ammonites, the son of Haṣṣalʾil king of the Ammonites, the son of Amminadab king of the Ammonites" (note the paponymy, that is, naming a grandson after a grandfather). This inscription is, of course, a royal inscription. The fact that it is inscribed on a bronze bottle demonstrates rather nicely the fact that royal inscriptions detailing public works were not always chiseled into stone (although this bronze-bottle inscription may have been a copy of a large monumental stone inscription). The contents of this royal inscription are consistent with the sort of memorializing that characterizes royal inscriptions: "May the produce of Amminadab … the vineyard, and the gardens, and the water canal, and cistern cause rejoicing and gladness for many days and distant years." The duty of a king to do public works is enshrined beautifully in the writing culture of ancient Iron Age Ammon.

The Siloam Tunnel Inscription of King Hezekiah of Judah (Old Hebrew) as a Public Work

The Siloam Tunnel Inscription is written in the Old Hebrew language, and in the Old Hebrew script of the late eighth century BCE. I do not believe that it is at all possible to date the Siloam Tunnel Inscription to the late ninth or early eighth centuries BCE (*pace* Ronny Reich and Eli Shukron).

The name of the Judean king responsible for the completion of the tunnel and the commissioning of the inscription was arguably King Hezekiah of Judah (r. 715–687

BCE). This conclusion is based upon paleographic dating (i.e., of the script) and upon the texts in the Hebrew Bible that associate this tunnel with Hezekiah (2 Kings 20:20; 2 Chr. 32:30; Sirach 48:17–18). The total length of the Siloam Tunnel is almost 600 meters, a fact that dovetails with the stated length in the inscription itself. It has often been stated that Hezekiah engaged in the building of the tunnel as one of his measures to fortify the city prior to the siege of the Neo-Assyrian King Sennacherib in 701 BCE. Ben Sira does use the term "fortify" (ḥzq) and this might suggest that the tunnel was completed in anticipation of Sennacherib's siege (since the following verse does refer to Sennacherib's campaign). Mostly, however, I view this reference as a word play on the name Hezekiah (ḥzqyh). But even if Ben Sira did connect the Siloam Tunnel with Hezekiah's siege preparations, he is writing some 500 years after King Hezekiah and so I do not believe that he can speak with independent authority regarding this. It is interesting that the Deuteronomist lists the building of the tunnel at the conclusion of his narrative about Hezekiah (2 Kings 20:20) and the Deuteronomist *does not connect* the building of the tunnel with fortifications of Hezekiah prior to Sennacherib's campaign. Strictly speaking, neither does the writer of Chronicles (2 Chr. 32:30). And it is not necessary to understand the references to Hezekiah's "stopping up the water courses outside the city" prior to Sennacherib's siege to be a reference to the Siloam Tunnel (2 Chr. 32:3–4; see also the essay by J. J. M. Roberts in this volume).

In any case, near the southern entrance of the Siloam Tunnel, an Old Hebrew inscription was found. It reads as follows:

> […] the tunneling. And this is the narrative of the tunneling. While the [stone cutters were wielding] the picks, each toward his coworker, and while there were still three cubits to tunnel through, the voice of a man was heard calling out to his coworker, because there was a fissure in the rock, running from the south [to north]. And on the (final) day of tunneling, each of the stone-cutters was striking (the stone) forcefully so as to meet his coworker, pick after pick. And then the water began to flow from the source to the pool, a distance of twelve hundred cubits. And one hundred cubits was the height of the rock above the head of the stone-cutters.

Although the king's name is not preserved, this massive engineering project was certainly royal in aegis and qualifies nicely as a public work. Of course, royal public works revolving around water are among the most common types, as reflected in the Mesha Stele and the Tell Siran Bronze Bottle Inscription, as well as the Tell Fakhariyeh Bilingual.

King Hadd-Yithi of Gozan: The Tell Fakhariyeh Inscription (Old Aramaic) and Public Works

This inscription is one of the most beautiful, elegant, and well-preserved statue inscriptions from the Iron Age Levant (Abou-Assaf et al.). The statue itself is life-sized, fully three-dimensional, standing nearly 2 meters in height. It was intended to be a representation of Hadd-Yithi, the king of Gozan, clothed in traditional garb. On the front of the statue is the Akkadian text, written in the Assyrian dialect. On the back of the statue is the Old Aramaic text, written in an archaizing Phoenician script. The inscription dates to the ninth century BCE. It was set up in the temple of Hadad-Sikanu. It is reasonable to understand this statue inscription to be connected with Hadd-Yithi's support of the temple of Hadad-Sikanu and probably with his donations to it or his renovations of it. Note in this connection, for example, the fact that the inscription refers to vessels in the temple marked with the name Hadd-Yithi, and a curse is pronounced upon anyone who may "remove my name from the vessels of the temple of Hadad."

Within this text are many descriptions of the activities of the god Hadad-Sikanu. For example, he is said to be the "lord of the water reserves of heaven and earth and the one who bestows wealth and who gives pasturage and watering places for all lands." And he is said to be "the lord of the water who reserves of all the rivers, the one who makes all lands lush." With regard to the character of Hadad-Sikanu, he is said to be "compassionate," using a tender word here that derives from the root word for "womb." Within this inscription, Hadd-Yithi requests for himself certain things, including good health, a long reign, and well-being for his family and for the people in his kingdom. He specifically requests that his "prayer be heard."

Of course, kings were often quite concerned about those who might attempt to destroy their monuments or desecrate sacred vessels which they had dedicated or inscribed. Along those lines, therefore, Hadd-Yithi states that if someone attempts to do such things, "may Hadad the Warrior be his accuser!" Several more curses follow: "May Hadad not accept his food or water from his hand" (i.e., offerings). And "May Sola, my Lordess, not accept his food or his water from his hand." As part of this divine rejection for any destruction and desecration, Hadd-Yithi also prays that the perpetrator might "sow a thousand kernels of barley, but not harvest a paris" (a very small unit of measure). In addition, "may one hundred ewes nurse a (single) lamb, but may it not be sated … and may a hundred women nurse a (single) child, but may it not be sated." Hadd-Yithi concludes the curses with these words upon anyone who destroys or desecrates something in the temple of Hadad-Sikanu: "And may Pestilence, the Plague of Nergal, not be removed from his land."

Of course, within the Hebrew Bible, there are references to the blessings and curses of Yahweh, and Kaufman has drawn attention to some of the closest parallels (e.g., Deut. 28:38–42; Lev. 26:26; Kaufman). Mention should also be made in this context of the blessings and curses on Mount Ebal and Mount Gerizim (Deut. 27). Further, much ink has been spilt through the centuries about the words "image and likeness of God" in the Priestly Creation Account (Gen. 1:26; see also the essay by David Carr in this volume). Both words occur in the Tell Fakhariyeh Inscription (lines 1 and 12) and they are used to refer to the physical representation of Hadd-Yithi in the stone statue. In short, the epigraphic references in this inscription demonstrate rather nicely that the priestly writer's point was to suggest that the physical appearance of human beings was modeled on the physical appearance of God (see also the essay by Theodore Lewis in this volume). With the words "image and likeness," therefore, the priestly writer was not emphasizing something about human rational faculties, human morality, or human capacity for religion, but rather the origins of the human form, the human body.

Royal Burial Inscriptions: The Ahiram Sarcophagus (Phoenician) and the Royal Steward (Old Hebrew)

Although kings and high officials prayed to the gods and goddesses for long life, and although they were often successful in battle and engaged in many building activities for the good of the nation, one fate befalls all of humanity, death. Therefore, as a final act the ancients often commissioned burial inscriptions. Among the oldest of the monumental inscriptions are the Royal Inscriptions of Byblos, a famous Phoenician port city, located on the Mediterranean Sea. Among the most impressive of the Byblian Royal Inscriptions is the Ahiram Sarcophagus Inscription.

This inscription dates to the early tenth century BCE (Rollston, "Early Royal Byblian") and was chiseled into a very finely made sarcophagus. Discovered in 1923 (Dussaud), the inscription reads as follows: "The sarcophagus which ['E]thba'l son of Ahiram king of Byblos made for Ahiram, his father, when committing him to eternity." This inscription has thus been made by a son for his deceased father. Ahiram, the father, was the king of Byblos and it is reasonable to contend that Ethba'l his son was also his successor. The inscription contains some of the traditional curse materials that are part of many royal burial inscriptions, namely,

> And if a king among kings or a governor among gov{er}nors, or an army commander should come up to Byblos and expose this sarcophagus, may the scepter of his rule be over-turned, and may the throne of his kingdom be in tumult, and may rest flee from Byblos. And as for him, may his royal record(s) be erased from By[blos].

From this inscription, it is apparent that kings were often very concerned about the future stability of their kingdoms and they were also concerned about the potential threat which conquerors or usurpers might pose for their own burial chamber and its sanctity.

This inscription is interesting for a number of additional reasons. First of all, the script is quite beautiful and reflects the presence of some very gifted Phoenician scribes and stonemasons during this early period of the Phoenician script. In addition, this inscription is also interesting because a letter was accidently omitted from the word for governor. Scribes and stonemasons were very careful, but they were not perfect. Sometimes a scribe or stonemason might notice an error after the fact and attempt to correct it (by writing a letter above or below the line, etc.), but in this case, there was no attempt to correct the mistake. I suspect that either the scribe or the stonemason (if the stonemason was literate) noticed the mistake but there was no elegant means of correcting it. In addition, because the sarcophagus was to be sealed in a burial chamber, few would see it. Moreover, literacy rates were low in antiquity and so few of those who might see it would be able to notice the problem. In any case, this inscription is among the most famous of the Old Byblian Phoenician inscriptions and it is a sterling demonstration of the sophistication of the Phoenician scribal apparatus in the Iron Age Levant of the tenth century.

The Royal Steward Inscription was found in the village of Silwan, a stone's throw from the walls of the ancient city of Jerusalem. It is a burial inscription written in the Old Hebrew language and script of the eighth century BCE and was deciphered by Nahman Avigad, after many had failed for decades before him (Avigad). Although it is the grave of a royal official (the term "who is over the house" is an official title attested in the Hebrew Bible), rather than that of a king, the burial inscription is very fine and contains a standard reference to the absence of anything of monetary value in the tomb, as well as a curse. The name of the owner of the tomb is not preserved, but it has often been proposed that it was that of Shebna, as he held the title "who is over the house" during the late eighth century and his tomb is mentioned in Isaiah (22:15–19; see also the discussion of Shebna's tomb in the essay of John Huddlestun in this volume). The inscription reads as follows: "This is the [grave of....]yahu, who is over the house. There is no silver or gold here [but rather his bones] and the bones of his maidservant with him. Accursed is the person who may open this [grave]!" Texts such as these demonstrate that the writers and readers of the ancient Levant were quite concerned about the disturbance of burial remains.

Inscribed Cultic Objects and Inscribed Prestige Objects: Inscriptions from Mudeyineh (Moabite) and Kefar Veradim (Phoenician)

During the Iron Age Levant, cultic objects and prestige objects were sometimes inscribed. These probably served a variety of purposes. For the inscribed cultic pieces, it seems reasonable to suggest (based on the evidence at hand) that these inscriptions contained some reference to the giver, or a statement about the function. For some of the inscribed prestige items, it seems reasonable to suggest that these were mantelpieces of some sort, intended to commemorate some aspect of the life or family of the giver. Because many of these are found in tomb contexts, it may be that at least some of these pieces were commissioned after the death of the deceased.

A magisterial inscribed incense altar was discovered at the site of Tell Mudeyineh (modern Jordan), a site that is some 20 kilometers southeast of Madaba, in ancient Moab (Dion and Daviau). Among the words of the inscription are the following: "The incense altar which Elishima made." The script and language of the inscription can be classified as Moabite. It can be dated with some certainty to sometime in the first half of the eighth century BCE. This incense altar would have functioned for some time in a cultic (temple) context and the name on it is, of course, of the person who made it. This inscription is reflective of the broader use of writing during the Iron Age, namely, for sacerdotal purposes.

The Kefar Veradim Bowl is a stunning artifact, made of bronze, and fluted (Alexandre). The inscription consists of just four words, all preserved quite well, with two word dividers present. It reads as follows: "The Bowl of Pesaḥ ben Shema." This inscribed bowl was found in a burial cave at Kefar Veradim (Israel). Moreover, the script is definitively Phoenician, even though this inscription was found in Israel. The script of this inscription reflects the work of a trained, consummate scribal hand. I consider this inscribed bowl to hail from the same basic chronological horizon as the Azarba'al Inscription from Byblos, that is, the late eleventh century or the very early tenth century BCE. It is quite probable that this was an heirloom piece, rather than something that was made at the time of the deceased's death. It is also important to mention in this connection that the Phoenician script was the prestige script during the tenth century BCE, and as such its usage is attested in multiple countries, including early Israel. Of course, during the early ninth century, the Old Hebrew national script rose and rapidly displaced the Phoenician script in the land of Israel. This piece is another nice example of the varied usages of writing during the Iron Age.

On the Bureaucracy of Kingdoms: The Samaria Ostraca and the Gibeon Jar Handles (Old Hebrew)

The Reisner Samaria Ostraca number in excess of one hundred. Some 60 were published (Reisner et al.). The remainder of the ostraca were not considered legible at the time. These inscriptions date to the first quarter of the eighth century BCE and are administrative in nature. Most contain reference to a year (arguably a regnal year of King Jeroboam II), with references to some place names, personal names, and some commodities. Scholars have disagreed about the precise function of these ostraca. Some have considered them to be records of commodities delivered to crown coffers. After all, Samaria was the capital of the Northern Kingdom. In such a case, the commodities might have been produced on royal farmland and production centers (e.g., olive presses) or the commodities might have been the "taxes" (in the form of commodities) coming to the crown. Conversely, some have argued that the commodities listed on the ostraca are the crown's expenditures, given as payment to those serving the crown. Two typical examples of Reisner Samaria Ostraca are as follows: "In the tenth year, to Gadyaw, from 'Aza, Abiba'l, Ahaz, Sheba, Meriba'l;" "In the tenth year, wine of the vineyard of the Tel (and) a jar of refined olive oil." Regardless of whether these are viewed as receipts of income or expenditures, these 60-some legible ostraca do provide some evidence for the bureaucracy of ancient Israel.

In addition, and at least as importantly, these ostraca reveal that there were two distinct dialects of Old Hebrew, namely, the southern dialect of Old Hebrew known from Judean sites such as Lachish and Arad, and the northern dialect which is attested on the Reisner Samaria Ostraca (a site in the Northern Kingdom of Israel). Although many of the differences between these two dialects will never be known, some are apparent. For example, in the northern dialect of Old Hebrew ("Israelite Hebrew"), the word for "year" was /šat/, to be contrasted with the southern dialect of Old Hebrew ("Judahite Hebrew") which used /šānāh/. In addition, within the southern dialect of Old Hebrew, the diphthong /ayi/ was preserved (hence the word for "wine" is written yyn (for yayin) in Judahite, but in the northern dialect of Old Hebrew, this diphthong was contracted and so this same word is written yn (for yēn) in Israelite Hebrew.

Perhaps a most striking irony of history is that ostraca, such as those of Samaria, Lachish and Arad, were intended to be ephemeral, but they have endured the vagaries of time. They were written in ink on broken pieces of pottery and served some short-term purposes. Many of the most important royal documents (in addition to those written on stone) would have been written on papyrus and vellum, materials that almost never survived from the Iron Age Levant.

Similar to, but different from, the Samaria Ostraca are the more than 60 Gibeon Inscribed Jar Handles in Old Hebrew (Pritchard, *Hebrew Inscriptions*; "Jar handles"). These come from the site of Gibeon, famous from the Hebrew Bible, and thus are from the Southern Kingdom of Judah. Some were inscribed after the pot had been fired and some were inscribed before firing. The jar handles can be dated to the late eighth century or the early seventh century BCE and are connected with the administrative apparatus of the Southern Kingdom of Judah. Two examples are as follows: "Gibeon, stone wall, 'Amaryahu" and "Gibeon, stone wall, Hananyahu." It comes as no surprise that ancient bureaucracies maintained written records, and this sort of data continues to augment our understanding of ancient writing culture.

Old Hebrew Epistolary Texts

The writing of letters is well attested in Iron Age Northwest Semitic. Moreover, the evidence demonstrates that there was a basic formula for writing letters, often with the writer providing his own name and the name of the recipient, and then a basic greeting, followed by the body of the letter (Pardee). For Old Hebrew letters, the sites of Lachish and Arad have been the most productive sites for epistolary materials. There is a fascinating letter from Lachish (Lachish Letter #3) in which a military official named Hoshaiah writes to his commander, a certain Ya'osh (Tur-Sinai et al.). After the standard greetings, "May Yahweh let my lord hear tidings of peace and tidings of good," Hoshaiah begins the body of his message. He begins by protesting part of the content of a letter Ya'osh had previously sent to him, a letter in which Ya'osh told Hoshaiah to "summon a scribe" because he "did not understand" some prior correspondence. Hoshaiah protests further, states that he is a literate person and that he has never needed to resort to summoning a professional scribe.

At long last, Hoshaiah finally moves on to discuss the subject at hand, military happenings. Namely, he states that "Coniah the son of Elnathan, the commander of the army has gone down into Egypt." He also mentions that he is forwarding to Ya'osh a letter of Tobiah, the servant of the king which had come to Shallum, at the insistence of the prophet. It said: "Beware!" This letter is written in the Old Hebrew language and script and it dates to the period immediately prior to the fall of Lachish and Jerusalem in 586 BCE. Some have suggested that the prophet mentioned in this letter was Jeremiah (famous from the Hebrew Bible). There is not enough evidence to state this with any certitude. It could be noted that this prophet was correct, as there was reason to "beware," with disaster lurking at the door of Judah.

This ostracon has also garnered substantial interest because the soldier states that he is able to read. Some have suggested that the person who responds must have been an ordinary soldier, not a mid-level or high-level officer, and they have used this text to argue for high levels of literacy among the populace. However, because this letter focuses on troop movements and high-level missives from the king himself, I would suggest that the person responsible for the correspondence is at least a mid-level officer. This letter may simply be evidence that those in the higher echelons of the Judean army had received at least a modicum of training in reading and writing. Of course, it should also be mentioned that this inscription makes it clear that scribes were recognized as the trained professionals in writing (at least Ya'osh felt this way!), distinct from even a bright officer with some capability in reading.

From the site of Arad is a cache of Old Hebrew inscriptions numbering in excess of one hundred (Aharoni). Some of these date to as early as the ninth century BCE and the latest Iron Age Hebrew inscriptions from Arad come from the early sixth century BCE. Some of these inscriptions are brief and poorly preserved, but many are preserved rather nicely. Here is a translation of Arad Ostracon 1: "To Elyashib. And now, give to the Kittim wine, (totaling) three baths. Write the name of the day. And the remainder of the flour from the first of the wheat, transport by horse one homer. And from the wheat flour make for them bread. From the wine of the large vessels give (them)." This letter is interesting at various levels. For example, we have here (as in Lachish Ostracon 3), the name of a military official who was the recipient of this military correspondence: 'Elyashib. We are not, however, given the name of the sender, but it is convincing to suggest that he was 'Elyashib's superior officer. After all, the sender commands 'Elyashib to provide the Kittim with wine and bread (not the sort of thing that a junior officer would command a senior officer). Significantly, as for the Kittim, they were arguably Cypriot or Greek mercenaries serving in the Judean fort of Arad. Also of interest is the fact that precise measures of flour and wine are specified for the Kittim and within this ostracon are also some hieratic signs (e.g., for bath and for homer). Rather importantly, hieratic numerals are well attested in Iron Age Israel, not only at Arad, but also at Lachish, Samaria and Kadesh Barnea. This is an additional datum that lends credence to the affirmation that there was a sophisticated scribal culture in the Iron Age Levant. After all, hieratic numbers are a foreign numeric system (from Egypt originally) and hieratic numerals are particularly difficult. Finally, it should be emphasized that in this letter 'Elyashib is commanded to "record the day" upon which he is providing these supplies, a further indication that records of expenditures were maintained rather carefully.

The Yavneh Yam Ostracon ("Meṣad Ḥashavyahu Ostracon") is among the most important of the Old Hebrew ostraca, because of its uniqueness in the corpus of extant Old Hebrew letters. It dates to the second half of the seventh century BCE and hails from the small Iron Age fortress near Yavneh Yam. In the vicinity of the fortress gate, several ostraca were found; most were short and poorly preserved, but one was large and consists of around 14 lines of preserved text (Naveh, "A Hebrew letter"; Cross, "Epigraphic notes"). In essence, this long ostracon is a petition for justice by a harvester. The harvester begins by saying, "Let my lord, the commander, hear (the petition) of his servant." The harvester proceeds to state that he was harvesting in a place called Ḥaṣar-'Asam, and he had harvested (grain), measured it, and then put it in storage. However, the harvester's supervisor had, before the Sabbath, taken the cloak of the harvester. The harvester provides the name of the supervisor, a certain Hoshaiah the son of Shobay. Presumably, the supervisor believed that the harvester had not been working hard enough. The harvester states that he is innocent and that there are witnesses willing to testify to this. The harvester petitions that the commander have Hoshaiah return the cloak, as he had apparently kept it for some time. It would be interesting to know all of the details, including the end result. But we do not. It has long been noted, however, that this ostracon is very reminiscent of some material in the legal material of the Hebrew Bible

(Exod. 22:25–26; Deut. 24:10–13; cf. Amos 2:8). These biblical texts command that in cases such as this the cloak must be returned prior to nightfall. Naveh suggests that the harvester had hired a scribe to write this letter. Because this was a band of military harvesters (it was a fortress and the recipient is referred to as a *śar*, that is, a commander), military scribes would have been present. In any case, I do not believe (as some have suggested) that the writer of this ostracon was some poor peasant. The script is carefully executed and the orthography is very nice as well. In any case, and most importantly, these epistolary documents help to "fill out," in very concrete ways, our understanding of Iron Age writing culture.

The Ubiquity of Religion in Ancient Writing Culture

Gods and goddesses, part of the fabric of the ancient Near Eastern world, are pervasive components of Iron Age Levantine epigraphic texts, and the Yeḥimilk Inscription provides a representative example. This Phoenician inscription, a temple dedication, dates to the tenth century BCE (Rollston, "Early Royal Byblian"). In this dedication, Yeḥimilk says: "May Baʻl-Shamēn and Baʻlat of Byblos and the Council of the Holy Gods of Byblos lengthen the days of Yeḥimilk and (lengthen) his years over Byblos." This inscription refers to the two heads of the pantheon, a god and a goddess, and to the divine council as well, a phenomenon also attested in the Hebrew Bible (Deut. 32:8–9, reading with the Qumran manuscript tradition; Job 1–2; see also the essay by Mark Smith in this volume). Similarly, the Abibaʻl Inscription (on a statue of Sheshonq I, who reigned ca. 945–924 BCE) is Phoenician and dates to the tenth century. It reads as follows: "[The statue which] Abibaʻl King of [Byblos, son of Yeḥimilk King of] Byblos brought from Egypt for Baʻlat [of Byblos, his Lordess. May Baʻlat of Byblos lengthen the days of Abibaʻl and (lengthen) his years] over Byblos." Of course, inscriptions such as the Tel Dan Stele and the Mesha Stele contain references to the actions of the gods as well. And within the Zakir Stele and the Panamuwa Stele there are references to the benevolent activities and the support of the gods, and Zakir even refers to prophetic "seers" sent to him by Baʼlshamayin in order to signal success and deliverance in all his pursuits. Within Old Hebrew literature, there is reference not simply to Yahweh, but also on several occasions to "Yahweh and his Asherah," a welcome epigraphic demonstration that early Israelite religion was more complex and rich than used to be assumed (Aḥituv et al.; see also the essays by Elizabeth Bloch-Smith and Mark Smith in this volume). The Old Hebrew Silver Amulets from Ketef Hinnom (Barkay et al.) demonstrate that even during the Iron Age certain texts familiar to us from the Hebrew Bible were already becoming sacred in some sense. In short, religion is a component of much of the epigraphic corpus.

Iron Age epigraphic evidence from the Levant is broad and deep. The genres of literature represented are impressive. Even the bureaucratic texts contribute to our understanding of writing culture. Furthermore, the evidence points to the impressively high caliber of the writing and the orthography. The mastery of the difficult hieratic numerals system by many scribes from various periods and sites is startling. The writers and readers of the Iron Age world of the Levant were gifted, and the texts that have been discovered to date reveal this in spades.

Bibliography

Abou-Assaf, Ali, Pierre Bordreuil and Alan R. Millard. *La statue de Tell Fekherye et son inscription bilingue assyro-araméenne.* Études Assyriologiques 7. Paris: Éditions Recherche sur les Civilisations, 1982. *Editio princeps.*

Aharoni, Yohanan. *Arad Inscriptions.* Jerusalem: Israel Exploration Society, 1981. *Editio princeps.*

Aḥituv, S., E. Eshel and Ze'ev Meshel. "The inscriptions." In Ze'ev Meshel (ed.), *Kuntillet 'Ajrud (Ḥorvat Teman): An Iron Age II Religious Site on the Judah-Sinai Border* (pp. 73–143). Jerusalem: Israel Exploration Society, 2012. *Editio princeps.*

Alexandre, Yardenna. "A Canaanite-Early Phoenician inscribed bronze bowl in an Iron Age IIA-B burial cave at Kefer Veradim, Northern Israel." *Maarav* 13 (2006): 7–41. *Editio princeps.*

Athas, George. *The Tel Dan Inscription: A Reappraisal and a New Interpretation.* London: T&T Clark, 2002. Reconsideration of *editio princeps.*

Aufrecht, Walter E. *A Corpus of Ammonite Inscriptions.* Lewiston, NY: Edwin Mellen, 1989. Standard reference for Ammonite.

Avigad, Nachman. "The epitaph of a royal steward." *Israel Exploration Journal* 3 (1953):137–52. Contains decipherment.

Barkay, Gabriel, Andrew G. Vaughn, Marilyn J. Lundberg, and Bruce Zuckerman. "The amulets from Ketef Hinnom: A new edition and evaluation." *Bulletin of the American Schools of Oriental Research* 334 (2004): 41–71. New edition and readings.

Biran, Avraham and Joseph Naveh. "The Tel Dan inscription: A new fragment." *Israel Exploration Journal* 45 (1995): 1–18. *Editio princeps.*

Cohen, Raymond and Raymond Westbrook. *Amarna Diplomacy: The Beginnings of International Relations.* Baltimore: Johns Hopkins University Press, 1999. Standard reference on diplomacy in Late Bronze Age.

Cross, Frank Moore. "Epigraphic notes on Hebrew documents of the eighth–sixth centuries BC: II. The Murabba'at papyrus and the letter found near Yabneh-Yam." *Bulletin of the American Schools of Oriental Research* 165 (1962): 34–46. Reprinted in Cross, *Leaves*, 116–24.

Cross, Frank Moore. *Leaves from an Epigrapher's Notebook: Collected Papers in Hebrew and West Semitic Epigraphy.* Harvard Semitic Studies 51. Winona Lake, IN: Eisenbrauns, 2003. The most exhaustive collection of this Harvard professor's epigraphic articles.

Dearman, J. Andrew (ed.). *Studies in the Mesha Inscription and Moab.* Society of Biblical Literature: Archaeology and Biblical Studies 2. Atlanta: Scholars Press, 1989. Collection of articles on this inscription, including a new edition of the text.

Dion, P. E., and P. M. M. Daviau. "An inscribed incense altar of Iron Age II at Khirbet el-Mudeyine (Jordan)." *Zeitschrift des Deutschen Palästina-Vereins* 116 (2000):1–13. *Editio princeps.*

Dussaud, René. "Les inscriptions phéniciennes du tombeau d'Ahiram, roi de Byblos." *Syria* 5 (1924): 135–57. *Editio princeps.*

Fitzmyer, Joseph A. *The Aramaic Inscriptions of Sefire.* Rev. edn. Biblica et orientalia (BibOr) 19/A. Rome: Editrice Pontificio Instituto Biblico, 1995. The most authoritative edition of this inscription.

Fox, Nili Sacher. *In the Service of the King: Officialdom in Ancient Israel and Judah.* Cincinnati: Hebrew Union College Press, 2000. Standard reference on officials in the Hebrew Bible.

Gitin, S., T. Dothan and J. Naveh. "A royal dedicatory inscription from Ekron." *Israel Exploration Journal* 47 (1997): 1–16. *Editio princeps.*

Green, Douglas J. *"I Undertook Great Works": The Ideology of Domestic Achievements in West Semitic Royal Inscriptions.* Tübingen: Mohr Siebeck, 2010. A fine treatment of royal inscriptions referring to public works.

Huehnergard, John and Christopher Woods. "Akkadian and Eblaite." In Roger D. Woodard (ed.), *The Cambridge Encyclopedia of the World's Ancient Languages* (pp. 218–87). Cambridge: Cambridge University Press, 2004. Synopsis of writing in Mesopotamia.

Kaufman, Stephen A. "Reflections on the Assyrian-Aramaic bilingual from Tell Fakhariyeh." *Maarav 3* (1982): 137–75. A very fine linguistic analysis of inscription.

Kramer, Samuel Noah. *History Begins at Sumer.* 3rd edn. Philadelphia: University of Pennsylvania, 1981. Good discussion of origins of writing and history.

Kutsko, John F. *Between Heaven and Earth: Divine Presence and Absence in the Book of Ezekiel.* Winona Lake, IN: Eisenbrauns, 2000. Study of divine presence in Ezekiel in the context of Assyrian and Babylonian deportation of divine images.

Loprieno, Antonio. "Ancient Egyptian and Coptic." In Roger D. Woodard (ed.), *The Cambridge Encyclopedia of the World's Ancient Languages* (pp. 160–217). Cambridge: Cambridge University Press, 2004. Synopsis of writing in Egypt.

Michalowski, Piotr. "Sumerian." In Roger D. Woodard (ed.), *The Cambridge Encyclopedia of the World's Ancient Languages* (pp. 19–59). Cambridge: Cambridge University Press, 2004. Synopsis of world's first written language.

Moran, William. *The Amarna Letters.* Baltimore: Johns Hopkins University Press, 2000. New edition of this diplomatic corpus.

Naveh, Joseph. "A Hebrew letter from the seventh century BC." *Israel Exploration Journal 10* (1960): 129–39. *Editio princeps.*

Naveh, Joseph. *Early History of the Alphabet: An Introduction to West Semitic Epigraphy and Palaeography.* 2nd edn. Jerusalem: Magnes Press, 1987. Superb introduction to history of alphabetic writing.

Niditch, Susan. *Oral World and Written Word.* Library of Ancient Israel. Louisville, KY: Westminster John Knox, 1996. Sophisticated analysis of orality and writing in antiquity.

Pardee, Dennis. *Handbook of Ancient Hebrew Letters: A Study Edition.* Society of Biblical Literature: Resources for Biblical Study 15. Chico, CA: Scholars Press, 1982. Edition of ancient Northwest Semitic epistolary texts.

Pritchard, James B. *Hebrew Inscriptions and Stamps from Gibeon.* Philadelphia: University Museum, University of Pennsylvania, 1959. *Editio princeps.*

Pritchard, James B. "More inscribed jar handles from El-Jib." *Bulletin of the American Schools of Oriental Research 160* (1960): 2–6. *Editio princeps.*

Reisner, George Andrew, Clarence Stanley Fisher and David Gordon Lyon. *Harvard Excavations at Samaria: 1908–1910,* vol. 1: *Text.* Cambridge, MA: Harvard University Press, 1924. *Editio princeps.*

Rollston, Christopher A. "Ben Sira 38:24–39:11 and the *Egyptian Satire of the Trades*: A reconsideration." *Journal of Biblical Literature 120* (2001):131–9. Synopsis of ancient statements about scribes.

Rollston, Christopher A. "Scribal education in ancient Israel: The Old Hebrew epigraphic evidence." *Bulletin of the American Schools of Oriental Research 344* (2006): 47–74. Discussion of epigraphic evidence for scribal curricula.

Rollston, Christopher A. "The dating of the Early Royal Byblian (Phoenician): A response to Benjamin Sass." *Maarav 15* (2008): 57–93. Synopsis of evidence for dates for earliest Phoenician inscriptions.

Rollston, Christopher A. "The Phoenician script of the Tel Zayit abecedary and putative evidence for Israelite literacy." In Ron E. Tappy and P. Kyle McCarter (eds), *Literature, Culture and Tenth-Century Canaan: The Tel Zayit Abecedary in Context* (pp. 61–96). Winona Lake, IN: Eisenbrauns, 2008. Discussion of literacy in ancient Israel.

Rollston, Christopher A. *Writing and Literacy in the World of Ancient Israel: Epigraphic Evidence from the Iron Age*. Archaeology and Biblical Studies 11. Atlanta: Society of Biblical Literature, 2010. Monograph on ancient writing in Levant.

Schniedewind, William M. *How the Bible Became a Book*. Cambridge: Cambridge University Press, 2004. Synopsis of origins of Hebrew Bible, using epigraphy and archaeology.

Tur-Sinai (Torczyner), H., L. Harding, A. Lewis, and J. L. Starkey. *Lachish I (Tell ed-Duweir): The Lachish Letters*. London: Oxford University Press, 1938. *Editio princeps*.

van der Toorn, Karel. *Scribal Culture and the Making of the Hebrew Bible*. Cambridge, MA: Harvard University Press, 2007. Focus on Mesopotamian writing and status of scribes.

Young, Ian M. "Israelite literacy: Interpreting the evidence, Part I." *Vetus Testamentum 48* (1998): 239–53.

Young, Ian M. "Israelite literacy: Interpreting the evidence, Part II." *Vetus Testamentum 48* (1998): 408–22. Tandem articles demonstrating that in the Hebrew Bible, it is elites who are said to have read and written.

Part II
Political History

A
Origins

Origins

CHAPTER 9

The Emergence of Israel and Theories of Ethnogenesis

Avraham Faust

From the mid 1920s – when Albrecht Alt published his monograph on the Israelite settlement in Canaan – to the mid-1990s, the most heated debate in biblical archaeology concerned the Israelite settlement in Canaan.[1] Various schools of thought – peaceful infiltration, military conquest, social revolution, evolution, and more – offered competing reconstructions of the process by which the Israelites settled the central hill country and its timing. From the mid-1990s, as a result of various developments that will be briefly addressed, doubts were cast on the identification of the highland settlers as Israelites. Consequently, one of the hottest debates in biblical archaeology today concerns Israel's first appearance on the historical scene as a group. From which point in history can we speak of an ethnic group by the name Israel?

Identity and Origins: A Cautionary Note

While the question of Israelite origins is, of course, interesting, it is, contrary to the prevalent view, not directly related to the issue discussed here and to the understanding of the nature and formation of Israelite ethnicity. As the vast anthropological and archaeological literature clearly indicates, from the moment the Israelites began to see themselves as distinct they became so, and should be treated accordingly by modern scholarship (cf. Barth; Emberling). The question of their origin – whether their ancestors were slaves in Egypt, seminomads in Transjordan or in the central highlands, Canaanite peasants, or a combination of some or all of the above – is of lesser importance for the present discussion, as interesting and important as it may be.

Past Research on the Emergence of Israel: A Brief Summary

The archaeological phenomenon which was viewed as the Israelite Settlement in Canaan is well known, and most of its components (though not its interpretation) are

The Wiley Blackwell Companion to Ancient Israel, First Edition. Edited by Susan Niditch.
© 2016 John Wiley & Sons, Ltd. Published 2016 by John Wiley & Sons, Ltd.

agreed upon. The following quote from Dever ("From tribe to nation," 215–16) nicely sums up the main points, and there would only be minor disagreements on the details:

> In the late 13th–12th centuries B.C. there occurred a major influx of new settlers into the hill country, especially from Jerusalem northward to Shechem. Hundreds of small villages were now established, not on the remains of destroyed or abandoned Late Bronze Age Urban Canaanite sites, but de novo. These villages are characterized chiefly by their hilltop location and lack of defensive walls; densely arranged "four-room" or courtyard houses of very stereotyped plan; an abundance of cisterns and silos for storage of water and foodstuffs; intensive cultivation of nearby terraced hillsides; a ceramic repertoire that is basically derived from Late Bronze Age Canaanite pottery types, but contains some new elements that are characteristic of isolated and poor rural areas; the increasing use of iron implements; and, above all, an "egalitarian" material culture that shows little sign of social stratification.

During the Late Bronze Age, Canaan was an Egyptian province. The locations and material remains of the Iron I agricultural villages indicate a rather different lifestyle from that of the Late Bronze Age, whose settlements were concentrated mainly in the valleys and plains and were highly stratified. The Iron Age settlements were rural and concentrated in an area that was relatively uninhabited in the preceding centuries (Finkelstein, *Archaeology*). Their inhabitants lived in the forerunners of a new type of building, called the three- or four-room house (see Francesca Stavrakopoulou's essay in this volume). The finds from the Iron Age hill country villages were poor and rudimentary. While pottery forms had Late Bronze Age antecedents, the assemblages typically included a limited pottery repertoire, consisting of cooking pots, bowls, and storage jars, which were mainly of the collared-rim type (Faust).

Until the 1990s, scholarly consensus held that these settlers constituted "early Israel," corresponding to the period of the Judges in the Hebrew Bible (Finkelstein, *Archaeology*, including references). This concept was based on the reasonable assumption that the settlement of the Israelite tribes as mentioned in the Hebrew Bible was synonymous with the material remains uncovered by archaeologists, a seemingly secure identification in light of the mentioning of Israel as an ethnic group in the Merenptah Stele, dating to the end of the thirteenth century BCE.

The material culture of these sites was seen, therefore, in the tradition of the dominant culture history school (discussed below), as representing the Israelites. This approach can be exemplified by the various attempts made to deduce the Israelite character of Megiddo Stratum VI from the presence of several characteristics, mainly the collared-rim jar.[2]

Gradually, however, serious doubts were cast on the direct equation of these material remains with the Israelites. Criticism focused on the discrepancy between the territories supposedly inhabited by Israelites, and the distribution of their assumed material markers. According to Ibrahim, for example, the presence of both four-room houses and collared-rim jars in Transjordan outside of the area of the Israelite settlement is clearly problematic evidence. Ibrahim believes that the appearance of the collared-rim jars in the Jordan Valley, the Ammonite region, and north of this area poses a problem for those who accept the proposal that these jars were associated with the Israelites (123). He concludes that the presence of the collared-rim jar cannot be attributed to any specific ethnic group, and that the long use of this vessel "ought to be considered in connection with a social-economic tradition" (124). However, Ibrahim did not offer any specific explanations for the distribution or longevity of the collared-rim jar.

Similar discrepancies were observed in the distribution of the four-room house. These houses have been uncovered both in Transjordan and in the coastal plain (e.g., Finkelstein, "Ethnicity," 204–5), leading many scholars to conclude that the unique connection between this building type and the Israelites is incorrect, and that the four-room house, just like the collared-rim jars, should be explained by its functionality and suitability for life in highland farming communities; however, since artifacts can be both functional and symbolic, the division between the two is artificial (Hodder and Hutson 71). These explanations were in implicit accordance with the adaptation spirit of the New Archaeology which began to exert some (usually indirect) influence on biblical archaeology. The New Archaeology, explored in detail below, eschewed normative approaches to culture, that is, that norms prescribe practices and behaviors of members of different groups, and so are responsible for the creation of different archaeological cultures.

This scholarly trend was also accompanied by a more cautious approach to the issue of identifying ethnic groups in the archaeological record – what has been called "pots and peoples." While a cautious and even negative approach was typical of the New Archaeology (e.g., Jones 5, 26–7; more below), it had only an indirect influence on Syro-Palestinian archaeology. Moreover, although these two lines of criticism – the problematic distribution of traits on the one hand and the indirect impact of the skepticism of the New Archaeology toward the study of ethnicity on the other – occurred together, it should be stressed that they are not complementary, and may even be contradictory, as we shall see below. Both, however, have gradually raised doubts over the once-popular identification of the Israelites with the above-mentioned material traits.

Various scholars have also pointed to the heterogeneity of early Iron Age society in the region, and to the fact that there is no evidence that the highlands' "material culture" was distinctively Israelite, as opposed to being Jebusite, Gibeonite, Kenite, Hivite, or belonging to any other group which, according to the Bible, inhabited the region at the time. The texts indicated that, although the area was inhabited only by Israelites during Iron Age II, there were other groups in the region during Iron Age I, such as the Gibeonites, Joshua 9; the Jebusites, Judges 19:10–11; 2 Samuel 5:5–7; and many others. Since the attempts to identify more than one "archaeological culture" in the region seem to have failed, many scholars concluded that the Israelites could not be identified.

Indeed, the problems with Iron I ethnic labels initially concentrated on the question of how to distinguish an Israelite from a member of any of the other groups who inhabited the region at the time according to the Bible. However, basic concepts of the "culture history" school were never questioned, and the dissatisfaction of many scholars with the Israelite label attached to the highland material culture stemmed from a culture history approach. That is, archaeologists were unable to differentiate between an Israelite culture and other archaeological cultures in the archaeological record.

In the late 1980s, London offered a more sophisticated solution to this problem. She suggested that the distinction between the "Israelite" and other settlements should be viewed as resulting from socioeconomic differences, such as rural versus urban. Variations, therefore, reflect diverse cultural elements within the same ethnic group. This is a more sophisticated solution since it is based on the understanding that material culture is not a direct and simple representation of an ethnic group and requires the consideration of other factors. On the other hand, London's work reflects unfamiliarity with the data from lowland villages at the time.

With these challenges, the validity of the Israelite ethnic label on the settlers in the highlands became increasingly doubted. Finkelstein suggested that we should treat all groups living in the Iron I highlands as Israelites on the rationale that regardless of their ethnic affiliation during Iron I, they became Israelite from the tenth century BCE onward after the formation of the monarchy(*Archaeology*, 27–8).

Finkelstein's solution was a subject of criticism, particularly by Skjeggestand. The critics based much of their argumentations on Finkelstein's misleading conclusion that the Iron Age pottery from the highlands was very different from its Late Bronze Age predecessor (Skjeggestand 170 n24; Dever, "Ceramics"; see also Faust 65–70). The assumption was that the similarity in pottery forms (and perhaps in other traits as well) between the Late Bronze Age and Iron Age I indicates continuity in population and culture, therefore invalidating the applicability of the term Israelite for these (Canaanite) settlers. Since, however, there is no reason to assume that pottery *forms* are necessarily ethnically sensitive (see below), this criticism was much less important for the present discussion than is usually thought, and led in a wrong direction.

In order to avoid the problem, W. G. Dever suggested calling the highlands' Iron I population "Proto-Israelite" (e.g., "Ceramics," 206–7). Dever's rationale seems to have been based on his awareness that this population had indeed constituted an ethnic group, and that this, together with the mentioning of Israel in the Merenptah Stela and the continuity of material culture from Iron I to Iron II in the hill country (when there is no doubt about the identity of the population), is sufficient justification to use the term. Like Finkelstein, he partially relied upon the consensus on the Iron Age II reality as a basis for conclusions on a previous period.

At the same time, however, the minimalist school was established, and questioned the relevance of the term Israel to Iron Age society, beginning with Iron I, but continuing this skepticism well into Iron II. The school is also referred to as the deconstructionist, nihilistic, and Copenhagen school, and is led by Niels Peter Lemche, Thomas L. Thompson, Keith W. Whitelam and Philip R. Davies. Although they differ on some matters, their views are similar enough to label them as a school. Even the existence of ancient Israel has been questioned, thus dragging the debate to other grounds. This is not the place for a detailed discussion of this school and its ideological views (see Faust for previous literature), but it should be emphasized that these scholars have usually offered no new evidence or even new insights into the discussion. None are archaeologists, and their writings usually show lack of familiarity both with archaeological theory and archaeological data (see Dever, *Archaeology*, 46; Faust, including references). They have greatly influenced academic discourse, however, especially in their denial of Israelite ethnicity.

Within this new intellectual environment, Finkelstein reexamined the archaeological evidence for Israel's existence in the highlands during Iron Age I and took a more critical stance. Referencing earlier papers by Dever – whose titles included the phrase, "Will the real Israel please stand up?" – he wrote a paper whose title included the question "Can the real Israel stand up?" There, he claimed that since the pottery forms continue Late Bronze Age antecedents and the characteristic architectural forms of the highlands are found in the lowlands and Transjordan, these cannot be seen as Israelite. He observed that the only criterion that can be used to infer the presence of Israelites at the time is the absence of pig bones (Finkelstein, "Ethnicity," 206). Yet, although this criterion was available, he concluded that the Israelites cannot be recognized in the Iron Age I archaeological record, but only in that of Iron II (209).

Views of Israelite ethnicity were thus increasingly skeptical until recently. Although those dealing with the archaeology of ancient Israel still work to a large extent in the tradition of the culture history school, ironically, it seems that the evaluation of ethnicity – the center of this approach – has changed. This is not so much a result of methodological changes, since, as noted above, the methodologies and approaches of the New (processual) Archaeology and subsequent schools did not have a direct impact on the archaeology of the Land of Israel (for more sophisticated treatments, see recently Bloch-Smith; see also Elizabeth Bloch-Smith's essay in this volume). The prevalent skepticism concerning Israelite ethnicity results more from an apparent failure of the conservative culture-history approach to account for the variability and distribution of the finds. This situation was exacerbated by the indirect influence of the negative views of the New Archaeology to the study of ethnicity in general. This skeptical approach is beginning to change (e.g., Elizabeth Bloch-Smith, Ann E. Killebrew, Avraham Faust) and as we shall see below is unwarranted.

Before developing the question of Israel's emergence in Canaan, however, a few words on the archaeology of ethnicity are in order.

Archaeology and Ethnicity: Background

The Culture History School

Archaeologists have always attempted to identify ethnic groups in the archaeological record. This endeavor was more or less the main agenda of the culture history school, the dominant archaeological paradigm during most of the twentieth century. Archaeologists working in this tradition equated "archaeological cultures," identified by their material culture, with ethnic groups (e.g., Trigger, Jones). Childe (v–vi) succinctly explains the rationale for this approach: "We find certain types of remains – pots, implements, ornaments, burial rites and house forms – constantly recurring together. Such a complex of associated traits we shall term 'cultural group' or just a 'culture.' We assume that such a complex is the material expression of what today would be called a 'people.'" This approach was based on a normative understanding of culture, that is, that norms or rules of behavior prescribe the practices and behaviors of members of any given group, as a result of shared ideas, worldviews, and beliefs (e.g., Jones 24).

The New (Processual) Archaeology

The New Archaeology, which evolved in the 1960s and later came to be known as processual archaeology, generally failed to direct much attention to the identification of ethnic groups (e.g., Jones 5, 26–7, 111). This school grew out of the dissatisfaction with the "unscientific" nature of the culture history school, specifically its inductive approach, its lack of rigorous scientific procedures, its descriptive nature, and, most important for our purposes, its normative approach to culture. Much discussion was devoted to adaptation. The new school believed that archaeological remains were the product of a range of complex processes and not "simply a reflection of ideational norms" (Jones 26). Furthermore, adherents of the New Archaeology school were interested in generalizations and laws, and disregarded the specific and the unique. Studies of differences and uniqueness, for example studies of specific ethnic identities, were consequently inconsistent with their scientific agenda (Trigger 312–19). It is further likely that the lack of interest in discussions of ethnicity also resulted from the horrifying outcome of the racial archaeology which was so prevalent in Europe until World War II. This so-called "archaeology" collaborated with the justification of the Nazi claims of racial superiority and, as a consequence, contributed to the extermination of millions. Ethnicity was relegated to a minor role as a part of discussions on style, which were in themselves not of great concern. As the New (processual) Archaeology came into favor, therefore, the methodological foundations of the culture history school and its normative approach to culture were heavily criticized and fell into disfavor (e.g., Trigger).

Changes in Anthropological Approaches to Ethnicity

At about the same time, however, revolutionary changes were occurring in the anthropological approach to ethnicity. The most important development in the study of ethnicity in general came with the publication of *Ethnic Groups and Boundaries*. In his introduction to the book, Fredrik Barth criticizes the conventional view of ethnic groups as "culture-bearing units", by which he means groups sharing core values that find representation in cultural forms (10–13). Barth defines ethnic groups as, in essence, a form of social organization; its critical criterion is an ability to be identified and distinguished among others, or in his words, allowing "self-ascription and ascription by others" (11, 13). Ethnic identity here is not determined by biological or genetic factors but is subject to perception and is adaptable. Barth's views had an immense impact in the social sciences, and probably even more so in archaeology, so much so that in Emberling's overview of the study of ethnicity in archaeology (295; see also Jones 60), works on the subject are referred to as B.B. (before Barth) or A.B. (after Barth). Following Barth, emphasis shifted from the shared elements or characteristics of a group to the features that distinguish it from others (also Eriksen, Wimmer). It was the contact between groups that was seen as essential for the formation of the self-identity of a group, which is thus clearly manifested in its material culture. Following these developments in anthropology and sociology, archaeologists have also come to understand that ethnicity is too complex to be merely identified with a material or an archaeological culture; it is fluid, it is merely one of several attributes of an individual's complete identity, and it is subjective (e.g., McGuire; Emberling; Jones, including bibliography). This new understanding of ethnicity also seemed appropriate for several postprocessual approaches to archaeology that were beginning to develop (e.g., Jones 5–6).

Archaeology and Ethnicity: The Response

The subjective and changing nature of ethnicity, as observed in existing groups, has led some scholars to question the ability of archaeologists to identify ethnic groups in the material record of extinct societies (see Jones 109–10, 124).[3] Yet in most cases, clear relationships between material culture and ethnicity can be identified, however complicated they may be (McGuire, Emberling, and others), and the potential of archaeological inquiry to deal with such issues should not be underestimated.

   Those new approaches to ethnicity were propagated at a time of change in archaeological thinking. New/processual archaeology, at least in its original orthodox version, was the target of increasing criticism, primarily by what came to be known as postprocessual archaeologists (e.g., on various grounds, Trigger, Hodder and Hutson). The postprocessual approaches (some of them at least) reinstated a different, yet normative approach to culture which did not seek to desert older approaches entirely (Hodder and Hutson). Today archaeology is much more responsive to the study of ethnicity, acknowledging its subjective nature.

Identifying Ethnicity in the Archaeological Record: Some Preliminary Observations

It is accepted today that groups define themselves in relation to, and in contrast with, other groups (Barth; Wimmer). The ethnic boundaries of a group are not defined by the sum of cultural traits it possesses but by the idiosyncratic use of specific material and behavioral symbols as compared with other groups (McGuire 160; see also Emberling 299; Barth 14, 15). McGuire points out that overt material symbols of ethnic identity (ethnic markers: e.g., yarmulke) are the clearest evidence of the maintenance of an ethnic boundary (163). However, such markers are scarce in the archaeological record. Furthermore, grasping the symbolic significance of artifacts can be extremely difficult. While all groups may communicate messages of identity through material culture, the vehicles used differ by group, message and context. Which artifact can express a boundary of a group depends on the ideas people in that society have about what "an appropriate artifact for ethnic group marking" is (Hodder and Hutson 3), but the selection may seem arbitrary to outside observers. One group might choose elements of clothing, while another might choose ceramics. Pinpointing those elements of material culture that were meaningful to any particular group, and determining when to attribute significance to an observed variation in the distribution of certain artifacts, is therefore a complicated endeavor.

Notably, in addition to ethnic markers, ethnicity can also be identified by "ethnically specific behavior," or more accurately, by the material correlates of such behavior. Such behavioral differences might include, in McGuire's words, "variations in rubbish disposal patterns … or differences in floor plans of dwellings, which reflect differing behavioral requirements for space" (163). This ethnic behavior is much easier to identify than ethnic markers, as archaeology is to a large extent a "behavioral science." As an instructive example one can consider the "Parting Ways" site in Plymouth, Massachusetts, which was inhabited by freed African slaves following the American Revolution (Deetz 187–211). Excavations at the site revealed a material culture generally similar to that of contemporary sites, but as observed by Deetz (210), there existed real differences in house construction, trash disposal, and community arrangement as compared to these sites – differences that could have been overlooked based on a "traditional" analysis of the artifacts themselves. So it is not the artifacts themselves that necessarily carry any ethnic importance, but the use made of these artifacts that is potentially important. Another, better-known example is the lack of pig bones in Israelite sites. This is not the place to discuss the relation between pig consumption and ethnicity (Hesse; Faust 35–40, and references; see more below), but it is clear that if they bear any connection, the absence of pigs is not an ethnic marker but a result of an ethnic behavior.

It should also be noted that in many cases there are elements (artifacts, decoration, etc.) that are used to convey messages to other members of the group, and are connected to intragroup communication. In many cases, however, those elements are not spread evenly across the human landscape, and are used by members of a specific group only – the group which uses them for its intergroup communication – hence, as a by-product, they "are likely to offer not only good but the best evidence of 'ethnicity' generally preserved in the archaeological record" (David et al. 378).

Notably, social dimensions such as economic status, prestige, religion, occupation, urban or rural setting, and other factors may all affect the symbolic content of artifacts (McGuire 164; see also London; Skjeggestand 179–80; Emberling 305–6, 310–11). Contradictions between different kinds of symbols may confound interpretations even further, such as when a member of an ethnic group characterized by a low economic status attains a higher status, or in elite dwellings, when the finds might include both symbols of solidarity with the local, ethnic group and symbols of solidarity with its social peers, although these latter symbols might be mainly associated with another ethnic group. The latter message might at times contradict the former.

In order to differentiate between the various "combinations of effects," a full examination of the society should be undertaken to identify all the social dimensions relevant to material culture production and symbolization. Only after the other elements have been identified can we attribute ethnic labels to some traits of material culture. The second step, of course, should be to find the tangible connection between those material traits and the ethnic group under discussion. The difficulties inherent in any attempt to identify symbolic traits in the archaeological record require the use of a very large database, but also that attention be given to written sources. Although sometimes quite problematic, a careful examination of these sources is needed in order to extract maximum information and gain insights into the society in question.

Many scholars have stressed that ethnicity is closely related to statehood. Emberling claims that while ethnic groups are not states they exist in some relationship with them, and he mentions the connection between processes of ethnogenesis and state formation and control (304, 308). For example, ethnic identity can develop when an area inhabited by an independent group or groups is incorporated into or conquered by a state. Shenan also refers to these relations (15), and believes that ethnicity is a product of the appearance of states, adding that ethnicity "does not exist outside the orbit of early states" (16–17).

While there seems to be a near consensus regarding the close relationship of ethnicity and statehood, the relations can take one of two forms: ethnicity as a form of resistance, and ethnicity as a direct product of state activity. Emberling mentions that ethnic identity often develops when independent groups are encompassed by a state; the emergence of ethnicity can therefore be seen "as a form of resistance" (308). Wiessner, too, believes that circumstances that might activate group identity include fear, competition or aggression among groups, need for cooperation, and imposed political control that necessitates "group action" (9). Most of these, particularly the latter, can be seen as a form of group resistance to outside control. According to Smith, "ethnicism is fundamentally defensive. It is a response to outside threats and divisions within" (55; see also 38–9, 54–7). Defining oneself in resistance to pressure from the outside is therefore clearly a major mechanism of ethnogenesis.

It is also true that states can actively encourage and develop the formation of ethnic groups. Ethnicity equals, in many instances, hierarchy or asymmetrical relations (more below). It should be noted, therefore, that in some cases "the ascription of ethnic identity to a particular group of people … has, in itself, been a major mechanism of political control" used by the state (Ucko xi). The Inca state created ethnicity and formed collective identities that provided an illusion of continuity with old practices and traditions in new contexts. The ethnic groups were vertically integrated, and emphasized the linkages between them and the emerging class structure of the Inca state (Patterson 79; see also the discussion of the Inca in David Schloen's essay in this volume). And Comaroff and Comaroff concluded that for a subordinate group, ethnic association could have originated by an ascription of collective identity by others. The Betsileo of Malagasy can serve as example, as they did not always view themselves as a distinct ethnic group. Before they were conquered by the Merina, there was no Betsileo identity as such, but only several chiefdoms and statelets which were located in what later became the Betsileo homeland. The Merina created the Betsileo province, and by so doing provided the basis for Betsileo self-consciousness. In sum, ethnic consciousness "increased throughout Malagasy as a function of political consolidation" (Comaroff and Comaroff 57). Thus it is clear that the attribution of ethnic affiliation on behalf of others (a state or a dominant group) is also a major mechanism of self-definition (this can be seen in the creation of most modern states in Africa).

The two mechanisms of resistance and state activity are by no means contradictory and can very well operate together, as can clearly be seen from the observation about the situation in Malagasy. A similar situation was also observed by Patterson: "at one level this cultural transformation may involve hybridization, fusion, or even replacement by state-imposed forms; at another, it may manifest itself in resistance or attempts to assert or invert tradition" (31). The activity of a central government can both "impose" an identity on a group of people, even if they did not have this identity before, and also promote the emergence of an identity as a form of resistance to its activities; these could very well be the "same" identity. The two processes can at times be one.

We are left to conclude that ethnicity results, one way or the other, from statehood. This is not to say that a certain group must live within the physical boundaries of a state in order to have ethnic identity. It must, however, exist within the orbit of a state.

While the importance and interrelation of statehood and ethnicity are well known and have received attention, we do not know much about the situation that preceded the emergence of ethnic consciousness. It seems that part of the analysis of ethnicity by Comaroff and Comaroff, and especially the distinction they draw between ethnicity and totemism, can shed more light on this process. They claim that, while past groups had some kind of self-identification, this is not always the same as an ethnic identity. They differentiate between totemic consciousness and ethnic consciousness (51ff.). Totemism, according to them, emerges when symmetrical relations between structurally similar social groups is established (whether those groups are integrated into a single political entity or not). Ethnicity, in contrast, is developed when groups which are structurally dissimilar are incorporated into a single political economy in an asymmetric fashion. They continue:

> more specifically, totemic consciousness arises with the interaction of social units that retain – or appear from within to retain – control over the means of their own production and reproduction. It is, in short, a function of processes in which autonomous groupings enter into relations of equivalence or complementary interdependence and, in so doing, fashion their collective identities by contrast to one another. (54–5)

According to Comaroff and Comaroff, ethnicity has certain qualities: (1) a subjective classification of the world into social entities; and (2) a stereotypical attribution of these groupings, usually in a hierarchical way, into niches in the social division of labor (52). Neither of these qualities is unique to ethnic consciousness. The first exists in totemism, while the latter in class. It is, however, in the combination of the two that the uniqueness of ethnicity lies. They add that for the subordinate group, ethnic affiliation may be ascribed to them by others (53). At times, the creation of such identities has no foundation in preexisting sociological reality, but even when a social identity has been assigned to them, subordinate groups usually classify their "new" identity as a symbol of a common predicament and interest, and this may lead to an assertion of shared commitment to a system of symbols and meanings (53).

It should be stressed that the difference between totemic consciousness and ethnic consciousness is not a chronological or an evolutionary one. There were ethnic groups in precolonial Africa, and totemism exists in the modern world. The difference lies in the context; in other words, the division of "us" versus "them" is primordial – and only the form of the division depends on the historical context (54). According to Comaroff and Comaroff, "ethnicity always has its genesis in specific historical forces, forces which are simultaneously structural and cultural" (50). It exists when there is inequality between groups (52–5).

Despite the differences, however, ethnicity and totemism share many qualities. Both are manners of social classification and social consciousness, denoting group identity (53). We should therefore stress that the dichotomy between totemism and ethnicity, as important an analytical tool as it is, is somewhat misleading. After all, we are dealing with a continuum, and there might be cases when it will be difficult to identify whether a certain group is an ethnic or a totemic one. Moreover, it is likely that the developmental process from one to another is not linear, that is, not a one-directional evolutionary process.

Finally, we should note that due to the prevalence of the European world-system, most groups with which anthropologists were in contact were already interacting with states, or in other words, were involved in asymmetrical relations. Hence, the reality before this interaction, for instance, that of totemic groups, is still far less understood. Thus, after evaluating a variety of evidence for the emergence of ethnicity in tandem with or prior to that of states, Emberling believes that this is an "empiric question" (308), since social boundaries in prestate societies are not well known (see also Smith 41). I believe that Iron I as a case study is sufficiently detailed, and can therefore contribute to these neglected aspects of research into the question of identity.

The Emergence of Israel in the Iron Age

Following these observations, we will try to identify ethnic traits during Iron Age II – a period in which practically all archaeologists agree that there were Israelites – and then we will go backward in time in order to identify the historical context in which those traits could have become ethnically meaningful (not their first time of appearance: Faust). In short, patterns of behavior and material items that seem meaningful during Iron Age II include the following.

It is well known that the Iron Age (both Iron I and II) highland pottery in particular and the pottery in Israel and Judah in general was nondecorated (e.g., Dever, "Ceramics," 205; Mazar 290; Bloch-Smith and Alpert Nakhai 76). While practiced already in Iron Age I, this characteristic is much more noticeable in Iron Age II, when many of the nearby polities/cultures did use decorated pottery, sometimes extensively (Faust 41–8). Decoration on pottery is used to convey messages of various sorts (David et al.; Faust, including references), and the *lack* of any decoration is a very suitable channel for a message of egalitarianism and simplicity. While a full discussion of style is beyond the scope of the present paper (e.g., David et al.), suffice it here to refer, as an illuminative example, to an interesting parallel. In his discussion of "early American life" James Deetz came to the conclusion that "Puritans' attitudes toward decoration of everyday objects might have had an effect on the delftware industry in the London area in the form of reduction of the amount of decorated pottery before the Restoration" (81). He, moreover, applied the same type of interpretation to the lack of decoration on various artifacts in Anglo-America, which was subsequently explained by Puritans' attitudes (81–2). I believe that we are witnessing a similar situation in which an ethos (of a different type, of course) is responsible for the "simple" pottery and for the lack of decoration. This trait is very noticeable already in Iron Age I, when it stands in contrast to the reality in the lowlands regions at the time, as well as to the situation during the closing phase of the Late Bronze Age.[4]

Another well-known trait is the lack of imported pottery in the highlands during Iron I, and throughout most regions of the kingdoms of Israel and Judah in Iron II (e.g., Dever, "Ceramics," 204; Bloch-Smith and Alpert Nakhai 76). Obviously, this trait is much more significant in the Iron II, following the resumption of trade in the eastern Mediterranean (Faust), but it is manifested in the Iron Age I by the almost total absence of Philistine pottery in the highlands, while it is found in areas much farther away from Philistia, for instance, in the northern valleys. Note that the lack of imports is not a result of the highlands' remote location, as can be seen in the wealth of importation during the Late Bronze Age. The lack of imported pottery, and for Iron I we are referring mainly to the lack of Philistine bichrome pottery, seems also to reflect the same ethos of simplicity.

Ever since the early studies by Hesse it has been well known that Philistines consumed large amounts of pork, while the Israelites did not. This cannot be attributed to ecology of course, as in other periods the highland population consumed pork (Faust and Katz), while the population in the coastal plain sometimes consumed much smaller quantities of pigs. Although they were not the only ones to avoid pork, it is clear that Israelites did not consume this type of meat, and whenever pigs are a significant part of the faunal assemblage one may deduce that the site was not Israelite. Notably, the significance of pork is accepted even by skeptical scholars, and Finkelstein, for example, notes that pig taboos appear to be the main – if not the only – trait that can be used to learn about the ethnic identity of the population during Iron Age I ("Ethnicity," 206). Interestingly, while the Israelites of the highlands avoided pork, the Philistines even enlarged its percentage in their diet during Iron Age I (see below). Notably, while this trait has received much discussion in relation to Iron Age I, it must be stressed that Israelites did not consume pork in Iron Age II either, and the question is in which historical context did this behavior became ethnically sensitive.

Turning to architecture, the four-room house is the dominant type of domestic building in ancient Israel from the beginning of the Iron Age until the Babylonian Exile. As such, numerous studies have been devoted to its origins and the ethnic identity of its inhabitants (see Bunimovitz and Faust, "Building identity"; Faust, including references). The high popularity of the four-room house was explained as expressing its close relation with the Israelites (without elaborating the reasons for this relation) and/or its functional suitability to the needs of the Iron Age peasants, regardless of their ethnicity. The former was viewed as simplistic and was abandoned by many in favor of the latter. Still, this functional explanation fails to account for the synchronic and diachronic dominance of the four-room house as a preferable architectural type in all levels of Iron Age settlement (from cities to hamlets and farmsteads), all over the country (both in highlands and lowlands), for almost 600 years(!). Moreover, the plan served as a template not only for dwellings, but also for public buildings, and even for the late Iron Age Judahite tombs. The fact that the house disappeared in the sixth century BCE seems also to refute any "functional" explanation, as no changes in peasant life and no architectural or agricultural inventions took place at the time. We have therefore suggested that an adequate explanation for the unique phenomenon of the four-room house must relate to the ideological/cognitive realm (Bunimovitz and Faust, "Building identity"; Faust, including references). Some of its architectural characteristics (a few of them revealed by Access Analysis, which is the analysis of spatial relationships in buildings) reflect Israelite values and ethnic behavior: for example, egalitarian ethos, purity, privacy, and cosmology. These are reflected in the spatial syntax of the house, as well as in the biblical text. Moreover, it appears that the Israelites were preoccupied with order, and hence once this kind of house became typical, it eventually became the appropriate and "right" one. It is thus the dialectic between function, process, and mind that created the "Israelite house" which, once crystallized, survived for hundreds of years and disappeared following the destruction of the kingdoms of Israel and Judah, when its creators and maintainers lost coherence and were dispersed. The house crystallized in its current form in Iron II, and it is quite clear that at this time it served the Israelite population, even if other people could still have used it (and evidence for that is very limited at best). It can, therefore, be labeled an Israelite house, and the key question is when it became part of Israelite ethnic behavior or an Israelite ethnic marker.

While there are also other markers/forms of ethnic behavior, suffice it here to state that the common denominator of many of the above-mentioned traits as well as others, such as burial in simple inhumations in the ground during most of this period and the limited use of royal inscriptions in the monarchic period, is an ethos of simplicity and perhaps even a form of egalitarian ideology. This ethos may well have been used by the Israelites to define their boundaries in relation to other, more hierarchical groups. In short, this ethos helped to differentiate them from others.

Can we trace these traits back into Iron Age I – the premonarchic period in biblical terms? When did those traits become ethnically sensitive and in what historical context? The answer will, it is hoped, allow us to determine when these people emerged as a group with a unique identity and self-awareness, negotiating its identity with or against other groups in Iron Age I.

The Historical Context for the Emergence of Israelite Traits: Israel and the Philistines

Some of the Israelite traits seem like a straightforward way to differentiate this group from the Philistines. The consumption of pork among the Philistines peaked in the final phases of Iron Age I: more than 20 percent of the diet in places where data are available. Canaanite sites exhibit either a low level of pork consumption, for example in Qubur el-Walaydah, or an avoidance of pigs, for example in Beth-Shemesh; cf. Faust and Katz. In most cases (Gath being an exception) this decreases dramatically during Iron Age II (Faust and Lev-Tov, including references). Therefore the time in which avoidance of pork could have become a meaningful ethnic trait must have been Iron Age I, and not later. Interestingly, while some question the sensitivity of even this trait for studying ethnicity in the Iron Age, it appears that new data further support its significance. Detailed data on the percentage of pork in a number of Iron I levels at Ekron show that while the Philistines consumed pork from the time of their arrival – no doubt food habits that carried no ethnic meaning at the time of their initial settlement – they gradually increased the percentage of pork in their diet during Iron I: from 14 percent to 26 percent in the course of some 150 years (see detailed discussion in Faust and Lev-Tov). Later, in Iron IIA, the percentage of pork in the Philistine diet shrank dramatically, hence pointing not only to its ethnic sensitivity in the Iron I, but also to the fact that Iron I was the only possible historical context for the emergence of this trait as an Israelite-specific ethnic behavior.

The tradition of not decorating pottery could also reflect an attempt to differentiate the Iron Age I highlands settlers from the Philistines, whose pottery was highly deco- rated. The Philistine decorated pottery of Iron Age I disappears during the transition to Iron Age II; hence, the absence of decorated pottery could have become an ethnic marker only in Iron Age I. Notably, Philistine pottery was clearly ethnically sensitive in Iron I, as can be seen in its very bounded distribution, that is, its complete absence in the Egyptian-Canaanite centers of the first half of the twelfth century BCE (Bunimovitz and Faust, "Chronological separation"). The fact that this pottery was ethnically sensi- tive is attested not only by its absence in Egyptian-Canaanite and, later, Israelite settle- ments, but also from sites within Philistia, as the percentage of this decorated pottery grew throughout Iron Age I, before completely disappearing in Iron IIA (Faust and Lev- Tov).

This is true for other traits as well, but these examples are enough to show that these behavioral patterns could not have been created after Iron Age I. These factors alone make it highly unlikely that Israelite ethnic identity was created only in Iron Age II, and clearly point to Iron I as the time of Israel's ethnogenesis.

It is worth mentioning briefly the issue of circumcision. This trait can hardly be dis- cussed on the basis of archaeological reasoning, but other lines of evidence clearly con- nect this trait with the Philistines. It is quite clear that the term "uncircumcised" is used in the Bible as an ethnic marker, and since many of the local population of the region practiced circumcision, the trait could have served as a marker only in relation to the Philistines who were foreign and uncircumcised (Bloch-Smith 415). Interestingly, the pejorative term "uncircumcised" is used only in texts that relate to Iron Age I; thus it appears that the Philistines adopted circumcision during Iron Age II as part of their acculturation process (see also Herodotus II:104). In other words, circumcision may have been practiced earlier but have become ethnically significant only as a result of the interaction with the Philistines, and this could have occurred only during the Iron Age I.

The Historical Background for the Israelite–Philistine Interaction

At the end of Iron Age I and during the transition to Iron Age II, that is, the eleventh and beginning of the tenth century BCE, many highland settlements were abandoned. The population became concentrated in fewer settlements that, as a result, became larger. All the famous small Iron Age I "settlement sites," such as Giloh, Khirbet Rad- dana, Ai, Izbet Sartah, Mount Ebal and many others, were abandoned, while sites like Tell en-Nasbeh (Mizpah), Dan, Bethel and others grew significantly in size, and eventu- ally became towns in Iron Age II. The explanation for this process of abandonment is, first and foremost, the Philistine military and economic pressure on the highlands, and especially in the hills of Judah and the territory of Benjamin and southern Samaria. The Israelite-Philistine confrontation reached a peak in this period. Although only the culmination of a long process, this appears to be the historical context in which the already-existing patterns of behavior that contrasted the Philistines with the Israelites could become ethnically sensitive and significant. This Philistine military and economic pressure simply added new meaning to Israelite customs. Traits like circumcision and avoidance of pork became symbols of ethnic identity that ethnically differentiated one group from the other. Facing the "enemy" or "other," such as the Philistines who came from the southern coastal plain (and originally from the Aegean world), the highland settlers reinforced a "contrasting" identity that stressed components that were very different from those of the Philistines. Since the latter consumed pork, the Israelites made the avoidance of pork into a "flag" that was used to show how different they were. The same is true for the tradition of using simple pottery. When facing the Philistine threat, the undecorated highland pottery became meaningful in contrast to the highly decorated pottery that the Philistines used.

This would seem sufficient to answer the question as to when Israelite ethnic identity existed: in the eleventh century BCE, within the context of the escalating conflict with the Philistines and the latter's encroachment from the coastal plain into the highlands. The highland settlers, who had a "simpler," totemic form of identity until then, developed an ethnic consciousness because of the asymmetrical confrontation with the much stronger and dominant Philistines (cf. Comaroff and Comaroff; see also McGuire; Emberling; Shennan).

Merenptah's Israel

There are a few problems with the above scenario, or, to be more precise, a few parts seem to be missing from the puzzle. While some ethnic patterns of behavior seem to result from the confrontation with the Philistines, there was a more appropriate "other" in Canaan in contrast to whom the avoidance of imported pottery, the usage of undecorated pottery, and the development of an egalitarian ethos, could have become meaningful (although all could be explained also against the Philistine background). All those traits (and others) could have resulted from interaction of the highland settlers with the highly hierarchical (Egyptian-ruled) Canaanite society in the closing years of the Late Bronze Age – namely, the Canaanite society and the Egypto-Canaanite political system.

Another factor that makes it difficult to attribute Israel's ethnogenesis only to the interaction with the Philistines in the eleventh century is the mention of Israel already in the late thirteenth century BCE in the Merenptah Stele. This indicates that in the thirteenth century the Egyptians were already familiar with a group by that name. Although the Merenptah Stele does not provide us with precise information regarding the location of this "Israel" or the size or composition of the group, it is more than tempting to connect it with the hundreds of settlements founded at this time in the highland regions of Canaan – exactly where the later Israel is agreed to have existed.

In the Late Bronze Age, the period just preceding Iron Age I, Egypt ruled Canaan. In this period, decorated pottery and imported wares were common in Canaan, indeed more common than in practically any other period, including the eleventh century BCE. At this time pottery was imported, mainly from the Aegean and Cyprus, but also from other places. It is found in large quantities throughout Canaan, at practically every site. Not only is most of this pottery decorated, but so is much of the local pottery. A similar situation prevails with respect to burials. We are familiar with hundreds of burials from the Late Bronze Age in Canaan, in dozens of different forms. This ends with Iron Age I – a period from which almost no burials are known in the highlands because the population was interred in simple inhumations.

In short, the lack of the Late Bronze Age Canaanite distinctive symbols in the highland settlements signifies a deliberate act of differentiation, and seems to indicate that the avoidance of traits like imported pottery or decoration on pottery, and even the emergence of the egalitarian ethos itself, gained their importance at that time. It appears, therefore, that the thirteenth century BCE is the best candidate for the emergence of "Israel," as attested not only in the Merenptah Stele, but also in the archaeological record. Circumcision and the avoidance of pork are the only patterns that seem to be associated only with the differentiation from the Philistines in a later period.

Israel's Ethnogenesis: A Chronological Summary

It appears that the beginning of the settlement process in the highlands (on both sides of the Jordan River), in the second half of the thirteenth century BCE, was accompanied by hostile relations between, on the one hand, the Egyptian rulers and administration in Canaan as well as the Canaanite city-states, and, on the other hand, the highland settlers. The latter were apparently pushed (or restricted) to the hilly and remote region by the Egyptian administration that strengthened its hold over Canaan at the time. The highland settlers had an asymmetrical relationship with the powerful Egyptian overlords and the Canaanite cities. Asymmetrical relations between groups typically result in the creation of groups with ethnic consciousness (Comaroff and Comaroff), and it is therefore to be expected that the highland settlers would develop a distinct ethnic identity under those circumstances. This is the Israel that is mentioned in the Merenptah Stele.

This highland group defined itself as egalitarian in contrast to the highly stratified and diverse Canaanite society, and avoided the use of imported or decorated pottery that was prevalent in Canaan at the time. Decorated and imported wares were a kind of nonverbal communication of Canaanite society in the Late Bronze Age. The differences were important to the various groups living there at the time. Complete avoidance of imported and decorated wares transmitted an even stronger message of difference.

During the twelfth century BCE the Egyptian rulers withdrew from the Land of Israel. The Canaanite city-state system that characterized the Late Bronze Age was weakened, and lost whatever influence it had had in the highlands. At this point the highland settlers had little interaction with the people of the lowlands. With the absence of any significant external "other," the highland settlers maintained a symmetrical relationship among themselves, that is, each group of settlers interacted mainly with similar groups, and had no connection with a larger or stronger group from outside the highlands. Since it is agreed that ethnic consciousness is promoted by asymmetrical, or hierarchical, relations between groups, it is likely that the symmetrical relationship that characterized this time period led to the stressing of "simpler" forms of identity (sometimes labeled totemic identities; Comaroff and Comaroff). In more daily language we can call those identities "local" or "tribal."

During the eleventh century BCE the highland population once again confronted a powerful external "other" – the Philistines. By that time the Philistines had an economic interest in various regions of Judah and probably also southern Samaria. This strong external pressure led the highlanders to stress their ethnic identity, in relation to the Philistine "other." In the new ethnic negotiation that ensued, many of the former relevant traits were renegotiated and were vested with new meanings (i.e., undecorated pottery, avoidance of imported pottery, and even the egalitarian ethos), along with new components that were deemed appropriate in the new context (e.g., circumcision and the avoidance of pork). All this left its mark on Israelite identity for hundreds of years, often through a repetitive process of negotiation and renegotiation, and some of those patterns are visible even today.

The "Israel" that is mentioned in the Merenptah Stele is indeed the "Israel" of the Iron Age. And it can be identified archaeologically. The rich archaeological database, and its analysis with appropriate tools, allow us to trace the Israelites and to decipher many of the internal and external processes that characterized the group from the beginning of the Iron Age onward.

Notes

1   This article has been developed from my 2006 volume *Israel's Ethnogenesis* (updated following subsequent research).
2   Most studies of Israelite ethnicity studied identity at the site level, e.g., whether the inhabitants of Megiddo VI were Israelites, Canaanites or Philistines. Many ancient sites, however, were inhabited by members of more than one ethnic group (the proximity of several groups at a single site often tended to increase boundary maintenance between them; Barth 9–10), and the study of ethnicity must be conducted on the household level.
3   Some claim that ethnicity is modern, but this view seems unfounded (e.g., Smith, Banks, Comaroff and Comaroff, and others), and need not be discussed here.
4   It had been claimed that Iron I pottery in the highlands was simple due to the harshness of the life in the region. This is a problematic explanation in any context, as decorating pottery was carried out also by simple societies and in very basic circumstances, and it is clearly untrue when addressing the reality in the Iron Age II.

Bibliography

Banks, Marcus. *Ethnicity: Anthropological Constructions.* London: Routledge, 1996. An anthropological study of the construction of ethnic identities.
Barth, Fredrik. "Introduction." In Fredrik Barth (ed.), *Ethnic Groups and Boundaries* (pp. 9–38). Boston: Little, Brown, 1969. An important article, which changed the way modern scholarship perceived ethnicity.
Bloch-Smith, Elizabeth. "Israelite ethnicity in Iron I: Archaeology preserves what is remembered and what is forgotten in Israel's history." *Journal of Biblical Literature 122* (2003): 401–25. An

updated attempt to study Israelite ethnicity on the basis of the biblical texts and archaeological finds.

Bloch-Smith, Elizabeth and Beth Alpert Nakhai. "A landscape comes to life: The Iron I period." *Near Eastern Archaeology 62* (1999): 62–127. A summary of the archaeological finds in Iron I Israel.

Bunimovitz, Shlomo and Avraham Faust. "Chronological separation, geographical segregation or ethnic demarcation? Ethnography and the Iron Age low chronology." *Bulletin of the American Schools of Oriental Research 322* (2001): 1–10. A study of the use of pottery to demarcate social boundaries between the Philistines and the Egyptian-Canaanite system in the first half of the twelfth century BCE.

Bunimovitz, Shlomo and Avraham Faust. "Building identity: The four room house and the Israelite mind." In W. G. Dever and S. Gitin (eds), *Symbiosis, Symbolism and the Power of the Past: Canaan, Ancient Israel and Their Neighbors from the Late Bronze Age through Roman Palestine* (pp. 411–23). Winona Lake, IN: Eisenbrauns, 2003. A study of the four-room house, its use and symbolism.

Childe, Vere Gordon. *The Danube in Prehistory.* Oxford: Oxford University Press, 1929. A classic archaeological work, representing the culture-history approach.

Comaroff, John and Jean Comaroff. *Ethnography and Historical Imagination.* Boulder, CO: Westview Press, 1992. An anthropological study which presents important insights into the study of ethnicity.

David, Nicholas, Judy Sterner, and Kodzo Gavua. "Why pots are decorated." *Current Anthropology 29* (1988): 365–89. Study of the significance of decoration on pottery, with important implications for the study of ethnicity.

Deetz, James. *In Small Things Forgotten: An Archaeology of Early American Life.* New York: Anchor, 1996. A classic study of historical archaeology that presents important insights into the way material culture reflects and shapes human behavior.

Dever, William G. *Archaeology and Biblical Studies: Retrospects and Prospects.* Chicago: Seabury-Western Theological Seminary, 1974. Brief series of lectures given on the relationship of archaeology and biblical studies.

Dever, William G. "From tribe to nation: State formation processes in ancient Israel." In S. Mazzoni (ed.), *Nuove fondazioni nel vicino oriente antico. Realtà e ideologia* (pp. 213–29). Pisa: Giardini, 1994. A study of Iron Age Israel.

Dever, William G. "Ceramics, ethnicity, and the questions of Israel's origins." *Biblical Archaeologist 58* (1995): 200–13. An attempt to understand Israel's origins.

Emberling, Geoff. "Ethnicity in complex societies: Archaeological perspectives." *Journal of Archaeological Research 5* (1997): 295–344. A major study of ethnicity from the perspective of archaeologists.

Eriksen, Thomas Hylland. *Ethnicity and Nationalism.* 3rd edn. London: Pluto Press, 2010. An updated study on the nature of ethnicity.

Faust, Avraham. *Israel's Ethnogenesis: Settlement, Interaction, Expansion and Resistance.* London: Equinox, 2006. A study of the development of Israelite identity in the Iron Age.

Faust, Avraham and Hayah Katz. "Philistines, Israelites and Canaanites in the Southern Trough Valley during the Iron Age I." *Egypt and the Levant 21* (2011): 231–47. Recent treatment of the detection of these ethnic groups in ancient Israel, and their interaction.

Faust, Avraham and Justin Lev-Tov. "The construction of Philistine identity: Ethnic dynamics in twelfth to tenth century Philistia." *Oxford Journal of Archaeology 30* (2011): 13–31. A study of the way Philistines, Israelites, and Canaanites interacted, and of the way they defined themselves in relation to each other.

Finkelstein, Israel. *The Archaeology of the Period of Settlement and Judges.* Jerusalem: Israel Exploration Society, 1988. A classic study of the Iron I remains in the highlands, and their association with the Israelites.

Finkelstein, Israel. "Ethnicity and the origin of the Iron I settlers in the highlands of Canaan: Can
the real Israel stand up?" *Biblical Archaeologist* 59 (1996): 98–212. A more skeptical study of
the Iron I remains and their connections to the Israelites.

Hesse, Brian. "Pig lovers and pig haters: Patterns of Palestinian pork production." *Journal of Eth-
nobiology 10* (1990): 195–225. A classic study of pork consumption in the Iron Age, and ethnic
sensitivity.

Hodder, Ian and Scott Hutson. *Reading the Past: Current Approaches to Interpretation in Archaeology.*
Cambridge: Cambridge University Press, 2004. A study of material culture, and its significance
for studying human societies.

Ibrahim, M. M. "The collared-rim jar of the early Iron age." In R. Moorey and P. Parr (eds), *Archaeology in the Levant: Essays for Kathleen Kenyon* (pp. 116–26). Warminster, UK: Aris & Phillips,
1978. A discussion of the collared-rim jars, and an attempt to disassociate them from the
Israelites.

Jones, Sian. *The Archaeology of Ethnicity: Constructing Identities in the Past and Present.* London:
Routledge, 1997. A fundamental study of the way in which ethnicity can be approached
archaeologically.

London, Gloria. "A comparison of two contemporaneous lifestyles of the late second millennium
BC." *Bulletin of the American Society for Oriental Research 273* (1989): 37–55. Argues that differences between archaeological assemblages in Israel have to do with socioeconomic class rather
than ethnicity.

Mazar, Amihai. "The Iron Age I." In A. Ben-Tor (ed.), *The Archaeology of Israel* (pp. 258–301). New
Haven: Yale University Press, 1992. A summary of the finds in Iron Age Israel.

McGuire, Randall H. "The study of ethnicity in historical archaeology." *Journal of Anthropological
Archaeology 1* (1982): 159–78. A classic study of ethnicity by an archaeologist.

Patterson, Thomas Carl. *The Inca Empire: The Formation and Disintegration of a Pre-Capitalist State.*
Worcester, MA: Berg, 1991. A study which offers some interesting insights into the nature of
power relations within the Inca empire, and the relations between states and ethnic groups.

Shennan, S. J. "Introduction: Archaeological approaches to cultural identity." In S. J. Shennan
(ed.), *Archaeological Approaches to Cultural Identity* (pp. 1–32). London: Unwin Hyman, 1989.
An archaeological study of the phenomenon of ethnicity.

Skjeggestand, M. "Ethnic groups in early Iron age Palestine: Some remarks on the use of the term
'Israelite' in recent literature." *Scandinavian Journal of the Old Testament* 6 (1992): 159–86. The
article questions what are usually identified as Israelite ethnic markers of the Iron Age.

Smith, Anthony D. *The Ethnic Origins of Nations.* Oxford: Blackwell, 1986. The book discusses how
modern nations evolved from preexisting groups.

Trigger, Bruse G. *A History of Archaeological Thought.* Cambridge: Cambridge University Press,
1989. A classic study of the development of archaeological thought.

Ucko, P. J. "Foreword." In J. Gledhill and B. Bender (eds), *State and Society: The Emergence of Social
Hierarchy and Political Centralization* (pp. vii–xii). London: Routledge, 1988. An introduction to
the study of the relations between societies and political complexity.

Wiessner, Polly. "Is there a unity to style?" In M. W. Conkey and C. A. Hastorf (eds), *The Uses of
Style in Archaeology.* Cambridge: Cambridge University Press, 1990. A classic study of style in
archaeology.

Wimmer, A. *Ethnic Boundary Making: Institutions, Power, Networks.* Oxford: Oxford University
Press, 2013. An updated study of ethnicity.

B

Monarchic Period

CHAPTER 10

The Early Monarchy and the Stories of Saul, David, and Solomon

Brad E. Kelle

In the main biblical presentation of Israel's past (Genesis–2 Kings), the period of the people's settlement as a tribal confederacy in the land of Canaan (Joshua and Judges) gives way to a dynastic monarchy ruled successively by Saul, David, and Solomon. The books of Samuel and Kings describe the formation of a united kingdom that ruled from a central capital, possessed a state bureaucracy, covered vast territory, and encompassed all of the Israelite tribes. According to conventional chronologies, this period of Israel's past covered the late eleventh and most of the tenth centuries BCE, with David coming to power around 1000 BCE and Solomon's death and subsequent division of the kingdom occurring around 930 BCE. Throughout most of the twentieth century, historians of ancient Israel used these texts as the primary, and often the only, source to reconstruct the early monarchical period of Israel's political history. Very few extrabiblical texts that date from this period exist and scholars typically looked to archaeological data simply to supplement the biblical description. These practices led many historians to accept the general historicity of the biblical description, especially for the reigns of David and Solomon (see Moore and Kelle 200–65).

Today's study of the early monarchy differs significantly from these older approaches and may be surprising to those who are new to research on ancient Israel or who were introduced to Israel's political history via scholarly works from the 1980s and earlier. Since that time, the so-called united monarchy period has received substantial reexamination and new historical portraits have been proposed that sometimes differ markedly from the biblical presentation. Recent trends in biblical studies, archaeology, and social scientific research have led many scholars to conclude that the traditional picture of the early monarchy generated by the biblical texts does not reflect the historical realities of the tenth century BCE. Some studies argue that the biblical depiction of a

The Wiley Blackwell Companion to Ancient Israel, First Edition. Edited by Susan Niditch.
© 2016 John Wiley & Sons, Ltd. Published 2016 by John Wiley & Sons, Ltd.

tenth-century united kingdom is a largely unhistorical creation of later writers attempting to address issues related to Judah in the Persian or Hellenistic eras (see the essays by Charles Carter and Matthew Goff in this volume), while others maintain that scholars can, at least to some degree, corroborate the biblical descriptions, however exaggerated, with archaeological and other extrabiblical data to reveal a historical, but more modest, tenth-century kingdom in Israel.

This essay traces the changes that have occurred in the study of Israel's early monarchy and explains the current reconstructions and the evidence on which they rely. Additionally, in the same way that Avraham Faust's essay in this volume broadened the discussion of Israel's origins to consider how contemporary studies of ethnicity and ethnogenesis might illuminate Israel's emergence, this essay also examines broader interpretive approaches for studying both the historical realities of eleventh- and tenth-century Israel and the literary texts that tell the stories of Saul, David, and Solomon. These broader approaches include anthropological theories of state formation as a new lens on how permanent government may have developed in ancient Israel and new reading frames that try to account in different ways for what the biblical narratives say and how and why they say it.

The Biblical Texts and the Political History of the Israelite Early Monarchy: Changing Assessments and Current Approaches

The period from the mid-1980s to the present has featured major changes in the historical study of the Israelite early monarchy and the assessment of the biblical portrayals of this period. Extensive extrabiblical evidence makes clear that the Iron Age kingdoms of Israel and Judah existed in the central hill country of Syria-Palestine by the time of the Omride Dynasty in Samaria in the ninth century BCE. What has been heavily debated, however, are the political realities that preceded the ninth-century kingdoms and the sources available to reconstruct those realities. Was there an Israelite monarchy before the ninth-century kingdoms and, if so, how long did it exist, what areas did it include, and what was its relationship to the later kingdoms? Moreover, do the biblical stories of Saul, David, and Solomon provide an accurate picture of Israel's political history before these later kingdoms? Comprehensive discussions of the debate over the early monarchy are available (e.g., Moore and Kelle 145–265; Dietrich; Finkelstein and Silberman; Knoppers; Handy; Miller), so the following section will only summarize the changes in research before outlining current interpretations.

Historical Reconstructions through the 1980s

Prior to the 1980s, reconstructions of the early Israelite monarchy depended heavily on the biblical texts. At that time, scholars widely shared the conviction that the texts describing the early monarchy were reliable historical writing. The Hebrew Bible (HB) contains two narrative accounts of the early monarchy under Saul, David, and

Solomon: 1 Samuel 8–1 Kings 11 and 1 Chronicles 10–2 Chronicles 9. Although differing in various details, these accounts give a fairly consistent portrayal: the emergence
of a sustained threat from the Philistines in particular led to the creation of a monarchy
that, within a few generations, achieved economic, political, and ceremonial aspects of
true kingship. The biblical texts present Saul (1 Sam. 9–31) primarily as a local ruler over
a limited group of Israelite tribes in the northern hill country, but they describe a tenth-
century kingdom in Syria-Palestine under David (1 Sam. 16–1 Kings 2) and, especially,
Solomon (1 Kings 1–11) that reached near-imperial proportions. According to this presentation, Solomon's kingdom took in massive amounts of goods, possessed an elaborate
administrative bureaucracy, and housed chariot and cavalry forces in specially identified cities. The portrayal includes the claims that Solomon used forced labor to fortify
cities such as Hazor, Megiddo, and Gezer (1 Kings 9:15), and exercised tribute-collecting
dominion over the whole of Syria-Palestine – "all the kingdoms from the Euphrates to
the land of the Philistines, even to the border of Egypt" (1 Kings 4:21).

The biblical depictions are part of larger literary works, each with its own complex
compositional history and particular theological aims. The Samuel–Kings account is
generally considered part of the so-called Deuteronomistic History (hereafter DtrH =
Deuteronomy, Joshua, Judges, 1–2 Samuel, 1–2 Kings). This work is thought by many
scholars to be a historiographical composition that originated in a first edition perhaps
as early as the time of Hezekiah or Josiah and continued to be supplemented in various
ways throughout subsequent years (see J. J. M. Roberts's essay in this volume). In its
final form, the DtrH appears to be an exilic or even postexilic (Babylonian or Persian
period) writing that incorporates putatively earlier sources, most apparent in explicit
references such as the "Book of the Annals of the Kings of Judah" (e.g., 2 Kings 21:17).
The Chronicles account postdates that of Kings, likely originating in the sixth century
BCE, with perhaps later editorial additions. It differs significantly at times from the DtrH,
and the historical usefulness of the distinctive material remains debated.

The use of these biblical texts for study of the early monarchy often focused on the
earlier sources thought to be within the DtrH. Scholars hypothesized that the DtrH
included several, originally independent, compositions that narrate the major events
of the early monarchy, interweaving them with various poems, administrative lists, and
geographical descriptions. Interpreters disagreed over the precise boundaries of the textual units but typically identified these compositions as the History of David's Rise (1
Sam. 15–2 Sam. 5), the Court (or Succession) Narrative (2 Sam. 9–20; 1 Kings 1–2),
and the Acts of Solomon (1 Kings 3–11). The common view was that these earlier compositions were written very close to the lifetimes of David and Solomon, primarily as
works to legitimize their reigns, and thus constituted reliable historical sources. In the
early 1920s, Leonhard Rost advanced the highly influential hypothesis that the Court
(Succession) Narrative was an originally unified composition (now found in parts of 2
Sam. 6–7; 9–20; 1 Kings 1–2) that was written to justify Solomon's accession to the
throne, most likely by a scribe in Solomon's court (Rost). Likewise, P. Kyle McCarter
advanced the influential theory that the David story was a tenth-century "apologia"
designed to defend David against accusations from his own day by showing David's innocence and righteousness in spite of the violent events that accompanied his rise to power
(McCarter).

These ways of evaluating the biblical texts led many historians before the 1980s to conclude that the HB provided a reasonably accurate picture of Israel's early monarchical period. Scholars operating in this older mode then looked to archaeology to bolster the biblical picture, especially evidence from excavations at particular sites where the excavators claimed they had found monumental architecture dating to Solomon's time (see Moore and Kelle 209–65; Knoppers). In the 1950s, for example, Yigael Yadin excavated Hazor, a sizable city in the Galilee, and found a monumental city gate that he dated to the tenth century BCE. The gate resembled one found earlier at Megiddo that had been dated to about the same time. Based on 1 Kings 9:15, which describes a tax that Solomon implemented in order to "build" Hazor, Megiddo, and Gezer, Yadin then searched old excavation reports from Gezer for a similar gate. He concluded that a structure there previously identified as a second-century BCE palace was, in fact, a gate dating from much earlier. For Yadin, these gates confirmed the HB's picture of Solomon's kingdom, since they fit locations mentioned in the text, and the construction of such large fortifications surely required a centralized government.

Scholars also found data that they concluded revealed a well-developed, functioning, central government that controlled major parts of Syria-Palestine in the tenth century BCE. Although the areas in Jerusalem where Solomon's temple and palace would have been are sacred to Muslims and thus have not been available for excavation, scholars compared the biblical descriptions of the temple with layouts of shrines and public buildings known from elsewhere in Canaan and Syria. Others identified the remains of several fortress-like structures and accompanying houses in the Negeb desert as tenth-century fortresses established by Solomon's central government in Jerusalem to protect the kingdom's southern border. Some early historians also interpreted the so-called Gezer Calendar, a tenth-century inscription describing agricultural patterns, as evidence of Hebrew literacy throughout the area that, in their view, suggested the sponsorship of a central government with scribal administration in Jerusalem.

Although no extrabiblical texts mention Saul, David, Solomon, or any Israelite kingdom in the tenth century BCE, earlier historians paid special attention to two Egyptian inscriptions that attest an invasion of Canaan by the pharaoh Sheshonq (see J. J. M. Roberts's essay in this volume). Egyptian chronology places this event in the tenth century, and accounts of the campaign appear on a fragmentary temple inscription at Karnak in Egypt and on a partially preserved victory stela at Megiddo. Neither of the inscriptions names Jerusalem, David, Solomon, or any peoples or kingdoms (but only particular towns and settlements), but 1 Kings 14:25–26 mentions the pharaoh's (there called Shishak) invasion, identifies Jerusalem as a target and dates it to the fifth year of the reign of Solomon's son, Rehoboam (ca. 925 BCE). Building on this convergence of biblical and extrabiblical texts, historians tried to link evidence of destruction layers at various sites with this invasion and posited that if Sheshonq felt compelled to invade the area, there must have been a burgeoning political entity like the united monarchy centered in Jerusalem described in the biblical texts. A more recent extrabiblical inscription that has played a similar role is the Tel Dan Inscription (discovered in 1993), an Aramaic text from a king of Aram-Damascus in the ninth century BCE that describes his defeat of the kings of Israel and Judah (see Christopher Rollston's and J. J. M. Roberts's essays in this volume). The inscription designates the southern king (Ahaziah) as the ruler of the "House of David." This is the only explicit reference to the name David outside the HB (although some scholars have tried to reconstruct a similar reference in the ninth-century Moabite inscription of King Mesha). While the appearance of David's name a century after the time the Bible locates him does not imply the historicity of the HB's stories about him, it does seem to indicate that David was the name of the eponymous ancestor of the Judean royal house, known even by outsiders.

By beginning with the framework of the biblical stories and incorporating these and similar assessments of extrabiblical data, historians before the mid-1980s widely proposed a reconstruction of the early monarchy that resembled the biblical depiction – namely, a significantly large, united monarchy ruled from Jerusalem and spanning most of Syria-Palestine in the tenth century BCE. The chapters on the early monarchy in Martin Noth's and John Bright's seminal histories of Israel exemplified this standard view (Noth 164–224; Bright 184–228). Bright's and Noth's reconstructions of Saul, David, and Solomon were basically paraphrases of the biblical narratives, with only minimal historical analysis consisting of explaining certain historical details (e.g., the nature of the Philistine threat). And scholars operating within this framework proposed that Solomon's reign was a cultural and literary "golden age" of enlightenment for Israel, a view articulated most clearly in the work of Gerhard von Rad, who linked the writing of the "Yahwist" source of the Pentateuch to the time of Solomon's accomplished kingdom.

Challenges and Reassessments

Beginning in the 1980s, new analyses challenged nearly every literary-critical, historical, and archaeological support for the older interpretations, opening the way for new reconstructions of the early monarchy that differed significantly from the biblical picture. The first challenges came from the changing climate among biblical scholars who, beginning especially in the 1980s, began to question the usefulness of the biblical texts for reconstructing Israel's history. Scholars increasingly emphasized that the relevant biblical texts were first and foremost literary constructions, produced many years after the events they purport to describe in order to serve particular political, ideological, and theological agendas. These considerations raised questions about whether historical reliability was a goal of the writers and whether readers can retrieve historically reliable information from biblical texts that were written in service of other aims. For some historians, this meant that scholars should not continue to privilege, or in some cases even use, the HB as a source for the early monarchical period. For others, the changing perspectives meant that while scholars need not assume an essentially skeptical stance relative to the HB's presentations, they must avoid overinterpreting the biblical text as though it were a historical source whose primary purpose was to transmit historical detail.

Along with these reassessments of the biblical texts, the primary challenges to the older consensus about the united monarchy were reassessments of the archaeological remains (see Handy; Knoppers 19–44). By the late 1980s, for example, several archaeologists concluded that the city gates at Hazor, Megiddo, and Gezer were actually built in different periods, with the Megiddo gate constructed later than the other two (see Finkelstein and Silberman 279). Others pointed to a lack of evidence that the fortifications were linked to a central government and objected that the only basis for associating them with Jerusalem was the biblical attribution to Solomon in 1 Kings 9:15. Archaeological assessments of tenth-century Jerusalem concluded that there was little evidence of significant building activity and the city was too small to sponsor building programs at other sites or to be the capital of a great empire. Moreover, archaeologists pointed to the discovery of similar six-chambered gates at sites that date no earlier than the end of the tenth century BCE (e.g., Lachish) and at non-Israelite locations (e.g., Ashdod), both of which suggested that the structures at Hazor, Megiddo, and Gezer might not be clear evidence for either the tenth century or ancient Israel (Knoppers 28).

Perhaps the most significant challenge, however, came from a new chronological sequence proposed for all of the material remains that had traditionally been dated to the tenth century BCE (Finkelstein, "Archaeology"). This sequence, known as the "low chronology," relied on a reinterpretation of the dates of certain kinds of Philistine pottery and the destruction layers at various sites in Syria-Palestine (see Moore and Kelle 212–15). As part of this new chronology, Israel Finkelstein concluded that markings on the ashlar blocks of the structures at Megiddo were identical to those at the later Omride palace in Samaria, and the pottery at Megiddo matched that of the Omride compound at Jezreel (less than ten miles east of Megiddo) (Finkelstein and Silberman 279). Since both of these Omride buildings date to the ninth century, the low chronology required that the monumental architecture at Megiddo (as well as Hazor and Gezer) that had traditionally been attributed to Solomon be reassigned to the time of the northern kingdom of Israel a century later. The low chronology remains at the center of nearly all current archaeological debates about the early monarchy because, if correct, it removes almost every artifact traditionally attributed to Solomon's reign and indicates that major territorial states did not develop in the Levant until the later time of the Assyrian empire in the ninth century BCE.

The other evidence typically marshaled for the older view of the united monarchy underwent similar challenges across the 1980s and 1990s (see Miller 13; Knoppers). Some scholars redated the fortresses in the Negeb that had been attributed to David or Solomon, with proposed dates ranging from the eighth to fifth centuries BCE, and with Israel, Judah, and Persia touted as possibly responsible for their construction. Others concluded that the Egyptian accounts of Pharaoh Sheshonq's invasion, which mentioned only individual towns, indicate that larger political entities did not even exist in the area at that time. Likewise, the use of comparative anthropological and sociological models in the 1980s led interpreters to expect that early "monarchical" Israel would more likely have been a limited chiefdom and that the apex of population growth in the Levant came later in the eighth century BCE (e.g., Frick; Coote and Whitelam).

The sum of these and other reassessments left historians with the seemingly untenable scenario that if there was a monarchy like that described in the HB, it had left no traces in contemporary inscriptions and only unclear or debatable evidence in archaeological remains. Hence, by the end of the 1990s, many interpreters decided that the united monarchy of the traditional reconstructions would have been out of keeping with the general circumstances of tenth-century Syria-Palestine and the older view could only be maintained by interpreting the imprecise epigraphic and archaeological evidence in light of the biblical texts (Miller 13–14). Some scholars dismissed entirely the historicity of the early monarchy, identifying the Saul, David, and Solomon stories as legendary constructions of scribes from the Persian or Hellenistic periods (Thompson 415–23). Most historians in the 1980s and 1990s, however, became more skeptical about the usefulness of the biblical texts but still identified a modest historical reality by extracting historically plausible materials from the HB that could be combined with archaeological and inscriptional evidence. In their view, David and Solomon were historical figures but primarily as local leaders who ruled over a limited chiefdom rather than an expansive monarchical empire (e.g., Miller and Hayes 160, 187–97).

Current Interpretations

In today's scholarship, historians remain divided over how to reconstruct the political history of Israel's early monarchy. Within the current discussion, several of the long-debated topics (e.g., the gates at Hazor, Megiddo, and Gezer) are receiving ongoing attention (see Dever; Becking). More recently, however, new evidence has generated different perspectives and more diverse options. For each of these items, some historians and archaeologists see them as supporting the more traditional view of the biblical united monarchy and others arrive at seemingly opposite conclusions. In Jerusalem, Eliat Mazar has interpreted the recently excavated remains of large walls made of undressed stones (the so-called Large Stone Structure) as part of a sizable, tenth-century BCE complex linked to the Stepped Stone Structure that had been excavated earlier on the slope of the same area. She dates the complex to around 1000 BCE and identifies it as David's royal palace. In her view, these remains provide the missing archaeological evidence that shows tenth-century Jerusalem was a developed administrative center. As noted above, however, there is little archaeological data in Jerusalem that can be associated with the early monarchy, even though there have been extensive excavations. Moreover, different assessments have challenged Mazar's interpretation of the pottery items used to date the remains, her dependence on biblical texts, and her claim that the different structures constitute one complex from a single era (Finkelstein et al.). Recent excavations have also yielded remains of an apparent copper mining industry at Khirbet en-Nahas, south of the Dead Sea (in the area of biblical Edom), including a citadel and administrative building. The excavators date the complex to the tenth century BCE and interpret the remains as evidence that Edom was a centralized polity, perhaps representing part of Solomon's expansion (Levy et al.). As with the Jerusalem remains, however, the dating of these finds is contested, and they may be from the eighth or seventh centuries BCE (Finkelstein, "A great united monarchy?" 15–16).

Perhaps the most significant new evidence for the early Israelite monarchy has been the interpretation of two extrabiblical texts from the tenth century BCE. Excavations in 2008 of the remains of a tenth-century fortress at Khirbet Qeiyafa (biblical Elah) uncovered an ostracon (inscribed potsherd) with five lines of a Hebrew text (see Becking 24–5). There is no agreement on how to read (right to left? left to right?) or interpret the inscription, but many consider it to be one of the oldest known Hebrew texts

(Galil). Additionally, recent excavations at Tel Zayit (biblical Libnah?) have discovered an abecedary (alphabet list) with 22 letters of the west Semitic alphabet (Tappy et al.). The assessment of these texts relates to the longstanding debate over the level of literacy in tenth-century Syria-Palestine (see also the Gezer Calendar mentioned above). Modern scholars have often argued that evidence of widespread, basic literacy in the tenth century BCE would suggest the existence of a centralized administrative system, since such literacy depends on a certain level of urbanization and economic development. For some, the Khirbet Qeiyafa and Tel Zayit inscriptions supply missing evidence of literacy that supports the existence of a centralized government and appeals to these texts have been increasingly prevalent in works arguing for more traditional reconstructions of the early monarchy. They may connect with the discovery of various bullae (clay impressions of seals used to bind written documents) at tenth-century rural pasturing sites (e.g., Khirbet Summeily) that might suggest governmental oversight. For others, however, the decipherment of the texts, dates of the structural remains (tenth or ninth century BCE?), and even ethnicity of the sites (e.g., was Tel Zayit Israelite or Philistine?) remain uncertain. And no clear evidence identifies these sites and texts as products of a centralized kingdom in Jerusalem rather than, say, products of local, even if governmental, structures caused by growth in trade and agriculture (Becking 24–5; Finkelstein, "A great united monarchy?" 16–17).

Today's scholarship features a range of views on the reconstruction of the early monarchy, mostly based on how different scholars assess the old and new evidence. The most common interpretation accepts a historical but more modest early monarchy in and around Jerusalem in the tenth century BCE (Israel as chiefdom; Solomon as a local ruler), finding some accurate reflections of this political reality within the biblical narratives of Saul, David, and Solomon (e.g., Miller and Hayes 187–97). The stories contain later, exaggerated, and unhistorical parts, but most scholars believe they can distinguish those from textual elements that have various degrees of historical reliability as authentic reminiscences, customs, or practices (e.g., Dietrich 106). The operative assumption is that "later compilation, composition, and redaction do not rule out the presentation of earlier material useful for historical studies" (Bodi 226). The task is to identify these elements and correlate them with archaeological, sociological, and anthropological data, but scholars often divide sharply over the extent to which this task is possible. For most interpreters today, the complexities involved in evaluating the available evidence do not permit the reconstruction of specific historical persons and events from the tenth century BCE, but may allow the identification of situations, customs, and practices within the biblical stories that fit plausibly in the tenth century BCE on the basis of other ancient Near Eastern sources. There may then be a basic historical plausibility (if not probability) for the HB's *general* description of the time, even if not its details. For example, there was a political vacuum in the tenth-century Levant that could have allowed smaller entities to expand into states. Likewise, certain historical and textual analogies suggest the biblical stories' plausibility. These might include accounts from eighteenth-century BCE Mari texts of the conflict between two clans as a "fitting historical analogy" for the biblical depiction of the conflict between the houses of Saul and David, or the rise of Zimri-Lim to power in Mari as an analogy to the HB's depiction of David's rise (Bodi 204–19). Still, some interpreters challenge that even more modest and plausible reconstructions are too dependent on the biblical narratives and not sufficiently supported by archaeology or contemporaneous records. This perspective leads to a more minimal view of any historical kingdom in tenth-century Israel (e.g., Davies 67–8). At the same time, some recent scholars mount a renewed defense of the traditional reconstruction of a wealthy and expansive tenth-century Israelite kingdom centered in Jerusalem, a developed imperial capital (e.g., Rainey and Notley 159–68).

Overall, today's interpretations of the early monarchical period take two major forms that can be conveniently illustrated by the arguments and reconstructions of Amihai Mazar and Israel Finkelstein (see Finkelstein, "A great united monarchy?"; A. Mazar, "Archaeology"; Finkelstein, "King Solomon"; A. Mazar, "The search"). Mazar concludes that although the biblical picture contains exaggeration and embellishment and cannot be taken at face value, the sum of all the evidence shows the plausibility of a more modest tenth-century united monarchy in Israel. He uses a "Modified Conventional Chronology" (in response to Finkelstein's Low Chronology) in which he claims the tenth and ninth centuries BCE constitute a single archaeological period, thus allowing evidence from Hazor, Gezer, and Megiddo to be plausibly related to the time before the sure existence of the two separate kingdoms of Israel and Judah. Finds such as the Stepped Stone Structure and its associated building in Jerusalem suggest that although Jerusalem was not the imperial capital of a large state, it could have been a power base for local rulers. And the few inscriptions reveal that literacy existed in the tenth century, which, in his view, indicates the presence of scribes and officials in the area. Mazar especially emphasizes that the extrabiblical accounts of Sheshonq's campaign (925 BCE) list sites in the central hill country north of Jerusalem (e.g., Gibeon). Hence, for him, there must have been a significant political power in that area at the time, and the most reasonable candidate was a kingdom established by David and Solomon. Mazar further contends that interpreters must consider the potential historical impact of individual personalities, leaders who possessed the charisma and ability needed to create temporary but significant political entities. He concludes that we might think of David on the analogy of earlier Apiru leaders (mentioned in the fourteenth-century Amarna texts) who succeeded in establishing political rule over an extended territory, though not to the level of the earlier Egyptian or later Assyrian empires.

Finkelstein assesses the key pieces of evidence differently (see especially Finkelstein and Silberman). He accepts David and Solomon as historical rulers from the tenth century BCE but allows only for a much more minimal Israelite monarchy at the time. David and Solomon were local potentates who ruled from Jerusalem, which was a modest settlement, over a territory that did not extend into the northern valleys or the lower Shephelah in the west (dominated by the Philistines). A centralized, united monarchy that spanned from Dan in the north to Beersheba in the south (to use the biblical description) came to exist only later under the Omrides in Samaria in the ninth century BCE, and the initial structures of statehood (e.g., the gates at Hazor, Megiddo, and Gezer) appeared only at this time, as well, and under Omride influence. Finkelstein sees the historical Saul as having been the leader of a northern Israelite tribal confederacy located in the Benjaminite highlands. In his view, the northern sites named on Sheshonq's inscriptions correspond to this location, suggesting that the campaign's target was Saul's northern confederacy (not some supposed power in Jerusalem) and that the biblical dating of the event to after Solomon's death (1 Kings 14:25) may be a later tradition. The biblical narratives developed over four centuries from these historical memories, especially during the time of King Josiah of Judah in the seventh century BCE.

As these representative examples show, much of today's research on the early monarchical period remains focused on the historical plausibility of the biblical presentation in light of the known political history of the tenth-century Levant. Historical interpretations are heavily shaped by what evidence is considered, how that evidence is evaluated in terms of its date and importance, and what role different evidence plays in larger reconstructions. To some, the united monarchy as portrayed in the HB looks plausible in an ancient Near Eastern context; to others the nature of the extrabiblical evidence seems not to support that plausibility; and to still others there are workable middle grounds.

The Early Monarchy as Israelite State Formation

As the above discussion shows, the most common approaches to the political history of Israel's early monarchy operate in one way or another within the framework of the biblical presentation – accepting, modifying, or rejecting it. More recently, however, a new trajectory is moving beyond this focus to offer broader ways to study Israelite history in the tenth century BCE and the emergence of the Israelite monarchy outside of the terms dictated by the biblical texts. If the study of this era does not have to revolve around the stories of Saul, David, and Solomon, what other kinds of historical inquiries might be interesting and beneficial? Avraham Faust's essay in this volume showed that current work on the origins of ancient Israel has shifted to the broader perspective of ethnogenesis, especially the material evidence of how a group defines itself over against others (see also the essay by Elizabeth Bloch-Smith in this volume). Likewise, one trajectory in recent research invites interpreters to reconceive the study of the early monarchical era as an inquiry into the dynamics and processes of Israelite state formation. This inquiry uses insights drawn from anthropological research on state formation as a lens for reconstructing the development of permanent government in early Israel. Following this approach means reframing questions about how to reconstruct the political history of Israel's early monarchy into questions about how and why societies like tenth-century Israel formed states, focusing on the social dynamics, environmental features, and societal patterns and considering how, if at all, these questions illuminate the biblical texts and archaeological realities.

Social scientists have developed various models and theories for the processes by which the complex organizational structures of permanent governments emerge in different kinds of political entities (e.g., agriculturally based territorial states). The classification of different states and state-like societies and descriptions of the means of and reasons for their formation have yielded models and comparative data for historians of ancient Israel to use. Social scientific models allow researchers to hypothesize "what kinds of governments or social systems could have plausibly inhabited the highlands, left the artifacts we have, been described in the way they were in the Bible, and later led to the historically verifiable kingdoms of Israel and Judah" (Moore and Kelle 208).

No single anthropological model has achieved dominance in histories of Israel, and successfully using such models depends on up-to-date knowledge of social scientific research concerning early states, often with technical jargon and classifications. Even so, social scientific models and anthropological theories are increasingly becoming the primary methodological tools scholars use to describe the formation of a permanent government in Israel.

Social scientific theories of state formation already played an important role in the new assessments and reconstructions of the united monarchy that appeared in the 1980s. For instance, Frank S. Frick used models of state formation developed by anthropologists and sociologists in the 1960s and 1970s to conclude that early "monarchical" Israel was more likely a "chiefdom" than a state ruled by kings. Likewise Robert B. Coote and Keith W. Whitelam argued that the monarchy was not an alien institution to early Israel but resulted from changes in the economic base of the central highlands, including the circumscription of resources and new levels of stratification and centralization. These earlier approaches found archaeological evidence for emerging statehood in the appearance of new tenth-century villages in harder-to-cultivate areas. The early stages of centralization and state formation may have resulted from the people's efforts to adapt to rougher environments by relying on larger social frameworks and new levels of centralized organization. Military pressure may also have been a catalyst for centralization and eventual state formation, just as the HB describes, since the new villages were in territories abutted by the Philistines and there may have been competition over resources and other forms of control. Already in the 1980s and 1990s, these kinds of social scientific perspectives led interpreters to the conclusion that what the HB pictures as the brand-new introduction of a royal kingdom was actually the middle phase in an evolutionary development from tribal society to chiefdom to monarchical state, the last phase of which did not occur in ancient Israel until a century or more later. Moreover, the wider archaeological and anthropological data suggested that the emergence of this kind of tenth-century polity in Israel was not unique but was part of long-term social patterns of growth in the area that featured complex chiefdoms rather than expansive monarchies (Coote and Whitelam).

In today's use of state formation theory on ancient Israel, the particular models and perspectives have changed, and there are new levels of complexity that offer potentially rich avenues of future research. In recent years, there has been much debate over the nature and types of states, the processes of their development, and the characteristics that accompany their existence. Significant challenges have emerged to the older view of chiefdom for ancient Israel, especially due to its connection with an evolutionary scheme wherein the chiefdom is seen as evolving from a kinship-based society and as the predecessor to the kingdom or state, which evolves from it. Social scientific research has shown that this is not always the case – chiefdoms may dissolve into simpler organizations and kingdoms and states do not necessarily exist earlier as chiefdoms (Master). Additionally, recent works stress that chiefdoms, states, and other more centralized organizations do not necessarily replace kinship structures but local kinship ties persist even in developed states, much as the biblical texts depict the importance of the lineages of Saul and David in establishing their rule. Kinship ties may remain as the base of some larger state and national structures, even though kinship then gradually ceases to be the only determining factor in social organization (Meyers, "Kinship," 168; Master 129; see also the essay by T. M. Lemos in this volume).

Perhaps most significantly, anthropological research has identified a new variety of types of states (e.g., territorial states, city-states, segmentary states, tribal states) that scholars have attempted to apply to early Israel. Interpreters debate what characteristics are needed to constitute a state (levels of population, bureaucracy, centralization, urbanization, hierarchy) and whether there is evidence of those thresholds in tenth-century Israel. A key to the discussion has been the identification of ancient Israel as a "secondary state" (as opposed to a "primary state"), a state formed under the influence of contact with existing state systems (Joffe). For some, this indicates a full-fledged state could have arisen in Israel in the tenth century BCE as a result of the collapse of earlier empires; for others, it means an Israelite state could only have emerged once there was contact with the Neo-Assyrian empire in the later ninth century BCE. Other identifications that scholars have adopted for understanding the government that existed under the early Israelite kings include "inchoative state," "early transitional state," "tribal state," and "patrimonial state" (see Moore and Kelle 226). Yet, some historians object to the use of "state" at all, noting that the kingdom was the dominant societal form in the ancient Near East.

One noteworthy upshot of this broader state formation perspective is that it allows historians of ancient Israel to explore the history of the wider Levant in the tenth century BCE without focusing solely on Israelite history and society or whether the biblical descriptions of David's and Solomon's kingdoms correspond to reality. Much of this work has its roots in the early study of social archaeology, which sought to provide a wider spatial and temporal framework for understanding the variety of historical and social developments in the Levant over the long period of the Bronze Age through the Greek and Roman periods (compare the "Annales" school of archaeology, an approach that originated outside biblical studies among French historians and emphasized the study of long-term social history). Historians working in this way can attend not only to archaeology, sociology, and anthropology, but to disciplines such as archaeozoology, geology, botany, and more. These broader perspectives have already led to creative reconstructions and new perspectives on older data. Concerning the remains of the monumental gates at Hazor, Megiddo, and Gezer, for instance, K. L. Noll believes they date to the tenth century BCE but reconceives them as evidence for relationships between these urban areas that featured a cultural unity, possibly centered in Gezer (Moore and Kelle 259). Likewise, Bob Becking investigates the tenth-century Levant by attending to the impact of landscape and climate. He identifies evidence for an increase in population and agricultural terraces for farming that accompanied a period of "global cooling" that produced increased rainfall (Becking 9–10). Other considerations that come into view through the use of broader state formation perspectives include the lifeways of tenth-century villagers as evidenced by the material remains and the population distribution in the central highlands and neighboring lands.

Overall, then, many current researchers are reconfiguring the study of the early monarchy into the exploration of the dynamics, structures, and patterns of state formation (or the formation of permanent government) in Israel as understood in the wider context of the social and political history of the tenth-century BCE Levant. This approach allows for a broader examination of the historical processes that were at work in Israel's early political development. Further, this approach allows interpreters to explore previously underemphasized dimensions of Israel's political history, including, for example, the moral issues involved in the formation of the Israelite monarchy and its biblical descriptions. These include the moral and ethical dynamics of the pooling of resources, the concentration of power in single persons and groups, the sanctioning of violence, and the nature and abuse of political power (Meyers, "Kinship," 166).

Other Reading Frames for the Stories of the Early Monarchy

Most historians today consider the biblical account of the early monarchy to be at least somewhat (if not far) removed from the historical realities of Israel's past in the eleventh and tenth centuries BCE. As a result, interpreters are increasingly turning to broader perspectives for this era, some of which are historical in nature (e.g., insights from state formation theory). Additionally, however, the historical controversies have generated a growing interest in new ways to engage and account for the biblical stories of Saul, David, and Solomon – what they tell, and how and why they tell it like they do, especially if they are not simply factual accounts of Israel's past. Recent scholarship has seen the emergence of several reading frames for the biblical narratives. Many of these associate the origins, or at least the main functions and purposes, of the Saul–David–Solomon stories with later eras than that of the period of state formation in the eleventh and tenth centuries BCE, moving beyond the strictures of the traditional debate over the united monarchy. The following provides a brief sampling of some of the emerging reading frames that offer new and creative ways to engage both the biblical stories of Saul, David, and Solomon and the dynamics associated with monarchy in ancient Israel's historical memory.

One such reading frame is the attempt to write a biography of David. A series of recent works aim to get behind the biblical presentation and elucidate the "real life" of David by looking for potential indications of past events in the stories while recognizing the stories' overarching message that David's reign was inevitable and desirable (McKenzie; Halpern; Baden). They resemble some approaches within the traditional history debate as they attempt to "dig through" potentially nonhistorical and propagandistic layers to get to the "seed" of historical truth, even while acknowledging that telling the "seed" from the "pulp" is sometimes difficult (McKenzie 44). They share a confidence that interpreters can bring the historical David to life by removing the "nonhistorical pro-Davidic elements" from the narrative and thereby "expose the basic events underneath" (Baden 10). The book-length examples of this reading frame that have appeared so far work from the older conviction (discussed above) that much of the biblical presentation of David originated as an apology (perhaps during or just after his reign) designed to defend his legitimacy as Saul's successor and exonerate him from accusations made by his contemporaries. The books focus heavily on David's character, often portraying David as a warrior of questionable morals (by our standards) who was power hungry and whose shortcomings were obscured by later authors who aggrandized his character and accomplishments. For many of these biographers, David began as a military chieftain or bandit-king before using intrigue and murder to gain power, albeit with more limited territory and accomplishments than the HB describes.

A second reading frame in recent scholarship moves away from this historical orientation and takes an entirely literary course (Gunn; Polzin). These readings shift their interest away from whether the biblical stories reported the past accurately or inaccurately, or talked about a real past in any way at all. They seek to illuminate the way the stories were written and how their characters, plot, and language function to create the story world. In this view, the writer of the DtrH was not merely an editor or compiler but a creative author who produced an artful and coherent composition. The analysis focuses not on the "genetic composition" of the text but on its "poetic composition" that reveals how the stories communicate as literature (Polzin 6). Read through this literary frame, one might consider the David narrative to be a "traditional story" – an artful work told in a traditional vein that functions as "serious entertainment" (Gunn 40, 62).

The third reading frame bridges the gap between literary and historical investigations. Some recent feminist scholarship draws upon comparative textual analysis, archaeological evidence, and anthropological models to explore the impact of the emergence of the monarchy on gender relations (particularly the status of women) within agrarian village settings like ancient Israel. Carol Meyers, for instance, concludes that the kinship-based village settlements of the prestate era featured relative parity between men and women in the control of resources and household authority (see the essay by Carol Meyers in this volume). However, the emergence of a new centralized government disrupted the traditional patterns, especially in urban settings, and contributed to the subordination of women (Meyers, "Kinship"; *Rediscovering Eve*). Although some women rose to political power, the rise of monarchical institutions typically paralleled the decline of women's authority.

The fourth reading frame in recent scholarship has the most exemplars and diverse approaches. Some interpreters seek to explore how and why the biblical stories of the united monarchy were composed and preserved within historical frameworks other than the tenth century BCE. Rather than limiting the use of these stories to questions about a possible tenth-century Israelite monarchy, these interpreters think creatively about when these stories might have been written and what purposes they might have served for those audiences. Several of these studies seek to identify compositional layers within the united monarchy stories and propose how each developing layer of the stories reflected and shaped the realities and aspirations of its era. Were the earliest written versions of the David tales composed in eighth-century BCE Judah as a unifying national story for Hezekiah's kingdom? Were the Solomon stories mainly developed in the seventh century BCE to present an Israelite ruler in the manner of an Assyrian emperor, as Manasseh may have aspired to be (Finkelstein and Silberman 26)?

At present, some of the most intriguing hypotheses about the time and function of the united monarchy stories place them in the sixth century BCE and beyond – that is, the time of the destruction of Jerusalem, the Babylonian exile, and the Persian period that followed. Some works focus particularly on the traumatic events of Judah's destruction and exile, noting that these events receive only the briefest mention in the DtrH and employing insights from contemporary trauma theory to read the stories of the monarchy through the lens of these catastrophes and their effects. David Janzen reads the entire DtrH as an exilic work designed to explain the destruction and exile. It contains a "master narrative" that explains the catastrophe as justified divine punishment for the people's worship of other gods (*The Violent Gift*, 3–5). At the same time, however, numerous stories interrupt this logic and dispute its claims, subverting the major concepts that the master narrative uses in its portrayals of God, Israel, justice, and punishment. By using trauma theory as a literary criticism, Janzen envisions a Judahite author who survived the destruction of Jerusalem and struggled to make sense of the experiences by exploring, rendering ambiguous, and even contradicting the typical ethical logic offered by the dominant narratives of his day. In the David and Bathsheba story (2 Sam. 11–12), for instance, the author portrays David as one who unjustly escapes the proper punishments because of God's preference for him and thus calls into question the master narrative's claim that established principles of justice underlie God's actions in history (Janzen, *The Violent Gift*, 178–80).

Other works within this reading frame have shifted the interpretive lens for the early monarchy stories to Persian-period Judean society centered in Jerusalem in the postexilic era (after 539 BCE). These works explore how the stories might have emerged or functioned in that community's struggles to envision what forms of government and society they should adopt for a postexilic future in the land, especially the question of whether monarchy as known from the past constitutes the ideal for the future. Joseph Blenkinsopp, for example, examines the David stories and other biblical texts to see how the theme of monarchy (especially the Davidic monarchy) impacted the collective memory and actions of the people. He suggests that different tellings of the David stories reflected the community's struggles with ongoing aspirations for a Davidic monarchy and some of the military and political elements of the traditional picture of David (Blenkinsopp 2).

John Van Seters also reads the David stories against the backdrop of postexilic Judah and begins with the long-observed presence of two contradictory pictures of David in the stories of 1 Samuel 16–1 Kings 2. Some texts idealize him as the model king, and some portray him negatively as a typical ancient despot. In a reversal of the common view, Van Seters argues that the story of David's rise and reign, especially the negative portrayals, was not an older source used to create the DtrH but was produced in the Persian period and added to the already existing DrtH, which had a more positive evaluation of the Davidic monarchy (Van Seters xii). In his view, this later court history was intended as the opposite of an apology; it was, in fact, an antimonarchy document – a critique of monarchy that subverted the positive view of David by depicting his acts of violence and unfaithfulness and thereby confronted the postexilic audience with the question of whether they should desire a revival of monarchy and royal ideology as the type of government for their future. By contrast, another of Janzen's works uses insights from postcolonial reading to arrive at nearly the opposite conclusion about the view of kingship within the stories of the early monarchy and the DtrH as a whole (see also Kim, *Decolonizing Josiah*; *Identity and Loyalty*). He sees the DtrH as written in and for a subaltern community in diaspora. However, postcolonial theory leads him to identify the text's presentation of the monarchy as reinscribing a "colonial discourse" designed to convince the people of their need for the monarchy (Janzen, *The Necessary King*, 3). The narrative depictions of the monarchy mimic the imperial discourse of the Neo-Assyrians and Neo-Babylonians by casting the Israelites as dangerous and chaotic "others" in need of a king to make them loyal to Yhwh. Although kings will commit unjust acts, they are necessary to enforce cultic loyalty, and the colonial rhetoric of the DtrH says that the people can flourish in the postdisaster era only if they submit to the vision of a future Davidic monarchy.

Also within this reading frame, Jacob Wright explores how the David stories might have served to address issues of identity and belonging in the formation of the people, especially in the wake of defeat and destruction. He compares the function of the David stories to the role that war memorials (commemorations) play in shaping identity and status in ancient and contemporary societies. He hypothesizes different compositional layers of the David story that grew over time and explores how the layers reflect issues of belonging and peoplehood in different eras long after David's putative reign (Wright 224). The larger goal of the David story is to respond to the catastrophic defeat and loss of statehood by imagining a new model of nationhood/peoplehood. To do so, the authors negotiate belonging and status among different groups in their society by using the David stories to show how different groups (through their ancestors from David's time) did or did not remain loyal to David during the events of his life. At the same time, the authors deliberately included stories that portrayed David as a flawed human character in order to offer a critique of monarchy and statehood. Overall, then, the David story is the product of a collective effort to envision a new future political community based on the model of nationhood and peoplehood (not monarchy and statehood) in the wake of defeat.

Detailed analyses of the stories of Saul, David, and Solomon along the lines of these recent, broader, and diverse reading frames are just beginning to develop. It seems likely that these emerging perspectives for understanding the stories about the early monarchy will have significant implications for using the texts as historical sources to reconstruct Israel's past in the eleventh and tenth centuries BCE. Even these brief examples suggest, however, that there are multiple ways to engage the biblical stories of Saul, David, and Solomon – what they tell, and how and why they tell it like they do – and multiple ways to explore the realities and dynamics of the early phases of ancient Israel's political history.

Bibliography

Baden, Joel. *The Historical David: The Real Life of an Invented Hero.* New York: HarperOne, 2013. A recent effort to write a biography of David by using the biblical texts.

Becking, Bob. "David between ideology and evidence." In Bob Becking and Lester L. Grabbe (eds), *Between Evidence and Ideology: Essays on the History of Ancient Israel Read at the Joint Meeting of the Society for Old Testament Study and the Oud Testamentisch Werkgezelschap, Lincoln, July 2009* (pp. 1–30). Oudtestamentisch Studiën 59. Leiden: Brill, 2011. A survey of emerging approaches to the historical and literary study of the early monarchy.

Blenkinsopp, Joseph. *David Remembered: Kingship and National Identity in Ancient Israel.* Grand Rapids, MI: Eerdmans, 2013. An examination of the David stories and other biblical texts to see how the theme of monarchy (especially the Davidic monarchy) impacted the collective memory and actions of the people.

Bodi, Daniel. "The story of Samuel, Saul, and David." In Bill T. Arnold and Richard S. Hess (eds), *Ancient Israel's History: An Introduction to Issues and Sources* (pp. 190–226). Grand Rapids, MI: Baker, 2014. Recent examination of the literary and comparative evidence for the biblical portrayals of the early monarchy.

Bright, John. *A History of Israel*. 4th edn. Louisville, KY: Westminster John Knox, 2000. Originally published Philadelphia: Westminster, 1959. Standard mid-twentieth-century history of Israel representing older approaches in the tradition of W. F. Albright.

Coote, Robert B. and Keith W. Whitelam. *The Emergence of Early Israel in Historical Perspective*. Sheffield: Almond, 1987. Early representative of the use of state-formation theory and anthropological research to study the early Israelite society and monarchy.

Davies, Philip R. *In Search of "Ancient Israel"*. Journal for the Study of the Old Testament, suppl. 148. Sheffield: JSOT Press, 1992. Groundbreaking revisionist ("minimalist") reconstruction of ancient Israel and the origins of the biblical texts.

Dever, William G. *What Did the Biblical Writers Know and When Did They Know It? What Archaeology Can Tell Us about the Reality of Ancient Israel*. Grand Rapids, MI: Eerdmans, 2001. A challenge to the revisionist interpretations of Israelite history based largely on archaeological data.

Dietrich, Walter. *The Early Monarchy in Israel: The Tenth Century BCE*. Society of Biblical Literature Biblical Encyclopedia 3. Atlanta: Society of Biblical Literature, 2007. A general introduction to the stories of the early monarchy from a variety of literary-critical, historical, and theological perspectives.

Finkelstein, Israel. "The archaeology of the united monarchy: An alternative view." *Levant 28* (1996): 177–87. A major articulation of the so-called "New Chronology" that redated material remains of the tenth century BCE to later periods.

Finkelstein, Israel. "King Solomon's golden age? History or myth." In Israel Finkelstein and Amihai Mazar, *The Quest for the Historical Israel: Debating Archaeology and the History of Early Israel*, ed. Brian B. Schmidt (pp.107–16). Archaeology and Biblical Studies 17. Atlanta: Society of Biblical Literature, 2007. Convenient summary of revisionist interpretation of united monarchy.

Finkelstein, Israel. "A great united monarchy? Archaeological and historical perspectives." In R. G. Kratz and H. Spieckermann (eds), *One God – One Cult – One Nation: Archaeological and Biblical Perspectives* (pp. 3–28). Beihefte zur Zeitschrift für die Alttestamentliche Wissenschaft 405. Berlin: de Gruyter, 2010. Convenient summary of revisionist interpretation of united monarchy.

Finkelstein, Israel and Neil Asher Silberman. *David and Solomon: In Search of the Bible's Sacred Kings and the Roots of the Western Tradition*. New York: Free Press, 2006. Extended popular treatment of revisionist interpretation of united monarchy.

Finkelstein, Israel, Z. Herzog, I. Singer-Avitz, and D. Ussishkin. "Has King David's palace in Jerusalem been found?" *Tel Aviv 34* (2007): 142–64. A critical reassessment of the archaeological data supporting the hypothesis of the large stone structure in Jerusalem as David's tenth-century BCE palace.

Frick, Frank S. *The Formation of the State in Ancient Israel*. Social World of Biblical Antiquity Series 4. Sheffield: Almond, 1985. One of the early applications of state formation theory and anthropological research to the formation of the Israelite monarchy.

Galil, Gershom. "The Hebrew inscription from Khirbet Qeiyafa/Neta'im." *Ugarit-Forschungen 41* (2009): 193–242. Description and analysis of the inscriptions from this site and their relevance for the question of tenth-century BCE Israel.

Gunn, David M. *The Story of King David: Genre and Interpretation.* Journal for the Study of the Old Testament, suppl. 6. Sheffield: Sheffield University Press, 1978. A pioneering narrative and holistic reading of the David stories outside of a historical frame of reference.

Halpern, Baruch. *David's Secret Demons: Messiah, Murderer, Traitor, King.* Grand Rapids, MI: Eerdmans, 2001. A recent effort to write a biography of David by using the biblical texts.

Handy, Lowell K. (ed.). *The Age of Solomon: Scholarship at the Turn of the Millennium.* Studies in the History and Culture of the Ancient Near East 11. Leiden: Brill, 1997. Representative compilation of essays illustrating the reassessments of the literary and historical evidence for Solomon in the 1980s.

Janzen, David. *The Violent Gift: Trauma's Subversion of the Deuteronomistic History's Narrative.* Library of Hebrew Bible/Old Testament Studies 561. New York: T&T Clark, 2012. Study of the Deuteronomistic History's explanation of destruction and exile from the perspective of trauma theory.

Janzen, David. *The Necessary King: A Postcolonial Reading of the Deuteronomistic Portrait of the Monarchy.* Hebrew Bible Monographs 57. Sheffield: Sheffield Phoenix, 2013. Examination of the Deuteronomistic History's rhetoric about kingship from the perspective of postcolonial theory.

Joffe, Alexander H. "The rise of secondary states in the Iron Age Levant." *Journal of the Economic and Social History of the Orient* 45.4 (2002): 425–67. Application of anthropology's category of "secondary states" to the emergence of the Israelite monarchy.

Kim, Uriah Y. *Decolonizing Josiah: Toward a Postcolonial Reading of the Deuteronomistic History.* Bible in the Modern World 5. Sheffield: Sheffield Phoenix, 2005. Examination of the Deuteronomistic History's rhetoric about kingship from the perspective of postcolonial theory.

Kim, Uriah Y. *Identity and Loyalty in the David Story: A Postcolonial Reading.* Hebrew Bible Monographs 22. Sheffield: Sheffield Phoenix, 2008. Examination of the Deuteronomistic History's rhetoric about kingship from the perspective of postcolonial theory.

Knoppers, Gary N. "The vanishing Solomon: The disappearance of the united monarchy from recent histories of ancient Israel." *Journal of Biblical Literature* 116 (1997): 19–44. Summary explanation of the reassessments of the historicity of the united monarchy that emerged throughout the 1980s and 1990s.

Levy, Thomas E. et al. "Reassessing the chronology of biblical Edom: New excavations and 14C dates from Khirbat en-Nahas (Jordan)." *Antiquity 302* (2004): 865–79. Report on archaeological work and interpretation of tenth-century copper mines in Edom.

Master, Daniel M. "State formation theory and the kingdom of ancient Israel." *Journal of Near Eastern Studies 60.2* (2001): 117–31. Critique of older anthropological approaches to the Israelite monarchy as a chiefdom that evolved and replaced kinship structures.

Mazar, Amihai. "The search for David and Solomon: An archaeological perspective." In Israel Finkelstein and Amihai Mazar, *The Quest for the Historical Israel: Debating Archaeology and the History of Early Israel*, ed. Brian B. Schmidt (pp. 117–45). Archaeology and Biblical Studies 17. Atlanta: Society of Biblical Literature, 2007. Convenient summary of traditional interpretation of the united monarchy in response to recent revisionist treatments.

Mazar, Amihai. "Archaeology and the biblical narrative: The case of the united monarchy." In R. G. Kratz and H. Spieckermann (eds), *One God – One Cult – One Nation: Archaeological and Biblical Perspectives* (pp. 29–58). Beihefte zur Zeitschrift für die Alttestamentliche Wissenschaft 405. Berlin: de Gruyter, 2010. Convenient summary of traditional interpretation of the united monarchy in response to recent revisionist treatments.

Mazar, Eliat. *The Palace of King David: Excavations at the Summit of the City of David: Preliminary Report of Seasons 2005–2007.* Jerusalem: Shoham Academic Research and Publication, 2009.

Interpretation of recent excavations of the large stone structure in Jerusalem as David's tenth-century palace.

McCarter, P. Kyle, Jr. "The apology of David." *Journal of Biblical Literature* 99 (1980): 489–504. Early interpretation of the Court Narrative in 2 Samuel as an apology for David written during or just after his lifetime.

McKenzie, Steven L. *King David: A Biography*. Oxford: Oxford University Press, 2000. A recent effort to write a biography of David by using the biblical texts.

Meyers, Carol. "Kinship and kingship: The early monarchy." In Michael D. Coogan (ed.), *The Oxford History of the Biblical World* (pp. 165–205). Oxford: Oxford University Press, 1998. Survey of the early monarchical period with special attention to social history and state-formation theory.

Meyers, Carol. *Rediscovering Eve: Ancient Israelite Women in Context*. Oxford: Oxford University Press, 2013. Examination of women in ancient Israelite society with special attention to social science perspectives.

Miller, J. Maxwell. "Separating the Solomon of history from the Solomon of legend." In L. K. Handy (ed.), *The Age of Solomon: Scholarship at the Turn of the Millennium* (pp. 1–24). Studies in the History and Culture of the Ancient Near East 11. Leiden: Brill, 1997. Classic explication of the reassessments of the historical and archaeological evidence for Solomon that emerged in the 1980s and 1990s.

Miller, J. Maxwell and John H. Hayes. *A History of Ancient Israel and Judah*. 2nd edn. Louisville, KY: Westminster John Knox, 2006. Originally published 1986. A comprehensive history of Israel and Judah that incorporated the reassessments of the united monarchy era that emerged in the 1980s and 1990s.

Moore, Megan Bishop and Brad E. Kelle. *Biblical History and Israel's Past: The Changing Study of the Bible and History*. Grand Rapids, MI: Eerdmans, 2011. A comprehensive survey of the developments in the reconstructions of Israelite history and the historical interpretation of the Bible from the 1970s to the present.

Noth, Martin. *The History of Israel*. New York: Harper, 1958. Classic example of the traditional reconstructions of the united monarchy based largely on the biblical texts.

Polzin, Robert. *Samuel and the Deuteronomist: A Literary Study of the Deuteronomistic History Part Two: 1 Samuel*. Indiana University Studies in Biblical Literature. Bloomington: Indiana University Press, 1989. A narrative interpretation of the stories of the kings in 1 Samuel.

Rainey, Anson F. and R. Steven Notley. *The Sacred Bridge: Carta's Atlas of the Biblical World*. Jerusalem: Carta, 2006. Comprehensive survey of the archaeological and literary evidence in the service of a traditional interpretation of the historicity of the united monarchy.

Rost, Leonhard. *Die Überlieferung von der Thronnachfolge Davids*. Beiträge zur Wissenschaft vom Alten und Neuen Testament 42. Stuttgart: Kohlhammer, 1926. In English as *The Succession to the Throne of David*, trans. M. D. Rutter and D. M. Gunn. Historic Texts and Interpreters in Biblical Scholarship 1. Sheffield: Almond, 1982. Classic interpretation of the Court Narrative in 2 Samuel 9–1 Kings 2 as an originally unified work dating from the time of Solomon.

Tappy, R. E., M. J. Lundberg, P. K. McCarter, and B. Zuckerman. "An abecedary of the mid-tenth century BCE from the Judaean Shephelah." *Bulletin of the American Schools of Oriental Research* 344 (2006): 5–46. Discussion of the recent inscription and its possible relevance for tenth-century BCE Israelite history.

Thompson, Thomas L. *Early History of the Israelite People: From the Written and Archaeological Sources*. Studies in the History of the Ancient Near East 4. Leiden: Brill, 1992. Comprehensive example of the revisionist interpretations of early Israel and the monarchy.

Van Seters, John. *The Biblical Saga of King David*. Winona Lake, IN: Eisenbrauns, 2009. Interpretation of the David stories in 2 Samuel as a later critique of the monarchy added to the already existing Deuteronomistic History for the sake of a postexilic audience.

Wright, Jacob L. *David, King of Israel, and Caleb in Biblical Memory*. Cambridge: Cambridge University Press, 2014. Examination of the function of the David traditions as war commemorations to negotiate political identity and belonging in a postdisaster context in Judah.

CHAPTER 11

The Divided Monarchy

J. J. M. Roberts

According to the chronology followed by the historian John Bright (469–71), the divided monarchy lasted ca. 335 years. Israel, the northern half of the divided monarchy, lasted only 200 years, from the split of David and Solomon's united monarchy under Rehoboam in 922 BCE until the north was terminated as a quasi-independent political entity by Shalmaneser V's conquest of Samaria in 722 BCE. Judah, the southern half of the divided monarchy, continued for another 135 years, until it was ended by Nebuchadnezzar II's second capture of Jerusalem in 587 BCE. Other historians sometimes follow different chronologies, but the differences are negligible. The split is sometimes dated up to four years earlier in 926 BCE, and the second capture of Jerusalem is sometimes dated a year later, in 586 BCE, but a five-year difference in the total length of the divided monarchy, whether 335 or 340 years long, is hardly significant, particularly given the many uncertainties in our knowledge of this period. In view of those uncertainties, it is important to deal with such preliminaries as how we know what we do know of this period before turning to a summary account of the main phases of this history.

Sources

The primary source for the history of these two states is contained in the relevant part (1 Kings 12–2 Kings 25) of the so-called Deuteronomistic History (hereafter DtrH = Deuteronomy, Joshua, Judges, 1 Samuel–2 Kings; see also Brad Kelle's essay in this volume). This is supplemented by the much later and more doctrinaire Chronicler's History (1–2 Chronicles), whose treatment of the divided monarchy is found in 2 Chronicles 10–36. Much of the Chronicler's History, however, is simply lifted from the earlier DtrH with slight stylistic changes. Where the Chronicler's History differs significantly from DtrH or adds significant additional material, the historical reliability of the differing or additional material is hotly debated. Does this material derive from other early, independent, and reliable source material still available to the Chronicler, or does it simply

The Wiley Blackwell Companion to Ancient Israel, First Edition. Edited by Susan Niditch.
© 2016 John Wiley & Sons, Ltd. Published 2016 by John Wiley & Sons, Ltd.

represent late hagiography, or even worse, is it simply the novelistic and theologically motivated creation of the Chronicler himself? In addition to DtrH and the Chronicler, there is also important supplemental material provided by the preexilic writing prophets. Moreover, a number of important Assyrian, Babylonian, Egyptian, Hebrew, Aramaic, and Moabite inscriptions give us a patchwork of important synchronisms and many additional, though sketchy, details for understanding the Israelite and Judean history of this period (see the essay by Christopher Rollston in this volume).

Determining the date of composition of the DtrH, our primary source, is not an easy task. The last event mentioned in 1 Kings 12–2 Kings 25 is the release of the Judean king, Jehoiachin, from a Babylonian prison in the first year (561 BCE) of Awīl/Amēl-Marduk, Nebuchadnezzar's successor on the Babylonian throne (2 Kings 25:28–30). Obviously, DtrH, in its present form, must have been written after the last event recorded in it. That, however, only dates the final form of the text. It does not answer the question of how many editions of the history were extant before being put into its final form. Frank Cross and others have argued persuasively that there was a major edition of DtrH published during the reign of the great reforming king Josiah (640–609 BCE), celebrating Josiah's restoration of the ideals of the Davidic golden age (Cross 274–89). As Cross pointed out, there are two themes running through this edition of DtrH. One is the theme of the sin of Jeroboam I, his own and that which he caused Israel to sin, that ultimately led to the destruction of the northern kingdom and the exile of its population (1 Kings 14:14–16). The other is the theme of God's chosen and faithful servant David, for whose sake God would preserve Judah and maintain the line of David, culminating in David's descendant Josiah, who would destroy the illegitimate sanctuaries of the north (1 Kings 13:2). At one point the work apparently reached its climax in the glorious description of Josiah's religious reform and his attempt at the reassertion of control over the former northern territories. The later material in DtrH, according to Cross, does not represent a thoroughgoing revision, but simply a series of ad hoc and very partial additions to the text to update it and provide some feeble attempt to explain why the hopes associated with Josiah failed.

This two-edition theory of DtrH has won many adherents, but others, like Robert Wilson of Yale University, have argued that there was an even earlier edition of the history. I first heard Wilson's views in a paper he presented years ago at the Colloquium for Biblical Research. Though that paper in its full form was never published, he has hinted at an early Hezekian edition of Kings in a number of his works (Wilson, *Prophecy*, 157; "Introduction," 590; "Former prophets," 91). Josiah's religious reform was preceded by Hezekiah's very similar religious reform almost a century earlier, ca. 715 BCE, only seven years after the final collapse of the north in 722 BCE, when Hezekiah also attempted to regain control over the north (2 Kings 18:3–8; 2 Chr. 29:3–31:21; on the historicity of the Chronicler's Hezekiah, see Vaughn). The theological explanation of the north's fall found in 2 Kings 17, though it has been reedited for the Josianic edition, was probably originally composed during Hezekiah's reform, and it is likely that there was a complete edition of DtrH composed for Hezekiah and in which Hezekiah was the heroic new David, much as the later edition assigned that role to Josiah. The later Josianic edition has obliterated some of the traces of this earlier edition, but it remains clear that both Hezekiah and Josiah followed Deuteronomistic principles in trying to restrict sacrificial worship to the temple in Jerusalem and in ridding the countryside and other cities of alternative cult sites, as well as outlawing and destroying such ancient cultic apparatus as stone steles, sacred poles or asherim, and other altars and incense altars. If Wilson's theory is correct, and I believe that it is, much of DtrH's account of the earlier history, both of the united monarchy and of the divided monarchy, had already assumed written form in the late eighth and very early seventh century BCE, little more than 200 years from the time of the split. This leaves untouched the related question of how many other earlier and relatively complete written sources the Hezekian editor simply incorporated into his historical account.

That earlier sources are incorporated in the account is clear from the contrast in theological outlook between the editors of DtrH and some of the earlier historical material that they include. The editors of DtrH judge former kings on the basis of the theological principles of the religious reforms of their own days. Almost every earlier king is judged on the basis of whether or not he did away with worship on the high places, stone steles (the pillars or *maṣṣēbôt*), and the stylized sacred poles or *'ăšērîm* representing sacred trees. Even the earlier good kings failed this test, for the obvious reason that the test was anachronistic. These earlier good kings had never heard of this Deuteronomistic requirement. Nonetheless, the editors of DtrH are troubled by this failure of the earlier good kings much as a modern American reader with sensibilities honed by modern political correctness might be troubled by the, judged by our standards, blatant racism one finds in outstanding American historians of the 1920s. Note DtrH's comment on Asa, "Asa did what was right in the sight of the Lord, as his father David had done … But the high places were not taken away. Nevertheless the heart of Asa was true to the Lord all his days" (1 Kings 15:11–14), or Joash, "Jehoash did what was right in the sight of the Lord all his days, because the priest Jehoiada instructed him. Nevertheless the high places were not taken away; the people continued to sacrifice and make offerings on the high places" (2 Kings 12:2–3); so also Amaziah (2 Kings 14:3–4) and Azariah (2 Kings 15:3–4). Of these four, pre-Hezekian reform, good kings, the most interesting religious detail concerns Asa. Despite the fact that he did not remove the high places and their cultic installations, DtrH does report that Asa "removed his mother from being queen mother, because she had made an abominable image for Asherah; Asa cut down her image and burned it at the Wadi Kidron" (1 Kings 15:13). This action does not seem to have stemmed from the later Deuteronomistic reform movement, since Asa failed the Deuteronomistic reform criteria, so it seems to have reflected an earlier theological concern. Asa put up with the high places, their stone steles, and their stylized sacred poles or *'ăšērîm*, but something about Maacah's image for Asherah was too much for a Yahwistic king of even the pre-Deuteronomistic period. The stylized sacred trees are often represented in Israelite art as a source of life, since they are often portrayed with wild goats standing or deer approaching from either side to eat from their leaves. A similar non-Israelite scene shows a female goddess, naked from the waist up, holding food in both hands, with wild goats in the same pose as on the Israelite scenes, eating from her hands (see Roberts and Roberts 183–5). The goddess is presumably the Canaanite Asherah, the mother goddess, and the ultimate background for the female principle embedded in the *'ăšērîm*, or stylized sacred trees, that were perfectly acceptable in Israelite worship prior to the Deuteronomistic reforms of Hezekiah and Josiah (see the essay by Elizabeth Bloch-Smith in this volume). My own view is that Maacah went too far in her worship of this female principle by abandoning the acceptable stylized tree for a clearly human female image, thus giving Asherah an independent existence alongside Yahweh. Even early Israel had a strong aniconic streak, and such a transgression of acceptable symbolic representations of divine powers was too much for the pious king (see the essay by Theodore Lewis in this volume). Asa had never heard of the Deuteronomistic demands, but even in his day, some things were just not done.

The Regnal Formulae

Even a casual reader of 1 Kings 12–2 Kings 25 will note the recurring feature of the regnal formulae. For the period when both the northern and southern kingdom existed, these formulae provide a synchronic framework for the reigns of both the northern and southern kings. Two examples will illustrate this. The regnal formula for the southern king Asa states, "In the twentieth year of King Jeroboam of Israel, Asa began to reign over Judah; he reigned forty-one years in Jerusalem. His mother's name was Maacah daughter of Abishalom" (1 Kings 15:9). The formula for the northern king Nadab says, "Nadab son of Jeroboam began to reign over Israel in the second year of King Asa of Judah; he reigned over Israel two years" (1 Kings 15:25). The regnal formulae continue for the southern kings even after the collapse of the north, but they obviously no longer contain the synchronic feature. Note the formula for Manasseh, "Manasseh was twelve years old when he began to reign; he reigned fifty-five years in Jerusalem. His mother's name was Hephzibah" (2 Kings 21:1). The fairly complete list of regnal formulae for the period of the divided kingdom, therefore, when linked with the absolute chronology provided by the Assyrian synchronisms, would appear to provide a nice reliable chronological framework for the history of the period. Unfortunately that expectation will not hold up.

I became aware of the problem at an early age. When I was barely in my teens, the women of my small West Texas church were studying the Books of Kings, and they decided to make a timeline, which they painted in bright colors on a white bed sheet that they hung up at the front of the auditorium. Apparently they supplied the dates from a standard history of Israel, but the numbers for the length of reign of each king came directly from the biblical text. Sometimes being bored in church, the colorful bed sheet drew my attention, and I started doing the math. I soon realized that if the figures for the lengths of reign were correct, neither kingdom could have ended as early as the historian's dates said they did. The figures did not add up. Years later as a professor at Princeton Theological Seminary, I directed a doctoral dissertation that focused a lot of attention on these regnal formulae. The student, Jeffrey Rogers, began with the assumption that these regnal formulae were derived from reliable ancient sources and provided the fixed framework on which the historian constructed his historical narrative. In thoroughly investigating the textual variants, particularly in the different Greek recensions, however, Rogers discovered that there was far greater fluidity in the numbers found in the regnal formulae than in the numbers of the synchronisms outside the regnal formulae. That led Rogers to the tentative conclusion that the regnal formulae were created from the narrative, not the other way around.

Even if he overstates his case, it is clear that these regnal formulae were subject to a great deal of alteration and reshaping to make them fit the different narrative demands of the different textual traditions. At the very least one must recognize that the figures in the regnal formulae do not deserve uncritical trust. Not only do they sometimes disagree internally with one another, a number of them contradict the absolute chronological framework provided by clear Assyrian synchronisms like Tiglath-pileser's conquest of Israel and Damascus in 733–732 BCE, or Sennacherib's third campaign against Hezekiah's Judah in 701 BCE. Sometimes the numbers in the Hebrew text are simply and undeniably wrong, even if we are not sure what the correct numbers should be. Sometimes the numbers can be logically adjusted to fit what on other grounds we know the chronology to be. At other times they appear to represent a tentative but, at least given our limited sources, a reasonably reliable framework for the history of the period. None of them deserve blind confidence, however.

Preexisting Prophetic Stories

Another structural feature of the narrative of DtrH is the insertion at several points of what appear to be fragmentary parts of independent written blocks of preexistent prophetic legends and stories. In 1 Kings 13:1–32 there is the very strange story of the unnamed prophet from Judah who bravely prophesied in the north at Bethel against Jeroboam I, and then broke the divine command by returning to the city to have dinner with the older northern prophet there, which resulted in the southern prophet being killed by a lion. This story has clearly been adapted by the Josianic editor of DtrH to make it point to the rise of Josiah, but the many oddities in the narrative suggest it is a much older story, perhaps of northern origin. Since the only southern prophet known to have given negative oracles at Bethel against a Jeroboam and his cult was Amos, against Jeroboam II in the middle of the eighth century BCE, and since the oracles of Amos are full of lion imagery, it may be that he was the historical prophet about whom this strange narrative originally crystalized. Prior to its southern reshaping, the story may originally have represented a critique of Amos as a false prophet by his northern prophetic opponents, but, if so, the complex editorial process has made any attempt to recover the actual form of the original story too hypothetical to be convincing.

In 1 Kings 17–2 Kings 8:15, 2 Kings 9:1–10, and 2 Kings 13:14–21, there is also a collection of stories, presumably of northern origin, about the northern prophets Elijah, Elisha, Micaiah ben Imlah, and a number of otherwise unnamed northern prophetic figures. Finally, in 2 Kings 18:17–20:19 there is a block of stories about the southern prophet Isaiah's interactions with the Judean king Hezekiah. The editors of DtrH used these prophetic stories to fill out their historical narrative, but it is highly unlikely that any of these editors was the actual author of these stories and legends, or even the first to put them into written form.

The Split and Its Aftermath (922–875 BCE)

The split in the kingdom took place because the northern tribes felt like they were bearing more than their "fair share" of the heavy burden of taxes and forced labor. When Solomon's successor, Rehoboam, refused to take their complaints seriously and threatened to increase their burden, the north revolted. Their revolt did give them a respite from Jerusalem's heavy demands, but from a longer-term point of view, the split in the kingdom was probably a disaster for both unequal portions of the former united kingdom. The northerners soon found that they had their own monarchy and their own royal sanctuaries to support with taxes and services. Both states now also had the expense and distraction of regular intermittent warfare with one another on their common border that drained the financial and manpower resources of both states. Moreover, after the split, neither kingdom possessed the united monarchy's power to keep all the surrounding states in submission and paying tribute. The Arameans of Damascus had already asserted their independence before the death of Solomon, perhaps the Edomites as well, and the Philistines were also soon independent. Despite the lack of sources, one may probably assume that Ammon and Moab also took advantage of Israel and Judah's internal struggle to stop paying tribute to either state.

In the struggle between Israel and Judah, the north controlled the larger and more fertile territory, had a larger population, and a larger portion of the former professional army was located in the north. Initially the north was less well organized, but prophetic opposition to a quick suppression of the revolt gave the north time to create a rival monarchal structure in the north, and, given this breathing room and their more abundant resources and population, eventually the northern kingdom would surpass the Judean kingdom in power. The larger territory and population in the north came at a price, however. There were major sectional and tribal rivalries in the north, particularly between the major tribes of Ephraim and Manasseh, that made the northern monarchy far more unstable than the Davidic monarchy in Judah. In the approximately 200-year history of the northern kingdom there were nine bloody dynastic changes, while in the 335-year history of Judah, despite the assassination of four kings and the foreign deportation of two, there were no dynastic changes apart from the brief interruption of Queen Athaliah's seven-year reign.

Moreover, as if the split were not disaster enough for the two kingdoms, in the fifth year of Rehoboam's reign the Egyptian king Sheshonq I, the biblical Shishaq, launched a major military campaign against Palestine, plundering areas of both Judah and Israel (see John Huddlestun's essay in this volume). His preserved accounts of this campaign are too fragmentary and unclear to reconstruct a detailed picture of the campaign, but he appears to have captured Megiddo and a number of other major Israelite cities in the wide and fertile valleys and plains that separate Samaria from Galilee (Pritchard 263–4). According to 1 Kings 14:25–26 Sheshonq also marched up against Jerusalem, where Rehoboam felt constrained to buy him off by stripping the royal treasury, the temple treasury, and the golden display shields of Solomon that had proclaimed the wealth and power of the united monarchy. Sheshonq's raid was a major economic blow to both kingdoms, and it would take time for both kingdoms to replenish their reserves. In the meantime the resource-draining intermittent border warfare between Judah and Israel continued into the ninth century BCE. Judah was eventually able to maintain a relatively stable northern border against the stronger north only by paying the Arameans of Damascus to open a northern front against Israel. This may have begun as early as Rehoboam, since Asa alluded to a treaty between his father and the father of Ben-Hadad (1 Kings 15:16–22), when Asa offered tribute to the Aramean king Ben-Hadad son of Tabrimmon to break his treaty with the Israelite Baasha. Ben-Hadad accepted the offer and attacked Israel's northern territories, forcing Baasha to withdraw from Judah's border to meet this northern threat, and that allowed Asa to mobilize his forces to further fortify his northern border with the building materials left behind by the withdrawing Israelites. The threat from Damascus and several years of civil war in the north after the murder of Baasha's son appear to have maintained this equilibrium until Omri was able to impose his reign on the north, eventually moving the northern capital to his newly founded city, Samaria.

Peace and Political Expansion (875–842 BCE)

With Omri and his son and successor, Ahab, the northern kingdom appears to have flowered and reached its full potential of strength. Unfortunately, the editors of DtrH considered the Omrides, Omri and Ahab, in particular, as paradigmatically evil kings, so their account of the reigns of these kings has little positive to say about them, and those positive things only slip through their negative spin by accident. Details of Omri's reign are very sparse, but it slips through that Omri founded and built the impressive new northern capital at Samaria (1 Kings 16:24). We know from the Moabite Stone (Pritchard 320–1) and from the admission in 2 Kings 3:4 that Omri reconquered Moab and took a huge yearly tribute from this country (see Christopher Rollston's essay in this volume). Ahab's diplomatic marriage to Jezebel, the daughter of Ethbaal, the king of the Sidonians (1 Kings 16:31), also suggests that Omri reestablished good relationships with the Phoenician monarchy, something that would have been important for his extensive building activity, as it had been for Solomon's. It is unclear what Omri's relationship to Asa of Judah was, but either under Omri or perhaps more likely Ahab (1 Kings 22:44), the long border war with Judah was resolved by Judah becoming a treaty partner with Israel. Jehoshaphat, Asa's successor, was clearly allied with Ahab, since Jehoshaphat's son and successor married a daughter of Ahab (2 Kings 8:18, 27), and the accounts of joint actions and state visits between Judah and Israel make clear that the two states were now at peace and on good terms.

Israel's relationship to the Arameans of Damascus during Omri and Ahab's reigns is less clear. During part of his reign, Ahab was clearly allied with Hadad-ezer of Damascus, the leader of a large anti-Assyrian alliance, since according to the Assyrian inscriptions of Shalmaneser III, Ahab contributed 10,000 infantry and 2,000 chariots to the allied effort at the battle of Qarqar in 853 BCE (Grayson 23 ii 89b–102). This was the largest chariot contingent of any of the allied participants in the battle, and the total number of Ahab's troops was only surpassed by Hadad-ezer's 20,000 infantry, 1,200 chariots, and 1,200 cavalry. This and Israel's previously mentioned domination of Moab suggests that Israel during Omri and Ahab's reign was a dominant power. Ahab appears to have been an independent partner in the anti-Assyrian alliance, not a subservient vassal of Damascus.

Judah under Jehoshaphat also seems to have regained some of its earlier strength. He appears to have reimposed Judean hegemony over Edom, since early in his reign Edom was a vassal without its own king, just a governor (1 Kings 22:47). Even later in his reign, when Edom once again had its own king, it still appears to have been Jehoshaphat's vassal, since it participated with him and Jehoram, the son of Ahab, in trying to subdue rebellious Moab (2 Kings 3:7). Jehoshaphat also tried to duplicate Solomon's earlier feat of sponsoring seaborne trade with Ophir from his port at Ezion-geber on the Gulf of Aqaba, though apparently unsuccessfully as his fleet was wrecked (1 Kings 22:48–49). The Chronicler also reports that Jehoshaphat instituted a major judicial reform in Judah (2 Chr. 19:5–11).

In the north, probably following Ahab's death, Moab revolted, and neither of Ahab's sons, the short-lived Ahaziah or Jehoram, despite Jehoram's major effort supported by Jehoshaphat's Judah and his vassal Edom, were able to restore Israelite hegemony over Moab. Notwithstanding this lack of success against Moab, however, Jehoram apparently maintained his participation in the anti-Assyrian coalition, since despite Shalmaneser III's failure to specifically mention Israel or its king, the same coalition of 12 kings fought against the Assyrian army again in 849, 848, and 845 BCE. When Shalmaneser marched west in 841 BCE, however, Hazael had replaced Hadad-ezer as king of Damascus, and Jehu had replaced Jehoram as king of Israel, suggesting that both these violent dynastic changes had taken place in 842 BCE.

DtrH's animosity toward Omri and Ahab may be partially responsible for a major element of confusion in the biblical accounts about Ahab's wars with Ben-Hadad's Arameans in 1 Kings 20 and Ben-Hadad's wars against Samaria and Hazael's murder of Ben-Hadad in 2 Kings 6:8–8:15. There was a Ben-Hadad, son of Tabrimmon, of Damascus, a contemporary of Asa (1 Kings 15:18), perhaps attested in an Aramaic inscription (Pritchard 655; see Christopher Rollston's essay in this volume), whose reign may have extended into the early reign of Ahab, but it is clear from the inscriptions of Shalmaneser III that the king of Damascus during Ahab's last years and into the reign of his two sons, between at least 853 and 845 BCE, was not a Ben-Hadad, but Hadad-ezer, whom the biblical text never mentions. Some have suggested that Hadad-ezer may have been succeeded by an otherwise unknown Ben-Hadad, perhaps a son of Hadad-ezer who had a very short reign, but Shalmaneser III implies that Hazael overthrew and immediately followed Hadad-ezer on the throne of Damascus (Grayson 118 i 25–ii 6). No Ben-Hadad who was king of Damascus after Hadad-ezer is clearly attested in the nonbiblical texts until Ben-Hadad, the son and successor of Hazael, is mentioned in the Aramaic inscription of Zakir of Hamath in the early years of the eighth century BCE (Pritchard 655–6).

Moreover, the account of Israel's abject weakness in 1 Kings 20 does not fit what we know of Ahab's reign, and while Israel was certainly weaker under Ahab's successors Ahaziah and Jehoram, the portrayal in 2 Kings 6:8–7:20 hardly fits the Israel of that period either. When Jehu's revolt begins in 842 BCE, the Israelite army is on the offensive, trying to wrest Ramoth-Gilead in the Transjordan from the Arameans. The stories in 1 Kings 20 and 2 Kings 6:8–7:20 are prophetic narratives that probably originally left the kings unnamed, but which fit far better in the period after Jehu's revolt, when Israel endured a long period of abject weakness, dominated first by Hazael and then for a time by his successor Ben-Hadad.

Even the account of Ahab's death in an attack on the same Ramoth-Gilead in 1 Kings 22 is problematic. Perhaps Ahab was actually killed in such an attack, but it is striking that Jehoram, the second of Ahab's sons to succeed him, was also seriously wounded in a battle at Ramoth-Gilead and that he was recovering at Jezreel from these earlier wounds when he was shot down in his chariot by Jehu's arrow in 842 BCE (2 Kings 9:15–26). The account of Jehoram's death in his chariot from an arrow is similar enough to the account of Ahab's death to raise questions. Could it be that the prophetic narrative in 1 Kings 22 was originally about Jehoram, but has been simplified and given a stronger narrative interest by making it about his more infamous predecessor Ahab? It should be noted that Jehoshaphat the Judean king participates in this battle at Ramoth-Gilead as an ally of the Israelite king, just as he participated in Jehoram's war against Moab (2 Kings 3:1–27).

Nationalistic Religious Retrenchment and Political Weakness (842–800 BCE)

Unfortunately the international and cosmopolitan outlook similar to that of the Solomonic period that helped Israel develop its full military and political strength under the Omrides also brought with it a religious syncretism that provoked a negative prophetic reaction similar to that which had undercut the continuity of Solomon's kingdom. At least from the point of view of conservative Yahwistic prophetic circles, like those who preserved the legends of Elijah, Elisha, and the story of Micaiah ben Imlah, Jezebel proved to be a rabid promoter of Phoenician religion in Israel, and the conflict between her views of religion and that of the Yahwists was so great that it provoked a bloody resistance to royal religious policy. This resistance and the resulting royal persecution of the Yahwists ultimately produced the prophetically inspired revolt of Jehu in 842 BCE. Jehu's revolt was extremely violent and bloody and extremely thorough. The presence of the Judean king in Israel on a state visit at the time of the revolt (2 Kings 9:16), and the ill-timed state visit of much of the Judean court to Israel during the subsequent blood-letting (2 Kings 10:12–14), resulted in the extermination of both the Israelite royal house and most of the Judean royal house. In addition to annihilating most members of both royal houses, Jehu also exterminated the majority of the experienced political and military elite in Israel, especially those who had, for reasons of real commitment or political necessity, supported the Phoenician syncretism favored by the influential Jezebel and her minions (2 Kings 10:18–28).

The religious result of this bloody coup in the north was the restoration of a more nationalistic form of Israelite Yahwism, but it came at a very high political price. The annihilation of the ruling class left Israel isolated from all its former allies and bereft of experienced political and top military leadership, and for the last half of the ninth century and the first years of the eighth century BCE, Israel suffered the consequences. Hazael of Damascus was battered by Shalmaneser III of Assyria in 841 BCE and again in 838 BCE, but after 838 BCE the Assyrian armies were occupied elsewhere, and by

830 BCE Assyria was in decline, Shalmaneser III's reign ending in 824 BCE in an internal revolt. This afforded Hazael the freedom to expand into the power vacuum left by the retreating Assyrians, and he took advantage of this opportunity with a vengeance. He crushed and humiliated Israel to the south, took tribute from Judah as well, and expanded his control far north into northern Syria. At one point he even crossed the Euphrates (Eph'al and Naveh 195–6).

Judah did not suffer the same degree of Phoenician-inspired religious syncretism prior to Jehu's coup, since Judah had no Jezebel, and Asa and Jehoshaphat had supported the Yahwistic and pro-Davidic priesthood in Jerusalem, but when Jehu's coup resulted in the death of the Judean king Ahaziah and most of the remaining royal heirs of Jehoshaphat and Jehoram, the Judean queen mother Athaliah, the widow of Jehoram and mother of Ahaziah, decided to wipe out the rest of Jehoshaphat's heirs and claim the throne for herself. Since she was a daughter of Ahab, during her seven-year interregnum the threat of a similar religious syncretism in the south increased, but she lacked the external success and the broad popularity arising from it that the Omrides had enjoyed in the north, and when a surviving infant son of Ahaziah, who had been hidden away with the help of the Jerusalem priesthood, was old enough, the priests led a palace revolt on his behalf to dethrone and execute Athaliah and restore the Davidic line (2 Kings 11:1–21). The young king, Jehoash, was under close priestly supervision, and the countercoup that elevated him to the throne involved a renewal of the covenant with Yahweh and a bloody suppression of the worship of Baal that Athaliah had been able to introduce. Nonetheless, the loss of Judah's ruling elite also left Judah politically weak well into the beginning of the eighth century BCE.

Limited Recovery (800–775 BCE)

It was only with the Assyrian Adad-nirari III's battering of Damascus in the very late ninth or beginning of the eighth century BCE (Grayson 207–13) that Israel under Joash and Judah under Amaziah began the recovery of both states from their earlier weakness. Joash of Israel was able to defeat the Aramean Ben-Hadad, the son of Hazael, in a number of battles and recover some of the territory that Hazael and Ben-Hadad had taken from Israel earlier. Amaziah of Judah was also successful in his war with the Edomites, but his pride in that victory overcame his good sense, and when he challenged Joash, Israel thoroughly defeated the Judeans.

Renewed Expansion (775–750 (738) BCE)

Despite this limited relief, however, real recovery for both states did not come until after 773 BCE, when Shamshi-ilu, the field marshal of the Assyrian king Shalmaneser IV, marched against Damascus and took heavy tribute from its Aramean king (Grayson 239–40). Following this campaign and its significant weakening of the Arameans of Damascus, the Assyrians also fell into major decline, and both Israel and Judah, who again seem to have been allied with one another, expanded at the expense of their neighbors. Jeroboam II of Israel captured a number of sites in the northern Transjordan, perhaps extending his control deep into former Aramean territory (2 Kings 14:25, 28), and his military successes against the Arameans and other eastern neighbors were impressive enough to create a new sense of national pride for Israel in their own military strength (Amos 6:13). In the meantime, Azariah of Judah, or Uzziah as he was also known, a somewhat younger contemporary of Jeroboam II, also built up the military strength of the southern kingdom (2 Kings 15:1–7; 2 Chr. 26). He appears to have been quite successful against the Philistines and some of Judah's southern neighbors. After Jeroboam II's death ca. 750 BCE, the north, torn apart by sectional rivalries and a bloody struggle for the throne, fell into a rapid decline, but Azariah's Judah apparently remained strong until his death ca. 738 BCE.

The international situation took a turn for the worse in 745 BCE, when Tiglath-pileser III seized the throne of Assyria, thoroughly reorganized the Assyrian state with a much stronger central government and much closer control over the provincial governors, and then began to reconquer former Assyrian dependencies. In 743 BCE he defeated the north Syrian anti-Assyrian league led by Arpad and their Urartian allies, and when Arpad fell after a three-year siege in 740 BCE, the members of the north Syrian league all rushed to pay tribute to Tiglath-pileser, including Kullani, biblical Calno or Calneh. To fill the sudden power vacuum in Syria, a certain Azariah created a south Syrian league to resist further Assyrian expansion into Syria, and by late 739 or early 738 BCE, this league seems to have persuaded Kullani and some 18 districts of Hamath to revolt against Tiglath-pileser. In 738 BCE Tiglath-pileser responded by defeating the southern league and capturing and sacking the city of Kullani. The identity of the Azariah who led this south Syrian league is disputed, but Tadmor originally argued that it was none other than Azariah of Judah (Tadmor 273–6), and I am still inclined to hold to that identification because of the major impact that the fall of Calno or Calneh had on both Amos's Israelite audience (Amos 6:2) and Isaiah's Judean audience (Isa. 10:9). With Kullani's fall, apparently in the same year as Azariah's death, most of the members of the south Syrian league, including Menahem of Israel and Rezin of Damascus, rushed to pay tribute to Tiglath-pileser, though Judah is conspicuously absent from these early tribute lists of Tiglath-pileser. After this event, however, Judah seems to have temporarily lost any appetite it may have once had for joining in any anti-Assyrian league.

Reaction to Assyria and the Fall of the North (735–715 BCE)

In contrast to Judah's reticence, by ca. 735 BCE, Rezin of Damascus, allied with the Phoenicians, Philistines, and Pekah the son of Remaliah of Israel, tried to reconstitute the south Syrian league against Assyria, urging first Jotham, Azariah's son, and then Ahaz, who apparently succeeded him on the Judean throne in 735 BCE, to join the league. Neither Jotham nor Ahaz would agree, however, and this led to the so-called Syro-Ephraimitic War of 735–732 BCE. To force Judah into the league Rezin and his allies made a surprise attack on Jerusalem in an attempt to quickly remove Ahaz from the Judean throne and replace him with a more agreeable ruler of their own choosing (2 Kings 16:5–9; Isa. 7:1–9). The surprise attack failed, however. Ahaz appealed to

Tiglath-pileser for help, and the besiegers soon had to abandon the attempt on Jerusalem in order to face the Assyrian threat to their north. Tiglath-pileser crushed Philistia in 734 BCE, and in 733–732 BCE he destroyed both the Arameans of Damascus and Israel. Only a small enclave around Samaria remained under the new Israelite king Hoshea, who had murdered Pekah and submitted to Tiglath-pileser; the rest of the former state of Israel was turned into Assyrian provinces under Assyrian governors and many of its former Israelite inhabitants were deported. The reprieve for Samaria and its environs was quite brief, however. Two years after the death of Tiglath-pileser in 727 BCE, Hoshea foolishly revolted in 725 BCE, hoping for help from Egypt, but he was taken prisoner and Shalmaneser V captured Samaria in 722 BCE. Many of the remaining Israelite inhabitants of Samaria were deported under Shalmaneser and Sargon II, but despite these moves there was another attempted revolt involving Samaria in 720 BCE led by Hamath and Gaza, but the revolt was quickly crushed despite the appearance of a Nubian/Egyptian relief force in southern Philistia that was put to flight by the Assyrians.

Again Ahaz remained loyal to his Assyrian overlords, and despite DtrH's refusal to say anything good about Ahaz, whom he regarded like Omri and Ahab as a totally bad king, Ahaz's policy probably benefited Judah in the long run. Early in the Syro-Ephraimitic War, Judah suffered some losses at the hands of Syria, Israel, and the Philistines, and early in the Hamath-Gaza revolt, Ahaz probably also suffered some losses at the hands of the Philistines. As those conflicts wore on with Assyrian involvement, however, Ahaz as a loyal Assyrian vassal probably more than made up his initial losses with territorial expansion at the expense of both Israel and the Philistines. In Judah he was celebrated as the staff that smote Philistia (Isa. 14:28–32).

Hezekiah's Revival (715–686 BCE)

In 715 BCE, when Hezekiah succeeded Ahaz on the Judean throne, there seems to have been great expectations of Judah recovering the greatness of the Davidic golden age, perhaps bringing the north back under the hegemony of Judah. These expectations were fed by a Deuteronomistic religious reform centralizing worship in Jerusalem and outlawing the other cult centers and local high places as well as their cultic paraphernalia like the stone stela and stylized sacred poles or 'ăšērîm. The Philistines, led by Ashdod, apparently feeling that the nationalistic Hezekiah would be more amenable to their plans than the dead Ahaz had been, were encouraging a revolt against Sargon, with the promised help of the Nubian rulers of Egypt. Nubia apparently sent their own embassy to the Judean court, but the prophet Isaiah demonstrated dramatically against this proposed revolt, appearing day after day before the palace barefoot and in the nude and proclaiming that the Assyrians would lead away any Nubian/Egyptian relief force just as barefoot and naked as the demonstrating prophet (Isa. 20:1–6). Though Isaiah had to maintain his embarrassing political theater for parts of three years before Sargon's field marshal arrived in Palestine to put down the Ashdod revolt in 711 BCE, apparently the prophet succeeded in dissuading Hezekiah from joining the revolt.

Judah dodged the bullet on this one, but in 705 BCE, when Sargon II was killed in a devastating ambush by mountain tribesmen, and his body was not recovered, rebellion broke out all over the empire – both in Babylon to the southeast of Assyria, and in Syria-Palestine to the west, with Nubian Egypt the major military power supporting the smaller states of southern Syria and Palestine. Apparently Hezekiah's court, with the bad taste of the Ashdod affair still in their mouth, tried to keep Isaiah outside the diplomatic loop. He complained that they were trying to hide their plans from God and refusing to seek oracles from God (Isa. 29:15; 30:1–2; 31:1). The prophet threatened that Judah's faithless reliance on Nubian Egypt would cause Yahweh himself to attack Jerusalem and bring it to death's door before, at the last moment, miraculously intervening to save God's chosen city (Isa. 29:1–8; 31:1–5).

In 701 BCE, when Sennacherib campaigned through Judah, capturing 46 of Judah's walled cities, deporting more than 200,000 of its inhabitants, and driving off the Nubian-Egyptian relief force, Isaiah's threatened judgment on Judah was vindicated. Nonetheless, despite Sennacherib's general success, he was unable to capture Jerusalem, and he returned to Assyria before receiving Hezekiah's promised tribute, which appeared to vindicate Isaiah's promise of last-minute deliverance. There is a great deal of uncertainty about the end of Sennacherib's campaign and why Jerusalem survived, but in Judah's historical tradition, already attested by the time of Jeremiah less than a century later, the survival of Hezekiah's Jerusalem was attributed to a miraculous intervention of Yahweh who struck many of the Assyrian troops dead. Nonetheless, Judah was once again an Assyrian vassal and remained such despite the renewed rebellion of Babylon in 691 BCE and the murder of Sennacherib by his own sons in 681 BCE.

Vassaldom (686–640 BCE)

With Hezekiah's death his religious reform withered away under his son Manasseh, a loyal vassal of Sennacherib, Esarhaddon, and Ashurbanipal, and a pagan syncretist of the order of an Ahab. During Manasseh's reign both Esarhaddon and Ashurbanipal invaded Egypt, Ashurbanipal quite successfully, even capturing Thebes in 663 BCE, so Manasseh had no real opportunity to assert his independence, even had the desire been present. During his reign many of the older syncretistic religious practices crept back in, and, though this is debated, some new religious practices, more directly related to Assyrian religiosity, may have crept in as well. Nor did things noticeably improve under his successor Amon, or even early in the reign of the eight-year-old Josiah.

Josiah's Revival (640–609 BCE)

It was only well into Josiah's reign, after he had reached adulthood and after Assyria's growing weakness and division in Ashurbanipal's last years opened up the opportunity, that Josiah began to push independence from Assyria and to promote his thoroughgoing Deuteronomistic religious reform. The reform was sparked by the discovery of an old scroll in the temple (2 Kings 22:8–13), and given the striking resemblances between Josiah's reform and the earlier religious reform of Hezekiah, it is likely that this old scroll, far from being a newly forged document made to look old, was a relic of Hezekiah's reform, deposited in the temple during his reign and then forgotten and neglected during the long reign of Manasseh, the brief reign of Amon, and the first 18 years of Josiah. Just as in Hezekiah's reform, there was an attempt to bring the northern territories of Israel back under Davidic rule, and for a time Josiah's program appeared to have a chance for success. The years from 622 to 609 BCE were heady days for Judah under Josiah, when it looked as though he might be successful in reestablishing the golden age of David in a manner that even the famous Hezekiah had not succeeded in doing. The total destruction of the hated Assyrian state between 615 and 610 BCE must have been seen in Judah as God's ultimate judgment on Assyria, and the joy in Judah is clearly reflected in the gloating oracles of the prophet Nahum. Unfortunately, the sudden and unexpected death of Josiah at the hands of the Egyptian king Necho at Megiddo in 609 BCE crushed these hopes and left Judah and its historians struggling for an explanation.

Collapse (609–586 BCE)

Judah's last days after Josiah's death were just one disaster after another. The Judeans put Jehoahaz on the throne in place of his father, Josiah, but when Necho returned from Carchemish, he took him away captive to Egypt. Necho replaced him with Jehoiakim, another son of Josiah, but Jehoiakim was thoroughly corrupt and despised by prophets like Jeremiah who held Josiah in high esteem. Jehoiakim remained a faithful vassal of the Egyptians, who had placed him on the throne, until the Neo-Babylonian Nebuchadnezzar II slaughtered the Egyptian army at Carchemish and Hamath in 605 BCE, and then invaded Palestine in 604 BCE. At that point, Jehoiakim had little choice but to change allegiance and swear loyalty to Nebuchadnezzar. When Nebuchadnezzar was checked at the Egyptian border in 601 BCE with heavy losses, however, Jehoiakim was quick to switch sides again, throwing his lot in with the apparently resurgent Egyptians to whom he owed his royal status. It was a bad choice. By 598 BCE the Babylonians had Jerusalem under siege, and Jehoiakim died before the end of the year.

Jehoiakim's son Jehoiachin succeeded him, but his effective reign was quite short. By March 15 or 16 of 597 BCE, he surrendered the city to Nebuchadnezzar, and he, his mother, and most of the nobility were exiled to Babylon. Nebuchadnezzar appointed Jehoiachin's uncle, Mattaniah, who received the crown name Zedekiah, as new king over Judah, but because Jehoiachin remained alive, many Judeans still considered Jehoiachin their legitimate king, undercutting the royal authority of Zedekiah. Zedekiah ruled in Jerusalem for ten years, but in his ninth year he rebelled against Babylon, putting his trust in Egyptian help, which again failed Judah. In 587 or 586 BCE, the city was breached. Zedekiah tried to flee, but was captured and brought to Nebuchadnezzar at Riblah. There the sons of Zedekiah were killed before his eyes, and then Zedekiah was blinded and taken to Babylon in fetters to face a miserable fate. The temple was burned, the city of Jerusalem thoroughly razed, and much of the remaining population of Judah was deported, leaving only the poor and scattered bands of refugees in the desolate land.

Nebuchadnezzar appointed Gedaliah as governor over this pitiful remnant, with his residence at Mizpah, north of the ruined city of Jerusalem, but that arrangement was short-lived. The gullible Gedaliah was soon murdered by Ishmael, the leader of one of the surviving militia groups, who took captive the rest of the remnant at Mizpah. These surviving captives were rescued by Johanan's band near Gibeon, though the murderous kidnapper Ishmael escaped to Ammon. Johanan's band and the large group of the survivors he had rescued from Ishmael then gathered near Bethlehem, where, fearful of Babylonian retaliation, they planned to flee to Egypt. They first consulted the prophet Jeremiah, promising to follow whatever word he received from Yahweh, but when he urged them to stay in Judah, promising God's protection and safety, they accused Jeremiah of lying, and forced Jeremiah and his scribe Baruch to accompany them into Egyptian exile. Their flight probably reflects the flight of many other bands of refugees to Egypt, with the result that Judah and its destroyed capital, Jerusalem, were left lying largely ruined and abandoned until Cyrus the Persian's conquest of Babylon and his edict allowing the return of the Jews to their homeland in 539–538 BCE.

The final editors of DtrH, apart from updating the history with the main events after Josiah's death, had little to offer in terms of overall interpretation. The two main themes of the earlier editions seem to have been dropped, and the only explanation offered seems to have been that the sins of Manasseh were so great that, despite the later reform of Josiah, God would not forgive them (2 Kings 21:10–16; 22:14–20). Nevertheless, after the release of Jehoiachin from prison in 561 BCE, a very late annotator included details about Jehoiachin's rehabilitation in the court of his conqueror, perhaps suggesting there was still some vague hope for the ultimate restoration of the House of David and the renewal of the eternal covenant that God had made with it (2 Kings 25:27–30).

Bibliography

Bright, John. *A History of Israel.* 3rd edn. Philadelphia: Westminster, 1981. Dated, but still solid history of Israel.

Cross, Frank Moore. *Canaanite Myth and Hebrew Epic.* Cambridge, MA: Harvard University Press, 1973. Discusses different editions of Deuteronomistic History.

Grayson, A. Kirk. *Assyrian Rulers of the Early First Millennium BC: II (858–745 BC).* Royal Inscriptions of Mesopotamia, Assyrian Periods 3. Toronto: University of Toronto, 1996. Annotated translation of Assyrian annals.

Eph'al, Israel and Joseph Naveh. "Hazael's booty inscriptions." *Israel Exploration Journal 39* (1989): 192–200 and plates 25–8. Covers Hazael's inscription mentioning his campaign beyond the Euphrates.

Luckenbill, Daniel David. *The Annals of Sennacherib.* Chicago: University of Chicago, 1924. Translation of these important texts.

Pritchard, James (ed.). *Ancient Near Eastern Texts.* 3rd edn. Princeton: Princeton University Press, 1969. Convenient collection of English translations of Near Eastern texts.

Roberts, J. J. M. and Kathryn L. Roberts. "Yahweh's significant other." In L. Day and C. Pressler (eds), *Engaging the Bible in a Gendered World* (pp. 176–85). Louisville, KY: Westminster John Knox, 2006. Discussion of Asherah and the *'ǎšērîm.*

Rogers, Jeffrey S. "Synchronism and structure in 1–2 Kings and Mesopotamian chronographic literature." Dissertation, Princeton Theological Seminary, 1992. Shows the textual fluidity in the regnal formulae in the Bible.

Tadmor, Hayim. *The Inscriptions of Tiglath-pileser III King of Assyria*. Jerusalem: Israel Academy of Sciences and Humanities, 1994. Edition and translation of these important texts.

Thiele, Edwin R. *The Mysterious Numbers of the Hebrew Kings*. Grand Rapids, MI: Eerdmans, 1965. Serious attempt to explain the chronology of the Israelite and Judean kings.

Vaughn, Andrew G. *Theology, History, and Archaeology in the Chronicler's Account of Hezekiah*. Atlanta: Scholars Press, 1999. Underscores the reality of Hezekiah's reform movement.

Wilson, Robert R. *Prophecy and Society in Ancient Israel*. Philadelphia: Fortress, 1980. Refers to Hezekian edition of Deuteronomistic History, as do the following works.

Wilson, Robert R. "Introduction and notes on 1–2 Kings." In Wayne A. Meeks et al. (eds), *The HarperCollins Study Bible*. New York: HarperCollins, 1993.

Wilson, Robert R. "The Former Prophets: Reading the Books of Kings." In James Luther Mays, David L. Petersen, and Kent Harold Richards (eds), *Old Testament Interpretation: Past, Present, and Future: Essays in Honor of Gene M. Tucker* (pp. 83–96). Nashville: Abingdon Press, 1995.

C

Postmonarchic Period: In the Land and Diaspora

CHAPTER 12

(Re)Defining "Israel"
The Legacy of the Neo-Babylonian and Persian Periods

Charles E. Carter

S een through the eyes of the Deuteronomic Historian and many of the prophetic
writers, the destruction of Israel by the Assyrians in 722 and Judah by the Babylonians in 586 were watershed events. The ten northern tribes of Israel were lost forever;
only the faithfulness of YHWH to the Davidic covenant made the survival of a remnant
of Judah possible (2 Kings 17:5–21). Given this assessment it is no surprise that both
biblical scholars and Levantine archaeologists focused their research and excavations
on periods and sites at the center of what they considered the most important traditions: the ancestors, the exodus, the emergence of Israel and Judah, and the rise and fall
of the monarchy. The years of Neo-Babylonian and Persian hegemony were deemed significant primarily because they demonstrated YHWH's judgment on Judah, and though
a limited restoration occurred, the prevailing opinion of scholars was that the religion
and social structures that emerged in the Persian period were as spiritually desolate and
empty as the smoldering ruins of Jerusalem. In this view, the religious impulse of the
prophets was reduced to legalism and ritualism and the priesthood gained power and
influence as the Persian period continued and the Hellenistic period began. Just as these
years were an add-on to earlier periods, they served as a prelude to the Second Testament
and the missions of Jesus of Nazareth and the Apostle Paul.

But what was once at the periphery of academic inquiry has shifted toward the center and is now recognized as pivotal, marked by multiplicity and creativity. The impetus
for this shift is perhaps more a result of newer methodologies and a gradual broadening
of perspectives than a singular discovery. There were, of course, some works that paved
the way forward: Olmstead's *History of the Persian Empire* (1948), Ackroyd's *Exile and
Restoration* (1968), and Stern's work on material culture of the Persian period (1982).
But the emergence of recent studies on the periods of Neo-Babylonian and Persian rule

The Wiley Blackwell Companion to Ancient Israel, First Edition. Edited by Susan Niditch.
© 2016 John Wiley & Sons, Ltd. Published 2016 by John Wiley & Sons, Ltd.

from 605 BCE through 332 BCE occurred in concert with broader interests in text as cultural artifact, application of the social sciences and attendant models, critiques of traditional male- and elite-oriented approaches, and a more nuanced set of historical and ideological questions. These, combined with new archaeological discoveries, renewed excavations and/or reviews of the remains from previously excavated sites and regional site-surveys, allowed for a more comprehensive understanding of these periods and their place within the broader history of "Israel."

In this essay, I address the most significant of these developments and discuss some of the pressing issues and questions in Neo-Babylonian and Persian period studies. How, for example, should we approach the idea and reality of "exile" and the biblical concept of an empty land? Are there methodological approaches that can guide our use of biblical texts and archaeological remains? How should we draw the physical boundaries of Yehud, map its sites and estimate its population? Just how significant was the province to broader imperial concerns? When and how did Jerusalem assume its central role within the socioeconomic and sociopolitical makeup of the province, and what sites may have rivaled the capital for regional influence? Is it possible to trace the religious movements of the Persian period, including the various groups competing for prominence?

The Problem of the Exile

The term "exile" is highly charged and its impact on biblical and later Jewish traditions cannot be overstated. The Deuteronomistic Historian, the prophetic traditions, and much of the Torah itself, are replete with references to the dangers of violating the covenant through worship of other deities, and the perils of intermarriage with its attendant ethnic and cultural diffusion, among others. In these traditions, whether before it became a nation, during the period of the "judges," the rise of the monarchy and throughout the history of Israel and Judah, these primary types of covenant unfaithfulness would result in the ultimate punishment: military defeat and forced exile. Just as the Israelites were called out of Egypt to become a people, so they could be disinherited, and return to Egypt or sent to unspecified places among the nations, where they would become an object of derision. YHWH is indeed a jealous god.

Added to this understanding of "gālût" and the attendant "gôlâ community" as at the same time curse and punishment was the notion that the exile "cured" Israel and Judah of their penchant to worship other deities. For several generations of biblical scholars the consensus was that not only did the punishment of exile fit the crime but it rehabilitated the criminal. Yeḥezqel Kaufmann's declaration regarding the "exile" and its effect is typical: "The Babylonian captivity is the great watershed in Israel's history, separating the age of idolatry from that of no idolatry … This time the strange gods are removed forever and buried finally …" (History, 12–13).

Neo-Babylonian and Persian period studies have offered a corrective to this view – rooted as it is in the perspectives of the biblical writers and editors. Those who challenge this traditional understanding of the exile are building upon the earlier, but initially rejected, observations of C. C. Torrey. In a series of articles Torrey claimed that there was no "exile" as such – that is, no singular event that marked the end of one era and the beginning of another. He viewed the traditions surrounding the fall of the southern kingdom as highly stylized, invented to explain the subservience of Judah to its Babylonian and Persian overlords. Population distribution in the form of deportations was common practice among ancient Near Eastern powers, experienced directly by the northern kingdom after its fall to Assyria; thus Judah's experience was not significantly different from that of Israel.

Watershed event or invention: how does one unpack these conflicting views? One approach is to recognize that "exile" is more a perspective than an event and is more accurately a series of events. The terms "deportation" and "repatriation" in place of the theologically laden "exile" and "return" come closer to the mark. That taking captives was a primary strategy of warfare in antiquity is established from some of our earliest texts from the ancient Near East and is well attested in public iconography (see, for example, the reliefs of Shalmanezer in Ninevah which show deportees from Lachish, and the Karnak reliefs depicting Shasu Bedouin as prisoners of Seti I). That people(s) – from the peasantry to the elite – were part of the spoils of war was not new or in any way unique. What made it so in Israelite and Judean traditions, and in subsequent biblical scholarship, was the concept of divine consequence seen from a particular (and particularistic) Yahwistic perspective.

Whatever term we use for the period at the end of the Judean kingdom and its early aftermath, there were at least three deportations (597, 587/6, and presumably after Gedeliah's assassination, either in 586 or 582; see J. J. M. Roberts' essay in this volume). Some of the vanquished remained in the land, and some fled to Egypt and other territories. In a relatively short time, instead of one geographically based people known as Judeans, at least three communities with cultural, ethnic, and ideological ties to the former (petty)-kingdom emerged: one in Babylon, one in Egypt, and one in Judea. If the term "exile" itself is problematic, the ensuing question of identity and authenticity became even more so, an issue to which we shall return.

Naming the period from 605–540/539 BCE is complicated by textual, archaeological and historical problems. Archaeologically, the normal markers of periods – technology and pottery – are difficult if not impossible to establish. As Avraham Faust correctly notes, there is not a clearly defined diagnostic pottery type and/or assemblage that we can identify as Neo-Babylonian (33). The period extended for less than a century, during which time Iron II and III pottery remained in use. Archaeologists continue to debate when a clearly Persian period ware emerges, which makes calibrating a settlement history with demographic patterns difficult. Jill Middlemas has proposed identifying the period as "the templeless age" – beginning in 587/6 with the destruction of Jerusalem and the temple, and ending in 515, when the second temple was completed. While using this term may remove the thorny issue of pottery typology and reduce the impact of the ideologically charged "exile," it still gives pride of place to the cultural/religious symbol most highly valued by the biblical writers – the Temple – and I am not certain that it is helpful to maintain what is essentially a Temple-centric viewpoint.

How Empty Is Empty?

Added to the question of defining historical and archaeological periods is the extent of disruption caused by the fall of Jerusalem and Judah. According to Robert Carroll and Hans Barstad nineteenth-century biblical scholarship accepted uncritically traditions that "all Judah was exiled from its land" (2 Kings 24:14; 25:21; Jer. 52:27) and the land lay in ruins for 70 years (2 Chr. 36:21). Added to these historical and prophetic memories of total annihilation, the writer of Leviticus proclaims that any (future) destruction of Israel/Judah will be a result of covenant unfaithfulness and the resulting expulsion and desolation will allow the land to "enjoy its Sabbath rest" (Lev. 26:27–35, 43).

Barstad and Carroll call this "the myth of the empty land" and suggest that traditions of the complete emptying of the land in the exile should be understood as suggestive rather than historical. That is, this "myth" demonstrates the severity and impact of these events on the psyche of the community and those who are reflecting on the significance of the fall of Judah. Both suggest we must differentiate between "what the exile *was* rather than what it *became* in later tradition" (Barstad 23). Like C. C. Torrey, then, exile and the exilic period are constructs of a community in crisis, with groups vying for authority and seeking to control identity. The historical events of destruction and deportation actually were far less serious and extensive than the biblical traditions and subsequent interpreters have averred. Instead, "with the great majority of the population still intact, life in Judah after 586 in all probability before long went on very much in the same way that it had done before the catastrophe" (Barstad 42). Thus, the collapse of Palace and Temple would have had little impact on the daily rhythms of life in the villages, allowing robust agricultural production to continue. This would have been in the interests of the Babylonian empire with its appetite for tribute, particularly in the form of wine and oil. By and large, the means of production remained intact – the primary difference was simply that the Babylonians rather than the Judean elite were extracting that surplus.

Textual and Archaeological Strata(gies)

The language of archaeological exploration lends itself well to the discussion and understanding of biblical texts. As the history of biblical scholarship amply demonstrates, we are frequently (if not always) dealing with traditions that have multiple levels, textual strata whose origin(s) and histories are complex, whose meanings are multivalent, whose shape and tenor often reflect earlier tropes, and which are themselves artifacts of culture. Like archaeologists, we approach our data – biblical texts and traditions – from multiple perspectives and methodologies – sometimes employing the equivalent of surface surveys, other times taking soundings, often carrying out more extensive and stratigraphic explorations, always taking care to be comparative and contextual. For some eras of Israelite and Judean prehistory and history the textual traditions may appear rich and closely relate to archaeological *realia*, but we must approach data from texts and tells in the Neo-Babylonian and Persian periods with a greater level of methodological care (see the essays by Elizabeth Bloch-Smith, Avraham Faust, and Brad Kelle in this volume). In addition to these important sources, we must appeal to geographic and environmental data, external texts and histories, archaeological surveys, excavation reports and comparative archaeological remains to put the province of Yehud in its appropriate historical and ideological context(s).

The Territory

Before we can examine issues such as settlement patterns, demography and population of the province of Yehud we must attempt to reconstruct its physical context – from boundaries, to size, to socioeconomic patterns, to its significance within the Neo-Babylonian and Achaemenid administrative structure. Once again we are faced with incomplete data sets that are subject to multiple interpretations. At issue are questions of the interpretation of biblical traditions, our understanding of imperial practice(s), shifts in the balance of power, and specific archaeological data. It is important, therefore, to use the term "boundaries" advisedly – any reconstruction of the size and extent of the province is tentative, at best, and suggestive and does not presume that Yehud's "borders" were fixed in the modern sense.

Why, then, even entertain such a notion? From a purely practical standpoint, proposing a general framework for the province may function heuristically: it allows rough comparisons with earlier and later archaeological/historical periods, an understanding of settlement patterns, and a view of broader socioeconomic developments. In short, a reconstruction, however provisional, is central to understanding peoples and cultures of specific periods and from the broader *longue durée*.

Five lists in Ezra-Nehemiah are the traditional starting point for a discussion of the size and boundaries of Yehud. Ezra 2//Nehemiah 7:6–73 are parallel accounts of the "first return" led by Sheshbazzar, ostensibly enjoying the authority and financial support of Emperor Cyrus. Nehemiah 3 describes the efforts to rebuild the walls of Jerusalem and identifies villages and territories that sent volunteers to assist in the project. As the only text that refers to specific districts or subdistricts within the province it comes closest to a description of the Persian period province. Nehemiah 11 is concerned with the repopulation of Jerusalem and ends with another list of villages. And Nehemiah 12:28–29 identifies settlements in which the singers of the Temple lived.

These traditions are best understood as an idealized rather than a realistic portrait of Yehud and its settlements. Taken at face value the texts lay a claim to towns, villages and cities that were part of the former kingdom of Judah at its height, as far afield as the central hill country, the tribal territory of Benjamin, the Shephelah, and the Jordan valley, extending into the coastal plain and even the Negev. They most likely refer to the social, political and religious aspirations of the returning *gôlâ* community and its attempt to define issues of identity and land tenure.

Ephraim Stern agrees that the lists are idealized and excludes sites in the Negev region from the province proper. However, his map of the province represents the maximalist tradition, and attempts to harmonize these biblical lists with archaeological finds (*Material Culture*). Specifically, he accepts as part of the province all sites mentioned in Ezra-Nehemiah at which Neo-Babylonian or Persian period coins or seal impressions have been discovered. And though these material markers are absent from the sites in the Coastal Plain (Lod, Hadid, and Ono), Stern includes this region with the territory of Yehud. He draws the western and southern boundaries based on a series of fortresses that have Persian period remains and, like most scholars, considers them evidence of Persian military interests within the province.

Many reconstructions follow roughly the list from Nehemiah 3 that purports to be a roster of districts and subdistricts that sent volunteers to assist the governor in rebuilding Jerusalem's walls. Surrounding the capital are the district of Mizpah to the north, Beth-haccerem to the west (perhaps including Gezer), Keilah to the southwest, and Beth-Zur to the south. Maps drawn by Avi-Yonah (181–4, map 6) and Lipschits (Lipschits and Vanderhooft 29, map 3) demarcate the districts, while Anson Rainey and Lester L. Grabbe follow the biblical outline but do not designate districts. (See the discussion in Carter, *Emergence*, 82–90 for more detailed discussion of the size and boundaries of the province as reconstructed by Stern, Avi-Yonah, Rainey and Grabbe.) The exact southern terminus is a matter of some debate, with some including and others excluding the important site of En-Gedi.

Carter and Lipschits approach the provincial boundaries from the perspective of environmental archaeology and historical geography, though Lipschits is more confident of, while Carter is more sanguine regarding, the reliability of Nehemiah 3. Both exclude the Coastal Plain sites of Lod, Hadid, and Ono from the province as they were most likely ceded to Phoenician control under the Sidonian Land Grant (Carter, *Emergence*, 97–8; Lipschits 173). The major differences in their reconstructions are the status of the Shephelah sites and the criteria each uses to determine the subdivisions of the province. Carter focuses on environmental and geographic features and identifies eight distinct areas oriented along a north–south grid. These environmental niches reflect differences in soil types, elevation, and rainfall patterns, among other factors, which may have influenced settlement patterns, and economic factors such as crop types and yields, and inter- and intraregional trade or commerce. Using Nehemiah 3, Lipschits identifies various districts (and subdistricts) of the province, and orients these more along a west–east grid. Lipschits includes the Shephelah sites mentioned in Nehemiah 3 whereas Carter proposes a western boundary that ends at the Central Hill country.

Imperial Context

Because most biblical traditions dating to (or set in) the Neo-Babylonian and Persian periods reflect a *gôlâ*-centric perspective, we must look to other sources to assess Yehud's place within the imperial system. Ezra-Nehemiah correctly situates the province within the Satrapy of Eber Nāri (*'ăbar nahărâ*), "across the river [Euphrates]." Similarly, many traditions recognize the presence and significance of the Community's enemies/rivals and suggest a somewhat fluid set of power relations among them. They do not, however, give any indication of the makeup or subdivisions of Eber Nāri. For that we turn to a variety of Babylonian, Persian and Greek texts, with Herodotus' *The Histories* considered by many to be one of the more reliable sources. It is commonly held that the satrapy had its origins in the period of Assyrian hegemony in the eighth century BCE and that the Babylonians and Persians after them simply adopted the Assyrian regional administrative organization and structures (Stern, *Archaeology*, 366–72).

Recently, D. Vanderhooft has challenged this near-consensus perspective, proposing instead that the Neo-Babylonian period was marked by a more diffuse, less centralized administrative approach (104–10). As we have seen, both Jeremiah and 2 Kings indicate that the Babylonians installed Gedeliah as ruler of the subjugated former kingdom of Judah with Mizpah as the seat of the territory. What is less clear, however, is the exact nature and extent of that short-lived rule and whom the Babylonians appointed to oversee the territory after Gedeliah's assassination. We do not know, therefore, whether or not the vanquished former kingdom was considered a province before the beginning of the Persian period.

By the end of the sixth century BCE the picture is much clearer: Yehud was granted provincial status, its capital had moved from Mizpah to Jerusalem, and its ruler held the title governor. The rest of the satrapy would have contained several provinces (many of which were larger and more important than Yehud), including Megiddo, Samaria, Damascus, Philistia (perhaps divided up into Ashdod and Lachish), Phoenicia (administered under the Sidonian Land Grant), and perhaps Cyprus (Carter, *Emergence*, 288–94; "Ideology," 301, fig. 105).

Settlements and Population

Understanding the sociocultural context(s) for any era is based in part upon the site distribution, settlement density and population of the area in question. This is a relatively easier task for periods that are well attested in both archaeological and textual traditions and that are the subject of sustained scholarly analysis. The recent interest in the Neo-Babylonian and Persian periods notwithstanding, these archaeological eras still lag far behind our knowledge of the Bronze and Iron Ages and the Hellenistic and Roman periods. Relying, as we must, more heavily on data sets that are less reliable introduces a higher level of speculation into our reconstruction, making any portrait of these periods provisional and subject to change as new data emerge.

From an archaeological standpoint we may identify the following hierarchy of sources. Controlled and sustained excavations are of course the most reliable. Salvage and/or emergency excavations often provide instructive, yet incomplete, data. Archaeological surveys are invaluable tools for mapping settlement history, but are more problematic for reconstructing site size and subsequently the significance and population of a particular city, village or region. This hierarchy is inverted for both the Neo-Babylonian and Persian periods. The majority of our data on site distribution/settlement history comes from surveys, comparatively less evidence from controlled excavations.

A look at the state of the data in the last 25 years is instructive. When I began my work on the province of Yehud in the late 1980s, only 12 of the 111 inhabited sites with remains dating to the Persian period had been excavated. Thus, a full 89 percent of the sites identified as part of the province are known primarily through three surface surveys, some of which were overlapping. When I revised my research for the publication of *The Emergence of Yehud in the Persian Period*, the number of settlements had

Table 12.1   Excavated sites in the Neo-Babylonian and Persian periods

Neo-Babylonian period	
Bethel I	Horvat Zimri (Pizgat Ze'ev 'D')
Tell el-Fûl (Gibeah of Saul)	El-Jîb (Gibeon)
Tell en-Naṣbeh	Kh. Er-Ras (S)
Persian period	
Bethel II	Tell en-Naṣbeh
Nebi Samwîl	Moṣah
Ras el-Kharrubeh	Kh. Er-Ras (W)
Jerusalem	Mamilla
City of David	City of David Archaeological Park
Ketef Ḥinnom	Rogem Gannim
Wadi Salim	Ramat Raḥel
Kh. Et-Tubeiqah (Beth Zur)	Kh. Abu et-Twein
Kh. Nijam (Har Adar)	'Ain 'Arrub
Tell es-Sultan (Jericho)	Ketef Yeriḥo
Tel Goren ('En Gedi)	

Note: Based on new excavations and Yehud seal impression typology, the sites of Kh. ʿAlmit and El-Ezariyah (Bethany), formerly included in my reconstructions, are excluded from this list.

increased to 125, primarily as a result of new salvage excavations and ongoing archaeological surveys. Still, the majority of our information on site distribution comes from surveys: only 16 inhabited sites – 13 percent – dating to the Persian period have been excavated. In the last decade, our understanding of the archaeological history of the province has changed yet again: new excavations at Moṣah, Nebi Samwîl, and several sites in and around Jerusalem, along with renewed excavations at Ramat Raḥel, have provided us with valuable new data and have in turn allowed us to refine our interpretation of material discovered in earlier digs.

One of the pressing problems that remain when attempting to use survey data to study and/or reconstruct settlement patterns and demographic tendencies is estimating with any degree of confidence the size of a site where remains from a period are discovered. Population estimates are based on applying a fixed coefficient of persons to the settled area (most commonly 250 persons per hectare = 25 per metric dunam). We are on more solid ground when studying excavated sites (see table 12.1), for stratigraphic analysis allows us to suggest the area of a site inhabited in a given period. For example, Tell en-Naṣbeh, which was established in the Chalcolithic period, will have had different contours during its history. The site has remains from the Early Bronze Age, Iron Age I and II, and the Neo-Babylonian, Persian, Hellenistic and Roman periods. Its maximal size is 34 dunams, but how does one estimate its size within specific eras? The density of pottery discovered at the site may provide a clue, but only a clue – for different surveys of a given site has sometimes yielded significantly different percentages of pottery and even archaeological periods. When dealing with salvage excavations and surveys, it is important to recognize that the overall size of the site and the area inhabited may be quite different. To date, no clear consensus has emerged on estimating the settled area of sites whose only (or primary) source of archaeological remains is based on surveys. Given these challenges, some scholars suggest that surveys only be used to map settlement history and site density, and that there are simply too many variables in methodology and inconsistencies in data to make meaningful population estimates (Faust 128–32). Others propose using paleodemography, available water supply, and potential carrying capacity (the amount of flora and fauna potentially available) as the basis to estimate maximal population of a specific area (Carter, *Emergence*, 195–9).[1] What is not always stated, but is particularly important for this study, is that any population estimates are at best provisional – intended to provide a starting point for broader socioeconomic analysis, but in no way exact.

It is also important to note that the mapping of sites may itself be somewhat misleading, because it appears that these sites are inhabited throughout an entire archaeological period. This obscures the reality that villages and towns, agricultural installations, and farmsteads may exist only for a part of the period in question. Accordingly, we must view any site map as maximal; at any given point during that era the number of villages/settlements may have been smaller.

With these caveats in mind, what can we say about the site distribution and population of Yehud? Given some of the difficulties regarding pottery types and periodization discussed above, we can only make general observations about the territory during the Neo-Babylonian period. Jerusalem remained desolate and uninhabited until after the initial return of the *gôlâ* community at the beginning of the Persian period. Destruction around Jerusalem and in portions of the Judean hills was extensive. The towns and villages in the former tribal territory of Benjamin seem to have been spared and show at least a measure of continuity between the Iron II and Neo-Babylonian periods. The territory was sparsely populated, though I expect that a certain level of agricultural productivity and attendant extraction of goods and surplus, however minimal, would have existed.

My previous studies attempted to draw a distinction between the early and later Persian periods, marked by the missions of Ezra and Nehemiah and archaeological evidence pointing to a measured, but strategic, increase in military installations. As Lipschits has pointed out, the evidence more typically used to determine periodization is pottery assemblages, which are notoriously absent for most of the years between 539 and 332 BCE. Three pottery designations are most common in dealing with this time period: Iron II/Persian, Persian, and Persian/Hellenistic. My approach drew on this general typology, and I presented the resulting proposal for population and site distribution in the Persian I period as hypothetical and provisional at best. But I would now agree that the lack of clear demarcation in pottery types brings into question the validity of making a clear distinction between Persian I and Persian II. It is more helpful to speak of general trends. My reconstruction in 1999 suggested a gradual increase in population within the province of Yehud, from roughly 13,000 in the first part of the period to roughly 21,000 by the fourth century BCE. Lipschits suggests a more cyclical pattern, with population peaking sometime in the late fifth–early fourth century followed by a gradual decline toward the end of the Persian period. He estimates the maximal population to be approximately 30,000. Two factors account for this difference of about 9,000

Table 12.2   Population distribution in Persian period Yehud

Territory	Carter	Lipschits
Benjamin	7,625	12,5000
Jerusalem (and environs)	1,500	2,750
Northern Judean Hills	8,850	9,750
Southern Judean Hills	2,150	–
Shephelah	–	4,875
Judean Desert/Eastern Strip	525	250
Total	**20,650**	**30,125**

Note: Lipschits data from O. Lipschits, *The Fall and Rise of Jerusalem*, 270, table 4.3.

persons. While I have excluded the region of the Shephelah from the province, Lipschits proposes that it was a part of Yehud and had nearly 5,000 inhabitants. Our methodology of population estimates also comes into play: while Lipschits seems to calculate a site's population based on its maximal size, I have attempted – however cautiously – to estimate a site's size based on the relative pottery distribution discovered in surveys and/or the extent of settlement that appears to be inhabited in excavated sites.

More significant for our understanding of the periods and their social and economic contexts is the level of agreement between Lipschits's and my own studies (see table 12.2). We both place the majority of the population and sites within the central hill country of Benjamin and Judah, with relatively few large sites. Jerusalem, with a population of between 1,500 and 2,750, is the only major city in the province, and the majority of sites would be smaller, unwalled villages. If one removes the Shephelah, our estimates are within 4,000 individuals, with my proposal at roughly 21,000 and Lipshits's at 25,000. Alternatively, if one adds the Shephelah to my reconstruction, Yehud's population would be approximately 26,000, compared with Lipshits's 30,000. In either case, we are dealing with a relatively small province, one that is accordingly relatively poor, however strategic it may have been to the imperial authorities.

Mizpah, Jerusalem and Ramat Raḥel: A Tale of Three Cities

In 605 BCE the petty-kingdom of Judah passed from Egyptian to Babylonian control; its status as a semi-autonomous state was dependent on subservience to Babylonian policies and payment of tribute. Even so, the kingdom extended northward toward Samaria, into the Shephelah in the west, the Judean desert in the east, and as far as the northern reaches of the Negev desert in the south. Jerusalem itself was home to a thriving temple and palace economy, with the bureaucratic support system and population of social and religious elites common to states in the ancient Near East at the end of the Iron Age. Other relatively larger cities and administrative centers remained vital to Judah, including Tell en-Naṣbeh (Mizpah), Lachish, Gezer (?), Jericho, En-Gedi, Bethel, Arad and Beer-Sheva, among others.

Mizpah's Ascent: Filling the Vacuum

The Judean rebellion of 597, begun by Jehoiakim and continued by his son Jehoiachin, was met with a harsh response from Babylon that included the first deportation of many of the elite from Jerusalem, the destruction of some of the capital city and looting of the temple. The king was removed from power and taken to Babylon, where he and his family were imprisoned, and Zedekiah appointed as the empire's client ruler. According to 2 Kings and Jeremiah both pro-Babylonian and anti-Babylonian constituencies (political, military and religious) competed for primacy during the next few years, and by roughly 590, Zedekiah led a second rebellion. The Babylonian response was devastating, involving the widespread destruction of much of Judah, an 18-month siege of Jerusalem, and the eventual dismantling of the city. There is no evidence for any settlement in Jerusalem from 587/6 until early in the Persian period. Whatever the nature of the former kingdom of Judah during those years, Mizpah became the primary administrative center – the appointed ruler, Gedeliah, evidently had the seat of his short-lived government there and it is one of a few sites that is occupied continuously from the Iron II period, into both the Neo-Babylonian and Persian periods. Several archaeological markers indicate its regional significance, among them architecture suggesting public building(s), Greek ware, indicating international trade, and the *m(w)ṣh* seal impressions (Zorn). Very likely, Bethel became the territory's primary cult center in the early years after Jerusalem's destruction, though both Blenkinsopp and Lipschits suggest that Mizpah may have been both a cultic and administrative center.

Jerusalem's Recovery

Explorers, surveyors and archaeologists have conducted surface surveys, trench soundings, salvage and full-scale excavations in and around Jerusalem almost continually since at least the middle of the nineteenth century. The first excavations with Persian period remains were conducted by R. A. S. McAllister and J. G. Duncan on the Ophel Hill from 1923 to 1925. Two years later, in 1927, J. W. Crowfoot and G. M. Fitzgerald excavated portions of the Tyropean Valley. The primary discoveries from these early digs were seal impressions dating to the Persian and Ptolemaic periods (mid-fifth through late fourth or early third centuries BCE). Dame Kathleen Kenyon carried out the first modern controlled excavations from 1961 through 1967. Perhaps the most important results from her work were the delineation of the Eastern and Western walls of Persian period Jerusalem and the discovery of a possible join of the city walls with the platform of the Temple Mount (a proposal that is no longer accepted).

Even more significant for our study are the City of David excavations directed by Yigal Shiloh for the Institute of Archaeology of the Hebrew University of Jerusalem between 1978 and 1982. Shiloh was only able to publish a preliminary report before his untimely death in 1987 and his students have collaborated on seven further studies on the excavations in the Qedem series.[2] The combination of refined archaeological methodology and advances in the dating of material culture – from pottery typology to paleography, from architectural patterns to construction techniques – allowed Shiloh to develop the most comprehensive stratigraphic analysis to date of Jerusalem from its earliest habitation in the Chalcolithic period through the early twentieth century CE. Of the 11 areas that Shiloh opened on the southeastern spur, four contained material remains from the Persian period, identified as stratum 9: areas E1, D1, D2 and G. It now appears that stratum 9 may be divided into two subphases, at least in area G. Stratum 9b consists of construction remains laid directly on top of the Iron II destruction layer, whereas stratum 9a seems to provide a base for Hellenistic period remains. The City of David excavations contained a wide array of ceramic evidence, at the time surpassing any assemblage of Persian period pottery discovered in Jerusalem, a significant number of stamped seal impressions, some Yehud coins, and both foreign and locally produced imitations of foreign ware.

Subsequent excavations in and around Jerusalem – on the Ophel, in the City of David Archaeological Park, the Givati parking lot, and Mamilla, among others – have added to our picture of Jerusalem in the Persian period. Together with the earlier excavations, we can say with confidence that during the Persian period Jerusalem comprised an acropolis that included not only the Temple complex and governmental buildings but also lodging for at least some of the elite and related officials. The majority of the settled area was on the eastern spur – the City of David. Other than some scattered squatting, the Western hill remained uninhabited throughout the Persian period. This would mean that from the middle of the fifth century until the last third of the fourth century, the maximal size of the city would have been between 130 and 140 dunams, of which 50 to 60 dunams were settled, with a population of between 1,200 and 1,500.

Related to the size, population and extent of settlement in Jerusalem are the date, purpose and significance of Nehemiah's wall. This is one of the central concerns of the so-called Nehemiah Memoir (generally understood as Nehemiah 1–7 and parts of chapters 11–13), one for which he claims royal support. Excavations in the areas of the Temple platform, the Ophel, and the City of David have sought to relate to the biblical description of the walls, and many scholars – my own work included – have created numerous reconstructions of the walls and their gates. The tendency has generally been to accept the veracity of Nehemiah's claims and date a wall-building and perhaps fortification program to the middle of the fifth century BCE. In the last decade this view has come increasingly into question, and a robust debate continues regarding the size and importance of Jerusalem. Some suggest that Jerusalem was very small throughout the Persian period, unwalled and unfortified, and that the Nehemiah traditions are an invention of the Hellenistic period. This is a minority view, but many seem ready to suggest a more modest level of settlement in the sixth through fourth centuries BCE: an acropolis that was largely unoccupied and sparse population in the central spur of the City of David.

Among the most important discoveries for our understanding of the socioeconomic and sociopolitical status of Jerusalem are the anepigraphic and epigraphic stamped-seal impressions. These have been present in many of the explorations and excavations since the early twentieth century, but only with the Shiloh City of David excavations did the stratigraphic implications of the impressions become clear. Early interpretations of these data lumped virtually all the impressions with the inscription *yehud* or any form of the provincial name, as well as the seals bearing the capital's name, *yršlm*, as either "Second Temple Period" or Persian period. Shiloh's excavations showed that only the impressions with the full spelling of the provincial name (*yhwd* in one or two lines), those with *yhwd* and a personal name, and those with the title *pḥw'*, "governor," date to the Persian period. All other *yehud* impressions are in later strata. In addition to the *yehud* seals, several anepigraphic lion seals are known from Jerusalem, as are at least four *m(w)ṣh* impressions.

Ramat Raḥel

Located 4 kilometers southwest of Jerusalem, the site of Ramat Raḥel was first exca-vated by Y. Aharoni in 1954, and then from 1959 to 1962. It was shown to have been a significant settlement in the Iron II period, with widespread reuse of buildings from that period during the Second Temple Period (the term Aharoni used to identify remains from the Neo-Babylonian through early Roman periods). It was clear from Aharoni's work that during the Persian period the site was a significant administrative center. In 2006 Tel Aviv University began a new series of excavations that have provided a more detailed stratigraphic analysis of the site. It is now clear that Ramat Raḥel was continu-ously occupied throughout the Iron II, Neo-Babylonian and Persian periods. Unlike Tell en-Naṣbeh, which saw a decline with the resurgence of Jerusalem, Ramat Raḥel grew both in size and evidently importance throughout the Persian period. This growth is evident both architecturally and by the large number of stamped seal impressions that date to the late Iron through early Hellenistic periods. While Aharoni had discovered that parts of the Iron II administrative building were reused in the Persian period, the renewed excavations show not only reuse but substantial expansion of the administra-tive complex later in the Persian period. Given the newly emerging data from Ramat Raḥel, Lipshits and Vanderhooft have concluded that it, not Jerusalem, was the central administrative site for the province of Yehud during the sixth through fourth centuries.

A comparison of the types and numbers of seal impressions found throughout the province is particularly instructive. Lipschits and Vanderhooft identify a total of 482 exemplars of *m(w)ṣh* and *yehud* seals dating from the sixth through the fourth cen-turies BCE, 84 percent of which were discovered at these three major sites (see table 12.3). As expected, the data for the types and percentages of the impressions is more or less inverted from the beginning of the Neo-Babylonian to the end of the Persian period. In the middle-to-late sixth century, when Tell en-Naṣbeh was the administra-tive center of the Babylonian territory of Judea, 86 percent of the *m(w)ṣh* impressions are from Mizpah, with only 11 percent and 3 percent from Jerusalem and Ramat Raḥel, respectively. During the Persian period, the number of impressions discovered at Tell en-Naṣbeh decreases markedly to 5 percent, while those discovered at Jerusalem and Ramat Raḥel increase to 20 percent and 74 percent respectively.

The question of the relative importance of the sites is another matter. Lipschits and Vanderhooft suggest that "current statistics do not favor viewing Jerusalem as the main administrative center represented in the corpus of the *yehud* stamp impressions, espe-cially among the early and middle types" (12). But does this statistical comparison truly measure the importance of each site? Do these percentages in fact suggest that Ramat Raḥel is more important than Jerusalem, perhaps even the economic center of gravity of

Table 12.3   Neo-Babylonian and Persian period epigraphic stamped seals

Seal type	Tell en-Naṣbeh	Jerusalem	Ramat Raḥel
m(w)ṣh	30 (86%)	4 (11%)	1 (3%)
Early Yehud (6th–5th century)	1 (1%)	17 (13%)	91 (84%)
Middle Yehud (5th–4th century)	18 (7%)	59 (22%)	186 (71%)
Total Yehud seals	19 (5%)	76 (20%)	277 (74%)
Total	**49 (12%)**	**80 (20%)**	**278 (68%)**

Note: Yehud seal numbers from O. Lipschits and D. S. Vanderhooft, *The Yehud Stamp Impressions*, 9–22.

the province? I would urge caution and suggest further assessment of the data as they emerge. What does seem to be clear – from the standpoint of the archaeological data as a whole, including architectural, pottery, seals and coins, among other artifacts – is that Tell en-Naṣbeh was the primary administrative center of Judea between the end of the southern kingdom through the early Persian period, and that Ramat Raḥel retained some administrative significance. With the reestablishment of Jerusalem as the capital of the province of Yehud during the late sixth century and into the fifth century, Tell en-Naṣbeh's importance declined significantly. Ramat Raḥel became the primary site for the collection and storage of taxes and other forms of surplus, but Jerusalem, not the latter site, was the political and religious center of the province.

Socioeconomic and Sociopolitical Contexts

As we have seen, the province of Yehud was relatively small, based in the Central Hill Country of Palestine, perhaps extending into the Shephelah, and comprised the former tribal territories of Judah and Benjamin. Aside from a few larger centers like Jerusalem and Ramat Raḥel and fortifications such as Beth Zur, Kh. Ez-Zawiyye and Kh. El-Qaṭṭ, the province was characterized by small to medium-sized villages. Hoglund has suggested that this village-based economy was imposed by the Persian empire as part of a strategy of ruralization, aimed in part at minimizing internal armed threats (54–68). He maintains that aside from Jerusalem and a few military outposts, no villages or towns in the province were walled, let alone fortified. It is in this context that land tenure became so important. However, Faust has recently questioned this assessment (66–8), seeing the village-based economy more as a function of the destruction associated with the Babylonian invasions, and the more natural tendency for resettlement to be relatively slower with outposts, small settlements and villages a common response to this physical degradation.

The texts in Ezra-Nehemiah also demonstrate another significant social development, one which ostensibly binds the Israelite and Judean pasts with the present realities in

Persian period Yehud. It is not entirely clear how or when it occurred, but by the middle of the fifth century BCE the *bêt 'ābôt* (literally "fathers' house") was established as a new identity marker, one presumably linked to the Iron I and II basic social unit, the ancestral household (*bêt 'āb*). Only those who are able to trace their genealogies to a Judean through the newly created (and almost certainly fictive) *bêt 'ābôt* are fully enfranchised citizens of Yehud and thus qualified to "reclaim" familial territory (see the essay by T. M. Lemos in this volume). All others, whether the often maligned "people of the land" or Judeans who are designated as "foreigners," are excluded not only from the *gôlâ* group but also from any meaningful role in governance and are subject to the whims of the newly established elite. Ironically, those who had inhabited the land since the Babylonian deportations in 586 – hence the insiders – became outsiders when an external power group exerted itself and claimed imperial authority from without.

Another social and religious adjustment of former Judean polity is the shared rule of governor and priest, identified by Meyers and Meyers as a dyarchy (*Haggai*, xl–xli and throughout commentary). The prophets Haggai and Zechariah together confirm the divine approval of the dual authority – and it is to both Zerubbabel and Yehoshua that many of their oracles are addressed. Further, it is likely that the former had Davidic ties, and the messianic tone of many of these prophetic oracles is without question. Although some have suggested that Zerubbabel or one of his close descendants led an unsuccessful revolt against Persia, there is no firm textual or archaeological evidence of this. Rather, it is more likely that prophet, priest and governor saw themselves as subject to and responsible to the emperors and their empire that YHWH ultimately established. It is widely assumed that as the Persian period progressed, at least from the late fifth century onward, the balance of power shifted and the high priest may have eventually also held the governorship of Yehud.

Commercialization and Trade

If Yehud is relatively small and relatively poor, as the evidence above suggests, how does one track the structure and impact of its political, social and cultic economy? Would the primary means of exchange and taxation remain in-kind? How widespread would an emergent moneyed economy become? How were taxes extracted from the family and village or town context and distributed to the elite in Yehud and the imperial coffers? How widespread was trade? Who were the mercantile partners and where do we see evidence of foreign influence? A brief examination of the archaeological evidence offers a preliminary understanding of these concerns.

Although the evidence points to a gradual shift toward a moneyed economy during the Persian period, traditional forms of in-kind and precious metal-based exchange almost certainly dominated commerce. The City of David excavations in Jerusalem, for example, unearthed both remains of scales and weights typical of the more traditional types of exchange/economic transactions. Neo-Babylonian, Persian, Greek and Egyptian pottery and/or luxury items have been discovered at Bethel, En Gedi, Tell es-Sultan (Jericho), Tell en-Naṣbeh (Mizpah), and Jerusalem, some in burial contexts, others in domestic and/or public settings. Notably, these finds are accompanied by locally produced copies of foreign vessels and materials. It is likely as well that the Persian period saw an increase in a mercantile class throughout the empire and expanded levels of both intraprovincial and more far-flung exchange of goods.

Yehud Coins

The earliest coin discovered in a controlled excavation within the territory of Judah dates to the late sixth century. This silver archaic Attic coin comes from Ketef Hinnom and though its stratigraphic context is early Persian period it may have been in circulation as early as the Neo-Babylonian period. According to the excavator it came from the mint of Cos (Carter, *Emergence*, 146). At least 17 coins dating to the sixth through fourth centuries have been discovered in Yehud, nine in Jerusalem and its environs and eight at Beth Zur. These include coins from some of the local minting authorities in Syria-Palestine, as well as both genuine and imitation Attic coins. It is apparent that there were three major types of coins: imperial mints, bearing the name of Mazday, who ruled Eber Nāri at the end of the Persian period; local mints, represented by coins from Tyre, Sidon, and Ashkelon, among others; and provincial mints, the Yehud and Samarian coins.

Most Yehud coins discovered to date are from the mid-fourth through early third centuries BCE; a relatively smaller sample is from the end of the Persian period and the majority from the Ptolemaic and early Hellenistic periods. As is the case with the seal impressions, some of the coins bear the provincial name alone, some have personal names with titular attribution, and some have personal name, title and territory. Perhaps the most interesting of the coins are those associated with Yeḥezqiyah – the one-time governor of Yehud – and those that are associated with the priesthood. One of the former coins was discovered at Beth Zur and reads *yḥzqyh* [*h*]*pḥh*, "Yeḥezqiyah [the] governor"; a second type reads *yḥzqyh* [*h*]*pḥh yh*, "Yeḥezqiyah [the] governor, Yeh[ud]"; a third type has only his name. Two coins are associated with the priesthood: one is generally read as *yhn*[*n*] *hkhn*, "Yohanan the Priest," and another bears the inscription *ydwʿ*, "Yadduʿa." Although the Yadduʿa coin lacks the title of priest, some have suggested that it was minted under the authority of the high priest Yadduʿa I or Yadduʿa II, who held that position in the late fifth and mid-to-late fourth centuries. Together, these coins are often considered to substantiate the theory that the high priest assumed a political role that included the authority to mint coins, or at least that the governor and high priest shared power.

The place of coinage in the overall economy within the empire and the province of Eber Nāri seems to develop gradually. The vast majority of coins discovered in controlled excavations date from the Hellenistic period and the practice of in-kind commerce and taxation persisted alongside the growing moneyed economy (see the essay by David Schloen in this volume). It is most likely that in the Persian period coins were used primarily in commerce (especially trade), to pay day-wages to laborers and soldiers, and perhaps in the collection of taxes (Carter, *Emergence*, 273–85).

Textual and Religious Constructs

Several questions arise when we address the biblical traditions themselves. What texts – books or portions of books – date to the Neo-Babylonian and Persian periods? Which of these are composed in their entirety, and which underwent major, or even minor, editing during this time frame? To what degree might they have been influenced by Babylonian and/or Persian imperial policy? How, if at all, did the material realities influence the ideologies and practices inherent in them? And, if we are able to identify the time of composition, venue, "author," or any combination of the above, are there any controls or guides to the use of the biblical texts to understand and reconstruct the historical and cultural framework(s) of the province of Yehud under Persian rule?

Some texts are best viewed as transitional; many reflect the writers' attempts to make sense of the deportations of 597 and 586, and the ultimate fall and desolation of Judah. Parts of Jeremiah and much of Ezekiel deal with the last decade of the Judean state and its early aftermath. Both critique cultic impurity, unfaithfulness to the covenant, and to some extent, political alignments. Both are written from a combination of Jerusalem-centric and diaspora experience, Jeremiah from Egypt, Ezekiel from Babylon, and both project a lengthy Judean presence in Babylon. The book of Lamentations and many psalms have a Neo-Babylonian period provenance. Most scholars posit a Babylonian editing of the Deuteronomistic History. And Second Isaiah is traditionally dated toward the end of the Neo-Babylonian and beginning of the Persian periods.

As impressive as this production is, there is a general consensus that the Persian period was marked by a level of literary activity that far exceeds what one might expect from a relatively small, relatively poor territory (see the essay by Tamara Cohn Eskenazi in this volume). It is apparent that much of what we now consider the Hebrew Bible bears the imprint of this era,[3] whether composed, slightly revised or thoroughly recast (see the essay by David Carr in this volume). And though some of these works reflect – or at least claim – imperial support and more importantly, authority, other texts are more sanguine regarding their relationship with their Persian overlords.

The variety of voices represented within these traditions are many and often strident, and each stakes its claim as the *vox Dei*. And although some traditions seem more formative of subsequent ideologies than others (Carter, "Syria-Palestine," 302–6), the fact that these multiple perspectives are represented within the texts from this era means that there is no one undisputed victor in these ancient "culture wars." In what follows I highlight several trends – some of which are interrelated and therefore defy strict or rigid categorization. Some are more characteristic of specific literary genres, others are represented across types.

The gôlâ Community

One of the most prolific, certainly the most doctrinaire, of the viewpoints that characterized the Persian period is that of the *bənê haggôlâ*, literally the "sons of the exile." Perhaps the clearest expression of this ideology is found in Ezra-Nehemiah. Whether one considers this work fictive or (quasi) historical it stakes the claim for authenticity and authority on both imperial and divine grounds. There are several levels of overlap, and several ways in which the *gôlâ* group connects with or co-opts earlier traditions. Even in Ezra-Nehemiah there are echoes of the prophetic tradition and Deuteronomistic perspectives, references to ideologies that reflect the Priestly and/or Holiness Code ideologies and a fully developed monotheism (see also the essays by Mark Smith and by S. A. Geller in this volume). It would seem therefore that the writer(s) had direct access to versions of the Torah, the Deuteronomistic History and many of the prophetic books associated with both Israel and Judah. Some examples of these connections include the assertion of the prophetic authority as divine interpreter of events, the place of YHWH as the primary shaper of history or events at whose whim emperors rise and fall, territorial claims based on tribal or ancestral ties, and a particularistic definition of community and identity.

The *bǝnê haggôlâ* (also rendered as *šǝbî haggôlâ*) are the "true seed of Israel", that is, the genuine extension of the "preexilic" Judeans. Though their ancestors were removed from Judah and deported to Babylon by divine decree, now Cyrus, emperor of Persia and moved by YHWH, authorized Jews in Babylon to return and rebuild the temple in Jerusalem. According to these texts, after Cyrus's oral and written edict, YHWH motivated leaders of the *gôlâ* community to return to Jerusalem, repopulate Judah and begin the divinely ordained task of temple building. This group was led by Sheshbazzar and enjoyed the economic support of the empire and those deportees who chose to remain in and around Babylon.

There is widespread skepticism about the reliability and/or historicity of the Ezra traditions in general and of the purported imperial edicts which were composed in Aramaic and included in the Book of Ezra to give it an air of authenticity. Some scholars even doubt the existence of Ezra as an individual, but whether or not he lived or the events the Book of Ezra portrays occurred, the book is an important artifact and offers considerable insight into the social and religious realities that obtained in Yehud. Ezra refers to himself as a "skilled scribe" (Ezra 7:6) and establishes the Torah of Moses as the normative "rule of law" for the province. This, he claims, is authorized by both YHWH and Artaxerxes (Ezra 7:11–25). This has led many interpreters to suggest that the (proto-)Torah was actually commissioned by the Persians and represented a co-opting of religious authority for imperial gain (Berquist; Watts). Nehemiah is less enthusiastic than the Ezra traditions regarding this divine/imperial authorization, but as governor of Yehud he recognizes Ezra's religious authority and supports his separatist ideology and policies (Neh. 8–10).

The primacy of the *gôlâ* community is seen in two distinct ways. The first is the forced divorce/separation of the returnees from their "foreign" wives (Ezra 9–10, Neh. 13:23–28). These traditions suggest that there was widespread failure of the people at all levels of Yehudite society to maintain their ethnic and religious purity. Because the people had not "separated themselves" from the various peoples of the land and had married "foreign" women, they faced exclusion from the *gôlâ* community and loss of their ancestral lands. I concur with the assessment of Tamara Cohn Eskenazi, Daniel Smith-Christopher and others who see the reference to foreign women and their ethnic and religious origins as code for anyone not agreeing with or adhering to the strictures of the *gôlâ* group. Foreign, therefore, does not necessarily mean non-Israelite or non-Judean, but anyone outside the narrow ideology represented by Ezra-Nehemiah.

A similar expression of the separatist ideology is seen in the series of disputes between the returnees and their various enemies. Ezra recounts repeated opposition from the "adversaries" from among the peoples of the land (perhaps, among others, Samaritans whose offer to help rebuild the temple was rebuffed), who in turn appealed to the imperium to intervene and stop the temple-building project (Ezra 4–5). Armed with the emperor's edict the officials prevail, the returning community is discouraged and work ceases. Ezra credits Haggai and Zechariah with encouraging the community to resume building, which was completed by roughly 516. Nehemiah likewise documents resistance from the surrounding peoples and territories as he and the people of Yehud seek to fortify and repopulate Jerusalem. Nehemiah names the Sanballat family from Samaria, a certain Geshem the Arab (likely representing the Edomite interests), the Ammonites and Ashdodites (Neh. 4:1–9; 6:1–7:4). By casting these ancient rivals as contemporary threats to the identity or survival of the *gôlâ* community, the writers of Ezra-Nehemiah reinforce its place as the true seed of Israel and reject the claim of other groups who also identify themselves as Yahwists.

An End of Idolatry?

The term idolatry itself is fraught – evoking various theological and/or ideological perspectives. Hence, the terms iconolatry or its opposite, aniconism, may be more appropriate for understanding this aspect of the Yehudite religious tradition(s) after the Babylonian incursion and the subsequent period of Persian rule. As discussed above, many historians proclaim Israel's penchant for worshipping other deities ended with the destruction of both the northern and southern kingdoms. Ephraim Stern approaches this issue from the context of archaeology and maintains that "in areas of the country occupied by Jews, *not a single cultic figurine* has ever been found despite intensive excavations and archaeological surveys of these areas" (Stern, "Pagan Yahwism," emphasis added). He concludes: "Upon the return from exile, the Jews purified their worship. Jewish monotheism was at last consolidated" (Stern, *Archaeology*, 29).

To evaluate Stern's assessment we must carefully define both the extent of the province of Yehud and what constitutes a "cultic figurine." Tell 'Erani, which Stern places within the province, on its southwest boundary with the Coastal Plain and the northwestern boundary between Idumea and Yehud (Stern, *Material Culture*, 375, fig. III.6), has yielded votive figurines. Their use is still a matter of debate, but their presence calls into question the interpretation that there are no material remains with cultic intent. These figurines have parallels at Lachish, Maresha and Tel Ḥalif. While these three sites are beyond even Stern's reconstructed boundaries they raise another question: are we to assume that Jews in Syria-Palestine only lived within the confines of Yehud's boundaries? Anson Rainey and Peter Ackroyd answered this question most succinctly: "Jewry is larger than Judah" (Carter, *Emergence*, 290).

Also pertinent to this issue are images on both seal impressions and on Yehud coins. Christoph Uehlinger analyses a number of seals found either within the boundaries or in close proximity to Yehud with Babylonian and Persian motifs. Many depict either human or divine heroes engaged in hunting or showing the hero with vanquished animals (sometimes portrayed as a *Mischwesen*, i.e., a composite figure with human and animal elements; see Theodore Lewis's essay in this volume). An impression from Tel Balaṭa dates to the late sixth–early fifth centuries. Images from Gezer and Tell es-Safi have astral motifs. Underneath a winged sun-disk (which may be related to Ahura Mazda) a hero holds vanquished winged beasts in each hand.

Many of the Yehud coins have Greek and perhaps even Persian decorative motifs. Several bear the portrait of a woman on the obverse and an owl on the reverse. The presence of the owl suggests that the woman should be identified as Athena. Another coin has the profile of the face of Athena with an inscription read alternatively as *yhd* or the name of the priest Yohanan. More controversial is a drachm in the British Museum. On one side is the portrait of a bearded male head. The figure wears a crown to which is attached a crest, perhaps of bay leaves. The other side depicts a robed, bearded male seated on a chariot. On his hand he is holding a bird, variously interpreted as a falcon, some type of Egyptian bird, or perhaps an eagle or hawk. Facing the seated figure is a disembodied head, sometimes interpreted as the Egyptian deity Bes. Who is this male figure that is seated on the chariot? Possible candidates have included Zeus, Dionysus, Hadranos, and even Ahura Mazda (this would evidently require that the winged chariot be interpreted as a stylized sun-disk that is generally associated with the Persian deity). The coin also has an inscription that appears to read *yhd*. Another interpretation of this coin is that the seated deity is intended to represent YHWH or perhaps Zeus, who is then syncretistically equated with YHWH. In her extensive discussion of this coin, Edelman mentions an onyx of unknown provenance with a portrait of a deity that resembles Zeus, but which has an inscription in Greek on the reverse, ΙΑΩ ΣΑΒΑΩ = Yahweh Sabaoth (Edelman 189–91 and 225, fig. 2).

These economic (coins) or cultural (decorated seals) artifacts may have several explanations. The coins may simply be an attempt to connote authentic mints – since Greek and Persian coinage were in some sense normative, those striking coins in Yehud may have intentionally used accepted international minting standards. The presence of semidivine hunters or the sun disk may be explained by claiming that the artifacts that bear them are owned by Babylonian or Persian officials, and thus have no bearing on a move toward monotheism and/or the presence or absence of an enforced aniconic tradition. But the onyx and the drachm argue against the notion – until recently accepted rather uncritically – that "the exile" cured "the true seed of Israel" of idolatry.

We need not base this conclusion on the archaeological data alone, though, for many texts from these periods themselves demonstrate a continued penchant for extra-Yahwistic worship. Note, for example, Jeremiah's pointed exchange with the leaders of the Judean community in Egypt (Jer. 44). The prophet warns them to worship YHWH exclusively and points to the fall of the kingdom as a consequence of their disobedience to the divine covenant. They respond by blaming the destruction of Jerusalem not on their unfaithfulness to YHWH but instead on their neglect of Asherah (Jer. 44:15–19).

Several passages that date to the Persian period also make either direct or oblique references to images and/or idols. In Zechariah 5:5–11 the prophet sees a vision of a basket containing a woman (called "wickedness" and equated with some form of heterodoxy) who is transported to Babylon to be placed in a temple being constructed for her. One interpretation of the passage is that the vision may be a call to remove idolatry from the land before Yahweh's temple is rebuilt in order to establish an orthodox form of Yahwism. Understood in this manner, the text may support the idea that idolatry ended *early* in the Persian period; even if this is the case, it is clear that the worship of other deities was not eradicated by the "exile."

Two texts in Second Zechariah may also point to the use of images. Zechariah 10:1–3 condemns the people for seeking "teraphim who speak wickedness." Are these teraphim household deities used in family worship, or perhaps "symbolic representations of humans – of deceased ancestors – who may have held quasi-divine or godlike status" (Meyers and Meyers, *Zechariah 9–14*, 184–8)? Likewise, Zechariah 13:2–6 proclaims that YHWH will cut off "the names of the idols" so they will no longer be remembered in the land.

Three passages in Third Isaiah also contain direct or veiled reference to idolatry. His adversaries are "children of a sorceress, offspring of an adulterous woman" whom YHWH will reject. In times of adversity, they will have to "turn to their assemblage" (presumably either idols or perhaps dead ancestors) who will be powerless to help (Isa. 57:3–13). Isaiah 65:3–7 accuses the people of offering incense on hills (forbidden sanctuaries) and practicing worship of the dead or incubation rites. Isaiah 66:1–4 contrasts those who "tremble at YHWH's word" with those whose worship is an abomination. Taken together, the texts in Jeremiah, Zechariah and Isaiah demonstrate that heterodox cultic practices, some of which are associated with idols/images of other deities, remained a problem well into the Persian period.

Alternative Visions

The *gôlâ* community and its strict religious and ethnic vision was but one of several voices we can discern in the Persian period. It is during this time that we see the initial movement toward apocalyptic as a worldview and characterized by specific symbolic and genre characteristics. Whether it was a result of social and religious deprivation (Hanson's hierocrats versus visionaries), or it emerged from frustrated bureaucrats seeking greater power (Berquist), or it was rooted in priestly, therefore, central power (Cook), we see its precursors in parts of Isaiah 56–66, First and Second Zechariah, Joel, and Ezekiel (see John J. Collins's essay in this volume). We also see a tension between the particularistic perspective of the *gôlâ* group, with its expectations of ethnic and ritual purity, Sabbath observance, and specific understandings of Torah observance, and a more universalistic orientation that would extend membership in the community of faith to the "nations" – characteristic of Ruth, Jonah and parts of Second Zechariah (see the essay by Tamara Cohn Eskenazi in this volume). Hero stories, such as the Joseph narratives in Genesis 37–50, Daniel and his compatriots, and Esther (however one interprets the book that bears her name), may have functioned to provide hope for the deported Judeans and those feeling under siege even after returning to Yehud (Smith-Christopher).

Retrospect and Prospects

This study demonstrates something of the fluidity and creativity that characterizes biblical scholarship in the twenty-first century. From the late nineteenth through the late twentieth centuries, an entire epoch of biblical history and religion was more or less written off as of little import at best, and as representing spiritual decline from prophetic creativity to priestly formalism at worst. The pioneering work of Ephraim Stern on the Persian period was pivotal in helping to change that perspective. From a textual standpoint, the early studies of C. C. Torrey and later works of Peter Ackroyd, in quite different ways, opened the way for a new and fresh approach to the Neo-Babylonian and Persian periods. Social science methodologies, archaeological studies, postcolonialist thought, and diaspora/forced deportation studies have shed considerable new light on these 200 years of Judean experience in Babylonian, Persian, Egyptian and Yehudite contexts. Indeed, the once peripheral has become a (but not the) focal point, or center, of Hebrew Bible scholarship.

One of the many impacts of this shift is the attempt to give a better name to the years from 605 through 332 BCE. Even though the majority of scholars continue to prefer the biblical terms of "exile" and "return" or "preexilic," "exilic" and "postexilic," to describe these years, I believe that to do so accepts the would-be dominant gôlâ ideology. Terms such as Neo-Babylonian and Persian (or both together) are perhaps more cumbersome, but they are, I have argued, more accurate. The destruction and forced deportations, the self-inflicted flight to Egypt, in short, the beginnings of diaspora, caused a profound identity crisis for all who survived, and these realities are embedded in both text and tell. Under Babylonian control, the geopolitical center within Judah seems to have been Tell en-Naṣbeh, though south of Jerusalem, Ramat Raḥel continued to serve as an administrative center. For those who remained in Judah after 597, 587/6 and 582, I expect that village life was similar to that during the last days of the Judean kingdom, but doubt that a full-fledged administrative system was put in place. It is only after Persia's conquest of Babylon that the former territory is made a province, and even in the late sixth century, Jerusalem was slow to rebound as a religious and political center. As the Persian period continued, however, the center of gravity shifted to Jerusalem.

The province of Yehud was small and poor. These conclusions are based on the foundation of various types of archaeological data: full-scale excavations, salvage or emergency excavations, and a number of archaeological surveys. With few exceptions, the province was made up of networks of small villages and towns, with only a few reaching either major size or status. There is still some debate regarding the extent or "boundaries" of Yehud, but beyond question is that the majority of people were settled in the central spur of the Judean hills, in the former tribal territories of Benjamin and Judah. Just as there were several deportations, so, during the sixth and fifth centuries, it is likely that there were several returns, though we cannot precisely date any of them. Lists in Ezra and Nehemiah, that claim well over 42,000 returnees with Sheshbazzar, are exaggerated and ideological.

Both the Neo-Babylonian and Persian periods were, despite (or perhaps because of) the upheaval and need for re-forming/reclaiming prior beliefs, periods of reflection and creativity. Much of what we now call the Hebrew Bible was either edited or composed during these eras, and a careful reading of these various texts demonstrates competing communities with sometimes different beliefs, all seeking and claiming sole legitimacy.

There are many opportunities for continued mining of these periods from textual and archaeological perspectives. One contribution would be a comprehensive analysis of settlements and demography for the entire areas that comprised the former kingdoms of Israel and Judah. Carefully conducted and using accepted models for population estimates, such a study would lay the foundation for a more precise understanding of the socioeconomic interrelationships among the various provinces of the satrapy "Across the River." There is great potential that archaeological finds will provide data that will change our understandings of the province, just as the renewed excavations at Ramat Raḥel have. In a similar way, a series of Babylonian texts that are to be published soon – among them those that speak of āl-Yaḫudu (variously translated as "the city of Judah" or "Judahville") – will shed light on the experience of Judeans in Babylon (Cogan; Pearce). A matter sure to continue to generate debate will be the relative status of the above-mentioned Ramat Raḥel and Jerusalem in the Persian period. To what degree can we accept the traditions of Nehemiah regarding rebuilding Jerusalem's walls and repopulating the city? Are there truly any archaeological remains for walls that we can date to the Persian period? Does the fact that the former site has produced more seal impressions than Jerusalem, and that there are remains of architectural expansion of the site, mean that it was the true economic capital of the province, outstripping Jerusalem in both size and significance? I expect that these and other similar issues will occupy both biblical scholars and archaeologists, enriching both the study of the period from 605 to 332 and its impact on our understanding of the Hebrew Bible as a whole for decades to come.

Notes

1   Those who do employ areal analysis (applying the formula of population to settled area) generally adhere to the following practices: for towns, villages, and urban centers, deduct at least 25 percent of the settlement's size to account for public space (streets, squares, religious and/or governmental buildings); and, depending on how exhaustive the survey is, add up to 20 percent to the settled area to account for sites not discovered or underreported.

2   See Shiloh, *Excavations*. The additional volumes by Shiloh's students are edited individually or jointly by D. T. Ariel, A. DeGroot and H. Bernick-Greenberg, see vol. 2, Qedem 30 (1990); vol. 3, Qedem 33 (1992); vol. 4, Qedem 35 (1996); vol. 5, Qedem 40 (2000); vol. 6, Qedem 41 (2000); vol. 7a, Qedem 53 (2012); vol. 7b, Qedem 54 (2012), all published by the Institute of Archaeology of the Hebrew University of Jerusalem, with the Israel Exploration Society.

3   I caution against a "pan-Persica" approach that would assign the initial writing of the majority of the biblical traditions to the Persian and Hellenistic periods – it seems no more defensible than the pan-Babylonian perspective many scholars advanced in the late nineteenth to early twentieth centuries.

Bibliography

Ackroyd, Peter R. *Exile and Restoration: A Study of Hebrew Thought of the Sixth Century BC*. Philadelphia: Westminster Press, 1968. An influential study of prophetic texts of the Neo-Babylonian and early Persian periods, including Jeremiah, Haggai, Zechariah, and Ezekiel. Also discusses Deuteronomic History and Priestly literature.

Avi-Yonah, Michael. *The Holy Land*. Grand Rapids: Baker, 1966. Classic work on the historical geography of Jerusalem and its environs, beginning with the exilic period.

Barstad, Hans M. *The Myth of the Empty Land: A Study in the History and Archaeology of Judah during the "Exile" Period*. Oslo: Scandinavian University Press, 1996. Most complete treatment of the empty land concept and comparison with the archaeological and textual traditions.

Berquist, Jon L. *Judaism in Persia's Shadow: A Social and Historical Approach*. Minneapolis: Fortress, 1995. Study of the social, religious, historical, and literary contexts and developments during the Persian period.

Blenkinsopp, Joseph. "Bethel in the Neo-Babylonian period." In Oded Lipschits and Joseph Blenkinsopp (eds), *Judah and the Judeans in the Neo-Babylonian Period* (pp. 93–107). Winona Lake, IN: Eisenbrauns, 2003. Analysis of the site of Bethel after the fall of Judah and its possible use as a primary cultic center during the Neo-Babylonian period.

Briant, Pierre. *From Cyrus to Alexander: A History of the Persian Empire*, trans. Peter T. Daniels. Winona Lake, IN: Eisenbrauns, 2002. The standard reference work on the Persian empire, its history, and imperial policies within the heartland and throughout its holdings.

Carroll, Robert. "The myth of the empty land." *Semeia* 59 (1992): 79–93. Introduces the concept of the empty land as a thematic creation of biblical writers that differs from the historical and cultural realities.

Carter, Charles E. *The Emergence of Yehud in the Persian Period: A Social and Demographic Study*. England: Sheffield Academic Press, 1999. Discussion of the history, archaeology, and social setting of the province of Yehud. Includes projections of settlement history, site distribution and population.

Carter, Charles E. "Ideology and archaeology in the Neo-Babylonian period: Excavating text and tell." In Oded Lipschits and Joseph Blenkinsopp (eds), *Judah and the Judeans in the Neo-Babylonian Period* (pp. 301–22). Winona Lake, IN: Eisenbrauns, 2003. Examines archaeological data for the former kingdom of Judah during the Neo-Babylonian period and the material impact on emergent ideologies.

Carter, Charles E. "Syria-Palestine in the Persian period." In Susan Richard (ed.), *Near Eastern Archaeology: A Reader* (pp. 398–412). Winona Lake, IN: Eisenbrauns, 2003. Brief summary of relevant archaeological and historical issues in Syria-Palestine from 539 to 332 BCE. Includes history of the region, pottery, architecture, burial practices, military developments, and discussion of Yehud, and its demography and economy.

Cogan, Mordechai. *Bound for Exile: Israelites and Judeans under Imperial Yoke: Documents from Assyria and Babylonia*. Jerusalem: Carta, 2013. Collection of texts pertaining to life under Assyrian and Babylonian rule after the destruction of the Northern and Southern kingdoms. Important information relating to Judean life in Babylon.

Cook, Stephen L. *Prophecy and Apocalypticism: The Postexilic Social Setting*. Minneapolis: Fortress. Critiques the deprivation model for the emergence of apocalyptic worldview and proposes apocalyptic is instead rooted in priestly circles.

Edelman, Diana V. "Tracking observance of the aniconic tradition through numismatics." In Diana V. Edelman (ed.), *The Triumph of Elohim: From Yahwisms to Judaisms* (pp. 185–225). Analyzes iconography on Yehud coins from the late Persian to early Hellenistic periods and identifies Persian and Greek decorative motifs on Judean coinage and other artifacts.

Faust, Avraham. *Judah in the Neo-Babylonian Period: The Archaeology of Desolation*. Atlanta: Society of Biblical Literature, 2012. Analysis of the archaeological remains and results from surveys in the former kingdom of Judah after the destruction of Jerusalem and Judah. Critiques views of Carroll and Barstad that downplay the level of disruption within Judea.

Hanson, Paul D. *The Dawn of Apocalyptic: The Historical and Sociological Roots of Jewish Apocalyptic Eschatology.* Rev. edn. Philadelphia: Fortress, 1979. Classic discussion of the development of apocalyptic literature in Isaiah 56–66 and Zechariah 9–14. Suggests conflict between priestly hierocrats and apocalyptic visionaries, a view rooted in the concept of social deprivation.

Hoglund, Kenneth. *Achaemenid Imperial Administration in Syria-Palestine and the Missions of Ezra and Nehemiah.* Atlanta: Scholars Press, 1992. Study of the relationship between Persian administrative policies and the province of Yehud in the mid-fifth century as expressed in Ezra-Nehemiah.

Kaufman, Yeḥezkel. *History of the Religion of Israel,* vol. 4: *From the Babylonian Captivity to the End of Prophecy.* New York: Ktav, 1977. Part of a multivolume, expansive history of Israelite religion, representing a maximalist view of biblical traditions and their reliability.

Lipschits, Oded. *The Fall and Rise of Jerusalem: Judah under Babylonian Rule.* Winona Lake, IN: Eisenbrauns, 2005. Treatment of Neo-Babylonian period and the fortunes of Jerusalem and the later province of Yehud in the aftermath of the destruction of 587/6 BCE. A comprehensive work that examines biblical traditions and history, archaeological data and significant extrabiblical documents pertaining to both Neo-Babylonian and Persian periods.

Lipschits, Oded and David S. Vanderhooft. *The Yehud Stamp Impressions: A Corpus of Inscribed Impressions from the Persian and Hellenistic Periods in Judah.* Winona Lake, IN: Eisenbrauns, 2011. Definitive study of the Yehud seals discovered throughout the province and beyond its purported boundaries. Divides impressions into three major periods (early, middle, and late) and discusses their distribution in historical and archaeological contexts.

Meyers, Carol L. and Eric M. Meyers. *Haggai, Zechariah 1–8: A New Translation with Introduction and Commentary.* Anchor Bible 25B. Garden City, NY: Doubleday, 1987. Interpretation of prophetic literature and historical context in early Persian period, specifically the role of both Haggai and Zechariah in temple rebuilding; social, political and religious contexts seen through the lens of archaeological, social science and literary perspectives.

Meyers, Carol L. and Eric M. Meyers. *Zechariah 9–14: A New Translation with Introduction and Commentary.* Anchor Bible 25C. New York: Doubleday, 1993. The significance of Second Zechariah for the community within Yehud during the Persian period. Like the previous volume, brings archaeological and social science perspectives to bear on central texts of the period.

Middlemas, Jill. *The Templeless Age: An Introduction to the History, Literature, and Theology of the "Exile."* Louisville, KY: Westminster John Knox, 2007. Critiques traditional notion of exile and the exilic period and suggests that a better assignation for the period between 587 and 515 BCE is a period without a temple, or Templeless era. Reviews literature of the period, including laments, Deuteronomic History, and prophetic traditions.

Olmstead, Albert T. *History of the Persian Empire: Achaemenid Period.* Chicago: University of Chicago Press, 1948. Until the publication of Briant's work, this was the standard study of the Persian period, used widely by biblical scholars in their analyses of the impact of the Achaemenid era on Judean history.

Pearce, Laurie E. "New evidence for Judeans in Babylon." In Oded Lipschits and M. Oeming (eds), *Judah and the Judeans in the Persian Period* (pp. 399–411). Winona Lake, IN: Eisenbrauns, 2006. Introduces the texts of Babylonian provenance that speak of inhabitants of a settlement, āl-Yaḫudu.

Shiloh, Y. *Excavations at the City of David I, 1978–1982: Interim Report of the First Five Seasons.* Qedem 19. Jerusalem: Institute of Archaeology, Hebrew University of Jerusalem, 1984. Important publication of pioneering work in Jerusalem.

Smith-Christopher, Daniel. *A Biblical Theology of Exile*. Minneapolis: Augsburg-Fortress, 2002. Uses social science models to examine biblical texts and traditions that reflect various responses to experience of "exiles."

Stern, Ephraim. *Material Culture of the Land of the Bible in the Persian Period, 538–332 BC*. Warminster, UK: Aris & Phillips, 1982. First comprehensive study of the archaeological record of Syria-Palestine in the Persian period. Significant for the emergence of Neo-Babylonian and Persian period studies within the disciplines of archaeology and biblical scholarship.

Stern, Ephraim. *Archaeology of the Land of the Bible*, vol. 2: *The Assyrian, Babylonian, and Persian Periods (732–332 BCE)*. New York: Doubleday, 2001. Assessment of the archaeological, historical, and political contexts of Israel and Judah in periods of imperial hegemony.

Stern, Ephraim. "Pagan Yahwism: The folk religion of ancient Israel." *Biblical Archaeology Review* 27 (2001): 20-9. Accessible article discussing heterodox religious practices in pre-monarchical Israel.

Torrey, Charles C. *Ezra Studies*. New York: Ktav, 1970. Collection of Torrey's essays concerning the "exilic" and "postexilic" periods; anticipates many of the currents of contemporary Neo-Babylonian and Persian period studies.

Vanderhooft, David S. *The Neo-Babylonian Empire and Babylon in the Latter Prophets*. Atlanta: Scholars Press, 1999. Study of the imperial perspectives and policies of the Neo-Babylonian rulers and their impact on the history and literary traditions of the sixth century BCE.

Watts, James W. (ed.). *Persia and Torah: The Theory of Imperial Authorization of the Pentateuch*. Atlanta: Society of Biblical Literature, 2001. Essays that assess the potential relationship between the composition/editing of the Torah and Persian imperial policies.

Zorn, Jeffrey. "Tell en-Naṣbeh and the problem of the material culture of the sixth century." In Oded Lipschits and Joseph Blenkinsopp (eds), *Judah and Judeans in the Neo-Babylonian Period* (pp. 413–47). Winona Lake, IN: Eisenbrauns, 2003. Examines the archaeological evidence for the site presumed to be biblical Mizpah. Zorn's study includes revised stratigraphy for the site, architectural and pottery analysis, and discussion of epigraphic remains.

CHAPTER 13

The Hellenistic Period

Matthew J. Goff

The Hellenistic period was an epoch of great change in Israel and the ancient Near East. The era is characterized not only by political strife and upheaval but also a striking degree of innovation and creativity. Hellenistic empires (the Ptolemies and then the Seleucids) exerted dominion over Israel, which led to the Maccabean Revolt and the rise of the Hasmonean Dynasty (142–63 BCE). These factors had profound political, cultural and literary consequences in Israel and the Diaspora. An article of this length cannot comprehensively address such a vast topic. This essay will focus on three of the most important issues for the Judaism of this era: Hellenism in Israel and the Diaspora, the Maccabean revolt, and the apocalyptic tradition (see John J. Collins's and Benjamin Wright's essays in this volume). The issue of Hellenism should be approached not only in terms of the spread of Greek philosophical ideas. The exchange of ideas and other forms of cultural knowledge needs to be understood in the context of the central political fact of the Hellenistic age – the loss of native autonomy by ancient civilizations across the Near East, which were conquered by, and kept under the dominion of, Hellenistic kingdoms.

Hellenism and the Hellenistic Age: Demarcations and Definitions

In a political sense the Hellenistic age lasted approximately three centuries, from 334 to 31 BCE. The advent of this epoch is justly associated with the Macedonian conqueror Alexander the Great (356–323 BCE) (Briant). In 334 he crossed into Anatolia with his army and launched an excursion against King Darius III (r. 336–330 BCE), king of the Achaemenid empire of Persia. After defeating Darius at Issus in Cilicia (southern Anatolia) in November 333, Alexander embarked upon numerous conquests. His military campaigns were remarkably successful. In 11 years he conquered a vast swath of land, around 2 million square miles, extending to the Danube River in Europe, the Nile in Egypt and the Indus River in what is now Pakistan (Waterfield 6). Much of this area was previously controlled by the Achaemenid empire.

The Wiley Blackwell Companion to Ancient Israel, First Edition. Edited by Susan Niditch.
© 2016 John Wiley & Sons, Ltd. Published 2016 by John Wiley & Sons, Ltd.

Alexander died in 323 BCE in Babylon without a male heir to assume control of his sprawling empire. This led to a bitter power struggle among his generals, the *Diadochoi* ("Successors"). They fought several wars against one another for control over various parts of Alexander's empire (Waterfield; Green 1–134). This immense area was eventually divided into several smaller, but still large, kingdoms. Ptolemy I Soter founded the Ptolemaic empire in Egypt, reigning as king from 305 to 285 BCE (Hölbl). Seleucus I Nicator (r. 305–281 BCE) began the Seleucid empire which, at various points in its history, had dominion in regions from Asia Minor to western India (Grainger; Sherwin-White and Kuhrt). Macedonia and parts of Asia Minor came under the control of other Macedonian leaders, such as Antigonus I Monophthalmus ("One-Eye"; d. 301 BCE) and Lysimachus (d. 281 BCE). In 31 BCE the sole remaining Hellenistic kingdom, the Ptolemaic Dynasty, ceased to exist after Marc Antony and the Ptolemaic queen Cleopatra VII were defeated at the Battle of Actium by Octavian (Augustus), who became the first Roman emperor in 27 BCE. The Hellenistic period is framed by Alexander the Great at its outset and Cleopatra at its close.

The designation of the Ptolemaic and Seleucid empires as Hellenistic denotes that they were dynasties based in the ancient Near East that were founded and ruled by Greek speakers who were steeped in Greek culture. The Seleucid kings, for example, understood themselves as descended from the god Apollo and they promoted this idea to legitimate their rule (Sherwin-White and Kuhrt 28). The Hellenistic rulers fostered the spread of Greek traditions in their kingdoms. The Greeks were by no means unknown in the ancient Near East before this. The biblical book of Ezra, for example, uses the term *darkəmônîm* (2:69), an adaptation of the Greek monetary unit *drachma* (in the genitive of price), and Greek mercenaries fought with the Assyrian and Babylonian armies in the seventh century BCE (Hengel 13, 33). But with the Hellenistic kingdoms, engagement with Greek culture took place on a scale heretofore unseen in the region. Numerous cities were founded, well over three hundred, that were often named after their Hellenistic founders, such as Alexandria in Egypt or Seleucia-on-Tigris in Babylon (Tcherikover 22). Greek and bilingual inscriptions, in Greek and a native language, are widely attested in this period, as are coins with Greek words. Near Eastern authors began to write in Greek. Berossus, for example, a priest of the Babylonian god Marduk, composed his *Babyloniaka*, a work about Babylonian myth and history, in Greek around 290 BCE.

The term "Hellenism" often signifies the spread of Greek philosophical ideas. The conventional usage of the word stems from the nineteenth-century scholar Johann Gustav Droysen, who coined it to denote the influence of Greek thought and language. It is implied that "Hellenism," as an "-ism," is an ideology or doctrine, but the transmission of Greek customs and culture should not be understood in solely abstract, intellectual terms. The discussion below considers concrete factors, including political, economic and social issues, when assessing the impact of Greek culture on Judaism, guided by Martin Hengel's astute perspective that Hellenism "must be treated as a complex phenomenon which cannot be limited to purely political, socioeconomic, cultural or religious aspects, but embraces them all" (3).

It should also be stressed that the rise of the Hellenistic kingdoms did not simply promote the advance of Greek culture in the Near East but also provided a context in which people learned about and interacted with other cultures under the dominion of these kingdoms. For example, Theopompus, a Greek historian who was a contemporary of Alexander, displays knowledge of Zoroastrianism, the ancient religion of Persia, especially its dualism of light and darkness (as preserved in Plutarch, *Isis and Osiris*, 47). Alexander himself promoted a kind of cultural syncretism. He wore Persian clothes and married Iranian women, including Roxane (Rauxana), a noblewoman from Bactria (in what is now Afghanistan). He also arranged a mass wedding that followed Persian customs between Macedonian officers and Persian women (Arrian, *Anabasis*, 7.4).

Hellenistic Kingdoms and Hellenism in the Land of Israel and the Jewish Diaspora

For much of the Hellenistic age, as in the preexilic period, Judea was a small, relatively weak political actor caught between more powerful forces: Egypt to the south and Syro-Mesopotamia to the northeast. The Ptolemies and Seleucids fought six wars with each other, the so-called "Syrian Wars" (fought intermittently between 274 and 168 BCE), for dominion over Coele-Syria, which included the small province of Judea. In 301 BCE Ptolemy I assumed control of Coele-Syria and it became part of the Ptolemaic empire, which sought a buffer state between it and the Seleucids. In 198 BCE the Seleucids, under Antiochus III the Great (r. 241–187 BCE), became the rulers of Judea.

The impact of the Hellenistic kingdoms on the land of Israel was extensive. There were several Hellenistic, non-Judean cities on the coast, such as Ptolemais-Acco and Jaffa (Tcherikover 90–116). According to the Maccabean literature, in the early second century BCE there was a gymnasium, a traditional center of Greek *paideia* (education), in Jerusalem (see further below). While direct evidence is lacking, if one assumes that the institution followed Greek customs regarding its curriculum, one can posit that Homer was taught in Jerusalem in this period.

There is a rich and abundant Jewish literature from the Hellenistic period. In addition to a large corpus of Jewish texts in Hebrew and Aramaic, attested in sources such as the Dead Sea Scrolls, there is a sizable body of Greek compositions from both Israel and the Diaspora written by Jews (for surveys, see Collins, *Athens and Jerusalem*; Gruen; see also the essay by Benjamin Wright in this volume). In Palestine a Jewish author by the name of Eupolemus, most likely the Maccabean official dispatched to Rome around 160 BCE (1 Macc. 8:17–18; 2 Macc. 4:11), composed a historiographic work in Greek about the biblical kingdom of Judea. In the second century BCE Theodotus retold the story of the rape of Dinah from Genesis 34, writing in Greek epic hexameter verse (Gruen 120). He has traditionally been regarded as a Samaritan author but he was probably a Palestinian Jew whose views reflect tension between Jews and Samaritans in the time of the Hasmonean king John Hyrcanus (r. 134–104 BCE) (Collins, *Athens and Jerusalem*, 59). There have also been ample discoveries in Palestine of ancient biblical manuscripts in Greek, such as a translation of the minor prophets found at Naḥal Ḥever. Even in instances where no explicit reliance upon Greek literature can be reliably posited, one can discern modes of thought and social organization in Palestine that can be attributed to cultural and economic exchange by disparate peoples brought under the common sphere of Hellenistic influence. For example, the sectarian community that produced some of the Dead Sea Scrolls demonstrates virtually no direct engagement with Greek learning but its organizational structure is similar to that of Hellenistic voluntary associations.

Still, while the impact of Hellenism in Palestine is substantial, one must make a distinction between Israel and the Diaspora in terms of the extent of Jewish engagement with Greek culture. Philo, living in Alexandria in the first century CE, produced an extensive corpus in which he reflects upon biblical traditions and Judaism in a way that shows a salient mastery of Greek philosophy. There is no comparable Palestinian Jew from the period, although familiarity with Greek learning may have influenced Palestinian Jewish traditions (see the discussion below on apocalypticism). The knowledge of Greek culture by Jewish authors is more extensive in the Diaspora than Palestine. Jews were living abroad before the Hellenistic period. The Babylonian exile in the sixth century BCE forcibly moved Judeans to Babylon, for example, and there they were exposed to influences from that region. Contact with other cultures did not originate in the Hellenistic period. But this is the first era in which we find a sustained effort by Jews to express and describe their religious and scriptural traditions in a non-Semitic language.

Much of the available evidence for Jews writing in Greek comes from the Diaspora (see the essay by Benjamin Wright in this volume). Jews lived in numerous locales throughout the Hellenistic world. They were settled in various places as mercenaries. There is evidence for synagogues in diverse regions such as Cyrenaica (Libya), Italy, Egypt and, as the travels of Paul described in the New Testament suggest, Asia Minor. The rise of Judaism in areas in which Greek was the common language is evident in the creation of the Septuagint, the translation of the Jewish scriptures into Greek. The Hellenistic Jewish *Letter of Aristeas* claims that the Torah was rendered into Greek in Alexandria during the third century BCE. The Jewish presence in Egypt was particularly vibrant. Many of the Diaspora texts discussed below are from Egypt. The campaign of Ptolemy I into Palestine resulted in many people from the region being deported into Egypt – over 100,000 people, according to the *Letter of Aristeas* (12–14, 35).

In a wide range of Diaspora texts Jews embraced Greek culture and drew from it to express and maintain their Jewish identity. Judaism is understood and valorized in a way that is compatible with its broader Hellenistic environment. Much of this literature was preserved not by Jews but rather Christians, in particular the Church Father Eusebius. In this material one finds scant references to classical Greek tropes, such as the Trojan War or the exploits of mythic figures like Hercules (Collins and Harlow 83). Rather, Jewish authors utilize Greek traditions to refashion and appropriate biblical figures and biblical narratives in new ways. One major concern is to portray the Jews as an ancient people who play a key role in the history of culture. A text by a Hellenistic Egyptian Jew by the name of Artapanus claims that Abraham taught the Egyptians astronomy (Collins, *Athens and Jerusalem*, 37–46). The author also hails Moses as the teacher of Orpheus and a culture hero to whom he attributes key elements of Egyptian civilization, including the invention of boats, the administrative structure of the country and hieroglyphs (fragment 3; Eusebius, *Praeparatio Evangelica*, 9.27.1–6). Writing in Greek in Palestine, an author known as Pseudo-Eupolemus (ca. 200 BCE), perhaps a Samaritan, similarly associates the spread of the knowledge of astronomy with Abraham, who learned it first in Babylon and, traveling west, taught it to the Phoenicians and then the Egyptians. This composition may appropriate the trope that Egypt is the source of much of Greek civilization (e.g., Herodotus 2.51, 104; Plato, *Timaeus*, 22b–e), denigrating the primacy of Greece in the history of culture. In these texts Judaism is celebrated not simply as important for Jews but also for its indispensable part in the transmission of culture that benefits all of humankind.

There is also in Hellenistic Jewish literature an impulse to cast the Jewish and Gentile worlds as compatible and harmonious. A core example of this phenomenon is the *Letter of Aristeas* (Gruen 206–22). This document, a product of Hellenistic Egyptian Judaism, is written in Greek and purportedly from the reign of Ptolemy II (r. 285–247 BCE), although it was composed somewhat later. The putative author, Aristeas, is dispatched by the king from Alexandria to Jerusalem to make arrangements for the translation of the Hebrew Bible into Greek (the Septuagint), which is to be included in the famous library of Alexandria (9–12). He tells the Ptolemaic king that the Jews "worship God the overseer and creator of all, whom all men worship including ourselves, O king, except that we have a different name. Their name for him is Zeus and Jove" (16). This statement, written by a Jewish author and placed in the mouth of a Greek, seeks common ground with Gentiles in the desire to worship a supreme deity, unambiguously identified as the God of the Jews. The Jewish philosopher Aristobulus similarly states that Zeus and the God of the Jews are one and the same entity, who goes by different names (fragment 4; Eusebius, *Praeparatio Evangelica*, 13.12.7). *Aristeas* extols the ritual and dietary laws of Leviticus for teaching moral truths allegorically, as one also finds in Philo. Birds that are not allowed for consumption, for example, are wild and carnivorous, so by not eating them Moses teaches one to be kind and not dominate others (*Letter of Aristeas*, 146–7). Moses as a lawgiver is praised as a philosopher, again as in Philo. The Jewish sages selected for the translation of the Bible, and the high priest Eleazar, are revered not only for their knowledge of the Torah but also for their *paideia* or Greek education (*Letter of Aristeas*, 121–7). The *Letter of Aristeas* stresses the compatibility of Jewish and Greek learning. The composition also asserts the superiority of Jewish monotheism over Gentile idolatry, in particular the paganism of Egypt (138).

The rejection of idol worship is a prominent theme elsewhere in Diaspora literature. The *Testament of Job*, a retelling of the biblical book, associates Satan with a pagan temple, which Job destroys. The author of *Joseph and Aseneth* apparently found it problematic that a biblical patriarch could marry a pagan Egyptian woman. The composition offers an elaborate retelling of the story of Joseph, who weds Aseneth, the daughter of a pagan priest (Gen. 41:45). The Book of Genesis mentions no controversy regarding this marriage, an odd silence given the prominence of the theme of endogamy in the text, stressed with regard to Abraham and Isaac. *Joseph and Aseneth* makes explicit that Joseph's wife converts to Judaism, legitimating a role in the religion for proselytes. The Diaspora literature of Hellenistic Judaism is characterized by a tension between universalism and particularism. Jewish authors turned to Greek idioms and values to make their traditions intelligible in Hellenistic terms, and worthy of respect in the wider Gentile world, while at the same time embracing the distinctive nature of Judaism as a monotheistic religion.

Political and Social Contexts: Economic Inequity and Native Revolts

Turning from the Diaspora, understanding Israel in the Hellenistic period involves not only surveying Jewish engagement with Greek ideas but also appreciating other factors of social change. In this section I address two issues: (1) economic reforms in Palestine undertaken by the Ptolemies, which led to widespread inequity (compare the essay in this volume by David Schloen for an earlier period); and (2) native revolts throughout the Hellenistic kingdoms.

The Ptolemaic administration of Coele-Syria in the third century BCE had a lasting impact on Judea. The Ptolemies, adopting a form of centralized state capitalism, focused on the economic development of Palestine in an aggressive and organized manner. They promoted an expansion of agricultural production and tax-farming, the outsourcing of tax collection by the state to a private entity (Hengel 18–55). An important source for these topics is the Zenon archive, discovered in Egypt in 1915. Zenon was an official who worked for Apollonius, a key advisor (the *dioikētēs*) for Ptolemy II Philadelphus. The papyri describe Zenon's travels on behalf of his employer to numerous locales, including Coele-Syria from 260 to 258 BCE. Zenon conducted this work to survey the land and establish trade relationships, reflecting Ptolemaic commitment to the economic utilization of the region. The papyri preserve two letters from Tobias to Apollonius, in which Tobias affirms his friendship with the powerful Egyptian official by sending him gifts, including slaves and rare animals. This Tobias is the same figure described in the famous Tobiad romance of Josephus (*Antiquities of the Jews*, 12.154–236). This narrative describes the meteoric rise of Tobias and his family, which achieved extraordinary wealth through possession of the right to farm taxes in Palestine. It is historically accurate to think of the Tobiads as extremely wealthy. This is confirmed by the archaeological remains of the impressive Tobiad fortress in the Transjordan, Iraq el-Amir. Josephus' account of this family, however, clearly has fictitious embellishments, as is evident, for example, in his story of Tobias's son Joseph's drunken exploits in Egypt (e.g., 12.187–8). There are also historiographic errors. Josephus, for example, places the story after the Seleucid takeover of Palestine in 198 BCE (Tcherikover 128). Nevertheless, the Zenon papyri endorse the view that Tobias became incredibly rich in part by cultivating good relations with the Ptolemaic court.

The Tobiads are important not only because they portray the elite class of Coele-Syria as reliant upon the largesse of the region's Hellenistic rulers. The economic expansion of the period produced a marked rise of inequity. The situation is not unlike that which the prophet Amos derided in the eighth century BCE – the efficient harness of economic resources through a centralized administration led not only to the creation of wealth, but also to its concentration in the hands of a small minority, who aggressively exploited the poor (see the essays by Robert Wilson and David Schloen in this volume). Ben Sira, writing in Jerusalem during the early second century BCE, himself in the employ of the upper class as a scribe, is critical of the situation: "A rich person does wrong and even adds insults; a poor person suffers wrong and must add apologies. A rich person will exploit you if you can be of use to him, but if you are in need he will abandon you" (13:3–4). He also writes: "What does a wolf have in common with a lamb? ... What peace is there between a hyena and a dog? And what peace between the rich and the poor? Wild asses in the wilderness are the prey of lions; likewise the poor are feeding grounds for the rich" (13:17–19; cf. 7:6; 8:1–2).

Other data support Ben Sira's characterization of his time as one of class disparity. Many Palestinians in his day were small-scale subsistence farmers. They were often in need of credit and dependent upon the vagaries of the agricultural season. Ben Sira urged his students, who were from an upper-class milieu, to be ethical creditors and lend money to people in need in order to help them, even though the funds might never be repaid (29:1–13). Few, it seems, heeded Ben Sira's teaching. Creditors with scruples were hard to find. A text from the Dead Sea Scrolls known as 4QInstruction (second century BCE) is, like Ben Sira, a wisdom text but written to people from much more humble backgrounds than the students of the Jerusalem sage. Several texts of 4QInstruction assume that the intended addressee is a farmer and he is repeatedly called "poor" (Goff 127–67). He is given extensive advice on borrowing and taught that indebtedness entails great risk. He is to avoid deceit when dealing with creditors, even though they could engage in heinous actions such as having him flogged (4Q417 2 i 21–5). Being taught to be honest and upright in the face of such treatment underscores the poor person's need to maintain good relations with creditors, reflecting his ongoing need for credit. 4QInstruction gives an impression of the economic difficulties that many Palestinian farmers faced at the time.

The scale of indebtedness in Judean society is also indicated by numerous debt contracts from the period that have been recovered (see, for example, 4Q344 and documents 18 and 144 from Murabba'at; cf. Goff 146). According to 1 Maccabees, the Seleucid king Demetrius I (r. 162–150 BCE) attempted to curry the favor of the people of Judea by offering them forgiveness of debts, suggesting that it was a wide-scale problem: "And all who take refuge at the temple in Jerusalem, or in any of its precincts, because they owe money to the king or are in debt, let them be released and receive back all their property in my kingdom" (10:43; cf. 15:8). Josephus, in his account of the Jewish revolt of 68–74 CE, describes pervasive class conflicts that came to a head after a long period of time. He claims, for example, that some Jewish rebels (a group known as the Sicarii) burned down the record office "to prevent the recovery of debts" (*Jewish War*, 2.427). There was substantial economic inequity in Israel during the Hellenistic period.

There was also considerable political resentment in the ancient Near East against the ruling powers. Native revolts were initiated and literature was composed that promoted the downfall of Hellenistic regimes (Collins, *Seers*, 59–74; Eddy). In Egypt uprisings against Ptolemy V Epiphanes (r. 204–180 BCE) were fueled by excessive taxation levied to fund wars (Assmann 376). The *Demotic Chronicle* is a Hellenistic Egyptian text that reviews the history of the kings of Egypt and shows disdain for the Ptolemaic kings. The document predicts the overthrow of the Ptolemaic dynasty and the advent of an indigenous king who is to lead a rebellion against the Greeks. The *Potter's Oracle*, an Egyptian text probably written in the third century BCE, proclaims that the goddess Isis shall send a "king from the sun" who will assume power and that the main city of Ptolemaic power, Alexandria, will be destroyed. In the Seleucid kingdom there were revolts in Asia Minor against Antiochus III. They were led by Greek generals but, as in Egypt, indicate native discontent toward the ruling class.

Dissatisfaction with Hellenistic rule was also expressed in Persia. The Iranian *Oracle of Hystaspes* (a Greek form of Vishtaspa), probably written in the second or first century BCE, predicts the arrival of a king from heaven who will defeat an evil ruler who has power over the world (Hultgård 74–6). The text asserts that a cataclysm of eschatological fire will burn all of humankind, destroying the wicked but leaving the righteous unharmed. Although its final form is much later, the Zoroastrian apocalyptic text *Bahman Yasht* (or *Zand ī Wahman yasn*) is also important for understanding Persian resistance to Hellenistic rule. Using imagery that recalls Daniel 2, chapters 1 and 3 of the work describe a tree of four branches, made respectively of gold, silver, bronze and mixed iron. Also as in Daniel 2, each metal denotes an epoch in which a kingdom rules (cf. *Sibylline Oracles*, 4.49–101). The fourth is an "evil race of wrath," called Yunan, a Persian form of the Greek term "Ionian" (Eddy 19). This is reasonably understood as a reference to Alexander and his Macedonian army, since they overthrew the Persian empire. In the *Bahman Yasht* numerous foreign barbarian tribes stream into Iran, causing great chaos and turmoil. The Persians eventually restore the proper religion of Iran (Zoroastrianism), with the help of the god Mihr (Mithra). Although a precise date of composition for this work is not available, the *Bahman Yasht* indicates, as does the *Oracle of Hystaspes*, that Persians adapted and reformulated their indigenous religious traditions to express political resentment against their Hellenistic rulers.

The Maccabean Crisis

The most well-known revolt of the Hellenistic age is the one led by the Maccabean family in Judea. As the preceding discussion illustrates, the Maccabean uprising is not an isolated incident but rather is consistent with widely attested dissatisfaction among Near Eastern peoples toward their Greek rulers. The economic issues reviewed above suggest that the causes for the Maccabean uprising were not simply religious and political but also were fomented by the economic inequity endured by many Judeans.

The Maccabean Revolt was a nationalistic uprising led by Mattathias and his sons, a priestly family from the Judean town of Modein (1 Macc. 2:1; cf. Josephus, *Antiquities*, 12.265–9). The chronology of the key events of this episode is often not certain because our main sources (1 and 2 Maccabees) do not always agree. Nevertheless, the revolt was triggered by the policies of the Seleucid king Antiochus IV Epiphanes (r. 175–164 BCE). According to the Maccabean literature, he launched several initiatives that were intended to expunge traditional forms of Jewish worship and piety. Jews were commanded to abandon the Torah, the practice of circumcision and the traditional sacrifices at the Temple (1 Macc. 1:41–50; 2 Macc. 6:1–2; cf. Josephus, *Antiquities*, 12.253). The pinnacle of these unpopular reforms was the erection of a "desecrating sacrilege" in the Jerusalem Temple in 167 BCE, which may be a reference to a statue of Zeus or perhaps a Syro-Phoenician deity, Baal Shamem ("Lord of Heaven"; 1 Macc. 1:54; cf. Dan. 9:27; 11:31). 1 Maccabees describes the situation in terms of a traditional biblical opposition between Israelites who remain loyal to their religious traditions and those who wrongly adopt foreign customs:

> In those days (ca. 175 BCE) certain renegades came out from Israel and misled many, saying "Let us go and make a covenant with the Gentiles around us" … and some of the people eagerly went to the king, who authorized them to observe the ordinances of the Gentiles. So they built a gymnasium in Jerusalem, according to Gentile custom, and removed the marks of circumcision and abandoned the holy covenant. (1 Macc. 1:11–15; cf. *Genesis Rabba*, 2:4)

2 Maccabees gives a fuller account of the same events, understanding the conflict as between "Judaism" and "Hellenism," terms that both first appear in this text (for the former, see 2:21; 8:1; 14:3; for the latter, see 4:13). In 175 BCE, the year Antiochus assumed the Seleucid throne, Jason (a Greek form of the name "Joshua"), brother of the high priest Onias III, bribed the king to take over the priestly office held by his brother. He promised Antiochus additional monies if he allowed Jason to create a gymnasium, a center of Greek learning, in Jerusalem and to "enroll the people of Jerusalem as citizens of Antioch" – perhaps an effort to curry favor with the king by renaming the city after him (2 Macc. 4:7–9; Portier-Young 102). Jason encouraged elite men to wear Greek hats and sent envoys to offer sacrifices to Hercules at quadrennial games in Phoenicia at Tyre (2 Macc. 4:12, 18). 2 Maccabees accuses him of promoting an "extreme of Hellenism" (*akmē tis hellinismou*) in Jerusalem (4:13). Traditional Jewish cultic life, according to the text, suffered as a result. Priests ignored their sacrificial duties, for example, to attend wrestling matches and discus-throwing events, traditional Greek sports. 2 Maccabees, on the other hand, places some of the blame for these developments on Antiochus, who sent an Athenian to encourage the Jews to abandon their traditions and rename the Jerusalem Temple "the temple of Olympian Zeus" (6:2). Jews were forced to pay homage to the Greek god Dionysus and women who circumcised their male babies were thrown off the city walls to their deaths (2 Macc. 6:7–10).

Three years after the ascension of Jason (172 BCE), a man named Menelaus offered the king a greater sum than Jason did to assume the office of high priest. Menelaus became high priest, even though he was not in the line of the priestly Oniad family. He forced Jason to flee to Ammon and had the previously deposed Onias murdered (2 Macc. 4:23–26, 34). A false rumor that Antiochus had died spread in Jerusalem, and Jason, viewing this as an opportunity to defeat his priestly foe, invaded the city with an army, which was successfully repulsed (2 Macc. 5:5–10). Antiochus, 2 Maccabees relates, interpreted this as meaning that Judea was in revolt and he used deadly force to restore order. He massacred many and defiled the Temple, stealing a massive amount of the wealth stored there (2 Macc. 5:11–21). He also fortified the Akra, a Seleucid military garrison in Jerusalem, to solidify his control of the city (1 Macc. 1:29–34; cf. Dan. 11:38–39). 2 Maccabees connects the rise of Judas Maccabee to Antiochus' bloodbath, from which Judas escaped into the countryside, where he began to organize military opposition against the Seleucids (5:27; cf. 8:1–4). This is the context, according to 2 Maccabees, of Antiochus' efforts to attack Jewish traditions and defile the temple (6:1–2).

It has been traditional to understand the Maccabean crisis in ideological and religious terms. This perspective is promoted by Elias Bickerman in his influential book *The God of the Maccabees* (in Bickerman, *Studies*, vol. 1). According to Bickerman, Jason and Menelaus were zealots for a radical reformulation of Judaism and the attacks on Jewish tradition should be primarily attributed to them. Comparing these policies to the modern Jewish reform movement of the nineteenth century, he argued that Jason and Menelaus attempted to eliminate circumcision and observation of dietary laws to expel from Judaism its distinctive and separatist elements in order to force it to be compatible with the religious traditions of their Seleucid overlords. The two men would have some precedent in the religious reforms of Ezra, who operated with the sanction of the Persian throne (as Menelaus and Jason did with the Seleucids). While it is certainly true that Jason and Menelaus were attracted to Greek customs (and that our most detailed source for these men, 2 Maccabees, despises them), their actions suggest that they were not grand visionaries of a new Judaism but rather Machiavellians who were hungry for power. The bribes of both men indicate a desire for great personal gain at the expense of venerable Jewish institutions. Their interest in Greek mores cannot be separated from their self-aggrandizing efforts to seek the favor of the Hellenistic rulers. Also, their battles against each other problematize any construal of the two men finding common cause. While knowledge of Greek customs and ways of life is clearly evident in Palestine in this period, as discussed above, the Hellenism of Jason and Menelaus took an extreme form that went beyond what many Jews in Palestine at the time considered acceptable. The members of Jason's own staff, for example, who were sent to Tyre to offer sacrifice to Hercules, refused to do so (2 Macc. 4:20).

Also, as Tcherikover has pointed out, Bickerman's view of Jason and Menelaus minimizes the role of Antiochus and his strategic thinking (Tcherikover 184). Antiochus shed blood to reassert control of Jerusalem – by no means a laudable decision, but, in terms of the logic of imperial rulers, not surprising. Antiochus successfully fought against Egypt in 169 BCE (during the Sixth Syrian War) but failed to take the Ptolemaic capital, Alexandria. He returned to Egypt again in 168 and the Ptolemies successfully lobbied the Roman Senate to intervene (Gera 164–6). Rome dispatched the legate C. Popillius Laenas to force Antiochus to leave Egypt, which he did, on the so-called "Day of Eleusis" (Dan. 11:30; Polybius 29.27; Portier-Young 129–34). While our sources are unclear as to whether Jason's revolt took place after Antiochus launched one or two Egyptian excursions (compare 1 Macc. 1:20 with 2 Macc. 5:1–3; cf. Josephus, *Antiquities*, 12.246), his activities in Egypt encouraged him to assert undeniably his control over Judea, part of the traditional buffer zone between the Ptolemaic and Seleucid kingdoms. In 165 BCE, a time of turmoil in Jerusalem, he began military campaigns to reestablish control over eastern portions of the Seleucid empire, triggered by the encroachment of King Mithridates I of Parthia (r. 170–138 BCE) (Sherwin-White and Kuhrt 223–5; Mittag 321–3). Antiochus' massive theft of monies from the Jerusalem Temple (1,800 talents according to 2 Macc. 5:21; cf. 1 Macc. 1:21–24) reflected his need for money to finance his eastern campaigns. 2 Maccabees 3 also reflects Seleucid interest in the holdings of the Jerusalem Temple, depicting a divinely rebuffed effort by Heliodorus, an official under Seleucus IV (r. 187–175), to take treasure from it. Antiochus also attempted to plunder several temples in Iran and he died in the east during these efforts (1 Macc. 6:1–4; 2 Macc. 1:13–17; 9:1–2; Polybius 31.9; Mittag 307–18). A recently published stele recounts correspondence between Seleucus and Heliodorus that reflects Seleucid interest in temples in their domain and imperial control over them (Portier-Young 80–6).

Jewish sources attribute to Antiochus the decision to initiate anti-Jewish policies (1 Macc. 1:41–44; 2 Macc. 6:1; 11:22–26; Dan. 11:31). Tacitus promotes a similar view, writing that the king wanted "to abolish Jewish superstition and to introduce Greek civilization" (*History*, 5.8.2). Such a policy of anti-Judaism is highly unusual and its rationale remains enigmatic. The move is in direct contradiction with the policies of his father, Antiochus III, who, according to Josephus, upheld the sanctity of the temple (*Antiquities*, 12.145–6). The strategy of Antiochus IV may have been motivated by his desire to show dominion over the rebellious city of Jerusalem and support worship there in a way that asserted the legitimacy of Seleucid control (Portier-Young 62). While the role of Menelaus in the reforms as formulated by Bickerman is generally discounted today, it nevertheless remains possible that Menelaus did to some extent encourage Antiochus to promulgate anti-Jewish decrees. According to 2 Maccabees 13:3–5, the corrupt high priest was killed by Antiochus V Eupator after Lysias, a Seleucid general, described him as "the cause of all the trouble," referring to the revolt in Judea. According to Josephus, Lysias told Antiochus V that Menelaus persuaded his father to make the Jews abandon their traditional religion (*Antiquities*, 12.384–5).

Both 1 and 2 Maccabees (the latter especially) emphasize a conflict between Judaism and Hellenism. It is fully reasonable to claim that there were Jews in Jerusalem who did not like the presence of the gymnasium in the city or that upper-class Jewish men were wearing Greek hats. But such concerns are not what triggered the violent uprising. As John Collins has stressed, one must make a distinction between cult and culture (Collins and Sterling 55). According to 2 Maccabees, the rebellion was ultimately caused not by Greek cultural innovations in Jerusalem but rather Antiochus' defilement of the temple and the accompanying state repression. The main significance of the Maccabean conflict for understanding the rise of Hellenism in Israel is not that there was an inherent conflict between Judaism and Hellenism but rather that the transmission of Greek ideas and customs cannot be separated from the power dynamics of the period. While Greek learning and culture were certainly appealing to some Jews, such an education was mediated at the time in Palestine during what was essentially a colonial occupation. The violent and eventually successful Maccabean uprising was prompted not by Greek cultural innovations but by the repressive policies of Judea's Hellenistic rulers.

Jewish Apocalypticism in Its Hellenistic Setting

Appreciating the broader context of the Hellenistic age is not only helpful for understanding political events such as the Maccabean Revolt. The Hellenistic context allows us to appreciate better the literary creativity of Jews in this period, in terms of how and why they developed new forms of expression. This is particularly evident in one of the most important Jewish developments in the period – apocalypticism (Collins, *Apocalyptic Imagination*; and see the essay by John J. Collins in this volume). The production of apocalypses flourished in the Hellenistic era, during which key representatives of the genre were composed – Daniel, *1 Enoch*, *2 Baruch* and 4 Ezra, for example. Apocalypticism constitutes a new reformulation of older traditions that draws upon and reformulates postexilic prophecy and ancient Near Eastern myth to interpret contemporary, Hellenistic events. The term "apocalypse" derives from the Greek *apokalyptō*, which means to uncover or to move back a veil. An apocalypse purports to contain knowledge that, while it is conveyed by a human visionary, has a supernatural source. Typically in apocalypses a person receives a heavenly vision disclosed by an angel. The emphasis on revelation provides a way to legitimate the knowledge contained in the text.

The two oldest Jewish apocalypses were incorporated into a noncanonical work known today as *1 Enoch* – the Book of the Watchers (*1 En.* 1–36) and the Astronomical Book (*1 En.* 72–82), both of which date to the third century BCE. While the term apocalypse often is equated with eschatology, relatively little of these two works is eschatological. The vast majority of the Astronomical Book conveys knowledge about the motion of heavenly bodies and transmits a large body of data about their movements in numerical form. Indicating the transmission of knowledge in the Hellenistic period, the astronomical information provided by the book (purportedly from the angel Uriel) can be often traced back to Babylonia, a traditional center of astronomy. The Book of the Watchers centers on an interpretation of the famously enigmatic biblical text Genesis 6:1–4, in which "sons of God" descend to earth, sleep with women and produce offspring. In the Book of the Watchers the "sons of God" are unambiguously angels who, in an innovation not found in Genesis, disclose illicit heavenly knowledge to their wives, including knowledge of astronomy, the ability to fashion metals in order to make weapons of war and jewelry for women, and how to make cosmetics for women such as eye paint (*1 En.* 8:1–3). These cultural innovations are associated with a rise in lawlessness and wickedness. The story of the Watchers has been understood as a Jewish adaptation of the Prometheus myth and, whether this is the case or not, its theme of illicit knowledge can be plausibly understood as a negative assessment of the spread of foreign learning and culture into Palestine in the Hellenistic age. The text's depiction of the sons of the Watchers as violent and destructive giants may be an allegory for the aggression of the Hellenistic kings in the fourth or third century (Nickelsburg 170).

The rise of determinism, the view that history and creation unfold according to a divinely ordained plan, is central to the Jewish apocalypses. Such a perspective is critical, for example, in the book of Daniel. Using various images, the visions of Daniel 7–12 all make the same essential point: a Gentile king will arise who shall defile the temple and oppress the faithful, and then God will come and vindicate his people at the eschatological judgment. The Animal Apocalypse of *1 Enoch* (85–90), which allegorically retells biblical and postexilic history with the key characters recast as animals, likewise purports to convey how historical events culminate in the final judgment in which the righteous shall be rewarded.

Determinism is evident not only in the apocalypses. The Community Rule, a text from the Dead Sea Scrolls, has a section known as the Treatise on the Two Spirits which asserts: "From the God of Knowledge stems all that is and what will be. Before they existed he established their entire design" (1QS 3:15). 4QInstruction teaches its intended audience that its members have access to the *rāz nihyeh*, an enigmatic phrase that can be translated "the mystery that is to be" (Goff 51–79). The expression denotes supernatural revelation and is associated with a tripartite division of time – the present, the future and the past (4Q417 1 i 3–5). By studying the mystery that is to be one can attain knowledge about God's guidance of events in all three spheres. God, the text claims, even created the world by means of this mystery. The *rāz nihyeh* signifies a divine plan that orchestrates the structure of history and created order, revealed to the addressee as a revealed truth. In ancient Judaism the rise of determinism goes hand in hand with claims of supernatural revelation.

These developments within Judaism reflect broader intellectual trends of the Hellenistic age. A demotic wisdom text from Hellenistic Egypt known as Papyrus Insinger, for example, reflects a deterministic perspective, asserting the frequent refrain "The fate and the fortune that come, it is the god who sends them" (e.g., 2.20; 8.20; 11.21; 15.6; see the essay by John Huddlestun in this volume). One of the most important Greek philosophical schools of the period is Stoicism, traditionally regarded as founded by Zeno of Citium in the third century BCE. Understanding the dynamic between free will and a deterministic cosmos is an important issue in Stoic thought. Cleanthes, a pupil of Zeno, proclaims in his *Hymn to Zeus* that the entire cosmos obeys Zeus and that he directs "the universal reason (*koinon logon*) which runs through all things" (Long and Sedley 1:326). The entire cosmos is structured according to and guided by Zeus' will. These Stoic ideas were known in Palestine. There were Hellenistic Semitic philosophers, such as Antiochus of Asheklon (ca. 130–68 BCE), who endorsed Stoic philosophy. It is reasonable to understand Stoic philosophy as an indirect factor that helped shape the determinism of Palestinian Jewish apocalyptic and wisdom texts written during the period (Hengel 86–7, 248). The theme of supernatural revelation is prominent not only in Jewish apocalypses but also consistent with their Hellenistic milieu (Hengel 210–17). Media such as otherworldly journeys, dream visions and secret books offered supernatural experiences and knowledge that gave people a fuller understanding of the cosmos and the heavenly world. The heavenly journey, in which a human is transmitted to heaven and shown secrets, is a crucial trope in *1 Enoch* and other Jewish apocalypses, and it is also found in Plato's *Republic* (Book 10) (Collins, *Apocalyptic Imagination* 34). The Cynic philosopher Menippus of Gadara (an ancient city located in what is now northern Jordan) satirized the trope of the heavenly journey in the third century BCE, suggesting that knowledge of the motif was popular and widespread in the region. Heraclides Ponticus (390–310 BCE) was a student of Plato who described a journey to the heavens by Empedotimus in which, not unlike Enoch, he is given secret knowledge about the movements of the stars. Appeals to supernatural revelation are prevalent throughout the Jewish literature of the period and common in the wider Hellenistic world.

The rise of determinism can at least in part be explained politically. The Hellenistic era, as discussed above, is characterized by the overthrow of native regimes and the political superiority of the new, Greek kingdoms over much older ancient civilizations in the ancient Near East. This produced a widespread sense of alienation, in which the world could be easily viewed as fundamentally out of balance (Festugière 40–1). In Palestine political crises and economic imbalance forced Jews to look not simply at the reality in front of them to discern the hand of God guiding events. They needed a theological context in which their arduous circumstances could be properly understood.

Deterministic conceptions of history provided a sense of order and understanding and helped make chaotic situations like the Antiochene crisis meaningful. Couching such views as divinely revealed knowledge gave them legitimacy and authority.

The general themes of alienation and loss of autonomy are expressed politically in the Maccabean crisis, a crucible in which the apocalyptic tradition is transformed. The two main pre-Maccabean apocalypses (the Book of the Watchers and the Astronomical Book) are not predominately eschatological works, as mentioned above, and do not focus primarily on explaining current events. Two apocalypses date to the Maccabean period – chapters 7–12 of the biblical Book of Daniel, and the Animal Apocalypse of *1 Enoch* 85–90. Both compositions show a marked interest in eschatology and contemporary political events. The imagery of the fourth beast in Daniel 7 alludes directly to Antiochus. The creature has ten horns, which, according to the angelic interpreter, signify kings (Dan. 7:24). One little horn in particular blasphemes God and attempts to "change the sacred seasons and the law" (Dan. 7:25). This is widely and accurately interpreted as a reference to Antiochus and his anti-Judaism edicts. The angel provides a cryptic length of time in which the horn has power – "a time, two times and half a time" (Dan. 7:26). This period of time, with each "time" denoting a year, signifies three and a half years. This is roughly the length of time in which the "desolating sacrilege" existed in the temple (167–164 BCE). The end of the book proclaims that after the defeat of the wicked king there will be a general resurrection of the dead and the righteous shall enjoy eternal life like the stars, a reference to joining the angels in a blessed afterlife (Dan. 12:1–3). A core message of the visions of Daniel, which were taught to Jews enduring the persecutions of Antiochus (11:35), was not to take up arms like the Maccabees but rather to endure for a short while longer and await God's eschatological deliverance.

The Enochic Animal Apocalypse, which took its final form in this period, tells a similar story with different imagery. *1 Enoch* 90:2–5 describes how the sheep, which represent the people of Israel, are attacked by various birds of prey – eagles, vultures and ravens. This is generally understood as a reference to the Macedonians and the conquest by Alexander the Great (Nickelsburg 395–6). A birth of lambs is described, that is, a new generation of Israelites (*1 En.* 90:6). Ravens come and attack the lambs, killing some of them. Then one sheep in particular sprouts a great horn (90:8). This is widely regarded as a reference to Judas Maccabee. The sheep fight against various animals and eventually God gives the sheep a sword and they kill all the enemy beasts (90:19). The Lord of the sheep sits in judgment, a new temple is created and the pious animals are transformed into white bulls, the same animal as Adam (85:3), indicating the eschatological restoration of Edenic paradise (90:20–38).

During the Maccabean crisis the present moment was very difficult – the pious were suffering and the wicked were powerful. One could easily conclude that God was not in control. The apocalyptic visions of *1 Enoch* and Daniel provided a way to make sense of the chaotic and dangerous situation. The divinely revealed plan discloses that there is *supposed* to be a period of time in which evil wins. Vindication is asserted but deferred to the final judgment. The current crisis does not mean that God is not in control but rather the opposite – everything follows a divinely ordained plan. The power of apocalyptic literature is in its ability to give people of faith hope amidst a bleak situation.

Conclusion

The Hellenistic age, roughly from the fourth century BCE to the first century CE, and its impact on ancient Judaism can be easily overlooked because this period is poorly represented in the Bible. But the political events and cultural developments that occurred during this period had a deeply lasting influence in Israel and the Diaspora. Many Jewish texts from this period are in Greek, engage aspects of Greek culture and respond to political developments set in motion by Hellenistic kings. Chief among these events is the Maccabean revolt, a pinnacle of Jewish resistance to oppression and occupation. Major traditions flourish in the Hellenistic age, such as apocalypticism, and along with it tropes such as eschatology, determinism and supernatural revelation. To comprehend the Judaism of this period, the crucible out of which both Christianity and rabbinic Judaism originate, one must recognize that it is, in both Israel and the Diaspora, Hellenistic Judaism, a designation that emphasizes that Jews in this period engaged with and responded to Hellenistic ideas and politics in diverse and creative ways.

Bibliography

Assmann, Jan. *The Mind of Egypt: History and Meaning in the Time of the Pharaohs*. New York: Metropolitan, 2002. A wide-ranging survey of ideas and traditions that were prominent throughout Egyptian history.

Bickerman, Elias. *Studies in Jewish and Christian History*. 2 vols. Leiden: Brill, 2007. A new edition of studies by this important scholar of Hellenistic Judaism, including his influential *The God of the Maccabees* (originally published in 1937).

Briant, Pierre. *Alexander the Great and His Empire*, trans. A. Kuhrt. Princeton: Princeton University Press, 2010. An informative and updated study of Alexander and his conquests, translated from the French original (1974).

Collins, John J. *Seers, Sibyls and Sages in Hellenistic-Roman Judaism*. Leiden: Brill, 1997. A collection of essays by a major scholar of Second Temple Judaism.

Collins, John J. *The Apocalyptic Imagination: An Introduction to Jewish Apocalyptic Literature*. 2nd edn. Grand Rapids, MI: Eerdmans, 1998. Originally published 1984. A leading and influential exposition of ancient Jewish apocalypticism.

Collins, John J. *Between Athens and Jerusalem: Jewish Identity in the Hellenistic Diaspora*. 2nd edn. Grand Rapids, MI: Eerdmans, 2000. An authoritative survey of the Hellenistic Jewish literature.

Collins, John J. and Daniel C. Harlow (eds). *The Eerdmans Dictionary of Early Judaism*. Grand Rapids, MI: Eerdmans, 2010. A new and richly informative encyclopedia of Second Temple Judaism.

Collins, John J. and Gregory E. Sterling (eds). *Hellenism in the Land of Israel*. Notre Dame, IN: University of Notre Dame Press, 2001. A collection of essays by leading scholars on Jewish adaptation of and responses to Hellenism that commemorates the substantial contribution of Martin Hengel to this topic.

Eddy, Samuel Kennedy. *The King Is Dead: Studies in Near Eastern Resistance to Hellenism: 334–31 BCE*. Lincoln: University of Nebraska Press, 1961. This book remains an important study of how peoples of the ancient Near East struggled against their Hellenistic rulers.

Festugière, André-Jean. *Personal Religion among the Greeks*. Berkeley: University of California Press, 1954. A classic study of personal piety in ancient Greek religion.

Gera, Dov. *Judaea and Mediterranean Politics: 219 to 161 BCE*. Leiden: Brill, 1998. A study of Judean history that emphasizes its international context, in particular Rome's encroachment in the eastern Mediterranean region.

Goff, Matthew J. *The Worldly and Heavenly Wisdom of 4QInstruction*. Leiden: Brill, 2003. An in-depth study of 4QInstruction, the lengthiest wisdom text of the Dead Sea Scrolls.

Grainger, John D. *Seleukos Nikator: Constructing a Hellenistic Kingdom*. London: Routledge, 1990. A useful and informative study of the founder of the Seleucid empire.

Green, Peter. *Alexander to Actium: The Historical Evolution of the Hellenistic Age*. Berkeley: University of California Press, 1990. A massive and richly detailed study of the Hellenistic period.

Gruen, Erich S. *Heritage and Hellenism: The Reinvention of Jewish Tradition*. Berkeley: University of California Press, 1998. An insightful and significant survey of the Jewish literature of the Hellenistic period.

Hengel, Martin. *Judaism and Hellenism*. Vol. 1: *Text*; vol. 2: *Notes and Bibliography*. Philadelphia: Fortress, 1974. A classic and indispensable study of the Judaism of the Hellenistic age.

Hölbl, Günther. *A History of the Ptolemaic Empire*. London: Routledge, 2001. A rich and extensive examination of the Ptolemaic empire.

Hultgård, Anders. "Persian apocalypticism." In John J. Collins, B. McGinn, and S. J. Stein (eds), *The Encyclopedia of Apocalypticism*, vol. 1 (pp. 39–83). New York: Continuum, 2002. An examination of Persian apocalypticism by a leading authority on the topic.

Long, A. A. and D. N. Sedley. *The Hellenistic Philosophers*. 2 vols. Cambridge: University of Cambridge Press, 1987. A standard edition of writings by Hellenistic philosophers.

Mittag, Peter Franz. *Antiochos IV. Epiphanes: Eine politische Biographie*. Berlin: Akademie, 2006. A thorough examination of the life of Antiochus and his reign as king of the Seleucid empire.

Nickelsburg, George W. E., *1 Enoch 1: A Commentary on the Book of 1 Enoch, Chapters 1–36, 81–108*. Minneapolis: Fortress, 2001. A standard commentary on most chapters of 1 Enoch, accompanied by its companion volume, G. W. E. Nickelsburg and J. C. VanderKam, *1 Enoch 2: A Commentary on the Book of 1 Enoch, Chapters 37–82*. Minneapolis: Fortress, 2011.

Portier-Young, Anthea E. *Apocalypse against Empire: Theologies of Resistance in Early Judaism*. Grand Rapids, MI: Eerdmans, 2011. A new and important examination of the Maccabean revolt that is richly informed by knowledge of the Seleucid empire.

Sherwin-White, Susan M. and Amelie Kuhrt. *From Samarkhand to Sardis: A New Approach to the Seleucid Empire*. Berkeley: University of California Press, 1993. A significant resource for understanding the history and structure of the Seleucid empire.

Tcherikover, Victor. *Hellenistic Civilization and the Jews*. Peabody: Hendrickson, 1999. Originally published 1958. A classic and highly recommended study of Judaism in the Hellenistic age.

Waterfield, Robin. *Dividing the Spoils: The War for Alexander the Great's Empire*. Oxford: Oxford University Press, 2011. A recent and authoritative study of the conflicts among Alexander's generals after his death.

Part III

Themes in Israelite Culture

A

God and Gods

CHAPTER 14

The Gods of Israel in Comparative Ancient Near Eastern Context

Neal Walls

T his chapter introduces some of the most prominent gods and goddesses worshipped in ancient Israel by examining their poetic descriptions in primary texts from Canaan and Israel. While Israel is renowned for its historic development of monotheism, the history of ancient Israelite religion presents a tremendous diversity of religious perspectives and practices across the centuries (see Zevit; Stavrakopoulou and Barton; and see the essays in this volume by David M. Carr, Francesca Stavrakopoulou, and Mark S. Smith), including the veneration of a host of divine beings. This essay explores the polytheistic context of preexilic Israelite religion, represented by the mythological literature of ancient Canaan, before turning to the Hebrew Bible's literary characterization of the Israelite god within this ancient Near Eastern religious environment.

"Who Is Like Yahweh?"

The Hebrew Bible introduces the controversial question of how the patron god of Israel compares with other divine beings in the heavenly assembly. The New Revised Standard Version (NRSV) of the Bible translates Ps. 89:5–7:

> Let the heavens praise your wonders, O Lord,
>   your faithfulness in the assembly of the holy ones.
> For who in the skies can be compared to the Lord?
>   Who among the heavenly beings is like the Lord,
> a God feared in the council of the holy ones,
>   great and awesome above all that are around him?
> O Lord God of hosts,
>   who is as mighty as you, O Lord?[1]

The Wiley Blackwell Companion to Ancient Israel, First Edition. Edited by Susan Niditch.
© 2016 John Wiley & Sons, Ltd. Published 2016 by John Wiley & Sons, Ltd.

Psalm 82 similarly depicts God taking his place within the divine council and issuing judgments against other divine beings, while the ancient Song of the Sea in Exodus 15 asks: "Who is like you, O LORD, among the gods? Who is like you, majestic in holiness, awesome in splendor, doing wonders?" (15:11, NRSV). Rather than reject the existence of other gods, these ancient Israelite poets and theologians appear to welcome comparisons and contrasts of their national god's power and character with those of rival deities.

The divine council of gods and goddesses is common in ancient Near Eastern mythological texts, and the Hebrew Bible shares the imagery of "the assembly of holy ones" (Ps. 89:5), "the assembly of El" ('*dt-'l*, Ps. 81:1), and the collective "sons of God" (*bny h'lhym*) (Gen. 6:1–4; Job 1:6) or "sons of El" (*bny 'lym*, Ps. 29:1) to depict supernatural beings. The "sons of God" seem to be autonomous agents in some texts, such as Genesis 6:1–4, where "the sons of God" married "the daughters of man" and had offspring with them. In this literary context, the phrase serves to describe divine beings who marry and breed with human women. In Job 1, on the other hand, the "sons of God" are more easily identified as the collective angelic host, clearly subordinate to the will of God, rather than autonomous deities. Indeed, the ambiguous Biblical Hebrew word '*ĕlōhîm* can denote gods, false gods, or the one true God of ancient Israelite tradition in different contexts.

The nationalistic god of ancient Israel and Judah is represented in the Hebrew Bible by the four consonants, *yhwh*. Although the Hebrew Bible attests the divine name over 6,800 times, later Jewish practice eventually refrained from pronouncing the sacred epithet. English Bibles have traditionally followed the Jewish practice and replaced *yhwh* with "the LORD," written in small capital letters to distinguish the divine name from the common Hebrew word for "lord." In order to emphasize the Hebrew text's use of the proper name of the Israelite God, and to further distinguish it from the generic word for God or gods, this chapter will deviate from that English practice and write out the name as Yahweh.

Although a case may be made for an original monotheism in early Israelite history, it is far more likely that monotheism was a relatively late theological development of Israelite religion, perhaps in the sixth century BCE (see also the essays by Avraham Faust and Mark S. Smith in this volume). The beginning of the Ten Commandments, for example, requires that Israelites serve no other gods rather than insist that there are no other gods (Exod. 20:1–2). Similarly, when Joshua prepares the wandering tribes to enter and possess the land promised to their ancestors, he refrains from denying the existence of other deities as he demands loyalty to the god of the exodus:

> Now therefore revere Yahweh, and serve him in sincerity and in faithfulness. Put away the gods that your ancestors served beyond the (Euphrates) River and in Egypt, and serve Yahweh. Now if you are unwilling to serve Yahweh, choose this day whom you will serve, whether the gods your ancestors served in the region beyond the (Euphrates) River or the gods of the Amorites in whose land you are living; but as for me and my household, we will serve Yahweh. (Josh. 24:14–15)

The cultic veneration of one deity to the exclusion of others, as seen in these texts, is properly called henotheism or monolatry rather than monotheism. Indeed, accusations of Israelites and Judeans worshipping other gods and goddesses are found throughout the Hebrew Bible, from early to late sources. It is no surprise, then, that the Bible repeatedly refers to Yahweh as a "jealous" or "zealous" (*qn'*) God who will tolerate no disloyalty (e.g., Exod. 20:5). Exodus 34:14 commands, "You shall worship no other god, because Yahweh, whose very name is Jealous, is a jealous God."

As a historical phenomenon, ancient Israelite religion encompassed a diverse set of practices before its eventual adoption of monotheism. 2 Kings 23:4–14 records that King Josiah's seventh-century BCE reform of Judahite worship rejected many polytheistic practices of earlier Israelite religion. He deposed priests "who made offerings to Baal; to the sun, the moon, the constellations; and all the hosts of the heavens. He brought out the image of (the goddess) Asherah from the House of Yahweh" (23:5–6). Josiah defiled the Tophet outside of Jerusalem's walls where Molech was worshipped with child sacrifice (23:10). He destroyed altars outside of Jerusalem which King Solomon had built for the foreign gods or "abominations," Ashtart, Chemosh, and Milcom (23:13). The Hebrew prophets also railed against these competing forms of Israelite religion. In his visionary tour of the defiled city of Jerusalem, the prophet Ezekiel describes forbidden rituals and cultic images (8:5, 10–11), women weeping for the Mesopotamian god Tammuz (8:14), and men worshipping the rising sun (8:16) within the Temple precincts. Jeremiah (7:17–18) describes families worshipping the Queen of Heaven with drink offerings and cakes in preexilic Judah, and again in exile in Egypt (44:15–19). Isaiah 57 uses strong language to describe illicit religious practices in the restored Judean community after 539 BCE. These biblical texts reflect the historical reality of the veneration of a host of gods and goddesses in ancient Israel. Accordingly, the current chapter will survey some of the most prominent deities of ancient Canaan and Israel within their ancient Near Eastern religious context before turning to the description of Yahweh within Israelite literary sources.

The Canaanite Pantheon

Although Israelite poets and prophets did not hesitate to contrast the power of Yahweh with deities from Babylon and Egypt (e.g., Isa. 19 and 46), the primary context for understanding Israelite divine imagery is the religious environment of ancient Canaan, understood here as the Late Bronze (ca. 1600–1200 BCE) and Iron Age (1200–539 BCE) cultures of coastal and southern Syria-Palestine other than Israel and Judah (see the essay by Song-Mi Suzie Park in this volume). The sources for reconstructing the Canaanite pantheon include cultic artifacts, artistic representations, and inscriptions in ink, stone, and clay from across the Levant and Egypt (see the essay by Theodore Lewis in this volume). Corroborating evidence comes from later Phoenician, Punic, and Hellenistic sources from around the Mediterranean coastlands. The most abundant and useful sources for exploring Canaanite religion, however, remain the Late Bronze Age archives from ancient Ugarit (modern Ras Shamra) on the coast of Syria near modern Latakia. This cosmopolitan urban site houses the only indigenous archive of extensive religious and literary texts from a Canaanite culture. The hundreds of texts written in a West Semitic dialect in alphabetic cuneiform script describe a pantheon of Semitic deities that overlaps substantially with the gods and goddesses mentioned by name in the Hebrew Bible. While the anti-Canaanite polemic within biblical texts must be judiciously weighed by the scholar, the Ugaritic tablets are primary sources that convey the religion and mythology of the Canaanites in their own voice. These religious texts, supplemented by the Bible and scarcer Iron Age and later sources, provide the most descriptive and substantive evidence of the religious and mythological world in which Israelite religion originated and developed. They also represent the poetic and literary traditions shared by later Hebrew poets and theologians.

Polytheistic mythological systems often include myths that portray the gods with all the limitations and vices of humans, including anger, drunkenness, sexuality, and arrogant pride. The Ugaritic texts accordingly describe a pantheon of gods and goddesses with individual mythological characters and literary roles. Like deities in ancient Near Eastern mythologies from Mesopotamia and Egypt, the Canaanite gods meet in a divine assembly for festive banquets, at times quite raucous, to adjudicate matters of cosmic significance, earthly governance, and their own political intrigues. The grey-haired god El (*'Ilu*) sits as the patriarchal head of the divine council that meets on his sacred mountain in Ugaritic mythological literature. Iconographic sources from Ugarit present "beneficent El, the kindly one" (*ltpn il dpid*) as an enthroned, bearded figure with his right hand raised in blessing. El is described as "holy" (*qdš*), "the father of the gods" (*ab ilm*), "the creator of creatures" (*bny bnwt*), and the "father of humanity" (*ab adm*). He communicates with humans through dreams, heals certain diseases, and grants the blessing of children in Ugaritic epics. Later Phoenician inscriptions (e.g., *COS* 2.31)[2] further acclaim him as "El, the creator of the earth" (*'l qn 'rṣ*). Unfortunately, no mythic narratives of El creating the earth or humanity have yet been recovered from the pre-Hellenistic period. El may also be the "king of eternity" (*mlk 'lm*), the divine leader of the underworld shades of deceased kings in the Ugaritic corpus, but this identification remains unsure.

Venerated as the wise "king" and "judge" among the gods, El receives homage and obeisance from the gods as he delegates spheres of sovereignty among his sons, resulting in the storm god Baal's power over the earthly realms and Mot's rule in the netherworld. No deity openly challenges El's authority without fear of losing his or her own position within the divine bureaucracy. Even Death, divine Mot, is subdued when the sun goddess Shapsh threatens him with El's displeasure: "Surely he will remove the support of your throne; surely he will overturn the seat of your kingship; surely he will break the scepter of your rule." The wise decrees of El carry ultimate authority among the quarreling gods of Ugaritic mythology.

El's most common epithet in Ugaritic texts, "the bull," communicates his political and sexual prowess. One Ugaritic myth, often called "The birth of the gracious gods" or "Dawn and Dusk" (*COS* 1.87), portrays El as a virile and lusty god who seduces and impregnates two goddesses at the seashore. They subsequently give birth to the celestial gods Dawn and Dusk, Shahar and Shalem. Indeed, El can be an intemperate personality, as shown in a surprisingly irreverent depiction of him drinking to excess at a divine banquet (*mrzḥ*) and trying to stagger home (*COS* 1.97). The drunken patriarch becomes incontinent and collapses in his own urine and feces as other gods insult him for his dissolute behavior. (This burlesque text appropriately concludes with a recipe for a hangover cure.) Nevertheless, the attributes of wisdom, judgment, and authority are most strongly associated with the presentation of the benevolent but elderly patriarch, El.

While El retains his authoritative position as the head of the pantheon, the storm god Baal Hadd exercises power over the earthly sphere of human life. The common Semitic word *ba'al* or *ba'l*, meaning "lord, master," is an appropriate title for any powerful god, but the epithet is intimately connected with the storm god Hadd or Hadad in Ugaritic and related religions. Baal is the divine patron of the Ugaritic royal house and protector of the city, as celebrated in a liturgical prayer that assures divine protection against military attack (*COS* 1.88). After the appropriate prayers, sacrifices, and festival procession in Baal's honor, "then Baal will listen to your prayer. He will drive the mighty one from your gates, the warrior from your walls." Baal's most frequent epithet in the Ugaritic texts is "Almighty Baal" (*aliyn b'l*). He is also "the mightiest of warriors" (*aliy qrdm*), "the rider of the clouds" (*rkb 'rpt*), and "the Prince, lord of the earth" (*zbl b'l ars*). A political rival to the "sons of El," he is the son of the grain god Dagan and the brother of the volatile Maiden Anat. Baal's palace is on Mount Saphon, the highest mountain in Syria, from which he controls the winds and storms on both sea and land.

As a god of both thunderstorms and fertilizing rains, Baal travels across the skies accompanied by storm clouds, roaring winds, thunder, and lightning. A rare hymn from Ugarit (Wyatt 388–90) celebrates Baal as firmly established upon his "mountain of victory," clutching "seven lightning bolts" in one hand and "eight bundles of thunder" in the other. The artists of Ugarit accordingly portrayed Baal as a young, bearded god, wearing a horned conical hat, brandishing a mace or battle-ax in his right hand and grasping lightning bolts in the left. Just as the storm god Marduk defeats the primordial dragon Tiamat in the Babylonian creation epic *Enuma Elish* (*COS* 1.111), so Almighty Baal defeats Prince Yamm, the primordial god of the Sea (*ym*), to become king over all the gods. He annihilates the draconic sea-monsters Litan (or Lotan) "the Fleeing Serpent," Tunnan, and the seven-headed "Twisting Serpent" in his epic battles (*COS* 1.86, tablet 5).

In addition to his warrior status, the storm god Baal provides for the fertility of the earth through his seasonal rains and daily dew. Baal "fattens gods and humans" and "satisfies the multitudes of the earth" with his fertilizing rains (Parker 137). The absence of Baal from the earth results in "no dew, no downpour, no swirling of the deeps, no welcome voice of Baal" to break the sweltering summer heat, according to the Epic of Aqhat (*COS* 1.103; Parker 69). Tablet 6 of the Baal Cycle (*COS* 1.86) reports that "the heavens rain oil and the wadis run with honey" in response to the renewed presence of Baal. A late ninth-century BCE Aramaic inscription from Tell Fekheriye in northern Syria (*COS* 2.34) confirms the continuity of Baal's role as "the regulator of the waters of heaven and earth, who rains down abundance, who gives pastures and watering-places to all lands" and who provides rest and food allotments to all the gods. Ugaritic myth also portrays Baal's close association with the fertility of domestic cattle by describing his impregnation of a cow through energetic sexual intercourse (see Parker 148, 181–7). While shocking to modern readers, this brutish depiction of divine bestiality provides an effective mythological metaphor for Baal's fertilizing power over livestock and wild herds.

Baal Hadd's rise to sovereignty among the sons of El is narrated by three related myths that constitute the six-tablet Baal Cycle, Ugarit's longest and most important extant mythological text (*COS* 1.86; Parker 81–180). In the cycle's first episode, Baal battles and defeats the primordial god Prince Yamm (Sea) for sovereignty as "king" (*mlk*) among the gods. In the cycle's second section, Baal eventually wins El's permission to build a palace as confirmation of his divine kingship. After Baal's enthronement and celebration as ruler of the earth, the cycle's third section describes Baal's conflict with the god Mot, the personification of Death, who challenges the fertility god's apparent attempt to enlarge his realm to subsume the land of death. Mot commands Baal to "enter the maw of Death" and descend into the underworld. A long break in the tablet obscures the plot at this point, but Baal defers to Mot's authority and either enters the netherworld or tricks Mot into believing that he has done so. Later, after the warrior goddess Anat overcomes the power of death, a revived Baal returns to the divine assembly and is again seated upon "the throne of his dominion." The Baal Cycle concludes with a political and cosmic compromise between the powers of Baal and Mot, life and death, as Baal retains kingship over the heavenly gods, the earth, and humanity.

Whether Baal is appropriately described as a seasonal "dying and rising god" remains unclear (see Smith, *Origins*, 104–31). Some later West Semitic texts hint at Baal's role in the revivification of the dead in a netherworld existence, but the fragmentary character of the relevant episodes in the Baal Cycle and other texts precludes any definite conclusion. Perhaps Baal is most accurately described as a "disappearing god" whose absence deprives the earth of his fructifying rains during the heat of summer and periods of drought. In any case, the Baal Cycle's focus on divine kingship, earthly fertility, and the specter of natural death reflects recurring themes in Canaanite mythology.

In contrast to the biblical tradition, divine feminine imagery and goddesses play prominent roles in ancient Canaanite art and mythology. Images and figurines of nude females and enthroned goddesses appear throughout the archaeological record from the Levant and Egypt. The best-known Canaanite goddess to later generations is Phoenician Ashtart (*'štrt*), usually called Astarte by the Greeks and Ashtoreth in the Hebrew Bible. There is a frustrating lack of mythological information concerning her character and divine responsibilities in Ugaritic and later sources. Although Greek sources equate Astarte with Aphrodite as a goddess of sexuality, the indigenous Canaanite texts only describe her as a goddess of the hunt and martial violence (Wyatt 370–4). A seventh-century BCE Assyrian treaty demonstrates the continuity of her martial violence: "May Ashtart break your bow in the thick of battle and make you crouch at the feet of your enemy." Her intimate relationship with Baal is reflected in her epithets, the "name of Baal" (*šm b'l*) and the "face of Baal" (*pn b'l*) in Ugaritic and Phoenician texts, as well as by her close association with Baal in the Hebrew Bible.

The Ugaritic goddess "Lady Athirat of the Sea" (*rbt aṯrt ym*) is El's consort and "the creator of the gods" (*qnyt ilm*), who are collectively called "the seventy sons of Athirat." Like "mother goddesses" in other ancient Near Eastern pantheons, Athirat does not play an especially active role in Ugaritic myth, but she is nonetheless a crucial figure in the divine politics of the Baal Cycle and in the plot of the Epic of Kirta (*COS* 1.102). As the divine queen mother, Athirat is an important political ally and intermediary for those who desire a favorable answer from El. This goddess appears in later Hebrew sources as Asherah (*'šrh*).

The Ugaritic pantheon also includes a rare but fascinating solar goddess, Shapsh or Shapash, who functions as a judge among the deities, the arbiter of magical powers, and an intermediary between the lands of the living and the dead. She is most likely the local form of the Mesopotamian sun god, Shamash, who manifests as female under the influence of Hittite religion's sun goddess of Arinna.

The goddess with the most fully developed persona in Ugaritic sources is the Maiden Anat (*btlt 'nt*), an adolescent figure with a volatile temperament who plays an especially prominent role in the Ugaritic Baal Cycle (*COS* 1.86) and the Epic of Aqhat (*COS* 1.103). Ugaritic myths identify her as a "maiden" or girl of marriageable age and presumptive virgin, "the loveliest of the sisters of Baal." Anat is the "Mistress of Kingship, Mistress of Dominion," and "Mistress of the High Heavens" (Wyatt 396). Fiercely independent, Anat is a staunch supporter of Baal's claim to divine kingship. Her loyalty to her brother is demonstrated by her extravagant grief over his disappearance in the Baal Cycle. She may be his sexual partner, but there is no clear evidence for their sexual activity in the Ugaritic corpus. Later Greek sources equate Anat with the virgin-warrior goddess Athena.

Like Ashtart, Anat is typically portrayed as a huntress and aggressive warrior in Ugaritic and Egyptian myth and iconography. Anat delights in the carnage of battle and "wades in [soldiers'] blood up to her thighs" in a famous scene from the third tablet of the Baal Cycle. She adorns herself with a garland of her enemies' severed heads and a sash of their severed hands before she exultantly plunges into the gore of battle a second time. This grisly scene portraying Anat's enthusiasm for violence is matched by her impassioned threats to drag her father El from his throne "to the ground like a lamb" for slaughter, to smash his skull, and to make his "grey hair run with blood and his grey beard with gore" unless he agrees to her demands. Similarly, when Death refuses her request to return her brother Baal to the land of the living, Anat responds with ferocious violence to utterly annihilate her opponent: "She seizes divine Mot; with a blade she splits him, with a sieve she winnows him, with fire she burns him, and with millstones she grinds him" (*COS* 1.86, tablet 6). Her violent overthrow of death allows for the return of Baal to the land of the living.

Although one must not assume a simple equivalence between the Late Bronze Age religion of Ugarit and the first-millennium Canaanite religions of the Phoenicians and the nations of southern Syria-Palestine, there is certainly continuity between the Ugaritic and Iron Age pantheons. El, Baal, Asherah, Ashtart, Anat and other significant deities of the Ugaritic literary texts continue to be venerated, as well as gods such as Resheph, Horon, and Athtar, who appear in ritual and magical texts. Indeed, there is cultural, religious, and linguistic continuity for over a thousand years of development from Ugarit's flourishing through the advent of the Hellenistic period in the late fourth century BCE in religious and poetic traditions. Evidence for the religions of the Iron Age nations of Moab, Ammon, and Edom is available in personal names with theophoric elements (onomastics), epigraphic inscriptions and cultic sites recovered by archaeological excavations, and the biblical record (see the essay by Song-Mi Suzie Park in this volume).

Each of the nation-states, including Israel, had its own patron god or gods, as well as a shared poetic tradition and common religious heritage reflected in the Ugaritic texts.

In its monolatrous rhetoric, the Hebrew Bible often refers to the Canaanite gods as the collective and generic "Baals and Asherahs" (e.g., Judg. 3:7) or "Baals and Ashtarts" (e.g., Judg. 10:6). Occasionally, however, the Bible names specific national deities and describes them as "abominations" (e.g., 1 Kings 11:7) or illegitimate rivals to Yahweh. In describing King Solomon's apostasy in his old age, for example, 1 Kings 11:33 identifies three local deities venerated by the lapsed king in deference to his many foreign wives. The text states that Solomon caused Israel to forsake Yahweh and to worship "Ashtart (*'aštoret*) the goddess of the Sidonians, Chemosh the god of Moab, and Milkom the god of the Ammonites" (1 Kings 11:33). Phoenician Ashtart (or Astarte) is well represented in Phoenician and Punic inscriptions as a powerful goddess, although literary myths concerning her character have not survived. Even less is known about the mythological character of Ammonite Milcom (*mlkm*) (*COS* 2.24). His possible relation to the abominable worship of Molech (*mlk*) through child sacrifice also remains unclear. The Moabite Chemosh, however, presents an interesting example of an Iron Age national god in competition with Israelite Yahweh.

The name of Moab's patron has come into English through the King James Version of the Bible as Chemosh (*kmš*). In the Moabite Stone or Mesha Stele (*COS* 2.23) from the late ninth century BCE, King Mesha praises Chemosh for delivering a military victory in a holy war (*ḥrm*) against Israel. Mesha explains that "Chemosh was angry with his land" and allowed King Omri of Israel to conquer it. Chemosh then commands his king to defeat and destroy enemy cities and dedicate them in his honor. Mesha claims to have set up the monument and a sacred high place after the holy war in which he slaughtered thousands of men, women, and children in honor of his god (cf. Josh. 6). Chemosh appears to be the local form of the god Ashtar, a male avatar of Ashtart, and he is equated with the chthonic and warrior god Nergal in Mesopotamian sources. (Athtar the Terrible appears in the Ugaritic Baal Cycle as an unsuccessful royal replacement for Baal.) The worship of Chemosh is attested in ritual texts from Ugarit and earlier Mesopotamian sources, but we have little information about the character of this deity beyond his militaristic and chthonic nature. The Hebrew Bible (2 Kings 3:27) also records Mesha's sacrifice of his royal heir to break the Israelite siege of Kir-haresheth, which further suggests Chemosh's militaristic function and provides a rare depiction of human sacrifice in Canaanite religion (cf. Ps. 106:36–38).

While 1 Kings 11:7 identifies the Phoenician goddess Ashtart in particular, the Hebrew Bible and archaeological artifacts together provide evidence for the veneration of various goddesses throughout Iron Age Syria-Palestine. Widespread archaeological discoveries of nude female figurines and plaques (called Astarte plaques) provide evidence for the Iron Age worship of goddesses in Israelite as well as Canaanite territories (see Hadley 188–205). Ashtart (or Astarte) is the most famous Phoenician deity, venerated by Phoenicians in general. Individual city-states also worshipped Ashtart or another goddess under the title of Baalat, "Lady," as a city goddess, in addition to named goddesses such as Tannit and Anat. The Phoenician princess Jezebel reputedly imported the worship of Phoenician Baal and Asherah into Israel as religious rivals to the Yahweh (1 Kings 18:19). The goddess Asherah (usually El's consort) or a symbol of her presence was also venerated in Judah, according to the Bible (e.g., 1 Kings 15:13; 2 Kings 21:7). In one revealing text, the seventh-century prophet Jeremiah (7:17–18) rails against people in Judah and Jerusalem who worship the Queen of Heaven as part of a domestic cult: "The children gather wood, the fathers kindle the fire, and the women knead dough to make cakes for the Queen of Heaven. They pour out drink offerings to other gods, to provoke me to anger." This anonymous goddess may be one of the Canaanite goddesses, named above, or an imported cult of the Assyrian Ishtar. Some scholars identify her with Anat, who is called the "Mistress of the High Heavens" at Ugarit. Anat is not explicitly mentioned elsewhere in the Hebrew Bible, but evidence for her worship appears in place names (Josh. 19:38, 21:18) and in the name of the hero Shamgar ben Anath (Judg. 3:31; cf. *COS* 2.84). Like Ashtart and Asherah, her name appears sporadically in non-biblical texts into the Hellenistic period.

In its list of foreign deities, 1 Kings 11:7 fails to mention the Phoenician storm god Baal, who was surely the most powerful rival to Yahweh in ancient Israel and Judah. The title Baal could be applied to various gods of the Canaanite pantheon, such as Melqart of Tyre, Baal Hammon, and Baal Shamayim. Tyrian Melqart (the "king of the city") may be the Baal of 2 Kings 18, whose prophets contested with the prophet Elijah, since Queen Jezebel is identified as a Tyrian princess and missionary of her native religion (cf. Ezek. 28).

In addition to the primary Ugaritic deities, numerous other gods were worshiped in ancient Israel and its neighboring nations. The Phoenicians worshiped a host of gods that go unnamed in the Hebrew Bible. The Philistines were Aegean immigrants who arrived at the beginning of the Iron Age (ca. 1200 BCE) and quickly adopted the language and religion of the Canaanites. The Bible reports that they worshiped the Semitic grain god Dagon (1 Sam. 5:1–5), and archaeological evidence from the site of Ekron (ca. 675 BCE) attests to their worship of the otherwise unknown goddess *ptgyh* (*COS* 2.42). The Edomites worshiped a god named Qaus or Qos, but like Ammonite Milcom there is scant evidence for his mythological character. The complexity of local pantheons and the wealth of lost literary materials are further demonstrated by the long but fragmentary inscription (ink on plaster) from the Jordanian site of Tell Deir 'Alla (*COS* 2.26). This tantalizing inscription, written in a mixed dialect and dated sometime in the eighth century BCE, refers to the cataclysmic visions of the prophet Balaam son of Beor (cf. Num. 22–24), who saw visions of the assembled gods (*'lhn*), the high god El, and the *šdyn*, the plural form of the biblical divine epithet Shadday (see Num. 24:4).

After the fall of the northern kingdom of Israel in 722 BCE, foreigners deported into Israelite territories brought with them the cults of numerous Near Eastern deities, listed in 2 Kings 17:29–34 (cf. Amos 5:26). These Samaritans "worshiped Yahweh but also served their own gods, after the manner of the nations" from which they had come, explains 2 Kings 17:33. The enigmatic Aramaic text in Demotic script called the Amherst Papyrus (*COS* 1.99) may offer another primary source for the religion of people from the Assyrian province of Samaria who had been removed to Egypt. This text, dated ca. 300 BCE, contains references to Yahweh (called Yaho) and numerous Canaanite, Mesopotamian, and Egyptian gods and goddesses (columns XI–XII) as it reflects a highly syncretistic religious community in Upper Egypt. Centuries earlier, by the fifth century BCE, Israelites who worked as mercenaries for the Persian army also settled in southern

Egypt around Elephantine Island (modern Aswan) and established a temple to Yahweh (called Yahu) next door to the local Egyptian temple to Khnum (see Modrzejewski 21–44). These and other texts convey the diversity of divine service in ancient Israel and in related communities abroad.

Literary Portrayals of Yahweh

The Hebrew Bible asks, "Who is like Yahweh?", but modern scholars have often sought to understand how Yahweh is like other ancient Near Eastern deities. Specifically, how does the Hebrew Bible's poetic description of Yahweh and his exploits compare with the literary depictions of other gods in Near Eastern (especially Ugaritic) mythological literature? The character of Yahweh avoids most of the dramatic excesses of polytheistic myth even as Hebrew poetry utilizes the divine imagery of Canaanite literature. Just as ancient Near Eastern hymns to any deity extol their many virtues in hyperbolic fashion, so the Hebrew Bible consistently portrays a dignified and admirable Yahweh, with few exceptions (e.g., Job 1–2). This section accordingly explores biblical and epigraphic sources for the literary characterization of Yahweh as the national god of Israel in the context of a common Near Eastern repertoire of divine imagery and poetic descriptions.

The definitive revelation of Yahweh's name occurs at Mount Horeb (or Sinai) in Exodus 3:13–16 when Moses asks in whose divine name he is to approach Pharaoh. Since Pharaoh ostensibly recognizes a pantheon of divine beings, which particular god has sent Moses? Yahweh's explanation of his eternal name, however, is more of a riddle than an exposition of the divine character. In interpreting his name, Yahweh offers Moses a folk etymology or pun by referring to a different Hebrew verbal root (*hyh*) than the divine name's actual root (*hwh*). The enigmatic statement, "I am that I am" (3:15), is a first-person play on the name Yahweh, understood here as the third-person verbal form, "He who is" (Exod. 3:16). This convoluted explanation does little to clarify who Yahweh is. Yahweh is further equated with El Shadday, the god of Abraham, Isaac, and Jacob (Exod. 6:2–3), who now makes himself known to Israel by intervening in history to free his chosen people from Egyptian slavery. Pharaoh will come to recognize Yahweh by his actions in history.

The intrinsic character of Yahweh is more fully expounded in the theophany of Exodus 34:6–7:

> Yahweh, Yahweh,
> a God merciful and gracious
> slow to anger
> and abounding in steadfast love and faithfulness;
> keeping steadfast love for the thousandth generation,
> forgiving iniquity and transgression and sin;
> yet by no means clearing the guilty …

This theological summary is quoted and reworked throughout the biblical literature (e.g., Num. 14:18; Ps. 103:8–14; Joel 2:13) as a definitive statement of Yahweh's faithful and compassionate nature. Indeed, the theological significance of this ancient Hebrew passage echoes throughout Christian tradition and in Muslim identifications of God as the Merciful and Compassionate.

While Exodus provides the traditional theological description of Yahweh as the one true God in Western religions, the biblical corpus also portrays Yahweh with diverse images shared by other ancient Near Eastern gods and goddesses. The identification of Yahweh with El Shadday in Exodus 6:2–3 is one of many examples of Yahweh's apparent identification with Canaanite El, with whom the Israelite god shares many divine attributes. The Hebrew Bible lacks any polemics or opposition to the worship of El similar to its denunciation of the worship of Baal and the host of heaven. It is most likely that Israelite theology equated the two gods, as confirmed by the phrase '*ēl 'ělōhê yiśrā'ēl*, "El, the god of Israel," in Genesis 33:20. The Hebrew Bible commonly denotes the God of Israel with the word '*ēl* and applies to him the titles El-Olam, "El the Eternal" (Gen. 21:33), and El-Elyon, "El Most High" (Gen. 14:22), as well as El-Shadday, "the Mountain God" (Gen. 17:1) (cf. Ps. 91:1–2).

Ugaritic El is "beneficent El, the kindly one" (*ltpn il dpid*), while Yahweh is "a compassionate and gracious god" ('*l rḥwm wḥnwn*) (Exod. 34:6). A Phoenician inscription invokes "El, the creator of the earth" ('*l qn arṣ*) (*COS* 2.31), similar to the biblical blessing of "God Most High, creator of the heavens and the earth" ('*l 'lywn qnh šmym w'rṣ*) (Gen. 14:19), whom Abram identifies with Yahweh (Gen. 14:22). El is the "father of humanity" and Yahweh is called "your father who created you" in Deuteronomy 32:6. Yahweh is closely associated with the blessing of children throughout Hebrew narratives. Like El, Yahweh is "the Holy One" (e.g., Isa. 1:4; 6:3) who communicates through dreams and visions (e.g., Gen. 37, 40–41). The divine figure of Daniel 7, the enthroned "Ancient of Days" ('*tyq ywmyn* in Aramaic) with white hair and beard, parallels the graybeard El of Ugarit, the "father of years" (*ab šnm*). Like Ugaritic El, Yahweh is portrayed as the wise judge who evaluates the fitness of other gods to reign in Psalm 82. "The sons of El" (*bny 'lym*) constitute the divine assembly in some Psalms (e.g., Ps. 29:1; 89:6, with enclitic *mem*).

While many attributes of compassionate El are shared by the Israelite god, the Hebrew Bible also describes Yahweh with poetic language and characteristics of Ugaritic Baal. Like Baal and other ancient Near Eastern storm gods, Yahweh "rides upon the clouds" (Ps. 68:4; cf. Isa. 19:1). In Psalm 18, Yahweh "bowed the heavens and came down, thick darkness beneath his feet. He mounted a cherub and flew. He came swiftly on the wings of the wind" (vv. 9–10), surrounded by dark storm clouds, thunder, and flashing lightning bolts (vv. 13–14). Nature convulses with earthquake and volcanic imagery when the god of the storm appears on earth in both Ugaritic and biblical poetry (Judg. 5:4–5; Hab. 3; Ps. 29). The prophetic competition between Elijah and the prophets of Baal in 1 Kings 18 demonstrates that Yahweh is alone responsible for the fertilizing rains commonly attributed to Phoenician Baal (cf. Hos. 2:8). Genesis 27:28 proclaims that Yahweh provides "dew of the heavens, the fat of the earth, and the abundance of new grain and wine." Indeed, Yahweh provides fertility to the land and flocks, and removes it in his anger, throughout the biblical literature (e.g., Deut. 28).

Ugaritic Baal annihilated the draconic sea-monster Litan (or Lotan) "the Fleeing Serpent" (*ltn btn brḥ*), the "Twisting Serpent" (*btn 'qltn*) (Parker 141) in his epic battles.

Similarly, Isaiah 27:1 portrays Yahweh defeating "Leviathan the fleeing serpent" (*lwytn nḥš brḥ*), "Leviathan the twisting serpent" (*lwytn nḥš 'qltwn*), and "the dragon (*tnyn*) that is in the sea" in eschatological battle (cf. Ps. 74:14). The monstrous Leviathan, described in poetic detail in Job 41:1–34, is merely a pet to the almighty Yahweh. Isaiah (51:9–10) likewise celebrates the cosmic victories of Yahweh: "Was it not you who hacked Rahab in pieces, who pierced the Dragon (*tnyn*)? Was it not you who dried up the Sea (*ym*), the waters of the great deep?" (cf. Isa. 30:7; Ps. 89:9–10). Like Baal, Yahweh battles Sea and River (Yam and Neharim) with his victorious chariot, bow, and arrows (Hab. 3:8–9). In contrast to the creation account of Genesis 1, Yahweh establishes the earth upon the conquered waters of primordial combat in these poetic traditions. Just as Baal is established as king of the gods in Ugaritic myth and Marduk is recognized as king in *Enuma Elish*, so Yahweh is celebrated as the enthroned divine monarch in some liturgical psalms of ancient Israel that profess, "Yahweh has become king!" (*yhwh mlk*) (Ps. 47, 93, and 95–9).

The wars of Yahweh are not restricted to the primordial past in canonical Hebrew literature, as noted in Exodus. Exodus 15:3 succinctly proclaims, "Yahweh is a warrior. Yahweh is his name!" A common epithet, Yahweh of Hosts (*yhwh ṣb'wt*), refers to Yahweh's army of human (or angelic) warriors (e.g., 1 Sam. 17:45). Deuteronomy 32:41–42 portrays the warrior Yahweh boasting that he will whet his "flashing sword" and declaring, "I will make my arrows drunk with blood – and my sword shall devour flesh! – with the blood of the slain and the captive …" Like Ugaritic myth's description of Anat's bloodbath, Isaiah 63:1–6 depicts the raging Israelite god spattered by the blood of his trampled enemies. Yahweh explains: "I trod [people] down in my anger and trampled them in my rage. Their lifeblood bespattered my garments and stained all my robes" (63:3). The bloody nature of warfare is also seen in the theology of holy war (*ḥrm*), which culminates in the slaughter of enemy men, women, children, and animals as the land is devoted to Yahweh (e.g., Josh. 6:21). This practice is also represented in King Mesha's inscription on the Moabite Stone in honor of Chemosh (*COS* 2.23). Yahweh is a warrior who is believed to engage in historic victories for his chosen people throughout the books of Joshua, Judges, and Samuel.

While Israelite divine imagery powerfully reflects its common heritage with Canaanite poetic and mythological traditions, Israelite literature is also influenced by Babylonian mythological literature of cosmic creation and the flood. When comparing the account of Noah's Flood in Genesis with older Babylonian flood accounts in *Atra-hasis* (*COS* 1.130; Dalley 1–38) and Tablet XI of the Epic of Gilgamesh (*COS* 1.132; Dalley 109–20), one sees the Hebrew adaptation of and interaction with older Mesopotamian mythological literary motifs. The polytheistic Babylonian texts explain the cause of the deluge as the anger of the storm god Enlil, who is deprived of sleep by the noise of the increasing human multitudes on earth. After numerous attempts to decrease the human population through disease, famine, and drought, the assembled gods agree to send a flood to wipe out humanity and end their tumultuous din. Only the intervention of the crafty god Enki, a friend to humanity, saves a remnant of humans from the gods' genocidal decision. Indeed, the Babylonian myth mocks the gods' capricious lack of forethought as it describes them cowering "like dogs" in fear of their flood's destructive power and, a week later, suffering from debilitating hunger and thirst since there are no humans to feed them sacrificial bread and beer. When the surviving humans (and their animals) disembark from their boat, the gods "swarm like flies" over the sacrificial meal and agree to tolerate human survival within their cosmos (Dalley 32–3, 113–14).

The Genesis flood account clearly shares a narrative structure and literary details with the older Babylonian texts, but the Bible's portrayal of the Israelite god often contrasts with the capricious and callous assembly of Babylonian deities. Since a single, just god propels the narrative, Genesis strives to convince the reader of humanity's utter and complete corruption of God's created order as the cause of the flood (Gen. 6:5, 11–13). In contrast to the cowering and famished Babylonian deities, Yahweh remains in complete control of the deluge and its results. The Hebrew Bible is careful never to depict the sacrificial cult as feeding Yahweh even as it criticizes foreign gods for being fed. Deuteronomy 32:38 thus mocks the impotence of foreign gods, "who ate the fat of their sacrifices and drank the wine of their libations." Yet, Genesis does depict Yahweh enjoying the pleasing odor (if not taste) of Noah's sacrifice and admitting that the flood did not ultimately solve the problem of human sinfulness (8:21). In fact, the creation and world-ordering accounts of Genesis 2–11 depict Yahweh engaged in a trial-and-error or experimental process in the organization of the world. Examples include the creation of animals as unsuitable companions to the first human (Gen. 3:18–20), the necessary expulsion of humans from Eden (Gen. 3:22–24), the need to wipe out creation and begin again after the flood, and additional alterations to God's created order (Gen. 9, 11). In these chapters God "regrets" or "repents of" his actions in a fully anthropomorphic manner on occasion: "And Yahweh regretted that he had created humans on earth and he was grieved in his heart" (Gen. 6:6). Such statements show the influence of a polytheistic literary context on the Genesis narratives even as they describe a single divine actor.

The creation account in Genesis 1 may represent a further development toward monotheism. In contrast with Marduk's defeat of the primordial sea-dragon Tiamat in *Enuma Elish*, the opening chapter of Genesis describes a transcendent God (*'ĕlōhîm*) speaking the universe into existence with neither aid nor opposition from other divine forces (cf. *COS* 1.15 for an Egyptian parallel). This theological statement likely "demythologizes" *Enuma Elish*'s theme of divine conquest by replacing Tiamat with the passive Deep (*tehôm*) of Genesis 1:2. Yet, even here, God speaks of creating humanity in "our image" (1:26) as though he is addressing a divine assembly or angelic court.

The development of monolatry in ancient Israel apparently resulted in the incorporation of the functions of other Canaanite deities into the literary portrayal of the Israelite god. With no other gods to blame for misfortune, Yahweh both sends and ends famines and plagues (e.g., 2 Sam. 24:15, 25). Deuteronomy 32:39 quotes Yahweh's confession: "I kill and I give life; I wound and I heal, and no one can deliver from my hand." Like the god Horon in Ugaritic texts (*COS* 1.94), Yahweh offers protection against venomous snakebite (Num. 21:6–9; cf. 2 Kings 18:4). Yet, Yahweh is not above sending an evil or lying spirit to torment someone who has fallen out of his favor in Hebrew literature (1 Sam. 16:14; 1 Kings 22:19–23). The archaic poem in Habakkuk 3 describes the march of the divine warrior Yahweh, with Pestilence (*dbr*) and Plague (*ršp*) in his train (3:5). A god of fever and plague in Ugaritic and later sources, Resheph has here been drafted into the service of the superior Israelite god. Yahweh also incorporates attributes of a solar cult and functions as a judge of the world similar to Shapsh in Ugaritic texts and Shamash in Mesopotamian tradition. Habakkuk 3:4 applies solar imagery to Yahweh as a divine warrior and Deuteronomy 33:2 declares, "Yahweh came from Sinai, and dawned upon us from Seir; he shone forth from Mount Paran" as a blazing warrior (cf. *COS* 2.47D). A rare example of influence from Egyptian texts is also seen in Psalm 104, which shares imagery with Akhenaten's "Hymn to the Aten (sun disk)" (*COS* 1.28; see also John Huddlestun's essay in this volume).

Just as Yahweh subsumes the functions of other deities in his narrative roles and poetic descriptions, some of the attributes or extensions of Yahweh's power are personified as hypostatic manifestations in the Bible. These include the Angel of Death or Destroyer (*mšḥyt*) in Exodus 12 and the semi-autonomous Angel of Yahweh in Hebrew narrative. Lady Wisdom (*ḥkmh*) is personified as God's "first creation" or the hypostatic manifestation of Yahweh's attribute in Proverbs 8:12–31 (cf. Sirach 24). Similarly, the figure of Satan appears to develop in the Second Temple period to absolve God of negative actions (contrast 2 Sam. 24:1 with 1 Chr. 21:1). "The accuser" also appears as part of the angelic cohort in the opening chapters of Job and as an adversary to the priest Joshua in Zechariah 3. Even without a divine assembly, Yahweh maintains an entourage of angels in the Hebrew Bible (e.g., Gen. 18; 2 Kings 22; Isa. 6) and late biblical and early Jewish texts introduce named angels (and demons) to take on roles that deities would play in polytheistic literature. Examples include the angel Michael in Daniel 10 and the angel Raphael and the demon Asmodeus in the apocryphal book of Tobit. The pseudepigraphical Enoch literature demonstrates the well-developed angelology and demonology of the Hellenistic period, when some angels are venerated with their own cults.

While Yahweh shares many attributes and poetic descriptions with other ancient Near Eastern gods, Israelite literature is also careful to distinguish Yahweh from other gods. One can thus ask, "How is Yahweh unlike other gods?" Hebrew sources refrain from presenting Yahweh in sexual, much less burlesque, activities. God may "rest" after creation (Gen. 2:2), but Yahweh, "the guardian of Israel, neither sleeps nor slumbers" (Ps. 121:4) as Babylonian gods do. Unlike Baal, whom Elijah mocks in 1 Kings 18:27, Yahweh is not a dying (or "dying and rising") god who disappears during the heat of summer. Yahweh never shrinks from battle with powerful foes, as Baal cowers before Mot in the Baal Cycle. Yahweh does not drink wine to excess like El and Enki, nor engage in sexual escapades like other ancient Near Eastern deities. As goddesses are rejected within the Yahwistic cult, traditionally feminine attributes are infrequently associated with Yahweh in the Hebrew Bible (Deut. 32:18; Hos. 11:3–4; Isa. 42:14; 49:15). Compared to other ancient Near Eastern religious traditions (e.g., *COS* 2.86), Yahweh gives almost no attention to combating demons in the Hebrew Bible (Lev. 16:26). The prophet Jeremiah (7:31) insists that Yahweh was unequivocally opposed to child sacrifice, but there is textual evidence for its practice by ancient Israelites in the form of stories, accusations, and prohibitions (e.g., Ps. 106:36–38; Judg. 11:34–40; 2 Kings 23:10; Ezek. 20:25–26; Lev. 20:2–3). One remarkable absence in the biblical portrayal of Yahweh is a concern with the life of the netherworld (e.g., Isa. 14:12–21). Other ancient Near Eastern religious traditions give significant attention to post-mortem existence, from Babylonian myths concerning netherworld deities (*COS* 1.108–10) to the extravagant

Egyptian portrayals of continued "life" (*COS* 1.26). Yahweh, by contrast, has no significant underworld associations (see Day 185–225).

Finally, any discussion of the literary characterization of Yahweh must acknowledge the complexity and diversity of ancient Israelite practices. Although the canon of the Hebrew Bible reflects the normative religious perspectives of its late Judean editors, there was undoubtedly a diversity of portrayals of Yahweh among ancient Israelites. The biblical texts reveal the existence of a geographical and temporal variety of cults and theologies prior to the Babylonian exile. The veneration of Yahweh in the southern kingdom of Judah, with its symbol of the Ark of the Covenant within the Jerusalem temple, differs from the cultic worship of Yahweh in the northern kingdom of Israel (ca. 922–722 BCE), with its symbol of the golden calf in the sanctuaries at Dan and Bethel (1 Kings 12:25–33). Similarly, David's son Absalom seems to be unable to fulfill a vow in Jerusalem made to Yahweh of Hebron (2 Sam. 15:7–8). These and other biblical texts suggest that some preexilic Israelites recognized different cultic or regional manifestations of the god Yahweh.

The epigraphic finds from the caravanserai at Kuntillet 'Ajrud (ca. 800 BCE) (*COS* 2.47) in the northeastern Sinai region demonstrate the complexity of ancient Israelite worship of Yahweh. These texts distinguish between localized forms of Yahweh as venerated in northern Samaria and in the southern region of Teman. Some archaic or archaizing poetry in the Hebrew Bible similarly associates the march of the divine warrior Yahweh from the region of Teman, Paran, and Seir (Judg. 5:4–5; Hab. 3:3; Deut. 33:2). Even more interesting from the Kuntillet 'Ajrud texts are the statements, "I bless you by Yahweh of Samaria and his asherah" (*COS* 2.47A) and "I bless you by Yahweh of Teman and his asherah" (*COS* 2.47B; see also the essays by Elizabeth Bloch-Smith and Francesca Stavrakopoulou in this volume). In the Hebrew Bible, the asherah is most frequently a wooden pole or stylized tree used as part of illicit worship (e.g., 2 Kings 21:7). It is most likely a cultic accoutrement of Yahweh that symbolized the goddess Asherah, the consort of Yahweh, according to a non-Deuteronomistic tradition. A similar blessing by Yahweh and "his asherah" is found in a late eighth-century BCE mortuary inscription from Khirbet el-Qom, near Hebron (*COS* 2.52). These texts affirm the biblical suggestion that Asherah was seen as Yahweh's consort in some Israelite religious traditions (e.g., 1 Kings 15:13). Such an association could be explained by Yahweh's identification with El, who was Asherah's consort, or a common polytheistic notion that all powerful gods had a consort and entourage. Fifth-century BCE Aramaic texts from the Jewish and Syrian communities around Egypt's Elephantine Island note a goddess named Anat-Yahu (*'ntyhw*), which may also identify Anat as the consort of the god Yahweh in that heterodox religious community (see Day 142–4). While the Bible's Judean editors would reject the pairing of Yahweh with any goddess, it is likely that some ancient Israelites believed that Yahweh had a consort.

Conclusion

The religion of ancient Israel is a complex historical phenomenon with divergent cultic practices and theological tendencies. In communicating their religious vision within this competitive environment, the poets and theologians of ancient Israel used the religious imagery of their broader Canaanite and Mesopotamian cultural context to praise and describe their own national god, Yahweh. The texts of the Hebrew Bible thus constitute a complicated and inconsistent presentation of supernatural beings other than Yahweh. In some poetic renditions (e.g., Ps. 89:5–7), other deities are subordinate to the power of the superior Israelite god. Psalm 96:4 declares that "all the gods" (*'ĕlōhîm*) hold Yahweh in awe, even as the next verse denigrates the gods of the nations as mere idols. Other texts clearly reject the reality of rivals to Yahweh's dominion. Deuteronomy 32:17 identifies the foreign gods (*'ĕlōhîm*) as "demons" (*šēdîm*) and "no-gods" (*lō' 'ĕlōah*) (cf. Lev. 17:7; Ps. 106:37). At times it is difficult to distinguish between theological candor and poetic rhetoric in the praise of Yahweh and the denigration of other deities. The historical evidence, nonetheless, records the worship of a host of deities other than Yahweh in preexilic Israel and later communities.

Eventually, a monotheistic theology that eschewed any comparison of the Israelite god with other, nonexistent divine powers developed in early Judaism. In a prophetic oracle that parodies the Babylonian gods, the exilic prophet called Second Isaiah recasts earlier texts as God's defiant challenge: "To whom would you liken me and make me equal, and compare me, as though we were alike? … For I am God, and there is no other; I am God and there is no one like me!" (Isa. 46:9). With declarations like this, one moves beyond the polytheistic context of preexilic Israelite religion, considered here, to the development of the monotheistic theology of early Judaism.

Notes

1   Unless otherwise noted, all translations of ancient texts are the author's.
2   Ancient Near Eastern texts are cited by Hallo and Younger and abbreviated as *COS*, followed by volume and text number.

Bibliography

Batto, Bernard. *Slaying the Dragon: Mythmaking in the Biblical Tradition*. Philadelphia: Westminster John Knox, 1992. The opening chapters provide an insightful analysis of Babylonian creation accounts and their relationship to Genesis 1–8.

Cornelius, Izak. *The Many Faces of the Goddess: The Iconography of the Syro-Palestinian Goddesses Anat, Astarte, Qedeshet, and Asherah c. 1500–1000 BCE*. 2nd edn. Gottingen: Vandenhoeck & Ruprecht, 2008. A very helpful compendium of goddess iconography.

Dalley, Stephanie. *Myths from Mesopotamia: Creation, the Flood, Gilgamesh, and Others*. Oxford: Oxford University Press, 1989. An accessible and reliable English translation of Babylonian mythological literature.

Day, John. *Yahweh and the Gods and Goddesses of Canaan*. Sheffield: Sheffield Academic Press, 2000. An excellent book-length study of this chapter's topic.

Hadley, Judith M. *The Cult of Asherah in Ancient Israel and Judah*. Cambridge: Cambridge University, 2001. An authoritative study of Asherah in ancient Israel.

Hallo, William W. and K. Lawson Younger, Jr (eds). *The Context of Scripture*. 3 vols. Leiden: Brill, 1997–2002. The most reliable and recent collection of texts from the ancient Near East in English translation, abbreviated as *COS*.

Keel, Othmar and Christoph Uehlinger. *Gods, Goddesses, and Images of God in Ancient Israel*, trans. Thomas H. Trapp. Minneapolis: Fortress, 1998. A landmark study of iconography and divine symbolism in ancient Israel.

Lipiński, Edward. *Dieux et déesses de l'univers phénicien et punique*. Leuven: Peeters, 1995. An extensive survey of Phoenician and Punic deities.

Miller, Patrick, D., Jr., Paul D. Hanson, and S. Dean McBride (eds). *Ancient Israelite Religion: Essays in Honor of Frank Moore Cross*. Philadelphia: Fortress, 1987. A dated but superb collection of articles about Israelite religion within its ancient Near Eastern context.

Modrzejewski, Joseph Mélèze. *The Jews of Egypt: From Rameses II to Emperor Hadrian*. Princeton: Princeton University Press, 1995. A useful survey of ancient Jewish communities in Egypt, including on Elephantine Island.

Parker, Simon B. (ed.). *Ugaritic Narrative Poetry*. Atlanta: Society of Biblical Literature, 1997. Excellent transcriptions and English translations of the Ugaritic mythological texts by a group of scholars.

Smith, Mark S. *The Origins of Biblical Monotheism: Israel's Polytheistic Background and the Ugaritic Texts*. Oxford: Oxford University Press, 2001. An excellent and thorough survey of the Ugaritic deities, diversity in preexilic Israelite religion, and the emergence of monotheism.

Smith, Mark S. *The Early History of God: Yahweh and the Other Deities in Ancient Israel*. 2nd edn. Grand Rapids, MI: Eerdmans, 2002. An excellent introduction with comprehensive bibliographic references to recent work on this chapter's subject.

Smith, Mark S. *God in Translation: Deities in Cross-Cultural Discourse in the Biblical World*. Grand Rapids, MI: Eerdmans, 2010. A detailed consideration of ancient attitudes toward polytheism and the rise of monotheism, from ancient Israel through the Greco-Roman period.

Stavrakopoulou, Francesca and John Barton (eds). *Religious Diversity in Ancient Israel and Judah*. London: T&T Clark, 2010. Insightful collection of essays on the diversity of religious traditions and practices in ancient Israel.

Tigay, Jeffrey H. *You Shall Have No Other Gods: Israelite Religion in the Light of Hebrew Inscriptions*. Atlanta: Scholars Press, 1986. An important study of names in nonbiblical inscriptions from preexilic Israel in which the author argues that there is relatively little evidence for worship of deities other than Yahweh.

Van der Toorn, Karel, Bob Becking, and Pieter W. van der Horst (eds). *Dictionary of Deities and Demons in the Bible*. 2nd edn. Leiden: Brill, 1999. An excellent scholarly resource with descriptions of almost every deity mentioned by name in this chapter.

Watson, W. G. E., and N. Wyatt (eds). *Handbook of Ugaritic Studies*. Leiden: Brill, 1999. A comprehensive introduction and guide to the study of Ugaritic society, culture, and literature.

Wyatt, N. *Religious Texts from Ugarit*. 2nd edn. Sheffield: Sheffield Academic, 2002. A bold translation and interpretation of Ugaritic mythological literature.

Zevit, Ziony. *The Religions of Ancient Israel*. New York: Continuum, 2001. An authoritative exploration of ancient Israelite religious practices and beliefs prior to the exile.

CHAPTER 15

Monotheism and the Redefinition of Divinity in Ancient Israel

Mark S. Smith

Monotheism, commonly defined as the belief in only one god, has long been thought to constitute one of the hallmarks of ancient Israelite religion. Roman authors singled out monotheism as one of Judaism's admirable features, and it has been identified as a feature of Israelite religion at least by the sixth century BCE. Several older scholarly works (Albright; Kaufman) viewed monotheism in biblical tradition as expressed by Moses on Mount Sinai: "you shall have no other gods before me" (Exod. 20:3 and Deut. 5:7). Many, if not most, scholars have surmised that this view of early biblical monotheism has been overstated, as monotheism would not acknowledge "other gods" who would be "before" Yahweh (or "besides," in some translations). Commentators have also pointed to Exodus 15:11 as a less than monotheistic understanding of divinity in Israel since the verse takes note of other "gods": "Who is like you, O Lord, among the gods?" The older view that monotheism is to be traced back to Moses has been replaced by a historical reconstruction that situates the emergence of monotheistic discourse in the seventh–sixth centuries BCE, based on the critical density of monotheistic texts at this time and later:

Deuteronomy 4:35: "there is no other besides Him."
Deuteronomy 4:39: "The Lord is God in heaven above and on earth beneath; there is no other."
1 Samuel 2:2: "There is no Holy One like the Lord, no one besides you."
2 Samuel 7:22 = 1 Chronicles 17:20: "there is no God besides you, according to all that we have heard with our ears."
2 Kings 19:15, 19 (cf. Isaiah 37:16, 20): "you are God, you alone, of all the kingdoms of the earth … You, O Lord, are God alone."

These and other biblical passages particularly in Isaiah 40–55 or "Second Isaiah" (Isa. 43:10–11; 44:6, 8; 45:5–7, 14, 18, 21; and 46:9) and other biblical works (Jer.

The Wiley Blackwell Companion to Ancient Israel, First Edition. Edited by Susan Niditch.
© 2016 John Wiley & Sons, Ltd. Published 2016 by John Wiley & Sons, Ltd.

16:19, 20; Neh. 9:6/Ps. 86:10; Ps. 96:5 = 1 Chr. 16:26) suggest an articulation of a monotheistic worldview in the seventh–sixth century BCE context and later (Smith, *Origins*, 149–94).

Discussion of the term not only involves the question of its ancient context. The issue also entails its modern history. Although the term "monotheist" is attested earlier in the work of the Cambridge Platonist Ralph Cudworth (MacDonald, *Deuteronomy*, 6 n4), the word "monotheism" is commonly considered to be the coinage of Cudworth's friend, another Cambridge Platonist, Henry More (1614–1687), in his 1660 work, *An Explanation of the Grand Mystery of Godliness; or a True and Faithful Representation of the Everlasting Gospel of Our Lord and Saviour Jesus Christ* (MacDonald, *Deuteronomy*, 5–58; Schneider 19–25). The term was developed in the Enlightenment to provide a comparative grid that could map various religions inside and outside of the European context. This terminology appeared "at about the time when 'deism' and 'theism' were first introduced into scholarly and popular parlance" (Moberly 95 n4). The same applies to the modern use of the term polytheism, although it appears to be older. Apparently first employed in antiquity by Philo of Alexandria, polytheism is thought to have entered modern vocabulary first with Jean Bodin in 1580 in French, who used the term in conjunction with atheism (Schmidt 9–60). In the seventeenth century, polytheism was, like monotheism, part of the discourse of philosophy of religion and interreligious polemics. Through the eighteenth and nineteenth centuries, monotheism continued to serve in scholarly efforts to classify religions worldwide. In this context, religions were labeled according to forms of divinity, which served as a universal grid. Additionally, these forms were assigned relative value or importance. In this approach, monotheism represented the highest form of religion.

For much of the twentieth century, monotheism continued to constitute a distinctive cornerstone in scholarship of ancient Israelite religion and the Bible. In the 1970s, the discussion shifted, with efforts made to locate biblical monotheism in the wider context in the broader ancient Near East. On the one hand, ancient Mesopotamian texts that represent other deities as the manifestations of one god or goddess came to be compared with biblical representations of monotheism (Smith, *Origins*, 87–8). On the other hand, social developments and political dynamics in the seventh and sixth centuries BCE came to be seen as influential in the development of Israelite monotheism (Smith, *Origins*, 163–6). These developments are important, and will be addressed in "The Context for Monotheistic Discourse in the Seventh–Sixth Centuries" below. First, however, we turn to objections to the application of the term monotheism to Israelite understandings of divinity.

Monotheism's Modern Discontents

In recent years, scholars have offered reasons to discard the term monotheism. First, the word is not a biblical or ancient Near Eastern term, but a modern anachronism. Second, the term is polemical and has figured in expressions of Western religious superiority over and against non-Western religions. Third, monotheism serves to construct a dualistic opposition with polytheism that tends to distort or flatten the ancient data, or least to overstate the contrast. Fourth, it reduces the understanding of divinity to a matter of form with insufficient regard for the "content" of divinity, the social and political contexts that produced such a notion, and the practices connected with it. Fifth, monotheism is difficult to define. Sixth, monotheism is a philosophical claim about divine being or ontology, and no real philosophical argument on these lines is made until the Hellenistic period. Seventh, biblical monotheism is not truly monotheistic; there are other divinities within the religion of ancient Israel. Eighth and perhaps most crucially, are the biblical texts claimed to be monotheistic truly monotheistic? These are serious objections, and there certainly are limitations to the term monotheism. At the same time, the case against this term is not so clear. We will deal with each objection in order.

Monotheism as an anachronism

Biblical scholars and historians of religion use several anachronistic terms, including Bible, religion, book, and monotheism. In reaction to the usual criticism of employing the term religion, Jonathan Z. Smith (193–4, 207–8) suggests its positive value when used critically:

> "Religion" is not a native term; it is a term created by scholars for their intellectual purposes and therefore it is theirs to define. It is a second-order, generic concept that plays the same role in establishing a disciplinary horizon that a concept such as "language" plays in linguistics or "culture" plays in anthropology. There can be no disciplined study of religion without such a horizon … it will not do … to argue that the modern sense of the word, as a generic term, bears no relation to its Latin connotations. It is the very distance and difference of "religion" as a second-order category that gives it its cognitive power.

The biblical field uses any number of anachronistic terms, both to serve as entry points into ancient cultures, and to gain a critical sense of the distance and difference between the modern and ancient contexts. Accordingly, anachronism does not constitute a serious objection in itself. Instead, it points to the importance of distinguishing indigenous understandings of the ancients (what anthropologists called the "emic") from modern interpretations of these indigenous understandings (the "etic"). Such a procedure provides a critical basis for probing the ancient cultural and religious contexts that suggest and inform the use of such terms in the modern context.

Monotheism used to assert religious superiority

The association of the term monotheism with biblical religion may encourage a championing of modern religious traditions that understand themselves as monotheistic. In addition, monotheism is part of the heritage of Western imperialism and colonialism, a polemical term that may seem unsuitable for scholarly use. The anthropologist of religion Daniel Dubuisson (192; see also 112–15, 151–3) traces monotheistic discourse back to early Christianity and argues that many of the terms used by historians of religion are informed by a particular theological orientation. The question is thus whether the term can be used critically in discussions of ancient religion, a question with serious ethical and intellectual implications.

From an educational – and ethical – perspective, there is a counter-consideration: avoiding the term may have the opposite effect of what is desirable, namely critical awareness and discussion. The issue is not simply a scholarly one. People outside the scholarly field are aware of this term. One might argue that its familiarity outside of academic settings suggests retaining it as part of a larger academic effort to engage society in a critical manner about ancient religion. The term's familiarity as well as its problems arguably provide a teaching moment about the religion of ancient Israel. How the term is handled can serve to educate people, professionals and nonprofessionals alike, about its methodological problems and the critical considerations faced by modern scholarship. Taking cognizance of the term's difficulties, in fact, serves to highlight the critical issues involved, thereby offering a deeper understanding of the ancient sources' bearing on divinity. This is a particular goal that scholars should not relinquish too hastily.

The polemical cast of monotheism as it was used in the modern religious context would seem to be a good reason for not using the term. At the same time, it is to be noted that the polemical use of monotheism also marks those texts in the Bible that understand Israel's national god as the only deity in contradistinction to the deities of other peoples. In other words, the ancient and the modern purposes correspond in a notable manner. As is evident from the contexts of Deuteronomy 4 and Second Isaiah, monotheistic discourse emerged as a polemical rhetoric aimed at attacking polytheism within ancient Israel's society and in other societies. Thus, it is arguable that the ancient polemical understanding of the term parallels the modern polemical use which asserts the superiority of Christianity over and against other religions. Scholars do well to recognize and underscore its polemical force in both contexts.

The dualistic opposition of monotheism versus polytheism

Many scholars object to the term's dualism as constructed with its counterpart, polytheism. Jonathan Z. Smith regards the two terms as one of "the host of related dualisms, all of which finally reduce to 'ours' and 'them'" (174). Elisabeth Schüssler Fiorenza would deconstruct the dualistic categories in these terms: "We also have to relinquish the colonialist-theoretical model that constructs the relation between *Monotheism* and *Polytheism* in oppositional dualist terms, valorizing either *Monotheism* as was done in the colonial period or *Polytheism* as is the case in post-modernism" (220). It is true that the terms monotheism and polytheism construct too sharp a contrast in the ancient data. As we will see below, there is something "mono" in ancient polytheism and something "poly" within ancient monotheism. Scholars have noted how the divine council and divine family serve as "mono-concepts" with multiple deities. In turn, scholars are giving thought to the problem of the many within a single deity.

Speaking from the opposite end of the theological spectrum as Schüssler Fiorenza, Brevard Childs remarked on the term's flattening of biblical data: "Although the historian of religion has every right to employ the term monotheism to the religion of Israel in contrast to polytheistic religions, the term itself is theologically inert and fails largely to register the basic features of God's self-revelation to Israel" (355). Childs is critical of history of religion and sociological reconstructions as reductionist not only on theological grounds, but also with respect to historical and literary issues. For Nathan MacDonald, monotheism is an intellectualized or philosophical term of the Enlightenment that does not speak sufficiently to the nature or character of the biblical God (*Deuteronomy*, 2, 4, 210). Despite these objections, it may be asked why a single term should be expected to cover the nature or character of any given deity. In short, the past history of the term need not be the meaning that it carries in present or future discussions.

As a related objection, it is claimed that theoretically in antiquity "monotheism" does not make sense until the term developed in opposition to "polytheism." It is assumed in the scholarly discussions that the use of these terms belies the ancient evidence. Depending on how the terms are used, there is truth to this claim. At the same time, it is possible to detect the emergence of monotheistic representations in the Bible alongside older expressions of Israelite polytheism. Deuteronomy 32 is sharply monotheistic (see "no god" in v. 21; "there is no god beside me," v. 39). Yet this passage contains the older world theology of the 70 gods in verses 8–9 (especially in the Greek version and the Hebrew version in the Dead Sea Scrolls). The opening of the book of Job uses an older polytheistic "mono-concept" of the divine council along with an assumed single God over all. In other words, sometimes in their expression of monotheism, biblical texts stand between the older, limited polytheism and the new monotheistic worldview. Even Deuteronomy 4:19, much heralded for its seeming acceptance of polytheism or concession to polytheism, seems to be drawing on the older family view of the gods of the nations to explain the idolatry around Israel that Israel must avoid. In short, monotheistic texts in the Bible draw on older polytheistic representations of divinity even as they resituate them within their monotheistic contexts.

Reductionism of divinity to a matter of form

Discussions of monotheism, especially when it is praised as the cornerstone of both ancient Israelite religion and modern Western religion, reduce the understanding of divinity to a matter of form. In this approach, Israelite divinity is reduced to an "-ism" with little or no reference to its content, such as truth-claims about a deity, or attendant praxis. A similar reductionism informs the uncritical correlation of monotheism with violence. In the ancient context, there is no correlation between monotheism and violence. Ancient monotheism and polytheism both entail violence, for example *herem*-warfare or "the ban." The tendency toward reductionism also is an underlying issue for the longtime comparison of biblical monotheism with the so-called monotheism of the Egyptian king Amenophis IV, better known as Akhenaten (Freud 27–43). However, the strongly differing content of the so-called monotheism of Akhenaten and Israelite monotheism makes for a dubious comparison (see also John Huddlestun's essay in this volume).

Modern biblical scholars do not wish to restrict the understanding of any particular deity to a form of theism. For W. F. Albright and Yehezkel Kaufman, monotheism as it relates to Yahweh includes features in addition to being one deity, for example, the deity's lack of mythology, sexuality, birth or death (Albright 271–2; Kaufman 29). Despite criticisms that might be raised concerning their particular positions, these scholars do well to point out that the term monotheism need not cover all aspects of a deity, but may refer to distinctive dimensions of that deity's profile.

A focus on the form of divinity risks ignoring the context of its production or the practices connected with it. A number of scholars, including Nathaniel Levtov and myself, have explored the expression of monotheism in Second Isaiah as more than polemic directed at rival deities and cultures in the environment of Second Isaiah's Judean audience. In addition, monotheism is not best presented as some sublime idea, as it has served at times in modern religious discourse. Instead, it is to be understood in a broader religious and cultural context involving a complex understanding of reality and a corresponding set of social and religious practices. Monotheism is only one part of the study of ancient Israelite divinity; it provides entry into a broader social and political context that informs Israel's self-understanding with respect to others and that is represented by a number of biblical texts. Monotheism was part of an innercommunity discussion that represented its concept of reality in contrast to the notions of other groups, reinforcing the identity of those whom monotheistic texts address.

Defining monotheism

Defining monotheism has been a challenging enterprise. In the Hebrew Bible, is it a belief, an idea, an abstraction, a worldview, a sort of rhetoric, an element of literary representation or some combination of these? The definitional difficulty in itself, however, does not seem to be a strong reason for discarding a term, as illustrated well by the reflections of the anthropologist Clifford Geertz on the problem of defining the word, culture:

> Everyone knows what cultural anthropology is about: it's about culture. The trouble is that no one is quite sure what culture is. Not only is it an essentially contested concept, like democracy, religion, simplicity, or social justice, it is a multiply defined one, multiply employed, ineradicably imprecise. It is fugitive, unsteady, encyclopedic, and normatively charged, and there are those, especially those for whom only the really real is really real, who think it vacuous altogether, or even dangerous, and would ban it from the serious discourse of serious persons. An unlikely idea, it would seem, around which to build a science. Almost as bad as matter. (9)

And yet, suggests Geertz, the challenging term "culture" has meaning and value. We would argue the same for monotheism.

Monotheism as a philosophical argument about divine ontology

It is sometimes thought that monotheism is at its heart a modern philosophical construct, one that should not be retrojected to the biblical context prior to Greek philosophizing. This view depends upon what constitutes philosophy. While biblical texts do not approach the question of reality with the sort of abstract reasoning characteristic of early Western philosophy, biblical texts do narrate and discuss reality. Within such representations of reality are embedded presuppositions or notions about reality: in other words, an implicit theory or theories of reality. Whether or not monotheism constitutes or embeds philosophy, it is the task of scholars to understand the worldview of the texts with their operating assumptions and procedures: in other words, their theories. Such biblical theorizing, whatever it is, entails biblical materials prior to the Greco-Roman philosophical enterprise. Indeed, the same point concerning theory applies to polytheistic representations of reality outside of the Bible, not to mention nonbiblical discourse focused on a single deity.

Biblical monotheism as a mistaken claim

The claim that ancient Israel is monotheistic seems misplaced, as there are other divinities within the religion of ancient Israel. This objection has gained a great deal of traction in recent discussions. However, the basic issue in this matter is not whether or not Israel's one-god discourse was characteristic of ancient Israel in general, but whether or not it is observable in texts of the sixth century BCE or later. The issue is in the first instance a textual issue. How it did or did not work itself out in Israel's society remains part of the research agenda. A further objection sometimes arises as a matter of definition involving the word 'ĕlōhîm ("gods, divinities") and its related forms. In other words, if other phenomena are labeled with this term, then as the objection goes, there is no monotheism. This approach misses the point about a number of important texts of the sixth century BCE and later. Second Isaiah (Isa. 40–55), Ezekiel, and Genesis 1, among other texts, make basic claims about Yahweh vis-à-vis other deities. For these texts, Yahweh is the only one who is indispensable in the picture of reality; other forms of divinity are at best relatively minor. Yahweh as god is beyond their power, and they have agency only because this one deity allows them power. In other words, from the perspective of such authors, if Yahweh is removed from the picture of reality, then the picture of reality does not stand.

The ongoing debate about the biblical texts claimed to be monotheistic

Some scholars object to the application of the term to ancient textual evidence claimed to be monotheistic. In recent decades, it has been popular to pick away at the monotheistic biblical passages cited at the outset of this essay. MacDonald complains about the term's appropriateness for characterizing certain biblical expressions found in these passages (*Deuteronomy*, 78–85, 209). These expressions, for MacDonald, are to be viewed not as claims concerning a single deity in, but instead as statements about Israel's singular allegiance to, one god. It seems, however, that both points are embedded in these biblical expressions. These texts represent all reality as dependent on the one deity, while additional biblical texts represent other deities as lifeless (Second Isaiah) or as missing from the picture of reality (Gen. 1). Such representations presuppose a monotheistic worldview.

The Context for Monotheistic Discourse in the Seventh–Sixth Centuries

Israel emerged between two periods of empire. At Israel's beginning was the end of the Late Bronze Age and at the other end was the rise of the Assyrians, Babylonians, and Persians beginning in the eighth century BCE and down through the seventh and sixth centuries BCE (see the essays by John Huddlestun and J. J. M. Roberts in this volume). The monotheism of Israel emerged in the context of these later empires that left their mark on Israel's expressions of monotheism. The period entailed several momentous events for Israel: the fall of the northern kingdom of Israel ("the lost ten tribes") to the Assyrians in the year 722 BCE; the deportation of over 200,000 Israelites in 701 BCE; the fall of Jerusalem and Judah to the Babylonians in 586 BCE; the exile of the Israelites in Babylonia in the 590s BCE and 580s BCE; the initial return and settlement of exiles under the Persians in 538 BCE; and the rebuilding of the temple in 518 BCE. These events produced some of the most heart-wrenching poetry of the biblical corpus, poetry of great trauma, such as the Book of Lamentations, the Book of Jeremiah with its own laments and the uplifting poetry of Isaiah 40–55 or Second Isaiah, with its references to Cyrus the king of Persia and the promise of God leading Israel home. This period also produced sustained reflections on God and reality, from the Book of Deuteronomy's reformulation of the Sinai covenant in Exodus–Numbers to the vision of reality in Genesis 1, produced by the priestly composer (see the essays by David Carr and S. A. Geller in this volume).

The biblical literature of the seventh and sixth centuries BCE was part of a wider international discussion concerning the nature of reality and the gods. Biblical authors, such as the priestly authors of Genesis 1 and Ezekiel, may have been familiar with some of these intellectual currents. The exceedingly literate book of Ezekiel, which reflects knowledge of various facets of Phoenician and Egyptian culture, is evidence of the ways in which biblical authors worked within the wider framework of international literature. A comparable case has been made for seeing Second Isaiah both as a priest and as a literate figure aware of international currents of thought. Broadly speaking, the priestly work of Genesis 1, Jeremiah, Ezekiel and Second Isaiah, works all rooted in the sixth century BCE, spoke to the same imperial world emanating out of Mesopotamia. All of these great biblical works also contain important creation accounts that probe the nature of God and God's power in a period dominated by foreign powers. These writings explore God's relationship with Israel, and all of them condemn or leave other deities out of the picture.

With the sixth century BCE and events surrounding the exile to Babylon, Israel stood at a major intellectual and political turning point, and not simply because its experience of the world was so different from that of earlier generations. The world was in the middle of dramatic change, and Israel was drawn into that change. Israel was part of a world of empire, a situation it had never experienced before and one that influenced its thinking about reality. The reality of empire not only influenced Israelite thinkers, but affected views of reality among the power-holders themselves. One feature of this international discussion is the focus on a single deity, on a one-god or one-goddess vision of reality. In most cases, it is "one-god" discourse envisioning a male deity, but in some cases the focus is upon a goddess.

Up to the time of the Assyrian expansion in the west in the eighth century BCE, ancient Israel had a national god, Yahweh, the great warrior-king. This male god was chief and monarch over the other divinities, who were minor divinities compared to Yahweh who seems to have been identified with El by this time (see Exod. 6:2–3). El's consort was Asherah, and perhaps as a result of Yahweh-El merger, this Yahweh-El was viewed to have Asherah as his consort (see the essays by Elizabeth Bloch-Smith and Neal Walls in this volume).

Other deities were regarded as secondary in status, such as Baal and Astarte, and the Sun and Moon; some seem to have dropped out of the picture, such as Anat; and still other deities became servants of Yahweh, such as Resheph and Deber in Habakkuk 3, where they are depicted as part of Yahweh's military force. Additional deities are known from personal names, such as "Dawn" and "Dusk." It is difficult to know how active these deities were considered to be.

As these deities underwent changes in status or acceptance, their language and imagery became associated with Yahweh, or one might say incorporated into the nature or character or Godhead of Yahweh. Even the language associated with Baal and with Anat was incorporated into the imagery of Yahweh, sometimes with considerable modification, and in other instances with only minor differences. The notion of the divine council or assembly of the gods led by the monarch Yahweh-El also remained in use, while divine family language was becoming more of a cliché. The divine council continued to serve as an expression of the chief god's status as the unrivaled monarch. At the same time, Israel recognized that other nations had their main, national gods who ruled over those countries. Just before the rise of the Assyrians in the west, Israelite cosmology suggested that the 70 countries of the world were ruled by a large royal family of gods consisting of the 70 gods, an image related to the later idea of the 70 guardian angels of the 70 nations found in the Book of Daniel (see the essay by Matthew Goff in this volume). Yahweh was the royal god ruling Israel (Deut. 32:8–9; cf. Ps. 82). As long as there was relative parity between Israel and its neighbors, this sort of "world theology" seemed to work. Thus in negotiations between Israel and its neighbors, the nations' gods are recognized as doing for them what Yahweh, the god of Israel, does for Israel. For example, in Judges 11:24, Jephthah sends a message to the king of Ammon and asks him: "Do you not inherit that which Chemosh your god gives you to possess? So we inherit everything that Yahweh our god gives us to possess."

The ascendancy of the Assyrian empire, however, changed this older world-theology of Israel. When the armies of Assyria moved west in the ninth and eighth centuries BCE, there was no longer parity. Assyria conquered and incorporated other lands to Israel's north, until the northern kingdom of Israel itself was swept into the Assyrian empire (see the essay by J. J. M. Roberts in this volume). Samaria, the capital city of the northern kingdom, fell to Assyria in the year 722 BCE, and about 28,000 Israelites were taken into captivity to Assyria; initially Jerusalem and the small kingdom of Judah survived the Assyrians. At first glance, it would seem that Judah managed fairly well, since it would last another 150 years until the fall of the city of Jerusalem in the year 586 BCE. However, this reading of history misses a crucial point in the history of Jerusalem and Judah. In the year 701 BCE, the Assyrian army led by Sennacherib himself swept into Judah and took over the country, with the exception of the besieged Jerusalem. When the Assyrians departed to deal with matters back in Mesopotamia, it seemed like a miraculous victory for Israel, as recalled in Book of Isaiah (37:36a, 37).

Despite this apparent divine intervention, however, Judea had suffered devastating consequences: according to Assyrian records, 201,150 Judeans were taken to Babylonia. If exile is understood to mean the loss of people and not only the loss of land, then the exile of Judah to Babylonia began already in the year 701 BCE, for the numbers of people lost were about seven times the number taken from the northern kingdom in 722 BCE. By occupying the northern kingdom of Israel and turning it into part of an Assyrian province, Assyria remained on the doorstep of Judah, which was required to produce monetary tribute to the Assyrian empire. Thus Assyria loomed very large over Judean society from 701 BCE until the fall of Assyria itself ca. 609 BCE; the Babylonians and Persians would follow in succession. One of the results of the loss of land and population was the loss of traditional family structure (see the essays by T. M. Lemos and Carol Meyers in this volume). The loss of family land and family members decimated Israel's traditional family structure, and significantly, the seventh–sixth centuries BCE witnessed the individual taking her or his place alongside the family as an important expression of social identity. The individual, according to changes taking place within Israelite society, was to be responsible for her or his own sins and no longer passed on sins to children or suffered for the sins of her or his parents. According to three great works on this period, "In those days, they shall no longer say, 'Parents have eaten sour grapes and children's teeth are set on edge.' But every one shall die for his own sins: whoever eats sour grapes, his teeth shall be set on edge" (Jer. 31:29–30; cf. Ezek. 18 and 33:12–20; Deut. 24:16). A society that would begin to see individual persons as responsible for their own actions in the sphere of human activity could also see a single national god as responsible in the sphere of divine activity, namely the universe as a whole. Understood within the sociohistorical framework of Israelite experience, monotheism was an assertion of identity in the face of tremendous loss.

Ideas of divinity among Israel's powerful neighbors responded to and reflected the realities of empire as well. The Assyrian empire developed a new worldview that corresponded to its role in the world; it would be followed by the Babylonian empire, which assumed Assyria's place by the end of the seventh century BCE. In both Assyria and Babylonia, texts emerged reflecting a one-god or one-goddess worldview. The best-known example of this worldview is found in the so-called Epic of Creation or Enuma Elish. According to Enuma Elish, Marduk defeats the personified cosmic waters, Tiamat, and then Marduk receives the acclamation of divine kingship from all the deities and builds the universe out of the dead corpse of Tiamat. In addition, the other deities are given their places in the universe that Marduk has now created. Crucial for this discussion, the final portion of Enuma Elish presents the names of the other gods as Marduk's own names. He is the sum of divinity relative to them.

Another text given its modern name based on its first line, "I will praise the lord of wisdom" (*Ludlul bel nemeqi*), shows Marduk's "supergod" status in a different manner. The "one-god" vision is expressed here largely in terms of the divine mind and thought:

> The lord [Marduk] divines the gods' innermost thoughts,
> > (but) no [god] understands his behavior.
> Marduk divines the gods' innermost thoughts:
> > Which god understands his mind?

The mind of Marduk penetrates into the minds of the other deities, but they cannot grasp even the external manifestation of his behavior. Marduk is far beyond all other deities. Elsewhere, other deities are understood as aspects of Marduk's supreme rule (see Smith, *Origins*, 87–8 for further discussion of the following texts):

> Sin is your divinity, Anu your sovereignty,
> > Dagan is your lordship, Enlil your kingship,
> Adad is your might, wise Ea your perception,
> > Nabu, the holder of the tablet stylus, is your skill,
> Your leadership (in battle) is Ninurta, your might, Nergal,
> > Your counsel is Nus[ku], your superb [minister],
> Your judgeship is radiant Shamash, who arouses [no] dispute,
> > Your eminent name is Marduk, sage of the gods.

Another text discusses all the deities as functions of Marduk:

Urash (is)	Marduk of planting
Luglalidda (is)	Marduk of the abyss
Ninurta (is)	Marduk of the pickaxe
Nergal (is)	Marduk of battle
Zababa (is)	Marduk of warfare
Enlil (is)	Marduk of lordship and consultations
Nabu (is)	Marduk of accounting
Sin (is)	Marduk who lights up the night
Shamash (is)	Marduk of justice
Adad (is)	Marduk of rain
Tishpak (is)	Marduk of troops
Great Anu (is)	Marduk …
Shuqamuna (is)	Marduk of the container
[] (is)	Marduk of everything.

Marduk was not the only deity who could be recast in these terms.

Parts of the bodies of a supreme god, whether it is Marduk or Ishtar or Ninurta, could be identified with other deities, as illustrated, for example, by depictions of the warrior-god Ninurta in the following hymn:

O lord, your face is the sun god, your hair Aya,
   Your eyes, O lord, are Enlil and Ninlil.
The pupils of your eyes are Gula and Belet-ili,
   The irises of your eyes are the twins, Sin and Shamash,
The lashes of your eyes are the rays of the sun that …
   The appearance of your mouth, O lord, is Ishtar of the stars
Anu and Antum are your lips, your command …
   Your tongue (?) is Pabilsag of the above …
The roof of your mouth, O lord, is the vault
   Of heaven and earth, your divine abode,
Your teeth are the seven gods who lay low the evil ones.

In these cases, the one-deity worldview remained grounded in traditional Mesopotamian polytheism; the other deities continued to be recognized, and the devotion to them in the form of sacrifices and temples was maintained. In these texts, the representations of their major deities as the one deity corresponded to the place of Assyria and Babylonia in the world. The other lands continued to exist, but as extensions of the empire. Correspondingly, other deities existed but as extensions or manifestations of the empire-god.

As this implicit paradigm shift concerning divinity took place in Mesopotamia, corresponding speculation was underway in Israel. What is the nature of reality and where does Israel's God belong with respect to this reality? As the Mesopotamian empires swept up the northern kingdom of Israel and then the southern kingdom of Judah, the world definitively changed for Israel. A vision of a more restricted pantheon, in effect a monotheistic vision, emerged in Israel at this time. Baal and Asherah were criticized; the sun, moon and the stars were not to be regarded as deities; there was no goddess, and the asherah became a symbol of blessing from God and God's teaching. As a result, there were now only two levels of divine reality, God and the angels. And these two were so different that in effect there was only one god. Angelic divinities were viewed as merely working for the one God, being entirely dependent on the one God. The notion of the 70 divine children found in the Ugaritic texts and prior Israelite traditions was no longer tenable; the divine children became instead 70 angels who guard the 70 nations (e.g., Dan. 10:13, 20–21), anticipating the role of guardian angels. In sum, for Israelite monotheism, the "head god" had become the "Godhead." Where Mesopotamian "one-deity discourse" allowed for the divinity of other deities even as extensions of a supergod, Israelite monotheism excluded the sacrifices and temples of such extensions.

Monotheism and the Redefinition of Divinity

Israelite monotheism did not simply redefine the profile of the older, traditional Yahweh-El. It also redefined divinity. First and foremost, all positive divine power and character resided in this God or Godhead. Whatever can be said positively about divinity in ancient Israel can be predicated only of Israel's god. In turn, other divinity was abolished. The older middle levels of the divine hierarchy were eliminated: sun, moon and the stars were not divinities. Angels served as divine accompaniment to humans (as opposed to the "personal god" or "household god"), and they were not regarded as divinities. The "seventy" gods became 70 angels. Divine military retinues were also identified as angels (see "angels" in Gen. 19:1 regarded as "destroyers" (*mašḥîtîm*), in 19:13). The divine council or assembly was believed to be populated only by angelic "sons of God" (see Job 1–2). In other words, "sons of God," formerly important members of the upper divine hierarchy, were demoted to angels, and the divine council became a new vehicle or stage for theological reflection on the divine agency of a single deity (again Job 1–2). Language of divine family became only residual as the oneness of divinity was located in a single divine figure.

As a corollary, all deities apart from Yahweh were defined in utter opposition to Yahweh; in short, they were redefined precisely as "*other* gods." The roots of this development can be seen already in the separate worship of Yahweh expressed in the Ten Commandments, mentioned at the outset of this essay. Stated differently, other deities were regarded as illusions or nothing. For Second Isaiah, God and not Marduk is the supergod in the universe. Isaiah 46:1 mentions Marduk (under his title Bel) as nothing other than a lifeless idol that weighs down those who carry it, in contrast to the living God who bears up the House of Jacob whom this God created (see vv. 3–4). This approach to other gods is consistent with the genericization of the names of some deities, for instance, Astarte as a term for fertility of flocks, Resheph as flame and Deber as pestilence. With the denial of "other gods" as not Israelite (see labeling such as "baals and ashtarot/asherot" in Judg. 2:13, 3:7, or "baals" in 10:10 and Hos. 11:2), claims emerged that older traditions formerly associated with Yahweh did not belong to Yahweh, for instance, the denunciation of asherah and of the "sun, moon and the stars." Similarly, symbols were divorced from other deities: asherah was no longer a symbol of the goddess but a symbol of Yahweh ("his asherah") and the divine torah (cf. the possible wordplay on the asherah in Prov. 3:18).

Apart from angels, other former divinities moved from the category of the uncreated to the created order. The sun, moon and stars were no longer viewed as lower-level divinities but as created (Gen. 1:16 and Ps. 148:2–3, 5). Angels were no longer regarded as lower-level divinities but as created (Neh. 9:6 and Ps. 148:2–5; see also *Jubilees* 2:1). Cosmic waters were no longer divine (much less personified as in Ps. 104:7), but created (Ps. 148:4–5; see also *Jub.* 2:2). Cosmic enemies such as Leviathan were represented as created (Ps. 104:26). The overall result suggests *a total polarity*: other deities appear as nondivine individuals or as mere illusions or idols, but in the case of Yahweh, we find total individualization of divinity and a complete and concentrated density of notions of divinity in one single God.

Monotheism may entail mystery or enigma involving ideas about divinity that were traditional at this time. Mystery, for example, is key to Ezekiel, with its visions of the divine chariot that moves in four directions at the same time to express the sense of God being able to be everywhere, to have knowledge and power everywhere at the same time (Ezek. 1–3). Enigma is likewise key to the exilic work Second Isaiah. In Isaiah 45:6–7, God is quoted as saying:

> I am Yahweh, and there is none else,
>> fashioning light and creating darkness,
> making peace and creating evil;
>> I am Yahweh who makes all these.

This statement tells Israel not only that God has power over all circumstances, with light and peace, but also that he is the very creator of all circumstances, even of darkness and evil. Darkness and evil somehow belong ultimately to God as ultimate cause. God can do anything and everything for Israel, and in bringing Israel home from Mesopotamia in the year 538 BCE, God was seen as demonstrating this truth. Images of light and peace for God are hardly unexpected, but the images of darkness and evil for God also suggest a notion that God is beyond what may be expected or known. God cannot be boxed into the attributes of divinity that are expected of God. This, it seems, is a central point of Job. God the divine reality is beyond the God of human theory.

This survey suggests that monotheism remains a reasonable label for some Israelite expressions of ancient Near Eastern one-deity discourse. This Israelite subset of ancient Near Eastern one-deity discourse argued for a redefinition of divinity via the one divine figure over and against other deities. The Israelite texts of the seventh–sixth centuries BCE may be capturing a shift that builds on many older strands. This subset of Israelite discourse differs from what was seen in Mesopotamia, with its continuation of the deities viewed as manifestations or parts of a single deity. In the polemics against other deities that accompany the expressions of monotheism in biblical works one glimpses a redefinition of major deities and of divinity itself which took place in Israel, Mesopotamia, and perhaps elsewhere as well. In ancient Israel, this development occurred in relation to a particular deity and that one deity alone, and this interpretive turn created new possibilities and new problems in understanding divinity. At this time, Yahweh seems to have become an individual with depth and difference. A number of literary critics speak of Yahweh becoming a real character in the Bible, and the representation of this deity relates to the larger literary and religious picture.

The one divinity/the divine appears as the divine paradox of ineffability and good, as known from older traditional divine roles, functions and emotions. Historians of religions have posited a three-dimensional structure of the divine world. For example, the Egyptologist Jan Assmann speaks in terms of "shapes" (cult images and representations of a deity in the temple cult); "transformations" (cosmic manifestations as sun, moon, stars and the like); and "names" (linguistic representations that include not only proper names, but also titles, pedigrees, genealogies and myths). According to the Assyriologist Beate Pongratz-Leisten, Mesopotamian polytheism is said to be focused on "imagery, concepts, roles and functions," which both delineate deities and suggest overlap between them (163, 166). These – and other – scholars see a multiplicity of alignments or even fluidity in a number of ancient Near Eastern contexts with divine names, titles, and posited characteristics shared by various gods and goddesses and evidently moving between gods and goddesses. In biblical monotheism, the fluidity across deities in divine representation flows to a single divinity, and in this sense monotheism reflects a process of differentiation or redefinition of prior norms for divinity (Smith, *Early History*, xxii, xxx, xxxvii, 189–90, 195–202; cf. Pongratz-Leisten 168). In the Israelite deity, features and titles available in the environment of ancient Israel became dimensions of this deity, even as they may also have been modified.

As a result, all the names of deity and all the roles properly identified for divinity in these biblical representations constitute a single reality of a single deity. The result is not simply a concentration of all divine names, titles and powers in a single deity. Other divine entities remain but are understood as having reality thanks only to this divine entity. The important corollary of this situation is that the one divine entity bears the range of character found elsewhere, spread across a number of deities; and no less importantly, this deity holds the range of character within its divine self or person. In other words, this deity is not only more divine in encompassing various divine characteristics, but this deity is also represented as more human than before, encompassing the human personalities seen across the range of other deities. The biblical God – and here I consciously am not suggesting that the "biblical God" is entirely the same as the Israelite God – seems both more divine and more human compared with earlier versions of the deity God and perhaps compared with other deities. If one may speak of a revolution in ancient Israel's concept of deity, it may involve not only the unity of the deity's roles and functions, but also the personality of the deity in the full range of divine and human roles that deities may exercise. There is not only one divine person; there is also only one order of divine personhood. Both are coterminous in the biblical God.

Bibliography

Albright, W. F. *From the Stone Age to Christianity: Monotheism and the Historical Process.* 2nd edn. Baltimore: Johns Hopkins Press, 1957. A classic study reflecting mid-twentieth century notions of religious progress culminating in Christianity.

Assmann, Jan. *Of God and Gods: Egypt, Israel, and the Rise of Monotheism.* George L. Mosse Series in Modern European Cultural and Intellectual History. Madison: University of Wisconsin Press, 2008. A judgmental casting of biblical monotheism that ignores Israel's ancient Near Eastern neighbors as well as its own cultural context.

Barr, James. "The problem of Israelite monotheism." *Transactions of the Glasgow University Oriental Society 17* (1957–8): 52–62. A critical and probing look at alleged biblical expressions of monotheism, especially in Second Isaiah.

Childs, Brevard. *Biblical Theology of the Old and New Testaments: Theological Reflections on the Hebrew Bible.* Minneapolis: Fortress, 1992. A subject-by-subject discussion of important theological issues in the Bible by a master of the field.

Dubuisson, Daniel. *The Western Construction of Religion: Myths, Knowledge, and Ideology*, trans. William Sayers. Baltimore: Johns Hopkins University Press, 2003. A thoughtful study of the modern construction of religion undertaken by historians of religion that express the very prejudices that they seek to criticize about religious adherents.

Freud, Sigmund. *Moses and Monotheism*, trans. Katherine Jones. New York: Vintage, 1939. A psychological classic on the topic that continues to be influential.

Geertz, Clifford. *A Life of Learning.* New York: American Council of Learned Societies, 1999. Reflections on academic life and work by a great anthropologist.

Geller, Stephen A. "The one and the many: An essay on the God of the covenant." In Barbara Porter (ed.), *One God or Many? Concepts of Divinity in the Ancient World* (pp. 273–319). Bethesda, MD: CDL Press, 2000. A probing and superb consideration of different textual expressions of covenantal monotheism.

Kaufman, Yehezkel. *The Religion of Israel: From Its Beginning to the Babylonian Exile*, trans. and abridged Moshe Greenberg. New York: Schocken, 1972. An old classic on the subject, with a concern for the Bible as Israel's great spiritual expression; there is little consultation of relevant comparative material.

Levtov, Nathaniel B. *Images of Others: Iconic Politics in Ancient Israel.* Winona Lake, IN: Eisen-brauns, 2008. This fine book seeks to understand biblical texts dealing with iconism in terms of their larger political and religious contexts.

MacDonald, Nathan. *Deuteronomy and the Meaning of "Monotheism."* Tübingen: Mohr Siebeck, 2003. This book questions the applicability of current definitions of monotheism for biblical texts.

MacDonald, Nathan. "The origin of 'monotheism.'" In L.T. Stuckenbruck and W. S. North (eds), *Exploring Early Jewish and Christian Monotheism* (pp. 204–15). London: Sheffield Academic Press, 2004. This essay traces the modern history of the term "monotheism."

Moberly, R. W. L. "Is monotheism bad for you? Some reflections on God, the Bible, and life in the light of Regina Schwartz's *The Curse of Cain.*" In Robert P. Gordon (ed.), *The God of Israel* (pp. 94–112). Cambridge: Cambridge University Press, 2007. A thoughtful response to liberal critiques of biblical monotheism.

Muffs, Yochanan. "On biblical anthropomorphism." In Kathryn F. Kravitz and Diane M. Sharon (eds), *Bringing the Hidden to Light: The Process of Interpretation: Studies in Honor of Stephen A. Geller* (pp. 163–8). Winona Lake, IN: Eisenbrauns, 2007. A work of religious thought on God, focused primarily on biblical representations of divinity.

Pongratz-Leisten, Beate. "When the gods are speaking: Toward defining the interface between polytheism and monotheism." In Matthias Köckert and Martti Nissinen (eds), *Propheten in Mari, Assyrien und Israel* (pp. 162–8). Göttingen: Vandenhoeck & Ruprecht, 2003. A thoughtful, comparative reflection on the categories of divinity that inform Mesopotamian polytheism and bear on biblical representations of monotheism.

Schmidt, Francis. "Polytheisms: Degeneration or progress?" *History and Anthropology* 3 (1987) = *The Inconceivable Polytheism.* This study questions the negative valuations attached to polytheism in modern history of religion discourse.

Schneider, Laurel C. *Beyond Monotheism: A Theology of Multiplicity.* London: Routledge, 2008. A theological probing of monotheism for its problems and possibilities.

Schüssler Fiorenza, Elisabeth. *The Power of the Word: Scripture and the Rhetoric of Empire.* Minneapolis: Fortress, 2007. A wide-ranging work, marked by a critical evaluation of the uses to which Scripture has been put.

Smith, Jonathan Z. *Relating Religion: Essays in the Study of Religion.* Chicago: University of Chicago Press, 2004. A collection of classic studies by a wonderful historian of religion.

Smith, Mark S. *The Origins of Biblical Monotheism: Israel's Polytheistic Background and the Ugaritic Texts.* Oxford: Oxford University Press, 2001. This study explores different structures and categories of divinity in ancient Israel and its West Semitic context and attempts to identify the conditions attendant on Israel's expressions of its one-god worldview.

Smith, Mark S. *The Early History of God: Yahweh and the Other Deities in Ancient Israel.* 2nd edn. Biblical Resource Series. Grand Rapids, MI: Eerdmans, 2002. A synthesis of what is known about deities in ancient Israel in light of biblical and extrabiblical sources and how this affects scholarly understanding of Israel's god.

Smith, Mark S. *God in Translation: Deities in Cross-Cultural Discourse in the Biblical World.* Tübingen: Mohr Siebeck, 2008, 2010. This book surveys how different cultures understood the reality of deities in other societies, from the Late Bronze Age through the Greco-Roman period (including the New Testament).

B

Mediation: Gods and Humans

CHAPTER 16

Priests and Ritual

S. A. Geller

Despite advances in archaeology and the comparative study of ancient Near Eastern religions, our primary source of information about priesthood and ritual in ancient Israel remains the Hebrew Bible, especially the books of Exodus, Leviticus and Numbers. The biblical sources, both inside and outside of the Pentateuch, reflect the ideological viewpoints of the major biblical theologies: the covenantal-Deuteronomic and the priestly. These dominant viewpoints have obscured actual religious practice in the ancient states of Israel and Judah during their existence, roughly from 900 to 600 BCE, as well as earlier stages. The theologies are mainly the product of the seventh–fifth centuries, in which the religion and culture of ancient Israel and Judah were reinterpreted and made to fit the newer idea of absolute monotheism and contemporary political and social conditions. This study explores the priestly and ritual dimensions of ancient Israelite religion as described in the Pentateuch, comparing and contrasting this material with information gleaned from the rest of the Hebrew Bible and relevant comparative evidence from Canaan and Mesopotamia. In this way, we can attempt a tentative historical reconstruction of the development of the priesthood and the cult. The essay is divided into the following sections: the Priestly Theology of the Tetrateuch; a brief discussion of the sacrificial system; a discussion of the priesthood in the biblical narrative of the Tetrateuch; and cult and priesthood in preexilic Israel and Judah.

The Priestly Theology of the Tetrateuch

Cultic matters, including sacrifice, priesthood, Sabbath and festivals, laws of ritual, and purity, make up about half the content of the Pentateuch. Most of these topics are found from Exodus 24, through all of Leviticus, to Numbers 9, the major exception being the laws of Passover-Unleavened Bread in Exodus 12–13. Most of this cultic material is ascribed by critics to the Priestly source(s) ("P"), a body of literature that consists of several priestly strands, as well as the material assigned by scholars to the related "Holiness Code" (mainly Leviticus 17–26). This work, attributed to a "Priestly School," also

The Wiley Blackwell Companion to Ancient Israel, First Edition. Edited by Susan Niditch.
© 2016 John Wiley & Sons, Ltd. Published 2016 by John Wiley & Sons, Ltd.

contains narratives, from the creation account in Genesis 1:1–2:4a, through assorted tales in Genesis, Exodus and Numbers.

The Priestly School in its latest form is responsible for the final editing of the Pentateuch, often associated with the work of Ezra around 450 BCE, and the bulk of the material is usually dated, in its present form, to the exilic and especially postexilic period of the sixth–fifth centuries BCE. Linguistic evidence may suggest that much of the P material is preexilic (Hurvitz); but, since cultic language tends to be conservative, early dating remains conjectural. The following discussion, with regard to form and theological content, is mainly based on the final form of the Pentateuch (for a source-critical approach, see Knohl and the essay by David Carr in this volume).

Priestly, cultic theology provides the overarching framework of the first four books of the Hebrew Bible; Deuteronomy completes the Pentateuch as a supplement. The Priestly theology ("PTh") represents a reinterpretation of Israel's older cult. It reflects an adaptation to the needs of the small postexilic Jerusalem community. The major new adjustment was to treat the cult, rather than the law, as the central aspect of the covenant with God at Sinai, in contrast to the earlier covenantal traditions. In the Tetrateuch older elements of nonpriestly religion, such as the "Covenant Code" of Exodus 21–23, appear encapsulated by priestly materials, so that the viewpoints of PTh dominate and provide the overall coherence of the work. But the association of cult with creation, basic to the ancient Near Eastern understanding of shrines, rituals and priesthood, is not given up. Rather, it is transmuted into a complex creation theology. Before examining individual aspects of the cult and priesthood, it is necessary to understand this overall structure and its theological framework.

The Priestly work of the Tetrateuch may be divided by basic content into six major sections. The first section, which consists of Genesis 1–11, may be termed the cultic *prehistory* whose central passages are the creation in Genesis 1:1–2:4a and the flood narrative of Genesis 6–9. The second section consists of the patriarchal narrative, in which the key P passage is the *covenant with Abraham* and his descendants. The third section is the account of the *Exodus*, the climax of which for P is the institution of the Passover sacrifice and the regulation of the festival of Unleavened Bread. The fourth and lengthiest section is the *Sinai revelation*, which for P consists primarily of the laws of the tabernacle and the sacrificial cult. The fifth section is the appointment of the house of Aaron to be the sole *legitimate priesthood* (Num. 17:21–26). The sixth section is a supplement including material from the "Holiness tradition," discussed in detail below.

In PTh's presentation, leading ideas appear in patterns of associations and recurring images rather than in explicit statements. The two most important of these involve light and blood: for example, the "Glory" (*kābōd*) of God, a refulgent light phenomenon representing the divine presence, and other manifestations of light in the cult, such as the fire on the altar, the menorah and the eternal light; and the blood of sacrifice, which effects atonement. Imagery involving light and blood reflects an epistemology that emphasizes the visual faculty. The result is a theology of allusions, associations, and other literary devices, the effect of which is more emotional than intellectual (see Edward Greenstein's essay in this volume). The Pentateuch thus presents a literary-religious program, an ideal of a cult, not the description of one that had actually existed earlier.

Cultic Prehistory: Creation and Flood

The first section is introduced by the creation story. PTh has written an account of origins, rejecting what seems to have been the older Israelite view of creation as the result of combat between Yahweh and a watery, sea-monster foe variously termed Leviathan, Tannin, Snake, River, Sea, or Tehom (Smith; see also the essays by Mark Smith and Neal Walls in this volume). It substitutes a process of ordering by divine commands, consisting of divisions and discriminations. Most significant is the initial creation of visible light as the first act of creation foreshadowing the role of sacred light in the cult.

The view of creation presented in Genesis 1 is related to PTh's later exposition of cult in at least two major ways. One is implicit: the revealed cult, like creation itself, will later be presented as a set of separations and divisions, both intellectual and, in the structure of the shrine and practices of the cult, physical. There will be carefully demarcated degrees of sanctity in all things, especially the shrine and its priesthood. The second way is explicit, although by foreshadowing, for PTh ends the account of creation in Genesis 2:1–4a with the blessing and sanctification of the seventh day on which God "ceased" work (*šābat*), a reference to the Sabbath. The Sabbath as an institution of sacred time will not appear explicitly until the covenantal laws in Exodus, where it is juxtaposed to the passages dealing with the erection of the tabernacle. There the Sabbath is declared to be a "sign" of creation, thereby linking creation to the shrine, sacred time to sacred space. This tactic is an excellent example of the way PTh expresses its ideas indirectly, through allusion and other literary devices. The linking of creation and cult is a feature of ancient Near Eastern priestly thinking also found in the myths of Egypt and Mesopotamia. PTh, however, accepts the viewpoint of developed biblical religion that all institutions, including cult, derive not directly from creation but from revelation in historical time at Sinai/Horeb. Yet while adhering to the new transcendent monotheism of biblical religion, PTh allows something of the ancient bond between created order and cult to be maintained. This creation theology underlies and unifies the entire later treatment of the shrine and cult in the Tetrateuch (see especially Smith).

The second key event to PTh in the introductory prehistory is the flood narrative, which ends with the manifestation of the divine Glory as the rainbow. The bulk of the flood story reflects Mesopotamian traditions, but PTh has bent it to its own theology. In the view of PTh, the flood was a return to the watery chaos that preceded creation, so that the emergence of dry land parallels the withdrawal of the waters at God's command in Genesis 1. Creation is renewed, but the second creation is inferior to the first. This pattern of an original dispensation, its disruption by human sin, and its restoration at a lower level, is used by P as a structuring device. In the original creation, which God had pronounced "very good," there was no consumption of flesh by animals or humans. Under the postdiluvian dispensation, meat eating is allowed, as a concession to human bloody-mindedness (Gen. 9), but blood, the "life" (*nepeš*) of the animal, must not be consumed. This focus on lifeblood anticipates PTh's picture of the Sinaitic sacrificial cult, in which blood is transformed into the means of atonement. The rainbow symbolizes the divine renewal of the world, corresponding to the light of Genesis 1, but also its inferior status, in that the bow is a weapon of war as well as a manifestation of the Glory.

Covenant with Abraham

In the covenant with Abraham and his descendants, a key institution is established in the command to Abraham to circumcise the males of his family (and himself), as a "sign" of the covenant between God and his seed. This is another example of PTh's reinterpretation of older ideas and cultic practices, because almost everywhere it is practiced, circumcision is a rite associated with puberty and sexual fertility (see the enigmatic story in Exodus 4). It is a *pars pro toto* sacrifice, in which the removal of the foreskin is intended to engender increased human fertility. But in PTh the foreskin is of less religious importance than the blood produced by the act. PTh has further disconnected circumcision from its association with sex and procreation by moving the rite close to birth. It is the only blood ritual PTh allows in the period before the Exodus. Abel's sacrifice (Gen. 4) and Noah's sacrifice (Gen. 8) are from another source.

Exodus from Egypt

The third section, the Exodus from Egypt, is mainly focused on the Passover sacrifice, the eating of unleavened bread, and some ancillary cultic matters, such as the status of the first-born as "belonging" to God. These are embedded in PTh's larger theological endeavor.

Sinai Revelation of the Covenant

The covenant focuses on the shrine, its cult and its personnel. The shrine is presented as an elaborate tent, the central function of which was intended to be a place for God to "tabernacle," that is, rest impermanently, in the Holiest Place on the Day of Atonement. The shrine is associated in PTh with the image of light, the divine Glory, a fiery nimbus (as seen in ancient iconography; see the essay by Theodore Lewis in this volume), which entered the Holiest Place of the Tabernacle at its dedication (Exod. 40:34). PTh's understanding of covenant as shrine and cult is laced with references to Genesis 1 and creation. The tabernacle is revealed to Moses as a model (*tabnīt*), a copy of the divine residence in heaven. The expression "Moses completed the commission" (*məlā'kâ*) echoes the phrase in Genesis 2 that "God completed his work (commission)." Light imagery pervades the shrine, especially in the menorah, the eternal light, the fire on the altar and the jewels of the high priest's breastplate. After the Golden Calf apostasy, God diminishes light by prohibiting lighting fires on the Sabbath (Exod. 35:3).

In Leviticus the various types of blood sacrifice are listed and described. The narrative logic may be that Israel proved itself so sinful in making the Golden Calf that God provided some regular means of remediation of sin. The older sacrificial cult is reinterpreted to center on the theological ideas of forgiveness and atonement for sin. This theme reaches its climax in Leviticus 16, the laws of the Day of Atonement, in which blood flung in the Holiest Place of the shrine by the high priest atones for the nation's sins. The atoning effect of sacrificial blood is explicitly described in Leviticus 17:11: "It is the life blood that works atonement." In effect, the older idea of sacrificial meat as food for the deity is replaced by a focus on the blood as a "ritual detergent" (Milgrom, *Leviticus*) cleansing from sin. This atonement is also indirectly linked to creation, because it restores the shrine to the purity of its day of dedication by Moses and Aaron (Lev. 9).

Additional references to creation are in the complex of ritual and purification laws in Leviticus 11–15. The first of these, the laws of permitted and forbidden animals, is a good example of PTh's strategy of theological presentation and imagery. The covenantal language of distinction evokes creation, as in Genesis 1, by making a new differentiation in nature, between animals that may and may not be eaten. The criteria cited involve the sense of sight, through direct empirical observation: only animals that chew the cud and have cloven hooves are allowed. Meat eating has negative connotations, as a concession to humans' propensity for violence (Gen. 9). In the new creation of covenantal cult, meat eating is sanctified by becoming the object of a new distinction, while blood is worked into the cult as the physical means of forgiveness. PTh never associates atonement or forgiveness with prayer, as in the Deuteronomic covenantal and prophetic traditions, but only with blood.

Other topics in Leviticus 12–15 are linked to creation indirectly, and make use of the tropes of sight and blood. Leviticus 12 deals with the purification of the woman made "unclean" by childbirth. Since verse 4 speaks of a rite of "blood purification," it is clearly the flow of blood that must be dealt with by the cult. The impurity engendered by childbirth is also related to the creation theme, in that women create new human life (cf. Gen. 4:1). This is also the case in Leviticus 15, which deals with men's emission of semen and the blood flow of menstruating women. In both cases, the perfection of humanity as the "image of God" seems to be violated, or at least threatened. The rites of the cult overcome the problem. (For other approaches, see especially Douglas; Frymer-Kensky.)

Violation of created human perfection may also be the case in the laws dealing with leprosy (or another skin ailment) in Leviticus 13, and the disfigurement of houses by fungus or mold in Leviticus 14. The diagnosis of the diseases by a priest emphasizes sight, through exact examination of the symptoms. It is significant that it is only this form-destroying disease, apparent to the eye, that is the object of religious horror, to be dealt with by cultic means.

The climax of the priestly cultic system and its underlying theology is in the laws of the Day of Atonement in Leviticus 16, where the categories of creation and forgiveness for sin come together (Geller). In an unparalleled density of sacrificial purification rites the high priest manipulates animal blood to attain forgiveness for the sins of himself, his family and the people as a whole. The special rites of the day are two. One is public, a unique example of vicarious atonement. The high priest places his hands on a goat that is then sent away to the desert, to Azazel. The latter is known from later literature (*1 Enoch*) as a rebellious angel, but in Leviticus his name seems to play on a word for "goat" (*'ēz*), and may indicate a kind of goat demon (note the reference at Lev. 17:7 to pagan gods as "goats"). Most important is that the location of Azazel in the desert, like the ocean before creation, can be used of chaos in the Bible (Deut. 32:10). Sin is thus banished from the world of order to the chaotic, empty desert. This ceremony, of uncertain origin, is thus woven into the creation categories of PTh.

The other rite more central to PTh is the climactic blood ritual. The high priest carries a bowl of sacrificial blood into the Holiest Place and flings it before the divine presence, which was believed to have become immanent in the Holiest Place by coming down from heaven to the throne formed by the cherubim lid of the Ark of the Covenant. How this unique blood rite attains atonement is not stated. On the contrary, it is essential that it remain a mystery of faith. But as the culminating blood rite of the cult it connects to all the other uses of blood in a ritual context. The role of the other main trope in PTh's religious epistemology, sight, is also prominent on the Day of Atonement, because it is only on this occasion that the very presence of God is said to become visible, "seen" in the Holiest Place, if only by the high priest (Lev. 16:2). The coming together in Leviticus 16 of the central interest of PTh in sin and atonement, with the dominant images of blood and the faculty of sight, mark the Day of Atonement as the supreme ritual act of re-creation.

The central ritual events in the five sections of the Tetrateuch as formed by PTh may be reduced to three: (1) the completion of the shrine (Exod. 40), built according to the model of the heavenly palace and linked to creation, especially by the Sabbath; (2) the main rituals of the cult ending with the dedication of the shrine in Leviticus 9, and the initiation of the ritual cult, confirmed by the descent of the divine "Glory" into the Holiest Place; and (3) the purification and renewal of shrine and cult in the yearly cultic-creation rite by which shrine, and cosmos, were restored to the state of being "very good," as creation was when perfect (Gen. 1:31). The theological structure of PTh is essentially complete in Leviticus 16. The fifth section of PTh, dealing with the Aaronic priesthood, is so large and complex, it will be discussed separately below.

Supplement and Commentary: HPTh

The rest of Leviticus and Numbers may be viewed mainly as supplementary to the dominant structure represented by the four sections listed above. Leviticus 17–26, the most important of these supplements, is assigned by scholars to a separate but related stream of priestly tradition, the "Holiness School" ("H"), which is dated earlier than P by some, but later by most (see especially Knohl). The completed work H acts as a supplement and partial commentary on PTh. Its theological climax is its definition of holiness at the end of chapter 20 (see below). Since it is a supplement to PTh, we shall refer to it as HPTh. Leviticus 17 with its emphasis on blood as atonement serves as an introduction to this pericope, and as a link to chapter 16.

The Definition of Holiness

Leviticus 18–20 forms a special section within HPTh. Chapters 18 and 20 form an envelope around chapter 19, which contains quite different material. Chapter 18 deals primarily with forbidden sexual relations, described as Canaanite perversions that resulted in that people's being "spewed out" by the land, which was then given to Israel.

Chapter 19 begins with an admonition to Israel to "be holy, as I, Yahweh, your God, am holy." Holiness is thus presented as a form of *imitatio dei*. There follows a series of commandments, some of which are cultic, but most of which are ethical in nature, echoing the Ten Commandments, and including the famous command to "love thy neighbor as thyself." Holiness is defined in terms of moral action, a fact that earlier led to H's being ascribed to prophetic influence (cf. Isa. 1:11–12), though demands for right action and thoughts were also aspects of ancient cultic tradition (see, e.g., Ps. 15 and 24). The logical relationship between the lengthy list of sexual crimes in chapter 18 and the moral requirements listed in chapter 19 is not clear. Chapter 20 clarifies the relationship, tying HPTh's argument together and offering a complex definition of holiness.

Chapter 20 begins with another list of crimes involving the family. The first is a longer exposition of the prohibition of offering children to Molech (probably a form of Baal), followed by an injunction not to consult ghosts and "familiar spirits," probably dead members of the family and ancient heroes. Verse 9 prohibits mistreating one's parents, completing a triad, children/living parents/ancestors. However, the bulk of the prohibitions (vv. 10–21) deal with the same kind of forbidden sexual relations as in chapter 18, forming an envelope.

The end of chapter 20 (vv. 22–26) offers the climactic definition of holiness, drawing together the sexual crimes of chapters 18 and 20 and the moral demand to "be holy as I … am holy" in chapter 19. The definition emerges not as a logical construct but literarily, through a juxtaposition of themes (see Edward Greenstein's essay in this volume). The sequence begins with a description of God as the one "who separated you from the nations." The text continues with the demand that Israel, for its part, separate clean from unclean animals for consumption, which God has "separated out" for them. The final statement is "You shall be holy to me, for I, Yahweh, am holy, who has separated you from the nations." The implication is Israel's separation from the nations must be maintained by the laws of forbidden and permitted animals and, of course, all the other ritual laws. By acts of separation, which themselves evoke God's acts of creation in Genesis 1, Israel displays its holiness, and thereby imitates God's holiness. This applies above all to the sexual distinctions that form the main topic in chapters 18 and 20. The HPTh definition of holiness as separation and acts of distinction is central to the theology and cultic structure of PTh as a whole, which is presumably why it appears as a supplement to PTh proper. The HPTh definition of holiness as separation and distinction is reflected in the layout of the shrine with its areas of ascending holiness, in the hierarchical divisions of the priests and Levites (see Jenson), in the functions of the sacrifices, the festivals and, above all, the Sabbath day, separated from the other days of the week, and in the status of the nation of Israel, distinguished from its neighbors by the covenantal mark of circumcision. This ritualistic and priestly view of holiness contrasts strongly with the viewpoint that associated holiness with God's "Glory filling the earth" (Isa. 6:3), and with the prophetic view associating holiness with righteousness (Isa. 5:16; see Robert Wilson's essay in this volume). This exclusionary view of holiness also reflects the particular historical and religious situation of the restored Judean community in the mid-fifth century BCE, when the Pentateuch was promulgated (see the essay by Charles Carter in this volume).

The Sacrificial Cult

The central rite of the biblical cult as presented by P in the Tetrateuch was animal sacrifice (Anderson). Nonanimal sacrifices consisted mainly of a meal offering (*minḥâ*, "gift") and offerings such as the first fruits. In other ancient religions, sacrifices were viewed as food for the deities. In the Akkadian flood story the famished gods, deprived of sustenance by the extermination of humanity, are pictured crowding around the first sacrifice after the flood "like flies." The biblical sacrificial cult still contains terms that seem to point to the rationale of sacrifice as food for the deity, for instance, the "pleasing aroma" (*rēaḥ niḥōaḥ*) of the smoke of burning meat, and the "bread of the Presence," set out daily before the deity in the shrine. But in PTh the "bread of the Presence" means not food for God, but rather food provided by God for Israel. Its etiology may be in the manna story in Exodus 16, where a container of the providential, heaven-sent bread is set out before the shrine as a memorial of the event. There is no hint that God eats manna.

Sacrificial rituals are multilayered in meaning. What the rationale was in earlier biblical religion we cannot know. However, in the sacrificial cult presented by PTh in Leviticus 1–4 and elsewhere, the primary reason for sacrifices is forgiveness and atonement (Janowski). The atoning ritual substance is not the meat, which in the case of expiatory offerings is either burnt as an offering to the deity or eaten by the priests in the shrine, but rather the blood of the animal, which must be manipulated in certain carefully prescribed ways.

Milgrom maintains that the blood of sacrifice acts as a "ritual detergent" to purge sin. He argues that the effect of the purgation offering (*ḥaṭṭā't*) is not to remove sin itself, but rather to counter the effect of sin on the offerer and the nation as a whole. Sin forms a "miasma" that is attracted to the shrine and, if left unpurged, would block the cult (Milgrom, *Studies*, 77). The rites of the Day of Atonement, in Milgrom's opinion, remove whatever miasma has accumulated in the past year that has escaped cleansing by the regular rituals of the cult. Milgrom rejects any direct link between blood manipulation and forgiveness for sin, despite the fact that Leviticus 17:11 seems to offer precisely such an explanation. If the ritual laws are viewed as part of a literary-theological complex including the narratives of Genesis, a rationale for blood does emerge. The key passage is Genesis 9, where the deity allows humans to consume meat provided they avoid the blood, in which lies the "life" of the animal. This permission is a concession to human sinfulness. But in the Sinai cult the same forbidden substance is transformed into the agent to purge humans of their sin, a reversal typical of cultic thinking.

In the Tetrateuch the animal sacrifices are the *'ōlâ*, the "burnt" or "whole offering" (in older translations, "holocaust"), the *šelem* (usually plural *šəlāmîm*), the "well-being offering" (older "peace offering"), the *ḥaṭṭā't*, the "purification" or "purgation offering" (earlier "sin offering") and the *'āšām*, the "reparation offering" (earlier "guilt offering" or "trespass offering"). All of these offerings are mentioned in earlier sources in the Bible, and have equivalents in the Ugaritic and Phoenician ritual lists. The burnt offering was entirely consumed by fire on the altar, but parts of the other meat sacrifices were the due of the priests. The difference between the purgation and reparation offerings is by no means clear, since there is overlap. Both were primarily for unintended sins which later became known to the individual or the community. However, the reparation offering seems to have been intended primarily for misuse of sacred property and therefore represented an "encroachment" on the divine (Milgrom, *Cult*). The Aaronide priests alone were allowed to eat the two expiatory sacrifices, after burning the fat and offal on the altar, a meal that had to take place in the sacred precincts. The ritual eating of these sacrifices was an aspect of the rituals of expiation and forgiveness of sin, and was therefore a kind of sacrament (Janowski). The well-being offerings were communal meals for the sacrificer and his family, but priests were assigned the right thigh and the breast, which might be consumed anywhere (Lev. 7; 10:12–15). In addition, priests were to receive most of the grain offering, as well as the first fruits of crops and flocks and tithes. The well-being sacrifice was prescribed for ceremonies of thanksgiving (*tôdâ*) and in the contexts of oaths (*neder*), a special type of which was the Nazirite oath. These functions of the well-being offering are certainly old, and played a major role in the religions of preexilic Israel and Judah.

Priesthood in the Tetrateuch

There could be no topic so important to the priestly writers as the origin and status of the priesthood itself. Yet there is a strange dichotomy in the Priestly narrative in regard to Aaron, the brother of Moses. On the one hand we have the exaltation of Aaron and his sons as the only legitimate priests, in opposition to the other members of the tribe of Levi, and on the other the fact that Aaron himself is a sinner, who made the Golden Calf. In the aftermath of that egregious apostasy, it is the Levites who rally to Moses and distinguish themselves by their zeal (Exod. 32). Yet later in the Pentateuch the Levites are demoted to being cultic servants of the Aaronide priests. A source-critical answer might be that Exodus 32, the account of Aaron's sin and the Levite zeal, is a document reflecting, not P, but sources opposed to the Aaronic priesthood, and supporting the Levites against them. We know there was such a struggle from the later seventh–fifth century, as reflected especially in Ezekiel 44. If, however, P is the redactor of the Tetrateuch as a whole one must still ask whether his inclusion of a story so destructive of Aaron, and by extension, the priesthood, was a mere oversight, or whether there was some larger theological issue. It appears there was a conflict between the ideal and the real: in this case, between the priests as the humans closest to God, in a state of holy separateness greater than ordinary mortals, and priests as humans, also subject to corruption and sin.

This theological tension is presented in the Tetrateuch in two threads: one involves the individual, Aaron, and the other, a more complex one, involves his descendants, the Aaronides and the priesthood as a whole. The Aaronic track consists of just two narratives. The first is Exodus 32, where Aaron sins in making the Golden Calf. This represents the pole of reality. Numbers 25 presents the opposite pole of the ideal. Here, people have abandoned Yahweh for Baal Peor, but Aaron's zealous grandson Phinehas intervenes, punishes the most egregious miscreant, and receives an eternal covenant for his priestly descendants.

The Aaronide track is more complicated, and consists of two major complexes of narratives and laws, one presented in Leviticus, the other in Numbers. The Leviticus pattern deals with the failure of the priests to live up to the divine ideal of priesthood. The Numbers pattern centers on the relationship between priests and Levites, which threatens the whole people with destruction and death. The overall movement both in Leviticus and Numbers is of increasing priestly exposure to danger, even as the holiness of the priests is confirmed and increased. A new equation is thereby established. Above we saw that the main theological endeavor of PTh was to set up the equation holiness = separation. The new equation is: holiness = danger. The theological message is that holiness is the medium of blessing for the people as a whole, but, simultaneously, holiness is a source of extreme danger to the priests themselves. PTh attempts to deal with this by presenting a set of rituals for the Day of Atonement in Leviticus 16 in which the sins of the priests and the people are purged, and, in Numbers 19, a ritual for purifying Israel from contact with the dead. Finally, PTh ends the entire narrative in Numbers 25 by combining the "Aaronic" and "Aaronide" threads to link the role and status of the priesthood to the track involving Aaron's apostasy and Phinehas's zeal. The final effect is to counter the general gloom of the picture of the priesthood in Leviticus and Numbers by a positive image, the covenant with Phinehas that counteracts Aaron's apostasy at Sinai. The whole priestly work thus ends on a priestly messianic note, looking forward to the Jerusalem temple and its Zadokite priesthood. We will now follow this complex structure in more detail.

The Aaronide Pattern: Exodus and Leviticus

An ideal stage in the Aaronide pattern is represented by the role assigned Aaron and his sons as priests in the first Sinai revelation of the cult (Exod. 25–31 and 35–40). This revelation is part of the heavenly model of the Tabernacle that God gives to Moses. It is clear that the high priest is a quasi-royal figure, since like kings he is anointed and his vestments and headdress are described as kingly. It is usually said that the description of Aaron as high priest reflects the theocratic priestly state of restored Judah after the exile, but as it stands in the Pentateuch, the function of Exodus 25–31 and 35–40 is to set up the divinely ordained ideal of the priesthood.

In this narrative thread, the disruption of the ideal of the priesthood is not in the tale of Aaron's apostasy in Exodus 32, which belongs to the other, Aaronic-Phinehas track, but rather in the ceremonies surrounding the dedication of the tabernacle in Leviticus 8–10. In the elaborate inaugural rites, where Aaron's, and the priesthood's, star seems to be at its apogee, a dreadful moment of disruption occurs: Aaron's two oldest sons, Nadab and Abihu, offer "strange fire," probably an unauthorized incense offering, and are incinerated by the divine fire. At its very beginning the priesthood is tainted by death. God's warning that he "must be sanctified by my holy ones" (Lev. 10:3) is an introduction to the danger of holiness.

The Aaronide Pattern: Numbers

In Numbers the narrative focuses on the relationship between Aaronide priests and Levites. At the time Aaron sinned by making the Golden Calf, the rest of the Levitical tribe rallied to God and punished the miscreants, all except Aaron himself. Their zeal extended even to killing their own brethren. In Numbers 3–4, the relationship between Aaronide priests and the rest of the Levites is clearly demarcated. The chapter opens with a reminder of the fate of Nadab and Abihu, as a link to the pattern in Leviticus, and a reminder that the pattern in Numbers starts where Leviticus left off: the pall of death already hovers over the priesthood. In Numbers 3, the situation will darken further. Moses is commanded to cause the tribe (*maṭṭeh*, "staff") of Levi to approach Aaron and stand before him as his, and the priesthood's, servants (*wəšērətū 'ôtô*). The Levites are to be "given" to the priests (Num. 3:9). The term used, doubled for emphasis, *nətūnîm nətūnîm*, "given ones, given ones," echoes the term *nātîn*, "one given," or devoted to the cult, a lower class of cultic functionary than the priests. The Levites are to do the maintenance work in the Tabernacle and guard its sacred vessels. The passage ends with the admonition, "the stranger who approaches (to serve in the cult) must be killed," language that evokes the fiery fate of Nadab and Abihu. The atmosphere of danger is increased in Numbers 3:11–13. The Levites stand in place of the first-born of the Israelites, who "belong" to God because the killing of the first-born of Egypt made the first-born of Israel open to danger as well. The Israelites are now freed by the substitution of the Levites.

The rest of Numbers 3 describes the duties of the Levites at the shrine. The patriarch Levi had three sons: Gershon, Kohath and Merari. The descendants of each are now given specific tasks in the shrine, but only the Kohathites may handle the most central and sacred objects: the ark, table, lampstand, altars and other sacred utensils. It is important to notice that in Numbers 3–4 the Aaronides appear not only as sole priests, but also as a clan of Levites. When the tabernacle is to be dismantled for travel, only the Aaronides, under the supervision of Eleazar, Aaron's son, can pack up the holiest vessels. The rest of the Kohathites must not be put in danger by approaching the most sacred things. They, like the Gershonites and Merarites, are allowed to handle such things as the curtains, poles and other appurtenances of the cult. Aaron's son and heir, Eleazar, is to be head of the Levites, in his capacity as a Kohathite, at the same time as he was destined for the high priesthood. In summary, a hierarchy is produced with ordinary Levites at the bottom, Kohathite Levites above them, and Aaronide Kohathites at the top.

The next element in the narrative pattern, a disruption by sin, is the rebellion of Korah in Numbers 16. The story of Korah's rebellion appears to be a composite of two originally separate challenges to Moses and Aaron. One is secular, involving the elders Dathan and Abiram, who presumably challenge the authority of Moses as sole leader. The other challenge involves Korah, of the Kohathite clan of Levites, and seems originally to have been directed against Aaron. The essential aspect of the challengers' claim is that all of Israel is holy, and Moses and Aaron have no right to "raise themselves above" the rest of Israel. On the surface, this claim is supported by the declaration that Israel as a whole is to be a "holy nation, a kingdom of priests" (Exod. 19:6). Moses and Aaron, however, regard the Levites' actions as a challenge to their authority and that of the Aaronide priests. Moses sets up a test, which again involves fire, specifically in the form of incense censers. The challenge is severe enough to require a new act of creation (*bərî'â*, Num. 16:30). The earth opens and Korah and his family, along with Dathan and

Abiram, fall into the chasm. But a fiery punishment, as in Leviticus 10, is also present, for a flame goes forth from God that consumes 250 men of the rebels offering incense. So the authority of Moses and of Aaron as priest is maintained.

The restoration of Aaron's priestly leadership follows, and his supremacy over the other Levites is established (Numbers 17). Yet immediately there is a new challenge. The people accuse Moses and Aaron of having brought death on the whole nation (Num. 17:6). God is so angry that he threatens to destroy the whole community, except for Moses and Aaron. In fact, he does send a plague that kills many. Aaron steps into the breach, the only time in his career that he does so. He takes a firepan, puts incense on it and stands between the dying and the rest of the people threatened by the plague. He makes expiation for them, so that only 14,700 (!) die.

Aaron's supremacy is finally confirmed by a new creative act. The head of each tribe is told to bring his staff (*maṭṭeh*) of leadership to the shrine. Aaron also does so as head of the tribe of Levi. The next day the staff of Aaron is found to have sprouted blossoms and almonds and is to be preserved in the shrine as a warning to any future rebels. The miracle wrought for Aaron technically confirms only the dominance of the Levites as a whole in the cult, but Aaron's supremacy over the rest of the Levites is implied.

So Aaron is restored and confirmed, but his restoration is at a lower level, because the level of danger to him and the priesthood as a whole is raised. The people are now even more fearful, and again cry out, "We are doomed to die! Anyone who even comes near the shrine dies!" The divine response increases the danger to the priesthood even beyond previous levels. God declares that Aaron and his sons alone are to bear any guilt connected to the sanctuary (Num. 18:1). The priests are to be sin magnets, as it were. By the end of this section, in Numbers 18, holiness is concentrated in the family of Aaron, but they are also uniquely liable to death for sins against God's holiness.

The relationship between leadership and doom is illustrated in Numbers 20. Moses and Aaron are both condemned to die for not having "sanctified" God before the Israelites. Asked to produce water for the thirsty people, Moses strikes a rock and says, "Shall we (i.e., Aaron and I) bring forth water for you?" They encroach upon God's sole authority over such miracles. God, at least, interprets their action as an act of rebellion. He does not smite them on the spot, but Aaron dies by the end of the chapter, and Moses is doomed to death before he can enter the Promised Land.

The pallor of death over the entire institution of the priesthood and the fear of the people at having such a dangerously holy God in their midst leads P to attempt a partial cultic repair and mitigation. Numbers 19 provides a parallel to Leviticus 16, the laws of the Day of Atonement. In Numbers 19, the focus is the contamination produced by contact with death. Laws are provided allowing those who touch a corpse, or anyone or anything polluted by death, to return to cultic purity. The medium of transformation is a concoction whose basic ingredient is ashes, produced by sacrificing and burning a red heifer (*pārâ 'ădummâ*). The redness echoes *dām*, "blood," and its expiating effect in the cult. Sprinkled on the impure, it removes the pollution of contact with death, at least temporarily, enabling the priests themselves to officiate in the cult, and the people as a whole to avoid the divine penalty imposed for contact with the dead. The placement of this chapter after the tumultuous events of Numbers 16–18 should be interpreted as PTh's attempt to lessen the gloom of its picture of the priesthood.

The final passage in the complex pattern constructed by the Priestly writer is in Numbers 25. At the end of the wandering in the wilderness, Israel duplicates its initial apostasy with the Golden Calf by worshipping Baal Peor, just before they are to enter the Promised Land. As part of the idolatrous celebration an Israelite has intercourse with a Moabite woman in public sight. Moses and all Israel stand by ineffectually, "weeping at the entrance of the Tent of Meeting," as the miscreants engage in (probably ritual) sex. Only one man intervenes, displaying the zeal of the Levites over the Golden Calf: Phinehas, the son of Eleazar, Aaron's heir. Phinehas himself will become high priest in the next generation. His act of zeal (*qin'â*) averts God's wrathful zeal, thus expiating their crime. In reward, God makes an eternal "covenant of peace" (*bərît šālôm*) with Phinehas and his descendants.

As noted above, in Numbers 25 the covenant with Phinehas contrasts with Aaron's gross breach of covenant in Exodus 32. The structure of Israelite apostasy–priestly reaction is intended to form an editorial frame around the desert period. In Exodus 32, however, the priest, Aaron, fails the test of zeal and loyalty (though the other Levites do not), and in Numbers Phinehas passes it. So a positive note concludes a pattern which portrays the priesthood as ever more exposed to danger and death. The eternal priestly covenant with Phinehas and his descendants may be viewed as the final and permanent repair of the defects in the ideal of the priesthood and the breach of covenant by the Aaronide founder in Exodus 32. Both threads, Aaronic and Aaronide, are brought together, completed and transcended by an ultimate repair that, unlike the Day of Atonement rituals (Leviticus 16) and the cultic rules of purification from contact with death (Numbers 19), is not temporary in its effect but permanent.

This new commitment by God also solves a dilemma. The cultic order of shrine and priesthood, revealed at Sinai before Aaron's apostasy, is an "eternal covenant" that cannot be abrogated even by an act of apostasy. It can only be overlaid by another eternal covenant, in this case with Phinehas and his descendants. Significantly, the main descendant of Phinehas and prime inheritor of his covenant of peace was to be Zadok, chief priest of Zion in Jerusalem under Solomon. According to the books of Samuel and Kings, Zadok displaced the sinful Elide priesthood, descendants of Aaron's other surviving son, Ithamar, to become high priests of the temple in Jerusalem under Solomon and his successors. The use of the term *šālôm*, "peace," for the promise to Phinehas evokes the name of Jerusalem, a city otherwise not mentioned in the entire Pentateuch, as well as the builder of the later temple there, Solomon (*šəlômô*). In a sense, a priestly messianic covenant corresponds to the royal messianic covenant. When royal leaders prove to be unworthy, the covenant cannot be abrogated, but is transformed by the prophets into an eternal promise that a perfectly worthy king would arise in the future. Phinehas is a priestly equivalent of David, and the eternal covenant with him looks forward to the later relationship between kings and priests in Jerusalem.

What larger theological messages did the priestly editors have in mind? First we shall consider the answer to the question with which we began: How can the founder of the priesthood, the source of its legitimacy, be presented as so passive, and in the case of the Golden Calf narrative, so sinful? One answer is historical, reflecting the age in which the priestly writers edited the Pentateuch, the sixth–fifth centuries BCE, a particularly tense era in which Persians gave political authority to a high priest and Persian governor, not to a native king (see Charles Carter's essay in this volume). As the books of Ezra and Nehemiah show, there was political, social and religious struggle on all levels of society. The mood of the age, as expressed in the speeches of Ezra (Ezra 9 and Neh. 9), was dark and threatened. To many, the Second Temple was a mere shadow of the first (Ezra 4:12). Ezra says that the Jews have but a tent peg in the holy land, a mere fraction of their preexilic glory. To maintain even that, total religious purity was necessary, lest the people sin again and be totally extinguished. Ezra was a priest and shared the viewpoints of P: purity and holiness were defined as strict separation of Jews from Gentiles and even Jews from other Jews, if they were thought to be polluted by foreignness.

In this atmosphere, inner-priestly struggles also became bitter. For a century, since the Deuteronomic reform of 621 BCE, the Aaronide priesthood of the Jerusalem shrine had claimed sole legitimacy. Priests of other shrines had been demoted, proclaimed to be ordinary Levites (cf. Ezek. 44). By the fifth century BCE the victory of the Aaronides was complete, but a problem still remained. Aaron had two surviving sons, Eliezer and Ithamar. Both were legitimately Aaronic, but the branch of the family represented by the high priests of the Jerusalem temple were descended only from Eliezer through Phinehas and Zadok. The only legitimate high priests were Zadokite. Descendants of Ithamar no doubt rebelled against this and continued their claims on the high priesthood. The authors of PTh were supporters of the Zadokites and present the priestly founder Aaron as a sinner, replacing him with his grandson Phinehas, the ancestor of Zadok, the model of an ideal priest, thus addressing contemporary inner-priestly struggles.

This historical explanation for the behavior of Aaron in the story of the Golden Calf does not, however, explain why the priestly writers use literary patterns characterized by an ever darkening sense of doom. Rather, these patterns have deep theological meaning in PTh's understanding of the priesthood and its religious standing, both in society and in the cosmos. Two critical themes emerge. The first is the priestly concept of holiness, which involves not only separation and exclusion, but also fear and danger. Even in the ideal presentation of the priesthood in Exodus 28, mention is made of the threat of death if the priests perform their functions incorrectly (v. 43). Yet contact with God's dangerous holiness allows blessing and its benefits to flow to the people. Priests are like workers in a nuclear power plant: a dangerous but crucial job.

The other theological aspect of the pattern has to do with PTh's position in relation to biblical religion. The dominant theology of the Pentateuch is covenantal, the Deuteronomic revelation of law to Israel at Sinai/Horeb. The religion of ancient Israel is tied to historical events in the real world. At the same time, priestly religions in the ancient world were viewed as timeless, rooted in the origin of the cosmos. The priestly writers share this viewpoint, as is made clear by their extensive use of creation theology in the Tetrateuch in regard to the Sabbath and the temple. To be sure, the ideal of the priesthood was revealed only at Sinai, in history, but as part of a heavenly, and therefore timeless, pattern presented by God. The term "eternal law" is used of the priestly and cultic order (cf. Exod. 28:43), something never said about the covenant in the Deuteronomic texts. The treatment of priesthood and cult in the Tetrateuch explains how the original, perfect ideal gradually became real through time. In this process the ideal was inevitably sullied, yet its original authority remains. A priest may be a sinner but he is still a priest, and may function as such.

The complicated and lengthy presentation of priests and Levites in the Tetrateuch is thus a prime site for PTh's expression of its theology and is, in fact, a predominantly theological document. After the Pentateuch was canonized, its regulations became the normative manual for the Second Temple. There the priests scrupulously followed the rules set out in the Torah. But the now sacred text was originally a programmatic ideal and expression of theology. It was not the description of a cult that had once existed but rather of one that should exist in the future.

Historical Reconstruction: Cult and Priesthood in Israelite and Judean Religions

We can now turn to the issue of what elements of the complex theological work of PTh in the Tetrateuch might actually reflect earlier religions of the small states of Israel (ca. 900–722 BCE) and Judah (ca. 900(?)–586 BCE) or earlier periods. To answer this question one must examine the sparse internal biblical evidence, archaeological finds and cross-cultural comparisons.

Yahweh was certainly the national deity both of northern Israel and southern Judah. The Israelite and Judean onomastica show little sign of deities other than Yahweh (Tigay). However, centralization of worship, so key to developed biblical religion, was not a feature either of the Israelite or the Judean cult. To be sure, both Israel and Judah had major shrines, supported by the monarchy (cf. Amos 7). In the north these were the shrines of Dan, which seemingly claimed a priesthood descended from Moses' son Gershom (see Judg. 18:30) and Bethel. 1 Kings 11 states that the cult at these royal shrines was established by the first king of northern Israel, Jeroboam, whom the Bible considers to be an apostate to idolatry. He set up two "calves" to be worshipped (the story of the Golden Calf in Exodus 32 reflects this event), and established a non-Aaronide priesthood. This view of the northern shrines and their cult as heretical reflects the prejudices of developed biblical religion. Most scholars think that the calves, that is, young bulls, were likely an animal pedestal for the deity to stand on when he descended to earth, on the model of Canaanite and Mesopotamian deities (see Theodore Lewis's essay in this volume). Thus the calves were the northern equivalent of the cherub throne that formed the lid of the ark in the Jerusalem temple.

Little is known of the cult in the royal shrines in the north, but the cult in the Judean Jerusalem temple seems to have been centered on the Davidic royal dynasty, with a focus on the eternal divine covenantal promise to the founder of the monarchy (2 Sam. 7; Ps. 89). As in the north, the Jerusalem temple on Mount Zion was viewed as a royal shrine, described in terms that are drawn, or inherited, from Canaanite mythology. The priesthood was Zadokite, and seems to have claimed descent from the Canaanite priest-king of pre-Israelite Jerusalem, Melchizedek (Gen. 14; Ps. 110). The Aaronic genealogy presented in the Pentateuch is likely much later. The Jerusalem temple was built by Phoenicians, and was a typical Canaanite structure in regard to its layout, furniture and, perhaps, ritual. The ark of the covenant, placed by David in the Holiest Place of the Zion temple, had been a kind of tribal palladium, carried into battle at the head of the tribal levies and linked to the practice of holy war (see, e.g., Deut. 20; Num. 31).

Outside the royal shrines, and for the majority of people, religious life centered on the cult of the "high places" (*bāmôt*) and local temples, such as that excavated at Arad in Judah (Zevit). Images as such seemed to have played no role in the cult of the royal shrines or the *bāmôt*, and there is a chance that Israelite religion was aniconic from an early period, though Judges 17–18 may describe an early image of Yahweh at Dan (see the essay by Theodore Lewis in this volume). Shrines had cultic pillars (*maṣṣēbôt*) and wooden poles (*'ăšērîm*) which were later viewed as idolatrous by biblical writers, as indeed were all local shrines after the centralization of worship in 621 BCE (see the essay by Elizabeth Bloch-Smith in this volume). Earlier, however, they seem to have been quite normal and acceptable (Exod. 20:24 even seems to mandate a plurality of altars). The wooden poles may have represented the tree of life and have been connected to the worship of the old Canaanite fertility goddess Asherah, who some even think may have been Yahweh's consort; but the supposed inscriptional evidence for this supposition is weak (Dever; see the essay by Elizabeth Bloch-Smith in this volume). One special image, the bronze snake (*nəḥuštān*), was even set up in the Jerusalem temple, and was removed only late in the eighth century BCE.

The cult of the local shrines seems to have involved sacrifice, of which the best attested are the communal meals. 1 Samuel recounts a yearly pilgrimage and sacrifice at the shrine of Shiloh, followed by such a communal sacrificial meal (*zebaḥ hayyāmîm*). Pilgrimages were made to shrines, sacrifices of thanksgiving offered, and communal meals eaten in the circle of one's family and friends. Such customs and beliefs seem to lie behind many of the "psalms of the individual" in the Psalter, although in their present form most such psalms are later and much reinterpreted. The Nazirite vow, described in Numbers 6, allows men and women to assume temporarily a special status as devotees. Cults of the dead may also have been practiced at local shrines. These rites involving a special communal meal with or for the dead (*marzēaḥ*) are attested at Ugarit and elsewhere, but references in the Bible are few (Amos 6:7; Jer. 16:5) and polemical in nature. Even more obscure is the role of child sacrifice, a custom known among the Phoenicians and later Carthaginians. The Bible calls it "making children pass through the fire to Molech." Biblical religion proscribed the practice, but the prophets claim that it was not infrequent, most notoriously at the tophet of Jerusalem in the Valley of Ben Hinnom. Whether the practice ever actually formed a part of Yahwism is unknown, but statements that all first-born "belong to Yahweh" may originally have meant that one acquired special merit by offering them.

Festivals

Pilgrimages were made to shrines on the three festivals enjoined by the old cultic calendars in Exodus 23 and 34: Passover-Unleavened Bread, Weeks and Booths, each of which was associated with a harvest (barley, wheat, and fruit and wine, respectively). Scholars can only speculate on the precise nature of such ritual activities. The "Songs of Ascents" in the Book of Psalms (Ps. 120–135) are often held to reflect pilgrimages, but the songs themselves are very late. Of the three major feasts, the best attested is Passover-Unleavened Bread. The largest body of laws concerning Passover is in Exodus

12–13, composed by the priestly writers, which conflicts in many regards with the version in Deuteronomy 16. The earlier history of the festival is conjectural. The dominant scholarly viewpoint is that Passover and Unleavened Bread were originally two separate cultic events, which at some stage became conjoined. Passover (*pesaḥ*) is likely related to the meaning of the root in the sense of "protect" (cf. Isa. 31:5), and in English would be more accurately termed "Watchover" than "Passover." The term originally was applied only to the sacrifice of a lamb or kid, held on the evening of the fourteenth of the first month, Abib (later Nissan). It is often conjectured that in pre-Israelite times the ritual event was an apotropaic sacrifice by shepherds, who offered a lamb on the full moon of the month in which they left winter pastures for summer ones. The offering was to ward off demons and other dangers on the journey. The later development of the tradition of an Exodus journey from Egypt made a good fit with the old tradition. In contrast, the eating of unleavened bread (*maṣṣôt*) marked a kind of Lent, a seven-day abstention from normal bread to eat the "bread of poverty" (Deut. 16:3). It is often supposed that it was a festival of settled farmers, marking the first harvest of the agricultural year, that of barley, from which the unleavened cakes would presumably have been made.

Weeks (*šābū'ôt*) was observed as a one-day pilgrimage feast 50 days ("Pentecost") after Passover-Unleavened Bread. It marked the wheat harvest and in the Pentateuch has no historical connection. The notion that it commemorates revelation, specifically the giving of the Ten Commandments on Sinai, is later. Booths (*sukkôt*) was held for seven days beginning with the fifteenth of the seventh month (the full moon), later Tishri. It marked the fruit and especially wine harvest. The historical link given by P is minimal: the temporary huts constructed for the festival supposedly commemorated the flimsy structures built by the Israelites in the Sinai desert. In fact, the booths were originally made to protect the vineyards.

Uncertainty surrounds the Sabbath, so central to the creation theology of PTh (Niels-Erik Andreasen). There is no evidence for a weekly Sabbath earlier than the late texts of the Pentateuch. The few references to it in earlier documents, such as the historical and prophetic literature, link it to the new moon (cf. 2 Kings 4:23). It is possible that the Sabbath is derived from a full moon ritual occasion, like the probably cognate Mesopotamian *šapattu*. If so, its observance and its prominence in PTh is entirely later and reflects developed biblical religion only, not its ancestor in Israelite and Judean religions.

The Priesthood

The origins of the priesthood are obscure. The distinction made in the Tetrateuch between the family of Aaron and the rest of the tribe of Levi represents the latest stage of the development in the fifth century BCE. Deuteronomy reflects an earlier situation, immediately following the Deuteronomic reform. It seems to know of no real distinction between priests and Levites. It regularly uses the term "Levitical priests" (*kōhănîm ləwiyyîm*) and represents the Levites as a clerical class dependent on donations for support, which the later Tetrateuch regularizes as a complex system of tithes (see the essay by Bernard Levinson and Tina Sherman in this volume). Cities were set aside for the Levites, where they had special grazing rights. It is clear that the clergy is privileged in theory and yet, not being part of the tribal system, is practically indigent and the object of charity.

The Hebrew term for "priest," *kōhēn,* seems to be the same as Arabic *kāhin,* a kind of seer. It does seem that priests offered oracles at shrines in response to people's queries. Another priestly function in the early period was to cast the Urim and Thummim, a kind of dice, which could give only a yes or no answer to a query. By the time of the Tetrateuch the Urim and Thummim became stones set into the breastplate of the high priest.

The etymology of Levite (*lēwî*) is unknown. It may be related to the root *lāwâ,* which has two basic meanings, "to accompany" and "to borrow, lend." The former sense would seem to refer to the Levites as assistants of the priests; but this status is very late. The other sense is perhaps more likely, implying that the Levite is "lent" to God, like Samuel. This interpretation may be supported by the fact that in Numbers the Levites are said to be "given" to God. It is also possible that the term Levite has no connection, except in later folk etymology, with either sense of the root *lāwâ.* The Bible claims there was originally a secular tribe of Levi, one of Jacob's sons, which was quite vigorous, even militaristic, aiding Simeon in the slaughter of the Canaanite Shechemites (Gen. 34) and killing the miscreants who worshipped the Golden Calf (Exod. 32). If there ever was such a tribe, it may have gained special prestige because of its link to Moses and Aaron, so that in the early period it was desirable to obtain a Levite to be a family priest (cf. Judg. 17). Certainly, being a Levite was not at this stage necessary for the priesthood. The child Samuel who was an Ephraimite was devoted by his parents to the priesthood, "lent" (*šā'ûl*) to God, in fulfillment of his mother's vow. David, a Judahite, is reported to have appointed his sons as priests. A Hebrew inscription from the seventh century BCE has a variant of a text associated with the priesthood in Numbers 6, the "Priestly Blessing." It is so far the only Hebrew inscription of the First Temple period that contains an actual biblical text (see the essay by Christopher Rollston in this volume).

The exaltation of the Aaronide Levites to the sole priesthood and the demotion of the other Levites, reflected first in Ezekiel 44, then in the Tetrateuch, was a process that began after the Deuteronomic reform and was completed by the time of the Book of Chronicles (ca. 400 BCE). There the respective priestly and levitical roles are set. The Chronicler assigns Levites the additional function of composing psalms, as well as some quasi-prophetic functions. Whether these roles go back to the Levites of the First Temple period is doubtful.

The contrast between the paucity of archaeological and even biblical evidence for both priesthood and cult before the exile contrasts with the dominant role these topics play in the Tetrateuch. The laws and theology in that work reflect the early Persian period, and are intended to set up the theocratic high priestly entity of Second Temple Judaism. Most striking is the complete absence of monarchy in the Pentateuch as a whole (except for Deuteronomy 17, which consists entirely of limitations placed on the kings). Even the image of God as king, so common in the rest of the Hebrew Bible, is almost absent, appearing only a few times in old poetic passages (cf. Exod. 15:18). Instead, the high priest is exalted into a quasi-royal figure. The religious structure of the Tetrateuch was intended to lay the groundwork for a kind of religion the Persians would allow, one that eliminated all hints of independent monarchy (see the essay by Charles Carter in this volume).

Closing Thoughts

To many the ritual laws and practices of the priestly literature, the blood-centeredness and its theology's obsession with sin and atonement, and its restrictive definition of holiness as separation and discrimination, must seem remote from their intellectual and religious concerns. But in fact it is the only theology in the Hebrew Bible that is presented systematically and thoroughly, though literarily rather than syllogistically. Although it contains much old material, its final form is a product of its time, primarily the fifth century BCE. The Pentateuch it constructed was intended to be the constitution of the restored Judean community in its tiny temple state ruled by an Aaronide high priest on behalf of foreign overlords. As such, it served as the base document for Jewish life until the destruction of the Second Temple by the Romans in 70 CE. Jews never wavered in their devotion to the temple and its cult, even as new religious ideas and forms of expression developed in apocalypticism (see the essay by John J. Collins in this volume) and the early rabbinic movement. Even when the actual cultic establishment mandated by PTh ceased to exist, the Rabbis cultivated its study as a kind of discrete messianic expression; and Christianity drew from its vocabulary of sacrifice, atonement by blood and priesthood to help formulate its own theology and religious practice. Even today many of the ideas of PTh are influential, for good or ill, especially in the sexual views of many Jews and Christians. Moreover, the priestly theology was indispensable as a counterweight to the intellectualism of the other main biblical religious expression, Deuteronomic covenantal religion. The latter was primarily a religion of the mind, of historical remembrance, education of the young, prayer and religious vigilance. Priestly religion was no less vigilant, but it tempered monotheistic zeal with a subtle reworking of myth, which provided an emphasis on the physical and the visual. The images of blood and sin connected directly to some of the wellsprings of human emotion in a way that simple adherence to covenantal law could not, while the pervasive creation theology provided an overall coherence of nature and revelation. The priestly work stands in its own right as a major religious expression in world religion, and one of the most influential.

Bibliography

Anderson, Gary A. *Sacrifices and Offerings in Ancient Israel: Studies in Their Social and Political Importance*. Harvard Semitic Monographs 41. Atlanta: Scholars Press, 1987. A detailed study of the sacrificial system and survey of scholarship. See also the author's article in the Anchor Bible Dictionary.

Carr, David M. *Writing on the Tablet of the Heart: Origins of Scripture and Literature*. Oxford: Oxford University Press, 2005. A study of writing, scribes, education, and the development of Israelite literary traditions.

Dever, William G. *Did God Have a Wife? Archaeology and Folk Religion in Ancient Israel*. Grand Rapids, MI: Eerdmans, 2005. An analysis of the biblical and archaeological evidence for Israelite popular religion, focusing especially on the issue of the role of Asherah.

Douglas, Mary. *Purity and Danger: An Analysis of Pollution and Taboo*. London: Routledge & Kegan Paul, 1978. Originally published 1966. A classic anthropological analysis that has been influential in the study of the biblical cult, especially in Leviticus.

Frymer-Kensky, Tikva. "Pollution, purification and purgation in biblical Israel." In Carol L. Meyers and M. O'Connor (eds), *The Word of the Lord Shall Go Forth: Essays in Honor of David Noel Freedman in Celebration of His Sixtieth Birthday* (pp. 399–414). Winona Lake, IN: Eisenbrauns, 1983. A study of the language and themes associated in Leviticus with ritual purification.

Geller, Stephen A. *Sacred Enigmas: Literary Religion in the Hebrew Bible.* London: Routledge, 1996. A literary and theological analysis of major biblical religious traditions.

Haran, Menahem. *Temples and Temple-Service in Ancient Israel.* Oxford: Clarendon Press, 1978. A major study of priesthood and ritual in ancient Israel.

Hurvitz, Avi. *A Linguistic Study of the Relationship between the Priestly Source and the Book of Ezekiel.* Paris: Gabalda, 1982. A study of the linguistic evidence for dating the priestly literature.

Janowski, Bernd. *Sühne als Heilsgeschehen: Studien zur Sühnetheologie der Priesterschrift und zur Wurzel KPR im Alten Orient und im Alten Testament.* Wissenschaftliche Monographien zum Alten und Neuen Testament 55. Neukirchen-Vluyn: Neukirchener Verlag, 1982. A study of the biblical rituals of the sin offering and atonement and their theological meaning.

Jenson, Philip Peter. *Graded Holiness: A Key to the Priestly Conception of the World.* Sheffield: JSOT Press, 1992. An analysis of the structure of the priestly view of the cosmos as reflected in the temple and cult.

Knohl, Israel. *The Sanctuary of Silence: The Priestly Torah and the Holiness School.* Minneapolis: Fortress, 1995. An examination of the relationship between the Priestly source (P) and the Holiness school (H).

Levine, Baruch A. *In the Presence of the Lord: A Study of Cult and Some Cultic Terms in Ancient Israel.* Leiden: Brill, 1974. An analysis of key aspects of the cult, primarily in Leviticus and Numbers, in preparation for the author's commentaries on these books.

Milgrom, Jacob. *Cult and Conscience: The Asham and the Priestly Doctrine of Repentance.* Leiden: Brill, 1976. A study of the practice and theology of the "guilt offering."

Milgrom, Jacob. *Studies in Cultic Theology and Terminology.* Leiden: Brill, 1983. Analysis of aspects of the cult in Leviticus and Numbers in preparation for the author's extensive commentaries on those books.

Smith, Mark A. *The Priestly Vision of Genesis 1.* Minneapolis: Fortress, 2010. A study of the background and theology of the creation account in Genesis 1 as an expression of priestly worldview.

Tigay, Jeffrey. *You Shall Have No Other Gods: Israelite Religion in the Light of Hebrew Inscriptions.* Atlanta: Scholars Press, 1986. A study of Israelite names as revealed from archaeological evidence and their bearing on the history of biblical religion.

Wright, David P. "The gesture of hand placement in the Hebrew Bible and in Hittite literature." *Journal of the American Oriental Society 106* (1986): 433–46. A study of this gesture and its implications for the biblical understanding of sacrifice.

Zevit, Ziony. *The Religions of Ancient Israel: A Synthesis of Parallactic Approaches.* London: Continuum, 2001. A detailed study of all aspects of the religions and cults of ancient Israel and Judah in terms of the archaeological evidence.

CHAPTER 17

Prophecy

Robert R. Wilson

Prophecy, as a religious phenomenon, is simply communication between the human and divine worlds. The agent or intermediary through whom this communication takes place is the prophet. Although some interpreters of the Hebrew Bible continue to maintain that the biblical prophets were in some way unique, in fact prophets have existed historically in many societies (and continue to exist), and prophecy has appeared in many cultures. Within the biblical world, figures having the same functions as the biblical prophets are attested in Mesopotamia at least a millennium before their Israelite counterparts, and similar figures seem to have existed as well in the cultures that immediately surrounded Israel. At about the same time that prophets appeared in Israel, they also appeared in Greece, and in fact the English word "prophet" is borrowed from Greek. Although all of these figures had distinctive features which need to be recognized, they all also had roughly the same religious functions and had family resemblances to each other. These common characteristics, patterns of behavior, and religious functions that are shared by ancient prophets are also exhibited by many modern prophets, and all of them can be usefully compared with the biblical prophets as a way of better understanding them, so long as their distinctive features are not overlooked.

However, it is important to recognize that this sort of comparative study is a fairly recent phenomenon. Since the biblical period, prophecy in general in the Western world has almost always been identified with, and understood with reference to, the examples to be found in the Hebrew Bible, and figures in other cultures were identified as prophets to the extent that they resembled the biblical prophets. Thus popular and scholarly understandings of the biblical prophets have deeply colored popular and scholarly understandings of prophecy in general and ancient Israelite prophecy in particular.

Although scholars throughout the history of biblical interpretation occasionally appealed to cross-cultural comparisons in order to understand Israelite prophecy more clearly, serious academic comparative studies of prophecy began only at the end of the nineteenth century, when the social sciences began to flourish in the universities. At that time a number of comparative studies were produced, but for various reasons scholars quickly lost interest in the new approach, and by the early twentieth century interpreters

The Wiley Blackwell Companion to Ancient Israel, First Edition. Edited by Susan Niditch.
© 2016 John Wiley & Sons, Ltd. Published 2016 by John Wiley & Sons, Ltd.

had reverted to more traditional treatments of prophecy that focused on prophetic theology and literature. These studies were based primarily on the biblical text itself, although occasionally efforts were made to set Israelite prophecy into a broader cultural context (Wilson, *Sociological Approaches*, 23–5). However, in general, research began to focus on the contents of the prophetic message and on its literary form, rather than on the religious phenomenon of Israelite prophecy itself. During this period several different aspects of ancient Israelite prophecy were highlighted, and all of these points of view have persisted in scholarly discourse to the present day.

First, expanding on an understanding of prophecy to be found in the biblical world itself, some scholars viewed Israel's prophets as being concerned mainly with predicting the future and therefore as dealing almost exclusively with events which were to come. Already in Deuteronomy 18:9–22, the writer suggests that a true prophet foretells events that actually come to pass, while a false prophet's predictions do not occur. This idea was picked up by the writers of the monarchical history in the Books of Kings, where the fulfillment of earlier prophecies is duly noted for the reader (see J. J. M. Roberts's essay in this volume). So strong was the belief that the words of true prophets would eventually turn out to be accurate predictions of the future that several biblical texts spend considerable time dealing with the problem of the apparent inability of true prophets to predict accurately what was about to happen (Jonah; Ezek. 29:17–20; cf. 26:7–14; Isa. 16:13–14; Jer. 28:8–9). The postbiblical interpretive tradition, of course, spends much time on this issue, trying to demonstrate how contemporary events fulfill ancient prophecies. However, while concern with the future is certainly an important feature of biblical prophecies, prophets sometimes spoke directly to situations in their own time and place. Prophets often urged changes of behavior and suggested that such changes could influence future events. A predicted disaster or judgment might be avoided if people in the present listened to the prophetic warning.

This recognition of the biblical prophets' interest in the present as well as in the future eventually led scholars to stress a second aspect of biblical prophecy, the concern of the prophets with theology and ethics. Israel's prophets could be viewed as having helpful advice to give about morality and religious life, and this advice could benefit modern communities of faith. Biblical scholars of the late nineteenth century, such as Heinrich Ewald, Bernhard Duhm and Julius Wellhausen, considered the ethical insights of the prophets to be the Bible's greatest contribution to Western thought, and twentieth-century theologians often attempted to abstract a "theology of the prophets" from biblical texts that were firmly anchored in particular historical and cultural contexts. The result of this effort was often a "theology of the prophets" that was thought to be shared by all of the biblical prophets but that was at the same time distinct from all other theological perspectives to be found in the Hebrew Bible. Furthermore, by removing prophetic theology from its historical and cultural contexts, scholars tended to consider the Israelite prophets to be unique religious geniuses, who had nothing in common with comparable figures in other cultures.

Finally, throughout much of the twentieth century, interpreters of biblical prophecy often reached their theological and ethical conclusions by applying various literary approaches to the biblical text. Like theological interpretation, literary study of the prophets has had a long history in biblical scholarship, but it rose to particular prominence early in the twentieth century in the work of the German scholar Hermann Gunkel, who stressed the oral origins of prophecy. In Gunkel's view it was possible to see within the written text of the prophetic books traces of the outlines of the original oral oracles of the prophets. Although Gunkel himself did not write much about prophecy, his students did, and throughout the century they produced a string of books seeking to recover the basic oral forms of prophetic speech and to locate that speech within its setting in the social life of ancient Israel. Thus, although Gunkel is primarily remembered for his literary work, he still recognized the importance of determining the sociological settings of prophetic activity. He was also strongly influenced by the work of Gottfried Herder, who argued for a close parallel between literary inspiration, which led to the creation of poetry, and prophetic inspiration, which led to the creation of ecstatic prophetic oracles, oracles which were eventually written down in poetic form. By looking at prophetic literature in this way, Gunkel inadvertently left the field with two sociological problems that plague it to this day. If oral prophecy functioned in the context of ancient Israel's social life, then how does the modern scholar identify that context and determine how prophecy functioned in Israelite society? Furthermore, if the oral oracles originated, as Gunkel thought, in an inspired ecstatic experience, how did the oracles become the written poetry, mostly intelligible, that we actually have in the biblical text? Gunkel's students, particularly Sigmund Mowinckel, worked on the first problem, but he and others could never come up with more than the suggestion that Israelite prophetic activity was socially located in the context of Israel's worship. The idea that all prophecy was cultic was somewhat attractive, but most scholars also thought that this view of the phenomenon was unduly narrow (Wilson, "Prophetic books").

As scholarship on the prophets progressed in the twentieth century, many of Gunkel's original insights gradually began to disappear from the discussion, and eventually studies of Israelite prophecy started to focus solely on the prophetic literature itself. In extreme versions of this approach, scholars have claimed that the biblical texts do not necessarily reflect any knowledge of the nature of prophecy in Israel. They are purely literary creations, the products of authors or scribes for whom the prophets themselves were more-or-less fictional characters or voices (Carroll; Davies).

Although most contemporary biblical scholars acknowledge ancient scribal participation in the creation of the prophetic literature, they have rejected the extreme view that Israelite prophecy was simply a literary creation. Furthermore, a growing number of scholars have recognized that while theological and literary approaches have made many valuable contributions to the study of prophecy, there is a danger that these approaches will obscure rather than contribute to a better understanding of the religious phenomenon of Israelite prophecy itself. In order to guard against this danger, scholars are increasingly focusing their attention on reconstructing the whole prophetic experience in Israel, from its inception to its later literary development. In order to do this, scholars are also increasingly using comparative materials to supplement the biblical evidence that has traditionally been employed. Such an effort requires a great deal of methodological caution, and scholars are wary of assuming that Israelite prophecy necessarily resembled similar phenomena to be found in other cultures. However, the comparative material can pose new and potentially fruitful questions to ask of the biblical materials, and it can also suggest a richer understanding of the nature and functions of prophecy that can then be explored and tested in the biblical texts (Wilson, *Prophecy and Society*, 1–19; Tiemeyer 161–4; Nissinen, "Comparing prophetic sources"; Grabbe 1–19).

In recent years, two sorts of comparative materials have been employed in order to understand more fully the nature of prophecy in ancient Israel. First, a number of scholars have turned to anthropological studies of contemporary societies where divine–human intermediaries resembling the biblical prophets have been active. These figures (prophets, shamans, witches, mediums, diviners, priests, and mystics) have a variety of culturally specific titles and operate in distinctive ways, but they also share a number of features in common. By abstracting these common features, scholars have been able to sketch a general account of how diverse societies think about the process of divine–human communication and how such communication functions in a variety of social contexts. Comparative studies of this sort suggest several common features of divine–human communication that might provide a fuller understanding of prophecy in ancient Israel.

First, intermediaries in modern cultures describe the means by which they receive their divine messages in different ways, but in general three sorts of processes are involved. Intermediaries may be possessed or taken over by a deity, who then communicates directly to the recipient of the revelation. Alternatively, an intermediary may travel spiritually or mystically to a divine realm (as in the case of soul flight or perhaps dreams), and the divine–human communication then takes place in this other world. Finally, the intermediary may provoke communication from the deity through the manipulation or interpretation of physical objects (as in the case of divination) or through the use of special techniques designed to cause possession or out-of-the-body experiences. Any or all of these processes may exist in a given society, although the society may have a preference for one means of communication or another. Similarly, a given intermediary may receive divine revelations in more than one way.

Cross-cultural studies of intermediation also suggest a second common feature of the phenomenon. The process by which an intermediary receives a divine communication is not open to public inspection, even though the audience may have a general intellectual understanding of what is taking place. Therefore, the people to whom the intermediary communicates the divine message must determine on their own whether the intermediary is genuine and truthful and whether the message is therefore reliable. This process of the accreditation of the intermediary is complex and may involve a number of factors. An intermediary such as a diviner or shaman, who is trained in certain technical skills, may be considered reliable because of the audience's respect for the individual's specialized training, but this method of accreditation does not work in the case of prophets or mediums, who generally do not undergo a period of training. In the case of these intermediaries, societies over time build up a commonly held picture of how such an intermediary behaves, and this social expectation plays a role in the accreditation process. Therefore, intermediaries who seek accreditation are under subtle pressure to make their words and actions conform to what the society expects. This social pressure may lead the speech and actions of intermediaries to become stereotyped within a given society. In short, the intermediaries talk and act in the ways that their audience expects them to act. Intermediaries who have built up a track record of giving true prophecies are more likely to be found creditable than those who do not, and successful prophets often attract support groups who are predisposed to believe the prophets even when their prophecies seem doubtful or even demonstrably false.

Third, in any society where intermediation is thought to be a possibility, the threat of false prophecy is always present. False prophecy may arise for a number of different reasons. The intermediary may be incompetent or may not hear or see the divine message clearly. An evil spirit or deity may become involved in the process and deliberately deceive the intermediary. In the worst case, the intermediary may lie about having received a divine message and may simply invent an oracle.

Finally, intermediaries function in societies in a variety of different ways, although their functions may change over time. Intermediaries on the periphery of the society usually advocate for social change that will remedy their peripheral status. This sort of peripheral intermediation often appears in the case of female intermediaries operating in male-dominated societies, although males can have peripheral status in such societies as well. On the other hand, intermediaries, both male and female, may operate in the power centers of a society to support and maintain central social structures. Such central intermediaries may still advocate for change, but they are likely to encourage gradual change rather than revolution (Wilson, *Prophecy and Society*, 21–88).

In addition to using comparative anthropological studies to understand biblical prophecy more clearly, modern scholars are also increasingly employing a second source of comparative material, the texts produced by Israel's neighbors in the biblical world. From ancient Mesopotamia, scholars have large numbers of texts dealing with divination, although so far little use has been made of this material in the study of Israelite prophecy. On the other hand, in recent years Mesopotamian texts dealing with various sorts of oracular speakers have attracted a great deal of attention, thanks to the appearance of new critical editions of this material. The largest number of relevant texts comes from the city of Mari, on the Euphrates. The texts are to be dated to the eighteenth century BCE and are primarily letters addressed to the kings of Mari reporting the messages of a number of oracular speakers and describing in some detail the contexts in which their messages were delivered and the means by which they were transmitted to the king. A smaller collection of Mesopotamian texts from the biblical period itself, from the seventh century BCE, contains prophetic oracles directed to the Assyrian kings Esarhaddon and Assurbanipal. In addition to this Mesopotamian material, scholars have a much smaller collection of first-millennium material from areas more geographically proximate to Israel (Nissinen, *Prophets and Prophecy*; *References to Prophecy*; Stökl).

While this material from the ancient Near East does not necessarily imply that Israelite prophecy was imported from elsewhere, the material does suggest that prophecy in Israel was a local example of a fairly widespread religious phenomenon and is best understood in this broader context. This sort of divine–human communication occurred in the biblical world at least as early as the second millennium BCE and continued well past the turn of the Era. Indeed, the phenomenon has continued in some Jewish and Christian communities down to the present day. In ancient Israel itself, the biblical texts suggest that prophecy existed at least as early as the ninth century BCE (the prophetic stories in the Books of Kings), and the superscriptions to the prophetic books suggest that oral prophetic oracles began to be recorded in writing as early as the eighth century (Amos 1:1; Hos. 1:1; Isa. 1:1). The production of prophetic writings continued through the Assyrian, Babylonian and Persian periods (seventh through the fourth centuries), with editorial revisions taking place even later.

In general, then, contemporary and ancient comparative materials suggest that prophecy is a complex religious phenomenon. For this reason any discussion of ancient Israelite prophecy must take into account the whole prophetic experience and not just its literary end product, even though that end product is now the initial means of access to the phenomenon itself. Therefore, the discussion that follows will sketch the stages of the prophetic experience in ancient Israel as best they can be reconstructed. The resulting picture will be based in the first instance on biblical sources, even though it must be recognized that these sources do not necessarily constitute a complete and unbiased record of all prophetic activity in ancient Israel. The reconstruction does assume, however, that the biblical texts actually reflect some understanding of the phenomenon of prophecy, even if what the biblical writers claim for it may not be fully accurate historically. In addition, material from ancient Mesopotamia and from a number of modern societies will be used to help fill out the picture. The result will not be a history of Israelite prophecy as a whole or an abstract of prophetic thought, but rather a reconstruction of the process through which every preserved biblical prophecy went from its inception to its final literary form.

The Perception of Divine Revelation

Every recorded example of prophecy in ancient Israel began with a perception of a divine revelation. Or, to put the point another way, the prophetic process began when the human intermediary, the prophet, received a communication from the deity. These communications were visual or auditory or both. According to the biblical texts, the prophets themselves said very little about what happened to them at the moment the communication took place. At most, they described what they saw or heard, but more often actual oracles were simply given with no indication of how or when the prophet received them. Sometimes the prophet prefaces an oracle with an introductory phrase, such as "thus God said" (Amos 1:3) or "this is what the Lord God showed me" (Amos 7:1), but in most cases even this minimal reference to the initial perception of a divine communication is lacking (Jer. 1:4).

Only occasionally does the prophet supply more detailed information about the experience of revelation. For example, the writers of the Books of Samuel provide an account of Samuel's initial call to be a prophet. According to the narrative, Samuel's mother dedicated him, while he was still a child, to the service of the temple of God at Shiloh. While he was serving there under the supervision of Eli the priest, the boy was sleeping before the ark of God when God called Samuel by name. Samuel did not recognize the divine voice, and, thinking that Eli had called, the child ran to him to ask what he wanted. Eli also did not realize that Samuel had heard God call and sent the boy back to his place before the ark. The same sequence of events occurred two more times, and after the third time Eli finally realized what was happening and told Samuel the appropriate response to such a divine summons. When God then called Samuel a fourth time, the child gave the correct response. God then gave him a long judgment oracle against the sanctuary at Shiloh, and from that point on Samuel was recognized as a prophet, delivering God's words to all Israel (1 Sam. 3:1–21). Although such detailed prophetic call narratives are rare in biblical literature, anthropological studies supply a number of examples of stories containing the same basic elements. Typically an individual becomes a prophet when a deity persistently calls or even afflicts the chosen person, who then has to be coached by specialists on the appropriate means of responding. After making the necessary responses, the individual becomes a servant of the deity and is able to function as an intermediary between the human and divine worlds.

A similarly detailed call account is found at the beginning of the Book of Ezekiel, although the details of the narrative are rather different from those in Samuel. Ezekiel did not initially hear a divine call but rather saw a strange vision, which is described in great detail. Ezekiel reports that he did not recognize what he was seeing but that the vision itself terrified him to the point that he fell helplessly to the ground. Ezekiel may not know what he has seen, but the educated reader of the book immediately recognizes what the vision represents. It is a vision of God's glorious presence, normally at home in the Jerusalem temple, but now being carried by its attendant cherubim and coming to rest on the ground in Babylon, where exiles from Jerusalem have been settled by the Babylonians. In this case the vision leads to the prophet's call, but it also symbolizes the message which the prophet is to deliver. God has deserted the temple in Jerusalem and left the city so that it can be destroyed by the Babylonians (Ezek. 1–3).

In contrast to the elaborate visual imagery in the narrative of Ezekiel's call, the call of the prophet Jeremiah is verbal and focuses on a conversation between the prophet and the deity (Jer. 1:1–19). Even more briefly, Amos simply reports that God singled him out to be a prophet (Amos 7:14–15). The Book of Isaiah includes a vision that resembles the one seen by Ezekiel, and the vision leads to a divine commission to the prophet, but given the placement of the narrative in the book, it is not certain that the narrative is a call narrative (Isa. 6). It may simply supply the background for a particular prophetic mission and may not mark the beginning of Isaiah's prophetic activity. If so, then the account would parallel the story of the prophet Micaiah, who describes a divine vision that led to a particular oracle (1 Kings 22:1–28).

Even when prophets recount the details surrounding their prophetic calls, individual prophetic books rarely mention the call stories more than once and never cite them to support the prophet's authority. Rather the literature portrays the prophets as receiving their revelations unexpectedly and often being forced to deliver divine messages against their wills (Amos 3:8; Jer. 15:10–21; 20:7–12). This view of prophetic revelation has parallels in the anthropological literature and also in the descriptions of prophetic activity at Mari, where intermediaries often receive their divine messages suddenly and are traumatized by the experience. At the same time, the modern and ancient comparative sources also recognize that in spite of the basic unpleasantness of the prophetic experience, intermediaries sometimes deliberately provoke their divine revelations. All of the sources know about the standard ways of doing this, and several such techniques are mentioned in ancient Israelite literature. The prophet Elisha summons a musician, whose playing causes the prophet to be possessed by the deity (2 Kings 3:15). Isaiah condemns the prophets of Jerusalem for overindulging in alcohol and then delivering misleading oracles (Isa. 28:7). The prophets of Baal use dance or repetitive motion to provoke a response from the god (1 Kings 18:26). Balaam and perhaps Jeremiah may have tried to encourage revelation through dreams (Num. 22:7–21; Jer. 31:26). In a number of instances prayer was used to provoke a divine response.

Although in the case of any given oracle the initial contact between God and the prophet was usually secret and not open to public observation, ancient Israelites had two primary explanations for what happened during the moment of revelation. Usually the biblical writers talk about the prophet being possessed by God's spirit. Frequently occurring idioms used to express this experience are to say that the "hand of God" was on the prophet (1 Kings 18:46; 2 Kings 3:15; Jer. 15:17) or that God seized the prophet (Ezek. 2:2; 8:3) or that the divine spirit entered the prophet (Judg. 6:34). Whatever the idiom, the point being registered is that the prophet ceased to be in control of bodily movements and speech and that the divine revelation being given to the prophet was the work of the deity alone. Less commonly, the Bible may talk about prophetic revelation occurring when the spirit of the prophet left the human body and traveled to a heavenly realm or entered a dream world, where it saw or heard a divine revelation. Such heavenly journeys are much more common in postbiblical literature than they are in the Hebrew Bible, but there are biblical examples of the phenomenon (Num. 12; Jer. 23; 1 Kings 22).

The Packaging of the Revelation

After a prophetic revelation has been perceived, it must be "packaged." The prophet must translate the revelation into human words or sometimes into actions, which can then be communicated to the appropriate audience. Without this communication by the prophet, the divine message would remain simply part of a mystical experience or a private revelation, and the prophet would not serve as an intermediary between the divine and human worlds. Descriptive evidence from the Hebrew Bible, as well as from stories about prophet-like figures in Mesopotamia, indicates that almost all oracles were delivered, at least initially, in oral form. The known Mesopotamian texts provide no examples of prophets writing out their own oracles. In the Hebrew Bible, prophets are seldom described as recording their own oracles in writing. To be sure, the Books of Chronicles do mention writings attributed to prophets, but these references seem to be to royal chronicles of some sort rather than to collections of oracles (1 Chr. 29:29; 2 Chr. 9:29; 12:15; 13:22; 20:34). Still, it is certainly possible that literate prophets could have simply written out their revelations, a phenomenon that would probably have become more likely after the exile of Judeans to Babylon. As a result of the exile, the Jewish community was dispersed, and oral communication would have become more difficult, so written prophecy would have become a more effective means of transmitting the divine word.

However, while "packaging" a revelation initially in writing remains a possibility, it is still true that narratives of prophets writing their own revelations are rare and mostly late (Hab. 2:2). The same is true of the narratives about prophets in Mesopotamia. In both locations there are instances of prophets dictating oracles to a scribe (Nissinen, *Prophets and Prophecy*, 74–5; Jer. 36), and Isaiah (8:16; 30:8), Ezekiel (2:8–3:3), and Zechariah (Zech. 5) mention written prophecies, but the idea of a prophet writing oracles without first delivering them orally is rarely attested. The most likely example of prophecy bypassing the oral stage and being recorded first in writing is the Book of Ezekiel, where the prophet is never described as delivering oracles orally and where the oracles themselves are so long and complex that oral transmission would have been a challenge. The exilic and postexilic portions of Isaiah and Jeremiah may also have moved directly from revelation to writing, although it is not clear exactly how the creators of this material thought about what they were doing (Petersen 1–36).

Rather than describing prophets writing their own oracles, most of the biblical narratives about prophetic activity and all of the Mesopotamian descriptions of prophecy suggest that the prophet's words and deeds were first reported by members of the audience who witnessed them (Nissinen, *Prophets and Prophecy*; Stökl). Most of the oracles preserved in the Hebrew Bible seem to be reported speech. What the prophets did and said was described and passed on by other people. A classic picture of the process may be found in Amos 7:10–17, where Amaziah, the priest of the royal sanctuary at Bethel, sends a message to King Jeroboam of Israel charging the prophet Amos with conspiring against the king and perhaps against the land itself. To support the charge, Amaziah quotes one of Amos's oracles: "Jeroboam shall die by the sword, and Israel must go into exile away from its land." The oracle that the priest quotes is not found in this form elsewhere in Amos but rather represents a paraphrase or summary of the oracles that the book contains. The quotation seems to represent what Amaziah has heard about the prophet's speech. The first part of the quote is a deduction from the end of Amos's vision report in 7:7–9, while the reference to exile at the end of the quote is repeated in a broader context in Amos's oracle that follows the narrative of the confrontation between prophet and priest (Amos 7:16–17). It therefore appears that Amaziah has heard an oral account of what Amos has been doing and saying and has perhaps already interpreted that activity in a particular way.

A more elaborate example of this process can be found in Jeremiah 26. In this chapter the prophet Jeremiah is told by God to deliver an oracle warning the people of Jerusalem to turn from their evil ways so that God can revoke the judgment planned for the city and its temple (cf. Jer. 7:1–15). The oracle is thoroughly conditional. If the people do not repent, then God will make Jerusalem like the old sanctuary at Shiloh, which God destroyed because of the sins that took place there. The priests, prophets and people, however, do not hear the oracle conditionally. Rather, they hear it as an announcement of judgment against the city. As a result of not hearing the oracle accurately, the priests, prophets and people charge Jeremiah with speaking against the temple and the city. At the subsequent trial for treason, various legal issues are raised and oral reports of other prophetic speeches are cited as precedents, but the legal issues are never sorted out, and Jeremiah eventually escapes with the help of some of his supporters.

Both of these examples also raise another complication of the packaging process. The necessity of packaging a divine revelation, whether on the part of the prophet or on the part of the audience, inevitably opens the door to the possibility of false reporting or misunderstood oracles that do not accurately reflect the actual revelation. In short, the very existence of human participation in the prophetic process carries with it the possibility of falsehood (Huffmon). The biblical texts recognize this possibility and take steps to combat it in various ways. The Book of Deuteronomy, for example, suggests that the contents of a prophetic oracle can provide the hearers with clues about its truthfulness or falsity. In Deuteronomy 13:1–7 the writer begins a discussion of treason against the Deuteronomic state. The first case considered is one in which a prophet or one who receives revelations through dreams advocates the worship of other gods. Even though the intermediary provides a confirming sign to guarantee the truthfulness of the oracle commanding this sort of worship, such prophets can be safely ignored because, from a Deuteronomic perspective, a true prophet would never deliver an oracle with this sort of content. A different approach to the problem of false prophecy is taken in Deuteronomy 18:9–22, where the writer bans intermediaries other than prophets and then holds up the figure of Moses as the paradigm of a prophet who is always true. Whenever a prophet like Moses delivers an oracle that conflicts with the oracles of other prophets, truth is to be found in the words of the Mosaic prophet, who always accurately delivers God's revelation. The word of a Mosaic prophet always turns out to be true, while the predictions of other prophets may not be reliable.

The Book of Jeremiah suggests that this prophet was particularly concerned about false prophecy and sometimes accused his rivals of lying or simply inventing the oracles that they delivered. Jeremiah felt that a true prophet, who has heard the divine word clearly and delivered it accurately, could be recognized because the word that the prophet delivered would achieve visible results. The word, said Jeremiah, is like fire, and like a hammer that breaks rock into pieces (Jer. 23:9–40). However, later in the book he seems to be less certain. When Jeremiah is confronted by the prophet Hananiah, who delivers an oracle that opposes one of Jeremiah's oracles, Jeremiah suggests that when oracles conflict in this way a survey of past prophecies may help to sort out the issue. In the case at hand, Jeremiah notes that his oracle of judgment has a long history of being correct, while Hananiah's oracle of well-being has in the past come true less often. Thus, in this case, Hananiah has the burden of proof. However, in the end none of the biblical solutions to the problem of false prophecy seem to have been adequate, and the threat of falsehood continued to plague the history of Israelite prophecy.

The Evaluation of Genuineness

In order to have an impact on a society, prophecies have to be taken seriously by the people to whom they are addressed. The audience needs to recognize and accept the authority of the prophet and to be able to sort out conflicting prophetic claims. In ancient Israel, as in every society in which prophets appear, this process of validation was complex and based on a subtle interaction between the prophet and the audience. Biblical and Mesopotamian texts say almost nothing about the process, but it is still possible to make a few generalizations.

On the one hand, an audience that witnesses a prophetic claim probably begins the validation process by determining whether or not the would-be prophet looks, talks and acts like other prophets that the audience has known. Each society in which prophets appear seems to have stereotypical ideas about prophetic behavior. These ideas have been built up over time, and all prophets are expected to conform to them. An intermediary who deviates too much from the norm risks rejection by the audience. Therefore, in the first instance the audience looks for signs of stereotypical speech and behavior. When these characteristics are present, the audience may be able to further categorize the intermediary by assigning one of several different titles to the individual. Such titles are well attested among the Mesopotamian oracular speakers, and several exist in the biblical record as well. In Israel some of the titles seem to relate to the means by which the figures received their revelations ("seer," "visionary"), although other titles seem more general ("man of God," "prophet"). Particular titles may also point to geographical or group preferences, with some titles being more common in Israel in the north and others being more prevalent in Jerusalem and Judah. Along with the different titles went different types of behavior. In some instances prophets were expected to exhibit ecstasy, with all of its usual physiological characteristics, while in other cases ecstasy was not expected and was even viewed as an abnormality (madness or illness). Throughout Israel the speech of prophets tended to be somewhat stereotypical. For example, judgment oracles tended to begin with an introductory formula identifying the divine speaker ("thus says the Lord") and then moved on to an indictment of the audience for a crime or sin. The indictment then led to an announcement of judgment, sometimes with another identification of the speaker at the end (Amos 1:3–5 and often). This common pattern occurs throughout Israel's prophetic corpus, and even the relatively late, highly developed judgment oracles of Ezekiel still follow the basic pattern. To be sure, there is much literary variation within the prophetic corpus, but stereotypical speech is still present.

On the other hand, because the audience was more willing to find credible prophets who resembled credible prophets in the past, intermediaries seeking accreditation were under subtle pressure to make their actions and words conform to what the audience expected. As the prophetic tradition continued to develop in Israel, some prophets not only made their behavior and speech patterns conform to audience expectations but actually borrowed the words of earlier prophets who had been judged genuine and truthful (Habakkuk), although prophets like Jeremiah condemned prophets who "stole" their oracles from other prophets (Jer. 23:30). However, it is important to note that in most cases the stereotypical character of prophets involved only behavior and speech. It did not extend to the content of the oracles, which varied from prophet to prophet and from occasion to occasion. Most Israelite prophets delivered judgment oracles, but on occasion they also spoke promises to the people or issued warnings in the hope of changing behavior. It would be misleading to think that the biblical prophets delivered only one kind of oracle.

However, it would be equally misleading to conclude that audiences paid no attention to the contents of an intermediary's oracle during the accreditation process. Like most people, ancient Israelites were more inclined to find credible those prophets whose oracles reinforced beliefs that the listeners already held. This thoroughly human characteristic caused great frustration for some of the Israelite prophets. Jeremiah in particular often complained that people were more interested in hearing a prophet proclaiming peace than they were in listening to Jeremiah's constant emphasis on judgment (Jer. 23:16–17). Similarly, Isaiah parodies his audience as asking the prophets not to prophesy what is right and to speak only "smooth things" and to prophesy illusions. There was also some variation within the audience of a given prophet. People who were on the fringes of society were probably more likely to find credible prophets who urged social change, while people in charge of the major social institutions, such as the palace and the temple, were probably wary of rapid change. Still, it is worth noting that the Israelite prophets whose words have been preserved spoke both good and evil to their audiences, which ultimately found them to be credible and passed on their words to future generations.

Preservation of True Prophecies

Oracles given by prophets considered to be truthful and reliable were eventually preserved and transmitted to future generations. In contrast, false prophecies were mostly forgotten, except when they were included in narratives for the purpose of contrasting them with true prophecies (Jer. 28:2–4). Initially reliable oracles were probably passed on orally, but eventually most prophetic words were recorded in writing, sometimes with a narrative indicating their original context. In recent years there has been a good bit of debate about how written Israelite prophecy developed. In Mesopotamia, the Mari letters suggest that prophetic utterances were heard by an audience, and prophetic behavior was observed. These observations formed the basis of oral reports, which were sometimes transmitted through several individuals before being included in letters that were sent to the king. Because the prophecies were all directed to the king, the letters were then included in a royal archive. It is not at all clear that this chain of transmission accurately preserved the prophets' words. Divine messages may have been condensed or summarized at the oral stage, and the letters themselves may have been further edited by the scribes who wrote them. In only one letter is there a report that an oracular speaker summoned a scribe in order to dictate an oracle, although there is still scholarly debate about whether or not this dictated letter has been preserved in the Mari archive (Nissinen, *Prophets and Prophecy*, 74–5). In the case of the Neo-Assyrian prophetic texts, individual prophecies seem to have been transmitted to the king in writing, although letters containing these prophecies have not yet been found. Once the letters reached the royal court, they were collected and copied by scribes onto single tablets, with all of the prophecies from a single prophet being grouped together. The royal archives also preserved narrative texts that indicate something of the context for some of the prophecies (Nissinen, *References*). In Mesopotamia the prophecies were written down and preserved in the first instance because they dealt with the king. In some cases they contained warnings or advice, and in some cases they predicted future events. In the latter instance, the prophecies may have been preserved in order to see whether or not their predictions came true. In the Neo-Assyrian collections, the prophecies are almost without exception favorable to the king and supported sometimes controversial royal policies. The archive therefore may have served to support the king's actions in the face of outside criticism.

On the basis of the Mesopotamian material, some scholars have suggested that written prophecy in Israel developed in much the same way (Davies). Oral prophecies were collected by temple or palace scribes and then copied onto scrolls, which were then archived in the palace or the temple. After the initial collections were made, the scrolls were periodically copied, and in the process the scribes edited and shaped the older prophecies and occasionally added new material. However, there are several difficulties with this scenario. First, it is not clear when this scribal activity might have taken place. If it began in the preexilic period, the palace and the temple could well have been involved. However, if this sort of scribal activity took place only in the exilic or Persian periods (or later), as many scholars have recently argued, then neither the palace nor the temple were in existence and could not have played much of a role in the process. Second, unlike the prophetic writings in Mesopotamia, the Israelite prophetic oracles that have been preserved are seldom directed to the kings, and only occasionally do they deal with the temple. Rather, biblical prophets seem to have considered groups of Israelites or Israel as a whole to be the audience for their communications. Finally, careful study of the prophetic books themselves suggests that they are quite different in the ways that they have been edited and shaped. Amos, for example, does give the impression of being a collection of individual oracles that might have circulated orally and that in the written text have been organized primarily on the basis of the oracles' literary structure. Jeremiah, on the other hand, contains oracle collections, along with at least two different types of narrative material that is in some way related to the poetic oracles. Isaiah is still more complex in its organization, with at least three varieties of fairly well-developed poetic oracles and occasional narratives that seem to come from several historical periods. All of these materials seem to be related to each other, but the actual arrangement of the book as a whole is difficult to describe. Ezekiel, on the other hand, is clearly organized as a book, and according to many scholars gives the impression of being a literary unity containing few signs of editorial activity. Clearly much more than simple copying and unified editing must have been involved in producing the prophetic corpus as it now exists.

In order to obtain a clearer understanding of how and why the transition from oral to written prophecy might have taken place in Israel, it will be helpful to begin the discussion with the only two accounts of the process that have been preserved, one in Jeremiah 36 and one centering on Isaiah 8. Both of these passages are suggestive, but they cannot necessarily be taken at face value, and they still leave many questions unanswered.

In Jeremiah 36, the unidentified narrator reports that Jeremiah was commanded by God to write in a scroll all of the oracles that the prophet had delivered from the beginning of his prophetic activities in the reign of King Josiah until the present moment, the fourth year of King Jehoiakim (ca. 605 BCE). Jeremiah therefore summons the scribe Baruch and dictates the contents of a scroll, as God had commanded. Jeremiah then orders that Baruch read the scroll in the temple before all of the people, in the hope that the people would repent and so avoid the punishment that God had decreed for them. Baruch does indeed read the scroll to the people, and it is overheard by two members of the royal court, one of whom comes from a family that had supported Jeremiah in the past. The courtiers inform the king and the royal court of the contents of the scroll, and the officials send for the scroll and ask Baruch to read it in the presence of the king and the court. The officials first verify that the scroll contains the words that Jeremiah dictated, and the scroll is then read before the king. As each column of the scroll is read, the king cuts off the section and burns it, perhaps to destroy its predictive power or simply to show his contempt for the prophet. Some of the assembled courtiers advise against this policy, but their advice is rejected. The king then orders the arrest of Baruch and

Jeremiah, but the order cannot be carried out because the two have been hidden. At the end of this incident, God commands Jeremiah to write a second scroll. This one contains all of the words included in the first scroll, but the first scroll is presumably brought up to date by including in it an oracle against the king who burned the first scroll, and the narrator comments that Jeremiah added additional words as well.

This story has an important role to play in the context of the Book of Jeremiah, but more generally it suggests how the narrator understood the relationship between oral and written prophecy and why prophetic texts were created. Several major points should be observed. First, just as oral prophecies are of divine origin, so also God commands the writing down of prophecies that were originally oral. The oral and written versions of Jeremiah's words are both understood to have the same authority. Second, both the oral and the written versions of the prophecies have the same function. Both types of divine communication are to warn the people (and the royal court) of the dangers they face if they do not repent. This fact suggests that one of the reasons for creating written prophecies was a belief that oral prophecies, which were created for a particular audience in a particular time and place, could function in the same way in the future for a larger and more scattered audience, if preserved in writing and circulated widely. Third, once the written collection of prophecies has been created, it can be transmitted either orally or in writing. The written text does not replace the oral oracles but supplements them, and both forms of the divine word can function in the same social context (Niditch, and see Susan Niditch's essay in this volume). Fourth, it is clear that supporters of the prophet play an important role in protecting the intermediary and in transmitting the oracles. This sort of support group is widely attested in anthropological literature, and Jeremiah 36 suggests that such groups existed in Israel as well. In this case, the support group, rather than the court or the temple, is responsible for the preservation and circulation of the prophet's words. Finally, the story is quite specific about the identity of the actors in this prophetic drama. This specificity may have had a role to play in postexilic Judah, when the descendants of the people mentioned in the narrative were competing for positions and power in the restored Jewish community.

The Book of Isaiah also provides insights into the creation of written prophecy in that particular tradition. The book itself seems to have grown over a long period of time, beginning with the activities of the prophet himself in Jerusalem around 738 BCE and continuing through the exilic period and well into the period of the return of exiled Judeans to Jerusalem. In this case, the carriers of the Isaiah traditions seem to have been the disciples of the original prophet, who are mentioned explicitly in Isaiah 8:16. In this verse the prophet issues an order to bind the prophetic testimony and to seal it among the disciples (literally "the ones who have been taught"). The language of binding and sealing suggests that the prophecies are on a written scroll, which will be unsealed at a future time (Isa. 8:17). The notion of sealing the prophecies suggests that the prophecies are not capable of being understood by the general public but require interpretation of some sort. The disciples, having been taught about the prophecies, are capable of understanding them and applying them to future situations.

While Jeremiah 36 suggests that written versions of the prophet's oracles can function in future settings in the same ways that they did when the prophet delivered them orally, the Book of Isaiah seems to suggest that future uses of the writings of the prophet require interpretation rather than simple repetition. The disciples of the original prophet apparently believed that they had identified a kind of eternal truth in Isaiah's words that could be applied to future situations in which the disciples found themselves. The growth of the book as a whole appears to reflect this belief. Oracles about God's fidelity to Jerusalem that were given by the original prophet in a particular situation, such as the Syro-Ephraimite War (Isa. 7), could later be applied to the Assyrian invasion of Jerusalem (Isa. 7:18–20; 33; 36–39; see J. J. M. Roberts's essay in this volume). Still later the disciples interpreted the same oracles as references to the preservation of the exilic community in Babylon and to its eventual return to a restored Jerusalem. In short, for the Isaiah community the preservation of the prophet's words in writing was to facilitate the process of interpretation, and the interpretive work of the disciples stimulated later expansions of the book itself.

Later Interpretations of Written Prophecies

The process of the interpretation of prophetic texts that is so marked in the Book of Isaiah can be seen in all of the prophetic books, a fact that suggests that later communities that copied prophetic texts, whether disciples of the original prophets or not, interpreted the texts to varying degrees as well. These interpretations initially became part of the prophetic corpus itself. At some point, however, the text itself was fixed, with the result that subsequent interpretations were no longer included in the prophetic writings themselves but were circulated separately. The date at which this shift took place is unknown, but in most Jewish and Christian groups it probably took place quite late. Communities in existence around the turn of the Era knew of various versions of some prophetic books, a fact which suggests that some of the texts of the prophetic corpus were not yet completely fixed. However, the interpretive processes that began in the biblical period continued and remain an important concern of religious communities today.

Bibliography

Barton, John. *Oracles of God*. Oxford: Oxford University Press, 2007. An introduction to prophecy in Israel after the exile.

Blenkinsopp, Joseph. *A History of Prophecy in Israel*. Louisville, KY: Westminster John Knox, 1996. The standard introduction to Israelite prophecy.

Carroll, Robert P. "Poets not prophets." *Journal for the Study of the Old Testament 27* (1983): 25–31. An argument that the biblical prophets were poets rather than religious figures.

Davies, Philip R. "'Pen of iron, point of diamond' (Jer. 17:1): Prophecy as writing." In Ehud Ben Zvi and Michael H. Floyd (eds), *Writings and Speech in Israelite and Ancient Near Eastern Prophecy* (pp. 65–81). Atlanta: Society of Biblical Literature, 2000. A discussion of the ways in which oral prophecies became written texts.

Grabbe, Lester L. *Priests, Prophets, Diviners, Sages*. Valley Forge, PA: Trinity Press International, 1995. A comparative study of religious figures in ancient Israel.

Huffmon, Herbert B. "The exclusivity of divine communications in ancient Israel: False prophecy in the Hebrew Bible." In C. L. Crouch et al. (eds), *Mediating between Heaven and Earth: Communication with the Divine in the Ancient Near East* (pp. 67–81). London: T&T Clark, 2012. A discussion of false prophecy in ancient Israel in the light of evidence from Mesopotamia.

Niditch, Susan. *Oral World and Written Word*. Louisville, KY: Westminster John Knox, 1996. A thorough study of the complex relationship between oral and written literatures.

Nissinen, Marti. *References to Prophecy in Neo-Assyrian Sources*. Helsinki: Neo-Assyrian Text Project, 1998. A study of the Neo-Assyrian oracle collections and references to prophets outside of that collection.

Nissinen, Marti. "Spoken, written, quoted, and invented: Orality and writtenness in ancient Near Eastern prophecy." In Ehud Ben Zvi and Michael H. Floyd (eds), *Writings and Speech in Israelite and Ancient Near Eastern Prophecy* (pp. 235–71). Atlanta: Society of Biblical Literature, 2000. A discussion of the transmission of oral and written prophecies in Mesopotamia.

Nissinen, Marti. *Prophets and Prophecy in the Ancient Near East*. Atlanta: Society of Biblical Literature, 2003. A critical edition and translation of all of the known prophetic texts from Mesopotamia and elsewhere in the biblical world.

Nissinen, Marti. "Comparing prophetic sources: Principles and a test case." In John Day (ed.), *Prophecy and Prophets in Ancient Israel* (pp. 3–24). New York: T&T Clark, 2010. A methodological study of the use of ancient Near Eastern comparative material in the study of biblical prophecy.

Overholt, Thomas W. *Prophecy in Cross-Cultural Perspective*. Atlanta: Scholars Press, 1986. A useful collection of anthropological sources dealing with prophecy.

Petersen, David L. *The Prophetic Literature*. Louisville, KY: Westminster John Knox, 2002. An introduction to the prophetic books of the Hebrew Bible, with an emphasis on their literary growth.

Stökl, Jonathan. *Prophecy in the Ancient Near East*. Leiden: Brill, 2012. A comprehensive study of the varieties of Mesopotamian prophecy in comparison with biblical prophecy.

Tiemeyer, Lena-Sofia. "Recent currents in research on the prophetic literature." *Expository Times 119* (2008): 161–9. A survey of recent trends in the study of biblical prophecy.

Wilson, Robert R. *Prophecy and Society in Ancient Israel*. Philadelphia: Fortress, 1980. A study of biblical prophecy in the light of anthropological and ancient Near Eastern evidence.

Wilson, Robert R. *Sociological Approaches to the Old Testament*. Philadelphia: Fortress, 1984. A study of the use of comparative sociology in the study of biblical texts.

Wilson, Robert R. "The prophetic books." In John Barton (ed.), *The Cambridge Companion to Biblical Interpretation* (pp. 212–25). Cambridge: Cambridge University Press, 1998. A survey of the various scholarly interpretations of the biblical prophets.

CHAPTER 18

Apocalypticism

John J. Collins

Identification of a Genre

The idea that apocalyptic literature constitutes a distinct genre in ancient Judaism was first formulated by the German New Testament scholar Gottfried Christian Friedrich Lücke in 1832. While such writings came to called *apokalypseis* in Greek, beginning in the late first century CE, there was no corresponding genre label in Hebrew or Aramaic (Smith). There was, of course, no systematic genre analysis of other categories of biblical literature, such as prophecy or wisdom, either, and the absence of a label does not mean that the works that came to be called apocalypses were not appropriately grouped together. The fact that the genre was not recognized in ancient Judaism, however, even in an embryonic way, contributed to the problems that have beset modern analysis of this literature.

Lücke's synthesis was prompted by the publication by Richard Laurence in 1821 of the Ethiopic Book of Enoch, which had been brought to England by a Scottish explorer, James Bruce, who found it while searching for the sources of the Nile. Lücke recognized the affinity of *1 Enoch* with Daniel, *4 Ezra* and the Sibylline Oracles, and grouped them together to clarify the literary context of the Book of Revelation, from which the loosely defined genre took its name. He considered this literature to be a special form of prophecy, with a strong eschatological component and a distinctive view of history as a unity. Later in the nineteenth century the corpus of apocalypses was expanded by the discovery of such texts as *2 and 3 Baruch*, the *Apocalypse of Abraham*, and the *Testament of Abraham*. All these writings (with the exception of parts of *1 Enoch*) are later in date than Daniel, and several are roughly contemporary with the Book of Revelation.

Apocalypticism in the Prophets?

From an early point, however, scholars also noted affinities between classic apocalyptic texts such as Daniel and Revelation, on the one hand, and passages in the Hebrew

The Wiley Blackwell Companion to Ancient Israel, First Edition. Edited by Susan Niditch.
© 2016 John Wiley & Sons, Ltd. Published 2016 by John Wiley & Sons, Ltd.

prophets, on the other. Already in 1847, Ferdinand Hitzig dubbed Ezekiel "der erste Apokalyptiker" ("the first apocalypticist"). Bernhard Duhm dubbed Isaiah 24–27 "the Apocalypse of Isaiah." Identifying such passages in the prophets did not always mean that the phenomenon was thought to be early. Duhm dated the "Apocalypse of Isaiah" to the Hasmonean period.

An important turning point in the study of this literature came with the work of Hermann Gunkel, at the end of the nineteenth century. Gunkel's study *Schöpfung und Chaos in Urzeit und Endzeit: Eine religionsgeschichtliche Untersuchung über Gen 1 und Ap. Joh 12* ("Creation and chaos in the primeval era and the Eschaton: A religio-historical study of Genesis 1 and Revelation 12"), published in 1895, pointed to the influence of ancient Near Eastern myth, especially the *Chaoskampf* or Combat Myth, on the Book of Revelation (see the essays of Neal Walls and Mark Smith in this volume). Gunkel relied on Babylonian myths, especially the Enuma Elish. The Ugaritic texts, discovered in 1929, would later provide closer analogies (see A. Y. Collins). The idea that the use of mythic motifs to refer to future catastrophes and judgment was the hallmark of apocalyptic literature would play an important role in the discussion of apocalypticism in the late twentieth century, and was one of the elements that encouraged scholars to find apocalypticism in the Hebrew Bible before Daniel.

With few exceptions, scholars have tended to view apocalypticism as a "child of prophecy," in the phrase of H. H. Rowley (15). This was true already of Lücke, and the view received classical expression in the English-speaking world from R. H. Charles. (The main alternative has been that it is derived from wisdom (von Rad 2.301–9). This view has never enjoyed much support, especially in the English-speaking world. Apocalyptic literature has sapiential aspects, but the kind of wisdom is different from what we find in Proverbs and Qoheleth. Compare 4QInstruction in the essay by Matthew Goff in this volume.) Opinions diverge, however, as to whether it is appropriate to speak of "apocalyptic" in the Hebrew Bible before Daniel.

On the one hand, Otto Plöger gave cogent expression to the view that a selection of postexilic eschatological passages such as Isaiah 24–27, Zechariah 12–14 and Joel could produce "a line, when joined together, that leads from the older restoration eschatology, which is certainly within the sphere of influence of the pre-exilic prophetic promises, to the rather different dualistic and apocalyptic form of eschatology, such as we find in a fairly complete form in the Book of Daniel" (108). Plöger related the whole development to the rise of the Hasidim in the Hellenistic period. Paul Hanson took issue with Plöger's late dating of these texts, but he also "views Daniel as one station along a continuum reaching from pre-exilic prophecy to full-grown apocalyptic, very much at home on Jewish soil and manifesting foreign borrowing only as peripheral embellishments" ("Old Testament," 53). Hanson does not posit a continuous social movement, but sees the later apocalypses as analogous to postexilic prophecy in their use of myth and their sociological matrix. He speaks of "early apocalyptic," in which "the central features of full-blown apocalyptic can be seen in an inchoate or emergent form." Within this literature he distinguishes different clusters: Isaiah 56–66; 24–27; Zechariah 12–14 and Joel 2:28–3:21, on the one hand, and a more priestly strand in Zechariah 1–6 on the other (Hanson, *Old Testament*, 35–8). Full-blown apocalypticism is exemplified in the Hebrew Bible only in the visions of Daniel 7–12.

Hanson placed great emphasis on the social alienation of the "early apocalyptic" writers, and drew on sociological theories of deprivation to make his point (*Dawn*). (Zechariah 1–6 is an exception, fitting uneasily in his category.) Stephen Cook's study of *Prophecy and Apocalypticism: Postexilic Social Setting* was formulated as a critique of Hanson's use of deprivation theory. Cook focuses on Ezekiel 38–39; Zechariah 1–8 and Joel, which he regards as "proto-apocalyptic" works produced by Zadokite priests at the center of postexilic society. But while his emphasis and his understanding of the social dynamics of apocalypticism are different, his "proto-apocalyptic" texts are essentially the same as Hanson's "early apocalyptic." These scholars view apocalypticism as an outgrowth and continuation of biblical prophecy, and see the prophetic texts of the Persian period as a transitional phase in that development (compare the essay by Robert Wilson in this volume).

On the other hand, many scholars start from the classic apocalyptic texts of Enoch and Daniel, and see apocalypticism as a new phenomenon that emerged in the Hellenistic period (see Matthew Goff's essay in this volume). In a seminal work that appeared in German under the title *Ratlos vor der Apokalyptik* in 1970, and in English as *The Rediscovery of Apocalyptic* in 1972, Klaus Koch noted the confusion generated by the German noun *Apokalyptik*, usually rendered in English as "apocalyptic," which could be used to refer variously to a literary form, a social movement or a kind of theology. Koch argued that these different senses should be distinguished, and argued persuasively that "if we are to succeed at all in the future in arriving at a binding definition of apocalyptic, a starting point in form criticism and literary and linguistic history is, in the nature of things, the only one possible" (23).

Definition of "Apocalypse"

Koch did not entirely heed his own advice. He continued to use the catch-all term "apocalyptic" and his preliminary list of features was not strictly literary. His challenge, however, was taken up by the Forms and Genres Project of the Society of Biblical Literature, which proposed a definition and master-paradigm of the genre apocalypse in the journal *Semeia* in 1979. An apocalypse was defined as "a genre of revelatory literature with a narrative framework, in which a revelation is mediated by an otherworldly being to a human recipient, disclosing a transcendent reality which is both temporal, insofar as it envisages eschatological salvation, and spatial insofar as it involves another, supernatural world" (J. J. Collins, *Apocalypse*, 9). The genre, so defined, is a macro-genre that encompasses various smaller literary forms, and allows the distinction of different subtypes (e.g., "historical" apocalypses with *ex eventu* prophecies of history, and otherworldly journeys; on the latter, see also Robert Wilson's essay in this volume). The visions of Daniel are the only part of the Hebrew Bible that fits this definition, but there is a fairly extensive corpus of noncanonical Jewish apocalypses (*1 Enoch* in its various parts, *4 Ezra*, *2* and *3 Baruch*, *2 Enoch*, *Apocalypse of Abraham*, *Apocalypse of Zephaniah*). The genre is well attested in early Christianity, and can also be found in Greco-Roman and Persian literature.

While various scholars have caviled over one or another aspect of this definition, it has been widely accepted as a workable definition of the literary genre (e.g., Reynolds

31). Even before the publication of *Semeia* 14, Michael Stone and Paul Hanson had drawn distinctions between "apocalypse" as a literary genre, apocalyptic eschatology as a religious perspective and apocalypticism as a social ideology or worldview (Stone 439–44; Hanson, "Apocalypse, genre" and "Apocalypticism"). Stone insisted that "apocalypticism" as usually understood "does not appear either to be the ideology of the apocalypses or to exhaust the contents of the apocalypses" (442). The implication of the *Semeia* volume, however, and even of Koch's original proposal, was that "apocalypticism" should be understood first of all precisely as the ideology of the apocalypses. The adjective "apocalyptic" is most naturally understood to mean "the kind of things we find in an apocalypse." The genre, in short, provides the touchstone for determining what other material may be called apocalyptic by analogy with it.

There has never been any dispute that many texts that do not fit the definition of an apocalypse have significant "apocalyptic" features. (The *Semeia* volume included a category of "related literature.") The so-called "proto-apocalyptic" texts resemble the apocalypses mainly in their use of mythic motifs and in the cosmic scope of their eschatology. But as Stone pointed out, the apocalypses are concerned with many things besides eschatology. To a great degree they are concerned with the revelation of heavenly mysteries, and the otherworldly journey type of apocalypse is greatly concerned with cosmology. If one looks only at the literary form, one may well trace a coherent development from Zechariah to Daniel, but it is not so easy to trace such a line to the Book of the Watchers in *1 Enoch* (Tigchelaar 259–62). Scholars who have seen a continuous development from "proto-apocalyptic" to "apocalyptic" have generally only taken Daniel into account, and have not attended to the full range of interests found in the apocalypses.

Persian Period Prophecy

That said, it is indeed true that there are lines of continuity from the later prophets to the visions of Daniel. On the one hand, the *angelus interpres* ("angel who interprets"), one of the characteristic features of the apocalypses, is found already in the visions of Zechariah, while the "man" who guides Ezekiel through the new Jerusalem in Ezekiel 40–48 anticipates the heavenly tour guides of the Book of the Watchers and the otherworldly journey type of apocalypses. On the other hand, Isaiah 24–27, like Daniel 7, draws on mythic motifs that are ultimately of Canaanite origin, in alluding to the destruction of Death (*Maweth* or *Mot*, Isa. 25:8) and the dragon that is in the sea (Isa. 27:1) (Millar). There are two issues in dispute in the discussion of this literature. The first is whether Persian period prophecy is significantly different from its preexilic counterpart (see the essay by Charles Carter in this volume). Second, is the similarity to Daniel and other apocalyptic texts sufficient to warrant the designation "proto-apocalyptic"?

Paul Hanson tried to map the transition from prophecy to apocalypticism on an axis of myth and history. He defined prophetic eschatology as "a religious perspective which focuses on the prophetic announcement to the nation of the divine plans for Israel and the world … which [the prophet] translates into the terms of plain history, real politics and human instrumentality" (Hanson, *Dawn*, 11). Apocalyptic eschatology focuses on the disclosure (usually esoteric in nature) to the elect of the cosmic vision of Yahweh's sovereignty – especially as it relates to his acting to deliver his faithful – which disclosure the visionaries have largely ceased to translate into the terms of plain history, real politics, and human instrumentality due to a pessimistic view of reality growing out of the bleak post-exilic conditions. (Hanson, *Dawn*, 11)

The visionaries, according to Hanson, "disillusioned with the historical realm, disclosed their vision in a manner of growing indifference to and independence from the contingencies of the politico-historical realm, thereby leaving the language increasingly in the idiom of the cosmic realm of the divine warrior and his council" (Hanson, *Dawn*, 12).

This way of formulating the matter, however, has been widely criticized (Grabbe 17–22). On the one hand, the "day of the Lord" in Amos is already a thoroughly mythological idea, as indeed is any conception of divine intervention in history. On the other, apocalyptic writers such as Daniel are not nearly so indifferent to the politico-historical realm as Hanson suggested. Neither were they blind to the role of human agency, as can be seen from the coded references to Antiochus Epiphanes, and to the wise teachers (*maskîlîm*) in Daniel 7–12.

Stephen Cook, drawing on sociological studies of millennial groups, argues that an apocalyptic worldview "combines a linear view of history with a futuristic eschatology that pictures an imminent radical change in the way things are. This radical change may involve the expectation of a coming judgment, often including world or cosmic destruction, or a least the destruction of a wicked enemy" (26). He does not explain what constitutes a radical change, but he argues that the visions of Zechariah qualify, because "in his view, historical processes are going nowhere and will accomplish nothing." The overthrow of the enemies of Israel and the turning of the nations to YHWH "are inconceivable without direct apocalyptic divine intervention from beyond history" (128–9). But might one not say the same about some passages in the preexilic prophets? Does the "Day of the Lord" in Amos or Isaiah not qualify as "direct divine intervention from beyond history"?

In a recent discussion of this issue, Antonios Finitsis argues that "the difference in the mythic motifs between pre-exilic and post-exilic eschatology is in degree but not in kind" (163). That there is a difference in degree should not be denied. When Isaiah 65:17 says that God is about to create a new heaven and a new earth, or when Isaiah 25 says that God will destroy death forever, these expectations are arguably more radical than anything found in the preexilic prophets. Isaiah 11, which speaks of a new order when the wolf will lie down with the lamb, is a difficult text to classify, as there is no consensus as to whether it is pre- or postexilic. The very possibility that it is preexilic, however, shows the difficulty of drawing a clear distinction between preexilic and postexilic prophecy either in the use of mythic motifs or in the radicalness of its expectations. Conversely, *pace* Cook, the eschatology of proto-Zechariah was not especially radical: it looked for the restoration of Judean monarchy and temple, essentially a return to the preexilic order (J. J. Collins, "Eschatology of Zechariah").

Scenes of universal judgment that are not evoked in response to a particular historical crisis are more common in postexilic prophecy than in the earlier period, although they do not occur consistently. Examples may be found in Joel 3, where all the nations are gathered in the valley of Jehoshaphat, or Zechariah 14, where all the nations are gathered against Jerusalem. The latter motif, however, is found already in Psalm 2, which most probably dates to the Assyrian period. Again, the radical character of the eschatology differs from that of the preexilic period only in degree.

Another difference is more notable. Plöger and Hanson attributed the heightened eschatology of the postexilic prophecies to tensions within the community. Finitsis notes that the eschatological message of Isaiah 56–66 and Malachi differentiates groups within the community (163–4). For example, Isaiah 65 makes a sharp distinction between "my servants," who will be blessed in the eschatological future, and "you" who will suffer the opposite fate. The servants, in this case, are clearly disenfranchised in the present, and the prophet hopes for a dramatic reversal in the future. For Plöger, and especially Hanson, this situation is paradigmatic for emerging apocalypticism. Cook argued for a broader social matrix that would include figures like Zechariah, who were close to the center of power in Judah. It should be noted, however, that Judah itself was in a marginal and vulnerable position in the Persian empire, so that even a prophet like Zechariah might be said to suffer relative deprivation. The insight of Plöger and Hanson that eschatology compensates for what is lacking in the present is true of most if not all Persian period prophecy, and retains explanatory value when we turn to the apocalyptic literature of the Hellenistic period.

The Hope for Resurrection

It is much easier to draw a clear distinction between Persian period prophecy on the one hand, and apocalyptic literature on the other, than between preexilic and postexilic prophecy. From a formal viewpoint, while there is continuity in the symbolic visions, the kind of prophetic oracles that we find in Isaiah 24–27, Isaiah 56–66 or Malachi disappear in the Hellenistic period. With regard to the eschatology, the sharpest difference appears in the apocalyptic belief in the resurrection and judgment of the dead (J. J. Collins, "Apocalyptic eschatology"; Finitsis 33–5).

The novelty of apocalyptic eschatology can be seen clearly in Daniel 10–12. The angel Gabriel explains to Daniel that earthly conflict must be seen against the background of struggles on the heavenly level. Gabriel and Michael, the prince, or patron angel, of Israel, are engaged in a struggle with the "princes" of Persia and Greece. This idea in itself was not new. When the Assyrian Sennacherib invaded Judah at the end of the eighth century BCE, his envoys asked: "has any of the gods of the nations saved their land out of the hand of the king of Assyria?" (Isa. 36:18; 2 Kings 18:33). He might more properly have said "out of the hand of the god of Assyria." The notion that peoples depended on their gods is deeply rooted in biblical tradition, and is modified in Daniel only insofar as the gods are demoted to the status of "princes."

The novelty of Daniel lies in what happens when Michael arises in victory.

At that time, your people shall be delivered, everyone who is found written in the book. Many of those who sleep in the land of dust shall awake, some to everlasting life, and

some to shame and everlasting contempt. Those who are wise shall shine like the bright-
ness of the sky, and those who lead many to righteousness, like the stars forever and ever.
(Dan. 12:2–4)

This is the only undisputed reference to the resurrection of individuals for judgment in
the Hebrew Bible (J. J. Collins, *Daniel*, 390–8). It does not promise universal resurrection: only the very good and the very bad will awake. Like many of the Persian period
prophecies, Daniel discriminates within the Jewish people. Only those found written in
the book (of life) will be saved. The wise, who are the heroes of the time of persecution
in Daniel 11, are lifted up to shine like the stars. In apocalyptic idiom, this means to
become companions of the host of heaven, as is clear from the parallel in the roughly
contemporary *Epistle of Enoch*, where the righteous are promised that they "will shine
as the lights of heaven and the portals of heaven will be opened to you" and that they
will "become companions to the host of heaven" (*1 Enoch* 104:2, 6).

The significance of this innovation can hardly be exaggerated. In biblical tradition
the goal of life was to live long in the land and to see one's children and one's children's
children. This was the reward promised to those who kept the law. For Daniel, the goal
of life is to live like the angels in heaven, who, as the Gospels would say, neither marry
nor are given in marriage (Matt. 22:30; Mark 12:25; Luke 20:35–36). The visions of
Daniel were written in the time of persecution in the Maccabean era, when people were
put to death for observing the traditional law (see Matthew Goff's essay in this volume).
The cognitive dissonance engendered by the persecution no doubt prepared the way for
acceptance of the belief in an afterlife, although that belief may be attested somewhat
earlier in writings attributed to Enoch. We should not suppose that those who hoped
for resurrection abandoned hope for an earthly restoration. Daniel also anticipates that
an earthly kingdom will be given to "the people of the holy ones of the Most High."
Later apocalyptic writings, such as *4 Ezra* and the Book of Revelation, would adjust their
eschatological scenarios to accommodate a messianic reign on earth before the judgment of the individual dead. But the shift in values was radical. Spiritual life with the
angels was now not only regarded as possible, but was prized more highly than mundane life on earth.

The hope for life with the angels was not peculiar to Daniel. In the Enochic Book of the
Watchers (*1 Enoch* 1–36) written perhaps a few decades before Daniel, Enoch is asked
by the Watchers, or Fallen Angels, to intercede for them. He is granted an audience with
the Most High, and told:

"Go and say to the watchers of heaven, who sent you to petition in their behalf,
'You should petition in behalf of humans,
and not humans in behalf of you. Why have you forsaken the high heaven, the eternal
    sanctuary
and lain with women, and defiled yourselves with the daughters of men;
and taken for yourselves wives, and done as the sons of earth;
and begotten for yourselves sons, giants?
You were holy ones and spirits, living forever …
and you have done as they do –

flesh and blood, who die and perish.
Therefore I gave them women,
that they might cast seed into them,
and thus beget children by them, …
But you originally existed as spirits, living forever,
and not dying for all the generations of eternity;
therefore I did not make women among you.'
The spirits of heaven, in heaven is their dwelling."

(1 Enoch 15:2–7; trans. Nickelsburg and VanderKam)

The Watchers and Enoch offer contrasting paradigms. The Watchers chose badly by giving up heaven for earthly women. Enoch, in contrast, is the paradigmatic human being who ascends to heaven to live with the angels. In a later apocalypse, the Similitudes of Enoch, his paradigmatic quality is made explicit, when he is told that "all will walk on your path … with you will be their dwelling and with you their lot, and from you they will not be separated forever and forever and ever" (1 Enoch 71:16).

Some scholars believe that the hope for resurrection is found already in the Persian period in the so-called "Apocalypse of Isaiah." Isaiah 25:8 says that God will swallow Death forever. This may mean that there would be no more death, but it does not mean that those who have already died would come back to life in any form. More plausibly, it is a symbolic way of saying that God will remove everything that is wrong with human life:

"and he will destroy on this mountain
the shroud that is cast over all peoples, the sheet that is spread over all nations."

Isaiah 26:19 is more controversial. In 26:13 the prophet says:

"O Lord our God, other lords besides you have ruled over us,
but we acknowledge your name alone.
The dead do not live; shades do not rise –
because you have punished and destroyed them and wiped out all memory of them."

Yet, a few verses further down he continues:

"Your dead shall live, their corpses shall rise.
O dwellers in the dust, awake and sing for joy!
For your dew is a radiant dew,
and the earth will give birth to those long dead."

Some scholars find here a hope for individual resurrection, not of all people but of "your dead" (e.g., Nickelsburg 31–2). The context, however, suggests rather an antithesis between the foreign lords who have ruled over us, and Israel. Babylon has fallen, and will not rise. Israel, in contrast, will come back from the dead. This understanding takes the passage as analogous to Ezekiel 37, where the dry bones represent the whole house of Israel. No doubt, the metaphorical use of resurrection in such texts as Ezekiel 37 and

Isaiah 26 facilitated the eventual acceptance of the hope for the resurrection of those who have died. But resurrection remains metaphorical in Isaiah 26.

The future hope typical of Persian period prophecy is set out most explicitly in Isaiah 65:18–25:

> "I will rejoice in Jerusalem
>   and delight in my people;
> no more shall the sound of weeping be heard in it,
>   or the cry of distress.
> No more shall there be in it an infant that lives but a few days,
>   or an old person who does not live out a lifetime;
> for one who dies at a hundred years will be considered a youth
>   and one who falls short of a hundred will be considered accursed."

This passage is no less mythical than Daniel 12, but it is a different mythical conception of a new creation. In the Isaian utopia, people will live longer and happier lives, but they will still die. There is no question of afterlife with the angels. The values implicit in Isaiah 65 are not essentially different from those of Deuteronomy. They concern the quality of earthly life. Daniel and Enoch, in contrast, are obsessed with the heavenly world. The visionaries converse with angels, and their ultimate hope is to join the angels in heaven.

It should be noted that the earliest apocalypses do not speak of bodily resurrection on earth, but of the resurrection of the spirit to heavenly life. This is also the case in the sectarian texts found at Qumran, where the Hodayot speak of life on the height in the company of the holy ones (J. J. Collins, *Apocalypticism*, 110–29). The idea of bodily resurrection appears just a little later in Judaism. 2 Maccabees 7 provides an early example. Later apocalypses try to accommodate both bodily and spiritual resurrection. But the spiritual, angelic character of resurrection in the earliest apocalypses shows that this conception did not evolve from postexilic prophecy.

A Hellenistic Phenomenon

Scholarship on apocalypticism has often been obsessed with finding the roots of the phenomenon in prophecy, or wisdom, or Iranian religion, or somewhere other than the phenomenon itself (see J. J. Collins, *Apocalyptic Imagination*, 19–21). This quest for external roots is misguided. The apocalyptic writers wrote to address the problems of their time. They drew motifs and ideas from many sources, including certainly prophecy, but what they produced was a new phenomenon, reflecting a new view of the world, where the boundaries between the heavenly and the earthly were much more permeable than they had seemed in Deuteronomy or Proverbs. It was a phenomenon of the Hellenistic age, not because it borrowed Greek ideas but because it reflected new assumptions about the way the world worked.

Most of the surviving Jewish apocalypses arose directly from a situation of crisis. Daniel and several sections of *1 Enoch* (The Animal Apocalypse, the Apocalypse of Weeks) can be related directly to the persecution under Antiochus Epiphanes. Several others (*4 Ezra*, *2 Baruch*, *3 Baruch*, *Apocalypse of Abraham*) were written in the aftermath of the destruction of Jerusalem by the Romans. In the latter case, the genre takes on the character of consolation for trauma. This is not to say that apocalyptic literature was always and necessarily crisis literature. The genre took on a life of its own, and the literature was retained and valued after the crises had passed. It now appears from the Dead Sea Scrolls that this kind of literature was more extensive than had previously been realized. Several fragmentary texts found at Qumran, 4Q243–44 and 4Q245 (Pseudo-Daniel), 4Q246 (the Son of God text), 4Q552–53 (Four Kingdoms), Apocryphon of Jeremiah C (4Q385a, 387, 388a, 389, 387a) and 4Q390, all have significant apocalyptic features (Reynolds 191–206, 253–374). Since the texts are fragmentary it is difficult to be certain of their literary genre, but at least they belong to the category of apocalyptic literature broadly conceived. It may be, then, that apocalyptic literature was more broadly dispersed and diverse than is apparent from the apocalypses preserved in the Pseudepigrapha.

Nonetheless, the available evidence lends credence to the view of apocalyptic sociology advanced by Hanson. This literature most often expressed dissatisfaction with the present order and the desire for a radical alternative. That much could also be said of much of Persian period prophecy, but in the apocalyptic literature proper the radical alternative was defined by the hope of resurrection and of heavenly life with the angels. In the words of *4 Ezra*, written after the destruction of Jerusalem, "the Most High has made not one world but two" (*4 Ezra* 7:50) and the two are qualitatively different. It is the hope that human beings could make the transition to the world of the angels and eternal life that constitutes the decisive difference in perspective between Persian period prophecy and the apocalypses of the Hellenistic age.

Bibliography

Collins, Adela Yarbro. *The Combat Myth in the Book of Revelation*. Missoula, MT: Scholars Press, 1976. The adaptation of Near Eastern and Greek mythology in the Apocalypse.

Collins, John J. "Apocalyptic eschatology as the transcendence of death." *Catholic Biblical Quarterly* 36 (1974): 21–43. Reprinted in *Seers, Sibyls and Sages in Hellenistic-Roman Judaism* (pp. 75–98). Leiden: Brill, 1997. Discussion of the difference between prophetic and apocalyptic eschatology.

Collins, John J. (ed.). *Apocalypse: The Morphology of a Genre (Semeia 14)*. Missoula, MT: Scholars Press, 1979. Definition of the genre "apocalypse," and outline of the corpus.

Collins, John J. *Daniel: A Commentary on the Book of Daniel*. Minneapolis: Fortress, 1993. Full historical-critical commentary on Daniel.

Collins, John J. *Apocalypticism in the Dead Sea Scrolls*. London: Routledge, 1997. Discussion of apocalyptic themes in the Scrolls, including dualism, messianism, the eschatological war, and life after death.

Collins, John J. *The Apocalyptic Imagination*. 2nd edn. Grand Rapids, MI: Eerdmans, 1998. Introduction to the Jewish apocalypses in their historical context.

Collins, John J. "The eschatology of Zechariah." In Lester L. Grabbe and Robert D. Haak (eds), *Knowing the End from the Beginning: The Prophetic, the Apocalyptic and Their Relationships* (pp. 74–84). London: T&T Clark, 2003. Argument that the eschatology of Zechariah is not apocalyptic in character.

Cook, Stephen L. *Prophecy and Apocalypticism: The Postexilic Social Setting*. Minneapolis: Fortress, 1995. Argument that postexilic prophetic texts, including Zechariah, have an apocalyptic character.

Finitsis, Antonios. *Visions and Eschatology: A Socio-Historical Analysis of Zechariah 1–6*. London: T&T Clark, 2011. Argument that Zechariah is not apocalyptic in character, but should be understood as prophecy in a particular context.

Grabbe, Lester. "Introduction and overview." In Lester L. Grabbe and Robert D. Haak (eds), *Knowing the End from the Beginning: The Prophetic, the Apocalyptic and Their Relationships* (pp. 2–43). London: T&T Clark, 2003. Argument that prophecy and apocalypticism should both be regarded as forms of divination.

Gunkel, Hermann. *Creation and Chaos in the Primeval Era and the Eschaton: A Religio-Historical Study of Genesis 1 and Revelation 12*, trans. K. William Whitney, Jr. Grand Rapids, MI: Eerdmans, 2006. Classic discussion of the ancient Near Eastern Combat Myth and its influence on Revelation.

Hanson, Paul D. *The Dawn of Apocalyptic: The Historical and Sociological Roots of Jewish Apocalyptic Eschatology*. Philadelphia: Fortress, 1975. Influential sociological analysis of a strand of postexilic prophecy deemed to be apocalyptic.

Hanson, Paul D. "Apocalypse, genre" and "Apocalypticism." In Keith Grim (ed.), *Interpreter's Dictionary of the Bible: Supplement* (pp. 27–34). Nashville: Abingdon, 1976. Influential definition of key terms in the study of apocalypticism.

Hanson, Paul D. "Old Testament apocalyptic reexamined." In P. D. Hanson (ed.), *Visionaries and Their Apocalypses* (pp. 37–60). Philadelphia: Fortress, 1983. Originally published in *Interpretation 25* (1971): 454–79. Argument that "apocalyptic" is rooted in ancient Near Eastern myth.

Hanson, Paul D. (ed.). *Old Testament Apocalyptic*. Nashville: Abingdon, 1987. Collection of essays by various authors on apocalypticism.

Koch, Klaus. *The Rediscovery of Apocalyptic*. Naperville, IL: Allenson, 1972. Seminal attempt to bring semantic clarity to the discussion of apocalypticism.

Millar, William R. *Isaiah 24–27 and the Origin of Apocalyptic*. Cambridge, MA: Harvard University Press, 1976. Discussion of the use of myth and of the social setting of Isaiah 24–27.

Nickelsburg, George W. E. *Resurrection, Immortality, and Eternal Life in Intertestamental Judaism and Early Christianity*. Rev. ed. Cambridge, MA: Harvard, 2006. Classic treatment of the diversity of Jewish conceptions of the afterlife.

Plöger, Otto. *Theocracy and Eschatology*. Richmond, VA: John Knox Press, 1968. Attempt to trace continuity between late prophecy and apocalyptic literature, marked by late dating of the prophetic texts.

Reynolds, Bennie H. III. *Between Symbolism and Realism: The Use of Symbolic and Non-Symbolic Language in Ancient Jewish Apocalypses 333–63 BCE*. Göttingen: Vandenhoeck & Ruprecht, 2011. Wide-ranging discussion of apocalyptic symbolism.

Rowley, H. H. *The Relevance of Apocalyptic: A Study of Jewish and Christian Apocalypses from Daniel to the Revelation*. London: Lutterworth, 1963. Dated discussion of apocalyptic literature, emphasizing its affinity to prophecy.

Smith, Morton. "On the history of *apokalypto* and *apokalypsis*." In David Hellholm (ed.), *Apocalypticism in the Mediterranean World and the Near East: Proceedings of the International Colloquium on Apocalypticism, Uppsala, August 12–17, 1979* (pp. 9–20). Tübingen: Mohr Siebeck, 1982. Incisive discussion of the use of key terms in antiquity.

Stone, Michael E. "Lists of revealed things in the apocalyptic literature." In F. M. Cross, Werner E. Lemke, and Patrick D. Miller (eds), *Magnalia Dei: The Mighty Acts of God: Essays on the Bible and Archaeology in Memory of G. Ernest Wright* (pp. 414–52). New York: Doubleday, 1976.

Argument that apocalypses are concerned with other things besides eschatology, notably cosmology.

Tigchelaar, Eibert J. C. *Prophets of Old and the Day of the End: Zechariah, the Book of the Watchers and Apocalyptic*. Leiden: Brill, 1996. Comparison and contrast of late prophetic and early apocalyptic texts.

von Rad, Gerhard. *Old Testament Theology*, trans. D. M. G. Stalker. 2 vols. Louisville, KY: Westminster John Knox Press, 2001. Notable argument that apocalypticism was derived from wisdom.

C

Social Interaction

CHAPTER 19

Religion at Home
The Materiality of Practice

Francesca Stavrakopoulou

The study of religion has for a long time been occupied with examining the household or dwelling as both a topographical and social location of religious beliefs and practices – in ancient and modern societies. For many scholars, it is in the domestic sphere that "the key elements of the human condition" might be most sharply perceived (Buchli) and constructions of family, gender, religion, economics, power and culture are exhibited (Bourdieu).

For scholars of ancient Israel and Judah, however, the designation "household religion" has particularly come to index a category of difference: on one level, it tends to be a label employed to describe and interrogate forms of religious practice that are distinct from religious activities associated with temples and other high-status religious sites. Scholars generally agree that worship at the temples of Israel and Judah was not only an urbanized, elite and highly specialized form of religious practice alien to most "ordinary" Israelites and Judahites, but many of its activities, ideologies and worldviews (such as kingship rituals and political cosmologies) were also quite unlike those experienced by the majority, whose primary locus of religious expression was the household in its agrarian context (see S. A. Geller's essay in this volume).

On another (though related) level of scholarly discourse, the term "household religion" is also employed to designate a category of difference concerned with distinguishing the "real" religions of Israel and Judah from the somewhat caricatured biblical portrayal of "ordinary" or "normative" religious practice in these ancient societies. According to the cultural memories of the religious past constructed in the Hebrew Bible, (male) Israelites and Judahites participated in regular pilgrimages to state-sponsored temples, celebrated "national" festivals, consulted priests and other professional religious specialists for ritual assistance, and were legally as well as religiously bound to a solitary national deity, Yahweh, by means of an ancient law-code enshrined in the Jerusalem temple (see the essay by S. A. Geller in this volume; on

The Wiley Blackwell Companion to Ancient Israel, First Edition. Edited by Susan Niditch.
© 2016 John Wiley & Sons, Ltd. Published 2016 by John Wiley & Sons, Ltd.

cultural memory in the Hebrew Bible, see Assmann and see also the essay by Steven Weitzman in this volume). At best, this biblical portrait might be considered selective, idealistic and anachronistic (Zevit, *Religions*); at worst, it might be thought to border on the schematized, imagined and fictitious (Liverani). Either way, biblical scholars tend to agree that the likely reality of household religion did not map directly onto its biblical portrait; instead, it was probably configured quite differently.

However, establishing what household religion is not (it is not elite, temple worship; it is not biblical religion) is somewhat easier than seeking to explore what might constructively be indexed by this category. Most acute is the problematic nature of the sources and theoretical paradigms on which scholars have tended to draw. Given the questionable reliability of the Hebrew Bible as an historical source, and its highly selective portrayal of the religious past, the scant details it offers of family rituals and other activities performed in or around the home cannot simply be lifted from the texts and applied uncritically to a scholarly reconstruction of household religion – despite the best efforts of (predominantly) older generations of biblical historians. While this is not to suggest that the biblical texts are wholly useless in this regard, it is to urge as a matter of priority critical rigor and care in employing biblical material. Configuring the robust assessment of biblical traditions alongside comparative, critically evaluated evidence from other ancient West Asian societies (whether textual, epigraphic, iconographic, or artifactual) is one way in which this might be more carefully achieved (cf. Schloen).

Another is the close analysis of the remains of Israelite and Judahite material culture, although this too is beset with difficulties, not least of which are the confessionally driven or nationalistic legacies of older generations of biblical archaeologists (Abu al-Haj), who were more concerned with locating and excavating the cities and towns associated with the heroes and villains of the biblical story than the agrarian settlements in which most of the population lived and worked (Davis). Until recently, material evidence from "ordinary" domestic dwellings was thus often not as well known, nor as extensive, nor as carefully managed, as that provided by long-lived urban excavations (Hardin).

But perhaps one of the more pervasive difficulties in discussing household religion derives from the continued privileging of certain theoretical ideals in discerning its nature and function. Many influential assumptions about the household as a foundational social and cultural unit derive from the post-Enlightenment rise of an intellectual interest in the dwelling place as a universal tool and measure with which to explore human nature, along with the politico-ideological reinvention of the "patriarchal" household as the beating heart of the European nation state (Buchli). These ideas formed a broader intellectual backdrop to the scholarly construction of the "household" among religious historians and biblical scholars of the nineteenth and early twentieth centuries, a construction that was already heavily distorted by the Western intellectual privileging of the Bible and its self-referential theological preferences, so that "written religion" is frequently valued above other, non-elite, nontextual forms of religious practice (Stavrakopoulou, "'Popular' religion"). Consequently, biblical scholars have often caricatured household religion in ancient Israel and Judah as a simplistic, diminished or even substandard form of assumedly "normative" religious expression (Zevit, "False dichotomies"); it is "nonofficial" or "popular" religion; it is "nonwritten" or "practiced" religion; it is the "folk" religion of the masses (Dever, *Did God?*).

But these assumptions, rooted as they are in what has traditionally been the Euro-American, Christianizing context of biblical scholarship, have been challenged from a number of directions in recent years – not least given the increasingly nuanced and valuable influence of the social sciences in religious studies and biblical criticism (see also the essay by Robert Wilson in this volume). In particular, the reconstruction of household religion in ancient Israel and Judah has been especially reinvigorated by a distinct social-scientific turn toward the "stuff" of the household itself. From the building to its occupants, and the places, spaces and activities they share, the materiality of the household itself – its people, places and objects – can be seen to be the very fabric of its religion.

Making a Household a Home

A house is more than a building. Like all objects and spaces, it is not a static entity, with an abstract, encoded meaning – it is socially constructed (Morgan); it is "practiced space" in which certain people, actions and objects come together to create a familiar locality: a home (Cieraad; Gray). And whether ancient or modern, a home is a continuously changing, dynamic space, (re)produced through a series of social and material practices (Miller).

However, this somewhat "holistic" understanding of the home as a dynamic socio-material construction has made little impact on those scholars interested in the religious cultures of households in ancient Israel and Judah. Instead, much has been made of the terminology employed by biblical scholars and religious historians to describe or refer to the religion of ancient Israel and Judah's non-elites, the vast majority of whom – perhaps as much as 90 percent of the overall Iron Age population (Stager; Meyers, "Household") – lived in an agrarian context.

For some, the term "family religion" is a preferable designation with which to refer to the rituals and other religious activities of the social group at the domestic level of these ancient societies. As a label, it conveys the essentially biological (and likely patrilineal) configuration of the basic socioeconomic unit in the sort of traditional, premodern agrarian society both ancient Israel and Judah appear to have been: a "nuclear" family configured around a conjugal pair – a father, a mother and their children – expanded to a limited degree by means of a few single adults of varying ages (unmarried or widowed members of the family), and perhaps even orphaned grandchildren or nephews and nieces (cf. Albertz and Schmitt 21–4). Indeed, archaeological evidence of the dwellings in which most Israelite and Judahite families lived (discussed further below) suggests most houses in rural areas could accommodate between five and eight people (for a summary of views, see Albertz and Schmitt 26–34). The term "family religion" thus refers to the practices of a group defined both in terms of its kinship and the socioeconomic interdependency of its members as a primary unit of subsistence (Albertz; Schloen; see also the essay by David Schloen in this volume).

But for other scholars – particularly Carol Meyers, whose work has been particularly influential in this area (Meyers, "Household religion"; see also the essay by Carol Meyers in this volume) – the term "family religion" is inappropriate because it fails to signal sufficiently the economic and material aspects of a family's domestic setting, such as its animals, crafts and other activities and products integral to its existence (such as food-stuffs and textiles); nor does it indicate the complexity of day-to-day shared living with nonblood members of the household (such as a laborer) or the extended family (such as a brother and his wife and children). Indeed, archaeological excavations suggest that a number of agrarian domestic dwellings shared a courtyard or other open-air spaces with at least one or two other houses, so that together they formed a small compound of dwellings (Brody). The term "household religion" might thus be preferable in that it refers to the spatial and material contexts of the socioreligious group, without limiting that group simply to the "nuclear" family.

But this designation too has its difficulties. For Saul Olyan in particular, it restricts the religious activities of the family group to the locus of the house itself, ignoring the possibility that other sites – including the family tomb – also played a key role in their religious experience, as did interactions with extended kinship groups or "clans" (Olyan). His views are influenced to a certain extent by those of Karel van der Toorn (*Family Religion*; "Nine months"), one of the major players in this debate, for whom assumed forms of "family religion" are virtually indistinguishable from "local" or "village" forms of religious activity, much of which engaged a large network of kinship groups.[1]

These differences in opinion highlight a perceived tension between the people of the household, its material aspects, and its spatial dimensions. But an alternative approach to thinking about the ways in which religious meaning might have been manifest in the experience of the domestic group views this "tension" differently; it reimages the dynamic interplay between people, materiality and space constructively, rather than problematically.

Indeed, the way in which space and place appear to have been constructed in the type of building in which most agrarian Israelites and Judahites lived itself would seem to encourage this. As is well known, the so-called "four-room house" appears to have been the more usual type of domestic dwelling throughout Iron Age Israel and Judah (Faust and Bunimovitz; see also Avraham Faust's essay in this volume). While some variation on this type is known (some houses were three-roomed, some two-roomed), and rural examples appear to have been larger (though not by implication more affluent) than their urban counterparts (Faust), most houses were set out in a broadly similar style: rectangular in its footprint, its entranceway was a wooden door set above a raised stone threshold, opening into a low-ceilinged central room. This room was partitioned by two rows of stone pillars making their way down its length, away from the door, creating two smaller rooms to the left and the right of the central room. Running across the back of the house was another room (sometimes known as the "broadroom"), access to which was only gained via the central room. Small slitted open windows provided some light and ventilation; some wall niches might have held lamps. The floor comprised hard-packed, beaten earth, with perhaps a cobbled section in one of the paralleled rooms, where animals might be kept in winter (King and Stager).

Very few features of the house were permanent fixtures: in the floor of the main room were a fire pit and a cooking pit, and one or two stone-lined storage pits; a small cistern might have been located in the back room. In contrast to the postindustrial modern West, where it is usual for families to live in buildings with clearly demarcated spaces for sleeping, eating, and working, the use of space in a typical four-roomed house was by necessity flexible and fluid, with the ground floor in particular fulfilling a variety of functions (Nakhai). Most of the space here was used to house animals (in the side rooms), to store foodstuffs and work equipment, to process, prepare and cook food, and to perform other daily household and craft tasks (Meyers, "Material remains"). Sleeping and other household activities, such as spinning or weaving, were likely performed above, either on an upper floor – accessed by a ladder or small wooden staircase from the central room – or on the roof (Albertz and Schmitt). There is some evidence to suggest that grain processing, beer-making, bread-baking and other craftworks may also have occurred outside the house in a courtyard or open area shared with other houses (Meyers, "Material remains"; Nakhai).

Among the material remains of domestic dwellings of the Iron Age period, objects unambiguously indicative of a ritual function have been found at a number of sites. These include cult stands and associated chalices or goblets, zoomorphic terra-cotta figurines or vessels, and libation vessels (Albertz and Schmitt). Model shrines and model furniture have also been uncovered at several sites, while the prevalence of (primarily female) anthropomorphic figurines (discussed further below) appears to have increased throughout the period. Among the numerous household vessels, bowls and burners associated with food preparation and consumption are frequently found certain assemblages which are strongly suggestive of a ritual function, to which the discussion will return presently.

In spite of this evidence for religious practices within the home, a number of scholars have remarked on the apparent scarcity in these houses of an obvious "cult corner" or "shrine": a dedicated place (a raised or plastered area or alcove; a small standing stone) at which to perform rituals (Ackerman, "At home"; cf. Hitchcock), along with the absence of any explicitly divine figurines. While both these characteristics are broadly in keeping with the wider West Semitic cultural context of domestic dwellings (Albertz and Schmitt), some argue they are suggestive of a limited form of household religion, and point instead to a preference for "local" religious practices within the neighborhood community (van der Toorn, *Family Religion*). But the fluidity and multifunctionality of space in the four-roomed house would suggest that a fixed place for any activity – including the performance of religious rituals and related actions – was not necessary (Nakhai).

Indeed, a notable characteristic of non-elite worship in traditional non-western societies appears to be the absence of a sharp distinction between the sacred and the profane (Verhoeven 124; compare S. A. Geller's essay in this volume). This would seem to be suggested by the archaeology of households in ancient Israel and Judah, for it is often only in finding an assemblage of cheaply produced, seemingly utilitarian vessels and objects (such as bowls, jugs and lamps) alongside objects with a more obvious "cultic" function (such as figurines, incense stands and amulets) that the religious use of domestic objects might be discerned (Albertz and Schmitt).

In one sense, this blurring of the sacred and the profane might be thought to reflect a constructed opposition between the "extraordinary" house in which the gods live (the local temple), and which demanded the careful marking and patrolling of ritual boundaries and objects, and the "ordinary" house in which people live, and in which they performed a changing variety of "mundane" tasks (Stowers). But it is also likely that the assumed distinction between the sacred and the profane is not only too simplistic in its application to traditional societies, but has also been overstated (Verhoeven).

By contrast, and as certain anthropologists and scholars of material culture increasingly argue, ritual and religious activities in these traditional societies are often deeply embedded in the social lives of the community as "strategic actions" (Bradley), so that religious meaning is constructed not only in the place but in the "doing" of activities: "by using objects, people gather them together spatially to form a place whose meaning derives from both actions and objects" (Gray 233). In other words, it is through the material manifestation and performance of actions that religious space is constructed, and religious meaning is accomplished (see also the essay by Theodore Lewis in this volume). Taken together, the people, places and objects of the household perform together as a dynamic whole to create or "do" religion – just as they do to create the "home."

The sociomateriality of the home can thus serve as a signpost for some of the more significant aspects of its religious culture. Taking cues from the most prevalent or distinctive features of the material remains of Israelite and Judahite households, the remainder of this discussion thus will focus on exploring some of the main characteristics of the religion of the home.

Setting a Meal

Of all household activities, the production, processing, preparation and consumption of food would have occupied a central place in day-to-day life. As Carol Meyers comments, "Survival depended upon the ability to raise crops and animals and to convert them into edible and wearable forms" (Meyers, "Household religion," 120; for the common foodstuffs of these ancient societies, see MacDonald). While much of this work was season dependent and variable in terms of its productivity, material remains indicate that much of the household's time, space and physical labor would have been taken up with its foodways: the paraphernalia of grain processing (grinding stones, smaller hand mills, sieves, grain pits), baking (clay ovens), beer-making (strainers), wine-making and olive-pressing (storage jars with both whole and perforated stoppers) are found commonly in domestic excavations (Ebeling; Meyers, "Material remains"; Albertz and Schmitt).

Excavations strongly suggest that household foodways also included a ritual dimension. Ritual objects, such as specialized libation vessels and ceremonial goblets, are often found assembled and arranged near fireplaces and cooking pits, along with other objects used for the consumption of food, such as bowls and spatulas (Albertz and Schmitt 224). In keeping with better-known (often temple-located) forms of religious practice in ancient West Asian societies, it thus seems highly probable that ritual meals formed an important part of household cult: food prepared, eaten and shared with those gods and/or ancestors credited with sustaining the agrarian productivity and well-being of the social group (Stolz).

The extent to which ritual meals would have comprised specialist foodstuffs is difficult to ascertain. While in temples ritual meals would have included regular and frequent meat offerings – as indeed the biblical portrayal of high-status animal sacrifice suggests – most scholars agree the ritual slaughter and consumption of animals (whether cows, sheep, goats or, in some regions and circumstances, pigs) was unlikely to have played as prominent and frequent a role in household religion (Bodel and Olyan), particularly given its costly impact on the household's economics (MacDonald 60–5).[2] It is more likely ritual meals instead comprised the regular or daily foodstuffs of the household – grain, bread or porridge; beer or perhaps wine (Ebeling) – and were rendered distinct from "ordinary" food by means of specialized actions and objects.[3]

In common with many traditional societies, and in keeping with the broader cultural landscape of ancient West Asia, the women of the household are likely to have played the dominant role in the processing and preparation of food – including ritual meals. This is suggestive of a more socioreligiously empowered aspect of women's lives than scholars have traditionally granted: in the home, women's religious experience and expertise was probably more highly valued than in certain other socioreligious settings, particularly those in which men played the dominant ritual roles (Meyers, "From household"; on the religious roles of higher-status women, see Marsman). For many scholars, especially those seeking to bring traces of women's religious lives out from the dark shadows cast by the male-centered traditions of biblical ideology (and indeed, biblical scholarship), the centrality of ritual meals offers powerful evidence that women are best regarded as the "ritual experts" (Meyers, "Material remains"; Ebeling; Dever, *Lives*) or even the "theologians" (Ackerman, "Household religion," 149) of household religion (see also the essay by Carol Meyers in this volume).[4]

However, although in the preparation and performance of the household's ritual meals it is likely women were considered the technical, religious specialists, attempts to rehabilitate them as religious leaders in the home may perhaps be a step too far toward contemporary Euro-American cultural preferences. Although household food-ways and other crafts and skills, such as spinning, weaving, midwifery and healing, probably formed the basis of women's informal religious networks within compounds and neighborhoods (Meyers, "Material remains"; Ebeling), it would be misleading simply to equate household religion with "women's religion."[5] After all, other members of the household, including fathers, husbands and sons, also played a key role in the production of the household's foodways, such as raising animals and crops and tending vines and olive trees. The household and its religion was thus a complex cultural matrix, socially constructed and rendered meaningful by means of the material interrelation of people, objects, actions and spaces. In a sense, the home was a site of reciprocal incorporation, both socially and materially. And ritual meals particularly expressed this.

As a daily social act, eating and drinking occupy a routinized place in the sociality of the household. As such, these activities lend themselves to meaningful investment as vehicles and manifestations of social identity and its religious expressions (Feely-Harnick). This is evident throughout the ancient West Asian cultures in which Israel and Judah were located, in which social engagement among and between worshippers and their gods was accomplished by means of ritual meals (Schmandt-Besserat). It is also reflected in numerous biblical traditions in which food and drink play a central role in the articulation and ritual manifestation of the relationship between humans and the divine.

Indeed, of all ritual activities, eating and drinking exhibit a particularly powerful religious materiality: as Michael Dietler observes, food and drink are "material objects produced specifically to be destroyed by a form of consumption that involves ingestion into the human body. This fact lends them a heightened symbolic and affective resonance in the social construction of the self" – and indeed in the construction of the socioreligious group (179).

It is the material "embodiment" of a ritual meal that is particularly effective in communicating the temporal dimension of household religion: a means of affirming and sustaining the existence of the social group, past, present and future. As is well known, the celebration and perpetuation of the generations is a primary concern of traditional household groups, and those of ancient Israel and Judah were no exception (cf. Stowers). Consequently, the dead – and perhaps those yet to be born – formed a part of the household alongside its living members (Stavrakopoulou, *Land*). And as vehicles of material embodiment, ritual meals likely played a major role in engaging and performing this temporal dimension of the household's social identity. As Paul Connerton argues, embodied or "incorporated" ritual performance functions as a means of conveying social memories, which in turn construct group identity (cf. Assmann). Drawing on Connerton's important work, David Sutton emphasizes that "remembering" in food creates a "cosmology of participation," in which the social group's past is brought into the present, and by which the "future" is indexed. It thus seems likely that the ancestors participated in the household's ritual meals, and were even recipients of food offerings in these contexts – a point to which the discussion will shortly return.

The powerful capacity for ritual meals to bring the past into the present by constructing and performing social "remembering" is well attested in a number of biblical traditions (see further Assmann; MacDonald; Altmann; Meyers, "Function of feasts"). Among the most prominent are those dealing with Passover, a ritual meal which in some texts is itself portrayed as a household activity (Exod. 12:1–28), but in others is seemingly co-opted and presented as a collective, "national" ceremony, performed at a central sanctuary to honor Yahweh (Exod. 23:14–17; Lev. 23:4–14; Num. 28:16–25; 2 Kings 23:21–23; 2 Chr. 30:1–27). While scholars disagree about the extent to which it was ever "originally" a household ritual, it is consistently promoted in the Hebrew Bible as a crucial means of "remembering" the ancestors and their relationship with Yahweh, who is presented in a number of Passover texts as the god of the household, as well as the god of the state.

Ritual meals thus represent one of the ways in which the very materiality of the home – its foodways, its bodies – functions as a mechanism for structuring and accomplishing socioreligious experience. Indeed, the high religious value of the materiality of the household is also well attested archaeologically in further features of the religion of the home, although it is not necessarily confined to the house itself.

Locating the Dead

The material remains of the dead and their burial places perhaps comprise the richest resource for understanding the religion of the home. In any society, mortuary practices and their associated rituals function just as much for the living as they do for the dead:

as numerous studies show, the methods and means of dealing with a corpse constitute a process effecting and maintaining the transformation of the deceased from a social person into a nonliving member of the household, enabling the living to negotiate and reframe their relationship with that individual (Bloch and Parry; Metcalf and Huntington; Hallam et al.).

Whilst there are some indications of regional variations, archaeological evidence suggests burial was the preferred means of dealing with the corpse in ancient Israel and Judah (Bloch-Smith). In particular, burial in cave, bench or chamber tombs, located outside settlements, is most typical of the Iron Age period.[6] Most archaeologists agree that the corpse would have been placed inside the tomb until the flesh had decomposed, leaving just the bones. The bones would then be gathered up and deposited in a niche in the wall of the tomb, or in a small pit or pile on the floor, often alongside the bones of the tomb's previous occupants, leaving space for the next fresh corpse.

The gathering of bones (often classed as "secondary burial") suggests the tomb was a locus of ritual activity beyond the initial burial itself – as might the presence of grave goods in virtually all tombs. In the main, these include terra-cotta jugs, storage jars, bowls and drinking vessels, lamps, amulets, rattles, beads, some anthropomorphic figurines (lacking obvious divine attributes) and jewelry (necklaces, bracelets, anklets, pendants, earrings, rings). While the jewelry, beads and rattles are likely to have held a magical or apotropaic (as well as ornamental) function for the dead, the presence of pottery vessels is more difficult to interpret: they appear not to have been specialized mortuary objects (although this does not mean individual items were not crafted especially for their mortuary use), but rather they are typical of the utilitarian domestic items used in the house. Scholars remain uncertain as to whether they were simply grave furnishings, or used solely in a funerary ritual, perhaps only by the mourners (Pitard), or were left for use by the dead, who might have been the recipients of food offerings (Lewis). However, in some ways, this is a moot point, for just as the social dynamics of eating and drinking among the living in the house likely allowed for the participation of the dead, so too a similar dynamic may well have pertained to the use of food and drink in the tomb as well. Either way, the presence of domestic vessels suggests the tomb was considered as much a part of the home as the house itself.[7]

What is more certain is the living community's concern to maintain the welfare of the material remains of the dead and their burial places. A handful of tombs from the Iron II period include (now damaged) inscriptions on their walls or at their entrances. Some of these simply identify the tomb's occupants, whereas others include a petition for a blessing from Yahweh (and "his Asherah," in two cases; see also Elizabeth Bloch-Smith's essay in this volume) or threaten a curse upon those who would enter the tomb with improper reason (Zevit, *Religions*; Lewis; Dever, *Lives*). The best known of these is the so-called "Steward's Inscription," which protected a high-status tomb in Jerusalem's Silwan Valley and has been dated to the latter half of the eighth century BCE. It identifies the tomb's occupant, a man with a Yahwistic name and who is described as "Over the House" – probably a technical term for a high-ranking official – before proclaiming: "There is no silver or gold, only [his bones] and the bones of his save-wife with him. Cursed be the person who opens this [tomb]!" (Avigad; cf. Isa. 22:25–28; see also the essays by John Huddlestun and Christopher Rollston in this volume).

In keeping with other examples from across ancient West Asia and the eastern Mediterranean, this tomb inscription attests to a fear of both the dead being disturbed, and the disturbed dead bringing a curse upon the living. Indeed, while the manipulation or removal of corpses or bones might be perceived in some circumstances as a socially appropriate or permissible activity,[8] the disturbance or unauthorized removal of remains from a tomb is in many societies (ancient and modern) often perceived negatively as an act of hostility toward the dead, displacing them not only from their graves, but also from their secure place in the underworld. This kind of disturbance would thus also destabilize both the post-mortem existence of the dead and fracture their relationship with the living. Warning off would-be tomb robbers and those seeking to do the dead harm is thus a primary function of tomb inscriptions – and significantly, also attests to a belief in the powerful social efficacy of the dead in the lives of the living (Lewis; Stavrakopoulou, *Land*).

Within this cultural context, it is unsurprising that an undisturbed burial in the ancestral tomb is thus idealized and celebrated in the Hebrew Bible and that the ritual "remembering" of the ancestors is heavily promoted – albeit in a way palatable to the monotheistic tastes of the biblical writers (Stavrakopoulou, *Land*). Although mortuary rites and other practices attesting to the care of the dead are not presented in any detail in the biblical traditions, a number of references to feeding the dead (Deut. 26:14; Isa. 57:6; 65:1–4; Ps. 16:3–4; 106:28; Tobit 4:17; Sir. 30:18; cf. Gen. 15:2), invoking and perpetuating their name (1 Sam. 28:15; 2 Sam. 18:18; cf. Prov. 10:7; Ps. 49:12; Ruth 4:10), and consulting the dead for their specialist knowledge (1 Sam. 28:3–25; Isa. 8:19–20; 19:3; 29:4) complement archaeological evidence suggesting they played a valuable religious role in ancient Israelite and Judahite households.

Corresponding anxieties about tomb disturbance, improper burial and corpse abuse also permeate the biblical traditions. In a number of texts, the aggressive exhumation of remains from tombs is presented as a punishment inflicted not only upon the dead, but upon their living descendants as a means of disrupting the social well-being of households (Jer. 8:1–4). Other texts threaten corpses or bones with violence or nonburial, and even annihilation by means of devouring by scavenging animals, or burning (2 Kings 23:15–20; Jer. 7:33–34; Ezek. 39:11–20).

The force of these biblical threats turns on the notion that the mistreatment of a corpse marks and manifests the social dislocation or abandonment of the dead. In some societies or in some circumstances, the material modification of corpses, the removal of organs, or the burning or devouring of the dead, is not perceived to be destructive to the dead or damaging to their post-mortem well-being; rather, it is often held to assist or manifest the transformation of the deceased and to regenerate the living community (Stephen). However, in other contexts, including those from which the biblical traditions emerged, the unwelcome damage or destruction of the corpse or its parts might be understood to render the deceased somehow socially unidentifiable, disabled, displaced or distressed in its post-mortem state, or even to limit or prevent the transition of the deceased individual beyond the living community (Stavrakopoulou, *Land*). Among some social groups, the communal impact of this is direct, for the distressed "spirit" of a mutilated corpse could harass or threaten the living, as is attested in certain Mesopotamian texts (Scurlock). There is also strong evidence to suggest that the dislocation of the dead, or the destruction of their grave and their remains, could similarly dislocate the living. In a number of societies, particularly (but not exclusively) those in a traditional or preindustrial cultural context, the dead perform a territorial function for the living, their burial places staking a claim to land on behalf of their descendants. Significantly, this perspective forms a deep-rooted seam running through the Hebrew Bible – indeed, even its highly specialized centrist ideology is framed around the territoriality of the dead (Stavrakopoulou, *Land*). Negative forms of corpse modification and displacement thus damage the living as well as the dead, as is well attested in the biblical traditions.

Both the archaeological and biblical material thus suggest not only that the tomb was a locus of ritual activity, but that the *material presence* of the dead was of great value to ancient Israelite and Judahite families. The burial site and the physical remains of the dead formed a part of the powerful materiality of the household, actively affecting the ritual remembrance of the ancestors (cf. Hallam and Hockey) and attesting to the continued and potent social efficacy of the dead in the lives of the living.

Ritualizing the Body

Of all artifacts widely considered indicative of household religion in ancient Israel and Judah, the so-called pillar figurines are perhaps the most distinctive (see also the discussion in Elizabeth Bloch-Smith's essay in this volume). Hundreds of examples have been found at sites dating from the tenth to the sixth centuries BCE throughout the areas identified as Israelite and Judahite, with the majority deriving from locations in Judah. Most have been found in domestic contexts, although their precise find-spots are variable: some are recovered from grain pits, cisterns or the rooms of houses; others are found in tombs (Kletter).

The artifacts themselves are stylized anthropomorphic baked-clay figurines, sometimes hollow, sometimes whole, portraying a woman holding or supporting her large, heavy breasts with her arms. The bodies of the figurines are hand-molded and stylistically sparse: with the exception of the arms and breasts, there are no distinctive features – nor any representation of the pubic triangle, labia or vagina. Instead, the trunk of the body is pillar-like in its presentation, broadening toward the bottom, which in some cases might allow the figurine to stand upright (Vriezen). In some cases, the heads of the figurines appear to have been made in a separate mold and subsequently attached to the body. Though simply produced, they share the same stylized features: clearly defined eyes and nose, and a short, tightly curled hairstyle or headdress. The heads of those figurines not made in two parts are less detailed again: a pinch of clay represents the nose; its hollows the eyes. In either case, the heads and faces exhibit very little variation. Although some figurines show traces of paint (usually whitewash, with red and black applied on top), the figurines tend to be devoid of decorative symbols or emblems (Byrne).

The seemingly standardized composition of the figurines, combined with their cheap production and widespread presence in domestic contexts, suggests these objects were reasonably common in households. Discerning their likely function and interpretation, however, remains a matter of some dispute among scholars.

Despite an apparent absence of divine emblems, many assume the pillar figurines are representations of the goddess Asherah, consort of Yahweh in the state cult of Judah, and a goddess widely argued to have been worshipped at local sanctuaries (van der Toorn, "Israelite figurines"; Ackerman, "At home"). Characterized by many scholars as a "fertility" or "mother" goddess, and a mediatrix and spouse of the high god, Asherah is often presented as one of the "approachable" members of the divine world, and a deity with a particular concern for fecundity – particularly that of women – in the earthly realm (Hadley). On the basis of her iconographical association with the "Tree of Life" motif, and in conjunction with the biblical portrayal of her cult symbol as a stylized (perhaps living) tree (for example, Deut. 16:21), some thus argue the pillar-shaped body of the figurine is best understood as a tree trunk, from which the goddess's supposedly bountiful breasts emerge (Keel and Uehlinger). The figurines are thus held to represent the worship of the Mother Goddess in the context of the home.

There are some problems with this interpretation, however. One is that the figurines are devoid of any obvious divine symbols, symbols which might reasonably be expected in view of goddess iconography attested in other West Semitic cultures (Albertz and Schmitt) and which might be expected if the figurines correspond in some way – perhaps as "souvenir" imitations – to the goddess's high-status cult statue in the Jerusalem temple, as some have argued (van der Toorn, "Israelite figurines"). Another is the broader methodological issue of what might teasingly be termed "Asherah-itis" in scholarship: while the acceptance of the goddess into the debating arena of the biblical academy is to be welcomed as an invaluable and paradigm-changing development in the scholarly understanding of ancient Israelite and Judahite religion, there is a tendency to see Asherah-worship everywhere as a matter of course, rather than considered and critical evaluation. Although this is not to belittle or diminish the role of Asherah in these ancient societies, it is to caution against an overreliance on this deity as an index with which to account for women's religious practice or elements of religion which appear focused on the female body.

Rather, the possibility that the pillar figurines represent a human woman should be taken more seriously. Given their overwhelming location in domestic contexts, and their cheap and relatively easy production from clay, it is possible that these figurines have been produced with some regularity and frequency, and that the heavy breasts emphasized on the figurines correspond not to the idealized body of a nurturing goddess, but to the bodies of their users themselves – the women of the household.

The large size of the breasts on the figurines, as well as the position of the figurines' arms, supporting or presenting the breasts, suggests that the breasts are the most significant aspect of the objects. While this is often taken as being generally indicative of female fertility, it is more probable that it is specifically lactation which is in view here – particularly given the absence of a pubic triangle or a womb motif on the figurines. Accordingly, some scholars prefer to interpret the figurines as magical or votive objects intended to bring about, sustain or petition for a steady flow of breast milk with which to feed a child (Hadley; Meyers, "From household"). Indeed, Ziony Zevit describes these and other votive objects as "prayers in clay" (Zevit, *Religions*, 274), and assumes they offer an insight into what is often termed the "personal piety" of mothers – and presumably expectant mothers – in the home.[9]

However, while it seems more likely that the figurines correspond to the bodies of human women, rather than that of a goddess, it cannot be taken for granted that each figurine indexes a concern for a specific individual's lactation in the way in which most scholars appear to assume.[10] In a number of village cultures and traditional societies, breast-feeding or its substitute with animal milk is often shared among women of the household – sometimes as a means of nurturing a child if for some reason (physical or practical) a mother is less able or unable to do so, but also as a means of sharing child-rearing activities, thereby constructing and maintaining the social, embodied fabric of the household (Maher). Indeed, at least one biblical tradition hints that a similar social dynamic pertaining to breast-feeding was not unknown (Ruth 4:1), although in most texts, given their higher-status contexts of composition, it is professional wet-nurses who appear more frequently (Gen. 24:59; 35:8; Exod. 2:9; 2 Kings 11:2–3).

A further clue to the use and function of the pillar figurines lies in considering more closely their materiality. In spite of their widespread presence in excavations of domestic sites, it is significant that very few examples have been found intact. Instead, most are broken. It might be thought these breakages are an inevitable consequence of a structural weakness in the figurines, but even those examples constructed from a single piece of clay tend to be broken across the trunk at the structurally strongest point of the object. This is suggestive of their being deliberately broken (Zevit, *Religions*, 271), which is often an action completing a ritual process, or accomplishing or manifesting a transformative religious reality, and is common to various cult objects throughout ancient West Asian cultures (Waraksa).

As such, the ritual breaking of the heavy-breasted figurines might point to a ritual concern more specific than only effective lactation; rather, the figurine might also have been used in a ritual marking the weaning of a child. In ancient Israel and Judah, as in many other ancient societies, children were probably breast-fed until they were at least three or four years old (Stol). As such, the weaning of a child was probably significant in a number of ways for the sociality of the home: not only was there a new member of the household, with whom the food and drink of the home (and its ritual meals) would be shared, but a weaned child was more likely to survive into adulthood and to become a productive member of the household as a socioeconomic unit. Moreover, the weaning of a child was more likely to herald or coincide with the woman's next pregnancy (Maher). This was a point in the life of both the woman and the child that was particularly transformative, as well as being of great significance for other members of the home. It seems unlikely that this was not marked as an important rite of passage in the life of the household. Indeed, some biblical traditions would appear to reflect an expectation that the weaning of a child was ritualized in some way (Gen. 21:8; cf. 1 Sam. 1:23). Thus, given the remarkable extent to which broken pillar figurines pepper the domestic sites of ancient Israel and Judah, it is not inconceivable that as a part of its ritual performance, the deliberate breaking of a pillar figurine accomplished the transformative rite of passage of a woman and a child, constructing in material form the shifting value of their bodies to the life of the home.

Summary

It has long been recognized that the writers of the Hebrew Bible offer a heavily distorted portrayal of the religious past. They are more concerned with the construction and promotion of an elite, idealized and "national" religious identity, than a representative portrait of the larger societies from which their traditions and texts emerged. In seeking to reconstruct a more plausible picture of the religious realities of ancient Israel and Judah, it is thus essential to examine the beliefs and practices of the agrarian households in which most Israelites and Judahites lived, worked and died.

In contrast to a number of studies, many of which rely too heavily on the biblical texts as a foundation from which to build their portraits of the past, this discussion has focused instead on some of the most representative or distinctive aspects of the material cultures of Israelite and Judahite households to argue that it is in the very materiality of the household that these ancient religious cultures are best perceived. The home, tomb and the body are each material entities, but each is at the same time socially constructed. As such, these are the sites at which household religion is manifest, exhibited and performed.

Notes

1   Acknowledging some of the difficulties and discrepancies in these definitions, Albertz and Schmitt suggest the compound term "family household" religion is used as an umbrella term with which to refer to three related forms of religion: the "domestic cult," which took place in or around the house, and in which the needs of the nuclear family were addressed; practices performed in and around the neighborhood, which were supported or engaged by members of the extended kinship group; and "public" cult, in which the family group participated in rituals and other celebrations alongside other kin, neighbors, and friends at regional or even state sanctuaries (45–6). While there are some attractive aspects of this model, it nonetheless reproduces (in an albeit condensed, repackaged form) Albertz's older and somewhat clunky tripartite model of ancient Israelite religious stratification, comprising family religion, local religion and "national" religion.

2   On the vexed issue of pork consumption and its possible ritual function, note Isaiah 65:1–4, in which its negative portrayal is nonetheless suggestive of pig sacrifice among some Judahites (see also the essay by Elizabeth Bloch-Smith in this volume).

3   Animal sacrifice with meat consumption is more likely to have been a high-profile component of neighborhood or local feasts – ritual events probably bound up with major transitions in the agricultural cycle; see further Meyers, "Function of feasts."

4   These views are further encouraged by biblical texts such as Jeremiah 7:17–18; 44:15–30, in which women appear to take the lead in performing rituals in a household cult of the Queen of Heaven (e.g., Ackerman, "Household religion").

5   This assumption is also heavily implied in the creative pieces offered by van der Toorn ("Nine months") and Ebeling, both of which focus on the religious behaviors of female characters.

6   While this might reflect in part the conventional privileging of certain (urban) sites over others (as discussed above), it is also due to the relative fragility of simple earthen graves, which are more likely to go undetected, disappear or suffer damage due to land management activities or erosion. As Albertz and Schmitt comment, the frequency of these types of burials is probably underrepresented in the archaeological record (439).

7   In higher-status areas, some tomb architecture would also indicate the tomb was similarly regarded as a part of the home: doorways with lintels, rooms and benches make up these burial places, and complement both comparative inscriptional evidence and biblical texts referring to the tomb as a "house" (cf. Job 17:13). Indeed, the common term for "grave" (*mškb*) can also mean "bed" (cf. Isa. 57:1–8).
8   Note, for example, the re-storage of bones in a tomb niche, pit or ossuary, or the transferral of bones from one tomb to another (Bloch-Smith).
9   Note, however, that Zevit leans toward the figurines representing the divine addressee of the prayers – a goddess (Zevit, *Religions*, 272).
10   In biblical scholarship, discussions of "personal piety" or the religion of "the individual" are often compromised by difficulties concerning ancient and modern constructions of the "individual" and "personhood." For a more nuanced discussion of these notions from the perspective of material cultural studies, see Fowler.

Bibliography

Abu el-Haj, Nadia. *Facts on the Ground: Archaeological Practice and Territorial Self-Fashioning in Israeli Society*. Chicago: University of Chicago Press, 2001. Critique of ideologies of some forms of Israeli archaeology.

Ackerman, Susan. "At home with the goddess." In William G. Dever and Seymour Gitin (eds), *Symbiosis, Symbolism, and the Power of the Past: Canaan, Israel, and Their Neighbors from the Late Bronze Age through Roman Palaestina* (pp. 455–68). Winona Lake, IN: Eisenbrauns, 2003. Examines biblical and archaeological evidence for the worship of Asherah in the home.

Ackerman, Susan. "Household religion, family religion, and women's religion." In John Bodel and Saul M. Olyan (eds), *Household and Family Religion in Antiquity* (pp. 127–58). Oxford: Wiley Blackwell, 2008. Biblical evidence for women's domestic religion.

Albertz, Rainer. *A History of Israelite Religion in the Old Testament Period*, trans. J. Bowden. 2 vols. London: SCM Press, 1994. A socioreligious approach to the biblical traditions.

Albertz, Rainer, and Rüdiger Schmitt. *Family and Household Religion in Ancient Israel and the Levant*. Winona Lake, IN: Eisenbrauns, 2012. A detailed analysis of archaeological evidence pertaining to family and household religion in Iron Age Israel and Judah.

Altmann, Peter. *Festive Meals in Ancient Israel: Deuteronomy's Identity Politics in Their Ancient Near Eastern Context*. Beihefte zur Zeitschrift für die Alttestamentliche Wissenschaft 424. Berlin: de Gruyter, 2011. The role of ritual meals in the construction of Deuteronomy's worldview.

Assmann, Jan. *Religion and Cultural Memory: Ten Studies*, trans. R. Livingstone. Palo Alto: Stanford University Press, 2006. Collection of essays exploring the formation of cultural memory in ancient Egypt, Israel and the Hebrew Bible.

Avigad, Nahman. "The epitaph of a royal steward from Siloam village." *Israel Exploration Journal* 3 (1953): 137–52. A key inscription from Iron II Judah.

Bloch, Maurice and Jonathan Parry (eds). *Death and the Regeneration of Life*. Cambridge: Cambridge University Press, 1982. Influential collection of essays about the anthropology of death.

Bloch-Smith, Elizabeth. *Judahite Burial Practices and Beliefs about the Dead*. Journal for the Study of the Old Testament, suppl. 123. Sheffield: JSOT Press, 1992. Classic work on Judahite mortuary practices, using archaeological and biblical data.

Bodel, John and Saul M. Olyan. "Comparative perspectives." In John Bodel and Saul M. Olyan (eds), *Household and Family Religion in Antiquity* (pp. 276–82). Oxford: Wiley Blackwell, 2008. A chapter by the editors in an excellent collection of essays on domestic religion in the ancient Mediterranean and West Asia.

Bourdieu, Pierre. *Outline of a Theory of Practice*. Cambridge: Cambridge University Press, 1977. Classic work of cultural theory.

Bradley, Richard. *Ritual and Domestic Life in Prehistoric Europe*. New York: Routledge, 2005. On the notion of ritualization.

Brody, Aaron J. "The archaeology of the extended family: A household compound from Iron II Tell en-Nasbeh." In Assaf Yasur-Landau, Jennie R. Ebeling, and Laura B. Mazow (eds), *Household Archaeology in Ancient Israel and Beyond* (pp. 237–54). Culture and History of the Ancient Near East. Leiden: Brill, 2011. A close analysis of archaeological evidence for domestic social groups.

Buchli, Victor. "Households and 'home cultures.'" In Dan Hicks and Mary C. Beaudry (eds), *The Oxford Handbook of Material Culture Studies* (pp. 502–17). Oxford: Oxford University Press, 2010. Interrogating the construction of "home" in cultural and social scientific debates.

Byrne, Ryan. "Lie back and think of Judah: The reproductive politics of pillar figurines." *Near Eastern Archaeology* 67 (2004): 137–51. Analysis of the political function of Judahite pillar figurines.

Cieraad, Irene (ed.). *At Home: An Anthropology of Domestic Space*. Syracuse, NY: Syracuse University Press, 1999. Essays on different constructions of the "home" in contemporary Western cultures.

Connerton, Paul. *How Societies Remember*. Cambridge: Cambridge University Press, 1989. Classic work on cultural memory and its sociopolitical functions.

Davis, Thomas W. *Shifting Sands: The Rise and Fall of Biblical Archaeology*. Oxford: Oxford University Press, 2004. Traces the paradigm shift in the use of archaeology in biblical studies.

Dever, William G. *Did God Have a Wife? Archaeology and Folk Religion in Ancient Israel*. Grand Rapids, MI: Eerdmans, 2005. The goddess Asherah in archaeological perspective (written for the general reader).

Dever, William G. *The Lives of Ordinary People in Ancient Israel: Where Archaeology and the Bible Intersect*. Winona Lake, IN: Eisenbrauns, 2012. An archaeological reconstruction of domestic life in eighth-century Israel and Judah (written for the general reader).

Dietler, Michael. "Feasting and fasting." In Timothy Insoll (ed.), *The Oxford Handbook of the Archaeology of Ritual and Religion* (pp. 179–94). Oxford: Oxford University Press, 2011. Archaeological and anthropological assessment of foodways in ancient cultures.

Ebeling, Jennie R. *Women's Lives in Biblical Times*. London: T&T Clark, 2010. Mixes fiction with archaeological and biblical data to reconstruct the life experiences of ordinary women in Iron Age Israel.

Faust, Avraham. "Differences in family structure between cities and villages in the Iron Age II." *Tel Aviv* 26 (1999): 233–52. Archaeological evidence for social diversity.

Faust, Avraham and Shlomo Bunimovitz. "The four room house: Embodying Iron Age Israelite society." *Near Eastern Archaeology* 66 (2003): 22–31. Domestic space as an index of Israelite identity and society.

Feely-Harnick, Gillian. "Religion and food: An anthropological perspective." *Journal of the American Academy of Religion* 63 (1995): 565–82. Anthropological study of the social role of foodways.

Fowler, Chris. *The Archaeology of Personhood: An Anthropological Approach*. London: Routledge, 2004. An archaeo-anthropological analysis of the notion of identity and personhood.

Gray, John. "Open spaces and dwelling places: Being at home on hill farms and in the Scottish borders." In Setha M. Low and Denise Lawrence-Zúñiga (eds), *The Anthropology of Space and Place: Locating Culture* (pp. 224–44). Oxford: Blackwell, 2003. Anthropological case study of constructions of "home."

Hadley, Judith M. *The Cult of Asherah in Ancient Israel and Judah: Evidence for a Hebrew Goddess*. Cambridge: Cambridge University Press, 2000. Detailed study of the goddess Asherah.

Hallam, Elizabeth and Jenny Hockey. *Death, Memory and Material Culture*. Oxford: Berg, 2001. Anthropological study of death and materiality.

Hallam, Elizabeth, Jenny Hockey, and Glennys Howarth. *Beyond the Body: Death and Social Identity*. London: Routledge, 1999. Excellent sociological and anthropological study.

Hardin, James W. "Understanding houses, households, and the Levantine archaeological record." In Assaf Yasur-Landau, Jennie R. Ebeling, and Laura B. Mazow (eds), *Household Archaeology in Ancient Israel and Beyond* (pp. 9–26). Culture and History of the Ancient Near East. Leiden: Brill, 2011. The social implications of domestic spaces.

Hitchcock, Louise A. "Cult corners in the Aegean and the Levant." In Assaf Yasur-Landau, Jennie R. Ebeling, and Laura B. Mazow (eds), *Household Archaeology in Ancient Israel and Beyond* (pp. 321–46). Culture and History of the Ancient Near East. Leiden: Brill, 2011. Evidence for small shrines in households.

Keel, Otto and Christopher Uehlinger. *Gods, Goddesses and Images of God in Ancient Israel*. Edinburgh: T&T Clark, 1998. Extensive collection and analysis of iconographical motifs.

King, Philip J. and Lawrence E. Stager. *Life in Biblical Israel*. Library of Ancient Israel. Louisville, KY: Westminster John Knox Press, 2001. Illustrated introduction to the material culture of Israel and Judah.

Kletter, Raz. *The Judean Pillar-Figurines and the Archaeology of Asherah*. Oxford: Tempus Reparatum, 1996. Important study of the Judahite pillar figurines.

Lewis, Theodore J. "How far can texts take us? Evaluating textual sources for reconstructing ancient Israelite beliefs about the dead." In Barry M. Gittlen (ed.), *Sacred Time, Sacred Place: Archaeology and the Religion of Israel* (pp. 169–217). Winona Lake, IN: Eisenbrauns, 2002. Excellent analysis of textual and archaeological perspectives.

Liverani, Mario. *Israel's History and the History of Israel*. London: Equinox, 2005. Minimalist and radical perspective on the historical reliability of the Hebrew Bible.

MacDonald, Nathan. *Not Bread Alone: The Uses of Food in the Old Testament*. Oxford: Oxford University Press, 2008. A social science approach to food traditions and motifs in the Hebrew Bible.

Maher, Vanessa (ed.). *The Anthropology of Breast-Feeding: Natural Law or Social Construct*. Oxford: Berg, 1992. Valuable cross-cultural collection of essays.

Marsman, Hennie J. *Women in Ugarit and Israel: Their Social and Religious Position in the Context of the Ancient Near East*. Leiden: Brill, 2003. Major study of the textual evidence for women's lives.

Metcalf, Peter and Richard Huntington. *Celebrations of Death: The Anthropology of Mortuary Ritual*. 2nd edn. Cambridge: Cambridge University Press, 1991. Classic and influential anthropological study of death practices.

Meyers, Carol. "From household to House of Yahweh: Women's religious culture in ancient Israel." In André Lemaire (ed.), *Congress Volume: Basel 2001* (pp. 277–303). Leiden: Brill, 2002. Social science approach.

Meyers, Carol. "Material remains and social relations: Women's culture in agrarian households of the Iron Age." In William G. Dever and Seymour Gitin (eds), *Symbiosis, Symbolism, and the Power of the Past: Canaan, Israel, and Their Neighbors from the Late Bronze Age through Roman Palaestina* (pp. 425–44). Winona Lake, IN: Eisenbrauns, 2003. Examines evidence for women's social networks.

Meyers, Carol. "Household religion." In Francesca Stavrakopoulou and John Barton (eds), *Religious Diversity in Ancient Israel and Judah* (pp. 118–34). London: T&T Clark, 2010. An excellent overview of the biblical and archaeological case for household religion.

Meyers, Carol. "The function of feasts: An anthropological perspective on Israelite religious festivals." In Saul M. Olyan (ed.), *Social Theory and the Study of Israelite Religion: Essays in Retrospect and Prospect* (pp. 141–68). Atlanta: Society of Biblical Literature, 2012. Feasting as social structure.

Miller, Daniel. "Behind closed doors." In Daniel Miller (ed.), *Home Possessions: Material Culture behind Closed Doors* (pp. 1–19). Oxford: Berg, 2001. Critical approaches to the analysis of domestic space.

Morgan, David. "Materiality, social analysis, and the study of religions." In David Morgan (ed.), *Religion and Material Culture: The Matter of Belief* (pp. 55–74). London: Routledge, 2010. Excellent essay on the value of materiality in religion.

Nakhai, Beth Alpert. "Varieties of religious expression in the domestic setting." In Assaf Yasur-Landau, Jennie R. Ebeling, and Laura B. Mazow (eds), *Household Archaeology in Ancient Israel and Beyond* (pp. 347–60). Culture and History of the Ancient Near East. Leiden: Brill, 2011. An archaeological approach to domestic religion.

Olyan, Saul M. "Family religion in Israel and the wider Levant in the first millennium BCE." In John Bodel and Saul M. Olyan (eds), *Household and Family Religion in Antiquity* (pp. 113–26). Oxford: Wiley Blackwell, 2008. Biblical and non-biblical evidence for the nature of family religion.

Pitard, Wayne T. "Tombs and offerings: Archaeological data and comparative methodology in the study of death in Israel." In Barry M. Gittlen (ed.), *Sacred Time, Sacred Place: Archaeology and the Religion of Israel* (pp. 145–67). Winona Lake, IN: Eisenbrauns, 2002. Critique of some assumptions in the debate about cults of the dead.

Schloen, J. David. *The House of the Father as Fact and Symbol: Patrimonialism in Ugarit and the Ancient Near East*. Winona Lake, IN: Eisenbrauns, 2001. Important comparative, social science study of patrimonialism.

Schmandt-Besserat, Denise. "Feasting in the ancient Near East." In Michael Dietler and Brian Hayden (eds), *Feasts: Archaeological and Ethnographic Perspectives on Food, Politics and Power* (pp. 391–403). Washington, DC: Smithsonian Institute Press, 2001. Useful overview of the social dynamics of feasting.

Scurlock, Jo Ann. "Death and the afterlife in ancient Mesopotamian thought." In Jack M. Sasson (ed.), *Civilizations of the Ancient Near East* (pp. 1883–93). New York: Scribner, 1995. Summary essay.

Stager, Lawrence E. "The archaeology of the family in ancient Israel." *Bulletin of the American Schools for Oriental Research 260* (1985): 1–35. Influential study.

Stavrakopoulou, Francesca. *Land of Our Fathers: The Roles of Ancestor Veneration in Biblical Land Claims*. Library of Hebrew Bible/Old Testament Studies 473. New York: T&T Clark International, 2010. The territorial value of the dead and their graves as ideological tools in the Hebrew Bible.

Stavrakopoulou, Francesca. "'Popular' religion and 'official' religion: Practice, perception, portrayal." In Francesca Stavrakopoulou and John Barton (eds), *Religious Diversity in Ancient Israel and Judah* (pp. 37–58). London: T&T Clark, 2010. Detailed critique of the "popular religion" paradigm in biblical scholarship.

Stephen, Michele. "Devouring the mother: A Kleinian perspective on necrophagia and corpse abuse in mortuary ritual." *Ethos 26* (1998): 387–409. On the social role of the corpse.

Stol, Marten. *Birth in Babylonia and the Bible: Its Mediterranean Setting*. Groningen: Styx, 2000. Comparative study.

Stolz, Fritz. *Einführung in den Biblischen Monotheismus*. Darmstadt: Wissenschaftliche Buchgesellschaft, 1996. Detailed introduction to the debate about monotheism in the Hebrew Bible.

Stowers, Stanley K. "Theorizing the religion of ancient households and families." In John Bodel and Saul M. Olyan (eds), *Household and Family Religion in Antiquity* (pp. 5–19). Oxford: Wiley Blackwell, 2008. Sharp, critical essay.

Sutton, David E. *Remembrance of Repasts: An Anthropology of Food and Memory*. Oxford: Berg, 2001. Anthropological study of the role of food and cultural memory.

van der Toorn, Karel. *Family Religion in Babylonia, Syria and Israel: Continuity and Change in the Forms of Religious Life*. Studies in the History and Culture of the Ancient Near East 7. Leiden: Brill, 1996. Influential study of the textual evidence.

van der Toorn, Karel. "Israelite figurines: A view from the texts." In Barry M. Gittlen (ed.), *Sacred Time, Sacred Place: Archaeology and the Religion of Israel* (pp. 45–62). Winona Lake, IN: Eisenbrauns, 2002. Case study in engaging biblical and archaeological approaches.

van der Toorn, Karel. "Nine months among the peasants in the Palestinian highlands: An anthropological perspective on local religion in the early Iron Age." In William G. Dever and Seymour Gitin (eds), *Symbiosis, Symbolism, and the Power of the Past: Canaan, Israel, and Their Neighbors from the Late Bronze Age through Roman Palaestina* (pp. 393–410). Winona Lake, IN: Eisenbrauns, 2003. Stimulating, creative piece.

Verhoeven, Marc. "The many dimensions of ritual." In Timothy Insoll (ed.), *The Oxford Handbook of the Archaeology of Ritual and Religion* (pp. 115–32). Oxford: Oxford University Press, 2011. Excellent essay on the concept and construction of ritual.

Vriezen, Karel J. H. "Archaeological traces of cult in ancient Israel." In Bob Becking, Meindert Dijkstra, Marjo C. A. Korpel, and Karel J. H. Vriezen (eds), *Only One God? Monotheism in Ancient Israel and the Veneration of the Goddess Asherah* (pp. 45–80). Sheffield: Sheffield Academic Press, 2001. Archaeological case study of evidence for goddess worship.

Waraksa, Elizabeth A. *Female Figurines from the Mut Precinct: Context and Ritual*. Orbis Biblicus et Orientalis 240. Göttingen: Vandenhoeck and Ruprecht, 2009. Detailed study of the socioreligious function of a group of ancient Egyptian figurines.

Zevit, Ziony. *The Religions of Ancient Israel: A Synthesis of Parallactic Approaches*. London: Continuum, 2001. Important and detailed analysis.

Zevit, Ziony. "False dichotomies in descriptions of Israelite religion: A problem, its origins, and a proposed solution." In William G. Dever and Seymour Gitin (eds), *Symbiosis, Symbolism, and the Power of the Past: Canaan, Israel, and Their Neighbors from the Late Bronze Age through Roman Palaestina* (pp. 223–35). Winona Lake, IN: Eisenbrauns, 2003. A critique of the "popular religion" paradigm.

CHAPTER 20

Education and the Transmission of Tradition

Raymond F. Person, Jr

In any society, education and the transmission of culture begins in the family home, where we learn our language from our parents and siblings and our culture through such everyday tasks as eating. Ancient Israel was no exception. In fact, because ancient Israel was primarily an agrarian society, this was even more the case, because formal education was strictly limited. With increasing urbanization and the related specialization, some ancient Israelites earned their living in various trades associated with artisan and craftsman guilds, but even in these settings education was primarily within the family business. Because of this, the vast majority of education and the transmission of culture in ancient Israel was oral, lacking any need of literacy.

An elite minority within the temple/palace bureaucracy received a formal education that included reading and writing. However, even their education was primarily oral in nature and the use of texts as a part of their curriculum was primarily as mnemonic aids for the internalization of the culture. Thus, even ancient Israelite scribes – the most literate members of their society – approached the task of reading, writing, and copying texts in ways that differ remarkably from how we moderns understand these same activities (see Susan Niditch's essay in this volume).

As the literate members of their society, scribes would have played an important role in the public education of the people by their recitation by memory and/or their public reading of traditional texts at various events such as religious festivals. Thus, even the illiterate, especially those in urban areas, nevertheless may have had some contact with literary texts in their public education at such occasional events.

Education in the Family Household

In ancient Israel, as now, the most basic social unit was the family and the task of education and the transmission of culture began in the family. In ancient Israel the family unit

The Wiley Blackwell Companion to Ancient Israel, First Edition. Edited by Susan Niditch.
© 2016 John Wiley & Sons, Ltd. Published 2016 by John Wiley & Sons, Ltd.

was referred to as the *bêt 'āb*, most literally the "house of the father." This term did not simply refer to the physical structure, but to all of the humans, animals, plants and land that together made up the basic socioeconomic unit. Thus, the most common translations are the "household of the father" or the "patriarchal household." Carol Meyers has made a good argument based on comparative anthropology of agrarian societies that a better translation is simply the "family household" ("Family"; see the essays by Francesca Stavrakopoulou, T. M. Lemos and Carol Meyers in this volume). Although the biblical text often describes the *bêt 'āb* in patriarchal ways, the social reality behind the text may not have been so patriarchal; rather, as in many other agrarian societies, even those in which gender roles are sharply defined, the *bêt 'āb* could only function well when the tasks of both males and females were highly and equally valued. The survival of the household required all family members to contribute significantly to the household's economy, including having important decision-making authority over the various gendered household tasks. Therefore, an androcentric denigration of work associated with women would have had serious negative consequences for the entire household and was probably not the reality in the typical *bêt 'āb*.

Like modern Israel, ancient Israel had a remarkable geographical diversity within its borders, so that various ecological niches existed and change from one to another could occur rapidly within short distances. Nevertheless, the general agricultural subsistence strategy throughout ancient Israel remained within the "Mediterranean agricultural pattern" that produced the major crops of grain, wine, and oil as well as a variety of legumes, fruits, nuts, herbs, and vegetables and included sheep and goat herding (Meyers, "Family," 10–11; see David Schloen's essay in this volume). Because of this tremendous ecological diversity, "virtually every family household experienced a different set of challenges in establishing a productive subsistence strategy" (Meyers, "Family," 19–20). The vital connection between the family's land and the knowledge concerning the best subsistence strategies for that land led to patrilineal and patrilocal traditions of ancient Israel, including levirate marriage (Deut. 25:5–6). Because of the close connections between the family and its land, "[t]he identity of any family unit was thus inseparable from its land, which was the material basis of its survival" (Meyers, "Family," 21).

The *bêt 'āb* depended on maximizing the labor of the entire family for its survival and this was differentiated to some degree according to both age and gender (Meyers, "Family," 22–32). Some seasonal tasks, such as the harvesting and storage of the main crops, required all able-bodied members of the household to assist; some ongoing tasks, such as tending orchards and vineyards or milking the animals, may have been shared. Other tasks were probably differentiated. Most likely the men were primarily responsible for the growing of the field crops, clearing fields, building terraces, constructing homes, and the making and repairing of tools. The women were primarily responsible for childcare, tending the gardens and livestock near the home, textile production, and food preservation and production. The children helped out with many of the light but time-consuming household tasks under the guidance of the women until they reached the age when they could assume their roles with the adults. This division of labor along gender lines meant that, on the one hand, the ecological knowledge necessary for growing the field crops was primarily male knowledge and, on the other hand, the technological knowledge of food preparation and textile production was primarily female knowledge. A patrilineal and patrilocal system strengthened both gendered realms of knowledge in that the male knowledge that was necessarily connected to the household's specific ecological niche remained on the land and the female knowledge that depended less on geographical factors was transported to the households of their husbands, thereby sharing any newfound strategies with other households. Both of these gendered realms of knowledge were closely interconnected – for example, the male knowledge that produced the grains in the field and the female knowledge that could store and prepare it for food – and both were necessarily valued highly, since the family's survival depended on them both.

The demands of subsistence farming meant that formal education – that is, the children leaving the home to attend a school taught by a professional teacher – was not only unnecessary, but strongly discouraged. The economics of the system simply did not allow for such formal education. Not only would the cost of losing the children's labor be devastating to the survival of the household, but the households in the villages would also not be able to afford the luxury of paying a teacher. Thus, the education and transmission of the culture occurred naturally in the context of the daily activities of the household and by extension to the village, the *mišpāḥâ*, especially when the various interrelated households came together for religious celebrations. Furthermore, even within agrarian societies, some degree of specialization probably existed within village life, so that, for example, midwives would have been important health care providers with some specialized skills not found in every household (Meyers, "Guilds," 164–5).

Because the Hebrew Bible is written by urban male elites, such specialists tend to be portrayed in ways that minimize how important women may have been in activities beyond the household. That is, even though some specialist roles may have been gender-specific – for example, "women singers, dancers, composers, mourners, and even reciters of proverbs or traditional sayings" (Meyers, "Guilds," 179) – such gender differentiation does not necessarily suggest a degradation of the value of such women specialists, at least within the village setting. Such specialists and their guilds, no matter how informal and occasional their "professional" gatherings may have been, certainly required at least some type of informal education within these guilds, most likely passing knowledge and skills from one generation to another within the family, while at the same time sharing any newfound knowledge from one practitioner to another.

Thus, within the agrarian households and villages of ancient Israel, education would have been an integral part of everyday life. In fact, James Crenshaw insightfully concluded, "Indirectly, the entire adult population contributed to moral training, for parents used communal insights, often formulated in maxims, to persuade their children that the teachings had wider sanctions than that of the individual household" (279). Societal norms were taught by parents to their children by drawing from the communal insights of the villages, and the professional skills were taught within the family and other informal groups within the villages.

Although it remained primarily an agrarian society throughout its history, ancient Israel also developed into something of a nation-state. As in other ancient Near Eastern societies, specialization developed further with increasing urbanization and centralization. Therefore, although the majority of the populace received their primary education in the agrarian *bêt 'āb*, not all household economies, especially in later periods, were based on subsistence farming, so that some families' primary source of income came from various trades, including pottery, textiles, stone masonry and carpentry, especially in the urban areas (Crenshaw 86; Rollston 123). New technological developments aided specialization. For example, the processing of grain into flour was an important task that women provided in the *bêt 'āb* by hand-grinding; however, with the development of milling technologies during the Hellenistic period this task that had been performed by women in the home became the task of men in a public business (Meyers, "Grinding"). Specialization did not always have the consequence of removing tasks previously associated with women in the home to those associated with men in the marketplace – for example, the specialization of midwifery continued as a women-only guild (Meyers, "Guilds," 164–5; "Grinding," 300) – but more often than not this was the consequence, at least within urban society.

Whatever the impact of the technology and the resulting specialization, the same principle for education remained – that is, the knowledge necessary for the continuation of the trade from one generation to the next and the success of the economic enterprise itself depended on the contribution and cooperation of various family members and the inheritance of the business from parent to child. Even for the vast majority of trades, formal education remained unnecessary and undesirable; rather, children learned from their parents in the natural environment of the family business, for just as the location of the family business of subsistence farming was the home, the location of the family business for most (if not all) of the specialized trades was also in the home or nearby.

Literacy in Ancient Israel

In the *bêt 'āb*, education did not require reading and writing, for subsistence farming does not require these skills. This would also be the case for the majority of the guilds, in which education was also primarily based in the family. For the vast majority of the populace, formal education, including literacy, was not only unnecessary but undesirable in light of the economic resources of time and money that it required. However, the development of a centralized state and its corresponding urbanization required various specialized skills, including the scribal skills of reading and writing. Even in the early monarchic period of ancient Israel, scribal guilds probably existed and scribal education occurred within the confines of these guilds. Much like the structure for the other trades, scribes most likely inherited the family business from their fathers. In contrast to some of the other trades, however, the scribal profession was more closely connected to the royal/temple administration of the capital city. Certainly, scribes could be found in some other urban areas and some may even have worked in private commerce, but even these scribes likely understood themselves and were perceived by others as having an origin in or close relationship to the central bureaucracy (Rollston 89, 113).

The discussion among scholars concerning literacy and especially the existence of schools open to the public includes, on the one hand, the argument that every major city in preexilic Judah had schools open to the masses so that literacy was widespread (Lemaire) and, on the other hand, claims that schools did not exist at all in ancient Israel, so that literacy was limited to a small elite group of bureaucrats (Whybray). Despite this variety, there appears to be a movement toward a more minimalist view of literacy and schools for instruction in ancient Israel, so much so that even as early as 1995 Graham Davies could conclude that "viewed as a whole, the tenor of scholarly discussion has moved from confident assertion [of the existence of schools] to doubt and even denial in recent years."

Nevertheless, most scholars have concluded that some form of scribal training, even as early as the monarchic period, was probable on the basis of the following types of evidence: (1) The Hebrew Bible contains narratives concerning professional scribes (for example, 2 Kings 22:8–13) (Carr, *Writing*, 112, 116–22; Rollston 88–90; van der Toorn, 76–7; Young), references to source materials, presumably from royal archives (for example, 1 Kings 14:19) (Carr, *Writing*, 112; P. Davies 86), and a technical vocabulary of scribalism (Rollston 112). (2) The complexity of the institution of the monarchy required scribal activity and, therefore, was necessarily involved in the education of scribes (P. Davies 15–19; Niditch, *Oral World*, 4; Dell 132). (3) Since scribal schools existed throughout the ancient Near East, ancient Israel by analogy may also have had scribal schools (Carr, *Writing*, 111–12; P. Davies 15–30; Rollston 85–8; van der Toorn 76). (4) Archaeological evidence, especially epigraphic sources, strongly suggests a professional class of scribes with standardized education (Carr, *Writing*, 112, 122–4; Crenshaw 34–5; P. Davies 7–78).

The recent contribution to the discussion by Christopher Rollston is the most judicious and thorough. Based to some degree on all four types of evidence but most significantly on the epigraphic data, Rollston concluded that literacy in ancient Israel was restricted to a small group of elites, who had received formal, standardized education in reading and writing as is evident in the epigraphic record, especially with regards to standardized practices of writing (see Christopher Rollston's essay in this volume). Rollston carefully avoids the problematic language of "schools," insisting rather that "formal, standardized education" most likely occurred within the scribal guilds themselves (94–5). In this sense, to some degree this "formal, standardized education" involving reading and writing is simply an extension of the type of education found in the other trades, in that scribal guilds were probably significantly based on "scribal families" (Rollston 122–5). So once again the family appears to be the primary context for education and transmission of cultural and professional knowledge.

In summary, the evidence strongly suggests that some type of formal education existed in ancient Israel, including during the monarchy, for the purpose of training a small cadre of professional scribes to serve the administrative bureaucracy of the state. Certainly some scribes would have been low-level functionaries involved in reading and writing more mundane, administrative texts (for example, letters, tax records, and inventories), but the comparative evidence from Mesopotamia and Egypt combined with the biblical evidence strongly suggests that scribes were also part of the royal officials, whose tasks were not only related to the act of reading and writing but also to providing advice and counsel (Blenkinsopp; Carr, *Writing*, 116–22; van der Toorn 51–108). Thus, Leo Perdue can conclude: "The scribes (*sōpərîm*) and sages (*ḥăkāmîm*) of Israel and Judah comprised a professional social class of intellectuals, composers, officials, and clerks from their origins in the monarchic period until the emergence of

Rabbinic Judaism during the early centuries of the Common Era (the Tannaitic and Amoraic periods)" ("Sages," 3).

This group of elites, most importantly the scribal guilds, produced the literature preserved in the Hebrew Bible. We must nevertheless note that some (if not most) of this literature has deep roots in the broader tradition of transmitting the culture in the context of the family and village, in the context of oral traditional culture. For example, although certainly the Book of Proverbs is elite literature, probably produced under the influence of ancient Egyptian wisdom literature for the purpose of training scribes and sages for the royal bureaucracy, the book itself is a compilation of proverbs and admonitions, many of which probably derive from the agrarian culture of the *bêt 'āb* and represent common wisdom (Perdue, *Wisdom Literature*, 37–76; see John Huddlestun's essay in this volume). Although the Book of Judges can be understood as literature undergirding the ideology of the monarchy, the book itself draws significantly from the genre of folktales that is most often associated with oral traditions (Niditch, *Judges*; see Susan Niditch's essay in chapter 5 of this volume). The urban literati had an influence on the preservation and transmission of the cultural legacy of ancient Israel, but to some degree their literature remained dependent on the rich oral traditional literature that not only preceded the written tradition but also probably dwarfed it in comparison. Even the scribes, the most literate individuals of ancient Israel, lived and worked in a primary oral society, so that they undertook even their most literate activities – that is, reading and writing texts – in ways that were significantly influenced by the primary orality of their culture (Person, *Deuteronomic History*, 41–68).

Texts as Mnemonic Aids

The vast majority of education and the transmission of culture occurred in the household, whether the family business was subsistence farming or one of the specialized trades. This would probably be the case for scribal education as well, for there is some evidence for scribal families – for example, 1 Chronicles 2:55 refers to "the families of the scribes that dwell at Jabez: the Tirathites, the Shimeathites, and the Sucathites" (Blenkinsopp 309–10; Rollston 122–6). Even though scribal guilds probably coincided significantly with scribal families, the formal education that scribes received was probably more state sponsored than that of the other trades. In fact, the epigraphic evidence, especially the consistency of the Old Hebrew script and the use of the Egyptian hieratic numeric system, strongly suggests the necessity of a formal, standardized educational system that most likely could only have come from a centralized state (Rollston 112–13). Rollston concluded, "I contend that those capable of conveying the necessary data to the Old Hebrew scribal students would have been a scribal teacher associated with the national Old Hebrew apparatus" (113). Though he avoids the term "school," Rollston nevertheless argues convincingly for state-sponsored formal, standardized education for scribes. Even though such formal education may have been extremely limited in terms of who the students were, the rest of this chapter concerns this formal education, probably the only education in ancient Israel that included the teaching of reading and writing. Before turning more explicitly to the form of this education, we should explore further the function of texts in the ancient world, especially since literacy is what sets such scribal training apart from the education of those in the other trades.

Even as the most literate members of their society, scribes lived and functioned in a primary oral culture, so that their understanding of written texts differed markedly from our own modern notions and more closely reflected the transmission of oral traditions. We will see that this is the case by examining comparative data on memory and its relationship to written texts, by observing that textual plurality and multiformity was the standard in the ancient world, and by contrasting our modern notion of "text" with the ancient understanding of writing.

In his comparative study of literature in the ancient Near East, David Carr concludes that the visual presentation of ancient texts required so much of the readers that they most likely were already familiar with the content of literature and may have even memorized it, especially with regards to the "long-duration texts like the Bible, Gilgamesh, or Homer's works" (*Writing*, 5). In fact, such literature represented the culture that should be internalized, which was the goal of scribal education. Carr writes that "such written copies were a subsidiary part of a much broader literate matrix, where the focus was as much or more on the transmission of texts from mind to mind as on transmission of texts in written form. Both writing and oral performance fed into the process of indoctrination/education/enculturation" (*Writing*, 5). Thus, the written texts functioned as mnemonic aids rather than the primary repository of memory (see also Steven Weitzman's essay in this volume). The primary repository was the collective mind of the community (preserved most carefully by the scribes) and the use of texts was simply one means to strengthen the transmission of culture, which was primarily oral in nature.

Carr's understanding of ancient literature as mnemonic aids relates well to the understanding of memory in the comparative study of oral traditions as summarized in the following five conclusions by John Miles Foley:

> First, memory in oral tradition is emphatically not a static retrieval mechanism for data. Second, it is very often a kinetic, emergent, creative activity. Third, in many cases it is linked to performance, without which it has no meaning. Fourth, memory typically entails an oral/aural communication requiring an auditor or audience. Fifth, and as a consequence of the first four qualities, memory in oral tradition is phenomenologically distinct from "our memory" (84).

Drawing upon the work of Foley and others, Raymond Person concludes that "the interplay between the oral and the written in the biblical description of oral instruction, writing, and memory … strongly suggests that Foley's five conclusions … also apply to the Hebrew Bible, including the role that texts played in the collective memory" ("Role," 547). For example, the oral and written characteristics of the Mosaic law work together to ensure the proper internalization of God's law, as is illustrated in Deuteronomy 11:19–20: "Teach them [these words] to your children, talking about them when you are in your house and when you are on the road, when you lie down and when you get up. Write them on the doorposts of your house and on your gates." Just as Moses recited the law to the people, the people should constantly recite them to their children, including settings in which it would be highly improbable for them to be carrying heavy scrolls. Since "these words" (Deut. 11:18) refers to God's "every commandment" (Deut. 11:13), the command to "write them on the doorposts" obviously is referring to selected commandments that symbolically represent the whole of the law. Furthermore, this quote brings us back to the above observation that education occurred within the family, even though the references here to writing probably reflect the ideology of the elite scribes more than common practice by a literate population. Therefore, this quote illustrates well how memory associated with the law is, in Foley's words, a "kinetic, emergent, creative activity … linked to performance … [that] is phenomenologically distinct from 'our memory'" (84; compare Person, "Role").

This phenomenologically distinct memory is also reflected in the textual plurality and multiformity of the extant texts of the Hebrew Bible. Carr introduces the term "memory variants," which are "the sort of variants that happen when a tradent modifies elements of texts in the process of citing or otherwise reproducing it from memory" such as "exchange of synonymous words, word order variation, [and] presence and absence of conjunctions and minor modifiers" (*Formation*, 17, 33; see similarly Person, "Ancient Israelite scribe"). He provides numerous examples from the Gilgamesh epic, the Temple Scroll, parallels between Samuel–Kings//Chronicles, and parallel proverbs. Based on comparisons of so-called "biblical" and "non-biblical" works at Qumran as well as the so-called "reworked" or "rewritten" texts, Sidnie Crawford concludes that most Jewish groups during the Second Temple period "did not insist upon a single textual tradition, but were willing to accept a certain amount of textual flux, even to the point of accepting two parallel literary editions of the same text as valid Scripture" (37). Similarly, Person concludes that both the Deuteronomic History and the Book of Chronicles "may best be understood as limited instantiations of the broader tradition in which an interplay of texts and communal memory exists, an ancient tradition that has been lost to us except as witnessed by these two competing historiographies and the textual plurality in which they exist" (*Deuteronomic History*: 160). The long-held consensus model of the textual production and transmission of ancient literature – that is, an authoritative text that determines future copies or becomes a "source" text for a "vulgar" text – has been seriously undermined by the thorough reexamination of text-critical evidence, especially in light of the study of the Dead Sea Scrolls. The ancient notion of literature, whether it exists primarily as "oral literature" or as written texts, differs significantly from our modern notion of a literary text, because it allows for a high degree of multiformity that led to what, from our modern perspective, is a plurality of texts but what, from an ancient perspective, might best be understood as a collection of texts, not one of which can re-present the tradition in its fullness but each one being nevertheless faithful to some degree to that tradition.

Scribal Guilds as Vehicles of Education and Transmission

Scribal education – that is, teaching both the writing and reading of texts – would have occurred primarily (if not exclusively) within the centralized bureaucracy of the state, most likely in the capital city, for the purpose of training scribes to effect the recording, storing and retrieving of administrative data as well as to provide a means for a certain degree of state-controlled propaganda through the selective transmission of cultural traditions, including religious texts. This statement is not inconsistent with the above observation that scribal training probably occurred within scribal families, for the scribal families themselves were situated within the central bureaucracy. Of course, the scribal families may have not always wholeheartedly accepted the cultural propaganda of the state, so that sometimes they may have written texts with ideologies critical of the (present or past) state bureaucracy (for example, 1 Sam. 8) or of the dominant ideology (for example, the Book of Job or the Book of Jonah). Nevertheless, the training of scribes served the administrative needs of the central government and thereby determined much of the curriculum. The curriculum then in turn determined to a large degree the public curriculum that the scribes as transmitters of culture presented in their recitations and education of the people.

Since the state sponsored scribal training to meet its own administrative needs, these very needs probably determined much of the curriculum. Scribes would thus learn about record-keeping and letter-writing as two of the most important administrative uses of reading and writing and these activities would have been standardized to ease the communication that they provided, especially since these are the types of texts that were less written as aids to memorization and were more like "static retrieval mechanism[s] for data" (Foley 84). The standardization would have included the script itself and the layout of the writing on the writing surface (margins, lines, letter size, spacing of letters) as well as learning certain formal characteristics, such as epistolary formulas (Rollston 91–115). Of course, in order to learn how to write, the ancient scribes must have had the knowledge of producing much of their own supplies, including pen and ink (Rollston 112). Furthermore, such administrative tasks often required the recording of quantitative data; therefore, the scribes must have learned some formal, standardized numeric system and from the epigraphic record this system was based on the Egyptian hieratic numerical system (Rollston 110). Thus, Rollston described the abilities of a trained scribe as follows: "the production of Old Hebrew texts in the standard script of the period, the standard orthography of the period, the capability of using a dominant numeric system, and the capability of employing a standard format (e.g., for letters, deeds, and so on)" (113; see also Tov 13–14 and Christopher Rollston's essay in this volume). Some scribes obviously must have been proficient in various foreign languages and scripts as well, since correspondence with other nation-states was necessary, especially when one was the vassal within a larger empire. The biblical text itself shows significant influence from other literature, even to the point of some literary dependence (Perdue, "Sages"; see John Huddlestun's and Neal Walls' essays in this volume).

The scribal skills necessary to serve these administrative purposes transferred well to the preservation and transmission of literature. Such cultural transmission may have been a secondary concern of the state, especially since the primary oral character of the society continued long after the introduction of writing (and arguably until the invention of printing presses with movable type); however, the state apparatus of writing may have been a somewhat effective tool for the centralization and standardization of the culture by the state. At least, the biblical text strongly suggests that this was attempted, even though Schniedewind and others make too much of this in their advocating that during the monarchic period "textualization" had already transformed the oral religious culture into a "religion of the book" (Schniedewind 135). For example, as noted above, Deuteronomy required every Israelite to write the law on their doorposts (Deut. 11:20), something that was probably beyond the writing skills of the populace. Furthermore, at times we see complaints about the efforts of scribes who are controlling the message, as when Jeremiah referred to the lying pen of the scribes (Jer. 8:8). Nevertheless, the comparative and biblical evidence strongly suggests that literary texts were primarily mnemonic devices for the purpose of the internalization/memorization of the tradition (Carr, *Writing*). We must constantly remind ourselves, however, that such memorization was not rote memorization, but an internalization of the meaning of the literature that allowed for a high degree of multiformity, so much so that our modern division between composition and transmission of texts is itself anachronistic.

The above distinction between administrative texts and literature must also not be understood as rendering them mutually exclusive. Administrative texts such as royal annals and letters may be some of the sources behind the literature of the Hebrew Bible. For example, the Deuteronomic History may include source material from preexilic royal archives. In fact, if the copying of texts was an important part of scribal training, then such examples suggest a close connection between such administrative documents and some of the religious literature that the Hebrew Bible later comprises.

Despite the widespread acceptance that such scribal training must have occurred in ancient Israel, little epigraphic evidence of the training itself exists. Nevertheless, Rollston discussed epigraphic evidence that he finds convincing, such as an abecedary and a student exercise text (111, 120–2). Although such earlier evidence is often lacking, Emanuel Tov has described such scribal exercises among the Qumran materials and concluded that similar practices must have occurred during the earlier periods, including the monarchy (14, 261).

As noted above, the scribes/sages were "a professional social class of intellectuals, composers, officials, and clerks" (Perdue, "Sages," 3) that served in various capacities (Rollston 129; Young). As was the case in Egypt (Williams), most likely the education one received within the Jerusalem bureaucracy began with a basic curriculum (emphasizing reading, writing and arithmetic), which led to more specialized studies, preparing for the different leadership roles within the temple and royal complexes such as priests, royal officials and possibly cult prophets. Which texts were memorized by the advanced students may have differed, depending on what specific leadership roles the students were preparing for within the different family guilds. For example, some subjects such as medicine may have been limited to specific specialists. Furthermore, the specific core texts that were taught most likely differed at least to some degree from one period to another. Such historical variety and the differentiation between the various guilds of specialists may help explain the variety of literary texts found in the collection we call the Hebrew Bible, many of which were likely produced in such educational settings. However, we must acknowledge that what has survived of the written curriculum of ancient Israel's scribal education is primarily (if not exclusively) those literary works that had meaning for the broader culture, so that they were much more than curricular materials. Those texts that were primarily used in the context of such scribal training (for example, exercise texts) have with very few exceptions been lost forever or remain buried in the vast area of Jerusalem that has not been excavated.

How did the teachers approach the task of teaching their students? We should remember that such education probably occurred within scribal families, so that the use of "father"/"son" imagery in Proverbs for instruction probably reflects such a setting. Just as raising children is portrayed in Proverbs as involving corporal punishment (Prov. 13:24), difficult students were probably beaten vigorously. In order to keep the students' interest, the teachers probably encouraged debate and dialog. Furthermore, since scribal students and their teachers were almost exclusively male, teachers spiced things up a bit with liberal uses of sexual innuendo (Crenshaw 117). In addition to internalizing literary texts and probably memorizing various proverbs and admonitions, students were encouraged to learn from their observations upon nature and human culture and by analogy to apply their observations to new situations (Crenshaw 120–6).

Those scribes who reached a higher level of training – that is, those who had been most successful in internalizing the cultural meanings of the (oral and written) texts and other forms of instruction – probably participated in some public educational events sponsored by the central bureaucracy. At least this can be inferred from the fact that all of the major characters of both the Deuteronomistic History and the Books of Chronicles are portrayed as having scribal skills and participating in the public recitation of important texts (Person, *Deuteronomistic History*, 51–65). For example, Moses (Deut. 32:45), Joshua (Josh. 8:32–35), Josiah (2 Kings 22–23//2 Chr. 34–35), and Ezra (Neh. 8:2–8) all recited the law to the people, taught them what it required and led them in their ritual obedience to the law. Therefore, the education that the scribes received also trained accomplished scribal leaders who in turn participated in the education of the masses by the public recitation of religious texts, especially during festivals in the capital city. In this way, the central bureaucracy could influence to some degree the primary oral culture of ancient Israel first through the formal, standardized training that specialists, especially scribes, received and then by the scribal leaders imparting the cultural traditions that they received within their guilds to the people on behalf of the temple and/or palace.

Bibliography

Blenkinsopp, Joseph. "The sage, the scribe, and scribalism in the Chronicler's work." In J. G. Gammie and L. G. Perdue (eds), *The Sage in Israel and the Ancient Near East* (pp. 307–15). Winona Lake, IN: Eisenbrauns, 1990. Analysis of the figure of sage/scribe in the Book of Chronicles.

Carr, David M. *Writing on the Tablet of the Heart: Origins of Scripture and Literature*. Oxford: Oxford University Press, 2005. Appraisal of the role of biblical texts as mnemonic aids with comparative evidence from the ancient Near East.

Carr, David M. *The Formation of the Hebrew Bible: A New Reconstruction*. Oxford: Oxford University Press, 2011. Criticism of current source-critical and redaction-critical approaches to the Hebrew Bible based on "empirical models," and proposals for moving forward.

Crawford, Sidnie White. *Rewriting Scripture in Second Temple Times*. Grand Rapids, MI: Eerdmans, 2008. Analysis of "rewritten scripture" focusing on Qumran documents.

Crenshaw, James L. *Education in Ancient Israel*. New York: Doubleday, 1998. Reconstruction of education in ancient Israel influenced significantly by the author's knowledge of wisdom literature, including that of Mesopotamia and Egypt.

Davies, Graham I. "Were there schools in ancient Israel?" In J. Day, R. P. Gordon, and H. G. M. Williamson (eds), *Wisdom in Ancient Israel: Essays in Honor of J. A. Emerton* (pp. 199–211). Cambridge: Cambridge University Press, 1995. Analysis of biblical and epigraphic evidence of schools in ancient Israel.

Davies, Philip. *Scribes and Schools: The Canonization of the Hebrew Scriptures*. Louisville, KY: Westminster John Knox, 1998. Reconstruction of the role of scribes and scribal schools in the canonization process in the Second Temple.

Dell, Katherine. "Scribes, sages, and seers in the First Temple." In L. G. Perdue (ed.), *Scribes, Sages, and Seers: The Sage in the Eastern Mediterranean World* (pp. 125–44). Göttingen: Vandenhoeck & Ruprecht, 2008. Discussion of the role of scribes, sages and seers in the First Temple period, focusing primarily on the Deuteronomistic History.

Foley, John Miles. "Memory in oral tradition." In R. A. Horsley, J. A. Draper, and J. M. Foley (eds), *Performing the Gospel: Orality, Memory, and Mark: Essays in Honor of Werner Kelber* (pp. 83–96). Minneapolis: Fortress, 2006. A comparative study of the role of memory in oral traditions.

Lemaire, André. "The sage in school and temple." In J. G. Gammie and L. G. Perdue (eds), *The Sage in Israel and the Ancient Near East* (pp. 165–81). Winona Lake, IN: Eisenbrauns, 1990. Reconstruction of widespread literacy and education in First Temple Israel.

Meyers, Carol L. "The family in early Israel." In L. G. Perdue et al. (eds), *Families in Ancient Israel* (pp. 1–47). Louisville, KY: Westminster John Knox Press, 1997. Reconstruction of the family household in premonarchic Israel.

Meyers, Carol L. "Guilds and gatherings: Women's groups in ancient Israel." In P. H. Williams, Jr and T. Hiebert (eds), *Realia Dei: Essays in Archaeology and Biblical Interpretation in Honor of Edward F. Campbell, Jr. at His Retirement* (pp. 154–84). Atlanta: Scholars Press, 1999. Reconstruction of guilds and other groups of women in ancient Israel based on archaeological and social scientific methods.

Meyers, Carol L. "From house to House of Yahweh: Women's religious culture in Ancient Israel." In A. Lemaire (ed.), *Congress Volume: Basel 2001* (pp. 277–303). Leiden: Brill, 2002. A discussion of how the change in technology from hand-grinding grain to mechanized mills influenced women's roles in the household.

Meyers, Carol L. "Grinding to a halt: Gender and the changing technology of flour production in Roman Galilee." In S. Montón-Subias and M. Sánchez-Romero (eds), *Engendering Social Dynamics: The Archaeology of Maintenance Activities* (pp. 65–74). Oxford: Archaeopress, 2008. Analysis of the connection between family households and the temple, especially focusing on the role of women in the religious culture of ancient Israel.

Niditch, Susan. *Oral World and Written Word: Ancient Israelite Literature*. Louisville, KY: Westminster John Knox Press, 1996. Reconstruction of literacy and the role of writing in ancient Israel, including discussions of the need to revise source-criticism.

Niditch, Susan. *Judges: A Commentary*. Louisville, KY: Westminster John Knox, 2008. Commentary on Judges drawing significantly from folklore studies and the comparative study of oral traditions.

Perdue, Leo G. "The Israelite and early Jewish family: Summary and conclusions." In L. G. Perdue et al. (eds), *Families in Ancient Israel* (pp. 163–222). Louisville, KY: Westminster John Knox Press, 1997. Editor's conclusion to a collection that contains essays on the history of the family in ancient Israel.

Perdue, Leo G. *Wisdom Literature: A Theological History*. Louisville, KY: Westminster John Knox Press, 2007. Introductory textbook for the wisdom literature of the Hebrew Bible.

Perdue, Leo G. "Sages, scribes, and seers in Israel and the ancient Near East: An introduction." In L. G. Perdue (ed.), *Scribes, Sages, and Seers: The Sage in the Eastern Mediterranean World* (pp. 1–34). Göttingen: Vandenhoeck & Ruprecht, 2008. Summary of the role of scribes, sages, and seers in Israel, drawing significantly upon comparative Near Eastern evidence.

Person, Raymond F., Jr. "The ancient Israelite scribe as performer." *Journal of Biblical Literature* 117 (1998): 601–9. Analysis concluding that ancient Israelite scribes copied their texts allowing for multiformity in ways analogous to oral epic performers.

Person, Raymond F., Jr. *The Deuteronomistic History and the Book of Chronicles: Scribal Works in an Oral World*. Atlanta: Society of Biblical Literature, 2010. Critique of the consensus model and new proposal for the relationship between Samuel-Kings and Chronicles.

Person, Raymond F., Jr. "The role of memory in the tradition represented by the Deuteronomistic History and the Book of Chronicles." *Oral Tradition 26* (2011): 537–50. Extension of Foley's arguments on memory in oral traditions to the relationship between Samuel–Kings and Chronicles.

Rollston, Christopher A. *Writing and Literacy in the World of Ancient Israel: Epigraphic Evidence from the Iron Age*. Atlanta: Society of Biblical Literature, 2010. The most definitive discussion of epigraphy on the issue of writing and literacy in ancient Israel.

Schaper, Joachim. "Tora als Text im Deuteronomium." In L. Morenz and S. Schorch (eds), *Was ist ein Text? Alttestamentliche, agyptologische und altorientalistische Perspektiven* (pp. 49–63). Berlin: de Gruyter, 2007. An argument for the textualization of Deuteronomy and scripture.

Schniedewind, William M. *How the Bible Became a Book: The Textualization of Ancient Israel*. Cambridge: Cambridge University Press, 2003. An argument for the textualization/standardization of scripture beginning in monarchic Israel.

van der Toorn, Karel. *Scribal Culture and the Making of the Hebrew Bible*. Cambridge, MA: Harvard University Press, 2007. Analysis of literacy and writing in ancient Israel within a comparative study of the ancient Near East.

Tov, Emanuel. *Scribal Practices and Approaches Reflected in the Texts Found in the Judean Desert*. Studies on the Texts of the Desert of Judea 54. Leiden: Brill, 2004.

Whybray, R. N. "The sage in the Israelite royal court." In J. G. Gammie and L. G. Perdue (eds), *The Sage in Israel and the Ancient Near East* (pp. 133–9). Winona Lake, IN: Eisenbrauns, 1990. An argument for a select group of elites as literate in a primarily illiterate society of ancient Israel.

Williams, Ronald J. "Scribal training in ancient Egypt." In J. G. Gammie and L. G. Perdue (eds), *The Sage in Israel and the Ancient Near East* (pp. 19–30). Winona Lake, IN: Eisenbrauns, 1990. Discussion of scribal training and schools in ancient Egypt.

Young, Ian M. "Israelite literacy: Interpreting the evidence." *Vetus Testamentum 48* (1998): 239–53, 408–22. Analysis of the amount of literacy in ancient Israel based on biblical, epigraphic, and comparative data.

CHAPTER 21

Kinship, Community, and Society

T. M. Lemos

I t is impossible to study any group of people without examining their customs surrounding kinship, their modes of building community, and their patterns of social organization. Kinship, community, and society are in fact overlapping categories of analysis, and even a cursory look at Israelite texts demonstrates the necessity of understanding these areas well in order to comprehend not only the earliest period of Israelite history – when kinship seems to have been the main organizing force within the society of ancient Israel – but all periods of Israelite and Judean history. The social history of ancient Israel and Judah was in no way static, and this essay, following a brief discussion of method and definitions of terms, will proceed in chronological fashion in order to make clear not only how this society was organized in different periods but also to demonstrate the very significant changes that occurred over the course of several centuries.

Methodological Issues and Terminology

The study of ancient Israel is plagued with historiographical problems of various kinds (McNutt 1–32). First, there are virtually no written sources dating from the Iron I period (1200–1000 BCE), the earliest era of Israelite history. While there is an abundance of archaeological evidence available, this evidence, like any data, requires interpretation and is not able to shed light on many aspects of the society. As pivotal as the evidence from the discipline of archaeology is, archaeological evidence cannot tell us how often the Israelites assembled for community events or whether they married non-Israelites, to provide just two examples. In light of this, many scholars use the more abundant literary evidence from the Iron II period (1000–586 BCE), or less frequently, from the preceding Late Bronze Age, to "fill in" the gaps left by archaeology. Yet, the biblical texts from the Iron II era present their own problems – biblical texts in general are often very hard to date, leaving some scholars questioning whether any biblical texts at all date from the Iron II period (see Davies; Thompson; see further Steven Weitzman's essay in

The Wiley Blackwell Companion to Ancient Israel, First Edition. Edited by Susan Niditch.
© 2016 John Wiley & Sons, Ltd. Published 2016 by John Wiley & Sons, Ltd.

this volume). Although this skeptical viewpoint is ultimately not compelling, the issues surrounding the dating of biblical texts are real ones. A related problem is that while some biblical texts purport to describe Iron I events and social realities, these works were written centuries after the era they discuss, leading to questions regarding the accuracy of the picture of early Israel they present. While reconstructing the society of ancient Israel can be a speculative enterprise, sufficient evidence does exist for reconstruction of Israelite social history to be performed, though the reconstruction will always be partial and in constant need of revision. The Israelites *were* a historically verifiable ethnic entity living in the ancient Levant, and it is possible to study the kinship patterns and other social structures of this entity, though we must be cautious and aware of the limitations of our enterprise.

In order to reconstruct with due diligence Israelite social history, it is necessary to consider the terms of analysis we are using. For example, what do we mean when we refer to "kinship"? The anthropologist David Schneider defines kinship in a rather limited fashion as "the social organization of reproductive activity" (268). Paula McNutt, who has written on the social history of ancient Israel, speaks more broadly: "Kinship systems and genealogies are ways of expressing relationships within a society. In the modern Middle East, a wide variety of personal relationships are expressed in the language of family relationships" (76). Two terms often used with "kinship" are "consanguineal," referring to genealogical or biological relatedness, and "affinal," meaning "related through marriage." While kinship does often express consanguineal relations or relations tied in with reproduction, kinship is also much more, becoming a vehicle for describing intimate non-consanguineal relations. The use of kinship language and symbolism can even be a tool for the creation of such relationships. At times, the origin of relations that are not consanguineal or affinal is masked through what is called "fictive kinship." Fictive kinship speaks of non-consanguineal relations as if they were consanguineal in nature in order to create social ties that may not have existed otherwise. However, as important as kinship was in ancient Israel and as much as it served as a model even for nonfamilial relations, kinship structures and ideologies were never the only form of social organization. No society is wholly organized by kinship relations or kinship language. Kinship relationships are always crosscut by non-kin relations, even if the former outstrips the latter in importance in some societies.

Another term that merits discussion is "community." One could ask of community the same question asked of kinship: What do we mean when we say "community"? In fact, even among social scientists "a precise definition of the term has remained elusive" (Rapport 114). Scholars have emphasized common interests, "smallness of social scale," and consciousness of group membership, as well as *how* community boundaries are drawn and sustained (Rapport 114–16). One could speak also of "sociality" or "sociability" as related concepts. This essay will speak of community as consisting of affective relationships that influence action and produce a sense of being tied with someone else. Communities can be primarily symbolic or have a major organizing and motivating role for individuals, groups and societies. Different institutions and rituals build community: kinship; marriage and affinity; cultic activities; agricultural festivals; and other ritualized events (see the essays by S. A. Geller and Francesca Stavrakopoulou in this volume). Communities are also built through rituals of exclusion rather than inclusion, through ethnic boundary-marking, in-group social hierarchies, and sectarianism. Military activities and collective violence, too, can serve to create community or reinforce communalties.

"Society" itself is a term that warrants some discussion. Society refers to a group of people living together in some organized way. While all groups of people have cultures and live in societies, this essay will speak primarily of "social structures" – the particular social institutions or groupings that organize the society, not just on the macro level but also on the level of everyday practices and decision-making. Kinship, one should remember, is one aspect of social structure. Others worth noting are: socioeconomic stratification; residential patterns, including urbanization; leadership and governmental structures; as well as cultic hierarchies and other types of ordered prestige ranking.

Kinship When There Was No King: The Social Structure of Early Israel (1200–1000 BCE)

Late in the thirteenth century BCE, the Pharaoh Merneptah claimed in a victory stele to have defeated a group living in Canaan called "Israel" (see the essays by John Huddlestun and Avraham Faust in this volume). This is the first historical mention of the Israelites and demonstrates that some ethnic polity with that name had arisen by this time. Nonetheless, one cannot assume that this "Israel" was the same "Israel" we read of in biblical texts. By that I mean that we cannot assume that this group had the same culture, social institutions, cultic practices or worldviews that the later Israelites had. For this reason, some scholars refer to this group as "proto-Israel" rather than "Israel" (Dever 194–6; see Avraham Faust's essay in this volume). The written evidence we have for this group is quite limited (McNutt 68). Yet, there is a plethora of archaeological evidence dating to this era. This evidence reveals hundreds of tiny, unwalled new settlements in the hill country of Canaan (Dever 98–9; Miller 127–36). These settlements were generally quite isolated, demonstrating few if any signs of having been governed by a centralized state or of trade with other groups (Finkelstein and Silberman 107–10; Lemos 161–8). The total population of these settlements numbered well under 100,000 (Dever 97–8). These "proto-Israelites" gained their livelihood through pastoralism and subsistence farming, including horticulture and the use of terraces to make the rocky hillsides cultivable (Stager 5–6). While some biblical texts present an image of the early Israelites as pastoralists, it is unclear what percentage of the population were engaged purely in pastoral activities, though it is unlikely it was the majority (Lemos 192–5).

What were the kinship patterns of this group? From archaeological evidence alone, it is difficult to state with certainty, but later biblical texts and cross-cultural evidence for groups with a similar combination of subsistence agriculture and lack of a central state fill in our knowledge to some degree. Based upon biblical texts, the Israelites were for the most part a patrilineal group, that is, a group that reckoned descent and inheritance through the male line. Their settlement patterns were correspondingly virilocal, meaning that at the time of marriage a woman would leave her own kinship group to go live with her husband's. Later Israelite texts typically show a preference for endogamy in both senses of that term – their authors preferred that Israelites marry within their own ethnic group, but also display a preference for marriage within families (cousin marriage, primarily). Since this preference cannot be verified archaeologically, it is unclear whether the early Israelites were like their descendants in preferring endogamy. In actuality, later biblical texts themselves contain cases of exogamy – marriage outside of one's family or ethnic group (Lemche 272–4) – so it is unclear what the rates of endogamy and exogamy were even in later Israelite history.

Some people refer to early Israel as a "tribal" society, echoing language that is used of some modern groups, as well. But what does this term actually mean? The usage of this term varies, sometimes referring to groups that have no centralized state, which was true of the Israelites in Iron I, and sometimes to groups for whom kinship structures are more important and have more symbolic and emotional value than other forms of social organization. While used often, the usage of the term is often orientalist and more obfuscatory than enlightening. Even in societies that have tribes and use specific terminology to refer to this kinship grouping, as the Israelites did, "the tribe appears to have existed more as a means of providing a range of potential identities than as a base for sustained collective action" (McNutt 81). It is important to remember that even for groups that have tribes, lower-order family groupings have more of an influence upon behavior and elicit more group loyalty.

Related to the matter of different orders of family groupings is the fact that various scholars have argued, based upon such biblical texts as Joshua 7:16–18, that early Israelite society was segmentary in nature (McNutt 78–94), utilizing a term from social anthropology. A segmentary society is one organized according to various levels of kinship, with each level successively larger than the next. A very simple diagram illustrating this would be:

nuclear family < extended family < minimal lineage < maximal lineage/clan < tribe

Complicating matters is that scholars sometimes use these kinship terms differently from one another. The term "minimal lineage" is sometimes used synonymously with the phrase "extended family," the latter of which refers to a family grouping comprising two to four generations (Lemche 71, 248). In some societies, a maximal lineage can include ten or more generations, and some groups also have lineages of intermediary sizes, that is, medial lineages. An Israelite clan was called a *mišpāḥâ*.

Scholars disagree over whether the nuclear or extended family was the most basic unit of Israelite society (McNutt 90; Faust 11). Stager has used both archaeological evidence and biblical texts, as well as comparative evidence, to argue that the clusters of dwellings found in Iron I villages represent extended families that lived together with their livestock, with a nuclear family occupying each unit of the cluster. He argues for the importance of the extended family in Iron I society and sees evidence for "multiple-family compounds" at Khirbet Raddana, 'Ai, and other sites (Stager 17–18, 22). Animals slept on the ground floor of each dwelling of the compound and families lived on the upper floor (Stager 12). Israelite land was held jointly by the extended family or lineage, with livestock possibly held by nuclear families (Stager 20; Bendor 135–40).

Even in Stager's reconstruction, there is a place for nuclear families. Relatedly, some scholars argue that it is more accurate to see nuclear, rather than extended families, as more basic (McNutt 90; Faust 11). The Hebrew term for extended family, generally speaking, is *bêt 'āb*, "house of (the) father," and the term for nuclear families is perhaps *bayit*, "house(hold)." Yet, the terminology used by biblical texts varies (Lemche 245–74). So does, too, the composition of families in biblical texts. For example, Samson's parents' household appears to have been a nuclear family, but Jacob's household was clearly an extended family (Lemche 257–8). Even if extended families were perhaps the ideal in ancient Israel, high death rates would mean a great deal of fluidity in family composition (Schloen 148, 150–1). It is worth noting, too, that each type of family presents certain advantages and disadvantages (see the essay by Carol Meyers in this volume). Agriculture in ancient Israel was back-breaking work. For such a labor-intensive endeavor, nuclear families would in many cases not be large enough to function as an effective productive unit, because a new family would not have children old enough to help with labor. In fact, childhood death rates kept a large proportion of children from ever reaching adulthood. On the other hand, extended families present their own disadvantages, being less mobile and more prone to fission. Biblical texts such as the patriarchal narratives in Genesis and the stories of David's family in 2 Samuel evince for us well that Israelite families were not any more likely to get along than are families today. The larger the family unit, the greater the tensions. It is also worth noting that even in our society today, where the nuclear family is considered normative, there exist many different types of households. Thus, it is arguably wrongheaded to focus upon the question of which type of family is the most basic or even the most idealized rather than upon what types of families are found and why families choose the types of living arrangements they do.

In either case, archaeological evidence by itself cannot tell us exactly which family members were living in a dwelling place or what the ideal family type was. Thus, making use of later biblical texts to reconstruct earlier Israelite history is unfortunately almost unavoidable. Of the biblical texts used to reconstruct early Israelite social history, many scholars utilize the Book of Judges in particular. This book is less suffused with monarchic and deuteronomistic ideologies than is the Book of Joshua, a text that is also set in the premonarchic, Iron I era. While it is important not to be too reliant upon Judges and other biblical texts to reconstruct Iron I history, one way these texts can be used in a methodologically useful manner is to corroborate reconstructions that are based primarily upon archaeological evidence. For example, the archaeological evidence demonstrates that the early Israelites did not have a centralized state. There is little or no evidence for state-level coordination of large building projects, of regional capitals or large population centers, or the social stratification typical of societies with states (McNutt 108–9; Lemos 180–3). Since it would be highly uncommon for a state to exist that left no archaeological traces of itself, it is only logical to conclude the Israelites had only local leadership. The Book of Judges matches the archaeological evidence in depicting the Israelites as lacking a monarchy. According to Judges, the Israelites were ruled by a series of charismatic leaders called "judges" and had a tribal militia rather than a regular army. They were also engaged in internecine fighting with other ethnic polities in the region – the Philistines and Canaanites primarily, but also the Ammonites, Moabites, and other groups – none of which rises to a position of real dominance. Interestingly, the ethnic fighting discussed in Judges is poorly attested in the archaeological record (Finkelstein and Silberman 109–10; see the essay by Song-Mi Suzie Park in this volume).

While some people may have had a higher social rank than others in early Israel – for example, a local chief versus his subordinates (Miller) – significant differences in wealth between families are not discernible in the archaeological record (Lemos 161–79). Based upon early Israel's major social features – lack of centralization and lack of entrenched social classes – one can tentatively reconstruct some social practices without recourse to later biblical texts. If there was no capital or major regional centers, cultic practices would have been at local shrines, and cultic functionaries, too, would have been localized (see Francesca Stavrakopoulou's essay in this volume). With the Israelites' livelihood being so centered on agriculture, agricultural festivals likely would have been important community-building activities. Considering the laborious nature of Israelite agricultural production, it is very probable that women contributed to agricultural and horticultural work (Meyers 56, 63; see the essay by Carol Meyers in this volume). In societies in which this is the case, polygyny is fairly common (Lemos 123). Cross-cultural evidence for societies like the Israelites' that are kinship-based and lack significant distinctions in wealth strongly suggests that Israelite marriages would have involved the giving of bridewealth – gifts from the bridegroom to the bride's father – what was previously referred to as "brideprice" (Lemos 89–158). Yet again, however, we must be cautious in our reconstructions, for the contemporary archaeological evidence does not explicitly provide this information.

The Social History of Iron Age II: A Changing Landscape

Major changes occurred in Israelite society in the Iron II period. This period spans from the time when the Israelite monarchy putatively began in the tenth century to the time when the Babylonian empire destroyed the Jerusalem temple and brought the Davidic monarchy to an end in the sixth century. Because the development of centralized governance in this period is the change that has generated the most interest among both scholars and lay people, it is appropriate to begin with this matter, though it is one that has sparked great controversy among scholars in recent years.

1 Samuel 8:4–5 reads: "Then all the elders of Israel gathered together and came to Samuel at Ramah, and they said to him, 'You have grown old and your sons do not follow in your ways. Appoint for us, then, a king to govern us like all the other nations'" (all biblical translations are my own). In the Book of Samuel, we read of a quick transition from a nonhereditary, charismatic chieftaincy form of leadership to the centralized, divinely appointed monarchic governance of Saul, and then of David. According to the Bible, the dynasty of the latter ruled over a united Israel for almost a century, and then over Judah in the south until the Babylonian exile – a total of over 400 years. The united kingdom of David and his son Solomon is depicted as being militarily successful and even quite wealthy, dominating much of the Levantine region (see the essay by Brad Kelle in this volume).

Increasingly, scholars have questioned whether or not such a quick transition to monarchy is plausible. Israel Finkelstein, for example, has argued that it was unlikely in light of the totality of the archaeological evidence that Israel achieved full statehood in the tenth century and that centralization would be centered in the south rather than in the northern region. This is because the more arid Judean region had very few settlements in the tenth century and was far less developed than the northern area of the central hill country of what had been Canaan. Consequently, Israel Finkelstein has proposed a "low chronology" that redates monumental building remains previously attributed to Solomon to the northern Omride Dynasty ruling in the ninth century (Finkelstein and Silberman 123–48; Moore and Kelle 214–15, 252–3; see the essays by Elizabeth Bloch-Smith and Avraham Faust in this volume). Other scholars have gone even further than Finkelstein, alleging that there was no historical David and no Solomon, thus no united kingdom (Davies; Thompson). Relatedly, some argue that ancient Israel was never a "true state," though these arguments sometimes border on the semantic. Still others have maintained that the biblical presentation of centralization is indeed correct, at least in its broad outlines. There is as yet no consensus that has arisen on these matters to replace the old consensus of scholars that was arguably too credulous of monarchic narratives in the books of Samuel and Kings (Moore and Kelle 200–65). Nonetheless, one can say that sometime in the first two centuries of Iron II, there emerged an overarching government entity responsible for monumental building projects, urban planning at such sites as Jerusalem, Dan, Samaria and Megiddo, and the military activities that are attested in Assyrian sources.

While discussions of social change in this era have often centered on questions of centralization, it is perhaps best to view the matter of centralization in light of an analysis of the many other changes that occurred in Iron II. First, there was a significant rise in social stratification – social classes based on differences in wealth – clearly discernible by the eighth–seventh centuries throughout Israel, north and south. Unlike the evidence for Iron I, archaeological evidence for Iron II includes luxury items, such as pottery imported from Cyprus, imitations of Assyrian palace ware, and the Samaria ivories. One also finds evidence for differential housing, with a small percentage of the population living in palaces or large houses, as well as differential burials, with some people being buried in ornate, finely cut tombs and others receiving far simpler burials (Lemos 179–90).

Contemporary biblical evidence also attests to wealth distinctions in this period. The eighth-century prophets rather famously decried social abuses carried out by the wealthy classes (see the essay by Robert Wilson in this volume). Amos 4:1 provides a good example:

> Hear this word,
> O heifers of Bashan
> who are on Mount Samaria,
> who extort the poor,
> who oppress the needy,
> who say to their husbands,
> "Bring something for us to drink!"

Isaiah 10:1 provides another example:

> Woe to you who make iniquitous decrees,
>> who write oppressive statutes,
> to turn aside justice from the poor
>> and rob the needy of my people of right judgment,
> for widows to become your spoil,
>> and orphans your prey!

Thus, biblical texts correspond with archaeological evidence in attesting an increase in social stratification.

A demographic change that put further strain on the region was the noteworthy increase in population that occurred over the course of just a few centuries. The population of the highlands grew from less than 100,000 at the beginning of Iron I to almost half a million by the mid-eighth century – roughly an eightfold increase (Broshi and Finkelstein)! One sees also a clear increase in the size of sites and the development of a settlement hierarchy, where, in addition to many villages and towns, one finds a few large administrative centers and a greater number of medium-sized sites (Faust 198; Lemos 180–1). While some of these features are correlated with government centralization and an increase in the importance of Israel and Judah, one should not think of the population increase as benign. It appears that population increases made land more scarce and increased ethnic tensions. Not only biblical texts (e.g., Amos 1:13; 2 Kings 12:17–18; 13:22–25; 16:5–9) but sources outside the Bible such as the Mesha Stele describe interethnic fighting involving land disputes occurring from the ninth century onward (see Christopher Rollston's essay in this volume). Some of these sources attest not just to fighting but to mass killing and brutal atrocities. Some biblical texts show a strong sense of difference between Israelites and other groups and a violent hostility toward the latter. This type of boundary marking not only serves to exclude others and justify actions against them, but also to *create* a sense of identity and community for the group doing the excluding (Rowlett 12–15, 69, 173; see Song-Mi Suzie Park's essay in this volume). In stating who was not Israelite, Israelite writers attempted to build a sense of pan-Israelite identity for groups that previously had not been joined under one centralized authority.

There has been some debate among scholars over whether this centralized monarchy itself had an impact on kinship and social structures in ancient Israel. Certainly, there is textual evidence for corruption, for example, the story of Naboth's vineyard in Kings, where Ahab seizes the lands of one of his subjects. The cultic centralization that 2 Kings describes Hezekiah and Josiah as performing in later centuries was a clear attempt to shift power from the local sphere to the capital – an attempt legitimated by theological discourses shrouding political intentions (see J. J. M. Roberts's essay in this volume). From the bluntly oppressive tactics of Ahab and other kings, the cultic centralization of such biblically vaunted figures as Hezekiah and Josiah, and the corvée labor and military conscription instituted by Solomon, it would not be unreasonable to conclude that the state slowly eroded or even attempted forcibly to displace local power structures. One could argue that authority tends to be a zero-sum game, and if the king and his officials had final say, then local leaders did not.

Yet, the situation is not so simple as this. While one cannot know for certain, it seems likely that the monarchy from the outset would not have rapidly displaced local structures of authority, centered often on kinship, but rather attempted to coopt their support. Some scholars argue that, if the authority of the king was based on patrimonial ideologies, there would in fact be no conflict between the king's having authority and the authority of local leaders and heads of household, which would be based on the same ideology (Schloen 360). Evidence that the monarchy did not displace kinship structures has been marshalled from archaeology as well (Schloen 136, 153; Vanderhooft 486–8). If Stager is right that the residential clustering one sees at Israelite sites represents extended families living together, it is noteworthy that this particular residential pattern persists for many centuries, even into the postexilic era at some sites (Stager 22). This would probably be the strongest evidence that the advent of centralized governance did not in itself radically change the course of daily life for most people.

One must maintain, however, a holistic view of the changes that occurred over the course of the Iron II era. While some residential patterns largely went unchanged, the rise in wealth-based social stratification, amply attested in both archaeological and textual sources, and marked population increases in all likelihood did greatly affect people's lives. It is hard to imagine such changes occurring without shifts in agricultural production, the concentration of resources in the hands of a few, and an attendant concentration of authority. Social changes were particularly pronounced in urban areas (Faust 270–1). These shifts did not occur rapidly, but once they took hold, Israelite authors themselves took notice. With the archaeological evidence and textual sources converging in their evincing of social change, we must ask not whether these striking changes occurred, but how a continuity in some residential patterns can be understood in light of the marked discontinuities in other areas of life.

An area of Israelite social history that relates to issues of social stratification is whether or not patron–client relationships were important in ancient Israel. A patron–client relationship, generally speaking, is one in which a person of superior status assigns part of his authority to a social inferior in exchange for loyalty or an acknowledgment of dominance that has real social consequences. J. David Schloen, in particular, has argued that the patrimonial ideology centered on the "house of the father" had a profound organizing force over both family structures and governmental structures throughout the Levantine region, with patron–client relations forming a kind of pyramidal social structure (see the essay by David Schloen in this volume). The king of course stood at the apex of this pyramid. Patron–client relationships are evident in ancient Near Eastern sources in treaty texts that encode relations of domination. One can also see this type of relationship in royal correspondence, the Amarna letters for instance, or in royal inscriptions. It is rather less obvious in other types of texts, however. Biblical texts, for example, do not speak of patron–client relationships as much as one might think, leading even a scholar who argues for their importance in ancient Israel to state that "patronage does not appear explicitly in ancient Near Eastern textual sources" (Pfoh 138). One might ask, then: Was socioeconomic stratification or patron–client relations more important for Israelite social organization? Which had more influence over behavior? In reality, biblical texts attest to both forms of social hierarchies. These hierarchies overlapped and crosscut each other, so that, again, the question for scholars is *how* they were interwoven, how they influenced people's lives and the relative status of individuals in different contexts. One must also ask how these types of hierarchies – those related to wealth and those related to kinship or patrimonial ideologies – intersected with other types of status ascription: for example, cultic hierarchies or gender hierarchies. Where women fit into patron–client relations is a question that has not been adequately addressed, in fact.

Despite the questions surrounding patron–client relations in ancient Israel, this form of social organization was clearly apparent in the first-millennium BCE political relations of the ancient Near East. The collapse of this region's empires and trade networks at the end of the Late Bronze Age left a power vacuum in the area that allowed various ethnic polities such as the Israelites to emerge and develop small-scale states displaying a sovereignty they could not have had in the second millennium BCE. Yet, the imperial power vacuum taken advantage of by these small Levantine groups would eventually be filled by the Neo-Assyrian empire, whose sway began to reach the Levant in the ninth century BCE (see J. J. M. Roberts's essay in this volume). The Assyrians had firmly established their political and military will over the region by the end of the ninth century, making Israelite kings accept a position of political subordination, and continued to do so until the mid-seventh century BCE. In 722 BCE, they in fact destroyed the capital of the northern kingdom, exiled some of its inhabitants, resettled foreign populations in the area, and made the region a province of Assyria (2 Kings 18; Moore and Kelle 305–9). In 701, military assaults were mounted, too, against Judah, though the Davidic king Hezekiah was in the end allowed to remain in power. In the late seventh century, the Neo-Babylonians displaced the Assyrians as the imperial force in the region. As brutal as the Assyrians had been, it was the Babylonians who would devastate Judah beyond the Judeans' own imagination – besieging and then destroying Jerusalem and the Temple of Yahweh along with it, bringing the centuries-old Davidic kingship to an end, exiling thousands of Judean elites to Babylon in 597, 587 and perhaps also 582, slaying thousands of Judeans in the capital and beyond, and leaving others to starve to death (2 Kings 24–25; Jer. 52:30; Lam.). In the wake of these horrors, Lamentations 2:20 asks plaintively: "Should women eat their own offspring, the children they have carried? Should priest and prophet be killed in the sanctuary of my lord?"

As obvious as the importance of these events is for reconstructing Israelite history, more directly relevant to this essay is the question of what effects these political shifts and military campaigns had on Israelite kinship, community, and social structure, apart from the glaring shifts in political structures. The effects are seen in various sources, although the evidence is sometimes indirect. As discussed above, population increases and a very significant rise in socioeconomic stratification apparently put strain on the ability of some Israelites to provide for their subsistence needs. The heavy tribute payments forced upon both northern and southern kingdoms of Israel must have further strained the region, likely necessitating the practice of cash cropping in which farmers focused their production upon the most lucrative products, such as olive oil and wine, at the expense of crops that were sometimes more important for subsistence needs (Finkelstein and Silberman 246; Routledge 208–9). These shifts in production could only go so far, and the difficulties of paying tribute were arguably one of the primary reasons that the Israelites, Judeans and other groups revolted time after time against the

Assyrians and Babylonians, despite the manifestly slim odds of success against these powers. The results were military campaigns that led to widespread death and destruction, destruction that is clearly seen archaeologically (Finkelstein and Silberman 295; Lemos 202–3). In fact, population estimates show that the population of the area fell dramatically between the eighth century and the Persian period, with Judah's population being halved or even cut to a third of what it had been at the end of the monarchic period (Lipschits 359–63; Lemos 203). This devastation and population decline affected some regions and some segments of the population more than others, but it is likely that all segments of the population in all areas were in some way affected. Clearly, the government and economic structures were completely disrupted. When the latter were reestablished, they were under the direct control of the Babylonians, who had their own imperial interests in mind rather than those of the remaining populace. Kinship structures were disrupted by the forced migration of some of the population and the death of many others. With the population cut in half, it is impossible to imagine how kinship structures could have been maintained exactly as they had been before. The Jerusalem-centered cult, too, was destroyed. Since Hezekiah and Josiah had attempted previously to shift local worship to the capital, the destruction of Jerusalem left many Judeans without a cult place to worship their deity. While there are many details about this period that are not perfectly understood, based upon the evidence we do have, it is in my view difficult to overestimate the profound nature of the disruptions of life that occurred in this region, first after the military campaigns of the late eighth century, and then in the early sixth century BCE (Lipschits 323–76).

The Beginnings of Diaspora: Judeans in Babylon and Egypt in the Sixth–Fifth Centuries BCE

What was life like for the Judeans exiled to Babylon? In addition to such biblical sources as the Book of Ezekiel and Psalm 137, we also have a cache of recently discovered documentary evidence for Judeans living in Babylon in the Neo-Babylonian and early Persian periods. Much of this corpus derives from a site called Al-Yahudu, "Village of Judea," or Alu-sha-Yahudaya, "Village of the Judeans" (Abraham, "Reconstruction"; Pearce). As Kathleen Abraham writes:

> The names of this village reflect the historical fact that most of its inhabitants originated from Judea, and probably even from Jerusalem itself, since Yahūd(u) was used in antiquity as a designation both for the province of Judea and for its capital, Jerusalem. Indeed, the practice of naming a village for the place from which most of its inhabitants originally came is well attested to in Babylonia. ("Reconstruction," 264)

The documents from this town record quotidian commercial activities, including loans, lease agreements, and receipts of transactions involving agricultural products, slave sales and marriage contracts. Documents of this kind are invaluable for reconstructing the life of a community, but unfortunately provide only indirect information on kinship and community practices. The Judean exiles were state dependents, at least some of whom worked a type of royal property called "bow-land" in exchange for performing military duties, perhaps as archers. The exiles seem to have been settled together. The documents contain evidence for around 200 people bearing Yahwistic names living in the same region. Their status was certainly not that of slaves – in fact, at least a few Judean exiles owned slaves themselves – but on the whole the social and economic status of the exiles was not particularly high – they " belonged to the lower echelons of society" (Abraham, "Reconstruction," 265). The later Murashu archives from Nippur in Mesopotamia also contain evidence for individuals with Yahwistic names taking part in ordinary Mesopotamian life, though the percentage of Yahwistic names is lower in those texts than in the Al-Yahudu corpus (Pearce 270–1). Between the maintenance of Yahwistic names over the course of generations of exile and biblical texts attesting to both a continuing sense of Judean identity and a continuing attachment to the Judean deity, we can conclude that at least a significant number of Judean exiles remained attached to their Judean roots and preserved communal ties with one another. The latter, though, was at least partially a function of settlement patterns set by the Babylonian state itself.

There are a few marriage documents from Al-Yahudu and Sippar involving Judeans or other Levantine migrants. These reflect a variety of practices, but are largely in keeping with Babylonian customs (Lemos 237–44). Like the other documents from this cache of texts, they are written almost exclusively in Akkadian, presumably by Mesopotamian scribes, a fact which may well have influenced their contents. There is some evidence for intermarriage (Lemos 241–2), but because no marriage documents survive from preexilic Judah and there is not a very large sample of marriage documents involving Judeans extant from Babylonia, it is very difficult to ascertain what the rates of intermarriage were and whether they were higher or lower than in other periods. In none of these marriage documents does the bride's father stand as a party to the document (Lemos 241), something which perhaps reflects low life expectancy, the fact that men married at an older age than women did, and possibly even the fact that some Judean men were conscripted into the Babylonian army and thus might perish in battle (Abraham, "Reconstruction," 263).

While these documents do not shed light on whether or not clan structures continued to exist in the exile or whether tribal identification was still meaningful, there does appear to be some evidence for extended families and patrimonial land holdings. Complicating matters is that these practices conform also to Babylonian custom. At least one text uses the term *bit abi*, the Akkadian equivalent of *bêt 'āb*, "house of the father" (Abraham, "Inheritance division," 208), but the term could reflect either Babylonian custom, Judean custom, or both. One sees in more than one text brothers, together with their mothers, serving as a party to their sister's marriage contracts in the absence of fathers (Lemos 241–4), demonstrating for us that at least some degree of cohesion existed among sibling units.

Further documentary evidence for Judeans living outside of Judah exists from Elephantine in Egypt. These documents, which date to the early Persian period, attest to the continuity of Judean identity and practices perhaps even better than those above. This group built a temple to Yahweh in Egypt – a violation of Deuteronomistic law but reflecting the plurality of sanctuaries existing for much of the monarchic era – celebrated the Passover, and maintained contact with Jerusalem and with Yahweh worshippers in the Persian province of Samaria. Part of what determined the boundaries of this group and created a sense of community among them, then, was the perpetuation of customs from Judah and an emphasis on their ancestral origins. Interestingly, however, this group was not strictly endogamous – marriage contracts clearly attest to one or more cases of intermarriage between Judeans at Elephantine and members of other groups. Also, both sexes could initiate divorce in this community (Porten 203, 223, 250, 258, 261).

Judah in the Persian Era: Social Disruption and the Fraying of Community Ties

Isaiah 40, a text written at the dawn of the Persian era when the Judean exiles were allowed to return home, displays a clear sense of hopefulness, describing how a path would be cleared in the wilderness for Yahweh to lead the exiles back to Judah. Yet, the optimism of this passage would soon give way to the tumultuous realities of Persian-era Judean life. Despite a seeming absence of political persecution and military assaults under the Persians, this era was one marked by deep community divisions and many social changes. One can infer from the biblical books of Ezra and Nehemiah that returned exiles sought to reclaim lands and influence from those who had not been forced to migrate. Ezra and Nehemiah draw communal boundaries in very rigid ways. The returned exiles seemingly become equivalent with the Judean community itself, with nonreturnees being relegated to the margins (Moore and Kelle 442–7). These books show much less tolerance for intermarriage than the Judean community at Elephantine did. In fact, they show a blatant intolerance, with Ezra 9 characterizing the practice as a "sacrilege" and banning it outright. Emblematic of the glaring social fissures of the Judah of the Persian era is the fact that Isaiah 56 clearly refutes the negative viewpoints held by Ezra-Nehemiah toward foreigners. The Book of Ruth was also likely written in this period, and it, too, promotes a tolerant attitude toward both intermarriage and foreigners. What these textual disagreements reflect is a fundamental uncertainty about issues of community membership and ethnic definition (see Charles Carter's and Tamara Cohn Eskenazi's essays in this volume).

These social disputes are particularly striking in light of the small population of Judah and the rural character of the region in this period. While social hierarchies are still evident archaeologically, the Judah of the Persian period and particularly of the early Persian period is a far less impressive one than had existed before the fall of Jerusalem (Lemos 201–13). It was also less urban and developed than were the coastal regions of Palestine in the same period (Lemos 202, 206–7). Yet, a smaller population and less pronounced socioeconomic stratification did not lead to fewer social tensions or to more homogeneous viewpoints about where to draw communal boundaries. In addition to the marginalization of those not exiled, people living in Samaria who were descended from Israelites and worshipped Yahweh were clearly excluded from the community advocated by Ezra-Nehemiah. Here, too, though, there is disagreement, for even the authors of Chronicles are more inclusive toward Samarians (Knoppers 43).

In addition to being concerned with matters of inclusion and exclusion, Ezra-Nehemiah and Ruth are both relevant to the study of kinship practices in this period. Ezra-Nehemiah uses kinship terminology differently from the way it had been used in the preexilic period and Ruth seems to demonstrate that some Judeans of the Persian era were unfamiliar with the specificities of the early Israelite kinship and marital customs that the book purports to represent. One finds used in Ezra and Nehemiah the phrase *bêt 'ābôt*, "house of (the) fathers" or "houses of (the) father," but the usage seems not to correspond exactly with the most typical preexilic sense of *bêt 'āb*, referring to extended families. In Ezra 8, the number of males included in the *bêt 'ābôt* units is far too large to comprise an extended family. Some of the kinship units number in the hundreds and would correspond with clans comprising several generations, that is, with the preexilic *mišpāḥâ*, not the *bêt 'āb*. Similarly, the Book of Ruth describes an older kinship practice in an odd way. This book narrates a tale of what appears to be levirate marriage – where a man is expected to marry the widow of his near kinsman – but its conception of this type of marriage is different from the one found in Deuteronomy 25, which is more likely to reflect an actual social practice. In either case, these divergences seem to reflect shifts in exilic and Persian-era kinship patterns.

Hellenistic Judea: Urbanization and Sectarianism

While treatments of Israelite social history do not normally cover the Hellenistic era, it is worth briefly examining the social structure of this period, not only because a few biblical texts were written then, but also in order to form a contrast with the exilic and Persian eras preceding it. Just as the Persian era was different from the late monarchic period in matters of social history, so, too, was the Hellenistic period different from the Persian. The rural character of Persian-era Judah gave way to the urbanization of Hellenistic Judea. Although there is evidence for wealth-based stratification in Persian-era Judah, such stratification was far more pronounced in the Hellenistic era, with disparities in wealth between classes and individuals becoming far more marked. For example, one sees in Jerusalem and Maresha ostentatious tombs featuring exterior monuments or frescoes presenting images of exotic animals and musicians. One also finds clear evidence of differential housing at various sites in Hellenistic Palestine. Ben Sira and other texts from this period attest to widespread debt, slavery, and abuse of the disadvantaged by the wealthy that would only increase further in the Roman era, contributing to the revolt of 66–73 CE (Lemos 213–27; see the essays by Matthew Goff and Benjamin Wright in this volume).

The debates over communal definition evident in the Persian era continued in the Hellenistic period, when sectarianism appears to have flourished. The disputes over Hellenization and acculturation to Greek practices have been addressed in detail by scholars (Grabbe 125–65). While some of the texts from this period – the Book of Jubilees, for instance – are very concerned with marking sharply the boundaries between Judeans and foreigners, others seem more concerned with marking *internal* boundaries between sect members and outsiders, or righteous Judeans and everyone else (see, for instance, various texts of the Dead Sea Scrolls, or even Dan. 12). For some at least, there was a diminishing sense of pan-Israelite or pan-Judean community, but sects provided their own community boundaries in the Greco-Roman period.

Corresponding to the xenophobia and sectarianism that various Hellenistic texts display is a continuing disparagement of intermarriage and a valuation placed upon endogamy. While it was generally ethnic endogamy with which texts were concerned, one also sees intrafamilial endogamy discussed by some texts. For example, the Book of Tobit seems to display a preference for cousin marriage and an interest in tribal affili- ations, though like Ruth it is set in a much earlier time than the one in which it was written and the author was perhaps attempting to depict earlier customs with which he was not entirely familiar. In any case, while tribal terminology was still sometimes used, tribal and clan structures no longer had any organizing role in the society of the area. Extended families, too, had lost much of their organizing importance, though some Judeans still lived in this family unit (Fiensy 128–32), as is sometimes the case even in our society.

Conclusion

The Israelites emerged at the transition between the Late Bronze Age and the Iron Age. While the Late Bronze was a time of great empires and city-states, the Iron I period was one of ruralization and isolation. The Israelites were one of many small ethnic groups that emerged in this period and the features of their social life fit the times: they were a simple group, subsisting in the highlands in tiny, unwalled settlements. They had no centralized state and were organized, it appears, according to segmentary kinship struc- tures and led by charismatic local rulers. Their society was agricultural and pastoralist in character and so their communal life was no doubt centered on family, subsistence, local worship and local festivals.

In time, however, things changed. This group came to have monarchic leadership, urban centers, wealth-based social stratification and more complex social groups. Kin- ship was still of great importance, but kinship and other local structures came to be strained and perhaps ultimately crushed by marked increases in population, differen- tiation in wealth, authoritarian leadership, foreign military assaults and imperialistic rule. Thousands died, and family, economic and political structures were uprooted in the eighth century and again in the sixth. The Persian era saw what the Hebrew Bible presents as a return both triumphant and tumultuous. While the exiles – or at least some portion of them – may have returned from Babylonia, a return to preexilic realities did not correspondingly occur. Instead, Persian Judah was rural and beset by disputes over community boundaries. The Hellenistic era would bring Judah back to the population levels and urbanization of the late monarchic era, but in a transformed landscape in which Judeans did not always see other Judeans as their brethren. Rather, increasing sectarianism led some to regard even most other Judeans as falling outside the margins of communities whose boundaries were drawn more and more narrowly. An examina- tion of the kinship patterns, community, and society of ancient Israel and Judah, then, demonstrates that it is not only in the modern world that radical social changes occur. In the ancient world, too, family and social structures shifted – so much so that it is unlikely that any proto-Israelites of the twelfth century BCE would have recognized the society of Hellenistic-era Judea as bearing any close relationship to their own.

Bibliography

Abraham, Kathleen. "An inheritance division among Judeans in Babylonia from the early Persian period." In Meir Lubetski (ed.), *New Seals and Inscriptions, Hebrew, Idumean, and Cuneiform* (pp. 206–21). Sheffield: Sheffield Phoenix, 2007. Presents a text that survives from the Judean exile community in Babylonia.

Abraham, Kathleen. "The reconstruction of Jewish communities in the Persian Empire: The Āl-Yahūdu Clay Tablets." In Hagai Segev (ed.), *Light and Shadows – The Catalog: The Story of Iran and the Jews* (pp. 261–4). Tel Aviv: Beit Hatfutsot, 2011. Brief summary of the important documentary evidence for Judean exiles in Babylonia.

Bendor, Shunya. *The Social Structure of Ancient Israel: The Institution of the Family* (Beit 'Ab) *from the Settlement to the End of the Monarchy*. Jerusalem: Simor, 1996. Assesses evidence for extended families in early and monarchic Israel.

Broshi, Magen and Israel Finkelstein. "The population of Palestine in Iron Age II." *Bulletin of the American Schools of Oriental Research 287* (1992): 47–60. Estimates the population of Palestine in Iron II (1000–586 BCE).

Davies, Philip R. *In Search of "Ancient Israel": A Study in Biblical Origins*. Sheffield: JSOT Press, 1992. Classic "minimalist" treatment of ancient Israel's history.

Dever, William G. *Who Were the Israelites and Where Did They Come From?* Grand Rapids, MI: Eerdmans, 2003. Presents clearly the evidence for the earliest period of Israelite history.

Faust, Avraham. *The Archaeology of Israelite Society in Iron Age II*. Winona Lake, IN: Eisenbrauns, 2012. Detailed examination of archaeological evidence for ancient Israel from ca. 1000–586 BCE.

Fiensy, David A. *The Social History of Palestine in the Herodian Period: The Land Is Mine*. Lewiston, NY: Edwin Mellen, 1991. Reconstruction of Hellenistic and Roman era social history of Palestine, based on multiple sources.

Finkelstein, Israel and Neil Asher Silberman. *The Bible Unearthed: Archaeology's New Vision of Ancient Israel and the Origin of Its Sacred Texts*. New York: Free Press, 2001. Clear presentation of Finkelstein's proposals regarding the redating of archaeological evidence.

Grabbe, Lester L. *A History of the Jews and Judaism in the Second Temple Period, vol. 2: The Coming of the Greeks: The Early Hellenistic Period (335–175 BCE)*. London: T&T Clark, 2008. Overview of the major historical issues concerning the Second Temple period.

Knoppers, Gary N. "Did Jacob become Judah? The configuration of Israel's restoration in Deutero-Isaiah." In József Zsengellér (ed.), *Samaria, Samarians, Samaritans: Studies on Bible, History and Linguistics* (pp. 39–70). Berlin: de Gruyter, 2011. Presents evidence for the Persian-era Judean community.

Lemche, Niels Peter. *Early Israel: Anthropological and Historical Studies on the Israelite Society before the Monarchy*. Leiden: Brill, 1985. Classic work applying anthropological ideas to the study of early Israelite social history.

Lemos, T. M. *Marriage Gifts and Social Change in Ancient Palestine: 1200 BCE to 200 CE*. Cambridge: Cambridge University Press, 2010. Work examining connection between marital practices and long-term changes in the social structure of ancient Palestine.

Lipschits, Oded. "Demographic changes in Judah between the seventh and fifth centuries BCE." In Oded Lipschits and Joseph Blenkinsopp (eds), *Judah and Judeans in the Neo-Babylonian Period* (pp. 323–76). Winona Lake, IN: Eisenbrauns, 2003. Provides archaeological evidence for destruction caused by Babylonians and other demographic changes occurring in the Neo-Babylonian and Persian eras.

McNutt, Paula M. *Reconstructing the Society of Ancient Israel*. Louisville, KY: Westminster John Knox, 1999. Excellent overview of social history of ancient Israel and methodological problems in reconstructing this history.

Meyers, Carol. *Discovering Eve: Ancient Israelite Women in Context*. Oxford: Oxford University Press, 1988. Seminal work that uses both archaeological and biblical evidence to reconstruct lives of Israelite women.

Miller, Robert D., II. *Chieftains of the Highland Clans: A History of Israel in the Twelfth and Eleventh Centuries BCE*. Grand Rapids, MI: Eisenbrauns, 2005. Work using a complex chiefdom model of state development to understand early Israel.

Moore, Megan Bishop and Brad E. Kelle. *Biblical History and Israel's Past: The Changing Study of the Bible and History*. Grand Rapids, MI: Eerdmans, 2011. Useful work that summarizes evidence and scholarly approaches to Israelite history.

Pearce, Laurie E. "'Judean': A special status in Neo-Babylonian and Achemenid Babylonia?" In Oded Lipschits, Gary N. Knoppers, and Manfred Oeming (eds), *The Judeans in the Achaemenid Age: Negotiating Identity in an International Context* (pp. 267–77). Winona Lake, IN: Eisenbrauns, 2011. Discusses evidence for Judean exiles in Babylonia.

Pfoh, Emanuel. *The Emergence of Israel in Ancient Palestine: Historical and Anthropological Perspectives*. London: Equinox, 2009. Recent work on Israelite social history discussing centralization and patron–client relations.

Porten, Bezalel. *Archives from Elephantine: The Life of an Ancient Jewish Military Colony*. Berkeley: University of California Press, 1968. Presentation of evidence for the Judean community at Elephantine by a scholar who has written much on the topic.

Rapport, Nigel. "Community." In Alan Barnard and Jonathan Spencer (eds), *Encyclopedia of Social and Cultural Anthropology* (pp. 114–17). London: Routledge, 1996. Overview of anthropological research on community.

Routledge, Bruce Edward. *Moab in the Iron Age: Hegemony, Polity, Archaeology*. Philadelphia: University of Pennsylvania, 2004. Archaeological treatment of Transjordanian region of Moab, addressing issues of wider Levant.

Rowlett, Lori L. *Joshua and the Rhetoric of Violence: A New Historicist Analysis*. Sheffield: Sheffield Academic, 1996. Analyzes the book of Joshua as product of Josianic monarchy.

Schloen, J. David. *The House of the Father as Fact and Symbol: Patrimonialism in Ugarit and the Ancient Near East*. Winona Lake, IN: Eisenbrauns, 2001. Study of patrimonial ideologies and social structure of ancient Israel.

Schneider, D. "Kinship." In Thomas Barfield (ed.), *The Dictionary of Anthropology* (pp. 268–70). Oxford: Blackwell, 1997. Brief reference article by a very important anthropologist specializing in kinship.

Stager, Lawrence E. "The archaeology of the family in ancient Israel." *Bulletin of the American Schools of Oriental Research 260* (1985): 1–35. Important article on archaeological evidence for family structures in preexilic Israel.

Thompson, Thomas L. *The Mythic Past: Biblical Archaeology and the Myth of Israel*. New York: Basic Books, 1999. Work by one of the major "minimalist" scholars of ancient Israel.

Vanderhooft, David S. "The Israelite *mišpāḥâ*, the Priestly writings, and changing valences in Israel's kinship terminology." In J. David Schloen (ed.), *Exploring the Longue Durée: Essays in Honor of Lawrence E. Stager* (pp. 485–96). Winona Lake, IN: Eisenbrauns, 2009. Discusses biblical and archaeological evidence for kinship structures in the monarchic and postexilic periods.

CHAPTER 22

Law and Legal Literature

Bernard M. Levinson and Tina M. Sherman

Despite the claim by Israelite authors for the divine origin of the legal collections, the archaeological remains of the ancient Near East demonstrate that biblical law was not created *ex nihilo*. The Near East bequeathed to ancient Israel a prestigious literary genre, the legal collection, that originated in the scribal schools (called *eduba*) of late third-millennium Sumer and then spread up the Fertile Crescent through Babylonia and Assyria into Anatolia and the Hittite empire. In the past century, archaeologists have uncovered about a dozen different cuneiform legal collections, written in Sumerian, Akkadian, and Hittite. Some of these documents are simply scribal school exercises, while others are extended, formal compositions. For example, Hammurabi's Code (ca. 1755 BCE), which was discovered in 1901, won such cultural prestige in ancient Mesopotamia that it was recopied for more than a millennium after its composition. Yet despite its widespread fame, scholars who have examined hundreds of thousands of actual court dockets that survive from the Old Babylonian period have found no evidence that its stipulations were ever implemented as actual law, let alone cited as prescriptive. Scholars now believe, therefore, that the great Near Eastern collections of law were not statutory "law codes" but were something closer to literary reflections on ethics and ideal forms of social organization.

At many points, biblical law closely corresponds to the great cuneiform legal collections in formulation, technical terminology, topos and range of sanctions. Yet the adoption of the literary form of a law collection was not simply an act of copying laws applicable to Israelite society into a new Hebrew composition. Rather, the biblical authors transformed the conventions of the genre, and in some cases the material in specific texts, in innovative ways to serve their ideological purposes. The result was a set of literary law collections composed over the course of several centuries and ultimately edited together into a single corpus, the Torah or the Pentateuch (see David Carr's essay in this volume).

While archaeologists have uncovered numerous court dockets and other legal documents from ancient Mesopotamia and Syria, no such extensive corpus of legal materials has been found in Israel. The Israelites typically used perishable materials for written

The Wiley Blackwell Companion to Ancient Israel, First Edition. Edited by Susan Niditch.
© 2016 John Wiley & Sons, Ltd. Published 2016 by John Wiley & Sons, Ltd.

documents, so most of the evidence of real applications of law is long gone. The legal material in the Bible is the best available direct evidence from Israel, but it must be used cautiously. Israelite authors almost never wrote propositionally; instead, they employed narrative, law and other conventional literary genres to express their ideas. Even when biblical writers sought to express new conceptions of religion, social structure or human values, their ideas assumed the forms of historical narrative and legal stipulation rather than the propositional formulations familiar to modern readers. The laws preserved in the Bible were carefully written and edited to align with the religious and cultural values of the authors. Moreover, as with their ancient Near Eastern precursors, there is no evidence of a real-world implementation of the stipulations in biblical law. However, the biblical texts can be used in combination with actual legal documents and literary collections of law from other ancient Near Eastern cultures to reconstruct, to some extent, the legal structures, practices and ethical thought of ancient Israel.

Biblical Sources of Law

The Pentateuch contains three formal literary collections of law: the Covenant Code in Exodus 20:22–23:33; the Deuteronomic laws in Deuteronomy 12–26; and the Holiness Code in Leviticus 17–26. Each of them begins with altar laws and ends with exhortations to obedience. In form, the three collections are similar to the cuneiform literary law collections, but in content, there are differences. While biblical law combines cultic, criminal and civil, and ethical law, in general the cuneiform collections, with the exception of the Middle Assyrian and Hittite Laws, rarely have such a mixture. The cuneiform collections primarily include only criminal and civil law.

Leviticus contains an additional collection of ritual and cultic laws attributed to the Priestly source (see also S. A. Geller's essay in this volume). The Holiness Code is embedded within this large block of material, so when scholars speak of the Priestly laws, they often include the Holiness Code within the boundaries of that material (Exod. 25 through Num. 10). The narrative plot of the Pentateuch presents the Covenant Code, the Priestly laws, and the Holiness Code as part of a single process of divine revelation to Moses at Sinai after the exodus from Egypt. Deuteronomy claims to be a retelling and rehearsal of this revelation of law, 40 years later, on the eve of the nation's entry into Canaan.

The three law collections and the Priestly laws are not the only legal material found in the Bible, however. Legal stipulations are also embedded within various biblical narratives. The Pentateuch is the richest source for this type of material. In addition, the condemnations of the prophets often refer to laws or legal principles that have been violated, Proverbs provides legal advice, the Psalms sometimes give insight into legal matters, and episodes within the narratives occasionally make reference to legal practices without specifically detailing the relevant laws. Because they come from a variety of sources, these laws and legal principles do not always agree with the stipulations of the legal collections in the Pentateuch. For example, the Book of Ruth mentions a former Israelite practice for concluding a contract in which "one man would take off his sandal and hand it to the other" (4:7). No such law exists in the Pentateuch, though there

Table 22.1 Categories of law

Legal form	Example
Apodictic (commands)	"Honor your father and your mother, *that you may long endure on the land that the Lord your God is assigning to you*" (Exod. 20:12, NJPS (excerpted from the Decalogue))
Casuistic (case law)	
Standard	"If a man strikes the eye of his slave, male or female, and destroys it, he shall let him go free *on account of his eye*" (Exod. 21:26, NJPS (modified))
Participial	"Whoever sheds the blood of man, by man shall his blood be shed; *for in His image did God make man*" (Gen. 9:6, NJPS)

is a reference to removal of a shoe in the context of a breach of law (Deut. 25:5–10). Given the inconsistent availability of evidence, and the occasionally conflicting legal stipulations within that evidence, the challenge is to assess the available information and attempt to determine whether, and to what extent, it reflects or suggests an actual Israelite legal practice.

Forms of Law

While the term "biblical law" may evoke the image of a series of "thou shalt not's," in reality, laws take several forms. Scholars generally categorize formal statements of law as either apodictic or casuistic. Apodictic laws are direct commands, addressed in the second person to the audience of the text, in which punishment for disobedience is not specified. Apodictic commands are universal and absolute: they apply in all circumstances and at all times without exception. In contrast, casuistic laws are case laws. They describe a specific situation and then give the legal consequences for one or more potential outcomes from that situation. Casuistic laws typically appear in an "if ... then" format, written in the third person, though second person address is also attested as a later development of the form ("if you ... then"). A subset of casuistic law is "participial" law, so named because the prohibited act is expressed using a Hebrew participle. Thus, participial law prescribes specific consequences for "whoever does ..." A statement of law will often be accompanied by a "motive clause," whose purpose is to encourage compliance, to provide a legal rationale for the law's stipulations, or to explain the origin or purpose of the law. Table 22.1 contains an example of each of the three legal forms. Each law also has a motive clause (in italics) corresponding to the types of motives listed above.

The participial law in table 22.1 is also an example of *lex talionis* or "talion," known colloquially as "an eye for an eye" or "measure for measure." The idea behind *talion*, which is also attested in the Laws of Hammurabi, is that proper redress for bodily injury or death requires a like injury to the guilty party. An injury to a legal person, in this view, cannot be corrected by means of financial compensation, because the person is considered infinite, not finite, in value.

Areas of Law

Israelite law operated in both the secular and cultic spheres. In the formulation of its stipulations, and in the determination of guilt and punishment, the relevant factors were the offense committed and the relative status of the offender and the individual harmed.

Legal Status of Individuals

Legal status had several dimensions in ancient Israel: status within the nation, status within clan and family, and status within society. National citizenship was determined by ethnicity or through marriage; it was not a matter of birthplace. That said, citizenship does not appear to have been a major criterion in most legal protections. In the Bible, it primarily arises only in the cultic and debtor laws. For purposes of taxation, the individual's place of residence was the determining factor, regardless of citizenship.

Clan affiliation was also a matter of genealogy or marriage (see T. M. Lemos's essay in this volume). Clans were extended families, and membership carried with it both rights and responsibilities in the areas of inheritance, criminal law and the social and financial welfare of other members of the clan. Within the family, which generally included several generations, a patriarchal structure was dominant, with a male most often holding the position of head of household, or paterfamilias. The legal standing of members below the head of household was determined by gender and marital status. A woman remained under her father's authority until she married, at which point her status changed from daughter to wife. A son remained under his father's authority while his father lived. Upon the death of the father, a son would receive his inheritance and could establish his place as head of his own household.

Social status often interacted with national and family status in determining an individual's legal standing. One of the most prominent distinctions was between slave and free person. There was no notion of race-based slavery comparable to what took place in American history or in South Africa under apartheid. Rather, a person could be born into slavery, could be enslaved in war or could become a debt-slave. In ancient Near Eastern practice, slaves were property to be bought, sold, and used for labor or sexual purposes. Yet biblical law takes pains to protect the human rights of slaves, especially in the case of debt-slaves. Oftentimes, to support a family that had fallen on hard times, one or more family members would be sold into slavery for a defined period of time. Biblical law is careful to restrict the rights of slave owners and stress their responsibilities to their slaves.

In addition to the distinction between slave and free person, for purposes of social justice biblical law highlights certain social groups. A special class of noncitizen living in Israel was the resident alien (the *gēr*). Resident aliens did not own land, and therefore presumably were at greater risk of social or financial reverses than landowners. The poor and individuals who lacked the support of a male head of household, such as widows and orphans, were similarly at risk of exploitation. Biblical law frequently establishes special protections for these vulnerable classes of individuals. Remarkably, the Bible even insists that resident aliens should enjoy equal protection under the law with native Israelites, without discrimination: "You shall have a single law for stranger and citizen alike ..." (Lev. 24:22).

Offenses against Individuals

Under biblical law, the punishment for major crimes such as homicide, injury or theft can take the form of either physical retribution (*talion*) or a monetary fine. Intentional homicide is punishable by death regardless of the status of the victim; even a slave may be avenged. The role of executioner apparently falls to the closest male relative of the victim. In cases of unintentional homicide, the accused may seek asylum until a legal judgment of guilt or innocence is made, presumably by the local elders. Some of the biblical evidence mentions designated cities where the accused could take refuge until the trial (Deut. 19:1–13; Num. 35:9–29), but the more likely model, one that is also supported in the extrabiblical evidence, identifies a temple altar as the place of refuge (Exod. 21:14; 1 Kings 1:50–53). If the accused is found guilty of intentional homicide, he loses his asylum rights and the family of the victim is free to exact retribution. If the verdict is unintentional homicide, then the accused is exiled from his home city instead of being killed (Josh. 20:1–9).

As in the homicide laws, intentional injury of another individual also calls for punishment in kind: "If anyone maims his fellow, as he has done so shall it be done to him: fracture for fracture, eye for eye, tooth for tooth" (Lev. 24:19–20). This is in contrast to the cuneiform law collections, which generally prescribe a monetary penalty for such offenses instead of the physical disfigurement. Minor physical injuries and cases of property damage call for monetary fines only. When the victim of an unintentional homicide or intentional injury is a slave, the penalties are monetary or monetary equivalents; either the slave's owner is paid, or the slave is freed (Exod. 21:26–27, 32). However, if a habitually goring ox kills a slave, in addition to the fine paid to the slave owner, the ox is killed. The idea behind this surprising requirement is not that the ox has killed intentionally, but that the created order has been overturned and needs to be restored; the slave is here clearly valued as a legal person.

In most cases, the punishment for theft is a requirement to repay a multiple of the value of the item stolen. For example, according to the Covenant Code, if a thief has stolen and slaughtered an ox, his penalty is five times what he stole (Exod. 21:37). This type of penalty is consistent with cuneiform law, though the multiple applied varies in both the biblical and cuneiform materials. An alternative punishment for theft in both biblical and extrabiblical sources is debt-slavery. One type of theft for which a harsher punishment is required in biblical law is kidnapping (where the theft of a person is for purposes of sale into slavery). In such cases, the death penalty is prescribed (Exod. 21:16).

Crimes committed by individuals of lower status against those of higher status carry harsh punishments. Offenses against God – violation of the Sabbath, apostasy, blasphemy – all require the death penalty (Exod. 31:14–15; Lev. 20:2–3; Lev. 24:15–16). On the human level, but in a similar vein, offenses against the king (1 Sam. 22:6–19; 1 Kings 21:1–16), disobedience to an order from a priest or a judge regarding a lawsuit

(Deut. 17:8–12), and neglect or disrespect of a parent by a child (Exod. 21:15; Lev. 20:9) are all capital offenses.

Sexual Offenses

Certain sexual acts, such as incest and bestiality, carry the death penalty in biblical law (Lev. 20:11–16). Rape and adultery comprise a special case of offense, however, because the nature of the offense and the punishment required depend on the status of the woman involved in the case. Adultery is defined as consensual extramarital sex between a wife and another man. Extramarital sex by a husband is not considered adultery unless his partner is a married woman. The Pentateuch stipulates that adultery is a capital offense requiring the death penalty for both participants (Lev. 20:10; Deut. 22:22). The fact that the husband did not have the right of disposition of his wife's fate, as he often did in Near Eastern law, shows that in biblical law, she was not considered his chattel, but an autonomous legal person. The offense was considered not a wrongdoing simply against the husband but against the larger moral order of the community. Outside of the Pentateuch, different solutions seem to be contemplated, including divorce or possibly even a monetary fine (Jer. 3:8; Prov. 6:32–35).

Rape of a married woman is not addressed in the law, but rape of a betrothed woman is considered a crime against the man to whom she is betrothed, and the punishment is death for the rapist (Deut. 22:25–27). For the woman, rape serves only as a defense against an accusation of adultery; it does not constitute an individual offense for which she can seek redress. Extramarital sex with a woman who is not betrothed calls for much milder penalties, generally involving payment of the standard bride price, and in some cases a requirement that the man and woman marry (Exod. 22:15–16; Deut. 22:28–29). The woman's consent is not a factor in determination of the penalty in these laws (see also the essay by Carol Meyers in this volume).

Property and Inheritance Law

Ownership of land carried with it risks and responsibilities in ancient Israel. Biblical law is silent about the property rights of kings, but biblical narrative and cuneiform sources suggest that a king had the right to confiscate the lands of a traitor or enemy, and to grant land to his supporters. Kings may also have had the right to tax landowners on the agricultural yield from their land (1 Sam. 8:14–17). The focus of biblical law is on tithes due to the Levites and priests, individuals who do not own land because their role in society is to maintain the cult. When the tithe amount is specified, it is set at one-tenth of the yield from flock or field (Lev. 27:30–33; Num. 18:25–32). The "firstfruits" of the field are also to be handed over to the priests (Exod. 23:19; Deut. 26:1–3). In addition to formal tithes, biblical law requires landowners to leave a portion of the produce from their fields for the poor. The laws reflect different mechanisms for accomplishing this: by direct gift from the annual tithe every third year (Deut. 14:27–29); by disregarding any produce remaining after the first pass at the harvest (Deut. 24:19–22); by not harvesting the edges of the cultivable land (Lev. 19:9–10); or by not harvesting the land every seventh year (Exod. 23:10–11). In the latter three cases, the poor – including the widow, the orphan, and the resident alien – may collect for themselves the produce that remains in the fields, vineyards and groves. There are no penalties for noncompliance with these laws in the biblical texts, however, and the extent to which these practices were customary is unclear.

The system of inheritance laws in the ancient Near East applied primarily to sons. In most cases, the property was divided equally among the heirs, by casting lots, upon the death of the head of household. Property division could be delayed if the heirs were unable to immediately take over management of their shares. In such cases, the property would be jointly held by all of the heirs until such time as division of the shares was feasible. Firstborn sons often received an enhanced portion of the inheritance, but otherwise, the property of the father was divided equally among the heirs. If a woman received an inheritance, it was generally by way of her dowry, which she would retain upon her husband's death. Based on the evidence from biblical and cuneiform sources, it appears that fathers had only limited ability to change these basic arrangements. A father could direct the apportioning of his property. He could assign the firstborn's share to another son, and he could choose to include his wife or daughters among his heirs, but he could not fully disinherit a lawful heir, nor could he designate individuals outside of his household as heirs. Similarly, while a head of household could sell a portion of his property, he could not irrevocably gift it to individuals outside the family. Gifted land apparently returned to the family upon the death of the head of household.

Biblical law seems to assume this basic inheritance system, and it then focuses on addressing special circumstances. For example, it details the line of succession should a head of household have no son, with the goal of retaining ownership within either the family or the clan (Num. 27:8–11). Another law sets limits around a father's ability to assign a firstborn's share to one of his brothers (Deut. 21:15–17). In addition, since women were generally excluded from direct inheritance, a widow with no dowry would be at particular risk of falling into poverty. Thus, the laws regularly include widows among the vulnerable in society who need special protections.

Contractual Law

The laws and customs governing contracts in the ancient Near East were designed to support a system of oral agreements. Contracts were sometimes written down for the purpose of retaining the details of the agreement, but they did not, by themselves, constitute an enforceable arrangement. Two types of oral contract are apparent from the available evidence. The first involves mutual obligations among parties to the agreement. This type of contract becomes enforceable as soon as one party to the agreement has completed his obligations. Agreements completed using this type of contract include sale of property, contracts for work to be performed, loans and deposits of valuables for safekeeping. The second type of contract takes the form of an oath, in which an individual curses himself to punishment by God should he fail to fulfill his obligations under the contract. Treaties and agreements whereby an individual is commissioned to perform a specific service appear to be the most common uses of this type of contract. As with inheritance law, biblical law seems to take the general ancient Near Eastern system of contracts for granted, and the authors then legislate for special circumstances, including providing special protections for society's most vulnerable members.

Legal Institutions

According to the most recent reconstructions, there were four major contexts for the administration of justice in ancient Israel: family and clan law, in the hands of the paterfamilias; local or town law, administered by the elders; sacral law, dispensed by the priests; and royal judicial authority. These four spheres most likely overlapped historically and competed with one another, but only the last three would generally be considered public legal institutions. Local justice was deeply rooted in the clan network of the Judean countryside and thus operated independently of any centralized state authority. Cases would be heard in important public locales such as the city gate (Deut. 21:19; 22:15; 25:7; Ruth 4:11) or the threshing-floor (Ruth 3:10–14; 1 Kings 22:10). The function of judge and jury in such legal proceedings was usually fulfilled by the elders, but sometimes fell to the public assembly. Such public hearings served to limit the right of the paterfamilias to take independent legal action against his wife or minor children. In addition, judicial oracles seem to have been proclaimed (Judg. 4:4–5) by the charismatic "judges" who may also have functioned as traveling "circuit-court" judges (1 Sam. 7:15–17).

In certain cases, the responsibility for dispensing justice fell to cultic officials instead of the elders or the public assembly. The various literary genres of the Bible, including each of the pentateuchal literary strata, point to the important role played by the priesthood (and with it the altar, the gate of the local sanctuary, and the casting of the priestly lots) in judicial activity (see S. A. Geller's essay in this volume). The sanctuary gate and the space directly before the altar constituted authoritative sites wherein legal proceedings could take place numinously in the presence of the divine (Exod. 21:6; 22:7; Num. 5:16; 27:5). Legal proceedings in this cultic context seem to have taken a number of forms, including the following: judicial oaths; judicial ordeals; priestly manipulation of oracular paraphernalia, such as the lots, in order to issue a judicial ruling; and priestly oracular rulings, apparently without recourse to the lots. What distinguishes these cases from those administered in a lay context was the nature of the case. Obviously, the priests were involved in all questions related to ritual purity and impurity, as the divine commission of Aaron and his sons makes clear (Lev. 10:10–11). Less obvious, and most important, the cultus played an essential role in cases in which a dearth of evidence or the absence of testimony by witnesses made reaching a clear determination of guilt or innocence impossible. Under such circumstances, the cultus granted the community access to a suprahuman agency of judicial decision-making. To resolve their dispute, the involved parties would repair to the local altar or sanctuary, and there, in the symbolic presence of the deity, they would swear a judicial oath or submit to the applicable ordeal (Exod. 22:8; Num. 5:11–31). In cases involving trial by ordeal, the divine determination of guilt became also, in effect, a death sentence.

While the elders and priests had an important role in local justice, ensuring justice in general within the nation was ultimately the role of the king. It was the responsibility of the king to prevent the oppression of those who lacked power – such as the widow and the orphan – by guaranteeing them access to the protections of the law. Kings directly and by delegation heard complex legal cases and entertained judicial appeals. Royal prerogative even entitled the monarch to pardon a capital offense that would otherwise legally require execution by the blood avenger (2 Sam. 14:1–24). Most important, in a responsibility that overlapped with the cultic sphere, the king would frequently preside over ambiguous legal cases involving only claim and counterclaim, with neither party able to summon witnesses or provide evidence in support of their account (1 Kings 3:16–28). As the broad powers of the king indicate, ensuring and dispensing justice was one of the defining attributes of kingship. This was true not only in Israel, but throughout the ancient Near East as well.

The Ideologies and Historical Contexts of the Law Collections

When rabbinic interpreters confronted the legal collections of the Covenant Code, Deuteronomy, the Priestly laws and the Holiness Code, they had no choice but to construct a coherent system by means of harmonistic exegesis. That exegetical system entailed certain assumptions about the nature of the biblical text: that it is everywhere coherent and that it is free of redundancy. Yet the attempt to resolve the legal incoherence illuminates neither the plain meaning of the texts nor their compositional history. The texts can be *read* that way but it is unlikely that they were *written* that way.

The Covenant Code

The Covenant Code is probably the oldest of the biblical law collections. The evidence suggests the Israelite scribes drew on a number of cuneiform legal sources, both directly and indirectly, in the composition of the text. Particularly useful to the dating of the Covenant Code is its close connection with the Laws of Hammurabi. The points of contact between the laws cannot be explained by cultural diffusion or oral transmission from second millennium Babylonia to first millennium Israel. The correspondence is best explained in terms of literary and textual dependence. After its composition in the Old Babylonian period, the greatest interest in the Laws of Hammurabi is in the Neo-Assyrian period. This accessibility of Hammurabi's Laws creates a possibility that the literary impact of that text upon the Covenant Code took place during the first millennium (most likely in the eighth or seventh century), when Judah became a vassal to the Neo-Assyrian empire (see J. J. M. Roberts's essay in this volume).

The Covenant Code has long been viewed as providing an important window into the preexilic history of ancient Israel. It has played a vital role in any reconstruction of Israel's cultus and sacrificial system, religious calendar, legal and ethical norms, and social structure. Though its selection of topics and laws is insufficient to serve as a comprehensive plan for a social and legal structure, the content of the laws suggests an agrarian society, with authority over the community residing with the chieftain, and with cultic observance practiced in the local communities. More significantly, the ordering of the laws demonstrates one of the primary ideological concerns of the Covenant Code: the protection of slaves.

No other ancient Near Eastern legal collection starts with slave laws. Usually, such material appears last in the law collections, an indication of the lowly status of slaves. Thus, the placement of the manumission laws at the beginning of the Covenant Code is a statement of human value. It is underscored by the content of the laws, which restrict the rights of the slave owner over the slave in terms of the length and conditions of service (Exod. 21:2–6). Even the laws governing female slaves may be interpreted in this light. Rather than releasing the female slave in a way that would leave her vulnerable in society, the law ensures her protection by requiring that she either be redeemed or wedded. And if the slave owner fails to live up to these responsibilities, the female slave is released without payment (Exod. 21:7–11). This concern for the status of slaves may reflect the respect the authors of the Covenant Code had for Israel's national origin story, in which Yahweh brought the Israelites out of slavery in Egypt.

Deuteronomic Law

The earliest literary strata of the Bible, including the Covenant Code and the narratives of Joshua through 2 Kings, clearly contemplate sacrificial worship of Yahweh at multiple altar sites throughout the land. Yet Deuteronomy rejects this practice as illegitimate, requiring instead that sacrificial worship be performed at a single sanctuary, "the place that the Lord will choose" (Deut. 12:13–14), a reference to the Jerusalem Temple, although the city itself is never explicitly named in Deuteronomy. The setting for Deuteronomy's innovation was a movement of major religious and social reform in Judah at the time of Neo-Assyrian hegemony in the Near East. As a strategic response to the Neo-Assyrian incursions, King Hezekiah all but abandoned the outlying countryside to the invaders. He contracted Judah into a rump state protected by fortress cities at the borders in defense of Jerusalem, the royal capital, at the center. To urbanize the population, he began to dismantle Judah's extensive rural cultus and the familiar clan structure that supported it. Josiah's so-called "reform" of 622 BCE (2 Kings 22–23) continued this process, centralizing the cultus and establishing the Jerusalem Temple as the exclusive site for legitimate worship of Yahweh. Cult sites outside of Jerusalem were demolished, while the Temple itself was purged of any elements not viewed as Yahwistic. Even previously legitimate Yahwistic shrines in the countryside were declared illegitimate, despite their associations with legendary patriarchal and prophetic figures (see S. A. Geller's essay in this volume). The legal corpus of Deuteronomy, which is intimately connected with this comprehensive transformation of Judean society and religion, provided divine sanction for the reform program necessitated by Neo-Assyrian encroachment into Judah.

Whereas the Covenant Code covered a range of topics relevant to a social and cultural environment that apparently preexisted its laws, Deuteronomy envisioned a radically different society. The Deuteronomic centralization of the cult and proscription of local ritual activity necessarily had to cover a broader range of topics. It required revision of essentially the entire apparatus of rituals and institutions that governed local religious activity. It also required secularization of many institutions of public and private life to replace the function of the local sanctuary in the resolution of ambiguous civil and criminal legal cases. Thus the first section (Deut. 12:1–16:17) of the legal corpus in chapters 12–26 primarily addresses technical cultic matters (such as sacrifice, tithes, and the festival calendar, with additional material added by way of association), while its second section (Deut. 16:18–18:22) lays out a plan for the complete restructuring of the major judicial, political and religious institutions of ancient Judah. The sequence of officials Deuteronomy names – judge, king, priest, prophet – reflects the priorities of the authors of the legal corpus itself as they systematically draw the consequences of cultic centralization for other spheres of public life, including judicial procedure and public administration. Even the conventional role of the king in Israelite society, as the highest civil and judicial authority, is fundamentally transformed on account of centralization. In this case centralization ironically leads to a decrease in royal power, as the Temple eclipses the king's authority. By means of this law collection, the authors subordinate the entire institutional life of ancient Judah, including the power of the king, to the authority of the Deuteronomic Torah.

At its core, Deuteronomy represents a radical and direct revision of the Covenant Code. In order to implement their unprecedented transformation of religion, law and social structure, the authors of Deuteronomy deliberately presented their new vision of the Judean polity as continuous with the abrogated past, and used the earlier textual material of the Covenant Code to sanction their own independent agenda. And though there is clear textual dependence, the Covenant Code did not constitute a source to which the authors of Deuteronomy were slavishly bound in language, scope or substantive legal content. Instead, the authors of Deuteronomy selectively transformed the Covenant Code to support their own very different religious and legal agenda.

While the reforms detailed in Deuteronomy fit logically within a seventh-century BCE historical context, it remains unclear whether these political, social and religious transformations were ever actually implemented. The law collections from the exilic or postexilic period do take cultic centralization for granted, but that does not prove that the full complement of Deuteronomic legislation was ever enacted in Israel. In its final form, Deuteronomy may well date to the exilic period, when its editors were held in Babylonian exile without any direct access either to political power or to their land. From these perspectives, the orientation of the text thus seems far closer to utopian political science, a revisioning of the possibilities of political, religious and social life, than to any immediate description of an existing status quo.

Priestly Law

In the study of biblical law, the Priestly corpus is unlike its peers. In contrast to the Covenant Code, Deuteronomy and the Holiness Code, Priestly law does not address civil law, social justice or political structures, except as these issues might intersect with cultic matters (see S. A. Geller's essay in this volume). Only in the Priestly patriarchal narratives are issues of social justice or moral-ethical law addressed. Otherwise, Priestly laws focus on the structure, management and practices of the cult. As such, they address such issues as maintenance of the Tabernacle, installation of priests, the cultic calendar, and a variety of sanctification, purification, and atonement regulations and rituals. The lack of civil and criminal law in Priestly legislation means it is also silent on legal institutions. As a result, the priest's role becomes one of spiritual caretaker for Israel, narrowly focused on Tabernacle duties, but without any responsibility for the administration of justice.

Precise dating of the Priestly laws (or of the Priestly source in general) is difficult because of a dearth of evidence for a direct literary connection to a datable source. Some scholars have attempted to date the text to the preexilic period based on linguistic evidence, but that opinion has not found widespread acceptance, in part because the Priestly laws are based on a centralized cult model. There is no polemic with Deuteronomic centralization in the Priestly laws, which suggests that centralization was an established fact by the time the Priestly laws were written. In addition, correspondences in themes between the Priestly material and exilic or postexilic texts like Ezekiel and Second Isaiah argue against a preexilic date for the Priestly source. Whatever the date of its composition, the content of the Priestly laws aligns with an exilic or postexilic reality. The Israelites no longer had the independent authority to define for themselves their system of justice. Only in the administration of their own cult would they likely have had some measure of freedom.

The Holiness Code

The Holiness Code is so named because of its characteristic phrase: "You shall be holy, for I am holy" (Lev. 19:2). The use of this phrase with both the moral-ethical and cultic laws of Leviticus 19–22 suggests that for the Holiness authors, there is no difference between moral-ethical sin and religious sin; both offend Yahweh and defile the offenders. As Israel Knohl puts it, "Holiness thus includes all areas of life and applies to the entire community of Israel and the land they inhabit." The concept of holiness in the Holiness Code is a clever blending of the cultic purity concerns of the Priestly laws and the cultic and moral-ethical concerns of the Covenant Code and Deuteronomic laws. As such, the Holiness legislation covers a range of cultic topics – regulations for priests, proper sacrificial practices, the cultic calendar – as well as a variety of moral-ethical concerns – sexual and criminal offenses, honesty and fairness in business and legal matters, protection of the weak. These laws are related to proper observance of the cult, in part, through the frequent repetition of the phrase, "I am the LORD," as an almost self-evident motive clause:

> You shall not pick your vineyard bare, or gather the fallen fruit of your vineyard; you shall leave them for the poor and the stranger: I am the LORD, your God. (Lev. 19:10, NJPS (modified))

> You shall not take vengeance or bear a grudge against your countrymen. Love your fellow as yourself: I am the LORD. (Lev. 19:18, NJPS)

The Holiness Code is as much a revision of Deuteronomic and Priestly law as Deuteronomy is a revision of the Covenant Code. The Holiness authors transformed their sources to support their idealized vision of society. For example, prior to Deuteronomy, all slaughter of domestic animals – even for purposes of food – was a ritual activity necessarily carried out at an altar. Deuteronomy's program of cultic centralization required the authors to separate cultic and secular slaughter so that the people could slaughter animals for food in their local communities (Deut. 12:13–16). The Holiness Code accepts the centralization of the cult, but its concern to subject all Israelite activity to cultic purity requirements means it cannot allow secular slaughter. Consequently in the Holiness laws, livestock slaughtered for food must first be presented as a sacrifice to God at the central sanctuary before it may be consumed (Lev. 17:2–7). Moreover, the challenge to Deuteronomy's authority operates both within the laws and in the narrative frame. With its frequent use of the first person for divine speech, the Holiness authors trump even the prestigious prophetic voice of Moses in Deuteronomy by attributing their laws to Yahweh himself as divine originator of the revised legislation.

Scholars have yet to identify a criterion by which an absolute date for the Holiness Code may be established. However, relative dating of the Holiness Code to some time after the Covenant Code, the Deuteronomic laws and the Priestly laws suggests an exilic or postexilic date for its composition (see the essay by Ohad Cohen in this volume). This dating is consistent with one of the primary concerns of the Holiness legislation: the separation of Israel from other nations. To preserve Israelite identity in the postexilic period when Judah as an independent nation no longer existed, the Holiness authors recast Israelite identity in terms of religion. Lacking a political identity, the Holiness Code created a cultural identity for the Israelites by using the law to establish the Israelites as "a 'holy' people, 'separated' from other nations" (Ska).

The Literary Frame of Biblical Law

The cuneiform precursors to the biblical law collections provided useful models of literary framing from which the Israelite scribes could draw inspiration. One important convention adopted from the cuneiform model was to set the series of legal provisions between a literary prologue and epilogue in which a royal speaker claims responsibility for promulgating the laws. King Hammurabi credits Shamash, the Mesopotamian sun god who is the custodian of the cosmic principles of justice, for granting him the ability to perceive the eternal truths encoded in his laws. However, the laws in their actual formulation are royal. Hammurabi repeatedly boasts that the laws are "*my* pronouncements, which *I* have inscribed on *my* stele" (xlix, 3–4, 19–21). Presented with the concept of divinely sanctioned royal law, the Israelite authors pushed the genre in a different direction. They transformed the royal speaker from a human monarch into their divine king, Yahweh. In so doing, the Israelite scribes introduced into the ancient world a new idea: the divine revelation of law.

Also striking in the biblical adaptation of the cuneiform model is that law is embedded in a larger narrative, without which it is incomplete: the covenant exists in history. The Pentateuch tells the story of how Yahweh revealed the law to the nation of Israel at

Mount Sinai. The narrative claim is that Israel was constituted as a people when Yahweh revealed himself as the God who enters into a covenantal relationship with his people:

> Now then, if you will obey Me faithfully and keep My covenant, you shall be My treasured possession among all peoples. (Exod. 19:5, NJPS (modified))

This divine proclamation of covenantal law is as much a moment of creation as when God spoke to bring the world into being in Genesis 1. It is through the Sinai/Horeb covenant that the nation gains its identity and history, both its past as a people redeemed from slavery and its future as a people wholly dedicated to and preserved by Yahweh.

This national originary moment – the moral and legal constitution of Israel – is completely separated from the account of universal creation in Genesis 1. Neither the nation nor its laws existed from the beginning of time. This model of national genesis tied to law is wholly different from the origin myths of the ancient Near East. For example, the Laws of Hammurabi were embedded in a literary frame in which the election of Babylon and its king, Hammurabi, represents divine destiny decreed from the beginning of time, independent of human history or agency. The radically different vision of the biblical narrative presents the existence of the nation as conditional upon the people's assent and ongoing commitment, generation after generation, to the covenant. The election of the nation, whereby it was brought into a special relationship to God, derives from history, not from cosmological destiny.

Legal Revision as a Means of Cultural Renewal

In addition to the broad selection of literary genres and *topoi* inherited from the Near East, specific techniques for collating, structuring, redacting and annotating law were a crucial part of the cuneiform patrimony of Israelite scribes. These are the techniques that the Covenant Code used to transform Hammurabi's laws, that Deuteronomy used to transform the Covenant Code, and that the Holiness Code used to transform the Deuteronomic and Priestly laws.

Yet the biblical authors' transformative actions did not operate exclusively at the empirical level. Indeed, their textual transformations cannot be understood apart from the larger problem of innovation in a culture in which the law is presented as divine revelation. There is a clear relationship between textual voice and textual authority, so that attributing a legal text to Yahweh literally gives that text ultimate authority. In any culture, social, economic and intellectual change occurs over time. How does a culture with a concept of divine revelation address the problem of legal change? How can legal texts, once viewed as divinely revealed, be revised to fit new circumstances without compromising their – or God's – authority?

In their own ways, the authors and editors of the legal collections confronted existing legal texts that enshrined the legitimacy of the laws the authors sought to change. Granted, those earlier collections may not have had the status of actual public law; they may have been only prestigious texts, part of the curriculum of scribal schools, but they were nonetheless texts that could not simply be ignored or dispensed with. The biblical authors, in one way or another, had to take account of these texts and justify their departure from their norms. These were sophisticated interpreters, or, better, reinterpreters of texts, both Israelite and cuneiform. They consciously reused and reinterpreted earlier sources to propound and justify their program of cultic and legal reform, even – or particularly – when those texts conflicted with the authors' agenda. Thus, in many cases, the composition of one text embeds the reception of other texts and responds to them, reediting and reorganizing their sequences and their substantive content. Yet the most striking thing is the way each text asserts its own originality. Each denies that it is in any way derivative. Far from appearing as a recondite or jejune rewriting of tradition, each text presents itself rather as more original than the tradition it both revises and expands.

The Decalogue

While it is not considered a law collection, the Decalogue is yet another set of biblical laws that demands explanation. On a compositional level, there are two main issues: how to explain the two versions of the text (Exod. 20:2–17; Deut. 5:6–18), and what is the relation of the text to Deuteronomy's narrative claim that these are the "Ten Words" God wrote on two stone tablets (4:13; 10:4). The two different versions of the Decalogue most likely derive from different historical contexts, with the repetition in Deuteronomy serving as a strategy for its competition with the Covenant Code. The reuse of the Decalogue helps to anchor Deuteronomy's religious and legal innovations to the tradition of divine revelation at Sinai. The actual enumeration of the Decalogue into ten commandments is complicated because there are no special numbers or names for each of the commandments in either Exodus 20 or Deuteronomy 5, and there are more than ten verbs expressing commands within each list. Because of this ambiguity, three different divisions of the text emerged in Jewish and Christian tradition.

The most remarkable thing about the Decalogue, however, is its message. In the existing corpus of ancient Near Eastern literature, there is no other text that represents a deity directly and publicly revealing his will to an entire nation, simultaneously, cutting across barriers of class, race and gender. In the divine proclamation of the covenant, God, speaking as "I," directly addresses each Israelite as "Thou," ungrammatically using the intimate singular form rather than the expected plural. Each addressee – or within the narrative structure, each former slave – thereby knows himself or herself to be directly addressed by God. That direct address requires a personal response – the creation of a moral self – on the part of the reader or hearer. But that self is not conceptualized as existing only in a relation of service to the deity. Indeed, the second half of the Decalogue stipulates rather the addressee's duties to other members of the community. The Decalogue creates the neighbor just as it creates the self. Adherence to the covenant brings into being a community of moral agents. The moral agent is also a historical agent: the future of the nation hangs upon how I treat my neighbor.

The radical formulation of this text goes beyond simply providing a sanction for socially disruptive actions. Here there are no sanctions or punishments. Instead, the actions themselves are simply prohibited. The goal of the text is not to regulate the status quo but to completely transform it, to create a new society altogether in which there is no longer murder, theft or adultery. Thus the commands of the Decalogue are transformative. They envision a new society, without precedent, and they seek to bring it into existence.

Deuteronomy's Draft Constitution: The Origins of Rule of Law and Separation of Powers

The Bible has survived and retained its relevance in the Abrahamic religious traditions for over two millennia, but a lesser acknowledged sphere of influence is in the Western legal tradition. Modern scholarship looks almost exclusively to classical Greece and Rome to reconstruct the history of constitutional thought, making exploration of the historical and cultural diffusion of Near Eastern law difficult. The attempt to recover this crucial lost chapter of intellectual history affords a different perspective not only upon the past but also upon the present.

Deuteronomy's laws of public offices provide a particularly instructive case (16:18–18:22). They introduce two innovations to transform the traditionally decentralized system of justice. The first is a professionalized judiciary that would assume responsibility for all routine legal cases in the local settlements, thereby eliminating the need for involvement of the local elders in judicial procedure (16:18). The second is the reassignment of ambiguous legal cases from the local sanctuaries to the Temple as a final authority (17:8–13). As a result, the dispensation of justice is completely taken out of the king's hands, denying him his traditional role in the judicial process. Taken together, these stipulations constitute a blueprint for a transformed society, one in which the key judicial, administrative, and cultic branches of government each have their separate spheres of authority defined and allocated by a single, sovereign text, to which each is equally responsible. Constituted by the law, they must also answer to it. This vision, moreover, provides a historical precedent for the later idea of a professional and independent judiciary, protected from the monarchy by virtue of its equal standing with it. The same concept would prevent Church or Temple from being reduced to a simple organ of the state, and at the same time preclude domination by either Church or Temple of the institutions in the public sphere.

The political structure that Deuteronomy envisioned was without precedent. Deuteronomy's subordination of the monarch to a sovereign legal text that regulates his powers and to which he is accountable has no known counterpart in the ancient Near East. It is equally distinct from the classical Greek ideology of kingship. Granted, Greek political theory of the fifth century BCE included a strong affirmation of respect for law over obligation to government, but even that differs from Deuteronomy's radical argument that the supreme political authority is himself accountable to the law, on an equal basis with other citizens. Deuteronomy's blueprint for a "Torah monarchy" arguably helped lay the foundations for the later political conception of a constitutional monarchy. The development of these revolutionary ideas in ancient Israel, has, for too long, gone unnoticed by legal historians and biblical scholars.

Conclusions: The Legacy of Biblical Law for the Modern World

The phenomenon of legal revision as a strategy for cultural renewal is another legacy of biblical authorship that has modern significance. Biblical Studies provides a way of critically engaging the ideological assumptions of contemporary theory, whose objections to the notion of a canon are certainly understandable: for being exclusive; for encoding class, race or gender bias; for silencing competing or less prestigious voices; for ignoring difference; for arresting social change; for enshrining privilege. In a similar vein, it opens avenues of dialog regarding assumptions of fundamentalist thinking. In both cases, the canon is taken to be a self-sufficient, unchanging entity, one that must be either wholly rejected or wholly accepted. The dynamic literary history of biblical law challenges that approach and demonstrates that the canon is radically open and embeds its own process of reflection and critique.

Just as Deuteronomy's program of social transformation introduced the concept of "separation of powers" that is central to the American Constitution, so the biblical scribes' approach to revision of authoritative legal texts in response to changing historical circumstances provides an analogy to modern constitutional interpretation. Precisely out of fidelity to their foundational canon, ancient Israelite scribes regularly found it necessary to update, revise and renew older laws. They did so while presenting those transformed laws as consistent with the very tradition they were revising and updating: they understood the renewal of tradition to represent the original intent of the tradition. Such a perspective calls into question the reductive and divisive debates that continue to take place in the context of American constitutional jurisprudence about two positions that are treated as mutually exclusive – the "original intent" position versus the "living constitution" position. In the case of ancient Israel, the "constitution" of the Pentateuch provided, from the very beginning, a model of ongoing renewal of its legal and religious heritage.

Bibliography

Barmash, Pamela. *Homicide in the Biblical World*. New York: Cambridge University Press, 2005. Includes an extensive analysis of biblical narrative and legal material relevant to homicide and a systematic analysis of actual documents of law from ancient Near Eastern sources.

Berlin, Adele and Marc Zvi Brettler (eds). *The Jewish Study Bible*. 2nd edn. New York: Oxford University Press, 2014. Contains a wealth of resources for exploring the biblical text, including a series of background essays for reading the Bible. Biblical passages quoted in this chapter use the New Jewish Publication Society translation (NJPS) that is incorporated in *The Jewish Study Bible*.

Bottéro, Jean. *Mesopotamia: Writing, Reasoning, and the Gods*. Chicago: University of Chicago Press, 1992. Includes a valuable essay on the literary nature of the Laws of Hammurabi and its role in the scribal curriculum.

Finkelstein, Jacob. *The Ox that Gored*. Philadelphia: American Philosophical Society, 1981. A brilliant monograph, published posthumously, contending that the conception of human value prevalent in modern Western culture corresponds to and derives from the ethical categories in biblical law.

Greenberg, Moshe. "Some postulates of biblical criminal law." In *Studies in the Bible and Jewish Thought* (pp. 25–41). Philadelphia: Jewish Publication Society, 1995. Greenberg's influential essay contrasts the Covenant Code's values with those of ancient Near Eastern legal collections, arguing that the differences in laws point to major cultural differences.

Greengus, Samuel. *Laws in the Bible and in Early Rabbinic Collections: The Legal Legacy of the Ancient Near East.* Eugene, OR: Cascade, 2011. Fascinating analysis of laws that are attested in ancient Near Eastern collections and rabbinic literature, but not in the Hebrew Bible, thereby suggesting an ongoing cultural tradition.

Jackson, Bernard S. "Reflections on biblical criminal law." In *Essays in Jewish and Comparative Legal History* (pp. 25–63). Leiden: Brill, 1975. Jackson challenges Greenberg's "Some postulates," arguing that pentateuchal laws represent ideal reflections upon social order and ethics rather than enforceable legal statutes.

Knohl, Israel. *The Sanctuary of Silence: The Priestly Torah and the Holiness School.* Minneapolis: Fortress, 1995. Knohl reverses the classic theory that the Holiness Code predates Priestly law and argues instead that the Holiness authors, as the final redactors of the Torah, both revised and supplemented the Priestly source.

Levinson, Bernard M. *Deuteronomy and the Hermeneutics of Legal Innovation.* Oxford: Oxford University Press, 1998. Levinson demonstrates how Deuteronomy's reform-minded authors defended their transformation of prevailing norms by reinterpreting earlier laws so as to lend authority to their new understanding of divine will.

Levinson, Bernard M. *Legal Revision and Religious Renewal in Ancient Israel.* Cambridge: Cambridge University Press, 2008. Examines the phenomenon of legal revision in ancient Israel using the principle of transgenerational punishment as a case study; an extensive bibliographic essay on innerbiblical exegesis serves as an additional resource for study.

Levinson, Bernard M. "The Right Chorale": *Studies in Biblical Law and Interpretation.* Winona Lake, IN: Eisenbrauns, 2011. Twelve studies exploring the relation between law and narrative, the connections between Deuteronomy and the Neo-Assyrian loyalty oath tradition, and the contributions of biblical law to later Western civilization.

Pressler, Carolyn. *The View of Women Found in the Deuteronomic Family Laws.* Berlin: de Gruyter, 1993. Comprehensive study of laws in Deuteronomy dealing with gender, challenging any too-confident notions of the text as enshrining women's rights.

Roth, Martha. *Law Collections from Mesopotamia and Asia Minor.* 2nd edn. Atlanta: Scholars Press, 1997. Roth provides an introduction and text edition for each of the major legal collections from ancient Mesopotamia and Anatolia.

Ska, Jean-Louis. *Introduction to Reading the Pentateuch.* Winona Lake, IN: Eisenbrauns, 2006. Ska places particular focus upon the biblical legal corpora and the interpretative issues they raise and provides a first-rate introduction to recent European theories on these issues.

Stackert, Jeffrey. *Rewriting the Torah: Literary Revision in Deuteronomy and the Holiness Legislation.* Tübingen: Mohr Siebeck, 2007. Fascinating analysis showing how both Deuteronomy and the Holiness Code redrafted and rethought their literary sources to meet new ideological goals.

Weinfeld, Moshe. *Deuteronomy and the Deuteronomic School.* Oxford: Clarendon, 1972. Weinfeld's groundbreaking study demonstrated the close relationship of Deuteronomy to cuneiform law and the thoughtful way the authors of the legal corpus reinterpreted earlier biblical law.

Wellhausen, Julius. *Prolegomena to the History of Israel.* Atlanta: Scholars Press, 1994. In his classical, brilliantly argued model of the Documentary Hypothesis, Wellhausen compared the legal collections of the Pentateuch both with one another and with the narrative works of the Deuteronomistic History (Joshua–Kings) and Chronicles.

Westbrook, Raymond (ed.). *A History of Ancient Near Eastern Law.* 2 vols. Leiden: Brill, 2003. A series of essays, arranged by millennium and by geographical region, using archaeological and textual evidence to reconstruct legal structures and practices in ancient Egypt, Mesopotamia, Syro-Palestine and the Hittite empire.

Westbrook, Raymond and Bruce Wells. *Everyday Law in Biblical Israel: An Introduction*. Louisville, KY: Westminster John Knox, 2009. Westbrook and Wells present a detailed reconstruction of ancient Israelite legal practices based on evidence derived from the biblical texts.

CHAPTER 23

Women's Lives

Carol Meyers

M ost Israelite women, like most Israelite men, lived in agrarian settlements. (This
essay uses "Israelite" and "Israel" in a general cultural sense, not as a political
or geographic designation). Their daily lives took place in the family household, which
was the smallest and most numerous unit of Israelite society (see the essays by Francesca
Stavrakopoulou, T. M. Lemos, and David Schloen in this volume). All the basic functions
of daily life, especially economic ones but also religious, social, and even political ones,
played out in the activities and interactions of the household members.

Women participated, to a greater or lesser extent, in all aspects of life in their
households, which consisted of the dwelling in which they lived, the people (usually
kin) who lived there, and its physical contents and also its lands and animals. Israelite
households were largely self-sufficient; women's daily lives thus centered on the myriad
activities necessary for survival. Anthropologists call these activities "maintenance
activities," a term referring to the processes required to sustain the household. They
encompass the production of basic commodities, reproduction (childbearing and
childrearing), sociopolitical interactions with others in the community, and religious
activities deemed essential for the well-being of the household. In addition, some
women had roles that transcended their households and served the larger community.

Sources

To achieve as balanced a view as possible of women's lives, a number of different
sources – biblical texts, archaeological remains, and ethnographic analogies and analyses – must be consulted, for no single source contains sufficient information (see Meyers,
Rediscovering Eve, 17–38). Each source, however, poses special problems.

The Hebrew Bible is an important source of information about Israelite women. However, its value has limitations for several reasons. The most obvious one is its andro-
centrism. Men are mentioned far more often than women; about ten times more men's
names than women's names, for example, appear in biblical texts. This imbalance is the

The Wiley Blackwell Companion to Ancient Israel, First Edition. Edited by Susan Niditch.
© 2016 John Wiley & Sons, Ltd. Published 2016 by John Wiley & Sons, Ltd.

result of the fact that most biblical authors were men, writing mostly for other men. Moreover, these men were mainly educated elites – priests, scribes, courtiers and most prophets – who were socially distant from the preponderance of women. This elite male bias is accompanied by an urban bias, for most biblical materials reached their final form in Jerusalem, a site unlike the smaller agricultural settlements in which most people lived. In addition, exceptional women appear more often than ordinary ones, and biblical texts often postdate by centuries the periods they are describing.

Because of these biases, the perspectives of biblical texts may differ from the social reality of daily life. One cannot assume unproblematically that the texts are reliable reflections of the lived experience of the average Israelite. Biblical materials, especially legal texts and narratives, are often taken as evidence of female subordination; but other evidence, presented below, points to areas of female authority and autonomy.

Despite its biases, the Hebrew Bible is an indispensable resource for certain kinds of information, namely, mundane aspects of everyday life. Biblical writings inevitably contain details about climate, crops, tools and other quotidian features of life in the Iron Age (ca. 1200–587 BCE). These details are likely to be reliable, for ancient authors produced texts with a degree of "verisimilitude" in order to be effective with their audiences (King and Stager 7). The Hebrew Bible also is an essential source of information about the positions women held outside the household.

Because of the scanty and sometimes misleading biblical information about average women, other sources are also important, archaeology chief among them. The excavation of Iron Age domiciles with their artifacts and installations provides primary data that, unlike biblical texts, have not been subjected to centuries of editing and modification.

Yet archaeology too poses problems. One is the matter of which sites are chosen for excavation and then which parts of the chosen sites are selected for the archaeologists' trenches. Until relatively recently, many excavators sought to recover information linking biblical "events" to facts on the ground. The biblical text seduced the excavators into concentrating on sites with a biblical connection: the larger ones mentioned in the Bible rather than the smaller ones in which most people lived. Moreover, in digging these sites, they inevitably sought to uncover monumental architecture – fortification walls and gates, temples and shrines, and palaces – associated with military personnel, the priesthood, and the royal bureaucracy, that is, male elites rather than average women. In other words, archaeology too often mirrored the elite, urban, male bias of the Hebrew Bible (see Elizabeth Bloch-Smith's essay in this volume). That said, virtually every major excavation has uncovered domiciles as well as community structures. And more recent projects have focused specifically on smaller sites and on the household contexts of daily life.

A related problem is that many projects have strong chronological interests, which often means a focus on the sequence of layers rather than the excavation of complete structures and the recovery of every artifact they contained, which is precisely the information needed to reconstruct people's lives. Moreover, in their publications archaeologists frequently group artifacts by type, making it difficult to identify exactly where objects were found or to determine the assemblage of items used in individual houses. To be sure, dwellings were often so disturbed in antiquity that all their tools and vessels cannot be recovered. Yet even a general idea of a household's items would be helpful, for they are vital clues to the lives of the women who used them. Fortunately, there are sufficient archaeological publications that present data in a way congenial to the task of reconstructing women's lives.

But how do we use archaeological materials, once relevant ones have been identified? A series of interpretive steps is necessary in order to determine who (i.e., women or men) used the various artifacts, figure out how the use of these items contributed to the various components of household life, and consider the social dynamics involved in women's activities. Reconstructing and evaluating women's maintenance activities thus draws upon the work of social scientists, especially ethnographers and gender archaeologists.

Economic Activities: Women at Work

As in virtually all traditional societies, some of the basic tasks necessary for survival in ancient Israel were generally performed by women and others by men. Still, there was likely some crossover in specific situations, with women helping with male-dominant activities and vice versa. In addition, women and men probably shared responsibility for some tasks. (For more details, along with references to relevant archaeological and ethnographic materials, see Meyers, *Rediscovering Eve*, 125–39.)

The most common and important task was food production. Men performed most of the activities needed for producing field crops, mainly grains and other basic foodstuffs (e.g., legumes, olives and grapes). Harvesting them was likely a family affair requiring the labor of all, children included, albeit with a gendered division of labor. For example, men reaped grains, and women (and children) gathered them into sheaves. Then, most crops required preparation in order to be edible, and women were the food processors. Many food-processing tasks were seasonal. For example, at the time of their fall harvest grapes were spread to dry so that they would be available as raisins later in the year.

However, the most time-consuming task – the transformation of grains into edible form – was performed by women virtually every day. Grains, in the form of porridge or gruel but more commonly bread, were the most important part of the Israelite diet, providing up to 75 percent of a person's daily caloric intake. In fact, bread was such an important part of the Israelite diet that the word for bread (*lehem*) is sometimes used more generally for food in the Hebrew Bible. Jacob, for example, invites his kin "to eat bread" (Gen. 31:54), that is, "to have a meal," just as "to break bread together" today means eating together.

Producing bread meant grinding the grain into flour, mixing it with water (and perhaps seasonings), kneading it to produce dough, and then baking it in an oven (see Gen. 18:6, which mentions kneading and forming "cakes," and 1 Sam. 28:24, which mentions kneading and baking). The first step was the hardest. Converting grains to flour meant placing them on a large concave stone tray (a lower grinding stone) and then rubbing them with a smaller stone (an upper grinding stone). These tools, probably represented by the Hebrew dual *rēḥayîm,* are mentioned in the Bible (e.g., Exod. 11:5; Deut. 24:6; Isa. 47:2; cf. Judg. 9:53; English translations vary and don't always convey the ancient reality of a pair of objects). In addition, they are found in the excavation of Iron Age dwellings, usually in the main activity area of the building. Moreover, multiple grinding tools are often found in a single dwelling – probably an indication that several women were grinding at the same time. This is hardly surprising, given that it took two to three hours a day to produce enough flour to feed a family of six. Tedious and time-consuming tasks are typically made tolerable when done in the company of others.

Baking too was likely a joint activity, with women from several households using a single oven. The Iron Age beehive-shaped clay ovens discovered in excavations are similar to ones still in use in age-old Middle Eastern contexts. Small ovens are found in individual dwellings; larger ones found in open spaces accessible to several dwellings were probably communal ovens, meant to serve several households, a practice common in traditional Mediterranean villages. Using a common oven is a fuel-conservation practice and also a social one, with women meeting as they gather to bake their loaves. Additional foodstuffs prepared mainly by women, such as stews of legumes and vegetables, would also have sometimes been cooked in shared ovens.

Other food preparation activities are more difficult to identify. Ethnographic evidence and occasional biblical references provide likely scenarios. The seasonal preparation of dried foods was a woman's task; the drying process (albeit of flax, not a foodstuff) is attributed to Rahab (Josh. 2:6). Lentils and chickpeas and other legumes also required drying and sometimes grinding, for legumes too were sometimes used for bread (see Ezek. 4:9). These tasks were almost certainly women's responsibility. Similarly, women collected and dried herbs, which, once dried, were ground in the small mortars and pestles often found near grinding stones in household spaces where women prepared food. The herbs served as condiments to flavor food and also had medicinal value, as noted below. Most milk was used to make cheese, with women doing the churning of milk and the subsequent boiling of the resulting curds (cf. Judg. 5:25).

Assigning gender to drink production is more difficult. Wine was the most common beverage, judging from the frequency with which grapes and wine appear in the Hebrew Bible. Women are linked with vineyards in the Bible (Prov. 31:16; Cant. 1:6), and the harvesting of grapes was probably a family affair. But it is difficult to determine who carried out the subsequent steps. Wine-processing was likely a male-dominated activity (perhaps indicated by Isa. 5:1–3). However, if beer was occasionally produced, women were probably the brewers, for beer-making technology in the ancient world, quite different from modern processes, was associated with bread-making.

The preparation of most crops for consumption in Israelite households depended on women's labor. The time-consuming and recurring nature of food-processing activities occupied a major position in the rhythm of their daily lives. Yet these tasks were not the only ones that fell mainly to women. Another important household activity was the production of textiles. In ordinary households fabrics were made of sheep's wool and sometimes goat hair, for the more costly linen was typically an elite fabric. Young boys and girls tended a household's animals (e.g., Gen. 29:6; 1 Sam. 16:19), and men sheared them (e.g., Gen. 31:19; 38:13). Women carried out the sequence of activities required to transform fibers to fabrics and then to garments and other items. Several of these activities are represented in the archaeological record: spindle whorls for spinning fibers to produce yarn or thread, loom weights from the vertical looms used for weaving in the Iron Age, and ivory or bone needles for sewing garments.

Textile tasks, although not daily activities, were no less time-consuming than bread production. Many hours were invested in washing the wool. Then, spinning enough wool to produce yarn for a single garment might take as long as 100 hours. The subsequent weaving of simple flat-weave fabric probably required several days' work, and sewing fabric into a garment meant similar long hours. Like the tedium of grinding grain, the monotony of spinning, weaving, and sewing was almost certainly relieved by women carrying out these tasks in the company of others. It is not unusual for several spindle whorls to be found in a single dwelling, although the labor of children and even old men may be represented by these multiple artifacts. However, the discovery of multiple sets of loom weights in the main activity area of a single dwelling (or in an outdoor space, where they would have been used in the warm summer months) suggests that weaving was a joint female activity. Ethnographic evidence supports this, especially because weaving together was not simply a matter of camaraderie; setting threads on a loom and manipulating them to produce cloth is best done by the cooperative effort of several women.

Another and little-recognized aspect of women's contributions to the household economy is their work as toolmakers and installation-builders. Ethnography provides compelling evidence that the people who used household implements and installations are typically the ones who make them. Thus men, who were likely professional craftsmen (see 1 Sam. 13:19), produced metal objects in workshops, as suggested by the attribution of the beginnings of metallurgy to a man (Gen. 4:22). However, most other household items could well have been made by women.

Certain food-preparation activities, for example, required appropriate vessels; and women, as the preparers of food, were best equipped to make those vessels. Professional male potters also produced wares, mainly in urban centers (e.g., Jer. 18:3). But women typically make handmade vessels for domestic use in traditional Mediterranean societies. Producing such wares required digging the clay, levigating it, and then forming and firing the vessels, activities rarely carried out by individual women. Rather, younger women would help an older, more experienced potter; and the forming of large vessels for domestic use required the joint efforts of several women. Ethnography also suggests that women built the clay ovens used for baking and cooking and that oven construction was typically a collaborative project. In addition, they likely produced other household items, including baskets, probably using plant fibers collected by their children, and even stone tools. And women no less than men contributed to the family project of house-building or renovation (see 2 Kings 4:10; cf. Neh. 3:12).

Women's numerous economic activities were necessary for survival. Several other features are important. One is that many had social aspects; that is, women often worked together to relieve tedium and also because some tasks required cooperative labor. Another feature is that most tasks were not only physically demanding and time-consuming but also technologically sophisticated. The requisite skills for producing fabrics or building ovens, for example, were transmitted by older, experienced women to younger ones – neighboring women, their own daughters, or both. The same would have been true for virtually every household task. Finally, women's responsibilities were generally complementary to those of men, as when they transformed the raw products produced by men into foodstuffs and textiles or participated in the labor-intensive efforts to harvest various crops (see also the essay by David Schloen in this volume).

Reproductive Activities: Women and Children

Biological reproduction was a central feature of women's lives (for more details and references, see Meyers, *Rediscovering Eve*, 97–102, 136–9). The Eden tale of Genesis 2–3 calls the first woman "the mother of all living" (3:20) and proclaims that she will have many pregnancies (3:16; see Meyers, *Rediscovering Eve*, 88–93); in her childbearing capacity the first woman represents all women. Having children was essential to survival: children were part of the workforce of every household (see Prov. 10:5; Jer. 7:18); adult children became caregivers for their aging parents (Exod. 20:12: this is the sense of the word translated "honor" in the fifth commandment; see also Deut. 5:16; cf. Prov. 23:22); and male children were the heirs to the family property (land, animals, dwelling, tools; see Prov. 19:14). As childbearers, women maintained their households and communities in an elemental sense.

Yet childbirth was fraught with dangers for most Israelite women (e.g., Gen. 35:16–18), as everywhere in premodern or developing societies. Although determining mortality rates for ancient populations is difficult, information from tomb excavations and from ethnographic and archival records consistently show life expectancies of women to be lower than those of men, probably because of the risk of death in childbirth. Estimated lifespans for women are as low as 20 to 25 years, with the chance of early death rising with the number of pregnancies. A description of the grim situation for women in early modern Europe could easily apply to non-elite women of the ancient Near East:

> A whole variety of conditions, such as haemorrhage, pelvic deformity, disproportion between the sizes of a child's head and the pelvis, severe abnormal presentations such as transverse lies, eclampsia and uterine inertia in labour, are likely to have posed problems which were beyond the capacity of those attending the birth to alleviate. (Schofield 235)

And other factors adversely influenced reproduction. New mothers were susceptible to infections that could be fatal. Inadequate nutrition – for the Israelite diet was often deficient in key nutrients and also because famines occurred sporadically – made women especially vulnerable to conditions negatively affecting prenatal health, childbirth and lactation. In addition, adulthood and motherhood were virtually coterminous. Girls were probably married by age 14, soon after puberty, and thus were young when they began bearing children. Very young women are at greater risk for childbirth complications than older ones.

Some biblical texts give the impression that Israelites had large families: Jacob, for example, has 12 sons; and some kings have many offspring. But the patriarchs and kings were elites, and their many children were the result of polygamy. Note that Jacob's 12 sons are borne by four women, an average of three children each, and three happens to be the average number of children in Israelite nuclear families according to ethnographic data and analysis of Israelite house size. And having three children entailed having as many as six pregnancies because of infant mortality rates: it has been estimated that only one in two children survived to the age of five (see 2 Sam. 12:14–18; Isa. 65:20). Newborns were particularly susceptible to infections, and young children had little immunity to the outbreaks of life-threatening infectious diseases that were a recurrent problem.

Bearing children was just part of a woman's reproductive responsibility; she was also responsible for reproducing social identities and teaching life skills (see also the essay by Raymond Person in this volume). Children become competent members of their culture only through the teachings of the people who raise them, and this is especially true in ancient cultures that lacked formal education (except perhaps for the elites). For women, reproduction thus entailed both creating new life and then socializing their offspring to become competent adults. Women were the primary educators of very young girls and boys, and they continued to teach daughters until they married and left home.

To a great extent, the educative process was embedded in a woman's daily routine. The skills required for most economic activities were imparted to children as they assisted their mothers in their daily tasks. This kind of persistent instruction in household technologies would be considered informal education; but it was no less important than what children in developed nations learn in schools. Similarly, in early childhood when children were cared for mainly by their mothers, both boys and girls began the process of being socialized into the norms and beliefs of their households and the larger community. Women played a pivotal role in teaching their children proper behavior (Prov. 1:8; 6:20; cf. 5:1; 31:26). The Proverbs 1 and 6 texts refer to both parents as teachers, for the parental educative roles were complementary; but they were not the same. As children became older, they learned gender-appropriate skills and behaviors from the same-sex parent. The role of mothers as educators was arguably greater than that of fathers because women dominated the educative process in a child's early years.

Children also learned family traditions and even gained historical knowledge from their parents (see Deut. 4:10; Josh. 4:21), with grandmothers (and grandfathers) likely instrumental in this regard. If they survived into old age, women probably performed fewer household tasks and took on more childcare responsibilities, including instructing their grandchildren in life skills. In addition, as members of the oldest living generation, grandmothers in traditional societies often are the ones to transmit family and community lore to the youngest members of the household. And they are frequently gifted storytellers. Some of the biblical narratives identified as folktales may well have originated in the storytelling skills of elderly women (see also Susan Niditch's essay in this volume).

Although probably done more intuitively than intentionally, imparting both technological and behavioral wisdom was an integral part of women's daily existence. Their comprehensive instructional role may be hard for us to grasp in today's industrialized world, where we give our children over to caregivers at ever earlier ages (unless we home-school them). Yet in biblical antiquity the continuity of household life depended on children learning modes of interacting with others as well as how to perform household tasks. The figure of personified wisdom – Woman Wisdom – in Proverbs (e.g., 1:20–23;

8:1–36) can be understood, at least in part, as a cultural expression of women's primary role in the teaching and socializing of young children.

Social and Political Activities: Women and Their Communities

An important but little-noticed feature of women's economic activities is that women often worked together (for more details and references, see Meyers, "Everyday life"; *Rediscovering Eve*, 139–46). In the process of sharing daily and seasonal tasks, they inevitably formed relationships. These connections constituted an informal alliance that contributed to the maintenance of individual households and also the larger community. Women's informal networks are virtually invisible in the formal records of a society, which typically mention formal (male) leadership and organizations. Although they operate differently than do the more visible male groups, women's alliances are no less necessary for the social and political functioning of their communities.

Only two biblical texts reflect the existence of women's networks. One is in the Book of Ruth, when the "women of the neighborhood" (*səkēnôt*) attend the birth of Ruth's son Oded (4:14-17; cf. 1 Sam. 4:20, where women gather at the birth of Ichabod). The women who assist in Oded's birth may well be the cohort mentioned at the beginning of Ruth (1:19), when women greet Naomi as she returns from Moab with Ruth. The other text (Exod. 3:22) describes Israelite women in Egypt seeking resources for their journey to the promised land. That the women ask for help from their female Egyptian neighbors (*səkēnôt*) suggests that relationships based on residential proximity were more important than the narrative interest in portraying Egyptians as the enemy. Asking neighbors for help also appears in an Elisha narrative, when a destitute woman borrows vessels from her neighbors, gender unspecified (2 Kings 4:1–3).

The theme of neighbors helping neighbors in these biblical passages resonates with what ethnographers have observed about the functions of informal alliances of women. Women who work together not only provide companionship and emotional support for each other in the face of drudgery; they also form bonds that obligate them to help each other when they or their households have problems. Women's networks thus serve as mutual aid societies. Households in premodern societies without community social services depend on these informal associations in order to meet some of the challenges that inevitably arise.

Sometimes the assistance women provide for each other is simple. They may help when a physical task is too difficult for a woman working alone. Or they may lend a utensil or a tool. Perhaps more important is that women who often spend hours together share information as well as tasks. Thus they know, for example, if someone's husband has been injured and can't sow seeds at planting time. Or they know if a daughter is ill and can't tend the family's goats. Or they know if a postpartum woman does not yet have the strength to perform all her tasks. Women respond to these and other problems by arranging for assistance to the household in need. It may mean deploying an older son to help the disabled man or an older daughter to shepherd the goats. Or it may mean sharing provisions with a household temporarily unable to feed all its members.

Illnesses, injuries and food shortages were common and could be resolved only through the helping hands of neighbors.

Women's networks were thus the conduits for the mutual aid necessary for survival. Sometimes these networks coincided with or overlapped with kinship connections. However, because ancient Israel was patrilocal, with a woman leaving her natal household and moving to her husband's household, kin were not always close by. The words of Proverbs (27:10) reflect the importance of relationships with neighbors – "Better is a neighbor who is nearby than kindred who are far away" (New Revised Standard Version (NRSV)) – and apply especially to women, whose work brought them together more often than did the work of men.

Women's alliances contributed to their communities in other ways. In their daily interactions women typically share technological knowledge with each other, passing along tips that could improve aspects of their food-processing or textile-producing tasks. This kind of knowledge sharing may have transcended individual communities because, according to ethnographic reports, women often maintained connections with kin in their natal households, perhaps reflected in the story of Jacob going to his mother's family to secure a wife (Gen. 28:2). These kinship connections, especially with nearby settlements, provided intercommunity contacts that might extend cooperative acts beyond a woman's immediate neighborhood.

Informal women's networks, both within a settlement and across settlements, also had political implications. In small Israelite communities and even in larger ones, issues or conflicts inevitably arose and were typically handled by (male) community leaders or elders. The deliberations and decisions of governing groups were part of the political dynamics of an ancient settlement. Most political decisions required information, and ethnography suggests that the communication channels formed by women working together were an important source of relevant information. Because of their regular interactions, women were privy to certain kinds of information that might be invaluable for dealing with community issues.

One example is access to installations, like threshing floors or olive presses, that were often used communally. Women would know which households had completed the olive harvest and were ready to process their olives; and they would be aware of the size of the yields. They would share this information with male household members and eventually community leaders, and the organization of work at communal installations would proceed efficiently. In short, women's shared tasks meant the formation of cohorts that participated in social and, albeit indirectly, political matters. In addition, because of their connections with kin in other communities, women could influence the kind of alliances made among settlements.

Women's Religious Activities: Regular and Occasional

Religiosity was an integral part of the lives of Israelite women (for more details and references, see Meyers, *Rediscovering Eve*, 147–70). Although belief in a god or gods is often thought of as the primary component of religion, in traditional societies belief is one of *two* main components. The other is the set of activities directed to supernatural beings in the hope of securing divine help for the many difficulties people confronted in their daily lives: recurring droughts and crop shortages, persistent hunger and malnutrition, chronic deficiency diseases and outbreaks of infectious diseases, and work-related injuries (see Meyers, *Rediscovering Eve*, 38–58). In addition, women faced infertility and death in childbirth.

A woman's connection to her god or gods was established and maintained by her religious activities. Those activities would have been more or less the same whether she believed in multiple deities or in the god Yahweh alone (which probably would not have been the case until relatively late in the period of the Hebrew Bible; for discussion, see the essay by Mark S. Smith in this volume). Sacrifice, especially at the national shrine (tabernacle or temple), is the dominant form of religious behavior mentioned in the Hebrew Bible; but a wide range of other kinds of activities took place in or near a woman's household. The Bible alludes to some of these practices, but mostly they are reconstructed on the basis of information from ancient or premodern peoples. In addition, the materiality of many religious practices means that traces of them have survived in the archaeological record.

Household religious practices are described in the essay by Francesca Stavrakopoulou in this volume. Here the focus is twofold: women's roles in practices involving all household members, and religious activities that were probably unique to women. The former are associated with regular and recurrent events (festivals and life-cycle functions). The latter include occasional rituals to deal with health problems or to address difficulties of pregnancy and birth and regular practices accompanying food preparation.

The most prominent regular religious events were festivals that took place at set calendrical times. Three major agricultural festivals (Booths, Passover and Weeks) marking significant economic moments, like the beginning or end of the harvest season, appear in the Hebrew Bible, where they are historicized to recall significant moments in the remembered past (see the essay by S. A. Geller in this volume). Biblical texts give the impression that these festivals took place only at the temple (e.g., Deut. 16:11, 15; see the essay by Bernard Levinson and Tina Sherman in this volume). Although only men are enjoined to celebrate, women apparently participated: the Deuteronomic texts mention daughters, female slaves and widows – but not wives, except for the inclusive language about the festival of Booths in the seventh year (Deut. 31:10–12). However, the texts omitting wives are addressed to the senior male of the family; and it is likely that, as in the Sabbath commandment (Exod. 20:8–11; Deut. 5:12–15), the senior female was subsumed in the address to her partner. In any case, these festivals were not limited to the central shrine but often, and perhaps typically, took place in a family's local community or household (e.g., Exod. 12:3–5, 46; Neh. 8:16), where women were surely among the participants. The same would be true for the monthly new-moon celebrations, which were apparently popular (Hos. 2:11; Amos 8:5) as local household or clan events (see 1 Sam. 20:5–29). And the weekly Sabbath likewise would have been observed in the household according to the Sabbath commandment.

These calendrical events served many functions: they contributed to community solidarity, provided Israelite agrarians with a welcome relief from their arduous daily life, and were an opportunity for people to spend rare leisure time with neighbors and kinfolk. Just as important, festivals were *feast* days – occasions for consuming foods and drinks not part of the everyday diet. Meat, for example, was not daily fare for most Israelites and thus would be a highly anticipated component of the three annual festivals, perhaps in the form of a portion of a sacrificial offering (see 1 Sam. 1:4). Meat was likely a component of monthly and perhaps weekly celebrations too, along with other special foodstuffs. The culinary dimension of Israelite festivals entailed the participation of women both as celebrants and as providers of the festal repasts. Families or neighbors would celebrate together (see Exod. 12:4; 1 Sam. 20:6, 29); and, as ethnographic sources indicate, women would share dishes and recipes much as in our contemporary potluck meals.

Women's culinary skills also provided essential components of recurrent life-cycle events, which were important social as well as religious occasions. Although marriages were not specifically religious in the preexilic period, like people everywhere Israelites surely celebrated marriages with festal meals (see Judg. 14:10, 17) and no doubt with prayers for the newlyweds to produce offspring (Ruth 4:11–12). Death rituals included mourners' feasts, judging from prophetic opposition to such practices (e.g., Jer. 16:5–8; see also the essay by Francesca Stavrakopoulou in this volume). In addition, because prayers to the dead were thought to help the living, food and drink offerings were offered at the graves of the deceased, perhaps as part of new moon festivals. The biblical prohibition against doing so (Deut. 26:14) indicates that Israelites indeed sought to connect the realms of the dead and the living by placing food and drink at burial sites. Thus women were probably both participants and providers of food for marriages and death-related events.

Family birth rituals – the celebration of a birth, or the circumcision of an eight-day-old male – would also have involved women. Hannah, for example, offers a sacrifice in gratitude to God for granting her a child (1 Sam. 1:24). Biblical texts have little to say about who performs a circumcision, although the mother carries out this procedure, perhaps as an apotropaic measure, in the only mention of someone circumcising an infant (Exod. 4:25). In addition, women name their offspring in about two-thirds of the biblical naming narratives (e.g., Gen. 29:32–35; Exod. 2:22; 1 Sam. 1:20), and the names typically invoke or acknowledge God's role in granting fertility. "Dan," for example, means "he [God] judged" in reference to God listening to Rachel's prayer and granting her a child (Gen. 30:6).

Household religious activities that were unique to women included both intermittent and regular practices. The former were healing practices and reproductive practices in addition to the birth rituals already mentioned; the latter were food-preparation rituals.

One kind of intermittent religious activity involved care for the all-too-frequent illnesses and injuries. In biblical antiquity these problems were understood to be within the divine realm. Thus human attempts to alleviate suffering and produce cures inevitably involved religious behaviors such as petitionary prayers (e.g., Ps. 38) and perhaps sacrifices at local shrines. Note that Leviticus 14 has people coming to priests to deal with certain skin ailments, and the Psalter mentions thanksgiving praises and sacrifices for the recovery from affliction (e.g., Ps. 69:29–30; 107:17–22). Still, the household was the primary arena of health care; and women were the likely caregivers for the ill and injured – as when a Shunammite man sends his ailing son home to his mother (2 Kings

4:19). The Hebrew Bible mentions various substances such as balm (Jer. 51:8) and oil (Isa. 1:6) as treatments for ailments, and women's food-preparation role afforded them familiarity with the healing as well as flavoring properties of various herbs. It is no accident that God's maternal care for Israel in Hosea 11:3–4 includes healing. Women were practitioners of what we would call folk medicine, and the requisite knowledge of medicinal substances, as well as the incantations likely to have accompanied their use, was passed on to younger women just as expertise in other aspects of household life was transmitted across generations.

As noted above, a birth was attended by a woman's network of friends who not only assisted in the birth but also offered appropriate prayers (e.g., Ruth 4:14); additional practices were also important. Because pregnancy and birth were fraught with difficulties in premodern societies, women typically engage in a variety of activities intended to secure successful childbirth. Prayers or sacrifices requesting an end to barrenness or celebrating ensuing fertility were surely offered by men (e.g., Gen. 20:17–18) as well as women (e.g., 1 Sam. 1:24–27), but the many folk-religion procedures surrounding reproduction were carried out by women. Some practices were meant to keep the evil powers or demons believed to threaten pregnant women and their infants at bay, and others were intended to ensure divine protection. Leviticus (12:6) indicates that women were to provide offerings to effect their purification after the birth of children, but it is uncertain whether this priestly regulation reflects a widespread practice.

Although measures to deal with reproductive problems other than infertility are rarely mentioned in the Bible, many are known from ethnographic reports. In fact, even in relatively recent times, women attending a birth used certain devices or procedures that go back to biblical days. The treatment of a newborn, alluded to in Ezekiel 16:4, involved anointing, rubbing with salt, and swaddling the infant – all acts believed to have apotropaic value and practiced well into the twentieth century by Jewish, Christian and Muslim women in traditional communities in the Middle East, Bulgaria and Macedonia. To this very day, some religious Jewish women hoping to become pregnant wear a red thread that has been wound around Rachel's tomb, a practice related to the use of red yarn as a protective measure according to some ancient Near Eastern texts and also found, although for a somewhat different function, in the narrative about the birth of Tamar's twins (Gen. 38:28).

Archaeology too provides evidence of women's practices relating to reproduction. For example, amulets, which were thought to protect a woman during pregnancy or keep a vulnerable newborn safe, have been found at many sites, sometimes even in household spaces associated with women's food-preparation tasks. The metal rings or bracelets that women wore were not simply items of personal adornment; their shiny surfaces reflected light to counteract the forces of darkness, which was considered the realm of danger and pestilence (Ps. 91:5–6). Oil lamps likely had a similar double function: providing light for household tasks, and serving to keep the demons of the dark away (Job 29:2–3). In this regard, note that until relatively recently women in some traditional Mediterranean societies would light lamps or candles near an infant to prevent supernatural beings from bringing evil.

Food-preparation rituals are much more difficult to identify, but ethnographic reports and indirect biblical evidence provide clues. Flour, especially the unrefined flour of biblical days, can easily go rancid; and tainted flour was attributed to evil spirits. Thus rituals accompanying bread preparation were meant to keep bread dough from spoiling. Consequently, the preparation of bread, the most important dietary staple, was thus a sacral task; note that mishandling dough (in some mid-twentieth-century Palestinian villages) was considered sacrilegious. The biblical instructions about dedicating a piece of dough to Yahweh (Num. 15:19–21) were probably intended to safeguard the dough and thus bring God's blessing to the household (Ezek. 44:30b). These texts may originate in a time-honored household ritual performed by women as part of their daily bread-producing tasks. (Other foodways, such as avoiding certain foods, are cast as religious stipulations in the Pentateuch but were unlikely to have originated as such.) Finally, archaeological evidence of cultic objects in household eating areas suggests that meals may have included token food offerings prepared by women and set aside for ancestors or a deity.

Outside the Household: Women's Community Roles

In addition to household roles, and perhaps even instead of them, a small number of women served their communities in specialized roles we might call "professions" (for more detailed information and further references, see Meyers, *Rediscovering Eve*, 171–9; and related entries in Meyers et al.). These varied and numerous professions – some carried out by women working alone, some by women in groups – are known mainly because nearly 20 of them are mentioned in the Hebrew Bible. They were often exclusively women's jobs, although a number were held by both women and men. Some would be considered menial labor, and others involved creative work or authoritative functions.

Women's household maintenance activities sometimes translated into trades or crafts serving the larger community. Their textile skills were used for making sumptuous cultic fabrics (Exod. 35:25–26; 2 Kings 23:7), and the woman of Proverbs 31 has a cottage industry producing garments (vv. 13, 18–19, 22, 24). The discovery of seals and scarabs with women's names likely attests to the existence of Israelite businesswomen. Similarly, although not mentioned in the Bible, the expertise of some women in producing utilitarian household objects (e.g., baskets or pottery) probably meant that some women marketed home-produced items. Proficiency in food preparation led to positions as herbalists (NRSV "perfumers"), cooks and bakers (1 Sam. 8:13) in the royal household or state industries. Familiarity with childbirth led some women, likely in their senior years, to function as midwives (Gen. 35:17; 38:28; Exod. 1:15–21), usually serving elite women rather than ordinary peasants. "Nurses" too (Gen. 24:59; 35:8; 2 Kings 11:2), probably wet-nurses, were typically employees of the wealthy.

Women had community religious roles that included menial positions – those enigmatic women serving at the entrance to the Tent of Meeting (Exod. 38:8; 1 Sam.

2:22) – and skilled ones involving sorcery (Exod. 22:18 (Hebrew 22:17)) or necromancy (1 Sam. 28:7–14). Women were also prophets, bringing God's word to the human realm (see Robert Wilson's essay in this volume). Some prophets are mentioned by name (Miriam, Deborah, Huldah and Noadiah); others are unnamed (Isa. 8:3; Ezek. 13: 17–23; Joel 2:28 (Hebrew 3:1)); and still others are probably represented in the use of the masculine plural "prophets" (*nəbî'îm*) as a designation for mixed-gender prophetic groups. Other religious activities were also part of the cultural realm. The composition and performance of songs with theological content are attributed to two named prophets (Miriam and Deborah) and also Hannah. Women also sang or performed with musical instruments in religious (e.g., Ps. 68:25) as well as secular (e.g., 2 Sam. 19:35 (Hebrew 19:36); Eccl. 2:8) contexts. Funerary performance and perhaps the composition of dirges were similarly attributed to women who specialized in lamenting the dead (Jer. 9:17–20 (Hebrew 9:16–19)), and the women "weeping for Tammuz" (Ezek. 8:14) were likely carrying out a mourning rite in the temple.

Several leadership roles are mentioned. Deborah is prominent as a military leader who also adjudicated. Two unnamed women were able to resolve national crises (2 Sam. 14:1–20; 20:14–22) because of their sagacity. A number of royal women (e.g., Athalya and Jezebel) exercised political power by virtue of their class; and several others, called *gəbîrâ* ("queen mother"), were court functionaries of some sort (e.g., Maacah in 1 Kings 15:13).

Several other roles bear mention. One is perhaps the least visible: women as couriers (2 Sam. 17:17; Prov. 9:3) or heralds (implied by the female gender of the word for "heralds," e.g., Isa. 40:9). Another is the profession mentioned most often: prostitution, which is discouraged (e.g., Lev. 19:29; Prov. 29:3) but never absolutely forbidden. In fact, one woman (Tamar) who disguises herself as a prostitute and one (Rahab) who is labeled a prostitute are depicted positively. In addition there are dozens of references to female servants and slaves, who performed maintenance tasks for the wealthy.

Conclusions

In evaluating the lives of Israelite women, it is important to avoid presentism. That is, current ideas and perspectives about women's activities cannot be anachronistically read into the past. To do so would risk misunderstanding how women experienced their lives, for the meaning and value of women's contributions to their households and communities in biblical antiquity diverged in fundamental ways from the way those activities would be viewed today.

Perhaps the best example comes in considering women's economic activities. Because most were carried out in or near their dwellings, we tend to label them "housework" or "domestic work," terms which today designate routine, unpaid labor. Moreover, because unpaid housework today is often considered supportive and secondary to work outside the home, it tends to be trivialized. Such views are largely the result of the industrial revolution and the concomitant separation of the workplace, the arena of (mainly) male economic activity, from the home, with little or no economic value assigned to women's housekeeping chores. The reality in premodern agrarian societies was quite different.

Women's maintenance tasks in biblical antiquity would have functioned in ways that challenge notions of women's work as inherently unimportant or less valuable than men's. Women's work in transforming agricultural products to edible or wearable form in Israelite households was an economic activity just as critical for family survival as was the growing of crops and animals. As such, it afforded women, especially senior women in extended family contexts, considerable household power. The female heads of households acted as COOs (chief operating officers) – organizing daily tasks, allocating resources and determining how household space would be used. In doing so, according to ethnographic studies, women exercised authority over young and even adult children, daughters-in-law and sometimes spouses. Several biblical passages attest to these power dynamics. Abigail (1 Sam. 25), the Shunammite woman (2 Kings 4:8–17; 8:1–6), the "strong woman" (NRSV, "capable wife"; Prov. 31:10–31), and to some extent Micah's mother (Judg. 17:1–6) are all depicted as having autonomy and agency in handling household resources. These are elite women, to be sure; but the lives of wealthy and peasant women were probably much the same, except that servants or slaves relieved the wealthy of some household labor.

Women's managerial powers call into question the idea of male dominance in all components of household life. Women's economic tasks complemented those of men, who dominated crop and herd management. Women and men were thus economically interdependent, and general female subordination would not have been a functional reality.

Evaluating the sociopolitical implications of the informal networks formed by women working together must likewise not succumb to presentist ideas. In premodern contexts, the indirect and less visible activities of women's groups are different but no less important than men's direct and visible ones. The community service resulting from women's connections is indicative of the interconnected and overlapping private and public realms of ancient life – very different from the separation of private and public into distinct spheres in the industrialized world.

Women's reproductive role must also be considered apart from the presentist idea, often found in feminist critiques of biblical texts, that bearing children served only male interests in producing heirs. Women no less than men were the beneficiaries of having children to assist them in household tasks and to care for them in their dotage. Just as important, the identity of premodern peoples tends to be more collective, with people seeing themselves embedded in families and communities, than individual. When a woman moved to her husband's household, she would quickly identify with *his* household (although probably remaining connected to her birth family); bearing children to inherit household property and continue the lineage thus served her interests too.

Many of women's religious activities involved food preparation, which today would not usually be considered a meaningful religious act. However, in traditional societies food-related contributions to divinely ordained religious celebrations have great positive value for women and their households. In addition, although they might be dismissed as superstition today, offerings or prayers to ancestors or deities had a life-death quality, for those offerings were linked to beliefs about obtaining divine assistance in securing fertility of the soil or the body. Rituals in handling bread-dough or other foods similarly had life-death importance, as did women's "medical" practices, especially those aimed at achieving successful childbirth. In these and other ways, the ritual expertise of women functioned virtually every day; it was a dynamic presence in household life, no less than priestly expertise at shrines.

Women's community roles also often involved expertise. Just as for household technologies, the skills or knowledge sets involved in many professions (e.g., musical performance, lamenting, prophesying, offering wisdom, as well as professions based on household technologies) were passed from experienced women to novices or apprentices. Thus there were hierarchies within these professions, especially those in which groups of women worked together. The senior women had the experience of exerting leadership, and all the women in these cohorts experienced the satisfaction of providing religiously or culturally important services to their community. (Similar hierarchies existed in women's informal networks, with some women taking the lead in organizing their assistance to households in need or in transmitting technical knowledge.) In short, women's hierarchies existed independently of the male-dominated ones operating in other arenas of Israelite life, thus again contesting the idea that men controlled all aspects of life.

In the aggregate, women's lives were more difficult and more complex than we might have imagined. Ancient Israel was not an egalitarian society with respect to gender, but women nonetheless had agency in significant areas of everyday life. And many women had ample opportunity to experience the satisfaction of contributing in vital ways to the welfare of their households and communities.

Bibliography

Bachmann, Mercedes L. Garcia. *Women at Work in the Deuteronomistic History*. International Voices in Biblical Studies 4. Atlanta: Society of Biblical Literature, 2013. An investigation of the contributions of female workers, mainly service ones, in Joshua through 2 Kings.

Brenner, Athalya. *The Israelite Woman: Social Role and Literary Type in Biblical Narrative*. Sheffield: Sheffield Academic Press, 1994 (reprint). This concise survey of the sociopolitical roles of Israelite women also includes literary analyses of several stereotyped images of biblical women.

Ebeling, Jennie R. *Women's Lives in Biblical Times*. London: T&T Clark, 2010. Part fiction and part scholarly reporting, this book reviews the life of a "typical woman" through the lifecycle.

Ebeling, Jennie R. "Puberty, marriage, sex, reproduction, and divorce, Bronze and Iron Age." In Daniel M. Master (ed.), *The Oxford Encyclopedia of the Bible and Archaeology*, vol. 2 (pp. 190–201). New York: Oxford University Press, 2013. A concise review of biblical and extrabiblical sources providing information about these lifecycle events.

Gruber, Mayer I. "Gender, Bronze and Iron Age." In Daniel M. Master (ed.), *The Oxford Encyclopedia of the Bible and Archaeology*, vol. 1 (pp. 453–60). New York: Oxford University Press, 2013. Texts (biblical and other) and archaeology provide data for this assessment of gender roles in ancient Canaan and Israel.

Gursky, Marjorie D. "Reproductive rituals in biblical Israel." Dissertation, New York University. UMI Microform 9997458, Ann Arbor, MI, 2001. Using mainly biblical sources, this study examines prayers and rituals that seek fertility and then mark the birth of a child.

King, Philip J., and Lawrence E. Stager. *Life in Biblical Israel.* Library of Ancient Israel. Louisville, KY: Westminster John Knox, 2001. Many illustrations and clear prose mark this comprehensive look at Israelite lifeways.

Meyers, Carol. "Everyday life in biblical Israel: Women's social networks." In Richard E. Averbeck, Mark W. Chavalas, and David B. Weisberg (eds), *Life and Culture in the Ancient Near East* (pp. 185–97). Bethesda, MD: CDL Press, 2003. Using archaeological and biblical sources, this article focuses on women's extrafamilial social networks and their function in village life.

Meyers, Carol. *Households and Holiness: The Religious Culture of Israelite Women.* Minneapolis: Fortress, 2005. Integrating archaeological, textual, and ethnographic sources, this booklet focuses on women's religious practices and their meaning.

Meyers, Carol. "Archaeology – A window to the lives of Israelite women." In Irmtraud Fischer and Mercedes Navarro Puerto, with Andrea Taschl-Erbele (eds), *Hebrew Bible – Old Testament: Torah*, vol. 1.1 of Jorunn Økland, Irmtraud Fischer, Mercedes Navarro Puerto, and Adriana Valerio (eds), *The Bible and Women: An Encyclopaedia of Exegesis and Cultural History* (pp. 61–108). Atlanta: Society of Biblical Literature, 2011. This article provides a concise look at the archaeological data relating to women's lives.

Meyers, Carol. "Women's religious life in ancient Israel." In Carol A. Newsom, Sharon H. Ringe, and Jacqueline E. Lapsley (eds), *Women's Bible Commentary*, 3rd edn (pp. 354–61). Louisville, KY: Westminster John Knox, 2012. This essay provides an overview of women's household and community religious activities.

Meyers, Carol. *Rediscovering Eve: Ancient Israelite Women in Context.* New York: Oxford University Press, 2013. Using multiple resources, this book examines the Eve narrative and also portrays the lives of ordinary women, in the process challenging "patriarchy" as a designation for ancient Israel.

Meyers, Carol. "Double vision: Textual and archaeological images of women." *Hebrew Bible and Ancient Israel 4* (forthcoming 2015). The disconnect between biblical texts and archaeological data relating to women's lives is explored in this essay.

Meyers, Carol, Toni Craven, and Ross S. Kraemer (eds). *Women in Scripture: A Dictionary of the Named and Unnamed Women in the Hebrew Bible, the Apocryphal/Deuterocanonical Books, and the New Testament.* Boston: Houghton Mifflin, 2000. This reference book has entries for every female figure – named and unnamed, human and nonhuman – in Jewish and Christian Scripture.

Montón-Subías, Sandra, and Margerita Sánchez-Romero (eds). *Engendering Social Dynamics: The Archaeology of Maintenance Activities.* British Archaeological Reports International Series 1862. Oxford: Archaeopress, 2008. The articles in this volume identify and interpret women's household maintenance activities.

Nakhai, Beth Alpert (ed.). *The World of Women in the Ancient and Classical Near East.* Newcastle upon Tyne, UK: Cambridge Scholars Publishing, 2008. Most of the essays in this collection show how archaeology provides otherwise unavailable information about the roles of ordinary women.

Perdue, Leo G., John Blenkinsopp, John J. Collins, and Carol Meyers. *Families in Ancient Israel.* The Family, Religion, and Culture. Louisville, KY: Westminster John Knox, 1997. The five essays in this volume consider family relationships and daily life from the premonarchic era to the Second Temple period.

Schofield, Roger. "Did the women really die? Three centuries of maternal mortality in 'The world we have lost.'" In Lloyd Bonfield, Richard Smith, and Keith Wrightson (eds), *The World We Have Gained: Histories of Population and Social Structure: Essays Presented to Peter Laslett on His Seventieth Birthday* (pp. 231–60). Oxford: Blackwell, 1986. This article looks at maternal mortality in early modern Europe.

Willett, Elizabeth Ann R. "Women and household shrines in ancient Israel." Dissertation, University of Arizona. UMI Microform 9927522, Ann Arbor, MI, 1999. Drawing mainly on archaeological materials, this study looks at women's rituals in household contexts and women's religious agency.

Zwickel, Wolfgang. *Frauenalltag im biblischen Israel*. Stuttgart: Katholisches Bibelwerk, 2005. This concise summary of the roles and activities of everyday women in the periods of the Hebrew Bible and New Testament includes 70 illustrations.

CHAPTER 24

Economy and Society in Iron Age Israel and Judah
An Archaeological Perspective

J. David Schloen

Archaeological Chronology and Political Context

The Iron Age in the southern Levant lasted from about 1200 to 600 BCE. The Israelite kingdoms described in the Bible were in existence during the second half of the Iron Age, from about 950 to 600 BCE, which archaeologists call the "Iron Age II." Archaeological periods do not necessarily correspond to political periods but in this case we have good reasons to associate the Iron Age II styles of pottery, architecture, and other artifacts with the economic and social life of the biblical kingdoms of Israel and Judah from the time of their formation until their demise at the hands of the Assyrians and Babylonians. These kingdoms were based in the highland territories west of the Jordan River and the Dead Sea, although they had a wider impact at times, dominating parts of Transjordan and projecting power to the Mediterranean coast.

In what follows, archaeological terminology for chronological periods will be used as a way to organize the evidence in a historical sequence, so it is worth explaining at the outset what is meant by these terms, especially since the archaeological periodization of the Iron Age has been modified in recent years (see the essays by Elizabeth Bloch-Smith and Avraham Faust in this volume). The geographical terminology currently used by archaeologists may also be a source of confusion. For example, the term "Levant," which can have a broad geographical meaning and in some branches of scholarship is used to denote the entire eastern Mediterranean region, has been appropriated by Near Eastern archaeologists to refer specifically to the far eastern shore of the Mediterranean and its habitable hinterland, the region that is also called "Syria-Palestine," which has natural boundaries and was the heartland of ancient West Semitic culture. The Levant is bounded by the Taurus and Amanus mountain ranges in the north, by the Euphrates

The Wiley Blackwell Companion to Ancient Israel, First Edition. Edited by Susan Niditch.
© 2016 John Wiley & Sons, Ltd. Published 2016 by John Wiley & Sons, Ltd.

River and the Syro-Arabian desert in the east, and by the Sinai Peninsula and the Red Sea in the south. In current handbooks of Near Eastern archaeology, the Levant is divided into two subregions: the "northern Levant," which extends from the Taurus Mountains to the latitude of Damascus, taking in parts of modern Turkey, Syria, and Lebanon; and the "southern Levant," which includes the State of Israel, the Palestinian territories, much of Jordan, and the southernmost parts of modern Syria and Lebanon.

The Bronze Age in the Levant ended not long after 1200 BCE with the collapse of the Hittite empire, which had ruled the northern Levant for the previous 150 years. At the same time there was a weakening of control of the southern Levant by the Egyptian empire, which had dominated Canaan for the previous 300 years. The collapse and weakening of these imperial powers permitted the invasion and colonization of the coastal Levant by Philistines and other "Sea Peoples" of Aegean and Anatolian origin, whose appearance marks the beginning of the Iron Age in the southern Levant.

As a result of these upheavals, the early Iron Age (Iron Age I) witnessed a population movement away from the coastal and lowland regions toward the highlands of the southern Levant with the founding of hundreds of new villages scattered over a wide area both west and east of the Jordan River (Stager; see also Avraham Faust's essay in this volume). During the Iron Age I, in the twelfth and eleventh centuries BCE, these highland villages were organized in small local polities about which we know little. They were eventually incorporated into larger kingdoms that emerged in the tenth century.

The beginning of the Iron Age II in the southern Levant coincides with the consolidation of the inland kingdom of David in the first half of the tenth century BCE and the simultaneous rise of the Phoenician kingdom of Tyre on the Mediterranean coast. This archaeological period continued through the break-up of the Davidic kingdom (the "united monarchy") into two separate kingdoms in about 925 BCE (the "divided monarchy"), after the reign of David's son Solomon (see Brad Kelle's essay in this volume). After 925, there was a northern kingdom called Israel, which had rebelled against the Davidic dynasty and was ultimately ruled from the city of Samaria (northwest of modern Nablus), and a smaller southern kingdom called Judah, which was ruled from Jerusalem by a long-lived dynasty that traced its descent from King David.

Until quite recently, the archaeological period called Iron IIA, the first phase of the Iron Age II, was thought to correspond to the united monarchy of David and Solomon, ending in 925 BCE. It is now understood to have ended much later, in about 830 BCE, on the basis of radiocarbon dating (see also Elizabeth Bloch-Smith's essay in this volume). The transition from the Iron IIA style to the Iron IIB style should now be associated, not with the splitting apart of the Israelite kingdom, but with the decline in Israelite power and the domination of the southern Levant by the Aramean kingdom of Damascus that began in the time of King Jehu of Israel in the late ninth century. However, the latest radiocarbon evidence still allows us to date the emergence of the Iron IIA pottery styles more than a hundred years earlier, in the first half of the tenth century BCE, during the united monarchy.

This is a much-debated issue in the archaeology of the southern Levant with important historical implications concerning the nature – and even the existence – of the kingdom of David and Solomon. The technical details are complex and beyond the scope of this article. It is sufficient here to note that the solution followed in this chapter is the one proposed by Amihai Mazar, a leading Israeli archaeologist at the Hebrew University in Jerusalem, in response to the "Low Chronology" espoused by Israel Finkelstein of Tel Aviv University. Mazar's "Modified Conventional Chronology" moves the end of Iron IIA from 925 to 830 BCE but still allows room for a kingdom of David and Solomon at the beginning of the Iron IIA period. Although the Iron IIA did not begin as early as 1000 BCE, as claimed in the conventional chronology, it must have commenced within a few decades of that date and probably no later than 950 (Mazar; Toffolo et al.).

In this modified chronology, the Iron IIB style came into vogue during the period of Aramean hegemony from about 830 BCE until the conquest of Damascus by the Assyrians in 732. The kings of Damascus had long been the leaders of Levantine resistance against the Assyrians; thus their demise opened the way for the Assyrian takeover of the entire Levant. By 720 the Assyrians had destroyed Samaria and brought the northern kingdom of Israel to an end. In 701 they besieged Jerusalem and devastated the kingdom of Judah, although they spared King Hezekiah and his dynasty, which ultimately outlived the Assyrian empire itself. Thus, the end of the Iron IIB period corresponds to the period of Assyrian conquests in the southern Levant in the final decades of the eighth century BCE (see J. J. M. Roberts's essay in this volume).

The last phase of the Iron Age, ushered in by the Assyrian conquests, is called Iron IIC in the southern Levant (the same period is usually called Iron Age III in the northern Levant). In the final decades of the seventh century the Egyptians made inroads into the Levant in the wake of the retreating Assyrians and there may have been a brief period of independence and even expansion on the part of Judah under the ill-fated King Josiah, who was killed at Megiddo by Pharaoh Necho II in 609 BCE. But the Iron IIC period was brought to an end with the conquest of the southern Levant by the Babylonians under Nebuchadnezzar II. This was accomplished in a series of devastating military campaigns from 605 to 597, followed a decade later by the final belated elimination of the kingdom of Judah and the destruction of Jerusalem in 586 BCE.

The economic impact of the Babylonian conquest on the southern Levant was severe (Faust, *Judah*). There had been major destructions and population displacements under the Assyrians but economic life continued in the Assyrian period and in some places there were economic innovations that were stimulated, intentionally or not, by Assyrian imperial policies. Under the Babylonians, however, population levels and economic production were at a low ebb. Major coastal cities like the seaport of Ashkelon were left abandoned and in ruins for several decades. Large numbers of people were deported to southern Mesopotamia, including many erstwhile inhabitants of Jerusalem and Judah, who experienced a "Babylonian exile" and established communities in Babylonia from which some exiles eventually returned to Jerusalem to rebuild the Temple and establish the province of Judea, ushering in the Second Temple period of Jewish history (see the essays by Charles Carter and Tamara Cohn Eskenazi in this volume).

For reasons of space, I will focus here on economic and social aspects of life in Israel and Judah during the Iron Age II, in particular. The highland villages of the Iron Age I established an economic and social pattern of agrarian life that continued for hundreds of years, until the Assyrian period. But relatively little is known about these villages archaeologically due to a lack of excavation and publication, although the general settlement pattern is clear from regional archaeological surveys (Stager; Faust, *Israel's*

Ethnogenesis). And it is a matter of debate whether these villages and their inhabitants should be characterized as "Israelite" already in the Iron I period. This raises complex questions concerning ethnic and religious identity that will not be dealt with here (see Avraham Faust's essay in this volume), including the question of whether the close association between Yahwism and Israelite national identity preceded King David or arose only in the wake of his conquests, when there was an expansive political kingdom called Israel that established a strong link between the worship of Yahweh and a new Israelite political identity – an identity that was fostered in regions where the southern god Yahweh, and even the name Israel, had perhaps previously been unknown.

The Iron I period also raises thorny questions of biblical criticism concerning the extent to which reliable information about this period might be contained in the biblical books of Joshua and Judges or in the patriarchal narratives of the Book of Genesis. If we argue that these sources contain reliable historical information about the early Iron Age, and perhaps even the Bronze Age, we are faced with the much-debated question of how this information could have been transmitted to the later biblical writers, orally or in writing, and what kinds of distortion it might have undergone in the process.

We are on firmer ground with respect to the Iron Age II because it is easier to understand how major events and personages of the day might have been recorded and preserved in royal annals of Israel and Judah from the tenth century onward, when the Phoenician alphabet became widespread. For this reason, many biblical scholars who doubt the historicity of Joshua and Judges are willing to accept the basic historical narrative in the Books of Kings while recognizing that this narrative is interwoven with fictional embellishments and editorial comments that reflect later political and theological concerns. In spite of later editing and reworking, political and economic realities of the Iron Age II are evident in the Books of Kings and in some other biblical books that pertain to this period, such as the prophetical books of Hosea, Micah, Amos, Isaiah and Jeremiah. This is shown by the fact that a number of different rulers, places, and events mentioned in the Books of Kings are also mentioned independently in nonbiblical textual sources from the Iron Age II, and in a way that demonstrates the basic correctness of the political geography and chronology found in the Books of Kings.

As for the Babylonian period that followed the Iron Age II in the Levant and lasted from 605 until 539 BCE, when Cyrus the Great of Persia captured Babylon, both biblical and archaeological evidence point to widespread devastation and abandonment, despite claims to the contrary (Faust, *Judah*). It is plausible to suppose that this was intentional on the part of the Babylonians, who were wary of the power and territorial ambitions of the Saite pharaohs of Egypt, whom they had met in battle in North Syria at Carchemish on the Euphrates in 609 BCE. After the failure of their attempt to invade Egypt in 601, the Babylonians apparently decided to create an empty no man's land in order to deprive the Egyptians of logistical support and allies along this imperial frontier. In any case, economic life in the southern Levant was at a low ebb and there are few archaeological sites of the period, limiting what can be said about it.

Finally, it would be worthwhile in a separate survey to discuss the economic and social life of the southern Levant and the province of Judea in later periods, during the Persian period from 539 to 332 BCE, when the Near East was ruled by the Achaemenid Persian empire, and during the subsequent Hellenistic and Roman periods, after the conquest of the Persian empire by Alexander the Great (see the essays by Charles Carter and Matthew Goff in this volume). It was in these periods that the Hebrew Bible was being compiled and edited into its present form. However, the economic, social, and political conditions of those periods differed greatly from those of the Iron Age, which is the focus of the present survey.

Sources of Evidence and Conceptual Frameworks

Quantifiable economic data about the Iron Age kingdoms of Israel and Judah are scarce. From archaeological investigations and written sources (including both the Hebrew Bible and occasional ancient inscriptions; see Christopher Rollston's essay in this volume) we know what kinds of goods were produced during the Iron Age II and we have an idea of how and where these goods were manufactured, distributed, and consumed. Most archaeological reports touch upon these topics in one way or another. In addition, there are useful handbooks and synthetic studies that discuss Iron Age Israelite agriculture, animal husbandry, domestic life, and craft production with reference to both archaeological and biblical evidence (e.g., Borowski; King and Stager; cf. Moorey).

The biblical evidence should not be used naively. From the perspective of biblical criticism it must be said that archaeologists often take insufficient care to distinguish different biblical sources and genres, some of which may tell us more about the Persian or Hellenistic period than about the Iron Age Israelite period to which they putatively refer, or may tell us more about the ideals and ideologies of the biblical writers than about what actually happened. This is a weakness, for example, of Roland de Vaux's classic work on the social and religious institutions of ancient Israel (de Vaux), in which he lumps together quite disparate biblical texts under thematic headings without discussing their respective dates of composition and literary purposes. The same defect is apparent in more recent works (e.g., Faust, *Israel's Ethnogenesis*; *Archaeology*).

Moreover, as I have said, despite the array of qualitative evidence derived from archaeological and textual studies, we lack data about quantities and relative proportions of various economic goods and services of the kind we would like to have in order to describe the structure and functioning of the Israelite economy. In particular, we find it difficult to quantify the relative importance of the three main modes of economic integration identified long ago by the economic historian Karl Polanyi, which are part of the conceptual toolkit of anthropologists and historians who study premodern economies. These modes of integration are: (1) *reciprocity*, which includes local exchanges among kinfolk who feel obliged to help one another, as well as personalized gift-exchange among elites, often conducted via long-distance trade, for the purpose of establishing and maintaining political relationships; (2) *redistribution*, which entails the stockpiling and disbursement of goods by political authorities to control resources and mobilize labor; and (3) *market exchange*, in which prices are established by the balance of supply and demand and economic actors respond to market prices in a utilitarian self-interested way by producing more or less of certain goods and exchanging them in a relatively depersonalized or "socially disembedded" manner, whether by simple barter or using some form of money as a medium of exchange (Halperin).

Ancient Israel is not unique in the paucity of quantitative economic data it has bequeathed to us. We lack such data for many other premodern societies, forcing us to infer the structural features of the economy and the relative importance of reciprocity, redistribution, and market exchange from ambiguous material remains and from scattered anecdotal evidence in written sources, which themselves are often difficult to interpret correctly. For some periods and places in the ancient Near East, a more detailed economic picture can be obtained from administrative archives that have survived to be unearthed and deciphered by scholars, especially in Mesopotamia, where inscriptions were made on durable clay tablets, and in Egypt, where the exceptionally dry climate has preserved texts written on papyrus, an organic writing material that was no doubt used extensively by Phoenicians, Philistines, Arameans and Israelites but has long since decayed in the wetter climate of the Levant. These kinds of documents can shed substantial light on ancient economic organization. However, few administrative inscriptions of this kind have been preserved in the Iron Age Levant and we cannot easily apply to the kingdoms of Israel and Judah the quite different economic and social features of Mesopotamia or Egypt. We are left with rather cryptic administrative notations on ostraca (inscribed potsherds), such as the Samaria Ostraca found in the capital city of the northern kingdom of Israel and dated to the reign of Jeroboam II in the early eighth century BCE, and other ostraca that were found in seventh-century contexts at Arad and Lachish in the kingdom of Judah.

This lack of detailed written data pertaining to economic activity should caution us to be aware of the interpretive models that scholars inevitably bring to the fragmentary evidence at their disposal in order to fill in the blanks whenever they make general statements about the Israelite economy. We should especially be on guard against anachronistic economic models that seem natural to us as modern people but are not necessarily applicable to Iron Age Israel and Judah. For example, it seems natural to us that economic production, distribution, and exchange should be coordinated by means of markets in which buyers and sellers respond to prices that are determined by supply and demand and in which they enter into transactions in a relatively depersonalized way, without regard to their familial or political relationships or lack thereof. It also seems natural to us that there should be an economic distinction between urban centers, in which specialized manufacturing and services are localized, and rural villages, in which primary agricultural production takes place.

However, there were many quite sophisticated premodern societies in which there was no urban–rural dichotomy of this kind and in which market exchange was relatively unimportant in the overall economy or was restricted to certain commodities. In particular, there are many cases in which various foodstuffs and craft products could be bought and sold on the market but there was no significant market in land, labor or capital goods (i.e., assets that enable useful work and the production of saleable goods) because access to these "factors of production" was embedded in political and social institutions that operated separately from the market. The lack of factor markets greatly limits the ability of market exchange to coordinate and integrate economic activity overall because wealth obtained from selling goods on the market cannot easily be converted to factors of production – land, labor and capital – that can be used to produce more goods to sell.

This was the case in the Aztec empire of precolonial Mexico, where there were thriving interregional markets in foodstuffs and craft products but little or no market for land or labor, and no credit mechanism to allow borrowing at interest for purposes of investment in productive assets. Although market exchange was important in some parts of the economy, the absence of factor markets prevented the integration of the entire economy by means of the market mechanism. The utilization of most land and labor was accomplished by nonmarket institutional mechanisms operating at the household level and at the governmental level: "almost all labor that was not performed by individuals for their own households' provisioning was recruited through corvée (labor taxation), seignorial rights on noblemen's landholdings, and kinship and neighborhood reciprocity" (B. Isaac, in Hirth and Pillsbury 437).

The pre-Columbian empires of the New World have been fertile ground for economic anthropology, in part because of the striking contrast between the Aztec empire and the Inca empire (see also Avraham Faust's essay in this volume). This contrast provides an instructive example of the danger of extrapolating the economic structures of one region to another, even in the same historical period, when the ecological setting was different and different political and cultural traditions were at work. In the vast Inca empire of the Andes region, market exchange seems to have been much less important than it was in the Aztec economy (Hirth and Pillsbury). The complex redistributive system of the Inca empire, in which political integration was achieved by the circulation of prestige goods over long distances, has prompted a fruitful conceptual distinction between "staple finance" and "wealth finance," a distinction that has been widely used in Near Eastern archaeology (Earle). These terms refer to two different mechanisms by which political followers are mobilized within a nonmarketized economy characterized mainly by reciprocity and redistribution.

Staple finance, a term adopted from the writings of Karl Polanyi,

> generally involves obligatory payments in kind to the state of subsistence goods such as grains, livestock, and clothing. ... Staples are collected by the state as a share of commoner produce, as a specified levy, or as produce from land worked with corvée labor. This revenue in staples is then used to pay personnel attached to the state and others working for the state on a part-time basis. (Earle 193)

Staples amassed by political rulers require governmental storage facilities, which can often be detected archaeologically. They are bulky and difficult to transport over long distances, so they are best suited for local mobilization of labor and to support military garrisons.

In contrast, wealth finance "involves the manufacture and procurement of special products (valuables, primitive money, and currency) that are used as a means of payment. ... They may be amassed as direct payment from subservient populations, or they may be produced by craft specialists attached to the central authorities" (Earle 193). There is a close connection between staple finance and wealth finance: "In Inka and other societies heavily dependent on staple finance to support state activities, wealth finance plays a complementary role. It economically integrates the managerial ranks, consisting primarily or partially of subject elites, into the central state authority structure" (Earle 207). Products used in wealth finance are high-value prestige items like fine clothing, vessels, and jewelry that are much more portable than staples and are suitable for conspicuous display. These items can be shipped efficiently over long distances to reward political followers and to serve as vehicles of personalized gift-exchange for establishing and maintaining political alliances. In effect, rulers use local redistribution to convert bulky staples obtained from agrarian households into portable prestige items for long-distance reciprocity in order to foster the political integration of their domain.

Prestige items that circulated for political purposes could in turn be used in market settings as forms of money to purchase other goods, if the political authorities permitted this. The rulers of the Aztec empire seem to have promoted market exchange, although marketplaces were tightly regulated and merchants were closely monitored to make sure they did not become too wealthy. But the rulers of the Inca empire seem to have discouraged market exchange and the construction of marketplaces, investing instead in facilities and personnel for large-scale storage and distribution (B. Isaac, in Hirth and Pillsbury 442).

The purpose of these New World examples is to show the range of possibilities in premodern agrarian economies and to introduce concepts that are useful for understanding the Bronze and Iron Age Levant in the period before the political and economic transformations of the Persian and Hellenistic periods, when new economic practices emerged that are visible archaeologically in the appearance of coinage, large cities, improved transportation technology, and other forms of capital investment. Market exchange seems to have increased in importance in the Persian and Hellenistic periods, although there is a longstanding debate among classicists concerning the degree of market integration that was actually present in the Greek world of the eastern Mediterranean in these periods, a debate which has echoes in scholarship on the pre-Hellenistic Near East (Finley; Manning and Morris; Scheidel et al.).

Market exchange was already becoming important in the economy of the coastal Levant during the late Iron Age, especially among the Phoenicians, who possessed very limited agricultural territory and established extensive maritime trading networks around the Mediterranean beginning in the eighth century BCE. But it is less clear that markets were a major part of the economy in the inland kingdoms of the Iron Age Levant. This is not to say that they were absent in the agrarian kingdoms of Israel and Judah. Most economic anthropologists today would agree that markets had a role to play in almost all complex "state-level" societies, rejecting Karl Polanyi's rather extreme view that they were absent in the early empires of the Near East and elsewhere (a view he himself qualified in his later writings). But the precise role played by market exchange and its importance in the overall economy remains an empirical question in each historical case. Local markets may have been limited to certain foodstuffs and craft items, being merely supplemental to the household-based production and consumption that occurred within largely self-sufficient agrarian towns and villages. And in the case of external trade, we must allow for "administered trade" in which prices (equivalencies) were set by custom, treaty or governmental decree and were not determined by market forces of supply and demand. The evidence at our disposal often permits this interpretation of ancient trade. In other words, the mere existence of trade does not prove the existence of market exchange. Likewise, an increase in trade does not necessarily indicate increasing marketization.

To be sure, market-oriented trade can coexist with administered trade. The same trader might be involved in both, depending on the context of the trade and the commodities involved. But political authorities normally have a great deal of control over the form of trade practiced in their territory and over the personnel who are engaged in it. We cannot simply assume, as some scholars do, that market exchange was actively encouraged by the rulers of Iron Age Israel and Judah or was even passively allowed to grow by default. And on comparative grounds we certainly have reason to be skeptical of the idea that the Israelite economy was organized and integrated overall by means of interconnected markets in land, labor, capital and commodities, as in the modern world.

Accordingly, we must go beyond the modern focus on markets and assess the importance of reciprocity and redistribution as modes of economic integration in Iron Age Israel and Judah in light of the available evidence and in light of comparative historical cases. Moreover, we have good reasons to believe that underlying all three modes of economic integration were self-sufficient farming households in which the vast majority of the population lived and worked. "Householding" is an important concept in Polanyi's work and is sometimes regarded as a fourth basic mode of economic integration in addition to reciprocity, redistribution and market exchange (Halperin 143–8). The economic features of traditional peasant households have been described by Marshall Sahlins, drawing on earlier work by the Russian economist A. V. Chayanov, as constituting a "domestic mode of production" in which the goal is production for livelihood ("use value") rather than production for exchange. This leads to systemic underproduction, a limited division of labor and low levels of capital investment. The basic elements of the domestic mode are "a small labor force differentiated essentially by sex, simple technology, and finite production objectives" (Sahlins 87). In tribal societies, in particular, the underproduction and simplicity of the domestic mode are continually reinforced because individual households are usually not the exclusive owners of farmland, pastureland or hunting and fishing territories, which are owned collectively by the larger kinship group. This inhibits capital investment and intensification of production. Individual households have customary rights of usufruct but are not free to expand their economic resources except by political means, by becoming chiefly or royal households that can extract goods and labor from subordinate households and redistribute them to support their political authority. And even then, paramount households must respect the customary rights of usufruct of the subordinate households whose members directly work the land in a largely autonomous fashion within a "patrimonial" hierarchy of households (Schloen). The households at the bottom of the hierarchy produce only what they need for their livelihood and to meet the demands of taxation imposed by their overlords.

This approach to the Israelite economy is not necessarily "substantivist" as opposed to "formalist," to use the labels that have been applied to Polanyi's school (the substantivists) in contrast to the opposing camp in economic anthropology (the formalists), who adopted the assumptions of neoclassical economics and tended to place strong emphasis on market exchange. Many formalists are now less insistent on markets and are happy to stress the political and institutional embedding of economic behavior, accepting this key tenet of the substantivist approach, now that the idea of the institutional embedding of the economy has been given a strong basis in formal economic theory by proponents of the "New Institutional Economics" (Furubotn and Richter). The substantivist emphasis on the social embedding of economic behavior in systems of reciprocity and redistribution has been given a formalist interpretation in terms of rational choice and individual maximization of utility by taking into account the "transaction costs" that inhibit market exchange (Ensminger; cf. Elardo). Formalists can argue on their own grounds that market exchange, which is the optimal economic strategy in a hypothetical situation of "unbounded rationality" and "zero transaction costs," is not optimal in many actual historical settings in which rationality is "bounded" (i.e., economic decision-makers have limited knowledge) and there are high transaction costs. For example, transaction costs are imposed by the lack of a legal mechanism to enforce contracts and property rights, which means that the legal institutions of a society will have a major impact on the overall structure of the economy (Frier and Kehoe). In such settings, there are economic incentives to supplement markets with other institutions and perhaps to replace them altogether with other modes of economic organization and exchange, such as reciprocity and redistribution, in order to maximize utility. This point was made long ago by Douglass North, one of the pioneers of New Institutional Economics, in a paper in which he engaged directly with Polanyi (North).

Thus, we can approach the Israelite economy from either a substantivist or a formalist perspective and arrive at the same conclusions concerning the role of markets. This does not mean that the debate between the two camps has ended. There is still a major methodological disagreement between substantivists and formalists concerning the proper unit of economic and social analysis. Formalists, following in the intellectual tradition of neoclassical economics, claim that human beings employ a universal economizing logic with respect to the need to choose among alternate means to achieve their desired ends and to maximize their individual utility in a context of scarcity, regardless of how utility and scarcity may be defined in a particular culture. This implies that all economies, ancient and modern, are susceptible to formal analyses in terms of marginal utility of the kind found in standard neoclassical economics and also in the New Institutional Economics, which shares many of the same assumptions (Furubotn and Richter 1–12).

Substantivists reply that describing the logic of economic choice in this way assumes methodological individualism – the view that atomized individuals and their actions are the proper units of sociological analysis rather than the collective structures in which individuals participate – and they note that methodological individualism has been rejected by many social theorists in favor of some form of methodological holism (Halperin 13ff.). The longstanding debate between methodological individualists and holists goes far beyond economic anthropology and rests on a fundamental philosophical disagreement about the nature of human society. Thus, despite the advent of the New Institutional Economics, which has helped to bridge the divide, there can be no resolution to the formalist–substantivist debate until the underlying philosophical issue is resolved.

Fortunately, we do not have to settle this philosophical question here. Whether we think in terms of transaction costs that affect incentives for individual maximizing behavior or think in terms of collective structures that enable and constrain individual behavior, we can remain sensitive to the institutional limits of markets as we construct a model of the Iron Age Israelite economy that is compatible with the available evidence. In my view, the most plausible model would give considerable weight to self-sufficient agrarian householding, local kin-based reciprocity, and governmental redistribution, for which we have many archaeological and textual indications, while making room for market exchange of some goods in some social contexts. We should also allow for structural changes over the course of the Iron Age II, especially in the Iron IIC period, in the wake of the Assyrian conquests and deportations of the late eighth century BCE, which had a major effect on the settlement pattern of the southern Levant, bringing in displaced foreigners from Syria and Mesopotamia who were settled in Israelite territory and displacing many people internally within the southern Levant.

In the remainder of this article, a number of issues pertaining to the economy and society of Iron Age Israel and Judah will be treated with these structural considerations in mind. The picture presented here is qualitative and impressionistic. We may never have sufficient data to quantify the relative importance of the three different modes of economic integration within the overall economy of ancient Israel and to determine when and where trade and prices were administered as opposed to market-driven. This does not mean that a more formal approach is impossible. The New Institutional Economics provides a method of formal analysis that does not depend on knowing quantities and prices but can nonetheless make use of fragmentary evidence to illuminate structural features of premodern economies. This is seen in the historically sophisticated work of the economist Avner Greif in his book *Institutions and the Path to the Modern Economy: Lessons from Medieval Trade*. In this work, he draws on textual evidence from the Cairo Genizah concerning the social relations among the medieval Jewish traders of North Africa in order to construct a game-theoretic model of the institutional dynamics of long-distance trade, building on earlier work in transaction-cost economics. Meanwhile, other social scientists have used the mathematical techniques of social network analysis to construct heuristic models of the institutional embedding of economic behavior in particular historical settings (Jackson; Scott). Increasingly, game theory and network analysis are being combined to construct models of socially embedded economic relationships and their development over time. These formal methods are often used in a way that treats atomized individuals as the basic units of analysis, in keeping with methodological individualism. However, the same methods can also be used in a way that focuses not on individual persons or organizations but on the dynamic networks of social relations in which these social actors are embedded and even constituted, an approach that is compatible with the phenomenological concept of "intersubjectivity" and thus may go some way toward satisfying substantivist concerns (Emirbayer and Goodwin; Mische).

Such methods are now attracting the attention of archaeologists and ancient economic historians (see, e.g., Knappett), so in the future we may see useful analytical forays in this direction by specialists who study the ancient Near East and ancient Israel, in particular. For now, we can use the broad conceptual framework presented in the preceding paragraphs to make sense of the archaeological and textual evidence. This evidence is compatible with the view that kings in Iron Age Israel and Judah accomplished the political and economic integration of their domains by means of a redistributive apparatus that employed staple finance, wealth finance and gift exchange in a way that is familiar from other premodern agrarian polities (Earle). There is clear evidence for royal storage and redistribution, on the one hand, and for local kin-based reciprocity, on the other. Furthermore, it is clear that self-sufficient agricultural households were the engines of the economy and supplied the staple goods and corvée labor that supported political elites, regardless of whether those households were located in walled towns or in unwalled villages. Thus, it is reasonable to suppose that most economic activity was deeply embedded in political and social institutions that determined how goods and services were produced, distributed and consumed.

There is some evidence for local markets in craft products and foodstuffs, as well as evidence for foreign trade, although we must be cautious in how we interpret this evidence because of the difficulty of distinguishing market trade from administered trade in the absence of detailed information about prices. But in the Iron Age IIA and IIB, in particular, before the Assyrian conquests and the massive population displacements they engendered, there is no evidence for an urban–rural dichotomy between economically specialized cities and unspecialized agricultural villages. This should cause us to doubt the importance of market exchange as a major mode of economic integration before the seventh century BCE.

Households, Villages, Walled Towns and "Urbanism"

If peasant householding, kin-based reciprocity, and governmental redistribution were the primary elements in the inland economy of the southern Levant before the Assyrian conquest, we would expect to find archaeological evidence of governmental facilities for military control, political administration, religious ritual, storage of staples and the production of prestige goods made by attached craft specialists for circulation as political payments in a system of wealth finance. We would also expect to find evidence of the decentralized production of subsistence goods within farming households characterized by a low level of economic specialization and a high degree of self-sufficiency. And we would expect to find a dispersed settlement pattern with no large cities, no large marketplaces, and no clear dichotomy between "urban" and "rural" sectors.

In fact, this is what we do find. Moreover, this view of ancient Israel – an agrarian society in which strong ties of kinship coexisted with centralized governmental institutions – is the view we obtain from biblical texts that purport to describe the monarchical period in Iron Age Israel and Judah (see the essay by T. M. Lemos in this volume). Economic and political interactions of a sort that typically arise in such a society are common in biblical narratives, laws, poetry and prophetic oracles that can be plausibly attributed to this period (in terms of their origin if not their final composition). These textual clues have led many scholars over the years to regard Iron Age Israel and Judah as economically quite simple societies in which foreign trade – which was the only large-scale trade – was a royal monopoly and local markets consisted of producers (farmers and craftsmen) selling directly to consumers, so there was no mercantile bourgeoisie (see, e.g., de Vaux 78).

There is no space here for a detailed review of the biblical and archaeological evidence, which I will present in a forthcoming book on *The Bible and Archaeology*. Here I will focus on the changing settlement pattern and the sizes and architectural features of the settlements. During the Iron Age I, several hundred unfortified agricultural villages of a similar type were established throughout the highlands of the southern Levant both west and east of the Jordan River (Stager; Faust, *Israel's Ethnogenesis*; see the essay by Avraham Faust in this volume). These villages were quite small, being a hectare or less in area. We can get a sense of the scale of the settlement by noting that the total number of settlements in several subregions that have been subjected to detailed surveys by archaeologists grew from 88 in the Late Bronze Age to 678 in the subsequent Iron Age I, increasing the number of settlements more than sevenfold and tripling the total built-up area from about 200 hectares in the Late Bronze period, with an estimated population of 50,000, to about 600 hectares in the Iron I period, with an estimated population of 150,000 (Stager 134). These figures exclude the Galilee region, so we must allow for an even larger population in the territory that was eventually incorporated into the kingdom of Israel sometime after 1000 BCE.

It is generally agreed, based on Middle Eastern ethnographic parallels, that most of these small villages, ranging in size from about 100 to 300 people, would have been inhabited by a single kinship group or small clan that claimed descent from a common ancestor, whether real or fictional. No doubt there were complex political alliances among villages that created larger clans and tribes of various sizes led by local chieftains or petty kings, as we might expect from reading the biblical narratives concerning this period in the books of Judges and Samuel. However, the enduring importance of tribal and clan identities in later periods should alert us to the possibility that these narratives are rooted as much in the "monarchical" period as in the "premonarchic" period and reflect a continuation of kin-based communities from the Iron Age I into the Iron Age II, when these communities were absorbed within larger polities but did not necessarily undergo significant internal transformations (see T. M. Lemos's essay in this volume).

During the Iron Age IIA there was a reduction in the number of small village settlements, although there is some disagreement about how drastic this reduction actually was and how quickly it took place (Finkelstein, "[De]formation"; Faust, *Archaeology*, 255–60). In any case, the Iron IIA period witnessed a concentration of the population within fewer, larger settlements, which in many cases were equipped with fortification walls. There seems to have been a shift away from isolated highland villages toward the fertile valleys and lowlands now controlled by the kingdom of Israel, which is not surprising in view of the fact that many highlanders would have fought in the Israelite army and may have been eager to relocate to regions with better farmland that they had helped to conquer. We can plausibly attribute the change in settlement pattern to the advent of a centralized polity during the reigns of David, Solomon and their successors, when political rulers took steps to establish and maintain control over an extensive territory and to make it easier to extract goods and labor from their subjects. Fewer settlements meant fewer locations to police and fewer collection points for taxation and conscription. Walled towns were necessary as royal centers of administration and military control.

But we must keep in mind that the vast majority of Iron IIA Israelite settlements were still rather small agricultural towns by comparative historical standards. They typically had only about 500–1,500 inhabitants. In this period Jerusalem itself, the royal capital, occupied only 4 hectares (10 acres), not counting the large temple and palace area that was added at some point and is attributed in the Bible to King Solomon. Tirzah (Tell el-Far'ah North), the first capital of the northern kingdom of Israel, was about 5 hectares in size (Finkelstein, *Forgotten Kingdom*, 67). Megiddo, which had been a major Canaanite city, was only 7 hectares (17 acres) in size in this period (Finkelstein, "[De]formation," 203). These towns were dispersed across the landscape and show little internal differentiation and no clear size hierarchy, casting doubt on the existence of an integrated economy based on market exchange between specialized settlements. Like many ancient towns, they were political phenomena and were not the result of economic "forces."

Furthermore, a politically inspired concentration of previously scattered clans within larger settlements does not give us reason to assume that their kin-based social organization and traditional agrarian householding practices disappeared simply because some clans now lived together in the same (small) town. Such an assumption rests on a discredited evolutionary stage model of a kind that was once popular in anthropology, in which kinship was thought to wither as tribes gave way to states. This stage model in turn is rooted in a misapplied organic metaphor in which social groups are conceived of as "organisms" whose quantitative growth necessarily entails specialization of function ("division of labor") and an internal structural transformation – a transition from mechanical solidarity to organic solidarity, to use Durkheim's terms. Sociological functionalism of this kind is deeply rooted in Near Eastern archaeology but it has been rejected by many social theorists since the 1970s and it flies in the face of Middle Eastern ethnography and history, which demonstrate the persistence of kinship and tribalism as organizing features of society even in large walled towns that are part of centralized states (Schloen 49–59, 194–200).

Similar considerations apply to the Iron Age IIB, the period from the late ninth century to the late eighth century when the Arameans of Damascus were dominant and before the Assyrians conquered the southern Levant. Most of our data about Israelite walled towns comes from this archaeological period and from the end of the period in particular, thanks to the wave of Assyrian destructions that encased Iron IIB architectural levels in rubble and preserved them for archaeologists to examine. There may have been some growth in the number of walled towns in the Iron IIB, but the basic pattern remained the same. Most towns were only a few hectares in size. Jerusalem, the capital of the kingdom of Judah, remained quite small for most of the Iron IIB until the final decades of the eighth century BCE, when it became hugely swollen with refugees, first from the destroyed northern kingdom and then from the Shephelah foothills through which Sennacherib, king of Assyria, rampaged in 701 BCE. Samaria, the capital of the northern kingdom of Israel, may have grown quite large in the Iron IIB period before the Assyrian conquest, but it had occupied only 3 or 4 hectares in the Iron IIA period and it is not clear that it exceeded 8 hectares in the Iron IIB, although many scholars assume without proof that it must have grown much larger due to its political importance (Finkelstein, *Forgotten Kingdom*, 94). This is a questionable assumption because there is no reason to think that a town's political importance is necessarily reflected in its size. There is no automatic link between political power and economic productivity.

The archaeological evidence concerning the walled towns and unwalled villages of Israel and Judah is summarized by Avraham Faust in his book on *The Archaeology of Israelite Society in Iron Age II*, which contains a wealth of data and many stimulating observations. Faust's work is singled out here because it is the most detailed current treatment of key aspects of the Israelite economy and because it raises theoretical issues that bear close examination. In this book and in his other publications, Faust posits an urban–rural dichotomy that is not warranted by the evidence. This dichotomy is a legacy of the outdated sociological functionalism that continues to infect archaeological studies of ancient Israel. Archaeologists rather casually describe any walled settlement as "urban" and refer to an increase in the number of walled settlements as "urbanization." But these terms carry theoretical baggage that is not appropriate for the case at hand. The term "urban" implies far more than a purely descriptive distinction between walled and unwalled settlements. It is not an architectural term but a sociological term that implies an economic contrast between specialized cities and unspecialized villages which are the locus of staple production but are dependent on urban centers for manufactured goods and professional services, creating an economic dynamic that was famously described (and wrongly assumed to be universal) by Adam Smith in his *Wealth of Nations*.

But the mere existence of town walls and nondomestic special-purpose buildings cannot be taken as evidence of a structural dichotomy of this sort in the absence of written evidence. These architectural phenomena may simply reflect the imposition of political control and related mechanisms of resource extraction on what continued to be relatively small and undifferentiated agricultural settlements, some of which were fortified by the king to serve as centers of power and were equipped with military garrisons, administrative buildings, and ritual facilities, and some of which remained unfortified. In such cases, the urban–rural dichotomy is meaningless as an economic distinction and ought to be recast as a purely political distinction between administrative and non-administrative settlements.

Faust acknowledges the criticisms voiced in the scholarly literature concerning the anachronistic application of the urban–rural dichotomy to premodern agrarian societies but he clings to the dichotomy nonetheless, citing functionalist-evolutionist sociological classics like the Lenskis' 1974 textbook *Human Societies* and the 1938 essay "On urbanism as a way of life" by the Chicago School sociologist Louis Wirth (Faust, *Archaeology*, 39–41, 129). Wirth, summarizing (approvingly) the functionalist understanding of urbanism that was already long established in his day, stated that: "The distinctive features of the urban mode of life have often been described sociologically as consisting of the substitution of secondary for primary contacts, the weakening of bonds of kinship, and the declining social significance of the family, the disappearance of the neighborhood, and the undermining of the traditional basis of social solidarity" (20–1).

Faust makes this venerable sociological dichotomy a central theme in his voluminous writings on Israelite society and he links it to his discussion of increasing social stratification that supposedly took place in the eighth century BCE (Iron IIB). Stratification is closely linked to urbanism in the functionalist paradigm, whereas villages are thought to remain more egalitarian and kin-based. I have criticized this approach else-where at considerable length, drawing on a large body of social theory and empirical data (Schloen), and I will discuss the Israelite evidence adduced by Faust in some detail in a forthcoming book. Here I will only remark that the variation in house sizes that Faust and others interpret as evidence of urban social stratification due to a functionalist divi-sion of labor (see Faust, *Archaeology*, 115, citing Lenski and Lenski) can be understood differently: partly in terms of political hierarchy, in the case of the largest and wealthiest houses, and otherwise in terms of changing agrarian family sizes over the course of the household life cycle, as patrilocal extended families progressed from the two-generation phase to three or four generations and back again, keeping in mind that the effects of the ancient Mediterranean mortality rate were such that at any one time the majority of such households were in the smaller two-generation stage consisting of a conjugal couple and their unmarried children (Schloen 135–83). I have argued that each house was inhabited by a patrilocal *bêt 'āb* or "father's house(hold)," which means that fami-lies swapped houses according to their space needs as the size of each lineage waxed and waned, or in some cases simply renovated their existing houses. Swapping houses is not at all unlikely (contra Albertz and Schmitt 39) because individual households did not have exclusive ownership of property, which was owned collectively by the clan (Hebrew *mišpāḥâ*). The households of a village or those in a particular quarter of a larger walled town constituted an endogamous clan that claimed descent (fictively or not) from a com-mon ancestor. The clan was the primary legal and juridical unit in ancient Israel, as in many traditional Middle Eastern societies. And just as clan elders reallocated the clan's farmland among its constituent households each year (a well-attested practice in the Middle East with respect to grain fields, as in the *musha* system of land tenure among the Arabs of Palestine) they could reallocate houses according to changing needs, keeping in mind that neighbors were cousins and were constantly engaged in reciprocal exchanges, being morally obligated to help one another. Some kinds of property, including livestock and perhaps olive groves and vineyards, which required multiyear investments of labor, unlike grain fields, might have been regarded as the patrimony of a particular lineage, as in the famous example of the vineyard of Naboth, who refused to alienate his hereditary land (1 Kings 21:1–24). But we should not infer from this that private ownership was widespread and applied to all kinds of property. The assumption by modern scholars that there was exclusive ownership of houses by individual Israelite families is another exam-ple of the insidious anachronisms that so often creep into our reconstructions when we project modern concepts of ownership and markets onto the distant past. And the exam-ple of Naboth's vineyard actually demonstrates the limitations of market exchange in ancient Israel because it was hereditary property that could not be sold.

From a hermeneutical perspective, the functionalist approach taken by Faust and others is overly objectivist and reductive. Another kind of objectivism is found in Faust's discussions of the Iron Age "four-room" house (Faust, *Archaeology*, 213–29) and of Iron Age pottery (*Archaeology*, 230–54; see Avraham Faust's essay in this volume). He gives a speculative, quasi-structuralist interpretation of the symbolism of specific material forms that links these forms to Israelite "ethnicity," which he treats in an essentialized way as a transpersonal reality somehow encoded in artifact styles rather than as a malleable identity expressed temporally in actual subjective narratives – a self-ascribed identity with many possible connections to particular material forms. This kind of interpretation reflects the persistent structuralist tendency in "postprocessual" archaeology, which coexists rather uneasily with an equally persistent "processual" functionalism. Structuralist interpretations of architecture and pottery are based on the questionable assumption that we can detect "material metaphors" inherent in physical objects, presumably because they reflect unconscious universal meanings. This structuralist assumption must be rejected on hermeneutical grounds. Neither functionalism nor structuralism grants sufficient analytical importance to the culturally specific forms of lived experience of social actors whose daily practices are shaped by – indeed, enabled by – a particular symbolic tradition, which is not functionally determined or somehow inherent in material objects but is expressed in native linguistic metaphors and narratives. An example of this is the symbolism of "the house of the father" that I have singled out as a key organizing principle in the ancient Levant (Schloen). This shared symbolism of social order was embodied in meaningful practices that continually reproduced the kin-based "domestic mode," which was not isolated in a stagnant rural sector ideologically opposed to the urban "state" but was the basis for the political (and thus the economic) integration of the whole kingdom. The kingdom was understood to be a single household that contained many other households, replicating the same structure at different scales and legitimizing royal rule by means of the very same patriarchal ideology that underpinned each ordinary household.

However, the cultural reproduction of the Israelite "house of the father" was interrupted by the massive shock of Assyrian conquest at the end of the eighth century BCE. As Faust has described very well, the Iron IIC period witnessed an unprecedented expansion of the population of Jerusalem, which now covered as much as 60 hectares (150 acres) in size, and there was a similar expansion of the Philistine cities near the coast. The once-flourishing Shephelah foothills were largely depopulated. In light of these changes it is not surprising that we find evidence of new economic (and religious) practices in this period, which were not triggered by organic economic growth but by the dissolution of large numbers of traditional clans, whose members had been resident for centuries in towns and villages that were now destroyed and not resettled. It is possible that the Assyrians had a conscious policy of preventing the resettlement of these places, forcing the survivors to live in a few large cities that could be more easily policed, which would also have saved them the trouble of mounting many different sieges in case of a widespread rebellion. In any case, the unintended consequence of the sudden displacement of many thousands of erstwhile clan members seems to have been a breakdown of the traditional economic system based on reciprocity and redistribution and an increase in specialized production and market exchange centered in large cities. This is shown by a noticeable increase in the use of weights for measuring quantities of silver as a means of payment – though, again, the mere fact that payments occurred does not necessarily mean that prices were set by supply and demand. Many such weights have been found in different shapes and sizes, indicating different systems in use in Judah, among the Phoenicians, and among the Assyrians themselves. Several hoards of silver pieces suitable for being weighed out as a medium of exchange (including broken-up bits of jewelry) have been found in seventh-century contexts in the southern Levant.

The Babylonian conquest at the end of the seventh century caused a dramatic reduction in population and economic activity, especially in Judah and Philistia, as Faust has now shown in some detail (Faust, *Judah*). Due to the lack of excavated evidence, little can be said about the Babylonian period in the southern Levant in the sixth century BCE. There was of course some agricultural activity to support the small population that remained and to support the Babylonian garrisons, but many elements of the Iron Age economy were gone. The one constant feature was the political embedding of the economy, which has been a recurrent theme in this article. The political rulers, in this case the Babylonian governors, no doubt demanded taxes and corvée labor to support their regime, employing a redistributive apparatus not much different from that which had existed for centuries. However, in the Phoenician world, at least, the steps toward market integration that had been taken in the seventh century continued throughout the sixth century and set the stage for the revival of economic life under Achaemenid Persian rule, when great seaports flourished along the entire coast of the Levant and Jerusalem and Judah were resettled.

Bibliography

Albertz, Rainer and Rüdiger Schmitt. *Family and Household Religion in Ancient Israel and the Levant*. Winona Lake, IN: Eisenbrauns, 2012. An exhaustive study of the textual and archaeological evidence pertaining to family and household religion in ancient Israel and neighboring regions.

Borowski, Oded. *Agriculture in Iron Age Israel*. Winona Lake, IN: Eisenbrauns, 1987. A useful survey of agricultural practices in Iron Age Israel and Judah based on information gleaned from the Hebrew Bible and from archaeological remains.

de Vaux, Roland. *Ancient Israel*, vol. 1: *Social Institutions*. New York: McGraw-Hill, 1961. A classic, but now quite dated, treatment of the social and economic institutions in ancient Israel, presented thematically by an eminent archaeologist of an earlier generation.

Earle, Timothy K. *Bronze Age Economics: The Beginnings of Political Economies*. Boulder, CO: Westview, 2002. A collection of essays published over the years by a leading economic anthropologist that present concepts and models useful for understanding premodern agrarian economies.

Elardo, Justin A. "Economic anthropology after the Great Debate: The role and evolution of institutionalist thought." In T. Matejowsky and D. C. Wood (eds), *Political Economy, Neoliberalism, and the Prehistoric Economies of Latin America* (pp. 53–83). Research in Economic Anthropology 32. Bingley, UK: Emerald Group, 2012. A survey of theoretical developments in economic anthropology since the 1960s, with particular reference to the impact of the New Institutional Economics.

Emirbayer, Mustafa and Jeff Goodwin. "Network analysis, culture, and the problem of agency." *American Journal of Sociology* 99 (1994): 1411–54. A seminal article on the relationship between formal methods of social network analysis and important theoretical issues in the social sciences with respect to the concept of culture and the role of individual agency.

Ensminger, Jean. "Anthropology and the new institutionalism." *Journal of Institutional and Theoretical Economics* 154 (1998): 774–89. An example of the reception within economic anthropology during the 1990s of concepts and methods derived from the New Institutional Economics, a branch of formal economics that emerged in the 1970s and 1980s and has become influential in recent years in the study of ancient economies.

Faust, Avraham. *Israel's Ethnogenesis: Settlement, Interaction, Expansion and Resistance*. London: Equinox, 2006. An interesting discussion of the emergence of the Israelites in Canaan during the early Iron Age in relation to the archaeological evidence.

Faust, Avraham. *The Archaeology of Israelite Society in Iron Age II*. Winona Lake, IN: Eisenbrauns, 2012. A wide-ranging survey of various aspects of Israelite society and its development over the course of the Iron Age in light of the archaeological evidence with particular emphasis on changing patterns of settlement and styles of architecture.

Faust, Avraham. *Judah in the Neo-Babylonian Period: The Archaeology of Destruction*. Archaeology and Biblical Studies 18. Atlanta: Society of Biblical Literature, 2012. A detailed discussion of the situation in Judah after the Babylonian conquests and deportations that took place from 604 to 586 BCE and culminated in the destruction of Jerusalem and its temple, emphasizing the abundant archaeological evidence for a widespread depopulation of the region and economic decline in keeping with the biblical portrayal of this period.

Finkelstein, Israel. "[De]formation of the Israelite state: A rejoinder on methodology." *Near Eastern Archaeology* 68 (2005): 202–8. A critique of Faust's view of the changes in the Israelite settlement pattern during the Iron Age IIA.

Finkelstein, Israel. *The Forgotten Kingdom: The Archaeology and History of Northern Israel*. Ancient Near East Monographs 5. Atlanta: Society of Biblical Literature, 2013. A useful survey of the archaeology and history of the northern kingdom of Israel during the Iron Age II.

Finley, M. I. *The Ancient Economy*. 2nd edn. Berkeley: University of California Press, 1985. An influential treatment by a leading scholar of the structural features of the ancient Mediterranean economy during Greek and Roman times.

Frier, Bruce W. and Dennis P. Kehoe. "Law and economic institutions." In W. Scheidel, I. Morris, and R. Saller (eds), *The Cambridge Economic History of the Greco-Roman World* (pp. 113–43). Cambridge: Cambridge University Press, 2007. A discussion of the relevance to the study of the ancient Greco-Roman economy of the "transaction cost" approach of the New Institutional Economics, which leads to an emphasis on the role of legal institutions in shaping the economy.

Furubotn, Eirik G. and Rudolf Richter. *Institutions and Economic Theory: The Contribution of the New Institutional Economics*. 2nd edn. Ann Arbor: University of Michigan Press, 2005. A detailed introduction to the approach in economics called the New Institutional Economics, which has become influential in scholarly work on premodern and ancient economies.

Greif, Avner. *Institutions and the Path to the Modern Economy: Lessons from Medieval Trade*. Cambridge: Cambridge University Press, 2006. A stimulating example of the application of New Institutional Economics in a premodern setting, namely, the long-distance trade conducted by Jewish merchants in Muslim North Africa during the medieval period, drawing conclusions about the development of the Western European market economy from comparisons of the structure and dynamics of the North African trade to contemporaneous trading activities of Genoese Christian merchants in Europe.

Halperin, Rhoda H. *Cultural Economies Past and Present*. Texas Press Sourcebooks in Anthropology 18. Austin: University of Texas Press, 1994. A stimulating discussion of concepts in economic anthropology by an advocate of Karl Polanyi's "substantivist" approach.

Hirth, Kenneth G. and Joanne Pillsbury (eds). *Merchants, Markets, and Exchange in the Pre-Columbian World*. Washington, DC: Dumbarton Oaks, 2013. A recent collection of essays on a range of topics pertaining to the economy of the pre-Hispanic Aztec empire in Mexico and the quite different economy of the Inca empire in South America, with special attention to the role of market exchange in each case.

Jackson, Matthew O. *Social and Economic Networks*. Princeton: Princeton University Press, 2008. An excellent introduction to the use of social network analysis, which was originally developed by sociologists, within the discipline of economics.

King, Philip J. and Lawrence E. Stager. *Life in Biblical Israel*. Louisville, KY: Westminster John Knox, 2001. A thematic survey of many aspects of daily life in ancient Israel that draws upon a wide range of textual and archaeological evidence.

Knappett, Carl (ed.). *Network Analysis in Archaeology: New Approaches to Regional Interaction*. Oxford: Oxford University Press, 2013. A recent collection of papers that provide examples of the use of network analysis in archaeology – a formal mathematical method increasingly being adopted by archaeologists to help explain spatial and temporal patterns of archaeological finds with the aid of computational tools that make it easy to analyze and visualize networks of ancient social and economic relationships that are inferred from the physical finds.

Manning, J. G., and Ian Morris (eds). *The Ancient Economy: Evidence and Models*. Stanford, CA: Stanford University Press, 2005. A useful collection of essays that shows a range of viewpoints on ancient Mediterranean economies, with some attention to the later periods in the ancient Near East.

Mazar, Amihai. "The Iron Age chronology debate: Is the gap narrowing? Another viewpoint." *Near Eastern Archaeology 74* (2011): 105–11. A convenient summary of the debate about the chronology of the Iron Age kingdom of Israel with reference to the radiocarbon dating of archaeological strata at various sites.

Mische, Anne. "Relational sociology, culture, and agency." In J. Scott and P. J. Carrington (eds), *The SAGE Handbook of Social Network Analysis* (pp. 80–97). London: Sage, 2011. A historical survey of the development of the use of social network analysis within a branch of sociology that tries to avoid both excessive individualism and excessive holism (structuralism) by emphasizing the importance of networks of relationship among individual social actors without denying individual agency and without denying the dynamic character of those networks.

Moorey, P. R. S. *Ancient Mesopotamian Materials and Industries: The Archaeological Evidence*. Oxford: Clarendon, 1994. An encyclopedic guide to craft production in ancient Mesopotamia that is also relevant to the ancient Levant.

North, Douglass C. "Markets and other allocation systems in history: The challenge of Karl Polanyi." *Journal of European Economic History 6* (1977): 703–16. An essay by a pioneer of the New Institutional Economics that engages with the institutional approach of the economic historian Karl Polanyi.

Sahlins, Marshall. *Stone Age Economics*. New York: Aldine de Gruyter, 1972. An influential set of essays by a leading anthropologist that introduced the concept of the "domestic mode of production" characteristic of agrarian households.

Scheidel, Walter, Ian Morris, and Richard Saller (eds). *The Cambridge Economic History of the Greco-Roman World*. Cambridge: Cambridge University Press, 2007. A large collection of essays about many different aspects of the ancient Mediterranean economy in the Greco-Roman era with attention to theoretical issues as well as descriptive summaries of the state of knowledge on various topics.

Schloen, J. David. *The House of the Father as Fact and Symbol: Patrimonialism in Ugarit and the Ancient Near East*. Winona Lake, IN: Eisenbrauns, 2001. An examination of the interplay between the resonant political metaphor of the father's house in the ancient Levant and actual social experience within patriarchal households as revealed in the archaeological and textual evidence.

Scott, John. *Social Network Analysis*. 3rd edn. London: Sage, 2013. A useful and relatively brief introduction to the methods of social network analysis and its role in the interpretation of various kinds of social behavior.

Stager, Lawrence E. "Forging an identity: The emergence of ancient Israel." In M. D. Coogan (ed.), *The Oxford History of the Biblical World* (pp. 123–75). New York: Oxford University Press, 1998. A discussion of the emergence of ancient Israel as a distinct national group in light of the archaeological evidence concerning the founding of many new village settlements in the high-lands of Canaan during the early Iron Age (ca. 1200–1000 BCE) and in light of the evidence for the invasion and colonization of the coastal region by Philistines and other "Sea Peoples" in the same period.

Toffolo, Michael B., Eran Arie, Mario A. S. Martin, Elisabetta Boaretto, and Israel Finkelstein. "Absolute chronology of Megiddo, Israel, in the Late Bronze and Iron Ages: High-resolution radiocarbon dating." *Radiocarbon* 56 (2014): 221–44. A recent technical study of radiocarbon evidence from the important site of Megiddo in Israel which indicates that the transition from Iron Age I to Iron Age II (corresponding to the rise of the kingdom of David, in political terms) had occurred by the middle of the tenth century BCE, in keeping with Amihai Mazar's "Modified Conventional Chronology."

Wirth, Louis. "Urbanism as a way of life." *American Journal of Sociology* 44 (1938): 1–24. A classic sociological essay that defines the concept of "urbanism" in a functionalist manner that is debatable with respect to many periods and places in the ancient Near East, and with respect to Iron Age Israel and Judah, in particular.

D
Artistic Expression

CHAPTER 25

Verbal Art and Literary Sensibilities in Ancient Near Eastern Context

Edward L. Greenstein

The Hebrew Bible emerged within a rich cultural milieu as a very mature and complex body of literature. It comprises a large number of genres, and virtually each of these exhibits a high level of sophistication. In calling the biblical texts "literature," however, I am making a number of assumptions about what it was that constituted what we call the literary in ancient Israel and the ancient Near East. How can we, who are so remote in time and place, and so different in our cultural norms, know what counted as verbal art in the ancient world? What, if anything, distinguished a literary text from another kind of text? Is there any way we can discern what the ancients found significant and effective in the many thousands of written works that have survived?

Extrinsic Considerations of Literariness: Marking the Literary Text

No culture of the ancient Near East has left us a poetics describing its own notion of the literary. The earliest extended comments in this vein come from classical Greece – occasional remarks on poetry by Plato, and Aristotle's *Poetics* of tragic drama. We do have some oblique indications that scribes in the ancient Near East had the sense that certain types of text were distinctive. For example, Mesopotamians used a single terminology for poems that were sung, with or without accompaniment. The category of "song" (Sumerian *šir*, Akkadian *zamāru*) included all manner of sung text, from a work song to a religious hymn. Lamentations were classified according to the manner of their instrumental accompaniment (Sumerian *balag, ershemma* – each signifying a different type of drum; see further Rubio 63–8). Such designations, therefore, do not relate to the content or character of a text but to the manner of its performance (cf. Miller 104–13). The

Hebrew term *māšāl* designates a variety of forms, from a proverb to a lengthy dissertation, and would seem to denote any discourse of an artful nature.

What we refer to as poetry was written in Mesopotamia on tablets of a distinctive size and shape, and each line on the tablet ordinarily contained a single line of verse. The physical disposition of the tablet attests accordingly to a sense of genre as well as prosody. Some poetic Egyptian texts were punctuated with red dots, apparently to segment phrases for oral performance, or red lines to separate stanzas.

Works of literature also tended to be written, in Egypt as well as Mesopotamia, in a classical, sometimes archaizing, language, using a different linguistic register from writing in more mundane genres, such as legal documents and letters. Some Sumerian poetry, lamentations in particular, used what the natives termed "fine" (literally, "female") language. From the mid-second through the first millennium BCE, Akkadian literature, encompassing such diverse genres as myths, prayers, epics, incantations and royal annals, employed an evolved form of Old Babylonian and its "hymnal-epic" language that we call Standard Babylonian. In Egypt a highly literary prose was developed alongside more consistently versified texts. The Hebrew Bible, like the Ugaritic (north Canaanite) verse that preceded it, reserved certain words (e.g., *təhôm*, "the deep," and *māḥaṣ*, "to strike") and forms (e.g., the otiose suffixes *-i* and *-o*) for poetry, in contrast to prose.

Egyptian scribes appear to have distinguished texts meant for entertainment from texts meant for intellectual stimulation by calling the former "forgetfulness of the heart" and the latter "searching of the heart" (Morenz 229). They understood that "beautiful speech" is more valuable than precious stones, and that it can be lowbrow as well as highbrow, finding expression even in women working (ironically) at "the grinding stone" (Morenz 230). The biblical book of Proverbs observes that "pleasant speech increases persuasiveness" (16:21, New Revised Standard Version). The prophet Ezekiel is advised by the Deity that the people flocking to hear his oracles are not moved by their message – rather, they regard his rhetoric as entertainment: "You to them are like a bawdy song, sweet of voice and well played" (33:32). In comparing prophetic speech to music, the verse does not necessarily imply that the prophet sang his oracles; but it does make clear that some discourse was artful and that artful language was enjoyed like popular music. A more dramatic attestation of the appreciation of literary effect is found in the Egyptian "Tale of the eloquent peasant" (*AEL* 1:169–84, edited by Lichtheim). A poor but eloquent man is denied justice by a court for an extended period just in order to have him return time and again and reformulate his appeal in elegant poetic discourse. Literary judgment and rhetorical know-how were meant to be cultivated among the scribes. An experienced Egyptian sage, in what is known as "The satirical letter," puts down a young colleague by telling him that he does not know whether a text he has recited is good or bad (Parkinson 52).

It should be admitted that definitions of art and the literary are culturally conditioned. Literature is what people regard as such. One may therefore take a reader-oriented approach to the question: literature is what we read according to our expectations of the literary. We look for certain phenomena that we associate with the literary, and if we find them, we apply the conventions by which we have learned to read literature.

Nonetheless, there are certain features that both generalists and scholars of ancient Near Eastern literature associate with the literary (cf., e.g., Eagleton; Groneberg; Loprieno, "Defining Egyptian literature"). Literary language is understood to proliferate meaning through punning, double entendre, connotation, allusion and intertextuality, and figuration, by contrast to everyday, or "scientific," discourse that is meant to convey only one specific sense. When an ancient ruler is identified figuratively as the shepherd of his people (said, e.g., of Hammurapi and David), the idea is not to locate him within a herd but to evoke an entire metaphorical domain entailing a complex of relationships between leader and led, caregiver and caregiven. Moreover, in a literary work, style and form are expected to convey or reflect the content of its message – the medium, to some degree or other, is the message. The opening of the book of Genesis, for example, is formulated in a rhythm of doubled discourse that helps convey the sense that creation is conceived as the division of things into twos: heaven and earth, dark and light, above and below, water and land, and so forth.

Literature is also thought to be aesthetic and not practical in function. Although some (e.g., Robertson 13–15) maintain that literature has the practical purpose of practicing for life by encountering a variety of fictitious situations and considering how to cope and not to cope with them, literature is generally thought to have its own purpose. In the ancient Near East and in the Bible, however, texts virtually always serve some practical function. An incantation, for example, may be highly troped; but it will manifest a practical purpose, like ridding a house of snakes or protecting you against demons. A sort of prose poem, abundant in parallelism, verbal repetition, sorites and other tropes, known as "The heart grass," is incorporated into a Babylonian medical procedure (Reiner 94–100). A proverb, which nearly always involves wordplay and often figuration as well, is not merely amusing but didactic. A prayer, an omen, a prophecy, a law and even a letter are likely to display a clear rhetorical structure and such tropes as parallelism, assonance and metaphor or simile (e.g., "I am trapped like a bird in a cage," Amarna letter 74; Moran 142–75). Narratives, too, are told for a reason.

Is there any way of isolating literary expression from its practical purposes? Without making any firm distinctions, it may be suggested that the literary function of a text becomes more dominant the more the text is extracted from its original functional setting and is used, copied, and taught outside that setting. When the laws of Hammurapi, for example, become a model of writing featured in the scribal school, they become literature (see Bernard Levinson and Tina Sherman's essay in this volume). When the Hebrew Song of the Well, which has Bedouin Arab parallels, was embedded in the narrative of Israel's travels in the wilderness (Num. 21:17–18), what probably originated as a kind of spell to raise water magically from a spring became a literary document of people's experience.

Some texts appear to have originated as literature. The Epic of Gilgamesh, composed in Akkadian around 1700 BCE, incorporates earlier legends and seems to serve more than one didactic purpose (edifying the audience with regard to the dangers of hubris, the human fate to be mortal, the whimsy of the gods, civilization and its discontents, and more; cf. the essays included in Foster, *Epic*; Kirk 132–52). The Epic, which was recreated in Standard Babylonian toward the end of the second millennium, became a model of writing in cuneiform schools throughout the Near East, but it seems even from the outset to have been primarily a literary expression. The Egyptian Tale of Sinuhe, composed around 1900 BCE but copied and disseminated for centuries throughout Egypt, relates the story of a palace official who, at a time of struggle for the throne, flees north to Canaan, where he prospers (Quirke 58–70). He longs to return to Egypt for an honored burial, and is delighted to receive a royal invitation to do so. The narrative is composed of many genres, poetry and prose, and it may be taken to serve a number of functions – political (how gracious is the monarch), didactic (there's no place like home), nationalistic (local boy makes good abroad), theological (the gods direct our lives), and self-serving (the subject of the story has been justified for honor). Nevertheless, the work is also, if not fundamentally, literature, and it seems to have been treated as such by the scribal community.

Texts of a primarily functional nature are written for practical use. Such, for example, are omens, which are consulted by specialized priests for purposes of divination; and contracts, which document a transaction and defend against legal claims. Literary texts may have practical functions, but they transcend them. Some are specifically intended to be perpetuated for all time. The Babylonian creation myth *Enuma Elish*, for example, written in the latter part of the second millennium BCE, says in its conclusion that it was written down "and preserved for the future to hear" so that the god Marduk would always be adored (Foster, *Muses*, 484). A long poem about the destructive Mesopotamian god Erra, from around 700 BCE, is unusually attributed to an author, Kabti-ilani-Marduk, who claims to have learned it in a revelation. Near the end of the poem, blessings are invoked for the scribe who commits it to memory and the singer who performs it. It is further wished that the "poem last forever, let it endure till eternity" (Foster, *Muses*, 911). Certain biblical poems, like the Song of Moses (Deut. 32) and David's Lament over Saul and Jonathan (2 Sam. 1:17–27), are also designated for teaching to the people for perpetuation (see Deut. 31:19–22; 2 Sam. 1:18). These texts, and others like them, are removed from their original settings and given a literary purpose. The fact that the language of the Song of Moses has a clear impact on later biblical compositions (see, e.g., Greenstein, "Parody") is proof positive that it was regarded as a classic of ancient Hebrew literature.

Mesopotamian scribes sometimes alluded to their literary classics. A line from *Enuma Elish*, for example, is paraphrased in a Neo-Assyrian text dealing with the river ordeal. The Epic of Gilgamesh is cited in a royal text from the same period. A lament for the "dying god" Tammuz alludes to the episode of Gilgamesh and Enkidu vanquishing the monster Humbaba in the Cedar Forest. An extreme example is an exercise by student scribes, who composed a mock letter to have been written by Gilgamesh, ordering the materials he would need in order to construct a tomb for and statue of his slain friend Enkidu – a parody on tablet VII of the Epic (Foster, *Epic*, 167–8). An Egyptian "harper's song" from ca. 1400 BCE, taking a cynical view of life and death, attests in a roundabout way to the influence of classical authors by asking, where are they now? Everyone uses their language, chants the harper, but no one (except the scribe-singer!) remembers their names (*AEL* 1:194–7). Conversely, another Egyptian text from ca. 1200 BCE (Papyrus Chester Beatty IV) recalls the names of these and other sages of old, adducing their immortality as a reason to be a scribe (*AEL* 2:175–8). The product of the scribe lives forever. In claiming this, the reference is clearly not to mundane texts, like receipts and sundry letters, but to what we – and apparently they – regard as literature.

Intrinsic Considerations of Literariness: Repetition

A close inspection of the language, rhetoric, and forms of ancient Near Eastern texts suggests a single principle that can broadly distinguish those that might count as literary from those that might not. Poetry in general may be understood to be a particular construction of language (note the derivation from Greek *poiēsis*, "to make") that features all manner of repetition, from the sound to the word to the phrase to larger structures (Mazur). Rhyme, assonance, alliteration, verbal repetition, parallelism, repetitive structures – all are characteristic of the literary. Repetition is the fundamental, though not necessarily the exclusive, criterion for distinguishing the literary in the ancient Near East as well. It is the basis of verbal art in the Hebrew Bible and in the surrounding cultures.

Consider the proverbial saying in Ecclesiastes 7:1: *tôb šēm miššemen tôb, wǝyôm hammāwet miyyôm hiwwālǝdô*, "Good (better) is a (good) name than good oil; and the day of death than the day one is born." The verse comprises two parts; thematically, they form an analogy: just as a good name is better than good oil, so is the day of death better than the day of birth. Both propositions have a moral thrust, but the first is immediately intelligible, whereas the second demands reflection, and perhaps an effort to get one's head around the idea. There is a structural, syntactic parallelism between the two statements (X is better than Y), and there is a certain morphological parallelism within each statement. Each pronouncement features verbal repetition, and in the former the pun between "name" (pronounced *shem*) and "oil" (pronounced *shemen*) doubles the phenomenon. Somewhat less obvious, but equally palpable, is the sound repetition within each line (the labials *b* and *m* and the vowels *e* and *o*; the labials *w* and *m*, the glide *y* and the vowel *i*, and the vowel *o*). Both lines have a preponderance of labials and the kindred vowel *o* in common, enhancing their formal coherence.

The very same phenomena that we observe in the verse from Qohelet (Ecclesiastes) may be found, to some degree, in literary expression from the single line to the epic throughout most bodies of ancient Near Eastern literature. (An exception may be the Hittite corpus, in which parallelism – the premier feature of ancient poetry, from Egypt to Mesopotamia – is rare, even in such ordinarily poetic genres as prayer.)

Take, for example, the Sumerian wisdom saying: "Nothing is precious; life should be sweet" (*nig-nam nu-kal, zi ku-ku-dam*; Alster, *Wisdom*, 269; trans. Rubio 59). The two half-lines are balanced in prosodic weight, which is the chief feature of parallelism in the biblical world (cf. O'Connor and Greenstein). The first half-line alliterates; in the second the syllable *ku* repeats. There are various repetitions of sound between the two half-lines: *i, u, am*. As in parallelism in general, the repetitive patterns between the two lines bind the two propositions semantically, leading one to consider the relation in thought between nothing having value and life being sweet. Is it cause and effect – because nothing is precious, one should be sure to make life sweet? Or is it a double protest: nothing has value, but life is supposed to be sweet? Either way, it is the intensive repetition on various levels between the two propositions that elevates the assertions from the pedestrian to the poetic.

The following line, admittedly exceptional, from the Egyptian Tale of the Eloquent Peasant relates its message, "When good is good, good is truly good," in nearly mantra-like repetition: *nfr nfrt, nfr rf nfrt* (see Loprieno, "Pun," 17). The slight differences in morphology, with their syntactic implications, and the pun between *nfr*, "good," and *rf*, "truly," produce difference of meaning within a pattern of likeness. The Old Babylonian epic myth of the flood, *Atra-xasis* (I am using *x* to indicate the sound *kh*), opens with a most poignant pun: "When the gods were man" – *inūma ilū awīlum* (Lambert and Millard 42; cf. Geller: 66–8). The assonance is evident. The repetition of sound calls attention to the resemblance of the word for "god," *ilum*, to the word for "man," *awīlum*, which seems to contain it. The irony is manifest: in the beginning the lower-ranking gods had to perform all the menial tasks, such as food-growing and feeding, which humans, who were not yet created, would eventually perform. The reason for creating human beings is expressed in a nutshell in this line. The pun is played upon later in the epic (tablet I, lines 223–8; Lambert and Millard 58), when the divine being who was slaughtered by the assembly of gods in order to create the first human is called *We-ila*, a name that alludes to both the term for "god" and the term for "man."

A comparable irony is conveyed by the assonance that characterizes the following expression of a paradox from the Ugaritic Epic of Kirta (tablet 3, column 1; Greenstein, "Kirta," 31): *'ū 'ilūma tamūtūna*, "Do gods, after all, die?" The irony may be enhanced by the fact that the verb "they die" subsumes the probably cognate noun denoting a mortal – *mutu*.

The Babylonian poets relished the repetition of sound and the pun. An extreme example may be found in the fourth tablet of *Enuma Elish* (line 57; Lambert 88), which relates the combat between the youthful divine champion Marduk and the old monster-goddess Ti'awat: "In an armored garment of awe is he (Marduk) garbed" – *naxlapti apluxti pulxāti xalip*. The two stems, *x-l-p*, denoting "garb," and *p-l-x*, relating "fear," are intermixed in a chiastic (ABBA) sequence; and the awesome aspect of Marduk's appearance is underscored.

In this line two very similar verbal roots are each repeated. Such a phenomenon is not at all unusual. Consider the following line from *Enuma Elish* (IV 12; Lambert 86): "In the place their temples are, let your place be there" – **ashar** *sagīshunu lū kūn* **ashru**kka. In addition to the multiple instances of assonance within the line, the term for "place" repeats with only a slight morphological change. Compare this example from Psalm 25:9: "He guides (**yadrēk**) the **humble** in judgment / And teaches the **humble** his way (**darkô**)."

Verbal repetition such as this was long regarded by modern biblical scholars as either a blemish or a copyist's mistake. In Psalm 1, for example, which abounds in forms of repetition of every type, the reiteration of the word *tôrâ*, "instruction," in verse 2 and of the word *derek*, "way," in verse 6 were often dismissed as textual errors. Even Kraus, who does not dismiss them, asserts that the importance of the ideas the terms convey overrides "the rules of poetry" (113). In other words, even from his point of view, verbal repetition is a defect and not a norm. In fact, however, repetition of words is routine in ancient Near Eastern poetry and has been shown to be very extensive in the Hebrew Bible (see Yona).

Extending the Line: Incremental Development

Verbal repetition is not a throwback but can be a progressive move in ancient poeticizing. In the early Babylonian flood epic, *Atra-xasis* (tablet III, column 1, lines 20–1; Lambert and Millard 88), the god Enki, trying to help the man Atra-xasis save life from destruction by flood, says: "Wall (*igāru*), listen up to me! / Reed wall (*kikkishu*), observe all my words!" When this bit of dialog is incorporated into the flood narrative as retold in the Gilgamesh Epic (Neo-Assyrian version, tablet XI, lines 21–2; Parpola 109), it is expanded: "Reed wall, reed wall (*kikkish*), wall, wall (*igār*)! / Reed wall (*kikkishu*), listen! Wall (*igāru*), pay heed!" The vocatives are each doubled, and they serve as a preliminary to the imperatives formulated in parallelism: wall/reed wall – listen/pay heed! This pattern of expansion is the most basic form of parallelistic expression in ancient Near Eastern verse (cf. Berlin, "Shared rhetorical features").

Compare the pattern called "forked parallelism," in which the topic of the first line is expanded in the next two (or more) lines. An example from Old Kingdom Egypt: "I am the eye of Horus; / more powerful than men; / stronger than gods" (quoted in Abbott 48). A somewhat more elaborate example: "My body speaks, my lips repeat / the music of a priest of Hathor, / the music of millions and myriads" (Abbott 48). A single proposition is articulated in a doubled, echo-like form. Compare this relatively late verse from Psalms 1:3, describing the fate of the righteous: "He will be like a tree well-planted / on water courses; / which gives its fruit in its due-season, / and its foliage does not wither, / and all it/he does prospers." The first couplet, unusually enjambed, presents the general picture; the next three lines elaborate that picture, spelling out the consequences of being well-planted in a series of parallel phrases.

In Ugaritic epic, a similar pattern can be used to advance the plot; for example: "The gods offer blessing, they go. / The gods go home to their tents, / the circle of El to their dwellings" (Kirta tablet 2, column 3, lines 17–19; Greenstein, "Kirta," 26). The pace of the narrative is typically halting; progress is in steps. The structure is one of particularization: an initial, general situation is extended by elaborating some of its details. While some (e.g., Kugel 1–58) have rightly laid stress on the particulars that are added in the process of elaboration within parallelism (cf. Kugel's formula "A, and what's more, B"), one should not lose sight of the fundamental structure of ancient verse in general and, as we shall see, of narrative verse in particular. The poet or narrator does not move ahead without pausing, without reviewing what has been said, without reiterating in the same or different words, without repeating on some level or on several levels. One does not take a step or two forward without taking a step backward or marching in place.

Compare these examples of particularizing structures from the archaic Psalm 29, which describes the eastward movement of the Israelite deity in storm god persona from the Mediterranean to the mountains of Lebanon to the Syrian Desert: "Hark! YHWH is (now) over the sea: / The venerable God thunders; / YHWH is (now) over the Great Sea!" (verse 3); "Hark! YHWH shivers the cedars; / YHWH shivers the cedars of Lebanon" (verse 5); "Hark! YHWH causes the desert to writhe; / YHWH causes the Desert of Kadesh to writhe" (verse 8). A single proposition – the deity is now performing act A in place P – is formulated not in one but in two or three lines and expressed by means of a lexically and syntactically repetitive structure. Repetition, to reiterate, distinguishes the poetic from the prosaic.

The Canaanite poets developed a unique pattern within this general structure. What has been called the "staircase" or "step" pattern comprises a unit of at least three lines of usually three major words each (Greenstein, "One more step"). The first line of each unit pauses the message by superfluously specifying the name of the person being addressed (a vocative) or the subject of the sentence. The second line begins by repeating the first two words of the first line and concludes with a new element. The third line is in some way parallel to the second line. Consider first Psalms 93:3: "The currents raise up, O YHWH; / the currents raise up their voice; / the currents raise up their pounding." In this instance, the progression is patently incremental. The second line only completes the interrupted first sentence. The third line only slightly modifies the characterization of the crashing of the waves. It adds nothing, putting the conveyance of information on hold. The following example (Ps. 77:17) has a similar structure and halting effect. It differs only in varying the vocabulary of the third line: "They see you, the waters, O Elohim! / They see you, the waters, they whirl; / Yes, the sea-depths roil." In a way the graduated variations in verbal repetition from line to line can be viewed as the genesis of parallelism, which, in its most prevalent form, maintains a similar syntactic pattern while diversifying the vocabulary; for instance, "Even the tallest man cannot reach heaven, / Even the widest man cannot cover the earth" (Sumerian proverb found in Gilgamesh and Humbaba with parallels in Akkadian and Hebrew literature as well; see Greenspahn).

In the Hebrew Bible poetry never narrates at any length; narrative is conveyed only in prose. (There are telltale signs of a prebiblical Israelite epic narrative – see, e.g., Cassuto – but this thesis cannot be elaborated here; nevertheless, see below concerning epic formulae.) Accordingly, "staircase" patterns in the Bible are not narrative in nature – they pause the discourse in order to focus attention, usually on the deity or another subject to be praised. In Ugaritic epic, however, the "staircase" pattern can serve to advance the narrative – albeit only in stages. Take, for example, King Kirta's tragic realization that his entire family has been wiped out (tablet I, column 1, lines 21–2; Greenstein, "Kirta," 12): "He sees his progeny, does Kirta; / he sees his progeny ruined; / his dynasty utterly sundered." This realization triggers the rest of the plot. In the Epic of Aqhat, the goddess Anat prods the young hero to trade his formidable bow in exchange for immortality (tablet 1, column 6; cf. Parker 61): "As for life, O Aqhat the Hero; / ask for life, and I'll give you it; / for no-death, and I'll endow you with it." Aqhat expresses disdain for the goddess's ruse and prompts her murder of him.

Incremental progress in narrative and in poetry in general is characteristic of the earliest Mesopotamian literature, that of (non-Semitic) Sumer. The classic wisdom text, The

Instructions of Shuruppak, begins not untypically with lines that tend only to gradually
extend those that precede them:

> In those days, in those far remote days;
> In those nights, in those faraway nights;
> In those years, in those far remote years;
> In those days, the intelligent one, the one of elaborate words, the wise one,
>> Who lived in the country;
> The man from Shuruppak, the intelligent one, the one of elaborate words,
>> The wise one, who lived in the country;
> The man from Shuruppak, gave instructions to his son –
> The man from Shuruppak, the son of Ubartutu –
> Gave instructions to his son Ziusudra
>
> (Alster, *Wisdom*, 56–7).

The variations add specification, but change the subject only once in several lines. The
typicality of the slow pace of presentation in these lines sheds valuable light on the aesthetic sensibilities of the ancient Near East. Lingering over an action or image is the
norm, and it is served by the diverse techniques of repetition, verbal repetition in particular, that make for the literary.

The very same patterns of delay and incremental development characterize Sumerian narrative. The text known as Dumuzi's Dream begins thus:

> Woe filled his heart, and he went out into the desert –
>> The lad, woe filled his heart, and he went out into the desert –
> Dumuzi, woe filled his heart, and he went out into the desert …
>
> (Jacobsen 28).

All that has changed from line to line is the increasingly specific identification of the
protagonist: from "he" to "the lad" to "Dumuzi." We find a similar pattern of incremental
expansion in this brief narrative passage in the biblical Song of Deborah (Judg. 5:4–5):

> O YHWH, when you went out from Seir,
>> When you marched from the plains of Edom,
> The earth quaked, / and the heavens dripped (*nāṭāpû*),
>> And the clouds dripped water;
> The mountains flowed (*nāzəlû*; i.e., shook)
>> Before YHWH, the One of Sinai, / Before YHWH, God of Israel.

Note also the recurrent imagery: the heavens rain and the mountains flow.

Repetition serves the poet and/or narrator not only in adding line to line but also
in the structuration of scenes. Epic-style narrative is often plotted by the addition of
scene to scene in a similar if not identical format. A case in point is the Sumerian mini-
epic Enmerkar and Ensuxkeshdanna, featuring an increasingly embedded competition
between city and city, king and king, witch and wizard (Berlin, *Enmerkar*). Another

example is the humorous and folktale-like verse narrative from Mesopotamia known as "The poor man of Nippur." In addition to the types of verbal repetition and formulaic expression that characterize epic (see below), key episodes in the plot are constructed similarly (see Cooper; Jason).

Many epic narratives employ verbatim repetition in command-fulfillment sequences: a god or another superior figure issues directions, and a subordinate executes them. The language of the execution recapitulates, sometimes word for word, the language of the instructions. A quite extended example is found in the Ugaritic Epic of Kirta (tablet 1; Greenstein, "Kirta," 14–23), in which the god El appears to the hero in a dream and tells him how to obtain a new wife and family. The instructions run on for about 100 lines. When the king awakens, he immediately begins to fulfill the instructions, with hardly a deviation in wording for another 100 lines.

A similar type of lengthy repetition is the delivery of a message. A protagonist recites a message to a messenger. The messenger then delivers the message, usually word for word, no matter the length, to the recipient. In the Epic of Gilgamesh, the longest of ancient Near Eastern narratives, several speeches are repeated several times. In tablet II, for example, both Enkidu and the city elders warn Gilgamesh of the hazards of his plan to overtake the monster Humbaba. In tablet X, Gilgamesh explains in virtually identical language to three different characters how his friend Enkidu's death has worn him down. Other set pieces of dialog may also be repeated. The hero Danel's plea for a son in the Ugaritic Epic of Aqhat is heard by the god Baal. Baal conveys the request to the father god El in a lengthy speech that includes a rationale extending 12 lines that delineate what are known as "the duties of the son" (e.g., he will support him when he's drunk and maintain his funerary rites after he's dead; Parker 53–6). El agrees to the request and blesses Danel in absentia, repeating the list of duties of the son. El then sends the happy news to Danel, reciting the duties of the son again. Danel receives the report in joy, and he too recites the duties of the son.

Let us pause and take note of an important point regarding the type of aesthetic being described. Lengthy verbal repetitions such as these are a clear mark of oral performance. An audience enjoying an aural experience appreciates verbatim repetition, just as a group will join in singing the chorus of a song after every stanza. Repetition facilitates the anticipation and participation of the audience. When reading, however, lengthy repetition is less tolerated. Accordingly, in the biblical prose account of the "battle" of Jericho, the narration of how the Israelites, led by priests carrying the holy ark and blowing rams' horns, encircle the walls of the city is first given in full. The narration of the second day's march is abbreviated: "They circled the city on the second day one time, and they returned to the camp." The same activities were to have taken place for the next four days, but instead of repeating the details, the narrator only summarizes: "Thus did they do for six days" (Josh. 6:12–14). If this were epic, oriented to the ear, the description of the first day's events would have been repeated verbatim five more times. In the prose narrative, which was clearly produced for the consumption of the reader, repetition is largely eliminated.

Repetition, however, need not be sequential, with the repeated wording or pattern closely following the earlier one; it can also be diffuse or cyclic. Many if not most ancient Near Eastern literary texts are rife with topoi or set-pieces and formulas (see Susan

Niditch's essay in this volume). These provide coherence and structure, on the one hand, and the kind of familiarity the audience enjoys – as is evident in verbatim repetition – on the other. The Ugaritic epics, for example, abound in formulas of greater and lesser length, from a typological description in several lines of a person (or god) falling physically apart in fear or distress to the single line introducing direct discourse. Such formulae as "He raised his eyes and saw," "She raised her voice and cried," become part and parcel of biblical narrative in prose (see Polak, "Epic formulas"; Avishur). The simplest formula is the word-pair (the ancient Near Eastern equivalent of rhymed words), by which conventionally established pairs of words are distributed between the two lines of a couplet in parallelism; e.g., "She opens up his *throat* for <u>eating</u>, / his *gullet* for <u>dining</u>" (Kirta, tablet 3, column 6, lines 11–12; Greenstein, "Kirta," 40).

The Egyptian "Tale of the shipwrecked sailor" features a number of recurrent patterns and formulas (Quirke 71–6). The framework is an implied situation, in which the sailor, now a high official, accompanies a governor on an expedition to the South. When the expedition fails, the sailor consoles the governor by recounting a similar expedition in which he participated. The entire crew was shipwrecked by a storm, and he alone survived. He was borne by a wave unscathed to an island, where he was confronted by a serpent, which bore him unscathed to his home. After the sailor retells the story of the shipwreck to the serpent, the latter tells how he alone among a large brood of serpents survived a burning fallen star. Several passages repeat, some in nearly identical wording, and several sections begin or are punctuated by similar formulae. Although the composition is not an epic poem, it features more than occasional parallelisms and is organized by various structures of repetition, from plot to description.

Full-scale epics (of a thousand lines or more) are, like the lines of Sumerian verse cited above, developed incrementally – scene by scene, episode by episode. Although episodes are rarely clones of those that precede, many scenes mirror earlier ones in structure and theme, and sometimes even in wording. In the Ugaritic Epic of Kirta, for example, when King Pabuli asks Kirta what he is after (silver, gold, horses, etc.) in laying siege to his town, he unknowingly echoes the very same questions that the god El had asked Kirta, when he was sobbing in bed (Greenstein, "Kirta," 13, 21–2).

Repetition in wording and structure can be very intensive, especially in the opening or at other key points of a text. Consider, for example, these opening lines of *Enuma Elish* (lines 1–2, 6–7; Lambert 50):

> <u>enuma</u> elish <u>la</u> nabu shamamu
> shaplish ammatum <u>shuma</u> la <u>zakrat</u> …
> <u>enuma</u> ilani <u>la</u> shupu manama
> <u>shuma</u> <u>la</u> <u>zukkuru</u> <u>shimatu</u> <u>la</u> <u>shimu</u>

> (When on high was not named the sky
> Below the earth its name was not said …
> When the gods had not emerged, not one
> Their name was not said, their fate was not fated.)

I have underlined those words that repeat (sometimes with a morphological difference), but it will be noted that nearly all the words display alliteration and assonance with other words in their vicinity. There is parallelism between the lines in each couplet, and repetition of structure from the former couplet to the latter one.

Intensive repetition of a somewhat different kind characterizes the opening of the book of Genesis (vv. 1–5). Virtually every word is echoed through rhyme, assonance, or alliteration in the succeeding phrase or sentence, and clause is linked to clause through verbal concatenation. Some examples, here transliterated phonetically, are: *bereishit bara'* ("In the beginning of creating"), *ha'arets we-ha'arets* ("the earth" – "and the earth"), *tohu – tehom* ("chaos" – "the deep"), *ruah – merahepet* ("wind/spirit" – "hovers"). There are more and subtler examples as well, for instance, *'elohim – shamayim* ("God" – "heavens"), *hayetah – tohu* ("was" – "chaos"). The echoes of sound, which are not at all atypical of ancient Near Eastern literature, make clear, as did the extent of lengthy verbatim repetition that was discussed above, that this verbal art is directed at the ear – it is first and foremost an oral art.

The Power of the Word and the Significance of the Pun

There is much more to it than that, however. Repetition is not only a circumstance of the oral-aural mode of communication. The repetition of words and of sounds, which creates verbal repetition through punning, rests on an ancient belief in the power of the word (cf. Schorch). Words have a mystique. In contrast to the modern notion that the relationship between a word and the concept it represents is arbitrary or conventional (Saussure), in ancient Near Eastern thought there is an inherent nexus between the sound of an utterance and its meaning. Perhaps for that reason the same term can denote both "vocable" and a "thing" or "matter" (e.g., Akkadian *awatu*; Hebrew *dābār*), and a term for "name" can denote an "image" as well (e.g., Akkadian *zikru*). The pronouncement of certain words, as in a magic spell, blessing, curse, prophecy or oath, is performative – it has a physical or metaphysical effect. The familiar magical formula *abracadabra* is apparently derived from Aramaic, in which it means something like, "I create (*'ebra'*) as I speak (*kə-dibra'*)" – the utterance produces a substantive result. Language, when intently articulated, performs.

By virtue of the link between word and object, words having similar sounds were often understood to have a semantic connection between them. A pun is therefore not an incidental resemblance but a meaningful association. The widespread use of puns in ancient Near Eastern texts of many types (see especially Noegel, "On puns") does not only produce irony or humor, as in modern literature (compare Job 7:6, in which the swiftly running – *qallū* – days of one's life run out – *wa-yikəlū* – without hope), but forges essential linkages between those things or concepts that the similar terms designate. Take, for example, the creation of the human *awīlu(m)* from the divine being *We-ila* in the Babylonian myth *Atra-xasis* cited above (tablet 1, lines 223–8). This *We-ila* is said to have possessed *tēmu(m)*, "intelligence." When he is slaughtered by the gods and his flesh and blood mixed with the clay from which the human body is formed, the human is invested with a living "spirit" – *etemmu(m)*, a meaningful pun on *We-ila*'s "intelligence."

The intrinsic relationship between a word and the thing that it names is best represented in the literary interpretation of, or simply punning on, a personal name. In virtually every culture of the ancient Near East we find serious paronomasia. This type of punning finds explicit expression in the name interpretation of David's nemesis Nabal. The latter's wife Abigail tries to excuse her rude husband as follows: "Pray, let my lord not pay heed to this feckless man, to Nabal; for he is just like his name: Nabal is his name, and he is a rogue (*nəbālâ*)" (1 Sam. 25:25). Job, feeling assaulted by the deity, finds new significance in his name – *'Iyyôb*. Confronting God, Job asks: "Why do you hide your face, and think of me as your enemy (*'ôyēb*)?" (Job 13:24). Only in light of his tragedy has Job painfully come to realize the implicit meaning of his name.

Many ancient heroes bear names that are appropriate to their character or fate. The Egyptian Sinuhe's name suggests "son of the sycamore tree" (Loprieno, "Pun," 11), which was sacred to the goddess Hathor, who welcomed the dead. It will be recalled that Sinuhe returns to Egypt from a long period abroad in order to be buried with honor at home. The Babylonian flood hero is Atra-xasis, whose name means "much in knowing"; to him was revealed the secret of the deluge, from which he saved the remnants of humanity. The Sumerian flood hero was called Ziusudra, "who sought life," and he indeed found life after the deluge. The Akkadian name of the Standard Babylonian flood hero, Uta-napishti(m), has a similar meaning. In *Enuma Elish* the god Marduk proves to be the champion of the pantheon. Toward the end of the composition the assembly of gods recite and interpret the 50 names of Marduk, giving them derivations in both Sumerian (e.g., Marduk = *Marutakku* = *amar utuk*, "buck of the sun") and Akkadian (e.g., *lu tukul mati*, "truly the stronghold of the land"; on Marduk's names, see also Mark Smith's essay in this volume).

Because puns can manifest essences, they reveal native insight and understanding. Thus, in ancient Egypt incense (*sntr*) is analyzed as "the scent of the god" (*stj-ntr*). The human condition could be explained by observing that "man" (*rmt*) was made from the "tears" (*rmj.t*) of the gods. A pun can link the literal and the figurative. It is said in a Ramesside poem concerning the king's chariot: "The weapons (*hmyt*) of your chariot are the steering oars (*hmyt*) behind the foreign land" (Loprieno, "Pun," 19). The pun has explanatory power. Accordingly, an Old Babylonian letter remarks that someone who is not trusted (*la taklu*) in his own locality will only be disrespected (*qallu*) in the palace (see Wasserman 165). A pun can provide sensible advice, as in this Sumerian proverb: "Build (*du*) like [a lord], walk (*du*) like a slave. / Build (*du*) like a slave, walk (*du*) like a lord" (Alster, *Proverbs*, 71).

The pun accounts for cause and effect. It is grounded in what James G. Frazer has called, in connection with sympathetic magic, the "law of similarity" – to produce a certain effect, one performs an act that resembles it (12–13; cf. Greaves). For that reason puns are commonly employed in prophecies, incantations, divination and dream interpretation (cf. Greenstein, "Hermeneutics"; Noegel, "On puns"). Observe the wordplays in this Old Babylonian incantation: "The dog (*kalbum*) – may he die (*limut-ma*), the man (*awilum*) – may he live (*liblut-ma*)" (see Wasserman 163). The death of the dog makes for the healing of the human. A thirteenth-century BCE Egyptian guide to dream interpretation predicts: If one sees in one's dream the capture (*ham*) of birds, people will take away (*nehem*) one's property. The Neo-Assyrian dream-book employs the same method: If one goes to the town of Aran, one's punishment (*aran-shu*) will be revoked. Or: If you eat raven (*aribu*), income will come in (*irbi irrub*) for you. Centuries later in the

Babylonian Talmud (*Berakot* 56b) we encounter the same interpretive practice (in phonetic transliteration): If one sees a cat in one's dream in a place where they pronounce
the word for "cat" *shunra*, one will enjoy lovely song (*shira na'ah*); but in a place where
they pronounce it *shinra*, one will suffer a change for the worse (*shinnui ra'*) (these references in Greenstein, "Hermeneutics").

The last example is of particular interest because the pun within it is bilingual: the
word for "cat" in either pronunciation is Aramaic, while the interpretations are Hebrew.
Connections between terms and sounds need not stop at the border between languages.
An Egyptian expression for "on earth" is "on the back of the god Geb." Why specifically,
the back of this land god? There is a pun between the name of the Egyptian god and
the West Semitic word for back – *gab* (Loprieno, "Pun," 10). The poet of the biblical
Song at the Sea (Exod. 15) creates a brilliant irony by producing a bilingual pun. The
singer opens by relating how the deity has "cast down" – *rāmâ* (Aramaic) – the Egyptian
enemy into the sea. He then presents in counterpoint his own exaltation (literally "elevation" in Hebrew) of the deity – *'ārōməmenhû* (v. 2). God is high, the enemy has been
brought low.

A remarkable poem that is essentially an amusing exercise in bilingual punning is
the early second-millennium Sumerian "Hymn to the hoe" (see Michalowski). The poet
constructs the poem out of one permutation after the other of the Sumerian word for
hoe (*al*). Typical are the following two lines (Michalowski 198):

> As for the heavens, the wren (*altigru*) is the divine (*ilum*) bird;
> As for the earth, it is the hoe (*al*), it is a beast (Sumerian *ur* has the Akkadian equivalent
> *kalbum* "dog") in the canebrake, a lion (*labbum*) in the thicket.

The Sumerian word for "wren" contains the syllable *al*; the term "divine" in Akkadian
(*il*) puns on *al*; the Sumerian word translated "beast" suggests the Akkadian word for
"dog" (*kalbum*), which includes the phonological sequence *al* – and it further suggests the
Sumerian word for 'dragon, lion' (*ushumgal*), which ends in the phonological sequence
al; and the word for 'lion' in Akkadian (*labbum*) contains the sequence *al* but backwards.
The poem may not be sublime, but it is an intricately crafted literary text.

Literary Art in Writing

It is important to note that some of the puns embedded in the "Hymn to the hoe" can
only be discerned visually – in recognizing a graphic pun between one cuneiform sign
and another. The component "man" in the word for "manhood" in line 97, for example,
is *ngurush*, which does not at first seem to contain the syllable *al*. The sign for *ngurush*
can also have the value *kal*, however, and therein one finds the sought-after syllable. The
implication is plain: although some, and perhaps most, ancient Near Eastern literature
was attuned to an aural reception, some texts can be fully appreciated only when read.
Certain texts and the literary tropes within them depend on being read in written form.
The most extraordinary example comes from an Egyptian text from about 1400 BCE in

which a blank space is left preceding a logogram (word-sign) having the value *'ntjw*. The text is written on a palette made of red wood, the word for which is *mrj*. The reader (a scribe) is expected to put the blank red space and the logogram together, make a pun, and produce the phrase *mrj 'ntjw* – "who loves myrrh" (Loprieno, "Pun," 4–5).

Another manifestly visual trope is the acrostic, in which the first letters or words of each successive line form a meaningful pattern when read as a series. In the Hebrew Bible the acrostic structure typically copies the alphabet, as each verse or half-verse begins with a succeeding letter: *aleph* …, *bet* …, *gimel* …, etc. Occasionally the name of the letter will be played upon by one of the words in the line; for example, "Come (*ləkû* begins with *lamed*), children, hearken to me; / the fear of YHWH I will teach you (*'ălammed*kem*; Ps. 34:12). The pattern can be extended by multiplying the number of lines beginning with the same letter; thus, Lamentations 3 uses the same letter of the alphabet three times in a row, and Psalm 119 does the same thing in batches of eight lines. A far more sophisticated acrostic is found in the early first-millennium Babylonian poem we call "The Babylonian theodicy" (Foster, *Muses*, 914–22) It comprises 27 stanzas of 11 lines each, and each line in the same stanza begins with the same cuneiform sign. When the 27 signs are combined in sequence they spell out a sentence identifying the composer of the poem: "I, Saggil-kinam-ubbib, am a devotee of god and king."

A special type of literary art that was oriented to the eye is the scribal joke (Foster, "Humor," 82–3; Civil 34–5). A cuneiform scribe might write a word in a surprising or punning manner for the amusement of his colleagues.

Such visual features as these make it clear that while most verbal art in the ancient Near East, including biblical Israel, was oral-aural in nature, some was intended for reading as well. Although most texts that were committed to writing were meant to be read out loud or declaimed (Carr), oral and written works coexisted for centuries and had an impact on one another (Niditch; Miller). Still, written texts, typically prose, assumed rhetorical qualities, such as embedded clauses and chains of noun-phrases (see Polak, "Oral"), that demanded sensibilities reaching beyond those developed for the hearing of literature alone.

In prose narrative, for example, the action is advanced more steadily, from clause to clause, eschewing the tropes of verbal repetition and parallelism that are so characteristic of ancient verse. Consider, for example, this excerpt from the Hittite prose narrative of Appu: "Appu's wife bore a son. The nurse lifted the boy and placed him on Appu's knees. Appu began to amuse the boy and to clean (?) him off. He put a fitting name upon him" (Hoffner 64). In the roughly contemporary Ugaritic Epic of Kirta, formulated in verse, virtually every new action would be restated; for example, "She conceives and bears him a son; / She conceives and bears to him two sons" (Greenstein, "Kirta," 26). Were this prose, the rhetoric would be economized: "She conceived and bore him two sons." To delve fully into this development, however, requires a discussion of its own.

I hope to have shown that in texts of many types in the ancient Near East words were appreciated for their rhetorical, if not magical, power. Words were combined artfully and effectively, and compositions in speech and writing, using repetition on every level, were crafted according to aesthetic, and not merely pragmatic, principles.

Bibliography

Abbott, Richard. "Forked parallelism in Egyptian, Ugaritic and Hebrew poetry." *Tyndale Bulletin* 62 (2001): 41–64. Illustrates a particular verse pattern.

Alster, Bendt. *Proverbs of Ancient Sumer: The World's Earliest Proverb Collections*. 2 vols. Bethesda, MD: CDL Press, 1997. Now standard edition.

Alster, Bendt. *Wisdom of Ancient Sumer*. Bethesda, MD: CDL Press, 2005. Now standard edition.

Avishur, Yitzhak. "Ten epic formulae common to the Ugaritic epics and the Genesis narratives." In Avishur, *Studies in Biblical Narrative* (pp. 199–223). Tel Aviv-Jaffa: Archaeological Center, 1999. Comparison of biblical and Ugaritic texts suggestive of the existence of lost Israelite epic.

Berlin, Adele. "Shared rhetorical features in biblical and Sumerian literature." *Journal of the Ancient Near Eastern Society* 10 (1978): 35–42. Illustrates the phenomena of expansion and particularization.

Berlin, Adele. *Enmerkar and Ensuḫkešdanna: A Sumerian Narrative Poem*. Philadelphia: University Museum, 1979. Text edition with literary commentary.

Carr, David M. *Writing on the Tablet of the Heart: Origins of Scripture and Literature*. Oxford: Oxford University Press, 2005. Important study of scribal purpose in all ancient Near Eastern cultures.

Cassuto, Umberto. "The Israelite epic." In Cassuto, *Biblical and Oriental Studies*, vol. 2, trans. Israel Abrahams (pp. 69–109). Jerusalem: Magnes Press, 1975. Reconstructs some early Israelite epic myth.

Civil, Miguel. "Sumerian riddles: A corpus." *Aula Orientalis* 5 (1987): 17–37. Standard edition and analysis.

Cooper, J. S. "Structure, humor, and satire in the Poor Man of Nippur." *Journal of Cuneiform Studies* 27 (1975): 163–74. Intratextual study of Akkadian satire on official corruption.

Eagleton, Terry. "What is literature? (1)." In Eagleton, *The Event of Literature* (pp. 19–58). New Haven: Yale University Press, 2012. A contemporary discussion of literariness.

Ehrlich, Carl (ed.). *From an Antique Land: An Introduction to Ancient Near Eastern Literature*. Lanham, MD: Rowman & Littlefield, 2011. Up-to-date surveys of literature from each ancient Near Eastern culture.

Enmarch, Roland and Verena M. Lepper with Eleanor Robson (eds). *Ancient Egyptian Literature: Theory and Practice*. Oxford: Oxford University Press, 2013. Important discussions of issues in the study of ancient Egyptian literature.

Foster, Benjamin R. "Humor and cuneiform literature." *Journal of the Ancient Near Eastern Society* 6(1974): 69–85. Detailed survey of the topic.

Foster, Benjamin R. *The Epic of Gilgamesh: A New Translation, Analogues, Criticism*. New York: Norton, 2001. The epic and kindred ancient texts translated with introductions and discussions.

Foster, Benjamin R. *Before the Muses: An Anthology of Akkadian Literature*. 3rd edn. Bethesda, MD: CDL Press, 2005. A broad collection of Akkadian literature in English translation, with notes for specialists as well.

Frazer, James G. *The Golden Bough: A Study in Magic and Religion*. Abridged edn. New York: Macmillan, 1958. A classic study of ancient folklore.

Geller, Stephen A. "Some sound and word plays in the first tablet of the Old Babylonian *Atraḫasīs* epic." In Barry Walfish (ed.), *The Frank Talmage Memorial Volume*, vol. 1 (pp. 63–70). Haifa: Haifa University Press, 1993. A sensitive study.

Greaves, Sheldon W. "Ominous homophony and portentous puns in Akkadian omens." In Scott B. Noegel (ed.), *Puns and Pundits: Word Play in the Hebrew Bible and Ancient Near Eastern Literature* (pp. 103–13). Bethesda, MD: CDL Press, 2000. Important treatment of the power of the word.

Greenspahn, Frederick E. "A Mesopotamian proverb and its biblical reverberations." *Journal of the American Oriental Society* 114 (1994): 33–8. Illustrates the diffusion of a conventional motif.

Greenstein, Edward L. "One more step on the staircase." *Ugarit-Forschungen* 9 (1977): 77–86. Study of a distinctive Canaanite verse pattern.

Greenstein, Edward L. "Kirta." In Simon B. Parker (ed.), *Ugaritic Narrative Poetry* (pp. 9–48). Atlanta: Scholars Press, 1997. Readable edition and translation of an Ugaritic epic.

Greenstein, Edward L. "Hermeneutics in the biblical world: From dream interpretation to textual exegesis." *Mo'ed* 13 (*Festschrift for Joseph Roth-Rotem*; Beit Berl College, Israel) (2003): 65–78 [in Hebrew]. A broad treatment of the place of wordplay and symbolism in ancient interpretation.

Greenstein, Edward L. "Parody as a challenge to tradition: The use of Deuteronomy 32 in the Book of Job." In Katharine Dell and Will Kynes (eds), *Reading Job Intertextually* (pp. 66–78). New York: Bloomsbury T&T Clark, 2013. Illustrates the intertextual use of a classic Hebrew poem in the book of Job.

Groneberg, Brigitte. "Towards a definition of literariness as applied to Akkadian literature." In Marianna E. Vogelzang and Herman J. J. Vanstiphout (eds), *Mesopotamian Poetic Language: Sumerian and Akkadian* (pp. 59–84). Leiden: Brill, 1996. A helpful perspective on Akkadian poetics.

Hoffner, Harry A., Jr. *Hittite Myths*. Atlanta: Scholars Press, 1990. Readable translations of the narrative Hittite texts.

Jacobsen, Thorkild. *The Harps That Once … : Sumerian Poetry in Translation*. New Haven: Yale University Press, 1987. Readable translations of numerous Sumerian poems.

Jason, Heda. "The Poor Man of Nippur: An ethnopoetic analysis." *Journal of Cuneiform Studies* 31 (1979): 189–215. Analysis of an Akkadian narrative as a folktale.

Kirk, G. S. *Myth: Its Meaning and Functions in Ancient and Other Cultures*. Cambridge: Cambridge University Press, 1973. An illuminating structural analysis of some Akkadian narrative poems.

Kraus, Hans-Joachim. *Psalms 1–59: A Commentary*, trans. Hilton C. Oswald. Minneapolis: Augsburg, 1988. A standard modern biblical commentary.

Kugel, James L. *The Idea of Biblical Poetry: Parallelism and Its History*. New Haven: Yale University Press, 1981. A fresh study of biblical parallelism.

Lambert, W. G. *Babylonian Creation Myths*. Winona Lake, IN: Eisenbrauns, 2013. The new standard edition of *Enuma Elish* and other Babylonian creation texts.

Lambert, W. G. and A. R. Millard. *Atra-ḫasīs: The Babylonian Story of the Flood*. Oxford: Clarendon, 1969. The standard edition of the Old Babylonian flood myth, including the creation of humanity.

Lichtheim, Miriam (ed.). *Ancient Egyptian Literature*. Vol. 1: *The Old and Middle Kingdoms*. Berkeley: University of California Press, 1973. Vol. 2: *The New Kingdom*. Berkeley: University of California Press, 1976. A standard translation of Egyptian literature. Abbreviated as *AEL*.

Loprieno, Antonio. "Defining Egyptian literature: Ancient texts and modern theories." In Antonio Loprieno (ed.), *Ancient Egyptian Literature: History and Forms* (pp. 39–58). Leiden: Brill, 1996. A helpful perspective on what counts as literature in the ancient world.

Loprieno, Antonio. "Pun and word play in ancient Egyptian." In Scott B. Noegel (ed.), *Puns and Pundits: Word Play in the Hebrew Bible and Ancient Near Eastern Literature* (pp. 3–20). Bethesda, MD: CDL Press, 2000. A finely illustrated discussion.

Mazur, Krystyna. "Repetition." In Roland Greene (ed.), *The Princeton Encyclopedia of Poetry and Poetics*, 4th edn (pp. 1168–71). Princeton: Princeton University Press, 2012. A standard and current account of repetitive forms in poetry in general.

Michalowski, Piotr. "Where's AL? Humor and poetics in the Hymn to the Hoe." In Alexandra Kleinerman and Jack M. Sasson (eds), *Why Should Someone Who Knows Something Conceal It? Cuneiform Studies in Honor of David I. Owen on His Seventieth Birthday* (pp. 195–200). Bethesda, MD: CDL, 2010. An illuminating study of a remarkable literary text.

Miller, Robert D., II. *Oral Tradition in Ancient Israel*. Eugene, OR: Cascade, 2011. Up-to-date treatment of the oral aspects of biblical literature.

Moran, William. *The Amarna Letters*. Baltimore: Johns Hopkins University Press, 1992. Standard translation of an important group of letters written mostly from Syria and Canaan to Egypt in the fourteenth century BCE.

Morenz, Ludwig D. "Egyptian life, by and with literary texts." In Roland Enmarch and Verena M. Lepper with Eleanor Robson (eds), *Ancient Egyptian Literature: Theory and Practice* (pp. 227–50). Oxford: Oxford University Press, 2013. Important study of the social contexts of Egyptian literature.

Niditch, Susan. *Oral World and Written Word*. Louisville, KY: Westminster John Knox, 1996. On the character of biblical writing within a context of oral performance and transmission.

Noegel, Scott B. (ed.). *Puns and Pundits: Word Play in the Hebrew Bible and Ancient Near Eastern Literature*. Bethesda, MD: CDL Press, 2000. Discussions of wordplay and its significance throughout the ancient Near East.

Noegel, Scott B. "On puns and divination: Egyptian dream exegesis from a comparative perspective." In K. Szpakowska (ed.), *Through a Glass Darkly: Magic, Dreams, and Prophecy in Ancient Egypt* (pp. 95–119). Swansea: Classical Press of Wales, 2006. On the connection between wordplay, divination, and dream interpretation in the ancient world.

O'Connor, M. P. and Edward L. Greenstein. "Parallelism." In Roland Greene (ed.). *The Princeton Encyclopedia of Poetry and Poetics*, 4th edn (pp. 997–9). Princeton: Princeton University Press, 2012. A current discussion of an important verse form.

Parker, Simon B. "Aqhat." In Simon B. Parker (ed.), *Ugaritic Narrative Poetry* (pp. 49–80). Atlanta: Scholars Press, 1997. A readable edition and translation of an Ugaritic epic.

Parkinson, R. B. *Poetry and Culture in Middle Kingdom Egypt: A Dark Side to Perfection*. London: Equinox, 2002. Important commentary on ancient Egyptian literature in its social settings.

Parpola, Simo. *The Standard Babylonian Epic of Gilgamesh*. University of Helsinki: Neo-Assyrian Text Corpus Project, 1997. An accessible edition of the greatest Mesopotamian epic.

Polak, Frank H. "Epic formulas in biblical narrative: Frequency and distribution." In R. F. Poswick et al. (eds), *Les actes du second colloque internationale Bible et informatique …* (pp. 435–88). Paris: Champion-Slatkine, 1989. Illustrates the extent to which ancient Canaanite formulas were employed in biblical prose.

Polak, Frank H. "The oral and the written: Syntax, stylistics and the development of biblical prose narrative." *Journal of the Ancient Near Eastern Society* 26 (1998): 59–105. Important criteria for distinguishing oral and written styles in biblical prose.

Quirke, Stephen. *Egyptian Literature 1800 BC: Questions and Readings*. London: Golden House, 2004. Bilingual presentation of important Egyptian literary texts.

Reiner, Erica. *Your Thwarts in Pieces, Your Mooring Rope Cut: Poetry from Babylonia and Assyria*. Ann Arbor: University of Michigan, 1985. Literary studies of select Akkadian poems.

Robertson, David. *The Old Testament and the Literary Critic*. Philadelphia: Fortress, 1977. Aspects of biblical literature from a comparative literary perspective.

Rubio, Gonzalo. "Sumerian literature." In Carl Ehrlich (ed.), *From an Antique Land: An Introduction to Ancient Near Eastern Literature* (pp. 11–75). Lanham, MD: Rowman & Littlefield, 2011. An in-depth survey of Sumerian literature and its art.

Saussure, Ferdinand de. *Course in General Linguistics*, ed. Charles Bally and Albert Sechehaye with Albert Riedlinger, trans. Wade Baskin. New York: McGraw-Hill, 1966. Classic treatment of language and its study.

Schorch, Stefan. "Between science and magic: The function and roots of paronomasia." In Scott B. Noegel (ed.), *Puns and Pundits: Word Play in the Hebrew Bible and Ancient Near Eastern Literature* (pp. 205–22). Bethesda, MD: CDL Press, 2000. On the significance of the spoken word in the ancient world.

Wasserman, Nathan. *Style and Form in Old Babylonian Literary Texts*. Leiden: Brill, 2003. Some chapters treat aspects of Babylonian poetics.

Yona, Shamir. *The Many Faces of Repetition: Basic Patterns of Repetition in Construct-State Expressions in Biblical, Post-Biblical, and Ancient Near Eastern Rhetoric*. Beer-Sheva: Ben-Gurion University Press, 2013 [Hebrew]. Illustrates the extent of verbal repetition in biblical literature.

CHAPTER 26

The Flowering of Literature in the Persian Period
The Writings / Ketuvim

Tamara Cohn Eskenazi

The Persian period saw a flowering of new texts and editorial activities that decisively shaped the Hebrew Bible/Old Testament. This chapter focuses on those books in the Hebrew Bible most readily recognized as stemming from this era. These books are now grouped together in the Hebrew Bible in a section known as "Writings" or "Ketuvim."

The Persian period (also known as the Achaemenid period) extended from 539 BCE, when King Cyrus of Persia conquered Babylon, to 333 BCE, when Alexander of Macedon toppled the Persian empire. King Cyrus had ushered in the largest empire the world had ever known at that time. Within 20 years, it extended from India to Turkey to Egypt, encompassing the entire Middle East and beyond. This empire became famous for its wealth and opulence. Its glorious remains are evident in today's Iran, with the towering columns and magnificent palaces in cities such as Persepolis, as well as from the surviving artifacts in the great museums throughout the world.

The province of Judah, from which the Bible emerged, lay at first at the western periphery of the Persian empire. The Persian conquest of Egypt in 525 BCE repositioned Judah strategically as it became part of the land bridge to Egypt, one of the empire's most lucrative and challenging territories. However, it took Judah many decades to begin to recover from the devastation caused by the Babylonian conquest of 587 BCE, when the Babylonians destroyed Jerusalem, burnt its temple, killed most of the royal house, and carted the rest to exile in Babylon and beyond, together with a significant portion of the population (see David Schloen's essay in this volume). This devastation, and the Babylonian exile that followed, continued as the central crisis in biblical history. It forced new questions about how to survive as a people when the institutions and geography that defined the nation – the king, the temple, and the land – were gone. Under the Persian empire, the survivors were able to rebuild Jerusalem and their life in Judah. According

The Wiley Blackwell Companion to Ancient Israel, First Edition. Edited by Susan Niditch.
© 2016 John Wiley & Sons, Ltd. Published 2016 by John Wiley & Sons, Ltd.

to the Bible (Ezra 1–6; 2 Chr. 36:20–23), King Cyrus of Persia permitted the Judeans to return to their land and to rebuild their temple. The Hebrew Bible or Old Testament as we know it is the product of this revival and reconstruction of Jewish life in the land. It is both a result and the strategy of such a survival.

Archaeology confirms that the province of Judah, or Yehud in the Persian period, remained in a dire economic condition during most of the Persian period as a result of the earlier Babylonian destruction (see, e.g., Edelman; Faust; Lipschits; see also Charles Carter's essay in this volume). It was very poor and sparsely populated, no doubt including peoples from the neighboring regions who moved into the vacuum created by war and exile. It also included survivors who were spared exile, as well as those who undertook the task of returning. Others remained scattered in foreign lands. In addition to expected economic and social challenges to individual survival, there was also the question of survival as a cohesive community. Living as a minority even in their homeland in a "multicultural setting" among larger and stronger nations, surviving Judeans needed to forge and sustain a shared identity so that they would not simply disappear as did other peoples. The issues were even more acutely present for those in Diaspora (Judeans scattered throughout the Persian empire, from Persia and Babylonia in the east, to Egypt in the west). Here new, additional questions needed to be addressed: How could they rebuild their life away from the home or homeland and still remain distinct as a people?

The flowering of literature in the Persian period, then, is a response to such questions. The Hebrew Bible is a project of rebuilding community and identity (see Wright, *Rebuilding Identity*). With its re-visioning of infrastructures and institutions, as well as hopes for a new future, the Hebrew Bible is both a key source as well as a strategy for this rebuilding (see Wright, "Commemoration").

As noted above, the Hebrew Bible/Old Testament was decisively shaped in this Persian period. Scholars continue to debate the date of the various editions of the specific books in the Bible. Spinoza in the seventeenth century credited Ezra in the fifth century BCE with the final edition of the Pentateuch. A version of this theory became entrenched in scholarship with the work of Julius Wellhausen in the nineteenth century, who did more than any other to present a widely acceptable model for the formation of the Pentateuch (the so-called "newer documentary hypothesis"). He too dated the final form to the Persian period. Versions of these scholarly views continue to be discussed, although some scholars suggest an even later date for portions of the Pentateuch and the Bible as a whole. The long editorial processes, evident in the formation of pentateuchal and prophetic literature (see the essays by David Carr and Robert Wilson in this volume), have led to dramatically different scholarly theories about the dating of this material. There is, however, a more widely shared scholarly agreement that those books included among the Writings or Ketuvim largely belong to the Persian period.

The Writings/Ketuvim is group of biblical texts that forms the third division of the Jewish Bible. The 11 books of Ketuvim appear in modern Jewish Bibles in the following order: Psalms (*Tehillim*), Proverbs (*Mishlei*), Job (*Yiob*), Song of Songs (*Shir Ha'shirim*//Song of Solomon), Ruth (*Rut*), Lamentations (*Aichah*), Ecclesiastes (*Qohelet*), Esther (*Ester*), Daniel, Ezra-Nehemiah (*Ezra-Nechemiah*) and Chronicles (*Divrei Ha'yamim*). This collection is the most heterogeneous part of the Bible, with the books, in addition, distributed differently in the various biblical canons, or versions, that is, Jewish, Protestant, Catholic and Eastern Orthodox Bibles/Old Testaments. In Christian versions of the Old Testament, some of these books are among the "Historical Books" (Ruth, Chronicles, Ezra, Nehemiah and Esther: Ruth is appended to Judges while the others follow each other after 2 Kings). Other books in this collection are placed among "Poetical or Wisdom Literature" (Job, Psalms, Proverbs, Ecclesiastes, Song of Solomon), with Daniel included among the "Prophetical Books."

In what follows, we explore the books in the Writings/Ketuvim and highlight the relevance of these writings to specific issues in the Persian period. Although some books in this collection (like Ruth and Chronicles) resemble material in the Pentateuch or narratives in prophetical literature, one must note an important difference. In the Pentateuch and the Prophets, the dominant voice is the voice of God, speaking through messengers, be it Moses or prophets like Jeremiah. In the Writings/Ketuvim, we hear mostly the voices of the people, of individuals or of the entire community, speaking back to God. In addition to this reorientation, these books show interest in the lives of ordinary people and concern themselves with the quest for the good life in family and work. The named and unnamed storytellers, singers, sages and seers in Ketuvim speak to each other and to God, seeking answers to the questions that preoccupy them. Our overview begins with the Book of Lamentations, which follows Jeremiah in the Christian Old Testament.

The Ketuvim in the Persian Period

The Book of Lamentations comprises five poems that respond to the destruction of Jerusalem and Judah in 587 BCE. The poems graphically describe the horrors of war and lament the terrible aftermath of the Babylonian destruction of Jerusalem and its attendant slaughter. The book captures the experiences of a community that has been devastated and now seeks to find a way to go on. The opening word, "How?" 'êkâ, which begins three of the poems (1:1; 2:1; 4:1), is an outcry in the face of incomprehensible horror (to be understood as "How could this happen!"). But as Wright observes (*We the People*), it is also a desperate attempt to cope (to be understood as "Now that this happened, how can I go on?").

The lamenting voices in the book recount in great detail the impact of loss, hunger, despair, pillaging, rape and deaths in war:

> My eyes are spent with weeping;
>   my stomach churns;
>   my bile is poured out on the ground
>   because of the destruction of my people,
>   because infants and babes faint
>   in the streets of the city.
>
> They cry to their mothers,
>   "Where is bread and wine?"

> as they faint like the wounded
>   in the streets of the city,
> as their life is poured out
>   on their mothers' bosom …
>
> (Lam. 2:11–12, NRSV)

The horror is everywhere in the life of the community that produces these laments. But the book does more than lament. It also begins a process of reconstruction. This gesture is evident in the manner with which Lamentations uses the alphabet to organize its outcry. Four of the five chapters take the form of an acrostic, articulating pain and loss from A to Z, as it were, by beginning the first verse or verses with *aleph*, the first letter of the Hebrew alphabet, and the last verse or verses with *taph*, the last letter of the alphabet. In so doing the laments introduce a measure of order into a world gone mad, and in that sense generate a mechanism for coping (see also Edward Greenstein's essay in this volume).

One can approach the rest of the Writings/Ketuvim as diverse responses to the "How" question. Directly or indirectly, much in Ketuvim seems to address questions such as: How can we now survive? How can we rebuild our lives? The books in Ketuvim then seek to guide and empower survivors to rebuild their lives as persons and communities, and many of these works, Ezra-Nehemiah, Chronicles, Ruth, Esther and Daniel, might be characterized as narrative responses to crisis (on Daniel as crisis literature, see John J. Collins's essay in this volume).

The Narratives in the Writings/Ketuvim as Responses to Crisis

Ezra-Nehemiah answers the "How" question by depicting a history of the return from exile and reconstruction of life in Judah. Although preserved as two distinct books in later Christian editions, "Ezra" and "Nehemiah" actually constitute a single book in the earliest manuscripts and are best interpreted as a unified work, Ezra-Nehemiah. The book picks up the thread of the national story roughly where 2 Kings ends, namely after Jerusalem's demise. Ezra-Nehemiah is the only biblical narrative that records a history of the return from exile to Judah in the Persian period. The book casts the return as an enthusiastic response to King Cyrus who commissions the Judeans or Jews to rebuild God's house in Jerusalem:

> In the first year of King Cyrus of Persia, in order that the word of the LORD by the mouth of Jeremiah might be accomplished, the LORD stirred up the spirit of King Cyrus of Persia so that he sent a herald throughout all his kingdom, and also in a written edict declared: "Thus says King Cyrus of Persia: The LORD, the God of heaven, has given me all the kingdoms of the earth, and he has charged me to build him a house at Jerusalem in Judah. Any of those among you who are of his people – may their God be with them! – are now permitted to go up to Jerusalem in Judah, and rebuild the house of the LORD, the God of Israel – he is the God who is in Jerusalem …" (Ezra 1:1–3, New Revised Standard Version (NRSV))

According to Ezra-Nehemiah, rebuilding took the form of three distinct stages, all guided by the Torah: the first stage saw the rebuilding of the temple (Ezra 3–6); the second stage concerned the rebuilding of the community itself (Ezra 7–10); and finally, the third stage saw the rebuilding of the city's walls (Nehemiah 1–7). When rebuilding was complete, the community celebrated the restoration with fanfare and reasserted its allegiance to the Torah of God (Nehemiah 8–13).

Although the historical accuracy of Ezra-Nehemiah is subject to debate, one can safely approach the book's narrative as a reflection of Persian period interpretation of the nation's history. The authors of this work illustrate a decisive Persian period shift in ideology of history and politics from what is represented in earlier works. For example, Samuel and Kings trace historical developments by focusing on the kings; they present the people as a group whose fate is largely determined by what kings do or do not do (see J. J. M. Roberts's essay in this volume). In contrast, Ezra-Nehemiah "spins" the record of events so as to highlight the people themselves as chief protagonists. Its narration creates a new type of infrastructure in which power is distributed among the citizens. Although individual leaders like Ezra and Nehemiah rise to the surface in Ezra-Nehemiah, the real hero is/are the people themselves. The people are the ones who rebuild the temple; they determine membership in the community; they build the city's walls, and they unilaterally and voluntarily undertake renewed obedience to the Torah.

Ezra-Nehemiah repeatedly accuses some peoples in the land(s) of sabotaging Jewish restoration (Ezra 4; Neh. 6:1–14), but it lauds the Judean community's perseverance in building. While the book underscores the enthusiasm of those who returned, it also discloses tension about membership in the community. One can surmise that enlarging the role of the community entails greater clarity about criteria for communal membership, and Ezra-Nehemiah is an example of a debate about the subject. Living under Persian rule, and as a minority among other peoples, the authors of Ezra-Nehemiah take the position that social and religious boundaries have to be rigorously maintained. In this book, the news that some people have married foreign women (Ezra 9–10; Neh. 13:23–30) results in a campaign to abolish intermarriage.

Ezra-Nehemiah bestows great significance on texts. In particular, it emphasizes the extent to which reconstruction was done in accordance with the book of the Torah. The Torah is publicly read in Nehemiah 8:1–12 in a ceremony that echoes the receiving of the Torah at Sinai. This time, however, it is not imposed from above. Instead, the entire community asks for it and vows to obey it (Neh. 10). With Ezra-Nehemiah, we witness the textualization of the tradition, in a sense establishing a new paradigm. The emphasis on written texts may reflect Persian imperial practices, given that the vast empire was managed via documents. In turn, however, the greater attention to writings stimulated the increased production of Judean texts that characterizes this period.

Chronicles is also a historiographic narrative, probably later than Ezra-Nehemiah (late Persian period). It retrojects the ethos and values of the Persian period to an earlier stage in Israel's history. Recounting largely the same events depicted in the books of Samuel and Kings (and often reproducing large portions of Samuel and Kings verbatim), Chronicles nevertheless reframes inherited traditions in a way that radically redefines the nature of the earlier monarchic period. The changes express an important feature of the literature in this period: the need to grapple with inherited *written* traditions in order to rebuild a society under changed circumstances. Thus past memories are now put into the service of a new type of community, and the pen or stylus is used to refashion the past in the service of the present and the future.

Consequently, King David is praised primarily for his role in building the temple, not for his wars or his uniting the nation (although these are recorded). Obviously Chronicles is aware that the Book of Kings credits David's son, King Solomon, with building the temple. And Chronicles acknowledges this tradition. But Chronicles claims that David planned all aspects of the temple and even appointed its personnel. All Solomon had to do was execute David's instructions. Indeed, most of the account of David's reign in 1 Chronicles 11–29 revolves around the cult (see 1 Chr. 15, 17 and 21–29).

In recasting the figure of David, Chronicles omits many of David's unsavory exploits. For example, Chronicles does not mention David's adulterous affair with Bathsheba or the rebellion of David's son Absalom against David. One readily sees the revision when comparing the two accounts of the war with the Ammonites in 2 Samuel 11–12 and 1 Chronicles 20. According to 2 Samuel 11:1 (NRSV), "In the spring of the year, the time when kings go out to battle, David sent Joab with his officers and all Israel with him; they ravaged the Ammonites, and besieged Rabbah. But David remained at Jerusalem." 1 Chronicles 20 begins the same way and continues with the conquest of Rabbah. However, Chronicles hastens to report in the very next verse what David did in Rabbah when it was captured:

> David took the crown of Milcom from his head; he found that it weighed a talent of gold, and in it was a precious stone; and it was placed on David's head. He also brought out the booty of the city, a very great amount. He brought out the people who were in it, and set them to work with saws and iron picks and axes. Thus David did to all the cities of the Ammonites. Then David and all the people returned to Jerusalem. (1 Chr. 20:2–3, New Jewish Publication Society (NJPS))

This sequence differs dramatically from the depiction in Samuel, which only records the capturing of Rabbah after a lengthy account of David's affair with Bathsheba and its deadly consequences. The verses that follow the introduction in 2 Samuel 11:1 linger on what happened to David in Jerusalem. Instead of a report about Rabbah, we are told that late one afternoon David sees from his roof a beautiful woman bathing (2 Sam. 11:2). He sends for her and lies with her. When the woman, Bathsheba, gets pregnant as a result, David unsuccessfully tries to cover up his role by recalling her husband from the front. When this loyal soldier refuses the luxury of going to sleep with his wife, David arranges for him to be killed in battle (2 Sam. 11:2–27). The deed is exposed by the prophet Nathan who castigates King David and foretells dire consequences to the House of David (2 Sam. 12). Only thereafter does the Book of Samuel record that David went to Rabbah to take over the final stage of the battle and vanquish its king.

When Chronicles reimagines the past, its overall agenda is to buttress the institutions of the present. Written when the nation was a colonized people under imperial rule, with no indigenous monarchy or political autonomy, Chronicles responds to contemporaneous needs and sets forth a new basis for national unity: what the monarchy provided in the preexilic period is replaced by the temple in Jerusalem. The temple now occupies the spatial center and functions as the main symbol of collective life for the inhabitants of Judah, and for Jews throughout the Diaspora.

This wrestling with, and revising of, the inherited tradition in Chronicles exemplifies an overriding theme that binds the other books in the Writings/Ketuvim. Moreover, the extent to which the authors of Chronicles feel free to revise ancient written traditions witnesses to a sense of the freedom that ancient authors exercised in retelling and reimagining. Yet the fact that Chronicles does not simply invent a story is likewise instructive: it illustrates the phenomenon that accounts for the abundance of literature in the Persian period, including the Pseudepigrapha and "Rewritten Bible." Like Chronicles, these writings anchor themselves in familiar biblical texts and elaborate on them in creative ways. The phenomenon illustrates the authoritative role that books like the Pentateuch and prophetical writings have come to possess in this period. Retelling biblical stories becomes the basis for affirming new and changing communal values through literature.

The Book of Ruth, which follows the Book of Judges in Christian Old Testaments, resembles family narratives in Genesis. But it radically differs from them in its casting of women, not men, as chief protagonists. Moreover, the book stands out as a "counterculture," in that its hero, Ruth, is a foreigner. Although the story is set at the time of the Judges, roughly the eleventh century BCE, internal clues indicate a later date for the book's composition (mid-fifth century BCE or later is the likely period for its composition: see Bush 18–30; Eskenazi and Frymer-Kensky XVI–XIX).

This book traces the (mis)fortunes of two widows, Naomi and Ruth, as they move from "futility to fertility" and from "famine to fullness" (see Trible 166–99). It shows how kindness, generosity and intelligence, together with effective collaboration with her mother-in-law, enable Ruth the Moabite to move from the position of a poor outsider to the very center of Judean society. Her marriage to the prominent, wealthy Judean man Boaz leads in due course to the birth of a great-grandson, David, who becomes the Bible's most beloved king. Although the book has only four chapters, it manages to accomplish some revolutionary things. At one level, the book's charm reminds one of Jane Austen's books, which gently offer sharp social critique while focusing on the romances of women at risk. At another level, one can discern how Ruth gently but effectively addresses a major political issue at the forefront in the Persian period – namely communal identity and membership.

The protagonist Ruth belongs to a people that the Book of Deuteronomy excludes permanently and unambiguously: "No Ammonite or Moabite shall be admitted to the assembly of the LORD. Even to the tenth generation, none of their descendants shall be admitted to the assembly of the LORD" (Deut. 23:3, NRSV). Despite such explicit prohibition in the Torah, the Book of Ruth nonetheless shows how a Moabite can in fact become a member of the community. It delineates the stages of Ruth's journey. In the first chapter Ruth famously commits herself to Naomi, Naomi's people and Naomi's God: "Where you go, I will go; Where you lodge, I will lodge; your people shall be my people, and your God my God" (Ruth 1:16, NRSV). At the end of the book, the entire community blesses the marriage of Ruth with Boaz of Judah (Ruth 4:11–12), a union that two generations later produces David. In this way Ruth's story paves the way to a new kind of inclusivity in the Persian period. The story, in which the worthy woman was welcomed into the community despite the prohibition, establishes a new model for integrating outsiders (see Neil Glover for a fine discussion of the process in Ruth). With the Book of Ruth as part of Scripture, inclusion was secured as a norm in Judaism, with subsequent laws of conversion showing this story's influence.

The issue of membership in the community appears to have been central in the aftermath of destruction and the prospects of reestablishing Jewish life anew. Isaiah 56:1–8 exemplifies such a concern with its welcoming proclamation concerning eunuchs and foreigners. In this debate, the Book of Ruth, likewise, functions as a possible response and a counterpoint to views such as those of Ezra-Nehemiah, which object to marriage with foreigners.

Another work featuring a female protagonist, the Book of Esther, transports readers from the periphery of the Persian empire in Judah to its very heart: the royal court in the capital city of Susa. The book is dated to ca. 400 BCE (Berlin XXXII–XXXVI) and is placed after Ezra-Nehemiah in Christian Old Testaments. In this book, the Persian monarch dismisses his disobedient queen and then seeks a new wife. A beautiful orphan Jewish girl is selected from among all the maidens in the land to become this new Queen of Persia. Her guardian and relative Mordecai instructs her not to disclose that she is Jewish. As the story unfolds, Mordecai enrages Haman, the king's chief officer/counselor, by refusing to bow to him. In revenge, Haman persuades the king to decree that all Jews should be killed. Haman describes Jews as "a certain people scattered and separated among the peoples in all the provinces of your kingdom; their laws are different from those of every other people, and they do not keep the king's laws, so that it is not appropriate for the king to tolerate them" (Esth. 3:8, NRSV). Mordecai, in despair, urges Esther to appeal to the king and save her people.

Reluctant at first, Esther finally consents. Using subtlety and charm, she successfully influences the king to countermand the decree and succeeds in saving her people. Haman is killed and Mordecai her guardian becomes the king's new chief officer. The book's happy ending includes a mandate to celebrate the feast of Purim in memory of these events.

In many ways, the Book of Esther resembles accounts in the historical books of Judges to Kings, where the people of Israel are endangered by foreign oppressors. Yet it stands in sharp contrast to these books. In those accounts the people typically reach a crisis point and turn to God, who then rescues them. The Book of Esther, however, makes no mention of God; it is the only biblical book with no reference to God. Furthermore, the hero of Esther is a woman. She not only saves her people; she also exercises unparalleled enduring authority. We read, for example, that "The command of Queen Esther fixed these practices of Purim, and it was recorded in writing" (9:32, NRSV).

Interpreters today focus on the fascinating gender twists in the story. In its own Persian period context, however, the gender bending in Esther was at the service of exposing the precariousness of life under Persian rule. Its messages pertain to cultivating strategies of survival. The Book of Esther highlights the vulnerability of life in exile even as it promotes an ethos in which all Jews are bound together by fate and circumstances, regardless of where or how they live. The story shows how a marginalized community, a subject people within a large empire and outsiders to the corridors of power, paves for itself a path to the throne room in order to secure protection and prosperity.

Access to royal power is deemed essential to survival, together with a commitment to one's Jewish identity and people. At one level one could say that the authors of this book recognize the important role women had to play in the life of the community, even though women ordinarily lacked authority in ancient societies. At another level, readers can see that Esther as a woman reflects the position of the Jewish community as it negotiates its place in the Persian empire (Avnery).

One final point about Esther. In common with Ezra-Nehemiah, the Book of Esther highlights the power of documents to shape history: the entire Persian empire is governed by means of letters and edicts as the decisive mechanism. This emphasis brings back the subject of literary production: an age in which written documents are deemed decisive sources of power is an age that will see a flowering of literary works (see Edward Greenstein's essay in this volume).

Also set in exile, the Book of Daniel offers some interesting contrasts with Esther. Placed with the Prophets in the Christian Old Testaments, where it follows Ezekiel, Daniel describes the misadventures of a pious and beautiful Jewish man in Diaspora. Its first part (1–6) narrates how Daniel's piety and wisdom both endanger his life and allow him to survive in the royal court in Babylon under Babylonian and Persian rule. The second part (7–12) contains apocalyptic visions that depict history allegorically down to the Maccabean era in 168 BCE. Because the decisive shaping of Daniel takes place in the Hellenistic period, it is discussed elsewhere (see John J. Collins's essay in this volume). However, it is useful to contrast the Book of Daniel with Esther. The Book of Daniel places God in the forefront. Daniel himself is constantly at prayer. His determination to honor specific Jewish practices repeatedly puts him in conflict with the surrounding culture. Whereas Esther (where God is never mentioned and no Jewish practices are noted) advocates clever and assertive human intervention to effect change, Daniel, reflecting a time of great political helplessness, advocates faith, reliance on God and perseverance, as well as readiness to die for fidelity to Israel's God.

Poetic and Proverbial Literature

The Hebrew Bible includes 150 psalms, organized into five so-called "books" which, in that sense, mirror the so-called "five books of Moses," that is, the Pentateuch/Torah (Genesis to Deuteronomy). Whereas the Pentateuch focuses on God's teachings and God's will for Israel, the Psalms are the human responses. The Psalms are filled with the outpouring of the heart. Tradition credits King David as author of many of these Psalms, but scholarly research, as well the content of some psalms, indicate a later period. Psalm 137, for example, depicts life during the Babylonian exile, over 400 years after David:

> By the rivers of Babylon –
>> there we sat down and there we wept
>> when we remembered Zion.
> On the willows there
>> we hung up our harps.

For there our captors
  asked us for songs,
and our tormentors asked for mirth, saying,
  "Sing us one of the songs of Zion!"

How could we sing the LORD's song
  in a foreign land?
If I forget you, O Jerusalem,
  let my right hand wither!

(137:1–5, NRSV)

Psalm 126 clearly depicts a celebratory return from exile during the Persian period:

When the LORD restored the fortunes of Zion,
  we were like those who dream.
Then our mouth was filled with laughter,
  and our tongue with shouts of joy ...

(126:1–2, NRSV)

The Psalms explore a full range of human experience from the perspective of an individual or a community in a manner that we would call religious. All the psalms, then, share with Lamentations the inscription of a people's voice or voices. All of them, in one way or another, address God or are about God, even when they challenge God.

Many psalms depict scenes from the nation's life, either bemoaning its plight, or celebrating God's protection. They question, petition, affirm, challenge and praise. In addition to collective laments or hymns about the nation's fortune, the psalms include highly personal prayers, reflecting an individual's intimate dialogs with God. The psalms express a person's longings, hopes, fear and joy. We hear the voice of an individual who struggles with God's absence at a time of great need (Ps. 22:1–22); this is followed by a voice of a person who experiences God's comforting and salvific presence (Ps. 23). Although the Psalms range across the broad landscape of human experience, the book is framed with affirmations of joy. The first word in the Book of Psalms is "happy," and the first Psalm seeks to define the ways of the happy person. The Psalms return to the subject of happiness more often than any other book, usually emphasizing social justice and piety as necessary components of human fulfillment. The book concludes with psalms of celebration that repeatedly proclaim "Halleluyah," a Hebrew word meaning "Praise Yah!" (typically translated as "Praise the LORD!").

Placed after the Psalms in both Christian Old Testaments and modern Jewish Bibles, the Book of Proverbs claims to offer reliable "recipes" for happiness. As its title indicates, this book is a collection of proverbs. It aims to persuade young men to seek wisdom and shun the danger posed by individuals who would lead them astray. The book's opening line credits King Solomon with authorship, but scholars recognize the book as a post-exilic document (Camp 233–8). Its teachings, the work of sages, are cast at times as parental teachings ("Hear, my child, your father's instruction, and do not reject your mother's teaching," Prov. 1:8, NRSV; see the essay by Raymond Person in this volume).

The book constantly warns against following fools or the wrong type of women (see below) and urges the young to cling to wisdom instead. Wisdom for Proverbs does not stand for philosophical, abstract thought but constitutes pragmatic lessons for a good life and material success. Proverbs, then, is a paradigmatic "How to" book with the goal of material security and a peaceful heart and hearth. The preoccupation with domestic, personal accomplishments, measured by successful work, pervades several Jewish writings from this period. Such a turning toward the home as the arena of significance can be viewed as a response to the loss of national pride. It reflects a withdrawal into more personal markers for success.

Another move that typifies the Persian period is the attention that Proverbs bestows on women. It views a loose or foreign woman as a major danger; but virtue is also emblematically dressed in feminine garb. Wisdom, a feminine noun, is the paradigmatic helper. Lady Wisdom should be pursued and followed. The book concludes (Prov. 31:10–31) with a long poem in an alphabetical acrostic, depicting the perfect wife from A to Z as it were (*aleph* to *taph* in Hebrew). Such a woman is far more precious than jewels. Interestingly, this praiseworthy woman is a working woman who runs the household for efficiency and profit. She produces food and fabrics, buys and sells merchandise, and is an independent manager. She is the household's mainstay and her activities are a source of pride to her husband and offspring. This depiction, like other perspectives on women in the Hebrew Bible, contradicts the tendencies to suppose that the Hebrew Bible presents women in inferior positions as helpless or weak (see the essay by Carol Meyers in this volume). Strong women are especially prominent in the Writings/Ketuvim (see Ruth, Naomi, Esther and the woman of valor in Prov. 31:10–31).

Proverbs accepts and affirms the status quo. It presumes an equitable world and maintains that correct behavior guarantees a good life. In Proverbs, God undergirds the system. Proverbs repeatedly urges reverence toward God. It is confident that God rewards the wise and righteous, and punishes the foolish and wicked. But the book's guidelines typically pertain to pragmatic wisdom, the know-how of managing effectively commercial and social business and other practical matters.

Domestic bliss counts as the arena for the best kind of life, in lieu of emphasis on the cult, social justice, or political and communal engagement. This feature is typical of Wisdom Literature as a genre, and is common in the ancient world. But its flowering in biblical Israel in the postexilic period may be influenced (as noted above) by the conditions under Persian rule where political aspirations were subsumed under imperial authority.

As if in protest against everything that Proverbs claims, the Book of Job, which follows in the Hebrew Bible (but precedes Psalms in the Christian Old Testament), dismantles precisely the kind of confidence that Proverbs expresses. The 31 chapters of Proverbs assure the reader that God-fearing people prosper when they live prudent and just lives. The 42 chapters of the Book of Job vehemently deny this. Job's protagonist is an impeccably righteous man. When disaster strikes him and all that is dear to him, Job begins to rail against God's injustice.

The Book of Job seems to challenge many basic tenets of the Bible. Its protagonist Job insists that the world we all see is unjust. He therefore demands that God explain why good people like himself suffer when the wicked prosper. As Job bewails his fate and howls out of his moral and physical pain, his three friends seek to comfort him by defending God. They argue that the wicked only seem to prosper but soon are punished, that humans are not perfect, that Job must have done something to deserve his fate, and that we are not to question God's justice:

> Can mortals be righteous before God?
> Can human beings be pure before their Maker?
> Even in his servants he puts no trust,
> and his angels he charges with error.
>
> (Job 4:17–18, NRSV)

God, says one of the friends,

> does great things and unsearchable,
> marvelous things without number.
> He gives rain on the earth
> and sends waters on the fields;
> he sets on high those who are lowly,
> and those who mourn are lifted to safety.
> He frustrates the devices of the crafty,
> so that their hands achieve no success.
>
> (Job 5:10–12, NRSV)

Many of the friends' arguments echo passages from elsewhere in the Bible. One is therefore surprised at the end of the book when God scolds the friends because, says God, "you have not spoken of me what is right, as my servant Job has" (42:7; NRSV). God at last responds to Job from the whirlwind (38:1ff.). But the message of this answer, and its capacity to placate Job or challenge his charges, remain obscure.

The book vividly portrays the traumas that afflict human beings: illness, abuse, loss of fortune and status. Although Job's own attitude is at odds with much in the rest of the Bible, this book occupies an incontestable place in human experience. It is especially fitting as an outcry in the Persian period, when some of the assumptions about collective retribution (such as those of Deuteronomy) had to be set aside or at the very least challenged due to historical events.

The most unusual biblical book may be Song of Songs, also known as Song of Solomon or Canticles (placed just before the Book of Isaiah in Christian Old Testaments). The Song celebrates sensuous love and proclaims that "Love is as strong as death." The Song of Songs shows no interest in theology or love as loyalty or as "loving-kindness," the forms of love that typify other biblical texts (especially Deuteronomy and Ruth). Instead it depicts love as erotic and passionate, a sentiment introduced in the book's opening lines when the woman exclaims: "Oh that he would kiss me with the kisses of his mouth!" (Cant. 1:2).

The introduction (Cant. 1:1) credits King Solomon as the one for whom or by whom the Song was composed. But even though the Song reflects some ancient traditions, its language, such as the use of Persian loan words, suggests that it originated in the Persian period or even later (Bloch and Bloch 22–7). In the Song, which is a poetic dialog, the reader encounters three main voices: the woman, the man, and a group addressed as

"Daughters of Jerusalem." The woman has the first word, the last word and most of the words in between. She announces that "I am black and beautiful" (1:6), confident of her beauty and her power. Her lover agrees, describing her with the most delicious metaphors, alive with abundance and energy:

> How beautiful you are, my love,
> how very beautiful!
> Your eyes are doves
> behind your veil.
> Your hair is like a flock of goats,
> moving down the slopes of Gilead ...
> Your lips are like a crimson thread,
> and your mouth is lovely ...
> Your neck is like the tower of David ...
> Your two breasts are like two fawns,
> twins of a gazelle,
> that feed among the lilies.
>
> (Cant. 4:1, 3–5, NRSV)

The lovers revel in each other's physical beauty (see her description of him in Cant. 5:9–16). Yet the love they express is both physical and spiritual. It is love that enables each partner to blossom in a relationship of reciprocity, mutuality, and equality.

Here is how the woman describes the relationship:

> My beloved speaks and says to me:
>   "Arise, my love, my fair one, and come away;
> for now the winter is past,
>   the rain is over and gone.
> The flowers *appear* [*are seen*] on the earth;
>   the time of singing has come,
>   and the *voice* of the turtledove is *heard* in our land.
> The fig tree puts forth its figs,
>   and the vines are in blossom;
>   they give forth fragrance.
> Arise, my love, my fair one,
>   and come away.
> O my dove, in the clefts of the rock,
>   in the covert of the cliff,
> let me *see* your face,
>   let me *hear* your *voice*;
> for your voice is sweet,
>   and your face is lovely.
>
> (Cant. 2:10–14, NRSV, emphasis added)

Although the passage begins by celebrating the beauty of nature in springtime, and is an invitation for the woman to enjoy it, we soon learn that the invitation is for the woman herself to bloom to her fullness. First the woman is invited to come forth because flowers are seen in bud, and birds' voices are heard everywhere (2:10–13). But what her lover longs for the most is her face and her voice: "let me see your face/let me hear your voice" (2:14). It is time for her to be seen and time for her to be heard (in 8:5 she awakens him to his potential).

Until the modern era, the majority of Jewish and Christian interpreters have read the Song as an allegory about the love between a divine being and a people. For such Jews, the Song depicts the love between God and Israel; for such Christians it is a love story between Jesus and the Church. But today's readers more readily acknowledge that the Song depicts human lovers who affirm both their spirit or soul and their body, and who celebrate the dialog of human love in sensuous terms.

The lovers in the Song conjure up a garden with lush flowers that are about to bloom, buds broadcasting their scent, with gentle animals – deer and doves – everywhere. The book speaks of bright red pomegranates, cheerful chirping of birds, the air dense with spices such as cinnamon and nard. As Phyllis Trible observes, the Song restores the primordial Garden of Eden as well as the primordial equality between male and female of Genesis 1:26–27, which were lost through disobedience (Gen. 3:16–17). Once again, a woman and a man are in a garden. Once again harmony reigns – between persons as well as in relation to the rest of the creation. This time there is no forbidden fruit, only savory fruit to be joyfully shared, and a relationship in which lovers cherish, sustain and empower one another (Trible 144–65).

Like Proverbs, Ecclesiastes (Qohelet in Hebrew) includes proverbial teachings about the good life and the ways to achieve it. Yet, placed before Song of Songs in Christian Old Testaments, Ecclesiastes like Job challenges traditional teachings such as those of Proverbs. The book's introduction attributes the composition to a son of David who reigned in Jerusalem; he is traditionally identified as King Solomon. Yet Ecclesiastes includes unmistakable late vocabulary and ideas, resembling Greek philosophical teachings. It is therefore thought to have originated in the late Persian period or early Hellenistic Age.

Ecclesiastes/Qohelet begins with an overarching declaration about the human condition (Eccl. 1:2), and repeats this declaration almost verbatim as the conclusion of Ecclesiastes' words (12:8). This framing declaration, as well as large segments of the book, depict life as fleeting and afflicted with toil and hardship. Yet the usual rendition of the opening phrase as "Vanity of vanities, says the Teacher, vanity of vanities! All is vanity" (1:2, NRSV) is misleading. The Hebrew word translated as "vanity" is *hebel*, which means "mist" or "vapor." What Ecclesiastes observes is that nothing lasts. Everything evaporates and vanishes. However, one errs when dismissing vapor and mist as futile. As water, vapor is a vital source for life.

The transitory nature of all life serves as a challenge that the book explores in detail. It prompts Ecclesiastes to pose the question: "What do people gain from all the toil at which they toil under the sun?" (1:3, NRSV). In other words, if nothing endures, what is the point of it all? To find the answers, Ecclesiastes embarks on a quest in which he tests different life options. He first explores the benefits of wealth, pleasure and wisdom, only to end in despair because each of these fails to guarantee security and longevity. Life, he concludes, is not fair. One famous conclusion that Ecclesiastes reaches is the recognition that life is always in flux, requiring changing responses:

> For everything there is a season, and a time for every matter under heaven:
> a time to be born, and a time to die;
> a time to plant, and a time to pluck up what is planted;
> a time to kill, and a time to heal;
> a time to break down, and a time to build up;
> a time to weep, and a time to laugh;
> a time to mourn, and a time to dance …
>
> (3:1–4, NRSV)

As Ecclesiastes' awareness unfolds, the advice he offers increasingly gravitates toward a greater appreciation of the preciousness of life. Awareness of life's fragility sharpens his sense of responsibility and inspires him to savor more deeply whatever good things happen, not to take them for granted or to overlook them. Repeatedly he affirms that there is nothing better than cultivating a capacity to enjoy whatever comes. People must "enjoy themselves as long as they live" because "it is God's gift that all should eat and drink and take pleasure in all their toil" (3:12–13, NRSV). Recognizing that life is neither predictable nor apparently fair, he urges his reader to find and love a companion and to celebrate the quotidian, the basic and simple pleasures of everyday existence, because "under the sun the race is not to the swift, nor the battle to the strong, nor bread to the wise, nor riches to the intelligent, nor favor to the skillful; but time and chance happen to them all" (9:11, NRSV). Such an uncertain future, Ecclesiastes exhorts, should guide us to make every day special.

> Go, eat your bread with enjoyment, and drink your wine with a merry heart; for God has long ago approved what you do. Let your garments always be white; do not let oil be lacking on your head. Enjoy life with the wife whom you love, all the days of your vain life that are given you under the sun, because that is your portion in life and in your toil at which you toil under the sun. (9:7–9, NRSV)

Not only this but also, importantly, one must do what one can with zest: "Whatever your hand finds to do, do with your might" (9:10, NRSV).

Like Proverbs, Ecclesiastes reflects a retreat from the grand sweep of history and its political, national and cultic aspects so emphasized in the Pentateuch and the Prophets. Instead, Ecclesiastes focuses on ordinary, pragmatic concerns, on the woes and joys of a life writ small, urging the reader to embrace it all.

Conclusions

What endures? Ecclesiastes wonders whether anything does. He begins and ends with the observation that all is vapor, all vanishes. Yet his book remains with us, as do many other Judean writings preserved from the Persian period. Destruction and deportation, and the opportunity to start again, challenged communities of Judeans and Jews in the Persian period to reenvision their life under imperial control. Survival demanded creative acts of recovery from a devastation that eliminated the age-old markers of identity and normality. The Bible is an enduring response to this trauma. The various books now included in the Writings/Ketuvim illustrate ways of coping, from mourning the loss (Lamentations) to celebrating renewal (Ezra-Nehemiah). The strategies embedded in these texts include greater attention to the quotidian: home became the arena of significance for some writers (Proverbs, Ecclesiastes). The past was re-visioned so as to legitimate and empower contemporary infrastructures such as the temple in Jerusalem (Chronicles). The plight of the individual as well as personal joy came to be expressed (Psalms and Job), and questions of communal identity (in the land and in Diaspora) were negotiated in new ways (Ruth, Ezra-Nehemiah and Esther). Above all, the written word became authoritative in a new way, with the Torah as the paradigmatic authority in lieu of the preexilic structures which relied on kings. The literature produced in this era enabled Jewish communities in Judah and in Diaspora to persist in the new circumstances, instead of vanishing in a sea of powerful nations. They became "the People of the Book." The blossoming of their literature continued to sustain them even when the temple was again destroyed in 70 CE, a crisis followed by centuries of exile. And the collection of these writings known as the Hebrew Bible, which began to assume its definitive form in the Persian period, laid the groundwork for formative ideas of Christianity and Islam as well, heavily influencing the writing of the New Testament and the Qur'an.

Note

1   I thank the National Endowment for the Humanities for the Fellowship that helped support the research for this essay.

Bibliography

Avnery, Orit. "The threefold cord: Interrelations between the Books of Samuel, Ruth and Esther." Dissertation, Bar Ilan University, 2011 [Hebrew]. I thank Dr Avnery for giving me the opportunity to read the manuscript; the work examines the literary, feminist, and political messages of the books of Ruth and Esther.

Berlin, Adele. *JPS Bible Commentary: Esther*. Philadelphia: Jewish Publication Society, 2001. A literary approach to the Book of Esther.

Bloch, Ariel and Chana Bloch. *The Song of Songs*. New York: Random House, 1995. A translation and commentary seeking to convey the power of the Hebrew poetry.

Bush, Frederic. *Ruth/Esther*. Word Biblical Commentary 9. Nashville: Thomas Nelson, 1996. A detailed and comprehensive commentary on the books of Ruth and Esther, with careful attention to issues of philology and a fine survey of diverse scholarship.

Camp, Claudia. *Wisdom and the Feminine in the Book of Proverbs*. Bible and Literature Series 11. Sheffield: Almond, 1985. Treatment of the varied images of women in the Book of Proverbs.

Edelman, Diana, *The Origins of the "Second" Temple: Persian Imperial Policy and the Rebuilding of Jerusalem*. London: Equinox, 2005. This book dates the building of the temple later than scholarly consensus proposes, but offers comprehensive archaeological data for the Persian period.

Eskenazi, Tamara Cohn. *In an Age of Prose: A Literary Approach to Ezra-Nehemiah.* Society of Biblical Literature Monograph Series 36. Atlanta: Scholars Press, 1988. The book examines the intricate ways with which the structure and themes of Ezra-Nehemiah convey the emphasis on community, the authority of documents, and the sanctity of the city and people, not merely the temple.

Eskenazi, Tamara Cohn and Tikva Frymer-Kensky. *JPS Bible Commentary: Ruth.* Philadelphia: Jewish Publication Society, 2011. Historical, literary and thematic approach to Ruth.

Faust, Avraham. "Settlement dynamics and demographic fluctuations in Judah from the late Iron Age to the Hellenistic period and the archaeology of Persian period Yehud." In Yigal Levin (ed.), *A Time of Change: Judah and Its Neighbours in the Persian and Early Hellenistic Periods* (pp. 23–51). Library of Second Temple Studies 65. London: T&T Clark, 2007. This essay describes the socioeconomic conditions of Persian period Judah as "a post-collapse society" by tabulating the settlements and population spread during this period.

Glover, Neil. "Your people, my people: An exploration of ethnicity in Ruth." *Journal for the Study of the Old Testament 33* (2009): 293–313. This article applies anthropological theory to gain insights on changing ethnicity in the Book of Ruth.

Lipschits, Oded. *The Fall and Rise of Jerusalem: Judah under Babylonian Rule.* Winona Lake, IN: Eisenbrauns, 2005. This study documents the conditions of the province of Judah in the aftermath of the Babylonian destruction, and challenges previous studies that minimized the effect of the Babylonian conquest of Judah.

Trible, Phyllis. *God and the Rhetoric of Sexuality.* Overtures to Biblical Theology. Philadelphia: Fortress, 1978. This early, foundational work of feminist scholarship remains a rich and sensitive source for how to read the Song of Songs and the Book of Ruth through literary and feminist lenses.

Williamson, H. G. M. *Ezra, Nehemiah.* Word Biblical Commentary 16. Waco: Word Books, 1985. Thorough technical commentary on these two books.

Wright, Jacob L. *Rebuilding Identity: The Nehemiah Memoir and Its Earliest Readers.* Beihefte zur Zeitschrift für die Alttestamentliche Wissenschaft 348. Berlin: de Gruyter, 2005. The book shows how the biblical text both reflects the development of communal identity and helps construct one by means of writing.

Wright, Jacob L. "The commemoration of defeat and the formation of a nation in the Hebrew Bible." *Prooftexts 29* (2009): 433–73. This essay illustrates how defeat and exile, rather than victory, provided the impetus for the composition of the formation of the Hebrew Bible.

Wright, Jacob L. *We the People* (working title; forthcoming). I thank Dr. Wright for the opportunity to see the manuscript.

CHAPTER 27

Hellenistic Period Literature in the Land of Israel

Benjamin G. Wright III

In the latter part of the fourth century BCE, a young Macedonian, Alexander the Great, and his army moved eastward from Macedon. Sweeping through Asia Minor, he advanced down the Mediterranean coast through the region that we know now as Israel and into Egypt, afterwards marching east to deliver the final blows to the once mighty Persian empire. His capture of the major Persian cities in the east brought all of Persian territory under his control. In his wake, Alexander established cities that became influential bearers of the Hellenistic culture that had shaped him, the most prominent of which was Alexandria in Egypt. Although he died young, in his early thirties, and despite the fact that his successors engaged in a protracted series of wars for control of his territories, Alexander's enduring legacy became the language and culture that he had spread throughout the East on his military conquests and that his successors continued to promulgate (see Matthew Goff's essay in this volume).

The ancient land of Israel, or Palestine as it was known in this period, was part of this Hellenistic empire and the elements of Greek culture, particularly the establishment of Greek cities with their constituent Hellenistic political institutions, language and religion, exerted a deep influence in this region just as elsewhere (Collins and Sterling; Hengel). By the time Rome became deeply entangled in Jewish politics in the first century BCE, the Greek way of life had become "deeply intertwined with Jewish life," and Roman rule in the East "was mediated through Greekness in a particularly noticeable way" (Rajak 3–4). This chapter will treat Jewish literature from the period of the advent of Alexander's conquests in the last part of the fourth century BCE to the beginnings of Roman rule in the first century BCE (and even a bit later), since the advent, establishment and entrenchment of Hellenism take place during these centuries.

A second introductory consideration has its genesis in the chapter's title: what are the geographical limits to be observed? In the period with which this chapter is concerned no entity known as Israel was recognized generally. If we take the approximate area of the

The Wiley Blackwell Companion to Ancient Israel, First Edition. Edited by Susan Niditch.
© 2016 John Wiley & Sons, Ltd. Published 2016 by John Wiley & Sons, Ltd.

Israelite united kingdom of the tenth century BCE, several smaller geographical regions make up this area in the Hellenistic period: primarily Idumea; Judea; Samaria; Galilee; the Trans-Jordan; and the Decapolis (in the period of Herod the Great). These regions compose the geographical boundaries of the chapter.

When we take into consideration the broad range of Jewish literature in this period, we observe one overarching characteristic: diversity. In fact, the texts from the Hellenistic period are so varied in content, themes and genre that some scholars refer to Judaisms in the plural to describe the tradition (Neusner et al.). Although I would not go so far as to use the plural noun, the broad diversity encountered in this literature is undeniable. One only has to consider the texts found in the caves near the settlement at Qumran to see how varied the literature belonging to one community could be. Even though not all the manuscripts were composed or even copied by the people living by the Dead Sea, the caves can safely be said to have constituted their collection, and from any perspective – genre or theology, for example – these texts represent something of a microcosm of the breadth and variety of early Jewish literature.

In order to make some sense of this literature, then, one of the pressing problems becomes how to categorize the texts, especially for a survey chapter such as this. Scholars generally have taken different tacks when approaching this task, sometimes combining more than one. So, for example, George Nickelsburg in *Jewish Literature between the Bible and the Mishnah* takes a chronological approach, since "texts are historical artifacts and not timeless entities" (xii). In the end, however, he concludes with a chapter that treats texts whose origins (Jewish or Christian), provenances and dates are not certain. While Nickelsburg is correct that the historical, social and cultural situatedness of texts argues for such an arrangement, we do not know with confidence the origins of a fair number of texts. In *The Old Testament Pseudepigrapha*, James Charlesworth arranges the texts according to general genre categories. While this method sets apocalypses with apocalypses, for instance, it also places next to each other texts whose origins might be worlds apart. Moreover, in the Hellenistic period, we encounter many mixed genres, and in some cases, such as wisdom, what counts as a genre and how to identify a genre are much debated (Collins; Newsom).

Two final issues complicate the way that we might categorize Jewish literature in this period. First, these texts are often labeled as "Apocrypha" and "Pseudepigrapha," terms that are not very helpful, since they are artificial designations that carry with them implicit value judgments about the texts' authenticity (VanderKam 56–8). Second, scholarship on Early Judaism has not quite reached a stage where the texts discovered at Qumran and elsewhere in the Judean Desert have been thoroughly incorporated into broader study of the tradition. So, if we look at survey literature such as Nickelsburg, or Schürer as revised by Vermes, Millar, and Goodman, the Dead Sea Scrolls, both texts composed by the community and those that were not, are grouped together rather than being distributed among whatever other categories are being employed. This situation, fortunately, has been shifting gradually as more scholars study the scrolls in the larger context of Judaism in the Second Temple period.

For this chapter, I propose to take a different tack to organizing the texts before us. Since there is a relatively large number of texts from this period and this region, I will not be able to treat them all in detail, but I will attempt to mention as many as possible.

In the Hellenistic period, Jewish writers had at their disposal a relatively large body of national literature and traditions that had been handed down from earlier times. Many, perhaps even a majority, of these texts would end up in the Hebrew Bible, even if we cannot speak about a Bible as such in this period. (I will use the term "scripture" or "authoritative books" in order to avoid any impression that there was a closed canon, a Bible as such, at this time.) While the "biblical" books were certainly not the only ones handed down, they compose the most important group, and some, even most, were authoritative for Jews in the Hellenistic period (Ulrich). The Pentateuch, for example, certainly was regarded as sacred, and it probably (although not necessarily for all Jews) formed a closed group. Yet, what order the books might have taken is not always definite, and the text of the Pentateuch was still in flux in this period, as, for example, the Book of Exodus in its last chapters demonstrates (cf. the Masoretic text and the Septuagint). George Brooke has argued convincingly that one of the primary characteristics of the Dead Sea Scrolls is their reception and use of this Israelite literary heritage. He writes, "Although some of the sectarian compositions allude to scripture only implicitly, the vast majority of literary works found in the caves can be seen either as biblical or as heavily dependent on biblical traditions" (Brooke 256).

Just as the scrolls witness to the breadth and variety of Jewish literature, they also are representative of Hellenistic Jewish literature more broadly. When we take an overview perspective of Hellenistic-period texts in Israel, we find, just as at Qumran, the vast majority of them in some relationship to earlier texts and traditions, and they frequently allude to, copy the form of, exegete, rework or even rewrite these earlier texts (see David Carr's essay in this volume). For the Qumran scrolls, Brooke suggests five categories of texts: (1) copies of "biblical" books; (2) texts related to the Law; (3) texts related to the prophets; (4) texts associated in some way with works found in the Writings; and (5) texts that cannot be readily seen as dependent on biblical antecedents. While this system avoids some of the pitfalls of categorizing by genre or theology or by a scroll's sectarian or nonsectarian character, it depends too heavily on canonical categories that are anachronistic and artificial for this period (although we do find Law and Prophets as categories in some texts, such as the Wisdom of Ben Sira).

I would suggest a slightly different approach, however, one that would organize the texts according to the general approaches that they take to relating to earlier scriptural materials. These categories cut across different genres, theologies and practices, and in sorting out the texts in this way, we can observe one significant consequence of such an organizing principle: despite all the possible ways that they might differ from one another, the writers and transmitters of these texts share the view that there exists a broadly shared and accepted font of texts and traditions, which they regard as possessing an authoritative status inasmuch as they perceive the need to relate to them in some way, and thus, this diverse set of texts witnesses to common elements in Judaism that obviate the need to talk about the tradition using the plural Judaisms. I will work with five categories: (1) the use of textual antecedents as a framing device or springboard; (2) implicit use of or allusion to earlier texts; (3) explicit citation and use of scriptural antecedents; (4) revision and rewriting of earlier texts; and (5) texts that relate to earlier texts but that complicate the previous categories. These categories are not necessarily mutually exclusive, however. For example, a text might take a feature of an older text and use it as a framing device and also allude to earlier literature as well. Furthermore, these divisions are quite broad and do not reflect the finer distinctions that one might want to make when studying exactly how the texts in each category relate to the scriptures they employed. I refer below to a number of studies that make distinctions within these categories, and the reader is encouraged to consult the bibliography for further reading.

Category 1: The Use of Older Literature as a Framing Device or Springboard

Jewish texts of the Hellenistic period often exploit perceived gaps or otherwise unclear aspects of scriptural texts to serve as a springboard for a new text. In some cases, the new text might also incorporate some of the antecedent text within it. This device appears in several different genres of texts, as we see in the examples below.

One widespread version of this type is the adoption of an ancient figure who becomes the pseudepigraphic vehicle for the new text or tradition. The best example is Enoch around whom an extensive literature developed. In our period, the primary texts are found in a collection of five booklets that make up the work known as *1 Enoch* (the Book of the Watchers; the Book of Parables; the Book of the Luminaries; the Animal Vision; and the Epistle of Enoch; see John J. Collins's essay in this volume). In the scriptural traditions in Genesis, Enoch does not figure very prominently. Indeed he has only four verses accorded to him. One of those verses, however, sets him up as a righteous and enigmatic figure whom God "takes": "Enoch walked with God after the birth of Methuselah three hundred years and had other sons and daughters. Thus, all the days of Enoch were three hundred sixty-five years. Enoch walked with God; then he was no more, because God took him" (Gen. 5:22–24, New Revised Standard Version (NRSV)). Of all the people given in the surrounding lists, Enoch is the only one who is not explicitly said to have died, and one obvious way to read the verse would be that Enoch was assumed into heaven. What did he do to warrant being taken, rather than dying? In the literature devoted to him, Enoch's righteousness enables him to ascend to heaven where God reveals to him the secrets of nature and the calendar as well as the end time (Nickelsburg 43–53).

One specialized type of literature, the testament, employs a figure mentioned in authoritative texts and around whom a new text is composed. These texts are often modeled on the testamentary speeches of scriptural figures, such as Jacob's in Genesis 49 or Moses' in Deuteronomy 31–34 (Dimant 416). Jews in the Hellenistic period produced a number of texts that purport to be the deathbed speeches of ancient patriarchs to their children. Thus, Amram, Moses' father, who only merits mention in the scriptures for his paternity (Exod. 6:18, 20; Num. 26.58–59), has a number of traditions build up around him in the Second Temple period, one of them a testament found in five copies (4Q543–548) in Qumran Cave 4. Known as the Visions of Amram, the work presumes to give Amram's last words to his children, particularly to Moses and Miriam, partly through the recounting of a dream vision he has had. Other examples are the 4QTestament of Qahat and 4QTestament of Naphtali. Another series of testaments, known as the Testaments of the Twelve Patriarchs, has each of Jacob's sons giving their final words to their sons. At least in their present form, they are clearly Christian, though some propose an originally Jewish document that underwent Christian revision (see Nickelsburg 302–15).

The Martyrdom and Ascension of Isaiah exemplifies how a perceived gap in scripture can result in a new narrative. This short book is a composite text that divides into about two equal parts. The first part, called the Martyrdom of Isaiah, itself comprises two sections. The first, 1:1–3:12, was likely written in Hebrew in Palestine, perhaps during the second century BCE (Knibb 149–50). It tells the story of King Manasseh's execution of the prophet Isaiah. No story of Isaiah's death is preserved in the narratives of Kings or in the work attributed to the prophet; the Martyrdom of Isaiah fills that gap and shows a clear relationship to the narrative found in 2 Kings 21 and 22. The bloodthirsty portrayal of Manasseh in the Martyrdom, which contrasts with the righteousness of his father, Hezekiah, seems to have sprung from consideration of 2 Kings 21:16: "Moreover, Manasseh shed very much innocent blood, until he had filled Jerusalem from one end to the other." One victim of that bloodshed according to the Martyrdom was Isaiah.

The Epistle of Jeremiah pretends to be a letter written by the prophet Jeremiah to Jews about to go into exile in Babylon in which he warns them about being seduced by the idols they will see there. It is neither from Jeremiah nor a letter, but rather it is a diatribe against gentile idolatry. The work takes its inspiration from the anti-idolatry poem in Jeremiah 10 and from the letter that Jeremiah wrote to those in Babylon preserved in Jeremiah 29 (Nickelsburg 35), which counsels the exiles to "seek the welfare of the city where I [i.e., God] have sent you into exile" (Jer. 29:7). This text, then, masquerades as a preparatory letter addressed to those heading into exile, written before the letter of Jeremiah 29. The date and provenance of the work are uncertain. The author of 2 Maccabees seems to know it, however, and a Greek fragment of it was found in Cave 7 at Qumran. At the least it was known in Palestine in our period.

Other Examples

Aramaic Levi Document, which served as an important source for the Testaments of the Twelve Patriarchs; Book of Giants from Qumran, another Enochic work; Prayer of Manasseh(?), which takes a different approach from the Martyrdom of Isaiah and gives the content of the prayer that 2 Chronicles 33:12–13 says Manasseh prayed; Testament of Moses.

Category 2: Implicit Use of or Allusion to Earlier Texts

The use of authoritative literature without any explicit formal marking or citation formulae constitutes the most common way that Jewish texts employ scripture, and for many of the texts of our period, this is the primary, and sometimes only way, that they interact with it. One can distinguish between implicit use, in which a text adopts the specific continuous wording from a recognizable source, and allusion, which "consists of interweaving into a new composition motifs, key-terms and small phrases" that can be recognized as deriving from a specific source text (Dimant 401, 410). Devorah Dimant establishes three words as the consecutive string necessary for implicit use of scripture, and indeed that would seem to be about as short as one could accept for identifying such use. For this category of uses of scripture, a writer usually draws on relatively short passages from the older text, and in both cases the older text is woven into the fabric of the new one. Thus, discovering the depth or richness of meaning that the implicit use or allusion imparts to the new text depends on the reader's knowledge of the source text and his or her ability to identify its intertextual presence (Dimant 400).

Within this category, we see several types of relationship to the older texts. In some cases, the newer text imitates or incorporates language from authoritative texts as a way of reasserting its authority and of shaping the identity of its readers. So, for example, the Hodayot or Thanksgiving Hymns from Qumran are replete with the language of scripture. They have a dense network of intertextual associations, and the work as a whole has a rich "biblical texture," as Michael Fishbane characterizes it (357). One type of implicit relation to authoritative literature is the use of models or motifs derived from those texts that appear without any obvious reference to the original context. A classic example would be the Book of Tobit (though there is a debate as to the geographical provenance of Tobit: see Fitzmyer 54 (Palestine) and Nickelsburg 34 (Diaspora)). Tobit's plot often follows that of Job, even to the point of Tobit's wife chastising him as Job's wife scolds him. Thus, although Job is never mentioned nor is there any unambiguous reference to the book, Tobit becomes a Job-like character (Dimant 417–41). The book of Tobit also employs explicit citation of scriptural texts (see 2:6, where Amos 8:10 is quoted), and is an example of a text that relates to earlier antecedents in multiple ways.

Methodologically for this category, it can be difficult sometimes to determine the extent to which a Jewish author is specifically drawing on a clearly identifiable *textual* antecedent. First of all, how close does close have to be to identify an allusion to an earlier Israelite text in a Hellenistic Jewish one? Second, although these authors certainly had access to written texts, to what extent did the traditions we find in these works come down to their authors in a stable, written form? What was the relationship between written and oral tradition and learning in this period and how might that affect the ways a writer might know and relate to traditional material? How we answer these questions will make us more or less confident in identifying possible allusions in our texts. We will begin by examining implicit uses of scripture.

Judith 9:2–4

O Lord, God of my father Symeon, to whom you gave a sword in hand for vengeance on aliens, the ones who ravaged the virgin's vulva for defilement and stripped naked the thigh for shame and polluted the vulva for disgrace, for you said: "It shall not be thus," and they did (it); therefore you handed over their rulers for slaughter, and their bed, which, deceived, felt ashamed at their deceit, for blood, and you struck down slaves with lords and lords upon their thrones, and you handed over their wives for pillage and their daughters for captivity and all their spoils for division among the sons loved by you, who also were zealous in zeal for you and detested the defilement of their blood, and called upon you as helper. O God, my God, listen to me, the widow. (New English Translation of the Septuagint (NETS))

Because the text of Judith 9:2–4 does not mention explicitly the key actors but only summarizes the story, I consider this passage an implicit use of Genesis, a judgment that differs from that of Dimant (396—7), who considers this an explicit use of scripture. Without naming the victim, Judith's prayer recalls the events of Shechem's rape of Dinah and her brothers' revenge on the Shechemites narrated in Genesis 34. As part of her prayer, Judith essentially inverts this event in her own plan to kill Holofernes, the general of the Assyrians, who are surrounding the city of Bethulia. Among other things, her recounting of Dinah's rape pins guilt on all the Shechemites and not simply on Shechem who raped her and characterizes what they did as deceit. In describing her own intended actions, she emphasizes the deceit by which she plans to defeat Holofernes and hence the Assyrian army (9:10, 13). Moreover, since her plan involved sexually seducing the Assyrian general, she herself, as a pious widow, might well end up in the position of Dinah, and her appeal to Dinah's rape emphasizes the sexual danger of her plan as well. (For a detailed discussion of the relationship between Judith 9 and Genesis 34, see Newman 123–8.)

4QWiles of the Wicked Woman (4Q184)

This short wisdom text from Qumran describes a woman who leads righteous men into sin and death. The figure of the woman is a development of the strange or foreign woman of Proverbs 2, 5, 7 and 9 (see Tamara Cohn Eskenazi's essay in this volume). Although the woman of 4Q184 differs from the strange woman of Proverbs, the poem throughout depends on Proverbs for its language and ideas. So, to cite two examples, Proverbs 5:5 warns that "her feet go down to death; her steps follow the path to Sheol." 4Q184 reflects this characterization as "her feet sink to act wickedly and to walk towards crimes" (line 3). In Proverbs 7, the woman beckons her prey, describing to him her couches "decked with coverings, colored spreads of Egyptian linen." 4Q184 retains the couches but transforms them into metaphors: "Her beds are couches of corruption … Her lodgings are couches of darkness and in the heart of the night are her tents" (lines 6–7). 4Q184 takes the overtly sensuous seductress of Proverbs who aims to seduce young men and, through use of the images from Proverbs and of metaphor, turns her into a much more dangerous and murky creature, who resides in Sheol and who can lead the unsuspecting there without them realizing it.

Wisdom of Ben Sira 38:5

"Was not water made sweet by wood in order that his (or: its) power might be known?"

The book of Ben Sira, written in second-century BCE Jerusalem, contains many implicit uses and allusions to scriptural texts (but the sage makes no formal citations of earlier literature). His relation to scripture is particularly clear in chapters 44–50, where he praises a series of famous persons from Israel's past, culminating in the praise of Simon II, the high priest during his time. Yet, Ben Sira evokes scriptural events elsewhere in his book. In chapter 38:1, the sage encourages his charges to honor the doctor, "for indeed God has established him," and in verse 4, he argues that the "sensible person" will not despise medicines, since God created them out of the earth. Verse 5 is part of the argument in favor of medicine. Here Ben Sira refers to the incident reported in Exodus 15:23–25, where Moses throws a piece of wood into bitter water, making it sweet and drinkable. Depending on whether we translate the Hebrew as "his power" or "its power," the point is either that medicine testifies to God's power manifest in the wonders of creation (cf. vv. 6, 8) or that this scriptural text demonstrates the power that inheres in natural materials to heal and to cure.

Turning to allusion, the examples below illustrate both the way that allusions to authoritative texts deepen and enrich the meaning of the new text and at the same time how difficult they can be to identify.

1 Maccabees 3:10–12

The book of 1 Maccabees is one of two texts that narrate events connected with the Hasmonean revolt against Antiochus IV Epiphanes. It survives in Greek, although scholars believe that it was written originally in Hebrew, and it contains explicit references to scriptural texts as well as allusions to them. Early on we are introduced to one of its heroes, Judas, son of a priest named Mattathias who has refused to perform sacrifices to non-Jewish gods and who instigated a rebellion. Early in his military campaigns, Judas defeats a certain Apollonius. The text employs language that recalls David's defeat of Goliath in 1 Samuel 17. As in the earlier text, a large force of Gentiles is marshaled against the Jews, and we read that Judas "went out to meet him, and he defeated him and killed him" (3:11). Although the latter part of verse 11 intimates that this clash engaged large forces, the beginning of the verse portrays it as a mano-a-mano encounter between two men, in the same way that David's contest against Goliath was one-on-one. In verse 12, Judas takes Apollonius's sword and wields it throughout his campaigns, which recalls David's use of Goliath's sword to decapitate him (1 Sam. 17:51) and his use of it later in battle (1 Sam. 21:9). Although 1 Maccabees nowhere refers to David or explicitly connects Judas and the earlier Israelite hero, the author of 1 Maccabees has used language that constructs Judas as a David-like figure, defending his people against the Gentiles.

2 Maccabees 9

This work, which narrates events from the Hasmonean revolt until about 161 BCE, is a condensation of a five-volume work by an otherwise unknown Jason of Cyrene (2 Maccabees 2:23). The passage that concerns us here reports the death of Antiochus IV. Several features of the narrative allude to the prophesy of the fall of the king of Babylon in Isaiah 14, again without quoting or otherwise pointing directly to that passage. So, Isaiah 14:4, "How his insolence has ceased," is transformed in the narrative of 2 Maccabees as, "Thus, he who only a little while before had thought in his superhuman arrogance that he could command the waves of the sea was brought down to earth and carried in a litter" (9:8). Antiochus, who is infested with worms and becomes so weak that he has to be carried, has fulfilled in his body the prophecy of Isaiah 14:10–11: "You too have become as weak as we … maggots are the bed beneath you and worms are your covering." Finally, the king of Isaiah 14, who dared to think that he could ascend to heaven and raise his throne above God's, "above the stars of God" (14:13), and is dashed down, becomes in 2 Maccabees the king, who "a little while before had thought that he could touch the stars of heaven" and whose stench prevented others from approaching close enough to carry his litter (9:10). By describing the dramatic and precipitous fall of Antiochus through an allusion to Isaiah 14, the epitomist of 2 Maccabees emphasizes the consequences of defying the God of the Jews and persecuting his people.

Other Examples

1QRule of the Congregation (1Q28a); 4QMysteries; 4QWords of the Luminaries; Songs of the Sabbath Sacrifice; 4QInstruction; Baruch; Psalms of Solomon 11. All the texts in this list only use scripture implicitly or allude to it.

Category 3: Explicit Citation and Use of Scriptural Antecedents

Explicit use of authoritative literature can take several forms in our literature. The most overt is the quotation of scripture, which cites continuous wording of the source text along with some special way of marking it as a citation. Introductory formulae such as "As it is written," "As it is written in the book of Moses," "And the Lord spoke to Moses, saying" or "As you [i.e., God] have said" make clear that the writer is quoting. Quite a number of texts from the Dead Sea Scrolls employ this device. In some cases, however, such as we will see below in 4QMMT, an introductory formula could just as well lead to a summary of the scriptural text, which also would constitute an explicit use, since the reader is expected to know the specifics of the reference.

In some other cases, however, explicit use of an earlier text might not carry specific introductory formulae, but citation is clear nonetheless. Two kinds of texts from Qumran work this way. The first, the *continuous pesher*, reproduces the running text of a prophetic work and then interprets it. The citation and accompanying interpretation are formally separated by the Hebrew word *pišrô*, "its interpretation is." For example, the *pesher* on Isaiah (3Q4) simply begins with a quotation of Isaiah 1:1 without any introductory formula. The other Qumran type is the para-prophetic work in which the text is presented as the prophecy of the scriptural prophet, often quoting or invoking sections of the scriptural text and including its interpretation as if the prophet gave it. A good example comes from 4QPseudo-Ezekiel (of which six fragmentary copies survive). The work is framed as a dialog between God and Ezekiel that uses the scriptural text of Ezekiel as a platform for the new text. In 4Q385 6, for instance, the text explicitly refers to "the vision that Ezekiel saw" and a version of the prophet's vision of God's chariot throne (cf. Ezek. 1 and 10) follows with interpretive details found only here. (Dimant also includes mention of biblical figures as part of her category of explicit use of earlier texts; I have included many of these in category 1.)

Daniel 9

"In the first year of his reign, I, Daniel, perceived in the books the number of years that, according to the word of the Lord to the prophet Jeremiah, must be fulfilled for the devastation of Jerusalem, namely, seventy years" (v. 2, NRSV) … (Daniel then prays to God for the people, and in verse 20 the angel Gabriel appears to him and says) … "Seventy weeks are decreed for your people and your holy city: to finish the transgression, to put an end to sin, and to atone for iniquity, to bring in everlasting righteousness, to seal both vision and prophet, and to anoint a most holy place" (v. 24).

The book of Daniel is a composite work supposedly authored by a certain Daniel, who lived in Babylon during the exile in the sixth century BCE. The first six chapters contain diaspora stories of Daniel's interactions with the Babylonian royal court (see Tamara Cohn Eskenazi's essay in this volume). The apocalypse of chapters 7–12 was written in the period of the Hasmonean revolt (see John J. Collins's essay in this volume). In this passage Jeremiah's prophecy of a 70-year exile preceding God's punishment of the Babylonians (Jer. 25:11–12 and 29:10) is interpreted as being weeks of years (Dan. 9:24–27), which are broken down into various periods that lead up to the time when "the decreed end is poured out on the desolator" (9:27). This interpretation of the older prophecy actualizes it in the time of the writer of Daniel and anticipates the destruction of Antiochus IV Epiphanes.

4QMMT (4Q394–399)

This significant text from Qumran explains differences in legal interpretation and practice (ḥălākâ in Hebrew) between the author and those who side with him, a "we" group mentioned in the text, and those who take an opposing approach, addressed as "you." The work treats a variety of subjects on which the two sides differ, including offerings in the temple, temple purity, those admitted into the temple precincts, and the purity of Jerusalem.

The following example illustrates how an authoritative legal text from the Mosaic Law is cited and explicated (see also the essay by Bernard Levinson and Tina Sherman in this volume). In lines 78–85 (of the composite text) the author addresses "fornications carried out in the midst of the people" (78). Our author is worried about marriages between priests and nonpriests. For the "we" contingent, priests should only marry within the priestly group. The justification for this position is based on a reference to Leviticus 19:19, which forbids breeding two different kinds of animals, sowing a field with two different kinds of seed or wearing garments with two different kinds of cloth:

> And concerning his [pure animal], it is written that he shall not pair off two species; and concerning clothing, [it is written that no] materials are to be mixed; and he will not sow his field [or his vineyard with two species] because they are holy. And the sons of Aaron are the [holiest of the holy], but you know that a part of the priests and the people mingle, and they squeeze each other and defile the [holy] seed … (lines 79–84)

In the author's opinion, because the law separates such things as animals, seeds and cloth, a principle is established about mixing unlike things. In the case of priests and the laity, the holiness of the priests must mean that they cannot mix with nonpriests, because these two groups of people are not alike.

4QFlorilegium (4Q174)

This text, extant in one copy from Qumran Cave 4, contains a string of quotations from the books of 2 Samuel, Exodus, Amos, Psalms, Isaiah, Ezekiel, Daniel and Deuteronomy (in that order) with interspersed interpretive commentary whose goal is to demonstrate the relationship among the texts. (For a similar type of excerpted text with brief commentary, see 4QTestimonia (4Q175).) Some scholars have characterized the work as a *thematic pesher*, since it introduces citations as proof texts that explicate the themes of the eschatological temple and messianic figures (Lim 14). The following passage highlights the text's use of scripture: "'[And] an enemy [will trouble him no mo]re, [nor will] the son of iniquity [afflict him again] as at the beginning. From the day on which [I established judges] over my people, Israel.' This (refers to) the house [which they will establish] for [him] in the last days, as it is written in the book of [Moses] …" Thereafter follows a quotation from Exodus 15:17–18.

Damascus Document

This foundational text, discovered originally among the medieval Cairo Geniza manuscripts and then later at Qumran Cave 4, provides us with a beautiful example of how the breadth of authoritative literature in the Second Temple period could extend beyond what we now recognize as the Bible. In column 16 of the Cairo text (= 4Q268 2 ii 4–5), the Book of Jubilees (see below) is referred to in the same manner as scripture is elsewhere: "And the exact interpretation of their ages about the blindness of Israel in all these matters, behold, it is defined in the book 'Of the Divisions of the Periods According to Their Jubilees and Their Weeks.'" Here readers are pointed to an authoritative text that will inform them about these matters. The context of the citation further emphasizes the scriptural status of Jubilees. Immediately preceding this citation, the text mentions the one who will "return to the Law of Moses," and after the reference, we read: "And on the day that the man has pledged himself to return to the Law of Moses …" A quotation from Deuteronomy follows this statement.

Other Examples

The Community Rule (1QS); New Jerusalem (2Q24, 4Q554, 4Q555, 5Q15, 11Q18); *Pesharim* on Hosea, Micah, Nahum, Habakkuk, Zephaniah, Malachi and Psalms; 4QPseudo-Moses; 4QApocryphon of Jeremiah (C and D).

Category 4: Revision and Rewriting of Earlier Texts

In recent scholarship the type of literature often called "rewritten scripture" has been the object of much debate, particularly around questions of whether there is a genre to be defined or whether this is a broader category of texts, which texts belong to it, and what authority these texts might claim for themselves. To explicate all these issues would take me far beyond the purposes of this chapter, but however these questions are resolved, all scholars recognize that taking earlier texts and extensively revising or rewriting them to create a new work constitutes a widespread phenomenon in our period (see David Carr's essay in this volume). The best working definition for my purposes is Sidnie White Crawford's: "These Rewritten Scriptures constitute a category or group of texts characterized by a close adherence to a recognizable and already authoritative base text (narrative or legal) and a recognizable degree of scribal intervention into that base text for the purposes of exegesis" (12–13).

For the most part, one of the distinguishing features of these texts is their scale. They take up and revise/rewrite large swaths of narrative or legal material. Since they often reproduce the exact wording of their sources, these texts might be considered a variation on those that use scripture explicitly. Yet, since they also do not cite the authoritative text with any kind of special marker and the rewriting usually results in a new text, they are akin to the para-prophetic works I discussed above. Perhaps the most familiar example of this kind of text comes from the Bible itself. 1–2 Chronicles, a work dating from the late Persian or early Hellenistic period, rewrites the books of 1–2 Samuel and 1–2 Kings in order to emphasize the importance and centrality of the temple for the postexilic Jewish community based on its preexilic significance, which is founded on the faithfulness of its first two kings, David and Solomon (see Tamara Cohn Eskenazi's essay in this volume). Thus, as he works out this agenda in the course of this rewritten text, the author tends to eliminate from his narrative negative or embarrassing events in the lives of these two kings, who become models of faithful obedience to God.

Jubilees

Before the discovery of the Dead Sea Scrolls, Jubilees would have been the parade example of this type of literature. Written in Hebrew, but only fully extant in the Ethiopic language Ge'ez, and most likely dating from the 160s BCE or slightly earlier, Jubilees reworks Genesis 1 through Exodus 14. It follows the sequence of the scriptural text fairly closely and often depends on its wording, even though it does not reproduce extensive sections. The narrative is framed as God's revelation to Moses on Mount Sinai mediated by the Angel of the Presence from heavenly tablets (1:26–29). The work shows a decided interest in *halakhah*, and it frequently portrays the patriarchs as observing the laws of the Mosaic Torah in the period before it was given to Moses. These observances form the basis for what is later written in the Law. So, for example, in Jubilees 16:20–31, Abraham observes the feast of Sukkoth (otherwise known as Booths or Tabernacles). He receives God's blessing as a result:

> And we [i.e., God] blessed him and his seed who are after him in every generation of the earth because he observed this feast in its time according to the heavenly tablets. Therefore it is ordained in the heavenly tablets concerning Israel that they will be observers of the

feast of booths seven days with joy in the seventh month, which is acceptable before the Lord as an eternal law in their generations throughout all time, year by year. (16:28–29)

The festivals throughout Jubilees follow a solar calendar, which was a subject of bitter debate in Judaism during this period. Another important theme is the levitical priest-hood, which Jubilees traces from Noah, who offers the first proper sacrifice after the Flood, through the patriarchs to Levi (Crawford 75–8; compare S. A. Geller's essay in this volume).

Temple Scroll

Found in Cave 11 and Cave 4 at Qumran, the Temple Scroll is arguably one of the most important discovered among the Dead Sea Scrolls. It purports to be the actual words of God spoken to Moses on Mount Sinai, and as such, it gives almost exclusively legal material with practically no narrative at all. The text begins with Exodus 34 and ends with Deuteronomy 23, although in between it shifts from book to book (Crawford 86–7). In this way it differs from Jubilees, which is narrative, and maintains the chronological order of the story from Genesis through Exodus.

The redactor of the Temple Scroll has employed several sources for his work (Craw-ford 89–94). One (cols 3–13, 30–47) focuses on the Jerusalem temple and depends for the most part on Exodus 25–27 (also using 1 Kings 6 and Ezek. 40–48). The second (cols 13–30) outlines the calendar of festivals and relies on Numbers 28–29 and Leviticus 23. The third (cols 48–51) concerns purity laws and draws on several sources, includ-ing Leviticus 12 and 15. The final source (cols 51–66) paraphrases material taken from the Book of Deuteronomy.

This scroll, then, does more than simply follow a scriptural text. Its redactor has taken material from several places and has incorporated them into a new text, which claims the authority of Moses. The scroll advocates a number of innovations that distinguish it from its scriptural sources. As part of the festival calendar, the scroll has four First Fruits celebrations to be observed at 50-day intervals – barley (cols 21:12–23:2); wheat (cols 18:10–19:9); wine (cols 19:11–21:10); oil (cols 21:12–23:2) – rather than the one, the Feast of Weeks, established in Numbers 28:26–31 and Leviticus 23:15–21. The rationale for these festivals probably comes from Deuteronomy 14:22–26, which commands that these four products be tithed (Crawford 91–2). Thus, the scroll's new configuration likely stems from a desire to harmonize scriptural passages. With respect to its purity regulations, the scroll, as a rule, extends purity demands beyond those of its source texts. As a result, Moses' command to the Israelites to refrain from sex for three days in order to prepare for God's appearance (Exod. 19:14–15) is now extended to the city of Jerusalem for all time (col. 45:11–12; Crawford 92–3).

Genesis Apocryphon

This fragmentary scroll, found in Cave 1 at Qumran, is written in Aramaic and reworks stories from the Book of Genesis, following that text's order. The scroll as we have it now is divided into three sections: Noah's birth (cols 0–5); a section on Noah, explicitly entitled "A copy of the book of the words of Noah" (col. 6:29; cols 6–17); and the story of Abram (cols 19–22). One example of how the Genesis Apocryphon rewrites the Genesis narrative exemplifies its approach. In columns 19–20, we see the same story narrated as in Genesis 12:10–20 in which Abram passes off his wife, Sarai, to the Egyptian Pharaoh, claiming that she is his sister. The account in the Genesis Apocryphon attempts to resolve potential problems in the Genesis story. So, in Genesis, after Pharaoh's officials see Sarai's beauty, she is taken into Pharaoh's house as his wife, and Pharaoh rewards Abram with gifts of animals and slaves. God then plagues Pharaoh, who somehow discovers the ruse. Pharaoh confronts Abram, gives Sarai back and sends them away. In the Genesis Apocryphon, after Sarai is taken, Abram beseeches God in sorrow about this development, and God sends a plague on Pharaoh that prevents him from approaching, let alone sleeping with, Sarai. After two years of this, the ruse is discovered, Abram prays for Pharaoh's healing, and Pharaoh sends Abram and Sarai away with many gifts. This rewriting removes any suspicion that (a) Abram has pimped his wife to Pharaoh, since the gifts that were given to Abram up-front in Genesis become in the Genesis Apocryphon presents from Pharaoh whom Abram's prayer has healed; and (b) Sarai has not slept with Pharaoh as his wife, a reading that Genesis not only makes possible but seems to encourage. Thus, the Genesis Apocryphon casts a much more positive light on this situation than Genesis might appear to.

Other Examples

Pseudo-Philo, *Book of Biblical Antiquities* (toward the very end of our period); Josephus, *Antiquities* (also at the limits of our period); Theodotus(?), fragments of whose poetry are preserved by the Christian church father Eusebius of Caesarea; Eupolemus(?), also preserved in Eusebius.

Category 5: Texts That Relate to Earlier Texts but That Complicate the Previous Categories

The texts treated in this section, while they use earlier scriptural texts, do not fit neatly into the previous categories, and they illustrate some of the complications that are implicit in them.

4QReworked Pentateuch (4QRP)

Some scholars have considered this Qumran text, preserved best in 4Q364 and 365 (along with 4Q158, 4Q366 and 367), as an example of rewritten scripture on a spectrum with the texts I discussed in section 4, and I could have included it there. Indeed, it shares a number of features with these texts, but it also differs in enough respects that I have placed it here. (For the most recent, detailed study of these manuscripts, see Zahn.) The complete work probably contained the entirety of the Pentateuch from Genesis to Deuteronomy, but rather than a copy of these books, 4QRP is characterized by many scribal interventions consisting mostly of harmonizations from other Pentateuchal books, small exegetical comments or the importation of some external material. In that sense, the name of the work is apt as a description of its contents. The issue concerns the nature of the reworking. Many of the exegetical comments are quite brief, and they resolve a perceived lack of clarity in the text. So, for instance, 4Q364 gives the text of Genesis 25:19, "[And these are the descendants of I]saac, the son of Abraham; [he begat Isaac]," and then comes additional text, "whom Sarah [his] wife b[ore] to him." This small addition makes clear that Isaac was Sarah's son, not Hagar's, and as such he should inherit God's promise to Abraham (Crawford 41). A good example of harmonization comes in 4Q364's version of Deuteronomy 2, which narrates the Israelites' journey through Edom. Before the last verse of this section, the redactor inserts from Numbers 20 Moses' request to the king of Edom to traverse his country, not found in Deuteronomy. The resulting text reads: "We will not c]ross in the field or in the vineya[rd and we will n]ot[drink water from the well; we will go on the King's road;] we will n[ot] swerve to the right or left [until we reach your border. But he (i.e., the King of Edom) said,] 'You shall not cro[ss over] me lest [with the sword I come out to meet you'…] (=Num. 20:17–18) Then we moved away from our brethren the children of Esau…" (= Deut. 2:8) (Crawford 44–5). Finally, the most famous addition of material comes in 4Q365 7, which contains the Song of Moses from Exodus 15. In the scriptural text, Moses' sister also sings a song (15:21), but hers is only reported as the first two lines of the song that Moses has sung already. The Qumran text attributes a real song to Miriam, and instead of repeating her brother's lines, we have preserved fragments of her own song: "you despised[…] for the majesty of[…] You are great, O deliverer[…] the hope of the enemy has perished, and he has cea[sed…] they perished in the mighty waters, the enemy[…] Extol the one who raises up, [a ra]nsom you gave[… do]ing gloriously […]."

11QPsalms^a (11Q5)

This large scroll from Cave 11 contains a series of psalms or hymns attributed to David. A short prose composition in column 27 ascribes 3,600 psalms and 450 "songs" to the king. The scroll itself contains a large number of psalms found in the Hebrew Psalter, the Hebrew versions of Psalms 151, 154 and 155, heretofore only extant in a Syriac translation, the eroticizing hymn to Wisdom from Ben Sira 51 and three previously unknown poetic compositions (Plea for Deliverance; Apostrophe to Zion; Hymn to the Creator). The "biblical" psalms do not come in their canonical order and some are interspersed among the other compositions. Thus, for example, columns 1–15 have the order Psalms 109, 105, 146, 148, 121–32, 119, 135–6, and columns 19–22 contain Plea for Deliverance, Psalms 139, 137, 138, Sirach 51, Apostrophe to Zion, and Psalm 93.

The scroll raises significant questions about and is an important piece of evidence for the development of the Psalter as it eventually looked in the Hebrew Bible, but for our purposes, we have in the same manuscript psalms that we know from the Bible, new works, and even a hymn that might have been excerpted from the book of Ben Sira, all ascribed to David, who was well known as a composer of psalms. All of these texts seem to have an equivalent status as Davidic compositions, and the manuscript defies categorization in the previous four sections.

Aramaic Targums

One feature of ancient use of authoritative texts that often gets overlooked is translation. While most of the Greek translations were made in Egypt, some were certainly executed in Palestine. Indeed, some of the Jewish works discussed above were written in Hebrew but their primary transmission has been in another language. A perfect example is 1 Maccabees, originally composed in Hebrew, now lost, but which survives in a Greek translation.

The practice of translating Hebrew scriptural texts in Aramaic began in the Hellenistic period and continued for long after. Some Aramaic versions of scriptural books were discovered at Qumran (4Q156 (Leviticus) and 4Q157 and 11Q10 (Job)). One of the well-known characteristics of the Aramaic Targums (*targum* means translation) is the frequent propensity to exegete the Hebrew text – in a way to engage in the same kinds of scribal interventions that we have seen above. However we categorize these texts, translations belong in any discussion of how Second Temple Jewish literature used earlier scriptural antecedents.

Although I have not been able to list every Jewish work produced in Palestine in the Hellenistic period – there are many more texts from Qumran in particular – those that I have examined provide a sufficient sampling of the literature that Jews composed. In the last 50 years, renewed scholarly attention has been directed to Jewish texts produced in the Second Temple period. Of course, the discovery of the Dead Sea Scrolls gave additional impetus to examining these texts anew. The results of that scholarly study have emphasized the vitality and dynamism of Judaism in this period, a vitality that is expressed in the diversity of literature that we have seen in this chapter. And yet, within that diversity a common thread emerges that bound Jews together as Jews – the acknowledgment of an authoritative national literature that set the broad terms for what it meant to be a Jew, despite how different individuals and groups grappled with and determined those texts' authority, meaning and implications.

Bibliography

Brooke, George J. "The Dead Sea Scrolls." In John Barton (ed.), *The Biblical World*, vol. 1 (pp. 250–69). London: Routledge, 2002. A short and accessible introduction to the scrolls.
Charlesworth, James H. *The Old Testament Pseudepigrapha*. 2 vols. Garden City, NY: Doubleday, 1983/1985. Introductions to and translations of many important nonbiblical Jewish works.
Collins, John J. "Wisdom reconsidered in light of the Scrolls." *Dead Sea Discoveries* 4 (1997): 265–81. A discussion of whether wisdom can be considered a literary genre in this period.
Collins, John J. and Gregory E. Sterling (eds). *Hellenism in the Land of Israel*. Notre Dame, IN: University of Notre Dame Press, 2001. Contains articles on aspects of Hellenism and Hellenistic Judaism.

Crawford, Sidnie White. *Rewriting Scripture in Second Temple Times*. Grand Rapids, MI: Eerdmans, 2008. A study of different ways that Early Jewish texts rewrite their scriptural antecedents.

Dimant, Devorah. "Use and interpretation of Mikra in the Apocrypha and Pseudepigrapha." In Martin J. Mulder (ed.), *Mikra: Text, Translation, Reading and Interpretation of the Hebrew Bible in Ancient Judaism and Early Christianity* (pp. 379–419). Compendia Rerum Iudaicarum ad Novum Testamentum 2.1. Assen: Van Gorcum, 1988. Discusses the ways that Apocrypha and Pseudepigrapha use and interpret "biblical" texts.

Fishbane, Michael. "Use, authority and interpretation of Mikra at Qumran." In Martin J. Mulder (ed.). *Mikra: Text, Translation, Reading and Interpretation of the Hebrew Bible in Ancient Judaism and Early Christianity* (pp. 339–77). Compendia Rerum Iudaicarum ad Novum Testamentum 2.1. Assen: Van Gorcum, 1988. Discusses the ways that the Qumran community used and interpreted "biblical" texts.

Fitzmyer, Joseph. *Tobit*. Commentaries on Early Jewish Literature. Berlin: de Gruyter, 2003. A detailed commentary on the book of Tobit.

García Martínez, Floretino. *The Dead Sea Scrolls Translated*. 2nd edn. Leiden: Brill, 1996. A convenient English translation of the most important Dead Sea Scrolls.

Hengel, Martin. *Judaism and Hellenism*. Philadelphia: Fortress, 1974. One of the most influential studies of the effects of Hellenism on Jews.

Knibb, Michael A. "Martyrdom and Ascension of Isaiah." In Charlesworth, *Old Testament Pseudepigrapha*, vol. 2 (pp. 143–76). A recent introduction to and translation of this text.

Lim, Timothy H. *Pesharim*. Companion to the Qumran Scrolls 3. London: Sheffield Academic Press, 2002. An accessible introduction to and study of the *pesher* texts from Qumran.

Neusner, Jacob, William Scott Green, and Ernest S. Frerichs. *Judaisms and Their Messiahs at the Turn of the Christian Era*. Cambridge: Cambridge University Press, 1987. A collection of articles on the idea of the messiah.

Newman, Judith H. *Praying by the Book: The Scripturalization of Prayer in Second Temple Judaism*. Society of Biblical Literature: Early Judaism and Its Literature 14. Atlanta: Scholars Press, 1999. A study of the way that early Jewish prayers incorporate and interpret scriptural texts.

Newsom, Carol. "Spying out the land: A report from genology." In Roland Boer (ed.), *Bakhtin and Genre Theory in Biblical Studies* (pp. 19–31). Semeia Studies 93. Atlanta: Society of Biblical Literature, 2007. A study of recent developments in genre theory in biblical studies.

Nickelsburg, George W. E. *Jewish Literature between the Bible and the Mishnah*. 2nd edn. Minneapolis: Fortress, 2005. An important introduction to Second Temple Jewish literature.

Rajak, Tessa. *The Jewish Dialogue with Greece and Rome: Studies in Cultural and Social Interaction*. Leiden: Brill, 2002. A collection of the author's essays on Jewish interaction with the larger Mediterranean world.

Schürer, Emil. *The History of the Jewish People in the Age of Jesus Christ*, rev. and ed. Geza Vermes, Fergus Millar, and Martin Goodman. 3 vols. Edinburgh: T&T Clark, 1973, 1979, 1986. A complete revision of a classic work on ancient Judaism.

Ulrich, Eugene. "The Bible in the making: The Scriptures at Qumran." In Eugene Ulrich (ed.), *The Dead Sea Scrolls and the Origins of the Bible* (pp. 17–33). Grand Rapids, MI: Eerdmans, 1999. A collection of Ulrich's essays on how the Bible took shape based primarily on the evidence from the Dead Sea Scrolls.

VanderKam, James C. *An Introduction to Early Judaism*. Grand Rapids, MI: Eerdmans, 2001. An accessible introduction to Second Temple Judaism.

Zahn, Molly M. *Rethinking Rewritten Scripture: Composition and Exegesis in the 4QReworked Pentateuch Manuscripts*. Studies on the Texts of the Desert of Judah 95. Leiden: Brill, 2011. A detailed study of 4QRP and its impact on how scholars talk about rewritten scripture as a category.

CHAPTER 28

Art and Iconography
Representing Yahwistic Divinity

Theodore J. Lewis

One of the most vibrant areas of interdisciplinary research on ancient Israelite culture has been the study of how divinity was represented through image and text. In recent years a plethora of studies combining archaeology, art history, textual studies (of the Hebrew Bible and epigraphic material), and especially iconography has focused on the ways in which the portrayal of Israelite divinity is similar to and different from the representation of divinity elsewhere in the ancient Near East (see the essays by Elizabeth Bloch-Smith, Christopher Rollston, Mark Smith, and Neal Walls in this volume).[1] Moreover, new data continue to be added to our corpus (e.g., a divine bull rider from Tel Dan and the large bronze figurine from Hazor (see Ornan, "Lady," "Ba'al")) as our understanding of older exemplars (e.g., the Bes figures from Kuntillet Ajrud (see Meshel 165–9)) continues to be refined.

A Concentration on the Anthropomorphic

What has been relatively constant throughout much of the debate has been a keen focus on whether Yahweh was represented anthropomorphically. Central to this discussion has been questioning the degree to which there was any carryover of the Late Bronze Age tradition of representing divinity anthropomorphically into the Iron Age. Late Bronze Age anthropomorphic figurines that have been considered to be divine males are attested at Hazor, Megiddo, Bet-Shemesh, Tel Kinneret and Tell-Balâṭah (see figure 28.1).

If we situate our study within the broader ancient Near East, it is easy to conclude that humans have always imagined their gods as humans. In Egypt, even the concepts of sky, air and earth are portrayed anthropomorphically through the deities Nut, Shu and Geb (figure 28.2). Ugaritic 'Ilu in ancient Syria even knows how to throw such a drinking

Figure 28.1   Male bronze figurine from Tell-Balâṭah.
Source: Photo by Lee C. Ellenberger; reproduced by permission of the Joint Expedition to Tell-Balâṭah and E. F. Campbell.

party that he falls down dead drunk – and perhaps he is portrayed on a drinking mug, cup in hand (figure 28.3).

The search for anthropomorphic representations of Yahwistic divinity is all the more understandable when one considers how anthropomorphic representation of Yahweh appears on almost every other page of the Hebrew Bible. Yahweh is a "*man* of war" whose right *hand* shatters his enemies, whose *nostrils* blast waters into a pile (Exod. 15:3, 6, 8). Isaiah seats Yahweh on a throne as does the Deuteronomist (Isa. 6:1–2; 1 Kings 22:19). Job's divine slayer gnashes his *teeth* and pierces with his *eyes* (Job 16:9). Apocalyptic literature will even dress the "Ancient of Days" with the appropriate white raiment and matching *hair* (Dan. 7:9)

At the same time, the ancients fully recognized that the gods were larger than life. Thus the common use of size such as Amun-Re who dwarfs his victims at Karnak (figure 28.4) or the ubiquitous use of horned headdresses (figure 28.5) helped distinguish gods from mortals.

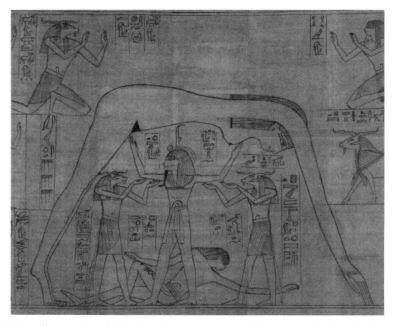

Figure 28.2   The Egyptian deities denoting the concepts of sky (Nut), air (Shu) and earth (Geb) were portrayed anthropomorphically as seen here in the Book of the Dead of Nesitanebtashru
Source: *The Greenfield Papyrus in the British Museum: The Funerary Papyrus of Princess Nesitaneb-tashru ... about B.C. 970. Reproduction ... with Introduction and Description* (London, 1912).

Figure 28.3   A scene from a drinking mug from Late Bronze Age Ugarit found in the so-called "house of the magician priest" in the south acropolis. The offering is presented before an enthroned bearded individual, perhaps representing the deity 'Ilu.
Source: Reproduced by permission of Mission archéologique de Ras Shamra-Ougarit.

Figure 28.4   A giant Amun-Re dwarfing his victims at Karnak.
Source: Reproduced by permission of Baker Publishing Group.

Symbols: Beyond the Anthropomorphic

Yet other ancient artisans and writers preferred to represent divinity symbolically. Here some scholars (e.g. Mettinger, *No Graven Image?* 20–3) have employed the insights gained from Peircean semiotics in describing the relation between the symbol and its referent, between the sign and the *significatum*. Other scholars have intentionally brought the field of iconography to bear. Of particular note is the work of Tallay Ornan (*The Triumph of the Symbol*) who documents the widespread use of abstract symbols from first-millennium Mesopotamia. The use of symbols such as Marduk's spade (figure 28.6) or his symbolic animal, the *Mischwesen mušḫuššu* dragon (figure 28.7), is ubiquitous. (The German term *Mischwesen* is frequently used by scholars to depict hybrid or composite

Figure 28.5   A procession of deities wearing horned headdresses and mounted on various animals coming before an Assyrian king. From Maltaya, located approximately 70 kilometers north of Mosul.

Source: Victor Place, *Ninive et l'Assyrie*, vol. 3 (Paris: Imprimerie Impériale, 1867), plate 45.

Figure 28.6   The god Marduk with his spade symbol and symbolic animal, the *mušḫuššu* dragon.

Source: L. W. King, *Babylonian Boundary-Stones and Memorial-Tablets in the British Museum* (London, 1912).

Figure 28.7   Marduk's symbolic animal, the *mušḫuššu* dragon.
Source: Reproduced by permission of Baker Publishing Group.

creatures of a fantastic nature: e.g., seven-headed dragons or cherubim creatures with mixed features of humans, lions, birds and bulls.) Consider too the Sippar tablet where the anthropomorphic image (*ṣalmu*) of a horned Shamash – twice the size of the three standing individuals – appears alongside the surrogate disk emblem (*nipḫu*) of the sun (figure 28.8).

From Sacred Stone to Sacred Emptiness

What I would like to explore with this short essay are greater degrees of abstraction, acknowledging at the outset that abstraction – a departure from concrete reality – exists along a continuum especially when mixing ideas and art. To what degree can iconography be used for highly abstract traditions? To what degree could such abstract images serve as "attention focusing devices" (à la Renfrew and Bahn 408–9) that served pragmatically in the Judean worship of Yahweh in the Iron Age?

There is no need to rehearse the data on sacred stones for they have been covered in detail in recent years. Of particular note is *No Graven Image?* by Tryggve N. D. Mettinger who introduced the term "material aniconism" to describe *maṣṣēbôt*. A few biblical texts give clear indication that *maṣṣēbôt* could indeed be used for divine symbols (e.g., 2 Kings 3:2; 10:26–27; see also the essay by Elizabeth Bloch-Smith in this volume). The best examples of standing stones being used within sacred space are at Shechem, the Bull Site, Arad, Tel Dan and Hazor. Granted, not all standing stones represent the divine, as can clearly be seen in other uses of the term *maṣṣēbâ* in the Hebrew Bible (e.g., marking a tombstone, Gen. 35:19–20; as a boundary marker, Gen. 31:44–49; as markers for the 12 tribes, Exod. 24:3–8; as a surrogate for a male heir, 2 Sam. 18:18). At a minimum, such conspicuous standing stones constitute "attention focusing devises" that

Figure 28.8   The anthropomorphic image of a horned Shamash appears alongside the surrogate disk emblem of the sun.
Source: Reproduced by permission of Baker Publishing Group.

focus attention to mark a theophanic experience, to signify the place where cult to a deity took place or to mark the ongoing presence of the deity residing in (or symbolized by) a standing stone.

Indeed, whereas most stone steles are anepigraphic, the abstract bull-headed warrior found at Bethsaida (figure 28.9) attests to the presence of either a lunar god with warrior features or a warrior god with lunar features (cf. Ornan, "Bull"). The discovery of a stele at Zincirli (figure 28.10) may help the modern reader with an analogy for how the ancients might conceive of a stone marking the immanent presence of the deity who was also thought to be transcendent. The inscription describes how the deceased person's "soul/essence" (*nabšu*) was envisioned as continuing to dwell <u>in the stele itself</u>! The text reads: "I established a feast at this (burial) chamber: a bull for Hadad … A ram for Shamash, a ram for Hadad … and a ram for my 'soul/essence' (*nbš*) that will be in this

Figure 28.9   A bull-headed warrior found at Bethsaida.
Source: Reproduced by permission of Bethsaida Excavations Project; photographer Hanan Shafir.

stele" (see Pardee). By analogy, just as a stele could house a human "essence" – localized in space and time – so too might it house a divine essence?

Resetting our Iconoclastic Clock: Sacred Emptiness

William Hallo (54) once wrote of "the perennial search" for a divine image of Yahweh. What is lost in such a search – be it via anthropomorphic statues or standing stones used in sacred space – is an exploration of "sacred emptiness." It is time to reset our iconoclastic clock and look at how abstract images are used to depict sacred emptiness in ancient Israel. Yet first a word on iconoclasm: iconoclasm involves the deliberate destruction of a culture's own religious icons. We cannot help but view it pejoratively – even more so if the 2001 destruction of the giant Buddhas of Bamyan by the ultra-iconoclastic Taliban of Afghanistan or the recent barbarous cultural atrocities of ISIS come to mind. The brutality of such acts should not be minimized. And yet, some depictions of the divine as "unseen" (dare we even say some iconoclastic visions) are born of poetry, artistry and/or a philosophy that prefers abstract thought as the best way to depict divine essence.

Perhaps one could say that humans hunger for the divine made visible. Sculptors and painters have given birth to this yearning. Yet for others, divine essence goes beyond such crafting. For them – to borrow the words from the Yale theologian-ethicist H. Richard Niebuhr (120) – abstract ideas "exercise a certain compulsion over the mind … known only by a kind of empathy or by an intuition that outruns sense [perception]." In the Hebrew Bible we come across a wide-ranging use of such abstract expressions: ethereal fire, solar imagery, divine "radiance" (hôd, hādār, kābôd, nōgah), (hypostatic) "name" theology, and empty-space aniconism.

Theoretical Framework

Theoretically, historians of religion describing this type of presence have used Rudolph Otto's categories of *fascinans* (the irresistible attraction of the numinous) and *tremendum* (the overwhelming, dangerous and lethal aspects of the numinous) from his *The Idea of the Holy*. Of special note is the work of ancient Near Eastern historians of religion employing such categories. These scholars would include Thorkild Jacobsen (16), Karel van der Toorn (363) and especially Benjamin Sommer's *The Bodies of God* (97). As a common example of *tremendum*, consider the category of divinity that Mark Smith (27–40) has termed "monstrous divinity." Mesopotamian *Chaoskampf* artisans were especially adept at using their imagination to create incredibly abstract *Mischwesen* representations of destructive divinity such as the seven-headed Tiamat dragon (see Lewis, "CT 13.33–34," for surrealist depictions of such monstrous divinity in text and iconography). Smith has astutely pointed out how benevolent deities are commonly represented by domesticated animals (e.g., bull, calf, bird, cow) whereas destructive deities are undomesticated (e.g., snake, serpent; see also the essay by Neal Walls in this volume). Yet abstract hybrid (composite) images such as *Mischwesen* were unimaginably surreal and therein lay their *tremendum*.

Divine Fire

In the Hebrew Bible, the numinous quality of fire is the most enduring image used to depict Otto's *fascinans* and *tremendum*. Divine fire appears in every Pentateuchal strand, most literary genres and throughout every chronological period. There is no need to detail these for they are extremely well known, especially the burning-bush episode in Exodus 3:1–6 with its unnatural fire that does not consume the bush, and the frequent "pillar of fire" ('ammûd 'ēš) used as a symbol of Yahweh's presence during the Exodus wanderings (Exod. 13:21–22; 14:24; Num. 9:15–16; 14:14; Deut. 1:33, Ps. 78:14; Neh. 9:12, 19). Other notable examples include the flaming torch in Abraham's covenant ceremony (Gen. 15:17), Yahweh's descent as fire on Mount Sinai (Exod. 19:18), and the divine fire in Elijah's Mount Carmel ordeal (1 Kings 18).

A survey of other theophanies in the Hebrew Bible reveals that fire together with associated storm images are the norm for depicting the active presence of Yahweh. Of special note is the theophany found in Psalm 18 (// 2 Sam. 22), where Yahweh descends with "fiery transcendent anthropomorphisms" (to turn a phrase from Ronald Hendel (223); I have added my adjective "fiery" to Hendel's astute phrase).

The earth heaved and quaked,	*wattigʿaš watirʿaš hāʾāreṣ*
foundations of mountains shook;	*ûmôsdê hārîm yirgāzû*
they reeled, because his (anger) burned.	*wayyitgāʿāšû kî-ḥarâ lô*
Smoke rose from his nostrils,	*ʿālâ ʿāšān bəʾappô*
fire from his mouth devouring;	*wəʾēš-mippîw tōʾkēl*
coals blazed forth from him ...	*gehālîm bāʿărû mimmennû ...*
He bowed the heavens and came down	*wayyēṭ šāmayim wayyērad*
Dark clouds beneath his feet	*waʿărāpel taḥat raglāyw*
He mounted the cherub and flew	*yirkab ʿal-kərûb wayyāʿōp*
He flew on the wings of the wind ...	*wayyēdeʾ ʿal-kanpê-rûaḥ ...*
Out of the brilliance before him	*minnōgah negdô*
his clouds broke through,	*ʿābāyw ʿābərû*
hailstones and fiery coals.	*bārād wəgahălê-ʾēš*
Yahweh thundered from the heavens,	*wayyarʿēm baššāmayim yhwh*
Elyon uttered his voice,	*wəʿelyôn yittēn qōlô*
hailstones and fiery coals.	*bārād wəgahălê-ʾēš*
He loosed his arrows and scattered them;	*wayyišlaḥ ḥiṣṣāyw wayəpîṣēm*
he discharged lightning and terrified them.	*ûbərāqîm rāb wayəhummēm*[2]

(Ps. 18:8–11, 13–15 (English 18:7–10, 12–14)) (cf. 2 Sam. 22:8–11, 13–15)

Notice the dramatic effect of the piling up of fiery images emanating from Yahweh: from fire (*ʾēš*) to coals (*gehālîm*) to brilliance (*nōgah*) to hailstones (*bārād*) to lightning (*bərāqîm*) together with verbs of burning (*ḥārâ*), devouring (*tōʾkēl*), blazing (*bāʿărû*), thundering (*yarʿēm*), and discharging (*rāb*). Isaiah 30:27–30 (also couched in storm language) expresses similar "fiery transcendent anthropomorphism" when it likens Yahweh's <u>tongue</u> to "devouring fire" (*ləšônô kəʾēšʾōkālet*) or conveys Yahweh's "majestic voice" (*hôd qôlô*)[3] and "the descent of his <u>arm</u>" (*naḥat zerôʾô*) through "devouring flames of fire" (*lahab ʾēš ʾōkēlâ*).

The Impossibility of Crafting the Essence of Fire

The essence of fire might provide a rationale to unpack various aniconic passages about not producing a sculptured image. Compare, for example, Deuteronomy 4:12, 15–16: "Yahweh spoke to you out of fire, You heard the sound of words, but saw no form of any kind ... so do not make sculptured images." One wonders whether those who prized

Figure 28.10   A stele from Zincirli whose inscription mentions that the deceased person's "soul/essence" (*nabšu*) was envisioned as continuing to dwell in the stele itself.
Source: Reproduced by permission of the Neubauer Expedition to Zincirli, University of Chicago.

the use of fire as an apt symbol for divinity advocated aniconism for the obvious reason: Ethereal fire <u>cannot</u> be sculpted without losing its essence. Once concretized, fire cannot burn with intense heat, give off light or instill the feeling of the numinous through flickering flames. A stone image of fire can be held in the hand – hence its inadequacy to represent *tremendum*. Nonetheless, pragmatists desire a focal point for worship and there are various ways in which real fire would have served as an attention-focusing device. Within sacred space, one need only think of the various lamps, some of which seem to have been lit perpetually. An even better symbol for divinity is the kindling of fires for sacrifices. Conceptually the "<u>continual</u> burnt offering by fire" (Exod. 29:41–45) was linked to Yahweh's promise to dwell among the people of Israel as their God.

The Use of "Radiance" to Depict the Presence of Yahweh

As with numinous fire, the concept of God being present via "radiance" is a prevailing theme conveyed through words such as *hôd*, *hādār*, *kābôd* and *nōgah*. These words are usually translated with the English equivalents of glory, majesty, brilliance, splendor, dignity, strength, and sovereignty. It is often overlooked that the word *kābôd* can also have a concrete meaning (e.g., Isa. 17:4; Ps. 16:9) and thus serve as a perfect vehicle for depicting a divine body that had substance (i.e. could take up space) and yet was also ethereal (cf. Sommer).

The antiquity of divine radiance in Israelite religion can be seen from poems such as Habakkuk 3:2–5, Deuteronomy 33:2 and Psalm 29 (cf. Ps 104:1–4). The "*kābôd* Yahweh" in P as well as in Ezekiel is one of the most notable phrases for designating divine presence via radiance (see the essays by David Carr and S. A. Geller in this volume). P portrays Yahweh's *kābôd* dwelling "like a consuming fire" on Mount Sinai (Exod. 24:16–17) as well as in the Tent of Meeting (Exod. 29:43–44) and within the newly constructed tabernacle (Exod. 40:34). Yahweh's *kābôd* appears to the priest Aaron and his sons Nadab and Abihu (Lev. 9) as well as to the people with Yahweh's fire consuming the offerings (Lev. 9:23–24). Note in particular P's articulation of divine lethality (*tremendum*) associated with the death of Nadab and Abihu for offering "strange fire" (Lev. 10:1–3). As Sommer notes, "it becomes brutally clear that holiness cannot be contained" (120).

As for the Book of Ezekiel, the opening theophany is filled with the imagery of radiance and fire. The piling up of vocabulary for radiance is simply overwhelming: "burnished bronze" (*nəhōšet qālāl*), 1:7; "burning coals of fire" (*gahălê-'ēš bō'ărôt*), 1:13; "torches" (*lappidîm*), 1:13; "radiant fire" (*nōgah lā'ēš*), 1:13; "lightning issued from fire" (*min-hā'ēš yōṣē' bārāq*), 1:13; "darting sparks" (?) (*rāṣô' wāšôb kəmar'ēh habbāzāq*), 1:14; "gleaming of chrysolite" (*kə'ên taršîš*), 1:16; "terrifyingly radiant" (*gōbah wəyir'â*), 1:18; "awe-inspiring gleam of crystal" (*kə'ên haqqerah hannôrā'*), 1:22; "sapphire" (*sappîr*), 1:26; "white-hot light" ('*ên hašmal*), 1:27; "fire" ('*ēš*), 1:27 (twice); "radiance" (*nōgah*), 1:27, 28; "rainbow" (*qešet*), 1:28; and "glory" (*kābôd*), 1:28.

The theophany culminates in the appearance of a "man" (*'ādām*) whose appearance is radiant fire from head to toe (Ezek. 1:26–28). Clearly Ezekiel's vision of the divine is no mere mortal despite his use of the word "loins" (*motnayĭm*). Human bodies are not made of fire and radiant brilliance; neither can they fly on the wings of cherubim.

What then are we to make of Ezekiel's use of such imagery? An obvious backdrop (especially with his Mesopotamian setting) is the concept of *melammu* used of gods like Nergal, who is described as "fire, wearing *radiance*" (*girru lābiš melamme*). Neo-Assyrian kings going to battle were assured of victory because they bore "the awe of the radiance (*pulḫu melamme*) of Aššur" that frightened enemies into submission even from afar (cf. Aster).

The depiction of the storm god Aššur from the time of the ninth-century BCE Tukulti-Ninurta II (figure 28.11) provides an apt analogy for the visual symbols found in Ezek. 1:26–28. The winged god is anthropomorphic from the waist up with taut bow in hand. Most importantly, he is encircled with flames of fire together with wavy lines depicting a radiance of some kind. It is thus not surprising that scholars have described this as

Figure 28.11   A depiction of the Mesopotamian storm god Aššur with radiant *melammu* and fire from the time of ninth-century BCE king Tukulti-Ninurta II.
Source: Walter Andrae, *Coloured Ceramics from Ashur and Earlier Ancient Assyrian Wall-Paintings* (London: Kegan Paul, Trench, Trubner, 1925), plate 8.

perhaps our best example of *melammu* being depicted in art. Radiant deities – be they Aššur or Ezekiel's – though anthropomorphic at a glance – can manifest their power and majesty by flying through the air engulfed in fire.

Solar Divinity

Space constraints prevent me from sketching the rich amount of literature on the solar imagery associated with Yahweh, both textual and pictorial (cf. Taylor). The relevant texts are well known, such as the following:

> Yahweh came from Sinai,
> He dawned (*zāraḥ*) from Seir,
> He shone forth (*hôpîaʻ*) from Mt. Paran.
> From his right hand fire flies forth.
>
> (Deut. 33:2)[4]

> For Yahweh is a sun (*šemeš*) and shield.
>
> (Ps. 84:12)

> Arise, shine, for your light has dawned (*bāʼ ʼôrēk*)
> The *kābôd* of Yahweh has shone (*zāraḥ*) upon you.
>
> (Isa. 60:1)

The iconographic representation of solar cults in the ancient Near East is well known too, with scholars giving particular attention to the Aten cult in Egypt. Aten is, after all, "the one who constructed himself with his own arms, the craftsman does not know him" (*p3 qd sw ds·f m'·wy·f bw rḫ sw ḥmw*). Indeed Aten never appears in the form of a statue; all that appears is a sun disk with rays ending in human hands (a "concession to anthropomorphism"). Donald Redford describes Akhenaten's iconography as "the most prominent act in a progressive move to rid concepts of the divine … of all anthropomorphic and theriomorphic forms" (75). According to Izak Cornelius, Aten was "not just another form of the sun god, or the sun disk, but the living sun best described as the light" ("Many faces," 29). Gay Robins underscores how "the actual sun in the sky served as the cult image of Aten" (4). (See John Huddlestun's essay herein.)

Obviously, one can never fully capture the sun, any more than one can contain divinity. Yet Judean artists used the winged sun disk to articulate the complex solar imagery of Yahweh. Here Joel LeMon articulates "striking areas of congruency where pictorial and literary images interact" (194). Though the question of whether we have empty space aniconism in register three of the Taanach cult stand (figure 28.12) is debated (cf. Taylor; Lewis, "Syro-Palestinian iconography," 77), we certainly have an iconic representation of a winged sun in register one.

Deuteronomistic Name Theology

The Deuteronomistic "Name Theology" was a reactionary theology in that it did not choose the rich vocabulary of "radiance" or divine fire. Nor was it comfortable with the anthropomorphism of divinity implied by Yahweh marching forth to battle or sitting as a king on a throne. Instead it advocated that Yahweh "chose for his name to dwell" (*yibḥar yhwh ləšakkēn šəmô šām*) as a representation of his presence within the Jerusalem Temple (Deut. 12:11; 14:23; 16:2; 1 Kings 5:5; 11:36, etc.). Thomas Staubli has argued that iconography can help us think in different categories about such a highly abstract concept. One of his best examples includes the name of Thutmosis IV represented as a fighting cartouche. Compare too a stele from Tell el-Borg depicting Athtartu's (Astarte's) name in a battle context contained in the excavation report recently edited by Hoffmeier (see also Lewis, "Athtartu's incantations").

I choose these military examples for comparison due to the way in which the Name of Yahweh was used hypostatically in passages such as Isaiah 30 to designate the presence of the deity.

> The Name of Yahweh (*šēm-yhwh*) comes from afar,
> In blazing wrath …
> His tongue like a devouring fire,
> His breath like a raging torrent …
> In raging wrath,
> In a devouring blaze of fire,
> In tempest, and rainstorm, and hailstones.

Figure 28.12   The terracotta tenth-century BCE Taanach cult stand depicts a winged sun disc above a quadruped in register one, caprids flanking a stylized tree in register two, cherub creatures in register three, and a nude female holding lions by the ears in register four. Some scholars suggest that register three represents a type of empty-space aniconism representing divinity.
Source: Reproduced by permission of the Israel Museum, Jerusalem.

> Truly, at the voice of Yahweh
> Assyria will be seized with terror
> As (Yahweh) smites with his staff.
>> (Isa. 30:27–28a, 30b–31; cf. Ps. 20:2–10)

Yet how was this envisioned in actual ritual? Was the actual name of Yahweh carved in a central location in the Jerusalem Temple? According to several passages, the Name that was thought to be Yahweh's practical presence was intimately tied up to the presence of the highly militaristic Ark. According to 1 Kings 8:16–21, the

Jerusalem Temple is described as both the <u>place</u> (*māqôm*) of Yahweh's Name and also "the <u>place</u> of the Ark" (*māqôm lā'ārôn*). Thus the Ark itself would represent a focal point for those who advocated Name Theology. According to John Van Seters, the Ark (with the two tablets of the Decalogue) housed the *inscribed name of the deity* deposited in the Temple (872; Van Seters is here responding to Sandra Richter's challenge to traditional understandings of Deuteronomistic name theology). Moreover, 2 Samuel 6:1–2 also contains a tradition wherein the Name of Yahweh was ritually invoked over the Ark.

One can also speculate about whether the very name Yahweh contributed to the development of aniconic traditions. Whatever one chooses for the etymology of this divine name ("He who is," "He who will be," "He who causes to be"), "Yahweh" is a god of "being" (cf. the essay by Neal Walls in this volume). How does a sculptor or painter craft an abstract concept such as "being"? It is far harder to craft a god of "being" than a god who is a lord and master (*ba'al*) and can be portrayed as a striding warrior with a weapon in his raised hand.

Sacred Emptiness

Finally we come to the most abstract tradition: sacred emptiness. Modern worshippers (especially in Judaism, Protestant Christianity, and Islam) are so accustomed to worshipping an invisible God that little thought is given to how revolutionary the idea was in its original ancient Near Eastern context. Throughout the ancient Near East, images of the deity were the focal point of religious ritual that included rites of fabrication, quickening, consecration, and procession as well as the use of images in an assortment of magic rituals (e.g., nurturing, healing, protection) and symbolic acts (e.g., capture, exile, spoliation, mutilation, and burial) (see Lewis, "Syro-Palestinian iconography," 83–102). In this context, to come across the sacred emptiness of the Jerusalem Temple is striking.

The Yahweh-Sabaoth traditions perceived Yahweh to be invisibly enthroned on *Mischwesen* creatures identified as cherubim (e.g., 1 Sam. 4:4; Isa. 37:6; Ezek. 10:18). The visual foundation for this is the common rendering of storm deities riding on the back of majestic animals including not just bulls but *Mischwesen* creatures such as the Neo-Assyrian depiction of Aššur depicted in figure 28.13. The *Mischwesen* sphinx-like (or cherubim) iconography is well attested in the Levant with well-known examples coming from Ayn Dara, Arslan Tash, Byblos, Sebastiyeh (biblical Samaria) and Megiddo. Certain biblical authors wed such images with sacred emptiness. In addition they used the language of size. According to 1 Kings 6, two colossal cherubim about 16 feet high were arranged "in the innermost part of the Temple" (*habbayit happənîmî*) serving symbolically to guard Yahweh's throne (1 Kings 6:27; 8:27). Such unmistakable focal points evoked divine wonder similar to viewing hybrid Neo-Assyrian human-headed, winged bulls called *aladlammu* (figure 28.14) that could also stand ~16 feet high. The existence of extant *aladlammu* sculptures can serve heuristically to help us imagine the wonder of seeing the monumental Cherubim that have not been preserved for us.

Figure 28.13   A Neo-Assyrian depiction of Aššur riding on the back of a *Mischwesen* creature. *Source*: bpk, Berlin/Vorderasiatisches Museum, Staatliche Museen, Berlin/Art Resource, New York; reproduced by permission of Art Resource.

Invisibility

As for invisibility, our most profound representation of abstract divinity from the Levant has gone largely unnoticed. I am referring here to the well-preserved (though poorly published) Syro-Hittite Iron Age temple of Ayn Dara (figure 28.15). As can be seen from the plans of the temple published by John Monson ("New Ain Dara temple," "Ain Dara temple"), a series of four, huge (bare) footprints was carved into three large limestone slabs that served as the elevated floor of the temple. That each of the footprints measures approximately three feet in length shows that the deity was portrayed as superhuman in size with estimates (based on the length of stride) approximating 65 feet tall! The layout of the footprints depicts the deity entering the temple and walking back to the inner sanctum where the statue of the deity would normally be found. At the portico entrance to the temple we find two footprints represented side by side on the first stone slab "as if some giant [deity] had paused at the entryway before striding into the building" (Monson, "New Ain Dara temple," 27). As one progresses forward, each

Figure 28.14   A hybrid Neo-Assyrian human-headed, winged bull called *aladlammu*.
Source: Reproduced by permission of Baker Publishing Group.

of the next two limestone slabs has a single carved footprint: first the left foot, followed
by the right. The length between second and third slab (depicting the right leg stride of
the deity) is approximately 30 feet long. The ancient artisans are portraying the deity
standing at the entrance to the temple and then walking right foot after the left, into the
inner sanctum. One knows the deity is present, not from embodying a physical, anthropomorphic statue, but from a type of sacred emptiness (i.e., the footprints left behind).
Such artistry evoked feelings of intimacy and wonder, about how the god was tangibly
present and yet also invisibly transcendent. In light of such imagery, Ezekiel's comments
about divine feet in the restored temple is striking: "Son of man, this is the place of my
throne and the place of the soles of my feet (*kappôt raglay*) where I will dwell in the midst
of the people of Israel forever."

Figure 28.15   The Iron Age Syro-Hittite temple at Ayn Dara in northern Syria has structural features that are very close to the Jerusalem Temple. A series of meter-long footprints were carved into the limestone threshold. They seem to depict a type of aniconic representation of a deity walking into the inner sanctum.
Source: Reproduced by permission of A. M. Appa.

Conclusion

In summary, in addition to celebrating the revolution that has happened in the study of anthropomorphic divine iconography in the last two decades, we should not lose sight of the ways in which ancient writers and artisans worked with "essence, ideas, concepts or images which are accessible only to <u>abstract</u> thought" (Niebuhr 120). In literature, abstract representations of Yahwistic divinity appear in a variety of ways: ethereal/divine fire imagery, solar imagery, divine "radiance" (*kābôd*), the divine (hypostatic) "Name" Yahweh, large-scale *kĕrûbîm* and invisibility. My suggestion in this paper

is that ancient artisans used their iconographic skills to echo what their scribal companions achieved via literature and to express how a god could take up real residence <u>via a
non-material presence</u>.[5]

Granted, physical iconography was not well suited to depicting fire. One would have
to rely on real fire in sacred space to express such ethereal divinity. Yet other attempts at
depicting radiance (at least by the Assyrians) and solar divinity were within reach. In a
world filled with tangible divine images, artisans at Ayn Dara used *size and empty space*
to depict a transcendent god larger than life. Though we cannot excavate a Jerusalem
Temple, the literary religion expressed in the Hebrew Bible echoes the use of size and
empty space to depict Yahweh as a transcendent god larger than life.

The relevance of the Iron Age Ayn Dara temple in neighboring Syria needs to be
weighed in any discussion of sacred emptiness in the Levant – including the Jerusalem
Temple. Such an artistic rendering provides a strong corrective to any who would
suggest that the religious ideas of the Iron Age Levant were narrow, small-minded
or conceptually primitive. Some scholars who advocate that there must have been an
anthropomorphic image of Yahweh in the Jerusalem Temple flirt with such pejorative
notions as they downplay any historical reality behind the various aniconic or abstract
streams of tradition. A priori, there should not be any barrier to assuming that Judean
sculptors (especially employing Phoenician artisans) were capable of similar abstract
representation. It is time to reset our iconoclastic clock such that our study of iconography appreciates those artists who used abstract images (in language and material
culture) to depict the divine.

Notes

1   The scholar most responsible for starting this wave of interest is Othmar Keel whose ground-
     breaking work, *The Symbolism of the Biblical World*, first published in 1972, is now in its fifth
     German edition. For a representative sampling of subsequent scholarship, see the following
     works included in the bibliography: Cornelius (*Iconography*; "Many faces"; *Many Faces*), Dick,
     Hendel, Keel and Uehlinger, Lewis ("Divine images" and "Syro-Palestinian iconography"),
     Mettinger (*No Graven Image?* and "Conversation"), Ornan ("Idols and symbols" and *Triumph*),
     Sommer, Uehlinger, and Walker and Dick.
2   On the root *hwm* designating divine terror, see Exodus 23:27.
3   The Hebrew word *qôl* is particularly apt for expressing such "transcendent anthropomor-
     phism" in that it can equally express the <u>voice</u> of Yahweh that speaks (and in Isa. 30:27–
     28, 30 with even the mention of his tongue (*ləšônô*), lips (*śəpātāyw*), and breath (*rûḥô*)) as
     well as the roar of divine <u>thunder</u>. It should be underscored that the metaphor of storm gods
     "thundering" with "voice" is found throughout the ancient Near East and Greece. See the
     many examples collected by Weinfeld (121–4; 141–3). A key example from Late Bronze Age
     Amarna Akkadian reads: "who gives forth his voice in the heavens like Adad, and all the earth
     is frightened at his voice" (*ša iddin rigmašu ina šamê kīma Adad u targub gabbi māti ištu rigmišu*;
     EA 147:13–15).
4   For this translation, see Lewis, "Divine fire."
5   It should also be underscored that the ancients certainly thought that one could speak about a
     god's "unseen" or "transcendent" presence. To do so only enhanced the majesty and mystery
     of the divine. The above examples did <u>not</u> resort to the language of the "ineffable" to describe

divinity. "Ineffable" (so well known via its later use with the name Yahweh) designates how adherents think that divinity is <u>incapable</u> of being expressed (due to the god's indescribable nature) and/or <u>unutterable</u> in nature (e.g., not to be spoken of due to potential misuse or irreverence). Rather, our ancient poets strained the limits of language to describe the *tremendum* of divinity. Likewise, ancient artisans used material culture to celebrate manifestations of divine glory.

Bibliography

Aster, Shawn Zelig. *The Unbeatable Light: Melammu and Its Biblical Parallels.* Münster: Ugarit-Verlag, 2012. A comprehensive study of the concept of "radiance" in Mesopotamian literature and its bearing on "radiance" in biblical traditions.

Cornelius, Izak. *The Iconography of the Canaanite Gods Reshef and Ba'al: Late Bronze and Iron Age I Periods (c. 1500–1000 BCE).* Fribourg: Fribourg University, 1994). A collection of many of the images of two of the most important deities in the Canaanite pantheon who are sometimes confused due to their overlapping traits.

Cornelius, Izak. "The many faces of God: Divine images and symbols in ancient Near Eastern traditions." In Karel van der Toorn (ed.), *The Image and the Book: Iconic Cults, Aniconism, and the Rise of Book Religion in Israel and the Ancient Near East* (pp. 21–43). Leuven: Peeters, 1997. A general overview of the many different ways in which ancient Near Eastern divinity was represented through iconography.

Cornelius, Izak. *The Many Faces of the Goddess: The Iconography of the Syro-Palestinian Goddesses Anat, Astarte, Qedeshet, and Asherah, c. 1500–1000 BCE.* Fribourg: Academic Press, 2004. A detailed collection of many of the images of four of the most important goddesses in the Canaanite pantheon who are sometimes confused due to their overlapping traits.

Dick, Michael B. (ed.). *Born in Heaven, Made on Earth: The Making of the Cult Image in the Ancient Near East.* Winona Lake, IN: Eisenbrauns, 1999. A collection of essays looking at how the manufacture of divine images was viewed in Mesopotamia and Egypt as well as prophetic (biblical) parodies against the making of such images.

Hallo, William W. "Texts, statues and the cult of the divine king." In John A. Emerton (ed.), *Congress Volume, Jerusalem 1986* (pp. 54–66). Vetus Testamentum, suppl. 40. Leiden: Brill, 1988. A study of the representation of royal cult in text and image.

Hendel, Ronald H. "Aniconism and anthropomorphism in ancient Israel." In Karel van der Toorn (ed.), *The Image and the Book: Iconic Cults, Aniconism, and the Rise of Book Religion in Israel and the Ancient Near East* (pp. 205–28). Leuven: Peeters, 1997. A provocative study that suggests new terminology ("transcendent anthropomorphism") that better matches what we find in the ancient record.

Hoffmeier, James K. (ed.) *Tell el-Borg I.* Winona Lake, IN: Eisenbrauns, 2014. Recent excavation report with important new evidence concerning Athtartu.

Jacobsen, Thorkild. *The Treasures of Darkness: A History of Mesopotamian Religion.* New Haven: Yale University Press, 1976. A classic in the field that explores the religion of ancient Iraq.

Keel, Othmar. *The Symbolism of the Biblical World: Ancient Near Eastern Iconography and the Book of Psalms.* Winona Lake, IN: Eisenbrauns, 1997. A groundbreaking work for using ancient Near Eastern iconography to understand the Hebrew Bible.

Keel, Othmar and Christoph Uehlinger. *Gods, Goddesses and Images of God in Ancient Israel.* Minneapolis: Fortress, 1998. A classic in the field that includes a treasure trove of data on the iconography of gods and goddesses.

LeMon, Joel M. *Yahweh's Winged Form in the Psalms: Exploring Congruent Iconography and Texts.* Orbis Biblicus et Orientalis 242. Fribourg: Academic Press, 2010. A dedicated study applying the study of iconography to a common literary motif.

Lewis, Theodore J. "CT 13.33–34 and Ezekiel 32: Lion-dragon myths." *Journal of the American Oriental Society 116* (1996): 28–47. A study of texts and images that were used to depict hybrid creatures in two well-known combat myths from Mesopotamia and the Hebrew Bible.

Lewis, Theodore J. "Divine images and aniconism in ancient Israel." *Journal of the American Oriental Society 118* (1998): 36–53. A detailed analysis of Mettinger's theory of "material aniconism" balanced with an analysis of other representations of divine images in ancient Israel.

Lewis, Theodore J. "Syro-Palestinian iconography and divine images." In Neal H. Walls (ed.), *Cult Image and Divine Representation in the Ancient Near East* (pp. 69–107). Atlanta: American Schools of Oriental Research, 2005. A survey of divine images found in ancient Syria (primarily Late Bronze Age Ugarit) and Iron Age Israel.

Lewis, Theodore J. "'Athtartu's incantations and the use of divine names as weapons." *Journal of Near Eastern Studies 71* (2011): 207–27. A study of the way in which the goddess 'Athtartu (also known as Astarte) was magically connected to mythological battles.

Lewis, Theodore J. "Divine fire in Deuteronomy 33:2." *Journal of Biblical Literature 132* (2013): 791–803. A solution to a famous biblical crux that explores the use of fire as an abstract representation of Yahweh.

Meshel, Ze'ev. *Kuntillet 'Ajrud (Ḥorvat Teman): An Iron Age II Religious Site on the Judah-Sinai Border.* Jerusalem: Israel Exploration Society, 2012. The final report of excavations that have had a major impact on the study of Israelite religion since the site was discovered in the 1970s.

Mettinger, Tryggve N. D. *No Graven Image? Israelite Aniconism in Its Ancient Near Eastern Context.* Stockholm: Almqvist & Wiksell, 1995. A comprehensive study of "standing stones" (Hebrew *maṣṣēbôt*) in ancient Israel set against its ancient Near Eastern backdrop.

Mettinger, Tryggve N. D. "A conversation with my critics: Cultic image or aniconism in the First Temple?" In Yairah Amit, Ehud Ben Zvi, Israel Finkelstein, and Oded Lipschits (eds), *Essays on Ancient Israel in Its Near Eastern Context: A Tribute to Nadav Na'aman* (pp. 273–96). Winona Lake, IN: Eisenbrauns, 2006. One of the most insightful scholars of divine images and aniconic traditions in dialogue with his critics.

Monson, John. "The new Ain Dara temple: Closest Solomonic parallel." *Biblical Archaeology Review 26* (2000): 20–35, 67. A very readable and beautifully illustrated summary of Monson's detailed 2006 article.

Monson, John. "The Ain Dara temple and the Jerusalem Temple." In Gary M. Beckman and Theodore J. Lewis (eds), *Text, Artifact, and Image: Revealing Ancient Israelite Religion* (pp. 273–99). Providence, RI: Brown Judaic Studies, 2006. A detailed examination of a Syro-Hittite temple with remarkable parallels to the Solomonic Temple depicted in the Hebrew Bible.

Niebuhr, H. Richard. *Radical Monotheism and Western Culture.* Louisville, KY: Westminster John Knox Press, 1960. A classic in the field by the important Yale Divinity School theologian and ethicist.

Ornan, Tallay. "The bull and its two masters: Moon and storm deities in relation to the bull in ancient Near Eastern art." *Israel Exploration Journal 51* (2001): 1–26. An insightful analysis of the abstract bull-headed warrior found at Bethsaida.

Ornan, Tallay. "Idols and symbols: Divine representation in first millennium Mesopotamian art and its bearing on the Second Commandment." *Tel Aviv 31* (2004): 90–121. A study of the importance of divine symbols in Mesopotamia and their importance for understanding biblical prohibitions against divine images.

Ornan, Tallay. *The Triumph of the Symbol: Pictorial Representation of Deities in Mesopotamia and the Biblical Image Ban*. Fribourg: Academic Press, 2005. A study of the widespread use of abstract symbols from first-millennium Mesopotamia that helps us better understand the polemics against using divine images in the Hebrew Bible.

Ornan, Tallay. "The lady and the bull: Remarks on the bronze plaque from Tel Dan." In Yairah Amit, Ehud Ben Zvi, Israel Finkelstein, and Oded Lipschits (eds), *Essays on Ancient Israel in Its Near Eastern Context: A Tribute to Nadav Na'aman* (pp. 297–312). Winona Lake, IN: Eisenbrauns, 2006. An analysis of a plaque depicting a goddess on the top of a bull coming from the biblical site of Tel Dan in northern Israel.

Ornan, Tallay. "'Let Ba'al be enthroned': The date, identification, and function of a bronze statue from Hazor." *Journal of Near Eastern Studies* 70 (2011): 253–80. A detailed analysis of a most remarkable large bronze figurine coming from the important archaeological site of Hazor.

Otto, Rudolf. *The Idea of the Holy: An Inquiry into the Non-rational Factor in the Idea of the Divine and Its Relation to the Rational*. London: Oxford University Press, 1952. A classic in the field of religious studies that theorizes about how the "numinous" is both *fascinans* (irresistibly attracting) and *tremendum* (overwhelming and dangerous).

Pardee, Dennis. "A new Aramaic inscription from Zincirli." *Bulletin of the American Schools of Oriental Research* 356 (2009): 51–71. A detailed study of an important inscription (excavated in 2008) that mentions a deceased person's "soul/essence" residing in his mortuary stele.

Redford, Donald B. *Akhenaten, the Heretic King*. Princeton: Princeton University Press, 1984. A study of the famous pharaoh from New Kingdom Egypt who was known for turning away from a traditional polytheism in favor of the worship of the sun deity Aten.

Renfrew, Colin and Paul Bahn. *Archaeology: Theories, Methods and Practice*. 3rd edn. London: Thames & Hudson, 2000. A widely used textbook on archaeology.

Robins, Gay. "Cult statues in ancient Egypt." In Neal H. Walls (ed.), *Cult Image and Divine Representation in the Ancient Near East* (pp. 1–12). Boston: American Schools of Oriental Research, 2005. A study of divine representation in ancient Egypt with attention to how gods were thought to be corporeal and noncorporeal at the same time.

Smith, Mark S. *The Origins of Monotheism: Israel's Polytheistic Background and the Ugaritic Texts*. Oxford: Oxford University Press, 2001. A comparative study of the way in which divinity was conceptualized in Late Bronze Age Syria (via the city of Ugarit) and Iron Age Israel.

Sommer, Benjamin D. *The Bodies of God and the World of Ancient Israel*. Cambridge: Cambridge University Press, 2009. An innovative investigation of the corporeal and noncorporeal ways in which God's body is portrayed in the Hebrew Bible with an emphasis on divine "fluidity."

Staubli, Thomas. *Bibel + Orient im Original: 72 Einsichten in die Sammlungen der Universität Freiburg Schweiz*. Fribourg: Academic Press, 2007. A commentary on an extensive collection of ancient iconographic art.

Taylor, J. Glen. *Yahweh and the Sun: Biblical and Archaeological Evidence for Sun Worship in Ancient Israel*. Sheffield: JSOT Press, 1993. A monograph arguing that Yahweh was perceived to have solar aspects with particular attention to analyzing the Taanach cult stand.

van der Toorn, Karel. "God (I) *'lhym*." In Karel van der Toorn, Bob Becking, and Pieter W. van der Horst (eds), *Dictionary of Deities and Demons in the Bible* (pp. 352–65). Leiden: Brill, 1999. A standard reference work that documents the many gods and other preternatural beings in the Hebrew Bible and the Levant.

Uehlinger, Christoph. "Anthropomorphic cult statuary in Iron Age Palestine and the search for Yahweh's cult images." In Karel van der Toorn (ed.), *The Image and the Book: Iconic Cults, Aniconism, and the Rise of Book Religion in Israel and the Ancient Near East* (pp. 97–155). Leuven:

Peeters, 1997. An attempt to see whether the biblical deity Yahweh might be represented in the iconographic record.

Van Seters, John. "Review of Sandra L. Richter, The Deuteronomistic History and the Name Theology: *Ləšakkēn šəmô šām* in the Bible and the Ancient Near East." *Journal of the American Oriental Society 123* (2003): 871–2.

Walker, Christopher and Michael B. Dick. *The Induction of the Cult Image in Ancient Mesopotamia: The Mesopotamian Mīs Pî Ritual.* State Archives of Assyria Literary Texts 1. Helsinki: The Neo-Assyrian Text Corpus Project, 2001. A technical study of the most important set of primary texts for articulating the way in which divine images were crafted, quickened, consecrated, and ritually used in ancient Mesopotamia.

Walls, Neal (ed.). *Cult Image and Divine Representation in the Ancient Near East.* Atlanta: American Schools of Oriental Research, 2005. A comparative study by various ancient Near Eastern historians of religions on divine representation in Egypt, Anatolia, Mesopotamia, and Syria-Palestine.

Weinfeld, Moshe. "Divine intervention in war in ancient Israel and in the ancient Near East." In Hayim Tadmor and Moshe Weinfeld (eds), *History, Historiography, and Interpretation: Studies in Biblical and Cuneiform Literatures* (pp. 121–47). Jerusalem: Magnes Press, Hebrew University, 1983. A study of the motif of gods as divine warriors including the way in which storm imagery was employed.

Index